# Case Problems in Finance

# Case Problems in Finance

*Tenth Edition*

Edited by

**WILLIAM E. FRUHAN, JR.**
Thomas D. Casserly, Jr., Professor of
Business Administration

**W. CARL KESTER**
Professor of Business Administration

**SCOTT P. MASON**
Professor of Business Administration

**THOMAS R. PIPER**
Industrial Bank of Japan
Professor of Finance

**RICHARD S. RUBACK**
Professor of Business Administration

All of the
Graduate School of Business Administration
Harvard University

**IRWIN**
Homewood, IL 60430
Boston, MA 02116

© RICHARD D. IRWIN, INC., 1949, 1953, 1959, 1962, 1969, 1972, 1975, 1981, 1987, and 1992

Case material of the Harvard Graduate School of Business Administration is made possible by the cooperation of business firms and other organizations which may wish to remain anonymous by having names, quantities, and other indentifying details disguised while maintaining basic relationships. Cases are prepared as the basis for class discussion rather than to illustrate either effective or ineffective handling of an administrative situation.

Sponsoring editor:   Michael W. Junior
Project editor:   Karen Smith
Production manager:   Greg Gallman
Designer:   Tara L. Bazata
Compositor:   Arcata Graphics Kingsport
Typeface:   10/12 Times Roman
Printer:   R. R. Donnelley & Sons Company

**Library of Congress Cataloging-in-Publication Data**

Case problems in finance/edited by William E. Fruhan, Jr.—[et al.].—10th ed.

   p.   cm.

  ISBN 0-256-08346-0

  1. Corporations—Finance—Case studies.   2. Business enterprises––Finance—Case studies.   I. Fruhan, William E.

HG4026.C279   1992

658.15—dc20                       91–31237

*Printed in the United States of America*
1 2 3 4 5 6 7 8 9 0 DOC 9 8 7 6 5 4 3 2

# Foreword

The publication of the tenth edition of *Case Problems in Finance* marks the fortieth anniversary of the first edition of this volume, published in 1951. Throughout this period *Case Problems in Finance* has been one of the leading books in its market niche, at times the only such book. The test of the marketplace provides the best evidence of the contribution that *Case Problems in Finance* has made over the years.

No one individual, or small group of individuals, can claim credit for its enduring success. From the beginning the book has been a cooperative effort. Counting the tenth edition, 17 members of the Harvard Business School faculty have served as editors of the volume. Typically, as in other phases of life, as the years have passed this responsibility has been transferred from older faculty to younger colleagues. The resulting renewal of vitality, technical skills, and sensitivity to evolving developments in the world of finance has enabled *Case Problems in Finance* to outlive by a wide margin the normal life expectancy of an academic publication.

The cases included in the tenth edition, as in earlier editions, draw on the work of many individuals other than the editors of this volume. The editors thank 23 individuals, not counting former editors, for their contributions to cases in this edition. Most of these individuals are current or former members of the Harvard Business School faculty. Anyone who has served as editor of *Case Problems in Finance* is keenly aware of the immeasurable contribution made to the quality of this volume by the varied expertise of so many colleagues.

*Case Problems in Finance* has been remarkably stable in its basic conception and emphasis throughout its existence. The tenth edition continues this tradition. It is still a casebook. Its focus continues to be managerial. Its orientation remains decisional. It is meant to complement theory, not to compete with it. The changes are evolutionary in nature. But the new material is extensive, timely, and innovative. Individuals familiar with the ninth edition can verify this fact by reading the Introduction and scanning the Table of Contents of this edition.

A hallmark of *Case Problems in Finance* has always been a very carefully prepared Teacher's Manual. The editors of the tenth edition share the conviction that the best possible Teacher's Manual is a matter of high priority. The editors have devoted as much care and energy to the preparation of the Teacher's Manual as to the book itself.

I have every confidence that the tenth edition of *Case Problems in Finance* will be an outstanding success. Professors Fruhan and Piper are veteran editors of the volume. They have made major, even dominant, contributions to the last several editions. Professors Kester, Mason, and Ruback are superbly qualified for the task they have undertaken. With these five individuals as editors *Case Problems in Finance* is in very competent hands.

J. Keith Butters

# Acknowledgments

To the business executives who contributed the material for the cases in this volume we express our sincere gratitude. In the development of these cases they gave liberally of their time, and in most instances they made available to us facts about their businesses that are normally held confidential.

We wish to acknowledge our debt to Pearson Hunt, Charles M. Williams, James T. S. Porterfield, Leonard C. R. Langer, Robert F. Vandell, Alan B. Coleman, Frank L. Tucker, James E. Walter, Erich A. Helfert, Victor L. Andrews, David W. Mullins, Jr., and J. Keith Butters, whose names have appeared as editors in earlier editions of this book. Their influence will be obvious to anyone who has used prior editions of *Case Problems in Finance*. We are particularly grateful to Keith Butters, whose leading role in five prior editions of the book represents the standard to which we all aspire.

Thirty members or former members of the faculty of the Harvard University Graduate School of Business Administration authored, coauthored, or supervised the writing of the cases used in this edition or earlier versions of these cases.

In addition to the editors of previous editions of this volume we wish to thank Robert N. Anthony, M. Edgar Barrett, Carliss Y. Baldwin, Robert W. Bruner, Dwight B. Crane, Jean de Menton, Michael Edleson, Robert R. Glauber, John Goldsberry, Bruce C. Greenwald, Steven E. Levy, George C. Lodge, R. L. Masson, John H. McArthur, Robert W. Merry, Ronald W. Moore, Kevin R. Rock, Erik Sirri, Jeremy Stein, Lawrence E. Thompson, Jonathan Tiemann, Richard F. Vancil, William L. White, and Harold E. Wyman for the use of cases for which they are responsible as author, coauthor, or supervisor. We also extend our thanks to the research assistants of the Harvard University Graduate School of Business Administration who assisted in the writing of the cases in this volume under the supervision of senior faculty members.

We are grateful to John H. McArthur, Dean of the Harvard University Graduate School of Business Administration, for encouraging us to undertake this task. Harvard Business School's Division of Research provided financial support for the development of the cases in this book. The copyright on all cases appearing here is held by the President and Fellows of Harvard College.

Most of all we should like to express our special appreciation to Alice Cheyer, Rita D. Colella, and Karen Smith for their invaluable assistance in the preparation of this volume. Their care and expertise in putting the manuscript into proper form for publication has contributed importantly to its quality.

The editors assume full responsibility for the contents of this edition, but they are keenly aware of their obligation to their predecessors and colleagues.

William E. Fruhan, Jr.
W. Carl Kester
Scott P. Mason
Thomas R. Piper
Richard S. Ruback

# Contents

**Mergers, Acquisitions, and Restructurings**

## PART IV: COMPREHENSIVE OVERVIEW

**Appendixes**

# Introduction

Many readers may be meeting the case method of instruction for the first time. More often than not the experience is a frustrating one, for cases typically end at the critical point—in the words of some, "just when they seem to be getting some place." At that point readers are left to make their own way. It may be helpful, therefore, to know from the outset what case problems are and what advantages we believe can be gained from their use.

The heart of the case method of instruction is the use of problems to train students to discover, and then to fix in mind, ways of thinking that are productive in the subject area. Appropriate use of theory and the acquisition of factual material and procedural skills are also important goals, but the main objective is an ability to handle different types of managerial problems intelligently.

The word *decisional* is sometimes used to contrast the case method with *expository* teaching. For example, most of the cases in this book are descriptions of actual business situations. The facts are those known to some executive; they present an immediate financial problem which that person had to decide. Some cases emphasize the preliminaries of decision making—the difficulty of isolating and defining the crucial problem or of determining whether enough information is at hand to make an intelligent decision. The majority of cases, however, are "issue" cases; they present reasonable alternative courses of action that might have been followed in the given situation. Sufficient information is given to place readers in the executives' position. From this vantage point students are challenged to analyze the problem and to decide on the course of action to be taken.

The cases themselves depict a wide range of financial problems and business situations. Reference to the Contents will show that problems have been drawn from most of the major areas covered in financial courses. Cases have been selected from a variety of industries and from different time periods. Cases are also included that illustrate different phases in the life cycle of business firms and problems of cyclical decline as well as of prosperity.

The ordering of materials reflects our decisional approach. We begin with Estimating Funds Requirements, a topic that is typically either omitted from a first expository course in finance or would occur at the end of the course. We begin with this topic because obtaining sufficient funds to maintain ongoing operations is the first responsibility of a financial manager. Although this subject is not glamorous, it enables students to focus on concrete problems that require decisions. This analysis naturally leads to a discussion of Managing Short-Term Assets and Liabilities and Capital Structure Policy. The cases in the Financing Decisions and Tactics section explore financial strategies and synthesize the earlier cases. After exploring short-term demands for funds, and the alternatives and issues associated with short- and long-term financing, our examination of liability management ends with a section on Distribution Policy.

We link the cases on liability and asset management with a new section, The Corporation in the Capital Markets. The four new cases in this section emphasize the link between financial markets and corporate investment policies. The material on Cost of Capital applies and extends these concepts to the problem of determining the appropriate discount rate to value risky investments. This leads to a section on Investment Decisions, which in turn leads to cases on Mergers, Acquisitions, and Restructurings. The book concludes with cases that provide a Comprehensive Overview of the course.

The order of the cases reflects our managerial focus, which contrasts with the capital market focus that underlies the organization of most expository textbooks and courses in finance. We believe that the ordering of materials from the managerial viewpoint is the most effective way to teach managerial corporate finance. One cost of this approach, however, is that it is often difficult to relate readings in popular textbooks to specific cases. We have therefore included several notes to provide students with essential background materials.

Twenty-seven of the 52 cases and notes in this edition are new. Of these 27 cases and notes, 17 are completely new and 10 are updates of notes and cases from the ninth edition. The new materials in this tenth edition of *Case Problems in Finance* reflect the changing financial environment as well as advances in the theory and practice of financial management. In our judgment, the materials in the sections on Estimating Funds Requirements, Managing Short-Term Assets and Liabilities, and Capital Structure Policy—all from the ninth edition—consist of well-tested cases providing a very teachable sequence that offers a good opportunity to stress fundamental techniques of analysis. We have added a ''Note on Bank Loans,'' which details the structure of credit agreements and loan facilities and describes common covenants. We have also added ''Colt Industries,'' which explores the issues involved in a leveraged recapitalization of a public corporation.

The Financial Decisions and Tactics section includes two new cases. ''Union Tank Car Company'' examines the lease versus buy/borrower decision. ''Novo Industri A/S 1981'' demonstrates how tapping the international capital markets can help a firm escape a capital cost disadvantage associated with being domiciled in a small country with segmented capital markets. The Distribution Policy section has two new cases: "Tandy Corporation" focuses on share repurchases, and "Avon Products" examines innovative payout policies.

The Corporation in the Capital Market section contains four new cases that stress the importance of the capital markets to corporate financial managers. "Valuation and Discounted Cash Flows" is a series of exercises on capital budgeting techniques. "Tom Paine Mutual Life Insurance Company" describes the various types of loans made by life insurance companies. "Metromedia Broadcasting Corporation" examines a financial institution's decision to purchase high-yield bonds. The "Anheuser-Busch" case focuses on the effects of insider trading on the cost of a major acquisition.

Two new cases in the Cost of Capital section highlight the relation between theory and practice. "Pioneer Petroleum Corporation" examines the advantages and disadvantages of divisional costs of capital. "Marriott Corporation: The Cost of Capital" applies the Capital Asset Pricing Model to calculate the corporate and divisional weighted average cost of capital.

The Investment Decisions section contains two new cases. "Economy Shipping" compares the costs of refurbishing a work boat to the costs of purchasing a new one. "Interco" applies valuation techniques to the problem of valuing a company in the midst of a hostile takeover. By providing details on the tender offer process, "Interco" is a bridge to the materials in the section Mergers, Acquisitions, and Restructurings, which includes the new cases "RJR Nabisco" and "Philip Morris." "RJR Nabisco" focuses on the leveraged buyout of that firm, and "Philip Morris" examines the merger of that company with Kraft. Together with "Gulf Oil Corporation," these cases describe the largest corporate control transactions to date and provide vehicles to explore takeover and defensive techniques and their implications.

Inevitably some instructors will regret that some of their favorite cases have been omitted in this edition. The editors share this feeling. If an instructor is especially eager to continue to use certain cases that were dropped in this edition, they can be ordered separately from the Harvard Business School Publishing Division, 145 North Harvard Street, Boston, MA 02163.

All these cases are designed to provide a basis for class discussion; as such they are not intended to illustrate correct or incorrect solutions to management problems. It need hardly be added that the discussion they provoke will move along more realistic lines if students also have a standard finance text or reference book available and use it freely for background information not provided by this casebook. In addition, students will need to acquire proficiency in a number of analytical techniques useful in handling the quantitative aspects of cases.

Case problems confront students with the necessity of making decisions, and this is perhaps their greatest value. Students cannot stop with an understanding of the facts and a listing of items that deserve consideration. Mastery of these matters is merely the jumping-off point for class discussion. To be effective, students must actually think the problem through to a decision, explain their analyses to classmates, and defend their ideas. The need to choose among balanced alternatives and to discuss the decision intelligently is a great force in learning. It helps to provide that elusive quality of judgment that is often missed when excessive reliance is placed on the application of theoretical models.

Since the cases present business situations that pose debatable alternatives of action, they contain problems that can be narrowed but not settled by the usual techniques of financial analysis. Judgment must enter into the process of decision making, so unanimous agreement as to the best decision is neither expected nor desired. This ambiguity also contributes to the initial frustration of many students who have been working with scientific and technical problems where a mechanistic approach can more frequently be counted on to yield a single "right" conclusion.

When analyzing case problems, readers should not overlook intangible human factors. The choice between financial alternatives in many, if not all, cases depends in part on the decision maker's disposition for risk taking and on other matters of judgment and taste.

Work with cases may require more student time than normal textbook reading assignments. However, the satisfaction of handling problems that introduce complexities involved in actual business decisions is normally sufficient to compensate for the extra time required.

# Part I

# Financing Current Operations

*Introductory*

# Assessing a Company's Future Financial Health

Assessing the long-term financial health of a company is an important task for outsiders considering the extension of credit and for insiders in their formulation of strategy. History abounds with examples of firms that embarked upon overly ambitious programs and that subsequently discovered that their portfolio of programs could not be financed on acceptable terms. The outcome frequently was the abandonment of programs in midstream at considerable financial and organizational cost to the company, its vendors, its employees, or its creditors.

The key issue in assessing the long-term financial health of a company is whether the corporate system of goals, product market strategies, investment requirements, and financing capabilities are in balance.

> At any given period every enterprise has a defined business mission which is realized in its established competitive positions in particular product markets. Corporate strategy centers on these competitive positions. This strategy may include a harvesting mode for a few mature and relatively unprofitable business units. But for most of the firm's product markets it is designed to maintain an existing market position or expand that position against primary competitors. Competitive strategy therefore dictates that the firm grow at least as rapidly as aggregate industry demand grows. The firm's targeted growth rate of sales must meet (or exceed) the expected growth rate of the industry.[1]

Thus, the starting point for assessing a firm's long-term health must be a thorough investigation of (1) management's goals for the company and for each of the product markets; (2) the strategy planned for each product market; (3) the likely response of competitors; and (4) the market, competitive, and operating characteris-

1. Gordon Donaldson, *Managing Corporate Wealth* (New York: Praeger, 1984), pp. 64–65.

tics of each product market. The analyst is well-advised to devote substantial time to exploring these areas, as the entire financial system of the company is driven by the economic and competitive environment of its established product markets. The firm's strategy and sales growth in each of its product markets will heavily determine the investments in assets needed to support these strategies; and the effectiveness of the strategies, combined with the response of competitors,

**FIGURE A**
Factors in Determining a Financing Plan

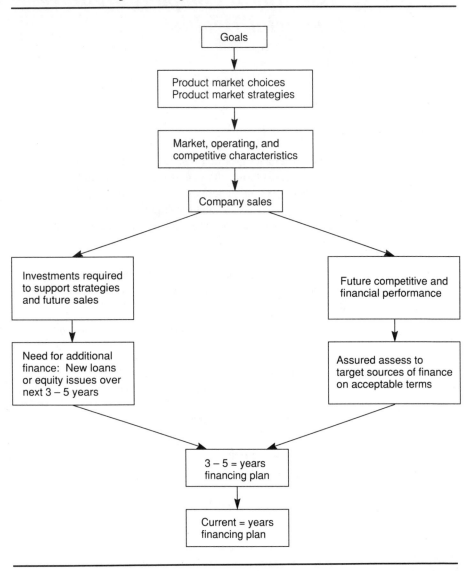

will strongly influence the firm's competitive and financial performance and its resultant access to funds to finance the investment in assets.

The following are some of the questions that seem important in assessing a company's future financial health. The sequencing of the questions corresponds to that suggested by Figure A.

1. What are management's goals for the company?
2. In which product markets does management plan to compete?
   a. What are management's goals in the various product markets?
   b. What is the strategy in each product market?
3. What are the market, competitive, and operating characteristics of each product market?
   a. What is the growth of primary demand in each product market? Are sales seasonal? cyclical?
   b. What are the strategies of the company's competitors?
   c. What are the company's operating policies?
   d. What are the main market, competitive, and operating risks?
4. What volume and nominal sales growth are likely for the company's units, individually and collectively?
5. What investments must be made in accounts receivables, inventory, and plant and equipment to support the various product market strategies? What will happen to the level of total assets over the next 3–5 years?
6. What is the outlook for profitability?
   a. What is the trend in reported profitability?
   b. What are the underlying financial accounting practices?
   c. Are there any hidden problems, such as suspiciously large levels or buildups of accounts receivable or inventories relative to sales?
   d. Is the level of profitability sustainable, given the outlook for the market and for competitive and regulatory pressures? (Figure B summarizes market and industry factors that can adversely affect a firm's future performance.)
7. Will the company need to raise additional finance over the next year, or over the next 3–5 years, to carry out strategically important programs?
   a. Does the company have a seasonal financing need? If so, how large is it, and what will be the perceptions of suppliers of finance at the time of the need?
   b. Does the company have a long-term need for additional finance? If so, how large is it, and what will be the perceptions of suppliers of finance at the time of the need?
   c. Will the company have a need for additional finance if it encounters adversity?
8. How soundly is the company financed, given its level of profitability, its level of business risk, and its future need for additional finance? (Access to target sources of finance depends on future competitive and financial

**FIGURE B**
Sources of Downward Pressure on Above-Market Returns

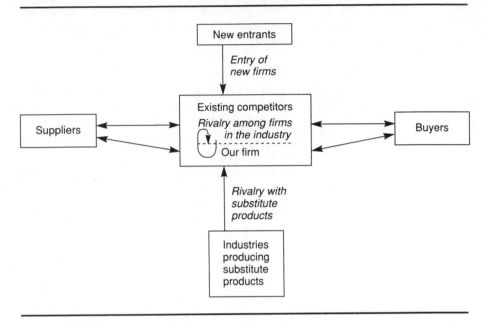

performance and on the soundness of the company's existing financial structure.)

    *a.* How current is the company in the payment of its suppliers?

    *b.* Is the company close to its borrowing limit according to restrictive covenants?

    *c.* Is the company within its capacity to service the debt? What is the maturity structure of existing debt?

    *d.* Are there any hidden problems such as unconsolidated subsidiaries with high debt levels or large contingent or unfunded liabilities?

**9.** Does the company have assured access on acceptable terms to external sources of funds in amounts needed to meet its seasonal, long-term, or adversity needs?

    *a.* Can the company raise equity funds?

      (1) Is there a market for the shares?

      (2) How many shares could be sold?

      (3) At what price could the shares be sold?

      (4) Would management be willing to issue new shares?

    *b.* Can the company raise long-term debt?

      (1) Who are the target suppliers?

      (2) What are their criteria for lending?

      (3) How well does the company meet these criteria?

      (4) How much additional long-term debt can the company raise on acceptable terms?

**FIGURE C**
Testing for System Balance

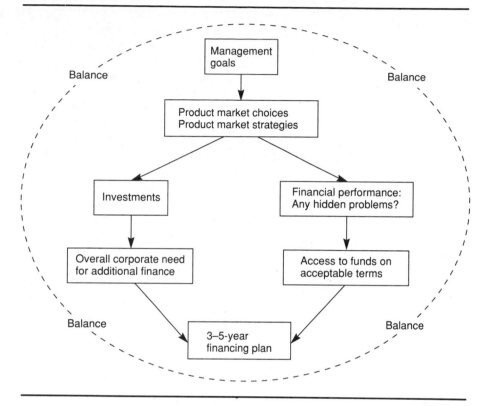

c. Can the company raise short-term debt?

d. Does the company have assets that could be sold to raise funds? How quickly could they be sold?

**10.** Are the company's goals, product market choices and strategies, investment requirements, financing needs, and financing capabilities in balance? (Figure C diagrams the interrelation of these management and financial considerations.)

**11.** Will the company's goals, strategies, investment requirements, financing needs, and financing capabilities remain in balance if the firm is struck by adversity?

a. What are the main regulatory, competitive, and operating risks? What combination of them might reasonably be expected to occur?

b. How would management respond in strategic and operating terms?

c. What would be the implications for future financing needs? For future financial performance?

d. Will it be possible to raise the finance needed on acceptable terms, given the financial suppliers' perceptions of the firm's strategic, competitive, and financial performance?

Clearly, many of these questions cannot be answered only by using the information contained in a company's published financial statements. Many require an understanding of (1) future industry structure and competitive behavior; (2) the competitive and operating characteristics of the business; (3) the long-term goals and plans of management; (4) the lending criteria of various segments of the capital markets; and (5) the soundness of management. Analysis of the published financial statements and their footnotes is only *one part* of a complete analysis of a company's future financial health.

It is also clear that the evaluation of a firm's financial health can vary substantially, depending on the perspective of the individual making the evaluation. A bank or supplier considering the extension of seasonal credit may consider a company a very safe bet, whereas a long-term lender dependent on the health and profitability of the company over a 15-year period may be very nervous.

The remainder of this note provides familiarity with the financial ratios that can be useful in answering some of the preceding questions. Exhibits 1 and 2 provide financial statements for 1986 and 1990 for a hypothetical company. The following section (Financial Ratios and Financial Analysis) presents four types of financial ratios and then asks a series of questions concerning the financial statements in Exhibits 1 and 2. Use the equations to answer the questions and fill in the blank spaces in the text. Your analysis of the statements should also answer two overall questions: Has the financial condition of the company changed during the 4-year period? What are the most significant changes, as indicated by the financial ratios?

## Financial Ratios and Financial Analysis

The two basic sources of financial data for a business entity are the income statement and the balance sheet. The income statement summarizes revenues and expenses over a period of time, e.g., for the year ending December 31, 1990. The balance sheet is a list of what the business owns (its assets), what it owes (its liabilities), and what has been invested by the owners (owners' equity) at a specific point in time, e.g., *at* December 31, 1990.

From the figures found on the income statement and the balance sheet one can calculate the following types of financial ratios:

1. Profitability ratios
2. Activity ratios
3. Leverage ratios
4. Liquidity ratios

### Profitability Ratios:   How Profitable Is the Company?

One measure of the profitability of a business is profit as a percentage of sales, as determined by the profitability ratio equation:

$$\frac{\text{Net profit after taxes}}{\text{Net sales}}$$

The information necessary to determine a company's profit as a percentage of sales can be found in the company's _____.

1. Magnetronics' profit as a percentage of sales for 1990 was $_____ divided by $_____, or ____%.

2. This represented an increase/decrease from ____% in 1986.

3. The deterioration in profitability resulted from an increase/decrease in cost of goods sold as a percentage of sales, and from an increase/decrease in operating expenses as a percentage of sales. The only favorable factor was the decrease in the _____.

Management and investors often are more interested in the return earned on the funds invested than in the level of profits as a percentage of sales. Companies operating in businesses requiring very little investment in assets often have low profit margins but earn very attractive returns on invested funds. Conversely, there are numerous examples of companies in very capital-intensive businesses that earn miserably low returns on invested funds despite seemingly attractive profit margins.

Therefore, it is useful to examine both the level and the trend of the company's operating profits as a percentage of total assets. To increase the comparability across companies within the same industry, it is useful to use profit before taxes and before any interest charges (earnings before interest and taxes, or EBIT). This allows the analyst to focus on the profitability of operations without any distortion due to tax factors or the method by which the company has financed itself.

4. Magnetronics had a total of $_____ invested in assets at year-end 1990 and earned before interest and taxes $_____ during 1990. Its operating profit as a percentage of total assets is calculated as follows:

$$\frac{\text{Profit before interest and taxes}}{\text{Total assets}}$$

In 1990 this figure was ____%, which represented an increase/decrease from the ____% earned in 1986.

From the viewpoint of the shareholders, an equally important figure is the company's return on equity. Return on equity is calculated by dividing profit after taxes by owners' equity:

$$\frac{\text{Profit after taxes}}{\text{Owners' equity}}$$

It indicates how profitably the company is utilizing shareholders' funds.

5. Magnetronics had $_____ of owners' equity and earned $_____ after taxes in 1990. Its return on equity was ____%, an improvement/deterioration from the ____% earned in 1986.

## Activity Ratios: Are There Any Hidden Problems?

The second basic type of financial ratio is the activity ratio. Activity ratios indicate how well a company employs its assets. Ineffective utilization of assets results in the need for more finance, unnecessary interest costs, and a correspondingly lower return on capital employed. Furthermore, low activity ratios or a deterioration in the activity ratios may indicate uncollectible accounts receivables or obsolete inventory or equipment.

Total asset turnover measures the company's effectiveness in utilizing its total assets and is calculated by dividing total assets into sales:

$$\frac{\text{Net sales}}{\text{Total assets}}$$

1. Total asset turnover for Magnetronics in 1990 can be calculated by dividing $ _____ into $ _____. The turnover had improved/deteriorated from _____ times in 1986 to _____ times in 1990.

It is useful to examine the turnover ratios for each type of asset, as the use of total assets may hide important problems in one of the specific asset categories. One important category is accounts receivables. The average collection period measures the number of days that the company must wait on average between the time of sale and the time when it is paid. The average collection period is calculated in two steps. First, divide annual credit sales by 365 days to determine average sales per day:

$$\frac{\text{Net sales}}{\text{365 days}}$$

Then, divide the accounts receivable by average sales per day to determine the number of days of sales that are still unpaid:

$$\frac{\text{Accounts receivable}}{\text{Average sales per day}}$$

2. Magnetronics had $ _____ invested in accounts receivables at year-end 1990. Its average sales per day were $ _____ during 1990 and its average collection period was ____ days. This represented an improvement/deterioration from the average collection period of ____ days in 1986.

A third activity ratio is the inventory turnover ratio, which indicates the effectiveness with which the company is employing inventory. Since inventory is recorded on the balance sheet at cost (not at its sales value), it is advisable to use cost of goods sold as the measure of activity. The inventory turnover figure is calculated by dividing cost of goods sold by inventory:

$$\frac{\text{Cost of goods sold}}{\text{Inventory}}$$

**3.** Magnetronics apparently needed $ _____ of inventory at year-end 1990 to support its operations during 1990. Its activity during 1990, as measured by the cost of goods sold, was $ _____. It therefore had an inventory turnover of _____ times. This represented an improvement/ deterioration from _____ times in 1986.

A fourth activity ratio is the fixed asset turnover ratio, which measures the effectiveness of the company in utilizing its plant and equipment:

$$\frac{\text{Net sales}}{\text{Net fixed assets}}$$

**4.** Magnetronics had net fixed assets of $ _____ and sales of $ _____ in 1990. Its fixed asset turnover ratio in 1990 was _____ times, an improvement/deterioration from _____ times in 1986.

**5.** So far, we have discussed three measures of profitability. They are
(a) _____
_____ (b) _____
_____ and (c) _____
_____ .

We have also discussed four activity ratios, which measure the effectiveness of the company in utilizing its assets. They are (d) _____
(e) _____
(f ) _____
and (g) _____ .

**6.** The deterioration in Magnetronics' operating profits as a percentage of total assets between 1986 and 1990 resulted primarily from _____
_____
_____
_____
_____
_____ .

## Leverage Ratios: How Soundly Is the Company Financed?

The third basic type of financial ratio is the leverage ratio. The various leverage ratios measure the relation between funds supplied by creditors and funds supplied by the owners. The use of borrowed funds by profitable companies will improve the return on equity. However, it increases the riskiness of the business and, if used in excessive amounts, can result in financial embarrassment.

One leverage ratio, the debt ratio, measures the total funds provided by creditors as a percentage of total assets:

$$\frac{\text{Total debt}}{\text{Total assets}}$$

Total debt includes both current and long-term liabilities.

1. The total debt of Magnetronics as of December 31, 1990, was $ _____, or ___% of total assets. This represented an increase/decrease from ___% as of December 31, 1986.

The ability of Magnetronics to meet its interest payments can be estimated by relating its earnings before interest and taxes (EBIT) to its interest payments:

$$\frac{\text{Earnings before interest and taxes}}{\text{Interest charges}}$$

This ratio is called the times interest earned ratio.

2. Magnetronics' earnings before interest and taxes were $ _____ in 1990, and its interest charges were $ _____. Its times interest earned was _____ times. This represented an improvement/deterioration from the 1986 level of _____ times.

A ratio similar to the times interest earned ratio is the fixed charge coverage ratio. This ratio recognizes that lease payments under long-term contracts are usually as mandatory as interest and principal payments on debt. The ratio is calculated as follows:

$$\frac{\text{EBIT + Lease payments}}{\text{Interest charges + Lease payments}}$$

3. Magnetronics had annual lease payments of $760. Its fixed charge coverage in 1990 was _____ times.

A fourth and final leverage ratio is the number of days of payables ratio. This ratio measures the average number of days that the company is taking to pay its suppliers of raw materials. It is calculated by dividing annual purchases by 365 days to determine average purchases per day:

$$\frac{\text{Annual purchases}}{\text{365 days}}$$

Accounts payable are then divided by average purchases per day,

$$\frac{\text{Accounts payable}}{\text{Average purchases per day}}$$

to determine the number of days of purchases that are still unpaid.

It is often difficult to determine the purchases of a firm. Instead, the income statement shows cost of goods sold, a figure that includes not only raw materials but also labor and overhead. Thus, it often is only possible to gain a rough idea as to whether a firm is becoming more or less dependent on its suppliers for finance. This can be done by relating accounts payable to cost of goods sold,

$$\frac{\text{Accounts payable}}{\text{Cost of goods sold}}$$

and following this ratio over time.

4. Magnetronics owed its suppliers $ _____ at year-end 1990. This represented __% of cost of goods sold and was an <u>increase/decrease</u> from ___% at year-end 1986. The company appears to be <u>more/less</u> prompt in paying its suppliers in 1990 than it was in 1986.

5. The deterioration in Magnetronics' profitability, as measured by its return on equity, from 15.2% in 1986 to 10.7% in 1990, resulted from the combined impact of _____

_____

_____ and _____

_____ .

6. The financial riskiness of Magnetronics <u>increased/decreased</u> between 1986 and 1990.

## Liquidity Ratios:   How Liquid Is the Company?

The fourth basic type of financial ratio is the liquidity ratio. These ratios measure a company's ability to meet financial obligations as they become current. The current ratio, defined as current assets divided by current liabilities,

$$\frac{\text{Current assets}}{\text{Current liabilities}}$$

assumes that current assets are much more readily and certainly convertible into cash than other assets. It relates these fairly liquid assets to the claims that are due within 1 year—the current liabilities.

1. Magnetronics held $ _____ of current assets at year-end 1990 and owed $ _____ to creditors due to be paid within 1 year. Its current ratio was _____, an <u>improvement/deterioration</u> from the ratio of _____ at year-end 1986.

The quick ratio, or acid test, is similar to the current ratio but excludes inventory from the current assets:

$$\frac{\text{Current assets} - \text{Inventory}}{\text{Current liabilities}}$$

Inventory is excluded because it is often difficult to convert into cash (at least at book value) if the company is struck by adversity.

2. The quick ratio for Magnetronics at year-end 1990 was _____, an <u>improvement/deterioration</u> from the ratio of _____ at year-end 1986.

## The Case of the Unidentified Industries

The preceding exercise suggests a series of questions that may be helpful in assessing a company's future financial health. It also describes several ratios that are useful in answering some of the questions, especially if the historical trend in these ratios is examined.

However, it is also important to compare the actual absolute value with some standard to determine whether the company is performing well. Unfortunately, there is no single current ratio, inventory turnover, or debt ratio that is appropriate to all industries, and even within a specific industry, ratios may vary significantly among companies. The operating and competitive characteristics of the company's industry greatly influence its investment in the various types of assets, the riskiness of these investments, and the financial structure of its balance sheet.

Try to match the following five types of companies with their corresponding balance sheets and financial ratios, shown in Exhibit 3.

1. Electric utility
2. Japanese trading company
3. Retail jewelry chain
4. Automobile manufacturer
5. Supermarket chain

In doing this exercise, consider the operating and competitive characteristics of the industry and their implications for (1) the collection period, (2) inventory turnover, (3) the amount of plant and equipment, and (4) the appropriate financial structure. Then identify which one of the five sets of balance sheets and financial ratios best matches your expectations.

**EXHIBIT 1**

Magnetronics, Inc., Consolidated Income Statements for Years Ending December 31, 1986 and 1990 (thousands of dollars)

|  | 1986 | 1990 |
|---|---|---|
| Net sales | $32,513 | $48,769 |
| Cost of goods sold | 19,183 | 29,700 |
| Gross profit | 13,330 | 19,069 |
| Operating expenses | 10,758 | 16,541 |
| Interest expense | 361 | 517 |
| Income before taxes | 2,211 | 2,011 |
| Federal income taxes | 1,040 | 704 |
| Net income | $ 1,171 | $ 1,307 |

**EXHIBIT 2**

Magnetronics, Inc., Consolidated Balance Sheets at December 31, 1986 and 1990 (thousands of dollars)

|  | 1986 | 1990 |
|---|---|---|
| Cash | $ 1,617 | $ 2,020 |
| Accounts receivable | 5,227 | 7,380 |
| Inventories | 4,032 | 8,220 |
| Current assets | 10,876 | 17,620 |
| Net fixed assets | 4,073 | 5,160 |
| Total assets | $14,949 | $22,780 |
| Notes payable, banks | $ 864 | $ 1,213 |
| Accounts payable | 1,615 | 2,820 |
| Accrued expenses and taxes | 2,028 | 3,498 |
| Current liabilities | 4,507 | 7,531 |
| Long-term debt | 2,750 | 3,056 |
| Stockholders' equity | 7,692 | 12,193 |
| Total liabilities and stockholders' equity | $14,949 | $22,780 |

**EXHIBIT 3**

Unidentified Balance Sheets

| | A | B | C | D | E |
|---|---|---|---|---|---|
| *Balance Sheet Percentages* | | | | | |
| Cash . . . . . . . . . . . . . | 7.3% | .8% | 13.5% | 7.2% | 11.3% |
| Receivables . . . . . . . . . | 22.5 | 5.4 | 5.8 | 60.3 | 10.9 |
| Inventories . . . . . . . . . | 8.3 | 2.8 | 35.8 | 8.7 | 61.5 |
| Other current assets . . . . . | 4.6 | .1 | 4.1 | 7.3 | 2.7 |
| Property and equipment (net) . . . | 35.0 | 83.0 | 23.6 | 4.3 | 8.3 |
| Other assets. . . . . . . . . | 22.3 | 7.9 | 17.2 | 12.2 | 5.3 |
| Total assets . . . . . . . | 100.0% | 100.0% | 100.0% | 100.0% | 100.0% |
| | | | | | |
| Notes payable . . . . . . . | 2.4% | 1.8% | 4.5% | 50.8% | 5.5% |
| Accounts payable . . . . . . | 7.9% | 3.2 | 14.6 | 15.2 | 14.3 |
| Other current liabilities . . . . . | 14.7 | 2.2 | 10.6 | 5.7 | 10.5 |
| Long-term debt . . . . . . . | 19.3 | 29.6 | 15.8 | 22.7 | 9.2 |
| Other liabilities . . . . . . . | 17.9 | 17.8 | 8.5 | 1.3 | 2.5 |
| Owners' equity . . . . . . . | 37.8 | 45.4 | 46.0 | 4.3 | 58.0 |
| Total liabilities and equity . . . | 100.0% | 100.0% | 100.0% | 100.0% | 100.0% |
| | | | | | |
| *Selected Ratios* | | | | | |
| Net profits/Net sales . . . . . . | .04 | .16 | .014 | .01 | .05 |
| Net profits/Total assets . . . . . | .05 | .06 | .07 | .01 | .06 |
| Net profits/Owners' equity . . . . . | .12 | .13 | .15 | .13 | .12 |
| Net sales/Total assets . . . . . | 1.2 | .38 | 5.6 | 2.1 | 1.5 |
| Collection period (days) . . . . . | 71 | 52 | 3 | 106 | 23 |
| Inventory turnover . . . . . . | 12 | 11 | 12 | 23 | 1.2 |
| Total liabilities/Total assets . . . . | .62 | .55 | .54 | .96 | .42 |
| Long-term debt/Owners' equity . . | .51 | .65 | .34 | 5.3 | .16 |
| Current assets/Current liabilities . . | 1.7 | 1.3 | 2.0 | 1.0 | 2.9 |
| Quick ratio . . . . . . . . . . | 1.4 | .9 | .8 | .9 | .8 |

*Estimating Funds Requirements—*
*Short-Term Sources of Finance*

# Butler Lumber Company

After a rapid growth in its business during recent years, the Butler Lumber Company in the spring of 1991 anticipated a further substantial increase in sales. Despite good profits, the company had experienced a shortage of cash and had found it necessary to increase its borrowing from the Suburban National Bank to $247,000 in the spring of 1991. The maximum loan that Suburban National would make to any one borrower was $250,000, and Butler had been able to stay within this limit only by relying very heavily on trade credit. In addition, Suburban was now asking that Butler secure the loan with its real property. Mark Butler, sole owner and president of the Butler Lumber Company, was therefore actively looking elsewhere for a new banking relationship where he would be able to negotiate a larger and unsecured loan.

Mr. Butler had recently been introduced by a friend to George Dodge, an officer of a much larger bank, the Northrup National Bank. The two men had tentatively discussed the possibility that the Northrup bank might extend a line of credit to Butler Lumber up to a maximum amount of $465,000. Mr. Butler thought that a loan of this size would more than meet his foreseeable needs, but he was eager for the flexibility that a line of credit of this size would provide. Subsequent to this discussion Mr. Dodge had arranged for the credit department of the Northrup National Bank to investigate Mr. Butler and his company.

The Butler Lumber Company had been founded in 1981 as a partnership by Mr. Butler and his brother-in-law, Henry Stark. In 1988, Mr. Butler bought out Mr. Stark's interest for $105,000 and incorporated the business. Mr. Stark had taken a note for $105,000, to be paid off in 1989, in order to give Mr. Butler time to arrange for the financing necessary to make the payment of $105,000 to him. The major portion of the funds needed for this payment was raised by a loan of $70,000, negotiated in late 1988. This loan was secured by Butler's land and buildings, carried an interest rate of 11%, and was repayable in quarterly installments at the rate of $7,000 a year over the next 10 years.

The business was located in a growing suburb of a large city in the Pacific Northwest. The company owned land with access to a railroad siding, and two large storage buildings had been erected on this land. The company's operations were limited to the retail distribution of lumber products in the local area. Typical products included plywood, moldings, and sash and door products. Quantity discounts and credit terms of net 30 days on open account were usually offered to customers.

Sales volume had been built up largely on the basis of successful price competition, made possible by careful control of operating expenses and by quantity purchases of materials at substantial discounts. Most of the moldings and sash and door products, which constituted significant items of sales, were used for repair work. About 55% of total sales were made in the six months from April through September. No sales representatives were employed, orders being taken exclusively over the telephone. Annual sales of $1,697,000 in 1988, $2,013,000 in 1989, and $2,694,000 in 1990 yielded after-tax profits of $31,000 in 1988, $34,000 in 1989, and $44,000 in 1990.[1] Operating statements for the years 1988–1990 and for the three months ending March 31, 1991, are given in Exhibit 1.

Mr. Butler was an energetic man, 39 years of age, who worked long hours on the job. He was helped by an assistant who, in the words of the investigator of the Northrup National Bank, "has been doing and can do about everything that Mr. Butler does in the organization." Other employees numbered ten in early 1991, five of whom worked in the yard and drove trucks and five of whom assisted in the office and in sales.

As part of its customary investigation of prospective borrowers, the Northrup National Bank sent inquiries concerning Mr. Butler to a number of firms that had business dealings with him. The manager of one of his large suppliers, the Barker Company, wrote in answer:

> The conservative operation of his business appeals to us. He has not wasted his money in disproportionate plant investment. His operating expenses are as low as they could possibly be. He has personal control over every feature of his business, and he possesses sound judgment and a willingness to work harder than anyone I have ever known. This, with a good personality, gives him a good turnover; and from my personal experience in watching him work, I know that he keeps close check on his own credits.

All the other trade letters received by the bank bore out this opinion.

---

1. Sales in 1986 and 1987 amounted to $728,000 and $1,103,000, respectively; profit data for these years are not comparable with those of 1988 and later years because of the shift from a partnership to a corporate form of organization.

In addition to owning the lumber business, which was his major source of income, Mr. Butler held jointly with his wife an equity in their home. The house had cost $72,000 to build in 1979 and was mortgaged for $38,000. He also held a $70,000 life insurance policy, payable to Mrs. Butler. Mrs. Butler owned independently a half interest in a house worth about $55,000. Otherwise, they had no sizable personal investments.

The bank gave particular attention to the debt position and current ratio of the business. It noted the ready market for the company's products at all times and the fact that sales prospects were favorable. The bank's investigator reported: "Sales are expected to reach $3.5 million in 1991 and may exceed this level if prices of lumber should rise substantially in the near future." On the other hand, it was recognized that a general economic downturn might slow down the rate of increase in sales. Butler Lumber's sales, however, were protected to some degree from fluctuations in new housing construction because of the relatively high proportion of its repair business. Projections beyond 1991 were difficult to make, but the prospects appeared good for a continued growth in the volume of Butler Lumber's business over the foreseeable future.

The bank also noted the rapid increase in Butler Lumber's accounts and notes payable in the recent past, especially in the spring of 1991. The usual terms of purchase in the trade provided for a discount of 2% for payments made within 10 days of the invoice date. Accounts were due in 30 days at the invoice price, but suppliers ordinarily did not object if payments lagged somewhat behind the due date. During the last 2 years Mr. Butler had taken very few purchase discounts because of the shortage of funds arising from his purchase of Mr. Stark's interest in the business and the additional investments in working capital associated with the company's increasing sales volume. Trade credit was seriously extended in the spring of 1991 as Mr. Butler strove to hold his bank borrowing within the $250,000 ceiling imposed by the Suburban National Bank.

Balance sheets at December 31, 1988–1990, and March 31, 1991, are presented in Exhibit 2.

The tentative discussions between Mr. Dodge and Mr. Butler had been in terms of a revolving, secured 90-day note not to exceed $465,000. The specific details of the loan had not been worked out, but Mr. Dodge had explained that the agreement would involve the standard covenants applying to such a loan. He cited as illustrative provisions the requirement that restrictions on additional borrowing would be imposed, that net working capital would have to be maintained at an agreed level, that additional investments in fixed assets could be made only with the prior approval of the bank, and that limitations would be placed on withdrawals of funds from the business by Mr. Butler. Interest would be set on a floating-rate basis at 2 percentage points above the prime rate (the rate paid by the bank's most creditworthy customers). Mr. Dodge indicated that the initial rate to be paid would be approximately 10.5% under conditions in effect in early 1991. Both men also understood that Mr. Butler would sever his relationship with the Suburban National Bank if he entered into a loan agreement with the Northrup National Bank.

**EXHIBIT 1**

Operating Expenses for Years Ending December 31, 1988–1990, and for First Quarter 1991 (thousands of dollars)

| | 1988 | 1989 | 1990 | 1st Qtr 1991 |
|---|---|---|---|---|
| Net sales . . . . . . . . . . . . . | $1,697 | $2,013 | $2,694 | $ 718[a] |
| Cost of goods sold | | | | |
|   Beginning inventory . . . . . . . . . | 183 | 239 | 326 | 418 |
|   Purchases . . . . . . . . . . | 1,278 | 1,524 | 2,042 | 660 |
| | 1,461 | 1,763 | 2,368 | 1,078 |
|   Ending inventory . . . . . . . . | 239 | 326 | 418 | 556 |
|     Total cost of goods sold . . . . . . | 1,222 | 1,437 | 1,950 | 522 |
| Gross profit . . . . . . . . . | 475 | 576 | 744 | 196 |
| Operating expense[b] . . . . . . . . . | 425 | 515 | 658 | 175 |
| Interest expense . . . . . . . . . . | 13 | 20 | 33 | 10 |
| Net income before income taxes . . . . . . | 37 | 41 | 53 | 11 |
| Provision for income taxes . . . . . . . | 6 | 7 | 9 | 2 |
| Net income . . . . . . . . . . . | $ 31 | $ 34 | $ 44 | $ 9 |

a. In the first quarter of 1990 sales were $698,000 and net income was $7,000.

b. Operating expenses include a cash salary for Mr. Butler of $75,000 in 1988, $85,000 in 1989, $95,000 in 1990, and $22,000 in the first quarter of 1991. Mr. Butler also received some of the perquisites commonly taken by owners of privately held businesses.

**EXHIBIT 2**

Balance Sheets at December 31, 1988–1990, and March 31, 1991 (thousands of dollars)

| | 1988 | 1989 | 1990 | 1st Qtr 1991 |
|---|---|---|---|---|
| Cash . . . . . . . . . . . . . . | $ 58 | $ 49 | $ 41 | $ 31 |
| Accounts receivable, net . . . . . . . . . . | 171 | 222 | 317 | 345 |
| Inventory . . . . . . . . . . . . | 239 | 325 | 418 | 556 |
|   Current assets . . . . . . . . . | 468 | 596 | 776 | 932 |
| Property, net . . . . . . . . . . . | 126 | 140 | 157 | 162 |
|   Total assets . . . . . . . . . . | $594 | $736 | $933 | $1,094 |
| Notes payable, bank . . . . . . . . . . . | – | $146 | $233 | $ 247 |
| Notes payable, Mr. Stark . . . . . . . . . | $105 | – | – | – |
| Notes payable, trade . . . . . . . . . . | – | – | – | 157 |
| Accounts payable . . . . . . . . . | 124 | 192 | 256 | 243 |
| Accrued expenses . . . . . . . . . | 24 | 30 | 39 | 36 |
| Long-term debt, current portion . . . . . . . . . | 7 | 7 | 7 | 7 |
|   Current liabilities . . . . . . . . | 260 | 375 | 535 | 690 |
| Long-term debt . . . . . . . . . . | 64 | 57 | 50 | 47 |
|   Total liabilities . . . . . . . . | 324 | 432 | 585 | 737 |
| Net worth . . . . . . . . . . . . | 270 | 304 | 348 | 357 |
|   Total liabilities and net worth . . . . . . . | $594 | $736 | $933 | $1,094 |

# Note on Bank Loans

Bank loans are a versatile source of funding for businesses. For example, these loans can be structured as short- or long-term, fixed- or floating-rate, demand or with a fixed maturity, and secured or unsecured. While each potential borrower's business is unique, reasons to borrow generally include the purchase of assets, including new fixed assets or entire businesses; repayment of obligations; raising of temporary or permanent capital; and the meeting of unexpected needs. Loan repayment generally comes from one of four sources: operations, turnover or liquidation of assets, refinancing, or capital infusion. This note describes traditional bank lending products, the role of the lending officer, credit evaluation, and the structuring of credit facilities and loan agreements. Specialized loan and credit products are described in the Appendix.

## Traditional Commercial Bank Lending Products

While increased competition has forced banks to develop innovative credit facilities and financing techniques, traditional products, which include short-term, long-term, and revolving loans, continue to be the mainstay of commercial banking.

### Short-Term Loans

Short-term loans, those with maturities of 1 year or less, comprise more than half of all commercial bank loans. Seasonal lines of credit and special-purpose

Research Associate Susan L. Roth prepared this note under the supervision of Professor Scott P. Mason and with the assistance of the Citicorp Institute for Global Finance.

loans are the most common short-term credit facilities. Their primary use is to finance working capital needs resulting from temporary buildups of inventory and receivables. Reflecting their use, repayment of short-term loans typically comes from the routine conversion of current assets to cash. These loans may be either secured or unsecured.

A seasonal line of credit is used by companies with seasonal sales cycles to finance periodic increases in current assets, such as inventory. The amount of credit made available is based on the borrower's estimated peak funding requirements. The borrower may draw on the seasonal line of credit as funds are required and repay the line as seasonal sales lead to liquidation of inventories. Interest accrues only on the amount of borrowing outstanding. A bank's commitments under lines of credit may exceed its ability to fund them all simultaneously, though simultaneous demand is unlikely to occur. So as not to have a legal obligation to lend its capital to a borrower in the rare case that demand for funds does exceed supply, the bank may structure this facility with a provision that allows the bank to terminate the facility at its option or provide funding subject to availability.

Businesses use special-purpose loans to finance, on a temporary basis, increases in current assets resulting from unusual or unexpected circumstances. Funding is based on the borrower's estimated needs, with the bank agreeing to fund either all or up to some percentage of the full amount. The credit facility is most likely to require full payment of accrued interest and principal at maturity, that is, a "bullet." The term for such a loan is usually fixed and is determined by approximating the point in time when repayment can be made. The bank's principal risk with a special-purpose loan is default because of a change in the circumstances on which the repayment plan had been based. Therefore, from the bank's perspective, it is important that the source and timing of repayment be clear at the time of funding. Identifying alternatives to routine asset conversion as a source of repayment will further protect the bank.

## Long-Term Loans

Introduced in the 1930s, long-term loans, or term loans, are relatively new in banking practice. Providing advantages in its flexibility to adapt to a borrower's special requirements, a term loan has the following characteristics:

- Original maturity of longer than 1 year
- Repayment provided from future earnings or cash flow rather than from short-term liquidation of assets
- Provisions of the loan arrangement detailed in and governed by a signed loan agreement between the borrower and the lender

Term loans are most often used for specific purposes such as purchase of fixed assets, acquisition of another company, or refinancing of existing long-term debt. The term loan may also be used in place of equity or a revolving credit facility to finance permanent working capital needs. The loan's amount and structure will closely match the transaction being financed. A term loan is typically fully funded at its inception, and principal and interest are repaid over a period of years from operating cash flows generated by the borrower. The tenor, or maturity, of term loans ranges from 1 to 10 years, with the average being from 2 to 5 years. Although the lender does not look to liquidation of the acquired assets as the primary source of funds for repayment, a term loan is likely to be secured. Most often the security will be a claim on the assets purchased with the proceeds of the loan.

### Revolving Loans

The revolving credit loan, a variation on the line of credit, has a commitment period often extending beyond 1 year, up to 3 or 4 years, and allows a business to borrow from a bank up to a maximum commitment level at any time over the life of a credit. The borrower's use of proceeds under a revolving loan tends to be not for an isolated transaction but to fund day-to-day operations, meet seasonal needs, or otherwise provide the borrower with a discretionary range of when and how much to borrow and when to repay the loan. Unlike a line of credit, a revolving loan is often used to finance permanent working capital needs when equity and trade credit are inadequate to support a company's sales volume.

Over the term of a revolving credit facility, the borrower has the right to repay a loan and later reborrow those funds. But this right to reborrow is effective only when the borrower is in compliance with the loan agreement's terms and conditions. The amount of commitment is based upon the value of the assets being funded as well as the borrower's creditworthiness. The borrower pays a commitment fee, based on the total amount of the revolving facility, to secure a formal commitment from the bank. Many revolving loans are structured to convert to term loans or to automatically renew at maturity. The latter structure, called an evergreen facility, automatically renews a revolving credit facility until either the bank or the borrower gives notice of termination. Like other credit facilities, a revolving line of credit may be secured or unsecured.

## Role of the Loan Officer

"Banks succeed when the risks they assume are reasonable, controlled, and commensurate with their resources and credit competence. Lending officers, in turn, must accurately identify, measure, and manage risk if their banks are to succeed."[1]

The loan officer must balance two often conflicting responsibilities: those of a marketing officer and those of a credit officer. While budget pressures require the loan officer to develop new banking relationships, credit responsibilities require that these new relationships not sacrifice credit quality for short-term profits. "The costliest mistake that a bank management can make is to book unworthy loans in

---

1. P. Henry Mueller, "Lending Officers and Lending," in *Bank Credit,* ed. Herbert V. Prochnow (New York: Harper & Row, 1981), p. 92.

order to achieve budget goals.''[2] The lending institution's credit policy should give loan officers guidelines to enable them to balance loan quality and quantity and achieve the bank's earnings objectives.

The lending institution and its shareholders expect loan officers to understand a credit thoroughly before approving the lending of the bank's capital. The credit proposal memo, described in Exhibit 1, includes the information and analyses used to evaluate a potential borrower's creditworthiness. Every commitment of a lending institution typically requires independent approval and the signatures of at least two senior lending officers, who are held directly accountable for the lending decision. Direct accountability is intended to make them more critical of any exceptions to the bank's credit policy.

## Evaluating Creditworthiness

Before a bank agrees to commit its funds to a company, its loan officers analyze the prospective borrower to determine creditworthiness. Loan officers have a responsibility to ''grasp the quantitative and qualitative details of each transaction thoroughly, analyze its variables, and make adequate allowance for their impact.''[3] Evaluation of a borrower's ability and willingness to repay a loan at maturity involves financial analysis, including forecasting and sensitivity analysis, a qualitative assessment of management's character and capability, due diligence, and an identification and analysis of risk.

### Financial Analysis

A thorough financial analysis requires preparation of the following:

- Year-to-year comparisons of financial statements
- Cash flow statements
- Liquidity analysis
- Capital structure analysis
- Projections and sensitivity analysis
- Estimation of asset values: market value and liquidation value
- Comparison of actual versus budgeted performance

A first step in the financial analysis of a potential borrower is a determination of the quality of earnings and the strength of the balance sheet. To make this determination the credit officer analyzes financial, operating, and leverage ratios, and trends in revenues and expenses over time, and compares such ratios to industry averages, looking for positive and negative changes in the company's profitability and industry position.

---

2. P. Henry Mueller, *Perspective on Credit Risk* (Robert Morris Associates, 1988), p. 18.

3. Mueller, ''Lending Officers and Lending,'' p. 40.

The historical financial condition of a borrower, however, is an incomplete indication of creditworthiness. Because the loan will be approved or denied based, among other essential criteria, on an assessment of a borrower's ability to repay the loan from future cash flow generated by operations, an estimate of a borrower's future financial condition is important to the lending decision.

Pro forma financial and operating statements are prepared so that the lending officer may assess the borrower's potential to generate sufficient free cash flow to make interest and principal payments when due. These projections and the underlying assumptions must be tested under various scenarios to establish the borrower's sensitivity to change. While one cannot possibly test for every possible event, worst-case scenarios will indicate just how poorly the business can perform before the borrower defaults.

## Qualitative Assessment

Credit evaluation also requires assessment of the character and capabilities of the persons to whom a loan may be extended, that is, the persons responsible for achieving the goals of the operating and financial plans. Lenders must determine the quality, breadth, and depth of the management team. Assessing its ability to implement operating and financial plans gives the lender insight into the management team's capability. Banks pay a high price for hasty credit decisions. Though gauging the integrity of a new customer takes time, integrity is a critical component of any lending decision. Management's interests should be aligned with the company's and with the bank's interests and expectations. Ownership and compensation systems indicate management's stake in the business.

## Due Diligence

Due diligence is the process of going out and "kicking the tires" of the potential borrower. While time-consuming, it is an important aid to understanding better how the prospective borrower does business. Due diligence can include plant tours, trade checks, and interviews with the borrower's competitors, suppliers, customers, and employees. Comprehensive due diligence also includes reviews of employee relations, compensation and benefits, management's planned capital expenditures, other debt obligations, and management information systems and technology. An environmental audit may also be necessary. Due diligence should also uncover any contingent liabilities that may materially affect the borrower's ability to repay the loan at maturity. Unfunded pension liabilities, pending or threatened legal proceedings, and guarantees by the borrower are some examples of contingent liabilities.

## Risk Assessment

Risk assessment is another component of the credit evaluation process. The credit officer must identify and analyze the key risks associated with a specific credit.

Some risks are associated with the borrower and his or her business; with potential changes in the environment; and with cyclical activity and regulatory or other unanticipated developments. The loan officer must make judgments about future conditions that could affect a borrower's willingness and ability to repay the obligation. Determining potential risks and assessing their level of severity, the probability that they will occur, and the estimated costs associated with their occurrence are critical. The structure of the credit facility and loan agreement attempts to minimize risk.

### Determining the Bank's Willingness and Ability to Lend

In addition to conducting a thorough credit evaluation, the loan officer must determine whether approving a loan application is in the bank's best interests and within regulatory capital and operating guidelines. A bank's ability to lend is restricted by banking regulations that limit the amount of loans that may be extended to any one borrower. A bank may also establish an internal limit (''house limit'') on the amount lent to a single borrower. What influences a bank's willingness to lend are its earnings targets and portfolio objectives. A bank attempts to maintain diversification in its portfolio of loans and investments to reduce its exposure to risk. These targets and objectives shape a bank's loan origination and acquisition strategy. Thus a potential borrower must not only meet the lending institution's credit standards but also be within its target lending market and legal lending capacity.

## Structuring the Credit Facility and Loan Agreement

Once creditworthiness is ascertained and the bank decides it is willing and able to extend credit to a company, the bank and the borrower can begin to structure an appropriate credit facility and loan agreement. The strength and the nature of a credit and the bank's credit policy help to determine the terms and conditions defined in a loan agreement.

Typically, short-term loans are not made pursuant to a loan agreement, or if so, the loan agreement is far less comprehensive than that used for long-term or revolving loans. The loan agreement discussed in this note applies to term and revolving loans and includes the following sections:

- Amount and terms of the credit facility
- Conditions precedent
- Representations and warranties
- Covenants of the borrower
- Events of default

### Amount and Terms of the Credit Facility

This first section of a standard loan agreement describes how much and when the borrower may borrow, the interest provisions, repayment terms and additional fees, the intended use of loan proceeds, and any security interest taken by the bank.

The amount of a bank's commitment under a credit facility may be stipulated or based on a formula, for instance, a percentage of accounts receivable. The interest rate charged for use of those committed funds may be based on either a fixed or a floating rate. The use of a fixed or a floating interest rate, the method for determining the floating rate and reset periods, if applicable, and the method for computing accrued interest are negotiable factors. Interest can be computed on the basis of a 360- or a 365-day year. Computation using a 360-day year yields a higher effective rate for the borrower.

Additional fees the bank may charge include commitment and closing fees. The borrower pays a commitment fee to compensate the bank for its use of the bank's capital over the duration of the commitment. This fee typically ranges from .25% to .75% per year. The borrower may also pay a closing fee on the day the loan closes, that is, the date the loan's legal framework is in place. This payment compensates the bank for work done thus far in evaluating the borrower's creditworthiness and setting up a credit facility for it. In a competitive situation this fee may be .25% to .375%; in a high-risk situation it can be as much as 2.00% to 2.50% of the amount of the commitment. A penalty or default rate of interest may also be stipulated. Applied in the event that payments are not made when due, this rate is set high enough so that it would not be to the borrower's economic advantage to delay payments.

The option to prepay and the option to reduce the total commitment are provisions negotiated in this section of the loan agreement for term loans and revolving loans, respectively. These provisions distinguish most bank financing from alternative sources of funds. Under a revolving credit facility, the right to reduce the amount of the commitment is valuable to the borrower should the company's financing needs change. Reducing the amount of the commitment will reduce the commitment fee paid by the borrower, since it is based on the total commitment.

In the case of a term loan, the loan agreement may provide for full or partial prepayment of the loan at the borrower's discretion, with or without a premium or upon occurrence of certain events. The option to repay provides a route of escape from covenants that may become overly restrictive. Prepayment also works in favor of the borrower should the cost of other sources of funds decline significantly over the term of the loan, making refinancing more economical. Recognizing the value of this right, a borrower may agree to tighter covenants or a higher rate of interest than if locked in by prepayment restrictions.

A description of the use of loan proceeds is also included in this first section of the loan agreement to assure the bank that the borrower intends to use the loan proceeds in the manner understood by the bank.

An additional provision negotiated in this section of the loan agreement is the taking of collateral or guarantees to secure a loan. A claim on certain assets of the borrower can mitigate the bank's loss should the borrower default. Assets used as collateral are typically those purchased with the loan proceeds; levels of collateral are typically commensurate with the creditworthiness of the borrower.

It is often to the bank's advantage to take as much security as possible against a loan.

If the borrower defaults on a secured loan, the bank has the right to take control of and liquidate the pledged assets. Funds from the liquidation are applied against the amount outstanding on the defaulted loan. If default is on an unsecured loan, the bank is only a general creditor of the business and recovery of the principal is less likely.

## Conditions Precedent

The conditions precedent are requirements the borrower must satisfy before the bank has a legal obligation to fund a commitment. These conditions may include any business transactions that must be completed or events that must have occurred. Other standard items in this section are the opinions of counsel, certificate of no defaults, the note, and resolutions of the borrower's board of directors authorizing the transaction. The conditions precedent will also include a material adverse change clause encompassing both balance sheet condition and operations (income statement and prospects). This clause serves an important protective function for the lender in the case that a material adverse change occurs prior to funding and is not yet reflected in the financial statements.

## Representations and Warranties

In considering a loan application, the lender relies on certain information furnished by the borrower and has thereupon made assumptions about the borrower's legal status, creditworthiness, and business position. It is upon these assumptions that the bank has agreed to lend money to the borrower. The representations and warranties section documents the information and assumptions relied upon. By executing the loan agreement, the borrower confirms the accuracy and truth of the information provided as of the date of execution. Misrepresentation constitutes an event of default. Principal representations and warranties include:

- Financial statements are correct, and there has been no material adverse change in the financial condition of the borrower
- The borrower is not subject to any litigation, pending or threatened, or party to a contract that could effect a material adverse change in the business position of the borrower
- Other facts pertinent to the credit judgment are correct
- No factual misstatement or omission in information furnished
- Due incorporation
- Continued existence
- The loan agreement will be legal, valid, and binding when signed
- No need for third-party consent
- Corporate authority
- No violation of existing agreements

- No violation of laws
- All tax returns have been filed; all taxes have been paid
- Collateral offered is owned by the borrower and free of liens

The material adverse change clause is designed to cover circumstances in which the borrower's ability to perform obligations under the loan agreement is thrown into doubt. With regard to the financial statements, the material adverse change clause is used to verify that there has been no material adverse change in the borrower's financial condition or operations since the date of the financial statements relied upon for the credit evaluation. This section may also contain a representation as to the accuracy of other information not included in the financial statements, including nonpublic information such as cash flow statements and projections, supplied by the borrower to the bank and fundamental to the credit decision.

The representations and warranties section also contains material adverse change standards with respect to actual or threatened legal proceedings where the outcome could significantly affect the strength of the borrower's credit standing in the eyes of the bank. These standards may also be broadened to include circumstances that may not be reflected immediately in the borrower's financial statements or result in litigation.

## Covenants of the Borrower

Covenants are a heavily negotiated part of loan agreements. As representations and warranties verify certain statements by the borrower at the date of execution of the loan agreement, covenants carry forward the representations and warranties, and establish the borrower's ongoing obligation to maintain a certain status for the loan's duration. Covenants set minimum standards for a borrower's future conduct and performance, and thereby reduce the risk that the loan will not be repaid. Violation of a covenant creates an event of default and gives the bank the right to refuse to make additional advances.

The use of certain covenants depends upon such factors as the nature of the borrower's business, the financial condition of the borrower, and the term of the loan. If credit risk is high, covenants may be tied directly to detailed financial projections provided by the borrower. If credit risk is low, a few general financial benchmarks may be sufficient. In any case, covenants should be no more restrictive than the policies any prudent manager would follow to maintain or build a solid credit rating, but they should be designed to give early warning of deterioration in the financial condition of the borrower. Covenants should also be drafted to allow for normal seasonal and cyclical variations of the borrower's business so that an event of default is not likely to occur.

**Affirmative Covenants.** Affirmative covenants stipulate actions the borrower must take, and would normally take even if the loan were not in effect. Generally they include the following:

- Application of loan proceeds to specified purpose
- Financial covenants
- Reporting requirements
- Compliance with laws
- Preservation of corporate existence
- Rights of inspection
- Maintenance of insurance
- Maintenance of properties
- Maintenance of records and books of account

As in the first section of the loan agreement, the borrower must assure the bank that the proceeds of the loan will be used in the manner the bank understood in its decision to extend credit.

Financial covenants are those based on information contained in the borrower's financial statements and focus on the borrower's financial position and overall operations. Financial covenants establish guidelines for operation of the borrower's business, carry forward the borrower's representations and warranties regarding its financial position, further help the bank to gather information about the borrower, and permit exercise of remedies upon default. Financial covenants establish minimum financial tests with which a borrower must comply. These tests can specify dollar amounts, such as (tangible) net worth and working capital, or ratios such as the current or quick ratios, net worth ratios, leverage ratio, and fixed-charge coverage ratio. Financial covenants should signal financial difficulty and be triggered long before liquidation or bankruptcy filing becomes necessary. They may be used like other affirmative and negative covenants to guide management decisions on an ongoing basis, or serve only as periodic tests.

To keep the bank informed of financial and operating performance, the borrower covenants that he or she will meet certain established reporting requirements and provide such information to the lender in a timely fashion. This information allows the bank's lending officer to monitor the borrower's financial condition and compliance with covenants.

**Negative Covenants.**   The negative covenants tend to be more significant and more heavily negotiated than affirmative covenants because they place clear restrictions upon managerial decisions. These restrictions are intended to prevent management decisions that might impair the borrower's liquidity or solvency, or jeopardize the bank's claim against the borrower's earnings and assets.

Negative covenants typically include the following:

- Restrictions on mortgages, pledges, or other encumbrance of assets (negative pledge)
- Limitation on total indebtedness
- Restrictions on payment of cash dividends
- Restrictions on repurchase of shares

- Restrictions on mergers
- Restrictions on sale of assets
- Restrictions on sale of subsidiaries
- Limitation on capital expenditure
- Restrictions on engaging in other businesses
- Restrictions on voluntary prepayment of other indebtedness
- Limitation on investment of funds
- Limitation on loans and advances
- Limitations on leasing arrangements

The negative pledge covenant is designed to prevent the borrower from creating liens on its assets or earnings for the benefit of other lenders. Its purpose is to provide a pool of assets that will be available for payment of unsecured creditors' claims equally, without preference of one over another in the event of default. The negative pledge is typically given to an unsecured creditor.

Restrictions on total indebtedness apply to a variety of debt instruments and often include capital lease obligations, deferred payment obligations, unfunded vested pension liabilities, guaranteed indebtedness, and indebtedness of others secured by property of the borrower. This restriction is usually stated as a specified amount or in the form of a ratio (total debt to total assets, to working capital, or to [tangible] net worth) and serves to limit the amount of additional indebtedness the borrower may incur over the term of the loan. The restriction may differ for short- and long-term obligations, and exceptions to the limit may be made for certain debt instruments such as subordinated debt.

In restricting the borrower's ability to merge or transfer a substantial part of its assets, the bank is ensuring the survival of the borrower's obligation. With reference to the sale or transfer of assets, those assets or subsidiaries fundamental to the bank's credit analysis should be specified as restricted from sale or transfer. Assets not involving the transfer of the borrower's business in or near its entirety should not be restricted by this covenant.

Restrictions on the use of funds for dividend payments, repurchase of shares, capital expenditures, or otherwise are included so that the bank may be further assured that cash will be available to make interest and principal payments when due. These restrictions and limitations also ensure the borrower's general adherence to its operating plan.

## Events of Default

The events of default section describes circumstances in which the bank has the right to terminate the lending relationship. Situations leading to the declaration of an event of default include the following:

- Failure to pay interest or principal when due
- Inaccuracy in representations and warranties

- Failure to abide by a covenant
- Bankruptcy, liquidation, appointment of receiver
- Entry of a judgment in excess of a specified amount
- Impairment of collateral, invalidity of a guaranty or security agreement
- Failure to pay other indebtedness when due or perform under related agreements: cross-default and cross-acceleration
- Change of management or ownership
- Extraordinary circumstances
- Expropriation of assets
- Material adverse change

Upon the occurrence of an event of default, the most common remedy lenders exercise is the renegotiation of the loan agreement. In some cases, usually where the circumstances are considered less significant, the loan agreement provides the borrower a period of time, referred to as a cure or grace period, to correct its breach of a covenant. If the default is cured, the bank is then required to continue providing the loan to the borrower.

In the case where the default is not cured and the loan agreement is not negotiable, the bank may accelerate the loan and terminate the lending relationship. The bank may also set off the borrower's deposits against its obligation to repay the loan and exercise its right to foreclose on security covered under a security agreement.

The cross-default provision gives the bank the right to declare an event of default when the borrower is in default on another obligation. This provision is designed to prevent the bank from being placed at a disadvantage if competition to obtain repayment begins among the borrower's creditors, that is, the borrower has defaulted under another loan agreement and the lender is demanding payment.

Although banks rarely exercise the right to accelerate loan repayment, having this right substantially strengthens a lender's negotiating position with the borrower and other creditors of the borrower if problems are encountered with the loan. Acceleration is used sparingly by banks, since use by one could cause its invocation by other creditors and precipitate a bankruptcy.

## Sale of Loans to Third Parties

No longer is the price of a loan set at the discretion of the loan officer guided by the lending institution. With increasing pressure to sell loans to third parties, the market is becoming the most influential factor in setting price.

Certain changes in the regulation of banks and in the business of commercial banking have precipitated increasing sales of loans. Regulatory changes, including new risk-based capital guidelines adopted by the Basle Committee on Banking Regulations and Supervisory Practices on July 11, 1988, require banks to be better capitalized (tangible net worth as a percentage of total assets). This is costly and restricts lending capacity. In addition to the risk-based capital guidelines, regulations and internal bank lending policies restricting the amount of loans a bank can make to one borrower or group of borrowers often force banks to sell off all or a portion of the loans they originate.

Several vehicles facilitate the sale of loans, some allowing an originating bank to maintain partial ownership of the loan or responsibility for its management. Participations, syndications, and asset sales are all examples of underwriting activities undertaken by banks.

## Participations

A participation loan is a single loan made to a large borrower by more than one lender. Participation loans are made when the lead lender cannot lend to a large borrower because of legal or internal lending limits restricting the amount of bank capital that can be loaned to one borrower or classification of borrowers. The lead bank originates the transaction and maintains responsibility for servicing the loan.

Many loan participations come about through correspondent banking relationships. A correspondent bank performs services for a bank in a market that is inaccessible to the other. Both banks must evaluate the creditworthiness of the borrower and independently decide to enter into the participation. While credit decisions are made independently, risk may not always be shared equally in participations. Some participations are structured on a last in, first out (LIFO) basis so that the originator, or first in, takes a larger portion of the risk associated with the participation loan.

## Syndication

Syndications are similar to loan participations, except that the syndicate members lend directly to the borrower. An originating bank, called the lead bank or manager, arranges a credit facility for a large borrower. The bank then sells off portions of the loan to other lenders.

Syndication has been used increasingly for several reasons, including the ability to spread risk across lenders, to lend to large borrowers when the size of the individual credit is larger than legal or internal standards would allow, and the ability to integrate the borrower's banking relationships. The syndicate members' obligations are separate; one lender is not responsible for the commitment of another; however, the rights and obligations of all the parties (the syndicate members and the borrower) are governed by one agreement, the syndicate loan agreement. Each participant in a syndication shares in the loan's risks and makes its own credit decision.

There are two types of syndicates: best-efforts and firm (or underwritten) commitment. In a best-efforts syndicate the manager will market the loan under the agreed-upon terms and conditions, but if the syndication is not fully subscribed, the loan will not be made and the manager retains no legal obligation to the borrower. In a firm commitment syndicate the lead bank agrees to make the loan regardless of its ability to fully syndicate it.

In a syndicate, a borrower pays certain fees in addition to interest on the loan: a commitment fee based on the amount of the credit and the undrawn portion; a management fee paid to the syndicate managers as compensation for assembling the syndicate and servicing the loan; and participation fees to syndicate participants based on the amount of their commitments. Participation fees range from .25% to 1.50% and are used to attract lending institutions to a syndicate. The agency fee paid to the bank servicing the loan can range from $5,000 a year for a routine transaction to $500,000 a year for a more complex transaction.

## Asset Sale

A relatively recent development has been the sale of loans to third parties. An asset or loan sale is similar to a syndicate except that the lead bank initially takes the credit on its books and then sells off most or all of the credit, retaining little or nothing for its own portfolio. In this transaction all risk from the sold portion is eliminated for the originating bank, and the loan is removed from its balance sheet. The bank earns a fee for its efforts in originating the loan. An asset sale typically occurs as a second phase to a syndication.

**EXHIBIT 1**
The Credit Proposal Memo

The credit proposal memo and presentation typically includes the following information and analyses:

- Company background and relationship with the bank
- Purpose of the credit extension
- Financial statement analysis, cash flow projections, and debt service capacity
- Assessment of management process, strengths, and weaknesses
- Assessment of major risks, including impact of forecasted economic trends and the strength of competitors
- Analysis of repayment sources for all facilities and timing for those with a tenor, or maturity, of greater than 1 year
- Summary of loan structure and repayment terms
- Summary of key covenants and repayment terms of other instruments that might materially affect the position of the bank
- Statement of adherence to credit policy guidelines or explanation of exceptions
- Analysis of collateral
- Listing of noncredit products
- Trade or bank checkings
- Comment on trustee relationships
- Account plans

*Source:* Citicorp Institute for Global Finance.

# Appendix

# Specialized Loans and Credit Products

## Trade Finance Products

Trade finance products are specialized bank products designed to reduce the risks and uncertainties associated with commercial transactions by substituting the bank's credit risk for that of the purchaser of the goods. Thus, they facilitate trade.

When entering into trade finance credit arrangements, the bank evaluates the obligor's creditworthiness in much the same way it evaluates other short-term credits. The most common trade finance products are letters of credit and banker's acceptances.

**Letters of Credit (L/C).**   A letter of credit represents a conditional promise to pay and is generally non-negotiable. It substitutes the bank's credit for that of its customers by providing a guarantee of payment to the third party upon the satisfaction of certain conditions. This differs from the banker's acceptance which, in effect, is payment.

In trade finance, a letter of credit is usually issued by the purchaser's bank, which agrees to pay the purchaser's obligation to a seller upon receiving proof that a specified delivery has been made. The bank has no obligation to delve into the content of the underlying commercial transaction (i.e., the sales agreement between the seller and buyer) except as specifically required by the terms of the L/C. The purchaser agrees to pay the bank the sales amount plus a fee.

The term of an L/C is generally related to the expected amount of time needed to complete the transaction. It may be revocable or irrevocable. A revocable L/C can be withdrawn, without notice to the beneficiary, at any time prior to actual performance of the transaction. An irrevocable L/C cannot be withdrawn before its expiration.

Stand-by letters of credit differ from trade L/Cs in that the issuing bank agrees to pay the L/C beneficiary only if its client defaults on payment to the beneficiary. So, in the above example, the seller would collect from the issuing bank only upon default of the purchaser.

**Banker's Acceptances.**   A banker's acceptance represents the bank's commitment to pay a specific amount of money on a specific date. This commitment arises when the bank agrees to pay the obligations of a purchaser to enhance its creditworthiness. The commitment is created when a seller prepares a time draft[4] ordering a buyer to pay for goods purchased upon their receipt. Once signed and acknowledged by the purchaser and "accepted" by the purchaser's bank, the draft becomes a banker's acceptance. The liability accepted by the bank is called acceptance liability.

The banker's acceptance is a short-term instrument generally with a duration of six months or less. The purchaser on whose behalf the banker's acceptance was accepted repays the bank under agreed-upon terms from the proceeds on the resale of the purchased goods. Since it is a negotiable instrument, the holder of a banker's acceptance may sell it to a third party or the bank, usually at a discount, to receive payment immediately. Thus, the banker's acceptance can be used as a form of accounts receivable financing.

## Factoring

Factoring is a method of accounts receivable financing in which the lender purchases the borrower's receivables. By purchasing a firm's accounts receivable, the bank assumes certain risks and activities it does not have with typical accounts receivable financing, in which a lender lends money to a company based on its accounts receivable balance. Factoring gives the bank legal ownership of the receivables and therefore the risk of accounts receivable defaults. The credit and collection functions formerly handled by the company may be undertaken by the bank. A lender may provide factoring services on a discount or maturity basis.

---

4. A time draft is one that is due upon presentation and acceptance by the purchaser's bank after a specified period of time, e.g., 30 or 60 days.

Discount factoring is a service in which the seller of the receivables receives payment from the bank before their expected maturities. The amount the bank is willing to lend is based on the accounts receivable balance less discounts and estimated returns and bad debts. Interest is charged based on the average daily balances owed.

Maturity factoring differs from discount factoring in that the lender performs the credit and collection functions and pays the borrower on invoice due dates. The factor receives a fee based on handling costs and estimated bad-debt risk.

## Asset-Based Lending

Traditional loans may be secured by the assets of the borrower, and repayment is assumed to come from operating cash flow or conversion of current assets to cash. Asset-based loans differ from traditional loans in that the borrower's ability to repay the borrowed funds from operating cash flows is less predictable. A lender making an asset-based loan looks mainly to the value of the assets securing the loan for repayment of the obligation. Asset-based loans are made against accounts receivable, inventory, and equipment.

In lending against accounts receivable, the asset-based lender agrees, after careful analysis, to lend up to a certain percentage of the accounts receivable. The percentage of face value the lender lends against will be based upon the age, quality, and concentration of accounts receivable, keeping in mind the liquidation value should the borrower default. Generally the lender will lend up to 80% of face value of the qualifying receivables amount. Qualifying receivables is the total amount less nonconforming receivables.

The analysis of inventory is similar to the analysis of accounts receivable, where current information and ongoing monitoring are key to successful lending. The lender will identify the percentage of inventory in raw materials, work-in-process, and finished goods inventories that qualify to be lent against based on their potential liquidation value. The advance rate against inventory is relatively low, sometimes 50% or less. This conservatism reflects the concerns for spoilage, technical obsolescence, and frequent deep discounts in disposing of inventories very quickly.

In lending against equipment, the asset-based lender has little concern for historical cost, fair market value, or replacement value. The lender instead wants to determine the value in a forced liquidation sale after related expenses, for instance, the cost of removing the equipment. Asset-based lenders will typically lend up to 80% of the forced sale value of machinery and equipment.

# Play Time Toy Company

Early in January 1991, Jonathan King, president and part owner of Play Time Toy Company, was considering a proposal to adopt level monthly production for the coming year. In the past, the company's production schedules had always been highly seasonal, reflecting the seasonality of sales. Mr. King was aware that a marked improvement in production efficiency could result from level production, but he was uncertain what the impact on other phases of the business might be.

Play Time Toy Company was a manufacturer of plastic toys for children. Its product groups included military toys, toy cars, trucks, construction equipment, guns, rockets, spaceships and satellites, musical instruments, animals, robots, and action figures. In most of these product categories the company produced a wide range of designs, colors, and sizes. Dollar sales of a particular product had sometimes varied by 30–35% from one year to the next.

The manufacture of plastic toys was a highly competitive business. The industry was populated by a large number of companies, many of which were short on capital and management talent. Since capital requirements were not large and the technology was relatively simple, it was easy for new competitors to enter the industry. On the other hand, design and price competition was fierce, resulting in short product lives and a relatively high rate of company failures. A company was sometimes able to steal a march on the competition by designing a popular new toy, often of the fad variety. Such items generally commanded very high margins until competitors were able to offer a similar product. For example, Play

Time's introduction of rock musician action figures in 1988 had contributed importantly to that year's profits. In 1989, however, 11 competitors marketed a similar product, and the factory price of the Play Time offering plummeted. In recent years, competitive pressures on smaller firms had also intensified with the rise of a number of large foreign toy manufacturers with low labor costs.

## Company Background

Play Time Toy Company had been founded in 1973 by Henry Richards after his release from naval service. Before his military service, Mr. Richards had been employed as production manager by a large manufacturer of plastic toys. Mr. Richards and his former assistant, Jonathan King, established Play Time Toy Company with their savings in 1973. Originally a partnership, the firm was incorporated in 1974, with Mr. Richards taking 75% of the capital stock and Mr. King taking 25%. The latter served as production manager, and Mr. Richards as president was responsible for overall direction of the company's affairs. After a series of illnesses, Mr. Richards' health deteriorated, and he was forced to retire from active participation in the business in 1987. Mr. King assumed the presidency at that time. In 1989 he hired Thomas Lindop, a recent graduate of a prominent eastern technical institute, as production manager. Mr. Lindop had worked summers in the plastics plant of a large diversified chemical company and thus had a basic familiarity with plastics production processes.

## Company Growth

Play Time Toy Company had experienced relatively rapid growth since its founding and had enjoyed profitable operations each year since 1976. Sales had been $7.4 million in 1990, and on the strength of a number of promising new products, sales were projected at $9.0 million for 1991. Net profits had reached $244,000 in 1990 and were estimated at $293,000 in 1991 under seasonal production. Tables A and B present the latest financial statements for the company. The cost of goods sold had averaged 70% of sales in the past and was expected to maintain

**TABLE A**
Condensed Income Statements, 1988–1990 (thousands of dollars)

|  | *1988* | *1989* | *1990* |
|---|---|---|---|
| Net sales | $5,198 | $5,950 | $7,433 |
| Cost of goods sold | 3,586 | 4,284 | 5,203 |
| Gross profit | 1,612 | 1,666 | 2,230 |
| Operating expenses | 1,270 | 1,549 | 1,860 |
| Profit before taxes | 342 | 117 | 370 |
| Federal income taxes | 116 | 46 | 126 |
| Net profit | $ 226 | $ 71 | $ 244 |

**TABLE B**
Balance Sheet at December 31, 1990 (thousands of dollars)

| | |
|---|---:|
| Cash | $ 175 |
| Accounts receivable | 2,628 |
| Inventory | 530 |
| Current assets | 3,333 |
| Plant and equipment, net | 1,070 |
| Total assets | $4,403 |
| | |
| Accounts payable | $ 255 |
| Notes payable, bank | 680 |
| Accrued taxes[a] | 80 |
| Long-term debt, current portion | 50 |
| Current liabilities | 1,065 |
| Long-term debt | 400 |
| Shareholders' equity | 2,938 |
| Total liabilities and shareholders' equity | $4,403 |

a. The company was required to make estimated tax payments on the 15th of April, June, September, and December. In 1990 it elected to base its estimated tax payments on the previous year's tax. The balance of $80,000 was due on March 15, 1991.

approximately that proportion in 1991 under seasonal production. In keeping with the company's experience, operating expenses were likely to be incurred evenly throughout each month of 1991 under either seasonal or level production.

Expanding operations had resulted in a somewhat strained working capital position for Play Time Toy Company. The year-end cash balance of $175,000 in 1990 was regarded as the minimum necessary for the operations of the business. The company had periodically borrowed from its bank of account, Bay Trust Company, on an unsecured line of credit. A loan of $680,000 was outstanding at the end of 1990. Mr. King had been assured that the bank would be willing to extend a credit line of up to $1.9 million in 1991, with the understanding that the loan would be completely repaid and off the books for at least a 30-day period during the year and would be secured by the accounts receivable and inventory of Play Time. Interest would be charged at a rate of 11%, and any advances in excess of $1.9 million would be subject to further negotiations.

The company's sales were highly seasonal. Over 80% of annual dollar volume was usually sold between August and November. Table C shows sales by month for 1990 and projected monthly sales for 1991. Sales were made principally to large variety store chains and toy brokers. Although the company quoted terms of net 30 days, most customers took 60 days to pay; however, collection experience had been excellent.

The company's production processes were not complex. Plastic molding powder, the principal raw material, was processed by injection molding presses and formed into the shapes desired. The plastic shapes were next painted at merry-go-round painting machines. The final steps in the process were assembly of the toy sets and packaging in cardboard cartons or plastic bags. Typically, all runs

**TABLE C**
Monthly Sales Data (thousands of dollars)

|  | Sales 1990 | Projected Sales 1991 |
|---|---|---|
| January | $ 70 | $ 108 |
| February | 88 | 126 |
| March | 98 | 145 |
| April | 90 | 125 |
| May | 88 | 125 |
| June | 95 | 125 |
| July | 98 | 145 |
| August | 1,173 | 1,458 |
| September | 1,390 | 1,655 |
| October | 1,620 | 1,925 |
| November | 1,778 | 2,057 |
| December | 850 | 1,006 |

begun were completed on the same day, so that there was virtually no work in process at the end of the day. Purchases on net 30 day terms were made weekly in amounts necessary for estimated production in the forthcoming week. Total purchases in 1991 were forecast at $2,700,000. It was the company's policy to retire trade debt promptly as it came due.

Mr. Lindop, the production manager, believed the company would be able to hold capital expenditures during the next year to an amount equal to depreciation, although he had cautioned that projected volume for 1991 would approach the full capacity of Play Time's equipment.

Play Time Toy Company's practice was to produce in response to customer orders. This meant only a small fraction of capacity was needed to meet demand for the first seven months of the year. Ordinarily, not more than 25–30% of manufacturing capacity was used at any one time during this period. The first sizable orders for Christmas business arrived around the middle of August. From August to December the work force was greatly expanded and put on overtime, and all equipment was utilized 16 hours a day. In 1990 overtime premiums had amounted to $165,000. Shipments were made whenever possible on the day that an order was produced. Hence, production and sales amounts in each month tended to be equal.

As in the past, pro forma balance sheets and income statements based on an assumption of seasonal production had been prepared for 1991 and presented to Mr. King for his examination. These appear in Exhibits 1 and 2.

## The Proposed Change to Level Production

Having experienced one selling season at Play Time, Mr. Lindop was deeply impressed by the many problems that arose from the company's method of scheduling production. Overtime premiums reduced profits; seasonal expansion and contraction of the work force resulted in recruiting difficulties and high training and quality control costs. Machinery stood idle for seven-and-a-half months and then was subjected to heavy use. Accelerated production schedules during the peak season resulted in frequent setup changes on the machinery. Seemingly unavoidable confusion in scheduling runs resulted. Short runs and frequent setup changes caused inefficiencies in assembly and packaging as workers encountered difficulty relearning their operations.

For these reasons, Mr. Lindop had urged Mr. King to adopt a policy of level monthly production in 1991. He pointed out that estimates of sales volume had usually proved to be reliable in the past. Purchase terms would not be affected by the rescheduling of purchases. The elimination of overtime wage premiums would result in substantial savings, estimated at $200,000 in 1991. Moreover, Mr. Lindop firmly believed that significant additional direct labor savings, amounting to about $235,000, would result from orderly production. A portion of the savings would be offset, however, by higher storage and handling costs, estimated at $100,000 annually. Mr. King speculated on the effect that level production might have on the company's funds requirements in 1991. He assumed that except for profits and fluctuations in the levels of inventories, accounts receivable, and accounts payable, funds inflows and outflows would be approximately in balance. To simplify the problem, Mr. King decided to assume that gross margin percentages would not vary significantly by month under either method of production; that is, cost of goods sold would be 70% of sales in each of the 12 months under seasonal production and would be 65.16% of sales in each of the 12 months under level production. The increased storage and handling costs of $100,000 would be included in operating expenses.

# EXHIBIT 1

Pro Forma Balance Sheets under Seasonal Production, 1991 (thousands of dollars)

| | Actual Dec. 31, 1990 | Jan. | Feb. | Mar. | Apr. | May | June | July | Aug. | Sept. | Oct. | Nov. | Dec. |
|---|---|---|---|---|---|---|---|---|---|---|---|---|---|
| Cash[a] | $ 175 | $ 787 | $1,366 | $1,110 | $ 924 | $ 794 | $ 587 | $ 428 | $ 175 | $ 175 | $ 175 | $ 175 | $ 175 |
| Accounts receivable[b] | 2,628 | 958 | 234 | 271 | 270 | 250 | 250 | 270 | 1,603 | 3,113 | 3,580 | 3,982 | 3,063 |
| Inventory[c] | 530 | 530 | 530 | 530 | 530 | 530 | 530 | 530 | 530 | 530 | 530 | 530 | 530 |
| Current assets | 3,333 | 2,275 | 2,130 | 1,911 | 1,724 | 1,574 | 1,367 | 1,228 | 2,308 | 3,818 | 4,285 | 4,687 | 3,768 |
| Net plant and equipment[d] | 1,070 | 1,070 | 1,070 | 1,070 | 1,070 | 1,070 | 1,070 | 1,070 | 1,070 | 1,070 | 1,070 | 1,070 | 1,070 |
| Total assets | $4,403 | $3,345 | $3,200 | $2,981 | $2,794 | $2,644 | $2,437 | $2,298 | $3,378 | $4,888 | $5,355 | $5,757 | $4,838 |
| | | | | | | | | | | | | | |
| Accounts payable[e] | $ 255 | $ 33 | $ 38 | $ 43 | $ 37 | $ 37 | $ 38 | $ 44 | $ 438 | $ 496 | $ 577 | $ 617 | $ 302 |
| Notes payable, bank[f] | 80 | 0 | 0 | 0 | 0 | 0 | 0 | 0 | 437 | 1,611 | 1,608 | 1,541 | 880 |
| Accrued taxes[g] | 50 | 27 | (24) | (153) | (235) | (286) | (369) | (419) | (334) | (260) | (128) | 18 | 25 |
| Long-term debt, current portion | 50 | 50 | 50 | 50 | 50 | 50 | 50 | 50 | 50 | 50 | 50 | 50 | 50 |
| Current liabilities | 1,065 | 110 | 64 | (60) | (148) | (199) | (281) | (325) | 591 | 1,897 | 2,107 | 2,226 | 1,257 |
| Long-term debt[h] | 400 | 400 | 400 | 400 | 400 | 400 | 375 | 375 | 375 | 375 | 375 | 375 | 350 |
| Shareholders' equity | 2,938 | 2,835 | 2,736 | 2,641 | 2,542 | 2,443 | 2,343 | 2,248 | 2,412 | 2,616 | 2,873 | 3,156 | 3,231 |
| Total liabilities and stockholders' equity | $4,403 | $3,345 | $3,200 | $2,981 | $2,794 | $2,644 | $2,437 | $2,298 | $3,378 | $4,888 | $5,355 | $5,757 | $4,838 |

a. Assumed maintenance of minimum $175,000 balance and included excess cash in months when company was out of debt.

b. Assumed 60-day collection period.

c. Assumed inventories maintained at December 31, 1990, level for all of 1991.

d. Assumed equipment purchases equal to depreciation expense.

e. Assumed equal to 30% of the current month's sales and related to material purchases of $2.7 million for 1991 as against sales of $9 million. This represented a 30-day payment period. Since inventories were level, purchases would follow seasonal production and sales pattern.

f. Plug figure.

g. Taxes payable on 1990 income were due on March 15, 1991. On April 15, June 15, September 15, and December 15, 1991, payments of 25% each of the estimated tax for 1991 were due. In estimating its tax liability for 1991, the company had the option of using the prior year's tax liability ($126,000) for its estimate and making any adjusting tax payments in 1992. Alternatively, the company could estimate its 1991 tax liability directly. Play Time planned to use its prior year's tax liability as its estimate and to pay $31,000 in April and September and $32,000 in June and December.

h. To be repaid at rate of $25,000 each June and December.

**EXHIBIT 2**
Pro Forma Income Statements under Seasonal Production, 1991 (thousands of dollars)

| | Jan. | Feb. | Mar. | Apr. | May | June | July | Aug. | Sept. | Oct. | Nov. | Dec. | Total |
|---|---|---|---|---|---|---|---|---|---|---|---|---|---|
| Net sales | $ 108 | $ 126 | $ 145 | $ 125 | $ 125 | $ 125 | $ 145 | $1,458 | $1,655 | $1,925 | $2,057 | $1,006 | $9,000 |
| Cost of goods sold[a] | 76 | 88 | 101 | 87 | 87 | 88 | 102 | 1,021 | 1,158 | 1,348 | 1,440 | 704 | 6,300 |
| Gross profit | 32 | 38 | 44 | 38 | 38 | 37 | 43 | 437 | 497 | 577 | 617 | 302 | 2,700 |
| Operating expenses[b] | 188 | 188 | 188 | 188 | 188 | 188 | 188 | 188 | 188 | 188 | 188 | 188 | 2,256 |
| Profit (loss) before taxes | (156) | (150) | (144) | (150) | (150) | (151) | (145) | 249 | 309 | 389 | 429 | 114 | 444 |
| Income taxes[c] | (53) | (51) | (49) | (51) | (51) | (51) | (50) | 85 | 105 | 132 | 146 | 39 | 151 |
| Net profit | $(103) | $ (99) | $ (95) | $ (99) | $ (99) | $(100) | $ (95) | $ 164 | $ 204 | $ 257 | $ 283 | $ 75 | $ 293 |

a. Assumed cost of goods sold equal to 70% sales.
b. Assumed to be same for each month throughout the year.
c. Negative figures are tax credits from operating losses, and reduced accrued taxes shown on balance sheet. The federal tax rate on all earnings was 34%.

# Dynashears, Inc.

On April 28, 1991, Mitch Winthrop, senior loan officer at the Wellington National Bank of New York, was reviewing the credit file of Dynashears, Inc. in preparation for a luncheon meeting with the company's president and treasurer. Dan Sheehan, treasurer of Dynashears, had recently informed Mr. Winthrop that the company would be unable to liquidate its outstanding seasonal loan as initially anticipated. Mr. Winthrop, while agreeing to extend the outstanding $1 million loan, had suggested that he would like to stop by and discuss the company's recent progress when he was next in the vicinity of Savannah, Georgia, where Dynashears' home plant and offices were located.

Dynashears manufactured a complete line of household scissors and industrial shears. Its quality lines were distributed through jobbers to specialty, hardware, and department stores located throughout the country. Cheaper products were sold directly to large variety chains. Although competition, particularly from companies in foreign countries, was severe, Dynashears had made profits in each year since 1958. Sales and profits had grown fairly steadily, if not dramatically, throughout the period.

Wellington National Bank had been actively soliciting the Dynashears account for several years prior to early 1990. Mr. Winthrop, after several unsuccessful calls, finally convinced the officers of Dynashears that association with a large New York bank offered several advantages not to be found with local banks. Mr. Winthrop was particularly pleased with the success of his efforts, because Dynashears historically held fairly sizable deposit balances in its principal banks.

The company had sufficient capital to cover its permanent requirements over the immediate foreseeable future. Its short-term borrowings from banks were typically confined to the period July–December of each year, when additional working capital was needed to support a seasonal sales peak. As a matter of policy the company attempted to produce at an even rate throughout the year, and this accounted in good part for the sizable need for seasonal funds.

In June 1990, Mr. Sheehan arranged a line of credit of $2.9 million with the Wellington National Bank to cover requirements for the fall. At the time, Mr. Sheehan anticipated that the loan would be completely paid off by December 1990. He gave Mr. Winthrop a pro forma estimate of the company's funds requirements over the forthcoming 12-month period to support his request. (These estimates are shown in Exhibits 1 and 2.) In addition to these requirements, the forecast showed a need for approximately $900,000 by June 1991. Mr. Sheehan attributed this increase in funds requirements (no funds were needed in June 1990) to a plant modernization program. He explained that the program, requiring expenditures of $5.2 million, was approximately half completed and would be finished by August 1990. Efficiencies resulting from the modernization program, once completed, were expected to save about $780,000 per year before taxes in manufacturing costs.

Mr. Sheehan called Mr. Winthrop in early September 1990 to let him know that the company would require $300,000 more than had been initially requested to cover peak seasonal needs. Mr. Sheehan explained that the principal reason for the larger requirements was higher expenditures for modernization than had initially been estimated. Mr. Winthrop informed Mr. Sheehan that the bank would be happy to accommodate the additional loan requirements.

In January 1991, Mr. Sheehan again contacted Mr. Winthrop. He noted that sales had slackened considerably since his previous call. He attributed this decline largely to the economic recession then in progress, not to any special conditions affecting his company or the shears industry. Slackening in sales demand, however, had created a need for additional short-term borrowing. Mr. Sheehan believed that additional funds would be required until the company could adjust to the new economic conditions. He envisioned that this adjustment probably would not occur until mid-April 1991 or thereabouts. Once more, Mr. Winthrop agreed to extend the necessary loan funds to Dynashears.

In April 1991, Mr. Sheehan phoned Mr. Winthrop a third time to inform him that Dynashears would probably not be able to repay its outstanding short-term loan of $1 million before the seasonal upturn in funds requirements in June. Mr. Sheehan explained that a further sales decline, occasioned by the recession, was largely responsible for the company's inability to liquidate the loan as anticipated. Mr. Winthrop, in reply, noted that the bank preferred seasonal loans to be ''off the books'' for at least two months of the year, but he saw no reason why he would not be willing to renew Dynashears' outstanding loan. He nevertheless thought it advisable to explore whether the inability to repay the seasonal loan in 1991 might be caused by a permanent change in the nature of the company's loan needs, such as might be occasioned by the modernization program. Mr.

Winthrop consequently suggested a meeting for April 29 to discuss the company's recent progress.

In preparing for this meeting, Mr. Winthrop examined carefully the various profit and loss statements and balance sheets that Mr. Sheehan had submitted to the bank over the course of the last nine months. (These data are shown in Exhibits 3 and 4.) He hoped this analysis might uncover the reasons for Dynashears' inability to repay its loan in accordance with original estimates.

**EXHIBIT 1**
Pro Forma Income Statements, Fiscal 1991 (thousands of dollars)

| | Actual June 30, 1990 | 1990 | | | | | | 1991 | | | | | | Total |
|---|---|---|---|---|---|---|---|---|---|---|---|---|---|---|
| | | July | Aug. | Sept. | Oct. | Nov. | Dec. | Jan. | Feb. | Mar. | Apr. | May | June | |
| Sales | $26,205 | $1,820 | $2,340 | $2,860 | $3,900 | $3,380 | $2,860 | $1,820 | $1,820 | $1,560 | $1,300 | $1,040 | $1,300 | $26,000 |
| Cost of goods sold | | | | | | | | | | | | | | |
| Materials and labor @ 60% of sales | 15,723 | 1,092 | 1,404 | 1,716 | 2,340 | 2,028 | 1,716 | 1,092 | 1,092 | 936 | 780 | 624 | 780 | 15,600 |
| Overhead (incl. depreciation $130) | 3,097 | 260 | 260 | 260 | 260 | 260 | 260 | 260 | 260 | 260 | 260 | 260 | 260 | 3,120 |
| | 18,820 | 1,352 | 1,664 | 1,976 | 2,600 | 2,288 | 1,976 | 1,352 | 1,352 | 1,196 | 1,040 | 884 | 1,040 | 18,720 |
| Gross profit | 7,385 | 468 | 676 | 884 | 1,300 | 1,092 | 884 | 468 | 468 | 364 | 260 | 156 | 260 | 7,280 |
| Selling and administrative expenses | 2,816 | 234 | 234 | 234 | 234 | 234 | 234 | 234 | 234 | 234 | 234 | 234 | 234 | 2,808 |
| Profit before taxes | 4,569 | 234 | 442 | 650 | 1,066 | 858 | 650 | 234 | 234 | 130 | 26 | (78) | 26 | 4,472 |
| Taxes | 1,553 | 79 | 150 | 221 | 362 | 292 | 221 | 80 | 80 | 44 | 9 | (27) | 9 | 1,520 |
| Profit after taxes | 3,016 | 155 | 292 | 429 | 704 | 566 | 429 | 154 | 154 | 86 | 17 | (51) | 17 | 2,952 |
| Dividends | 1,300 | | | 260 | | | 260 | | | 260 | | | 520 | 1,300 |
| Retained earnings | $ 1,716 | $ 155 | $ 292 | $ 169 | $ 704 | $ 566 | $ 169 | $ 154 | $ 154 | $ (174) | $ 17 | $ (51) | $ (503) | $ 1,652 |
| Cumulative retained earnings | — | $ 155 | $ 447 | $ 616 | $1,320 | $1,886 | $2,055 | $2,209 | $2,363 | $2,189 | $2,206 | $2,155 | $1,652 | |

**EXHIBIT 2**
Pro Forma Balance Sheets, Fiscal 1991 (thousands of dollars)

| | Actual June 30, 1990 | 1990 | | | | | | 1991 | | | | | |
|---|---|---|---|---|---|---|---|---|---|---|---|---|---|
| | | July | Aug. | Sept. | Oct. | Nov. | Dec. | Jan. | Feb. | Mar. | Apr. | May | June |
| Cash | $ 1,844 | $ 640 | $ 640 | $ 640 | $ 640 | $ 640 | $ 1,006 | $ 2,280 | $ 2,774 | $ 2,108 | $ 1,952 | $ 1,536 | $ 640 |
| Accounts receivable[a] | 1,812 | 2,470 | 3,250 | 4,030 | 5,330 | 5,330 | 4,550 | 3,250 | 2,730 | 2,470 | 2,080 | 1,690 | 1,820 |
| Inventories | 7,049 | 7,280 | 7,228 | 6,864 | 5,876 | 5,200 | 4,836 | 5,096 | 5,356 | 5,772 | 6,344 | 7,072 | 7,644 |
| Current assets | 10,705 | 10,390 | 11,118 | 11,534 | 11,846 | 11,170 | 10,392 | 10,626 | 10,860 | 10,350 | 10,376 | 10,298 | 10,104 |
| Net plant | 21,360 | 22,660 | 23,960 | 23,960 | 23,960 | 23,960 | 23,960 | 23,960 | 23,960 | 23,960 | 23,960 | 23,960 | 23,960 |
| Total assets | $32,065 | $33,050 | $35,078 | $35,494 | $35,806 | $35,130 | $34,352 | $34,586 | $34,820 | $34,310 | $34,336 | $34,258 | $34,064 |
| Bank loans payable | $ 0 | $ 853 | $ 2,410 | $ 2,816 | $ 2,062 | $ 528 | $ 0 | $ 0 | $ 0 | $ 0 | $ 0 | $ 0 | $ 940 |
| Accounts payable[b] | 749 | 647 | 676 | 676 | 676 | 676 | 676 | 676 | 676 | 676 | 676 | 676 | 676 |
| Taxes payable[c] | 0 | 79 | 229 | 70 | 432 | 724 | 565 | 645 | 725 | 389 | 398 | 371 | 0 |
| Misc. other | 234 | 234 | 234 | 234 | 234 | 234 | 234 | 234 | 234 | 234 | 234 | 234 | 234 |
| Current liabilities | 983 | 1,813 | 3,549 | 3,796 | 3,404 | 2,162 | 1,475 | 1,555 | 1,635 | 1,299 | 1,308 | 1,281 | 1,850 |
| Mortgage 8% | 10,400 | 10,400 | 10,400 | 10,400 | 10,400 | 10,400 | 10,140 | 10,140 | 10,140 | 10,140 | 10,140 | 10,140 | 9,880 |
| Common stock | 10,000 | 10,000 | 10,000 | 10,000 | 10,000 | 10,000 | 10,000 | 10,000 | 10,000 | 10,000 | 10,000 | 10,000 | 10,000 |
| Earned surplus | 10,682 | 10,837 | 11,129 | 11,298 | 12,002 | 12,568 | 12,737 | 12,891 | 13,045 | 12,871 | 12,888 | 12,837 | 12,334 |
| Total liab., net worth | $32,065 | $33,050 | $35,078 | $35,494 | $35,806 | $35,130 | $34,352 | $34,586 | $34,820 | $34,310 | $34,336 | $34,258 | $34,064 |

a. Assumes collections lag sales by 45 days.

b. Assumes 30-day payment period, in accordance with trade terms.

c. Estimated taxes are paid in four equal installments of $380,000 each in September, December, March, and June based on pro forma earnings calculated the previous June.

*(continued)*

**EXHIBIT 2** *(concluded)*
Inventory Subsidiary Data (FIFO)

| | 1990 | | | | | | 1991 | | | | | |
|---|---|---|---|---|---|---|---|---|---|---|---|---|
| | July | Aug. | Sept. | Oct. | Nov. | Dec. | Jan. | Feb. | Mar. | Apr. | May | June |
| *Raw Materials* | | | | | | | | | | | | |
| Opening balance | $ 705 | $ 676 | $ 676 | $ 676 | $ 676 | $ 676 | $ 676 | $ 676 | $ 676 | $ 676 | $ 676 | $ 676 |
| Plus: Purchases | 647 | 676 | 676 | 676 | 676 | 676 | 676 | 676 | 676 | 676 | 676 | 676 |
| Less: Trans. to work in process | 676 | 676 | 676 | 676 | 676 | 676 | 676 | 676 | 676 | 676 | 676 | 676 |
| Closing balance | $ 676 | $ 676 | $ 676 | $ 676 | $ 676 | $ 676 | $ 676 | $ 676 | $ 676 | $ 676 | $ 676 | $ 676 |
| *Work in Process* | | | | | | | | | | | | |
| Opening balance | $2,704 | $2,704 | $2,704 | $2,704 | $2,704 | $2,704 | $2,704 | $2,704 | $2,704 | $2,704 | $2,704 | $2,704 |
| Plus: Raw materials additions | 676 | 676 | 676 | 676 | 676 | 676 | 676 | 676 | 676 | 676 | 676 | 676 |
| Plus: Labor additions | 676 | 676 | 676 | 676 | 676 | 676 | 676 | 676 | 676 | 676 | 676 | 676 |
| Less: Trans. to finished goods | 1,352 | 1,352 | 1,352 | 1,352 | 1,352 | 1,352 | 1,352 | 1,352 | 1,352 | 1,352 | 1,352 | 1,352 |
| Closing balance | $2,704 | $2,704 | $2,704 | $2,704 | $2,704 | $2,704 | $2,704 | $2,704 | $2,704 | $2,704 | $2,704 | $2,704 |
| *Finished Goods* | | | | | | | | | | | | |
| Opening balance | $3,640 | $3,900 | $3,848 | $3,484 | $2,496 | $1,820 | $1,456 | $1,716 | $1,976 | $2,392 | $2,964 | $3,692 |
| Plus: Work in process additions | 1,352 | 1,352 | 1,352 | 1,352 | 1,352 | 1,352 | 1,352 | 1,352 | 1,352 | 1,352 | 1,352 | 1,352 |
| Less: Cost of goods sold | 1,092 | 1,404 | 1,716 | 2,340 | 2,028 | 1,716 | 1,092 | 1,092 | 936 | 780 | 624 | 780 |
| Closing balance | $3,900 | $3,848 | $3,484 | $2,496 | $1,820 | $1,456 | $1,716 | $1,976 | $2,392 | $2,964 | $3,692 | $4,264 |
| Total closing inventory | $7,280 | $7,228 | $6,864 | $5,876 | $5,200 | $4,836 | $5,096 | $5,356 | $5,772 | $6,344 | $7,072 | $7,644 |

**EXHIBIT 3**
Balance Sheets, 1990–1991 (thousands of dollars)

| | 1990 | | | | | | | 1991 | | |
|---|---|---|---|---|---|---|---|---|---|---|
| | June | July | Aug. | Sept. | Oct. | Nov. | Dec. | Jan. | Feb. | Mar. |
| Cash . . . . . . . . | $ 1,844 | $ 832 | $ 497 | $ 609 | $ 606 | $ 723 | $ 559 | $ 986 | $ 936 | $ 601 |
| Accounts receivable . . | 1,812 | 2,467 | 3,169 | 3,822 | 4,914 | 4,805 | 4,846 | 3,442 | 2,756 | 2,493 |
| Inventories . . . . | 7,049 | 7,285 | 7,220 | 6,924 | 6,242 | 5,829 | 5,652 | 6,020 | 6,233 | 6,410 |
| Current assets . . | 10,705 | 10,584 | 10,886 | 11,355 | 11,762 | 11,357 | 11,157 | $10,448 | 9,925 | 9,504 |
| Net plant . . . . | 21,360 | 22,698 | 24,063 | 24,216 | 24,224 | 24,211 | 24,248 | 24,211 | 24,183 | 24,184 |
| Total assets . . | $32,065 | $33,282 | $34,949 | $35,571 | $35,986 | $35,568 | $35,305 | $34,659 | $34,108 | $33,688 |
| Bank loans payable . . | $ 0 | $ 1,104 | $ 2,398 | $ 3,197 | $ 2,673 | $ 1,634 | $ 1,917 | $ 1,131 | $ 611 | $ 995 |
| Accounts payable . . | 749 | 686 | 673 | 733 | 762 | 725 | 595 | 608 | 572 | 447 |
| Taxes payable . . | 0 | 58 | 177 | (56) | 252 | 480 | 266 | 310 | 313 | (80) |
| Misc. other . . . | 234 | 239 | 276 | 247 | 252 | 239 | 234 | 231 | 226 | 224 |
| Current liabilities . . | 983 | 2,087 | 3,524 | 4,121 | 3,939 | 3,078 | 3,012 | 2,280 | 1,722 | 1,586 |
| Mortgage 8% . . . | 10,400 | 10,400 | 10,400 | 10,400 | 10,400 | 10,400 | 10,140 | 10,140 | 10,140 | 10,140 |
| Common stock . . | 10,000 | 10,000 | 10,000 | 10,000 | 10,000 | 10,000 | 10,000 | 10,000 | 10,000 | 10,000 |
| Earned surplus . . | 10,682 | 10,795 | 11,025 | 11,050 | 11,647 | 12,090 | 12,153 | 12,239 | 12,246 | 11,962 |
| Total liab., net worth . . | $32,065 | $33,282 | $34,949 | $35,571 | $35,986 | $35,568 | $35,305 | $34,659 | $34,108 | $33,688 |

*(continued)*

**EXHIBIT 3** (*concluded*)
Inventory Subsidiary Data (FIFO)

| | 1990 | | | | | | 1991 | | |
|---|---|---|---|---|---|---|---|---|---|
| | *July* | *Aug.* | *Sept.* | *Oct.* | *Nov.* | *Dec.* | *Jan.* | *Feb.* | *Mar.* |
| *Raw Materials* | | | | | | | | | |
| Opening balance | $ 705 | $ 708 | $ 659 | $ 662 | $ 691 | $ 717 | $ 678 | $ 664 | $ 656 |
| Plus: Purchases | 684 | 676 | 728 | 754 | 697 | 598 | 600 | 567 | 450 |
| Less: Trans. to work in process | 681 | 725 | 725 | 725 | 671 | 637 | 614 | 575 | 523 |
| Closing balance | $ 708 | $ 659 | $ 662 | $ 691 | $ 717 | $ 678 | $ 664 | $ 656 | $ 583 |
| *Work in Process* | | | | | | | | | |
| Opening balance | $2,704 | $2,722 | $2,778 | $2,799 | $2,801 | $2,726 | $2,637 | $2,564 | $2,414 |
| Plus: Raw materials additions | 681 | 725 | 725 | 725 | 671 | 637 | 614 | 575 | 523 |
| Plus: Labor additions | 686 | 686 | 671 | 686 | 650 | 686 | 686 | 598 | 562 |
| Less: Trans. to finished goods | 1,349 | 1,355 | 1,375 | 1,409 | 1,396 | 1,412 | 1,373 | 1,323 | 1,300 |
| Closing balance | $2,722 | $2,778 | $2,799 | $2,801 | $2,726 | $2,637 | $2,564 | $2,414 | $2,199 |
| *Finished Goods* | | | | | | | | | |
| Opening balance | $3,640 | $3,855 | $3,783 | $3,463 | $2,750 | $2,386 | $2,337 | $2,792 | $3,163 |
| Plus: Work in process additions | 1,349 | 1,355 | 1,375 | 1,409 | 1,396 | 1,412 | 1,373 | 1,323 | 1,300 |
| Less: Cost of goods sold | 1,134 | 1,427 | 1,695 | 2,122 | 1,760 | 1,461 | 918 | 952 | 835 |
| Closing balance | $3,855 | $3,783 | $3,463 | $2,750 | $2,386 | $2,337 | $2,792 | $3,163 | $3,628 |
| Total closing inventory | $7,285 | $7,220 | $6,924 | $6,242 | $5,829 | $5,652 | $6,020 | $6,233 | $6,410 |

**EXHIBIT 4**

Income Statements, 1990–1991 (thousands of dollars)

| | 1990 | | | | | | 1991 | | |
|---|---|---|---|---|---|---|---|---|---|
| | July | Aug. | Sept. | Oct. | Nov. | Dec. | Jan. | Feb. | Mar. |
| Sales | $1,799 | $2,265 | $2,678 | $3,536 | $2,933 | $2,434 | $1,529 | $1,511 | $1,303 |
| Cost of goods sold | | | | | | | | | |
| Materials and labor @ 60% of sales | 1,134 | 1,427 | 1,695 | 2,122 | 1,760 | 1,461 | 918 | 952 | 835 |
| Overhead (incl. depreciation $130) | 257 | 252 | 296 | 270 | 263 | 250 | 255 | 325[a] | 281[a] |
| | 1,391 | 1,679 | 1,991 | 2,392 | 2,023 | 1,711 | 1,173 | 1,277 | 1,116 |
| Gross profit | 408 | 586 | 687 | 1,144 | 910 | 723 | 356 | 234 | 187 |
| Selling and administrative expenses | 237 | 237 | 255 | 239 | 239 | 234 | 226 | 224 | 224 |
| Profit before taxes | 171 | 349 | 432 | 905 | 671 | 489 | 130 | 10 | (37) |
| Taxes | 58 | 119 | 147 | 308 | 228 | 166 | 44 | 3 | (13) |
| Profit after taxes | 113 | 230 | 285 | 597 | 443 | 323 | 86 | 7 | (24) |
| Dividends | — | — | 260 | — | — | 260 | — | — | 260 |
| Retained earnings | $ 113 | $ 230 | $ 25 | $ 597 | $ 443 | $ 63 | $ 86 | $ 7 | $ (284) |
| Cumulative retained earnings | $ 113 | $ 343 | $ 368 | $ 965 | $1,408 | $1,471 | $1,557 | $1,564 | $1,280 |

a. Includes special cost for laying off personnel.

61

# Hampton Machine Tool Company

On September 14, 1979, Jerry Eckwood, vice president of the St. Louis National Bank, was considering a loan request from a customer located in a nearby city. The company, Hampton Machine Tool Company, had requested renewal of an existing $1 million loan originally due to be repaid on September 30. In addition to the renewal of the existing loan, Hampton was asking for an additional loan of $350,000 for planned equipment purchases in October. Under the terms of the company's request, both loans, totaling $1.35 million, would be repayable at the end of 1979.

Since its establishment in 1915, Hampton Machine Tool Company had successfully weathered the severe cyclical fluctuations characteristic of the machine tool manufacturing business. In the most recent cycle Hampton had experienced record production and profitability during the mid- and late-1960s. Because Hampton's major customers included the military aircraft manufacturers and automobile manufacturers in the St. Louis area, the company's success in the 1960s reflected a strong automobile market and the heavy defense spending associated with the Vietnam War. Hampton rode the 1960s boom into the early 1970s. Hampton, along with the rest of the capital goods industry, experienced a severe decline in sales and profitability in the mid-1970s. Precipitous declines in the production of automobiles in St. Louis facilities reflected the Arab oil embargo, subsequent increases in the price of gasoline, and the 1974–1975 recession. Massive reductions in defense spending in the post-Vietnam War period had a severe adverse impact on Hampton's other major customer segment, military aircraft manufacturers. Hampton's sales had bottomed out in the mid-1970s, and the several years prior to 1978 had seen a steady rebuilding of sales. Hampton's recovery was due primarily to three factors. First, military aircraft sales had increased substantially, reflecting both an expanding export market and a more benign domestic market. Secondly, though the automobile manufacturers in the area were not expanding, this segment of Hampton's market had at least stabilized. Finally, the adverse economic conditions in the mid-1970s had taken their toll in the regional capital goods industry. Consequently, Hampton's market share increased as many thinly capitalized competitors had been forced out of the industry. Hampton's recovery had suffered a mild setback, as 1978 sales were far below capacity. However, with a substantial backlog of firm sales orders, Hampton entered 1979 expecting its first year of capacity sales since 1972.

Hampton's conservative financial policies had contributed to its survival and success in the volatile capital goods industry. The company had traditionally maintained a strong working capital position as a buffer against economic uncertainty. As a result, the company had no debt on its balance sheet during the 10 years prior to December 1978. In a meeting in early December 1978, Benjamin G. Cowins, president of Hampton, requested the initial loan of $1 million to facilitate purchasing the stock of several dissident shareholders. While Hampton had some cash in excess of that required for normal operations, excess cash was not sufficient to effect the stock redemption. Therefore, Mr. Cowins had asked Mr. Eckwood for a loan from the St. Louis National Bank. The loan of $1 million was to be taken down at the end of December 1978. Hampton would make monthly interest payments at an interest rate of 1½% per month (approximately 18% on an annual basis) on the principal which would be due at the end of September 1979. In support of his request, Mr. Cowins had submitted a forecast of monthly shipments for 1979 (see Exhibit 1), a balance sheet dated November 30, 1978 (first column of Exhibit 2), and documentation of Hampton's backlog of sales orders. Mr. Eckwood felt at the time that the documentation provided by Mr. Cowins was sufficient to support favorable action on the request. Furthermore, Hampton had traditionally kept its ample cash balances on deposit at the St. Louis National Bank, and the bank's management knew Mr. Cowins well. Mr. Cowins, then 58 years old, had succeeded his father-in-law as president of Hampton in 1963. He was widely respected in the business community as an energetic and successful executive. In mid-December 1978, Mr. Eckwood had approved the loan to Hampton.

Hampton took down the loan at the end of December 1978. The proceeds of the loan plus $2 million in excess cash were used immediately to repurchase 75,000 shares of Hampton's $10 par value stock from several dissident shareholders at an aggregate cost of $3 million.

After the loan was made, Mr. Cowins regularly sent the bank profit and loss statements and balance sheets documenting Hampton's financial condition. In preparing his analysis of Mr. Cowins' request, Mr. Eckwood focused on the documents presented in Exhibits 1, 2, and 3. In examining Hampton's financial statements, Mr. Eckwood recalled that Hampton's selling terms were 30 days net. Occasionally a customer placing a large order would make an advance payment to help Hampton finance the construction of the machines ordered. Because Hampton's products were largely made to order, the construction period involved five to six months for some of the larger, more complex types of machines. Upon completion and shipment of orders against which advances had been paid, Hampton deducted the amount of the advance from the amount billed to the customer. Also, Mr. Eckwood understood that the company purchased its materials on terms of net 30 days.

In a letter to Mr. Eckwood, Mr. Cowins had made his request for the extension of the existing Hampton note until the end of the year plus an additional loan of $350,000 to finance equipment purchases. The additional loan would be needed by the end of October and would be payable at the end of the year with monthly interest payments remaining 1½% of principal. In his letter, Mr. Cowins commented at some length on the company's financial condition, the reasons for the shortfall of actual from projected 1979 shipments, and Hampton's substantial backlog of firm sales orders. In addition, Mr. Cowins stated that he expected to be able to repay both loans in full by December 31, 1979. Mr. Cowins' letter is presented in full as Exhibit 4. Although Hampton would not need the additional $350,000 loan until the end of October, the maturity date of the existing note was fast approaching. Therefore, Mr. Eckwood needed to decide upon a response to Mr. Cowins' request.

**EXHIBIT 1**
Shipments at Selling Price (thousands of dollars)

|  |  | As Forecast Dec. 1978 | Actual | As Forecast Sept. 1979 |
|---|---|---|---|---|
| 1979 | January | $ 1,302 | $ 861 | |
|  | February | 1,872 | 672 | |
|  | March | 1,635 | 1,866 | |
|  | April | 1,053 | 1,566 | |
|  | May | 1,293 | 873 | |
|  | June | 1,479 | 1,620 | |
|  | July | 1,488 | 723 | |
|  | August | 1,797 | 507 | |
| Eight months total |  | $11,919 | $8,688 | |
|  | September | $ 1,299 | | $2,163 |
|  | October | 1,347 | | 1,505 |
|  | November | 1,311 | | 1,604 |
|  | December | 2,298 | | 2,265 |

**EXHIBIT 2**
Balance Sheets, 1978–1979 (thousands of dollars)

|  | 1978 | | 1979 | | | |
|---|---|---|---|---|---|---|
|  | **Nov.** | **Dec.** | **Mar.** | **June** | **July** | **Aug.** |
| Cash . . . . . . . . . . . | $2,520 | $ 491 | $ 505 | $1,152 | $1,678 | $1,559 |
| Accounts receivable, net . . . | 1,245 | 1,863 | 1,971 | 1,893 | 1,269 | 684 |
| Inventories . . . . . . . . | 2,601 | 2,478 | 3,474 | 3,276 | 3,624 | 4,764 |
| Current assets . . . . . | 6,366 | 4,832 | 5,950 | 6,321 | 6,571 | 7,007 |
| Gross fixed assets . . . . . | 4,010 | 4,010 | 4,010 | 4,010 | 4,010 | 4,010 |
| Accumulated depreciation . . . | 2,998 | 3,010 | 3,040 | 3,070 | 3,080 | 3,090 |
| Net fixed assets . . . . . . | 1,012 | 1,000 | 970 | 940 | 930 | 920 |
| Prepaid expenses . . . . . | 62 | 40 | 39 | 24 | 24 | 42 |
| Total assets . . . . . . | $7,440 | $5,872 | $6,959 | $7,285 | $7,525 | $7,969 |
| Notes payable, bank . . . . . | — | $1,000 | $1,000 | $1,000 | $1,000 | $1,000 |
| Accounts payable . . . . . | $ 348 | 371 | 681 | 399 | 621 | 948 |
| Accruals . . . . . . . . | 561 | 777 | 849 | 678 | 585 | 552 |
| Taxes payable[a] . . . . . . | 150 | 74 | 373 | 354 | 407 | 479 |
| Customer advance payments . . . . . . . | 840 | 1,040 | 1,040 | 1,566 | 1,566 | 1,566 |
| Current liabilities . . . . | 1,899 | 3,262 | 3,943 | 3,997 | 4,179 | 4,545 |
| Common stock ($10 par value) . . . . . | 1,178 | 428 | 428 | 428 | 428 | 428 |
| Surplus . . . . . . . . . | 4,363 | 2,182 | 2,588 | 2,860 | 2,918 | 2,996 |
| Net worth . . . . . . . . | 5,541 | 2,610 | 3,016 | 3,288 | 3,346 | 3,424 |
| Total liabilities and net worth . | $7,440 | $5,872 | $6,959 | $7,285 | $7,525 | $7,969 |

a. Tax payments in 1979 include $75,000 due March 15 on underpayment of 1978 taxes and four equal payments of $181,000 due on the 15th of April, June, September, and December for estimated 1979 tax liability with any underpayment of 1979 taxes due March 15, 1980.

**EXHIBIT 3**

Income Statements, 1978–1979 (thousands of dollars)

| | Fiscal Year Ending 12/31/78 | Dec. 1978 | 1979 | | | | | | | | Eight Months Ending 8/31/79 |
| --- | --- | --- | --- | --- | --- | --- | --- | --- | --- | --- | --- |
| | | | Jan. | Feb. | Mar. | Apr. | May | June | July | Aug. | |
| Net sales . . . . . . . | $7,854 | $1,551 | $861 | $672 | $1,866 | $1,566 | $873 | $1,620 | $723 | $507 | $8,688 |
| Cost of sales[a] . . . . . | 5,052 | 1,122 | 474 | 369 | 1,362 | 1,137 | 567 | 1,197 | 510 | 276 | 5,892 |
| Gross profit . . . . . | 2,802 | 429 | 387 | 303 | 504 | 429 | 306 | 423 | 213 | 231 | 2,796 |
| Selling and admin. expenses . | 1,296 | 248 | 103 | 61 | 205 | 172 | 96 | 130 | 87 | 66 | 920 |
| Interest expense . . . . | – | – | 15 | 15 | 15 | 15 | 15 | 15 | 15 | 15 | 120 |
| Net income before taxes . . | 1,506 | 181 | 269 | 227 | 284 | 242 | 195 | 278 | 111 | 150 | 1,756 |
| Income taxes . . . . | 723 | 87 | 129 | 109 | 136 | 116 | 94 | 133 | 53 | 72 | 842 |
| Net income . . . . . | $ 783 | $ 94 | $140 | $118 | $ 148 | $ 126 | $101 | $ 145 | $ 58 | $ 78 | $ 914 |
| Dividends . . . . . | $ 50 | $ 25 | – | – | – | – | – | $ 100 | – | – | $ 100 |

a. Includes depreciation charges of $150,000 in 1978, $12,000 in December 1978, and $10,000 per month in 1979.

**EXHIBIT 4**

HAMPTON MACHINE TOOL COMPANY
East St. Louis, Illinois

September 12, 1979

Mr. Jerry Eckwood
Vice President
St. Louis National Bank
St. Louis, Missouri

Dear Mr. Eckwood:

I enclose the company's August 31 financial statements. While these statements show our cash balance as $1,559,000, you will note we have an obligation to a customer for cash advances of $1,566,000, and we expect to ship this order over the next three months. With respect to our note for $1,000,000 due September 30, we request that you renew it until the end of 1979. We also wish to borrow an additional $350,000 to be available at the end of October to be repaid by the end of the year with interest at the rate of 1½% per month on the principal. This additional loan is required to purchase certain needed equipment. At the end of the year, as you can see for yourself, we expect to be able to have enough cash on hand to retire our obligations in full.

For the past month or more we have been producing at capacity and expect to continue at this rate through the end of the year and beyond. On August 31, our backlog of unfilled orders amounted to about $16,500,000—approximately 90% of annual capacity. I should stress that these are firm orders from respected customers.

Despite our backlog, our shipment schedule has been upset, particularly the last several months, because we have had to wait on our suppliers for shipment of electronic control mechanisms. On August 31, we had seven machines with an accumulated cost of about $1,320,000 completed except for the installation of these electronic components. The components were finally received last week and will enable us to complete a number of machines in the next few weeks. After this imminent reduction in work in progress of about $1,320,000, the remainder of our work in progress inventories will probably remain stable for the foreseeable future because of our capacity rate of production.

We bought raw materials beyond our immediate needs in July and August to be assured of completing our orders scheduled to be shipped by the end of the year. We have accumulated about $420,000 worth of scarcer components above our normal raw materials inventories. The extra $420,000 will be used up by the end of the year, bringing our raw materials inventories back to normal levels for capacity production. Because we bought ahead this way, we expect to cut raw materials purchases to about $600,000 a month in each of the four remaining months of 1979.

Our finished goods inventories are, of course, negligible at all times since we ship machines within a day of completion.

Our revised shipment estimates (at selling price) are as follows:

| | | |
|---|---|---|
| September | . . . | $2,163,000 |
| October | . . . . | 1,505,000 |
| November | . . . | 1,604,000 |
| December | . . . | 2,265,000 |
| | | $7,537,000 |

*(continued)*

**EXHIBIT 4** *(concluded)*

The shipment estimates include the $2,100,000 order for the General Aircraft Corporation. We are now scheduled to ship against this order as follows: September, $840,000; October, $840,000; November, $420,000. Since we obtained a $1,566,000 advance from General Aircraft on this order, we will be due nothing on these shipments until their $1,566,000 credit with us is exhausted.

You will note the decline in our accrued expenses. As I mentioned to you last month when you visited us, we have been paying off commissions due to our three principal sales people (who are also large stockholders in the company). Last year when we needed funds to redeem part of our capital stock, these people agreed to defer their commissions until the funds could be more easily spared. In August, we paid off the last of these back commissions. This has been the principal cause of the decline in accruals, which, like prepaid expenses, normally do not change much from month to month. Assuming accruals will stay about the same as on August 31, our monthly outlay for all expenses other than interest and raw materials purchases should be around $400,000 per month.

Due to poor economic conditions and our desire to conserve cash, we have spent very little on new equipment in the last several years, and this has contributed somewhat to the difficulties we have had in maintaining production at a capacity rate this year. We feel that we should not further postpone replacing certain essential equipment if we are to avoid a possible major breakdown at an inconvenient time. Therefore, we think it necessary to purchase additional equipment costing $350,000 in October to maintain production efficiency. The proceeds from the additional loan we have requested will be used at the end of October to pay for this equipment. This equipment has an estimated life of eight years, an estimated net salvage value of zero, and the $350,000 purchase price will be depreciated on a straight-line basis.

Our tax people tell us that the equipment will qualify for a 10% investment tax credit (ITC). However, the tax savings of $35,000 will not affect our scheduled tax payments this year. We are scheduled to pay $181,000 in taxes on September 15 and to make another payment of the same amount on December 15. As I understand it, the ITC savings of $35,000 will reduce both our tax liability and the taxes payable on our balance sheet as well as increase reported earnings. However, the cash flow impact of this savings will not be felt until March 1980 when we make our final settlement with the government on 1979 taxes.

Despite temporary bottlenecks which reduced shipments, our profits for the year to date have been quite satisfactory. With raw materials and components supply assured and the efficiency provided by the new equipment we plan to purchase, we feel confident we can meet our shipment forecasts for the rest of the year. Furthermore, the business which we expect to ship in the next four months is on our books on profitable terms. While our profit, as you know, varies with the item involved, our engineering estimates indicate that we expect to earn a profit before taxes and interest of about 23% of sales on these shipments. Even after taking into account our tax rate of 48% and the interest we must pay on our notes, 1979 looks like a very good year. Because of these good results and in view of our conservative dividend policy during the last several years of economic uncertainty, we plan to pay a dividend to our stockholders. Our dividend disbursements in 1979 have continued to be quite modest, and we want to be sure that those stockholders who stood by us last December have no cause to regret their action. Under the circumstances, we feel that a dividend of $150,000 payable in December is the least we can do in view of our high earnings and our stockholders' patient support.

If there is anything further you need to know, please do not hesitate to write or phone.

Sincerely yours,
*(Signed)* B. G. Cowins
*President*

# Science Technology Company (1985)

Early in March 1985, Bill Watson, president of Science Technology Company (STC), was reviewing a 5-year financing plan prepared for the company by Harry Finson, the chief financial officer. Mr. Finson intended to discuss the plan at the forthcoming board meeting. If both the plan and the premises on which it was based were endorsed by the board, the plan would greatly influence the financial policies and the total development of the firm.

After some study, Mr. Watson identified several questions for further consideration and resolution:

1. In view of the uneven growth in sales, inventories and receivables, and earnings in the past, were Mr. Finson's 5-year forecasts useful?

2. What impact would a resurgence of inflation, fueled by massive budget deficits, have on STC?

3. Was the company well-positioned to finance the rapid sales growth that was anticipated?

## Description of STC

Science Technology Company was a leading manufacturer of computer-controlled automated test equipment (ATE) that was used to monitor and manage quality over the life cycle of electronic products. With 31% market share, the company was the dominant firm in the design and manufacture of testers and test software for printed circuit boards. Its second largest business was its semiconductor test operation, which manufactured complex systems that cost in excess of $1 million and were used to test state-of-the-art very large scale integrated (VLSI) circuits. Other products included a system to test electronic products in the field; systems used to test a product's mechanical and structural integrity under stress; and computer-aided engineering software used to test and verify designs before they were physically built, by creating electronic models and simulating their performance in the software version.

STC was headquartered in Minneapolis, Minnesota, and had plants in Minnesota, Colorado, and Arizona. Customers were supported by a sales and service network with offices and representatives across the United States and more than a dozen countries in North and South America, Europe, Africa, Asia, and Australia. Total sales were $227 million.

## STC's Objectives and Strategy

STC's primary objective was to be the recognized international leader in providing integrated quality management systems to manufacturers of electronic devices and equipment. This objective required maintaining its leadership in creating new test technologies and new products for all segments of the design and test markets. This commitment to maintain a fundamental superiority in test expertise required very heavy spending on research and development.

To be viable financially, the company sought to spread the cost of its research and development across a large number of sales. Its strategy was to pursue aggressively most major segments of the semiconductor and electronics manufacturing industries throughout Europe, North America, and the Pacific basin.

## Market for Automated Test Equipment

During the period 1975–1984, computer-related technologies changed swiftly and dramatically. Technological breakthroughs inspired the development of new products that consumers and users eagerly acquired. Examples include personal computers, cordless telephones, video cassette recorders, microprocessor-based home appliances, solar-powered calculators, mainframe computers, automated teller machines, and automated offices and factories. Consumers demanded and could expect products of high quality at low prices. Consequently, electronics manufacturers had critical test requirements at every stage of the product cycle from engineering to manufacturing to service.

So rapidly were new technologies developing that the introduction of a new silicon chip could quickly make the competition obsolete. There was no longer time to follow the traditional product development process of designing, building a prototype, testing, redesigning, building a new prototype, and so forth. It would also have been cost-prohibitive to put each design iteration of a complex circuit on a silicon chip. Any change in the design would require making a new chip.

STC provided software products that let design engineers know how well a new circuit would work without the costly necessity of building a prototype.

Getting a highly competitive product to market on time, with high quality and within budget, depended on the speed with which a new design was moved into manufacturing. This speed depended on testability. New products could not be made unless they could be tested. The electronic circuitry was contained in small devices mounted on printed circuit boards of varying size and complexity. These devices must work well if a product was to perform well; and cost considerations required electronics manufacturers to be able to sort out good components from bad *before* they were mounted on printed circuit boards, and to spot production problems early.

Automated test equipment was also of increasing importance in the field. High-quality, fast, low-cost repair service must be provided by the electronics manufacturer after the product was sold.

The growth of the worldwide ATE market was tremendous between 1978 and 1984 (see Table A). Sales increased from $359 million in 1978 to $1.6 billion in 1984. This rapid growth of 28% per year was spurred by the rapid growth of electronic products, powered in part by technological breakthroughs in computers and in miniaturization.

ATE firms were also helped by the steady increase in labor rates, which pushed electronics manufacturers to automate their testing. A second important trend was the move by electronics manufacturers away from the design and manufacture of their own test equipment. In the early 1960s, when the ATE market was just emerging, most ATEs were produced in-house by the electronics manufacturers. One of the main reasons for this was the absence of standard test equipment, especially for testing state-of-the-art semiconductor devices. Later, as semiconductor components increased in number and complexity, most of the major semiconductor and electronics manufacturers found it too difficult and expensive, in view of their limited in-house production volume, to build their own testers. A third trend that spurred the sales of firms specializing in ATEs was the dramatic improvement in testing technology and changes in the devices to be tested. Much of the electronics manufacturers' in-house testing capacity was made obsolete by these forces.

**TABLE A**
U.S. Factory Shipments, Electronics (billions of dollars)

|  | 1978 | 1979 | 1980 | 1981 | 1982 | 1983 | 1984 |
|---|---|---|---|---|---|---|---|
| Consumer products | $ 9.1 | $ 9.4 | $ 10.9 | $ 12.5 | $ 12.5 | $ 14.6 | $ 17.8 |
| Communications | 21.7 | 25.7 | 30.8 | 35.7 | 39.1 | 41.4 | 46.1 |
| Computers | 15.1 | 19.7 | 24.3 | 29.1 | 33.3 | 37.9 | 45.0 |
| Industrial | 10.6 | 12.7 | 14.7 | 18.1 | 21.0 | 20.5 | 22.6 |
| Components | 17.1 | 21.4 | 25.6 | 28.8 | 29.6 | 32.9 | 41.1 |
| Total | $74 | $89 | $106 | $124 | $136 | $147 | $173 |

## STC's Performance, 1980–1984

With one of the broadest lines in the industry, STC benefited from the strong ATE market. Sales increased by 58%, from $144 million in 1980 to $227 million in 1984, a compound annual growth rate of 12%. Exhibits 1 and 2 show STC's income statements and balance sheets for 1980–1984.

While sales increased each year, profits were erratic. Net profits of $10 million in 1980 were followed by a $3 million loss in 1981. Profitability then improved dramatically, to $16.3 million in 1983. With the ATE market strong, management and investors anticipated strong sales and earnings growth. The price of STC shares soared from $10 at the beginning of 1982 to a high of $42 in June 1983. Management responded by selling 1,650,000 shares of common stock at a price of $11½ in June 1982 and another 1,800,000 shares at $26 only nine months later.

The optimism of mid-1983 soon faded. STC's profits were disappointing in 1984, falling to $10 million. Several factors accounted for this poor performance. First, the company increased the number of employees and the amount of plant capacity in anticipation of a stronger sales growth than the 10% realized. Second, market opportunities and competitive pressures required that research and development spending be increased by 32% to a level equal to 16% of sales. Third, the company had significant problems with a new product at the largest division, requiring expensive product recalls and repairs. And finally, the company had major manufacturing problems with a line of very large and complex testers at its semiconductor test division, resulting in divisional losses of $18 million in 1984.

## Prospects for the ATE Industry and for STC

Mr. Watson was optimistic about the long-term prospects for the ATE industry. Industry sales were forecast to reach $4 billion in 1988, a compound annual growth of 26% from the $1.6 billion in 1984.

Competition was intensifying, however. There were a large number of competitors, including Teradyne, Zehntel, Takeda Riken, Ando, Marconi, Fairchild, Hewlett-Packard, and LTX. Furthermore, many of these firms were broadening their product lines and the range of markets they served. The VLSI test market was a good example. When STC decided in 1977 to enter, two firms, Fairchild and Tektronix, dominated the market with a combined market share of 80%. After spending approximately $75 million to develop its VLSI testers, STC was faced with a totally different competitive situation in 1985 as the result of the unexpected entry of Teradyne, Takeda Riken, Ando, Megatest, and LTX.

Mr. Watson believed that STC had a number of strengths that would help it during the coming period of intensified competition. It had a large customer base, extensive software, a broad line of testers, a dominant share of the printed circuit board test market, and a fair position in VLSI testing. Quality problems affecting an in-circuit tester that was expected to be a mainstay product over the next few years had been solved; and a high performance new tester, representing a break-through in test technology, would be introduced in mid-1986. These two develop-ments were expected to halt the recent decline in STC's share of the printed circuit board segment. The company also was making substantial progress in the VLSI test market and had been selected by the U.S. Department of Defense for a major program.

On the strength of these developments, STC's sales were forecast to reach $295 million in 1985 and $843 million in 1989 (see Exhibit 3).

## Financial Pressures

The sale of 3.45 million shares of common stock in 1982 and 1983 raised $66 million and established a strong financial base for the planned growth. STC's financial strength in 1985 matched that of its competitors and seemed sufficient to obviate the need for additional equity issues (see Exhibit 4). Mr. Watson was concerned, however, by the past difficulties in forecasting and by the very substantial increase in debt that Mr. Finson's forecasts assumed.

**EXHIBIT 1**
Consolidated Income Statements, 1980–1984 (millions of dollars)

| | 1980 | 1981 | 1982 | 1983 | 1984 |
|---|---|---|---|---|---|
| Net sales | $144 | $154 | $171 | $206 | $227 |
| Cost of goods sold | 66 | 73 | 79 | 90 | 104 |
| Gross profit | 78 | 81 | 92 | 116 | 123 |
| R&D expense | 13 | 19 | 22 | 28 | 37 |
| Selling, general, administrative exp. | 42 | 50 | 57 | 65 | 76 |
| Other expense (income) | – | 1 | – | (1) | (3) |
| Interest expense | 3 | 7 | 3 | 2 | 2 |
| Profit before taxes | 20 | 4 | 10 | 22 | 11 |
| Taxes | 9 | 2 | 3 | 6 | 1 |
| Profit after taxes, continuing operations | 11 | 2 | 7 | 16 | 10 |
| Loss from discontinued operations | 1 | 5 | – | – | – |
| Net income | $ 10 | $ (3) | $ 7 | $ 16 | $ 10 |
| *Selected Financial Ratios (% of sales)* | | | | | |
| Cost of goods sold | 46% | 47% | 46% | 44% | 46% |
| R&D expense | 9 | 12 | 13 | 14 | 16 |
| Selling, general, administrative exp. | 29 | 32 | 33 | 32 | 33 |
| Profit after taxes, continuing operations | 7.6 | 1.2 | 4.1 | 7.8 | 4.4 |

**EXHIBIT 2**
Consolidated Balance Sheets, 1980–1984 (millions of dollars)

| | 1980 | 1981 | 1982 | 1983 | 1984 |
|---|---|---|---|---|---|
| Cash | $ 4 | $ 4 | $ 4 | $ 25 | $ 3 |
| Accounts receivable | 40 | 45 | 46 | 68 | 74 |
| Inventories | 56 | 46 | 49 | 68 | 86 |
| Tax claims | 1 | 7 | 4 | 5 | 1 |
| Other | 2 | 5 | 2 | 7 | 10 |
| Current assets | 103 | 107 | 105 | 173 | 174 |
| Net fixed assets | 32 | 32 | 30 | 36 | 62 |
| Other | 1 | 2 | 2 | 5 | 6 |
| Total assets | $136 | $141 | $137 | $214 | $242 |
| Notes payable, banks | $ 7 | $ 9 | $ 5 | $ 6 | $ 14 |
| Accounts payable | 11 | 9 | 11 | 17 | 13 |
| Accrued taxes | 2 | 1 | 4 | 8 | 1 |
| Accruals | 12 | 14 | 17 | 17 | 18 |
| Current liabilities | 32 | 33 | 37 | 48 | 46 |
| Long-term debt | 35 | 41 | 7 | 8 | 25 |
| Other | 1 | 2 | 2 | 4 | 7 |
| Net worth | 68 | 65 | 91 | 154 | 164 |
| Total liabilities and net worth | $136 | $141 | $137 | $214 | $242 |
| *Selected Financial Ratios* | | | | | |
| Accounts receivables as % of sales | 28% | 29% | 27% | 33% | 33% |
| Inventories as % of cost of goods | 85 | 63 | 62 | 76 | 83 |
| Net fixed assets as % of cost of goods | 48 | 44 | 38 | 40 | 60 |
| Accounts payable as % of cost of goods | 17 | 12 | 14 | 19 | 13 |
| Accruals as % of cost of goods | 18 | 19 | 22 | 19 | 17 |

**EXHIBIT 3**
Five-Year Capital and Financing Plan

Permanent new capital requirements for Science Technology Company depend almost entirely on sales growth, retained profits, and the efficiency with which corporate assets are employed. Our growth has been moderate—12% per year since 1980. Our net profits have ranged from a deficit (including the loss from discontinued operations) in 1981 to 7.8% of sales in 1983. Profits have not increased our equity rapidly enough to keep up with requirements. However, the absence of any cash dividend and our two share issues, which raised a total of $66 million in new equity, allowed us to avoid excessive debt financing.

At the end of 1984 total assets were $242 million, or 106% of sales. Much of the growth of assets occurred in 1983 and 1984 as (1) the mix of business shifted toward more complex systems; (2) capacity was expanded to accommodate anticipated strong orders; and (3) production run rates were based on forecasts that proved optimistic in 1984.

| | *1980–1984 Range* | *1984* | *Competitors' 1984 Range* |
|---|---|---|---|
| Accounts receivable as % of sales . . . . . . | 27–33% | 33% | 19–39% |
| Inventories as % of cost of goods . . . . . . | 62–85 | 83 | 48–50 |
| Net fixed assets as % of cost of goods . . . . . | 38–60 | 60 | 67–90 |
| Total assets as % of sales . . . . . . . . . | 79–106 | 106 | 82–100 |

The accompanying five-year financial projection (Table 1 on the next page) shows a 30% annual growth rate for sales, a 7.5% profit margin on sales, and an improvement in the turnover of total assets. The projections are based on the forecasts prepared by the divisional managers and are consistent with the industry sales growth that was discussed during our strategic planning sessions.

From 1985 to 1989 sales are projected to grow from $295 million to $843 million, and net profit from $23 million to $61 million. By 1989 total debt will be 35% of total capital—still in line with the debt levels of competitors. Earnings per share grow from $1.45 in 1985 to $3.84, and the possible market price of the stock reaches $77, assuming a multiple of 20 times.

It is extremely interesting to note the relations among net profit, total debt, and earnings per share.

| *Net Profit as % of Sales* | *5-Year Cumulative Profit ($ millions)* | *Net Worth 1989 ($ millions)* | *Total Debt 1989 ($ millions)* | *Total Capital 1989 ($ millions)* | *Debt as % of Capital 1989* | *Earnings per Share 1989* |
|---|---|---|---|---|---|---|
| 5.0% | $133 | $297 | $265 | $562 | 47% | $2.56 |
| 7.5 | 199 | 363 | 199 | 562 | 35 | 3.84 |
| 10.0 | 266 | 430 | 132 | 562 | 23 | 5.12 |

Obviously, the higher the profit rate, the lower the need for additional debt financing and the higher the earnings per share. This demonstrates the importance of our programs to reduce manufacturing costs and to correct the problems at the semiconductor test division.

The price-earnings ratio for the stock seems likely to be influenced by the growth of sales and earnings. The following table, based on a profit margin of 7.5% and an asset-to-sales ratio of .80, considers the implications for stock price of different levels of sales growth. While no one knows with certainty the price-earnings ratio at which a stock will sell 5 years hence, the table does suggest the importance of maintaining a strong sales pattern.

| *Annual Sales Growth* | *Earnings per Share* | | *Annual % Increase* | *Price-Earnings Ratio 1989* | *Stock Price 1989* | *Debt as % of Capital 1989* |
|---|---|---|---|---|---|---|
| | *1985* | *1989* | | | | |
| 10% | $1.18 | $1.73 | 8% | 12 | $21 | 0% |
| 20 | 1.29 | 2.65 | 15 | 15 | 40 | 16 |
| 30 | 1.45 | 3.84 | 22 | 20 | 77 | 35 |

*(continued)*

**EXHIBIT 3** *(concluded)*

**TABLE 1**—Financial Projections, 1985–1989 (millions of dollars)

|  | 1985 | 1986 | 1987 | 1988 | 1989 |  |
|---|---|---|---|---|---|---|
| Net sales | $295 | $384 | $499 | $648 | $843 | +30 % per year |
| Cost of goods sold (COGS) | 121 | 157 | 204 | 266 | 345 | 41% of sales |
| Gross profit | 174 | 227 | 295 | 382 | 498 |  |
| R&D expense | 41 | 54 | 70 | 91 | 118 | 14% of sales |
| Selling, general, administrative exp. | 91 | 119 | 155 | 201 | 261 | 31% of sales |
| Interest expense | 3 | 4 | 6 | 11 | 17 |  |
| Profit before taxes (PBT) | 39 | 50 | 64 | 79 | 102 |  |
| Taxes | 16 | 20 | 26 | 32 | 41 | 40% of PBT |
| Profit after taxes | $ 23 | $ 30 | $ 38 | $ 47 | $ 61 |  |
| Cash | $ 2 | $ 3 | $ 4 | $ 5 | $ 6 |  |
| Accounts receivable | 94 | 123 | 160 | 207 | 270 | 32% of sales |
| Inventories | 70 | 91 | 119 | 154 | 200 | 58% of COGS |
| Other | 4 | 4 | 4 | 4 | 4 |  |
| Current assets | 170 | 221 | 287 | 370 | 480 |  |
| Net fixed assets | 70 | 82 | 106 | 138 | 180 |  |
| Other | 8 | 8 | 8 | 8 | 8 |  |
| Total assets | $248 | $311 | $401 | $516 | $668 |  |
| Notes payable | $ 1 | $ 28 | $ 69 | $122 | $194 | Plug |
| Accounts payable | 16 | 20 | 27 | 35 | 45 | 13% of COGS |
| Accruals | 21 | 27 | 35 | 46 | 59 | 17% of COGS |
| Current liabilities | 38 | 75 | 131 | 203 | 298 |  |
| Long-term debt | 21 | 17 | 13 | 9 | 5 |  |
| Other | 2 | 2 | 2 | 2 | 2 |  |
| Net worth | 187 | 217 | 255 | 302 | 363 |  |
| Total liabilities and net worth | $248 | $311 | $401 | $516 | $668 |  |

**EXHIBIT 4**
Financial Information on Primary Competitors

| | Teradyne[a] | Fluke[b] | LTX[a] | STC |
|---|---|---|---|---|
| *Size ($ millions)* | | | | |
| 1984 sales | $ 389 | $ 208 | $ 90 | $ 227 |
| 1984 assets | 350 | 171 | 91 | 242 |
| *Five-Year Growth* | | | | |
| Sales | +136% | +62% | +186% | +94% |
| Net income | +280 | +97 | +299 | +67 |
| Earnings per share | +170 | +86 | +219 | +31 |
| *Profitability, 1984* | | | | |
| Cost of goods sold as % of sales | 45% | 44% | 46% | 46% |
| R&D expense as % of sales | 16 | 10 | 15 | 16 |
| Selling, general, and administrative as % of sales | 20 | 33 | 27 | 33 |
| Earnings before interest and taxes (EBIT) as % of sales | 19 | 14 | 12 | 6 |
| Net income as % of sales | 11 | 9 | 7 | 5 |
| Return on equity | 19 | 18 | 15 | 6 |
| Return on capital | 15 | 6 | 11 | 6 |
| *Financial Condition, 1984* | | | | |
| Current ratio | 3.6 | 3.4 | 2.5 | 3.8 |
| Acid ratio | 2.0 | 1.9 | 1.7 | 1.9 |
| Total liabilities as % of total assets | 35% | 39% | 52% | 33% |
| Bank and long-term debt as % of equity | 28% | 27% | 61% | 24% |
| EBIT ÷ interest expense | 14 | 8 | 8 | 7 |
| *Per Share Data, 1984* | | | | |
| Market price | $21–39 | $23–31 | $14–22 | $13–37 |
| Earnings per share | $ 1.87 | $ 2.39 | $ .86 | $ .63 |
| Dividends per share | — | — | — | — |
| Earnings multiple | 16 | 11 | 21 | 40 |
| Book value | $ 10 | $ 13 | $ 6 | $ 11 |

a. Teradyne and LTX design, manufacture, and sell computer-controlled systems for testing semiconductor integrated circuits and electronic components.

b. Fluke designs, manufactures, and sells commercial electronic test and measurement instruments and systems.

# Advanced Medical
# Technology Corporation

Early in April 1986, Tom Winter, vice president and loan officer of the Western National Bank of San Francisco, California, was reviewing a loan request for $8 million from Peter Haskins, president of Advanced Medical Technology Corporation.

Advanced Medical Technology Corporation (AMT) developed, manufactured, and sold scientific medical instruments, needles, and catheters that allowed rapid and less invasive access to a number of different organs and vessels. These products represented an alternative to traditional surgical procedures and allowed analysis or corrective treatment with less risk and trauma and at lower cost. An example of the products were catheters that could be introduced into a blood vessel and then manipulated through partially closed arteries or into the heart itself.

AMT had experienced extraordinary growth, fueled by heavy spending on research and development and a rapid expansion of its sales force. Its technical staff was very well regarded for developing new products with a wide range of applications. The combination of state-of-the-art products and a rapidly expanding market resulted in sales growth in excess of 30% per year. Mr. Haskins believed that industry sales would continue to grow at this rate and that any failure to maintain AMT's market position would be damaging in terms of competitive position and internal morale.

Sales volume, which had grown continuously from the start, was always large in relation to the available capital. The situation was exacerbated by large operating losses as AMT entered new markets aggressively.

Management met the financing pressures by heavy reliance on short-term credit, by leasing some manufacturing facilities, and by establishing a connection with Biological Labs, Inc., a leading pharmaceutical firm. Biological Labs had been eager to participate in the large and rapidly expanding medical instrumentation market but had failed in its internal efforts to enter the business. By 1983, Biological Labs had fallen behind in catheter and instrumentation technology. Management abandoned its internal efforts and entered into an agreement with AMT. At the initial closing on June 2, 1983, AMT received a cash payment of $7 million in exchange for 5% of the outstanding shares and the right to purchase an additional 13% of the outstanding stock over a 5-year period ending June 1988 for $12 million. If Biological Labs purchased the $12 million of additional stock, it would also have the right to require AMT to merge into Biological Labs in 1992. The price would be based on a multiple of average earnings in 1990 and 1991. Subsequent to the agreement, Biological Labs made four purchases of stock, as shown in Table A.

On April 14, 1986, at the suggestion of his public accountant, Mr. Haskins visited the Western National Bank to discuss the possibility of securing a line of credit. He met with Mr. Winter, vice president and loan officer of the bank. Mr. Winter explained that although he was unfamiliar with AMT's products, he had handled the accounts of several similar types of technology companies. Exhibits 1 and 2 present the financial statements that Mr. Haskins brought to the bank.

Mr. Haskins was thoroughly dissatisfied with the company's current loan arrangement with the Sunnyvale Bank, from which it had a credit line of $6 million with accounts receivable and inventory pledged as security. He thought that Mr. Flint, the loan officer at Sunnyvale, made no effort to understand the company and was constantly making suggestions that seemed inappropriate. He routinely visited AMT once every six months. While the visits were cordial, they were of very little value to Mr. Haskins. Furthermore, Mr. Haskins felt that the bank had been quite arbitrary in selecting the receivables that it would accept as collateral and in setting the percentage of inventory that it would advance as a loan. The restrictive attitude on the bank's part was limiting the company's ability to expand at exactly the time that increased volume seemed to be the key to profitability.

Mr. Haskins was perfectly willing to pledge the company's accounts receivable, inventory, or anything else that the bank thought would be desirable security as long as the arrangement was fair to the company and specific enough so that he could count on having the funds available when he needed them.

Mr. Winter explained that the bank was always interested in sound loan proposals from companies that showed the promise of developing into good accounts.

**TABLE A**
Equity Investments by Biological Labs

| | April 1985 | June 1985 | October 1985 | May 1986 |
|---|---|---|---|---|
| | $4,000,000 | $2,000,000 | $2,000,000 | $4,000,000 |

He promised to study the request and said that he hoped to visit the company in the near future.

Before going to the company, Mr. Winter telephoned Mr. Flint, head of Sunnyvale's asset-based lending operation, and learned that his experience with AMT had been thoroughly unsatisfactory. According to Mr. Flint, the company had maintained extremely low balances and on several occasions had overdrawn its account. The pattern of losses, despite excellent products that were well received in the trade, seemed to be the direct result of Mr. Haskins' determination to spend heavily on research and development and on marketing. Lastly, the receivables pledged as security and counted in the borrowing base did not always measure up to the bank's definition of acceptable collateral.

Mr. Flint pointed out that AMT was a familiar name to two other major banks in San Francisco and suggested that Mr. Winter might consider seeking the insights of the loan officers involved. Summaries of their comments are provided in Exhibit 3.

Upon visiting the AMT plants, Mr. Winter noted that the production process was primarily an assembly operation, involving several hundred products typically produced in small lots. It took an average of eight weeks to complete the processing of medical instruments. Ten to twelve weeks of finished-goods inventory was maintained to ensure immediate response to orders. However, Mr. Haskins hoped that significant savings in inventory could be realized. A computer-based inventory control system, linking purchasing, production, and sales, had been installed in late 1984. While the pressures to push product development and sales had prevented Mr. Haskins from becoming directly involved, he sensed that important headway was being made.

Sales were made to over 3,000 hospitals, clinics, and doctors. These accounts had been extended open lines of credit on net 30 terms without investigation. Although Mr. Haskins believed that some of the customers tended to be undercapitalized, collection experience had been excellent. However, slow payment seemed to be a competitive reality. Accounts receivables on AMT's books as of December 31, 1985, included $1.8 million due from foreign customers, representing 27% of the total. An aging of the receivables was as shown in Table B.

Mr. Winter also raised questions over the history of operating losses. Mr. Haskins provided full access to the divisional figures. Two of the three divisions

**TABLE B**
Aging of Accounts Receivable at December 31, 1985

| Month of Shipment | Age (days) | Outstanding Receivables | Sales |
|---|---|---|---|
| December 1985 . . . . . . | 0–30 | $2,598,000 | $2,917,000 |
| November . . . . . . . . | 31–60 | 1,890,000 | 2,657,000 |
| October . . . . . . . . | 61–90 | 627,000 | 2,730,000 |
| Prior . . . . . . . . . | 90 | 881,000 | |
| Total . . . . . . . | | $5,996,000 | |

were close to break-even in 1985, with plans to turn profitable in 1986. The third division, which represented a huge growth opportunity, was still incurring major losses as management tried to build a product and market position rapidly. All three divisions had dedicated research, production, sales, and marketing organizations.

When Mr. Winter returned to the bank, he immediately solicited the help of the loan officer who handled the Western National Bank's very substantial relationship with Biological Labs. A meeting was arranged with an executive vice president who assured Mr. Winter that Mr. Haskins was a strong operating manager whose aggressiveness and hard-driving entrepreneurial nature were important in building a major presence in this rapidly evolving industry. Biological Labs was prepared to provide a comfort letter stipulating that it "supported the efforts of AMT for which it had important plans." However, company policy made it impossible to guarantee the debt.

On May 8, 1986, Mr. Haskins returned to the Western National Bank to explain that the Sunnyvale Bank was unwilling to increase the percentages that it would loan against the assets. While Biological Labs had made a final investment of $4 million at the beginning of the month, AMT was rapidly exhausting its $6 million credit line. Mr. Haskins hoped that the Western National Bank would provide an $8 million line, with the agreement that all borrowings from the Sunnyvale Bank would be fully repaid.

Mr. Winter promised to let Mr. Haskins know the bank's decision within a few days.

**EXHIBIT 1**
Income Statements, 1983–1985 (thousands of dollars)

|  | 1983 | 1984 | 1985 |
|---|---|---|---|
| Net sales | $13,198 | $21,624 | $30,848 |
| Cost of products sold | 6,825 | 9,682 | 13,989 |
| Gross profit | 6,373 | 11,942 | 16,859 |
| General, selling, and administrative expenses | 6,299 | 11,374 | 14,478 |
| Research and development | 1,168 | 2,839 | 4,182 |
| Operating earnings | (1,094) | (2,271) | (1,801) |
| Interest expense | 501 | 611 | 634 |
| Sale of patents and technology | 0 | 1,370 | 627 |
| Other income | 103 | 336 | 321 |
| Earnings before taxes | (1,491) | (1,176) | (1,487) |
| Income taxes | (202) | 0 | 0 |
| Net earnings | $ (1,289) | $ (1,176) | $ (1,487) |

**EXHIBIT 2**
Balance Sheets at December 31, 1983–1985 (thousands of dollars)

|  | 1983 | 1984 | 1985 |
|---|---|---|---|
| Cash | $1,243 | $ (80) | $ (652) |
| Accounts receivable | 2,549 | 3,359 | 5,996 |
| Inventories | 3,305 | 6,782 | 9,762 |
| Other | 520 | 2,249 | 2,605 |
| Current assets | 7,617 | 12,310 | 17,711 |
| Net fixed assets | 906 | 1,494 | 1,802 |
| Capital leases[a] | 321 | 374 | 212 |
| Investment[b] | 0 | 1,943 | 1,049 |
| Other | 301 | 322 | 303 |
| Total assets | $9,145 | $16,443 | $21,077 |
| Notes payable to Biological Labs | $ 0 | $ 2,260 | $ 1,735 |
| Note payable to bank | 1,307 | 5,628 | 4,900 |
| Note payable to vendor | 47 | 0 | 0 |
| Accounts payable | 725 | 1,926 | 1,853 |
| Accrued expenses | 740 | 1,086 | 1,331 |
| Current portion, long-term debt, capital leases | 124 | 119 | 90 |
| Other | 22 | 37 | 33 |
| Current liabilities | 2,965 | 11,056 | 9,942 |
| Deferred income | 0 | 627 | 0 |
| Long-term debt | 254 | 0 | 0 |
| Capital lease obligation | 267 | 277 | 139 |
| Total liabilities | 3,486 | 11,960 | 10,081 |
| Net worth | 5,659 | 4,483 | 10,996 |
| Total liabilities and net worth | $9,145 | $16,443 | $21,077 |

a. In addition to the capital leases, the company has entered into noncancellable operating leases in the amount of $2.5 million per year for each of the next 10 years. These leases relate to the company's main manufacturing facilities.

b. Investments represent partial ownership in two small private companies.

**EXHIBIT 3**
Loan Officers' Comments

### Bank of San Francisco (Asset-Based Lending Division)

"Peter Haskins is a very likable, magnetic person who puts you through challenging but enjoyable mental gymnastics during negotiations. He is also a grinder who comes back once a week with a new request. He never lets up when he wants something; just keeps coming at you and grinding away. Peter also tries to get to the highest possible authority, even on mundane issues. He left Bank of San Francisco because of our unwillingness to add to AMT's highly leveraged position. We simply didn't believe that the quality of the assets warranted higher lending limits."

### Bank of the West (Technology Lending Group)

"Haskins is extremely honest and made AMT an open book. The bankers were invited to the strategic planning meetings and were kept informed of developments at the company. Haskins is well trained, with an MBA from Wharton, and is a tough, effective operating manager. He is a doer and a shaker. The relationship with Biological Labs is an important plus."

# Managing Short-Term Assets
# and Liabilities

# Allen Distribution Company

On June 16, 1967, William McConnell of the mid-Atlantic office of the Allen Distribution Company was considering whether his company should extend a credit limit of $1,000 to the Morse Photo Company of Harrisburg, Pennsylvania. Mr. McConnell had recently transferred from his job as credit representative in one of the company's western branch offices to become credit manager of the mid-Atlantic branch office, where he assumed full responsibility for initiating and supervising the branch's credit policies. When he assumed this position, Mr. McConnell had asked the five credit representatives who had been handling the branch's accounts on their own to submit to him for review a few borderline credit accounts waiting the establishment of credit limits. Mr. McConnell believed that his decision and method of analysis might prove helpful in setting the tone of future operations in the credit department. Therefore, he planned to write out his analysis and decision so that it could be circulated.

The Allen Distribution Company, a subsidiary of the Allen Electric Company, one of the nation's largest manufacturers of electrical appliances and lighting equipment, was a national wholesale distributor of the parent company's products. Merchandise sold by the Allen Distribution Company ranged from refrigerators and television sets to electric light bulbs. Its competition included other nationally known wholesalers and small regional wholesalers of the Allen line as well as wholesalers of a number of competing product lines.

The parent company sold goods to the Allen Distribution Company on the same terms as to independent wholesalers. Allen Distribution in turn usually sold its merchandise at the wholesale prices and on the terms suggested by the parent company, as did most other wholesalers of the Allen line. However, Allen Distribution maintained the right to set its own prices, and occasionally, when price competition developed in local areas, prices were reduced for short periods.

Since wholesale prices for competing products tended to be uniform, the intense competition for retail outlets and intermediary wholesale houses handling the Allen line caused the company to give major attention to the services offered these customers, including cooperative advertising, store displays, inventory control, and credit arrangements. However, the slight differences in the quality of services rendered by the large wholesalers of Allen products were not fully appreciated by customers, and sales often depended more on the personal relationships developed between the customer and company salespeople. For this reason, Allen Distribution's sales force tended to concentrate on maintaining current accounts and on expanding sales by securing outlets carrying competing product lines where brand differentials could be emphasized.

These salespeople were paid a straight commission of 1% for net sales in their territory. An additional 1% commission was given on net sales to new accounts during the first year. The sales force was not held responsible for bad debt losses resulting from their sales efforts, although they sometimes helped in collecting overdue receivables.

Sales during the first four months of 1967 for the entire company, as well as the mid-Atlantic branch, had decreased 2% in comparison with the similar period in 1966, even though the number of customers serviced remained relatively unchanged. In late May 1967 the president of Allen Distribution had called together the branch managers and announced an intensified sales campaign for new outlets to offset the sales decline. Sales quotas by branch and by salespeople were established, and a prize system was devised to reward sales personnel for successful efforts. Mr. McConnell knew that the mid-Atlantic branch manager was actively supporting the program and wanted the branch to make a good showing.

The mid-Atlantic branch office of Allen Distribution had net sales of $78 million in 1966. A percentage analysis of the branch's 1966 income statement is shown in Table A.

**TABLE A**
Percentage Income Analysis, Allen Distribution Mid-Atlantic Branch, 1966

| | | |
|---|---|---|
| Net sales | 100.0% | |
| Cost of merchandise | 92.0 | (All costs variable) |
| Gross profit | 8.0% | |
| Operating and other expenses | | |
| Warehouse | 4.1 | (Variable portion: 1.2% of sales) |
| Selling | 1.4 | (Variable portion: 1.1% of sales) |
| Administrative | 1.1 | (Variable portion: .1% of sales) |
| Bad debt loss | .13 | |
| Interest expense | .27 | |
| Total | 7.0% | |
| Net profit before taxes | 1.0% | |

Mr. McConnell found that throughout 1966 the branch's outstanding receivables had averaged $5.6 million, of which approximately $150,000 represented overdue amounts. The active accounts, numbering 15,000, were turning over approximately every 25 days. Twelve people were employed in the credit department, and its operating expenses (included in the administrative expenses) were $150,000 per year. This did not include bad debt losses, which were .13% of sales in 1966 and had averaged .14% of sales in recent years. These bad debt losses derived principally from the marginal accounts and were therefore approximately 1.4% of sales to the marginal accounts.

In Mr. McConnell's belief, a credit department should have little difficulty in approving good accounts and rejecting the bad ones. The real core of the credit department's operation rested in the evaluation of marginal accounts. Although Mr. McConnell had not made a study of the branch's operation, it was his opinion that the good accounts covered Allen Distribution's total operating and overhead costs, whereas the selection and handling of marginal accounts made the difference between profit and loss. Furthermore, Mr. McConnell believed that the purpose of a credit department was not to minimize credit losses but rather to maximize profits. He thought it was significant to recognize that an increase in sales volume for Allen Distribution usually meant increased sales for the parent company.

In evaluating a marginal account, Mr. McConnell considered the cost of handling the account, the current and potential profitability of the account, and the inherent risks. Although Mr. McConnell did not know how much more it cost a credit department to maintain a marginal account, he knew the credit department spent at least twice as much time maintaining credit files and collecting overdue amounts on marginal accounts as on good accounts. He estimated that 20% of the branch's accounts, representing nearly 10% of sales, were marginal firms. Nevertheless, collections from these companies tended to be on the average only five to ten days slower than collections from good accounts. Mr. McConnell had not determined an appropriate basis for distributing these costs to marginal firms, but he thought they should bear a substantial portion of the credit department's operating expenses. He also believed that the 7% interest charge on bank loans, which roughly paralleled the size of the accounts receivable balance, was a cost factor chargeable to his department. Although Mr. McConnell was not certain how it might apply, he knew that management of the parent company expected new investments to promise returns of 20% or more (before taxes) before the investment was considered acceptable.

Although Mr. McConnell hesitated to define a good account in specific terms, he generally considered that companies with a two-to-one current ratio and with an equity investment greater than outstanding debt fitted into this category. He also examined, when appropriate, acid test ratios, net working capital, inventory turnover, and other balance sheet and income statement relations but found it difficult to establish rules to cover every situation. Unsatisfactory credit requests were also difficult to define in terms of specific ratios. With experience, a good credit analyst was able to handle good and bad accounts in a routine manner. Real judgment, however, was required to select from the marginal applications those worthy of credit. In evaluating a marginal account, Mr. McConnell thought the principal's character, although difficult to ascertain, was as important as the company's financial status. In an analysis of a credit application, two factors were considered important: (1) the risk of losing all or part of the outstanding receivable balance through bankruptcy; and (2) the cost of having to carry the amount due beyond the net period. Since the credit department screened almost 1,000 new requests for credit annually, Mr. McConnell knew that the evaluative procedures would have to be streamlined.

Mr. McConnell thought that the most difficult aspect of his new job would be translating any changes in credit policy into appropriate action by the credit representatives. Consequently, he planned to analyze a few selected marginal accounts so he might set forth the reasons for accepting or rejecting the accounts as a step toward establishing new credit standards. The Morse Photo Company was the first situation he had decided to review.

A credit file on the Morse Photo Company had been established on the basis of the following memorandum, dated May 16, 1967, from the company's Harrisburg salesman:

> Have sold Anthony W. Morse, president of Morse Photo Company, 280 Carlisle Avenue, Harrisburg, Pennsylvania, on the idea of switching from Oliver Electric Company's flash bulbs to ours. Sales would be $5,000 a year on current volume, and the Morse company is a real grower. Tony Morse is a terrific salesman and should sell a whale of a lot of bulbs for us. He wants $1,000 worth (net cost to him) of bulbs as a starter.

Photographic flash bulbs were not a major product item and for statistical purposes were grouped with electric lighting equipment, which accounted for 25% of Allen Distribution's sales volume. These electrical lighting supplies normally carried gross margins of 7–10% for Allen Distribution, but photo bulbs, one of the highest profit items sold by the company, had a gross margin of 17% after cash discounts. In addition, the parent company earned a "contribution" profit margin of 20% (before taxes) on its sales of photo bulbs.

The Morse Photo Company was similar to a number of Allen Distribution's customers. Almost half of Allen Distribution's 15,000 credit accounts purchased only lighting supplies from the company. Many of these accounts were small wholesale houses or regional chain stores whose annual purchases were in the $5,000–20,000 range.

Largely in order to control the retail price, photo bulbs were sold only on a consignment basis, but the practice had possible financial significance. Although a supply of bulbs was delivered to a customer, Allen Distribution remained the owner until the bulbs were sold by the consignee and hence was entitled to recover its bulbs at any time from the consignee's stock. To ensure recovery, segregation of inventory was agreed to by the customer. This meant that the stock of Allen bulbs should be plainly marked and physically separated from the remainder of inventory.

After a sale of bulbs, the consignee was supposed to keep the resulting receivables or cash separate from other accounts or funds until payment was made to Allen Distribution. Therefore, if the prescribed procedures were followed, it was possible to identify, as Allen Distribution's, the total value of a consignment in inventory, receivables, or cash. Thus, in the event of liquidation, no other creditor could make claim against these items.

Owing to the inconvenience of keeping separate stocks, accounts, and funds, the safeguards associated with these consignment shipments were not often observed in practice. Allen Distribution made little effort to verify whether a separate inventory was actually maintained by its photo bulb customers. Nevertheless, it was believed that the company might have some protection in recovering consigned merchandise in the event of a customer's bankruptcy, since the bulbs carried the Allen brand name. More significantly, Allen Distribution made no effort to enforce segregation of funds after bulb sales were made by the customer. In consequence, it stood in the same general position as other creditors from the time the bulbs were sold by the consignee until remittance was made. Mr. McConnell therefore concluded that the consignment method afforded little financial protection in practice and appraised these accounts in the same way as open accounts.

At each month's end, the consignee inventoried the bulb supply and made payment in the amount of actual sales, less 25% trade discount. Credit terms were 5% 10 E. O. M. All photo bulb consignees were on a 1-year contract basis, whereby the customer agreed to sell Allen bulbs exclusively, and Allen Distribution agreed to supply the customer's needs up to a predetermined limit ($1,000 in the case of Morse Photo Company), provided payments were made within terms.

In the credit file Mr. McConnell found a credit report containing balance sheets and income statements of the Morse Photo Company (Exhibits 1–4) and four letters in reply to credit inquiries by a branch credit representative (Exhibit 5).

**EXHIBIT 1**
Associated Credit Agency Report, May 27, 1967

| | |
|---|---|
| *Company:* | Morse Photo Company, 280 Carlisle Avenue, Harrisburg, Pennsylvania. |
| *Rating:* | Limited (unchanged from previous report). |
| *Business:* | Commercial developing and photographic finishing. Also does a small volume of wholesaling films and camera supplies. Its distribution includes about 300 drug and periodical stores within a 130-mile radius of Harrisburg. |
| *Management:* | Anthony W. Morse, president and principal stockholder. |
| *History:* | Business started as proprietorship in May, 1961, with limited capital. On November 12, 1962, present owner purchased the assets but did not assume the liabilities for a reported $11,000; $2,000 was derived from savings and the balance was financed through a bank loan. On April 30, 1965, the proprietorship was succeeded by the present corporation, which corporation took over assets and assumed liabilities of the predecessor business. |
| *Sales terms:* | 2% 10 days, net 30. |
| *Employees:* | Twelve individuals, of which three are salespeople. |

This 7-year-old concern has expanded rapidly since its founding. This has been accomplished by expanding from a local territory to a radius of 130 miles and by giving 24-hour service to its customers. In order to accomplish this, there has been a substantial increase in fixed assets and approximately a 60% increase during the last year under review. This has been made possible in part by acquiring the Meade Photo Company in September 1966. While the net earnings transferred to surplus have been small, there has been an increase in

*(continued)*

**EXHIBIT 1** (*concluded*)

capital. During 1965 an 8% preferred stock issue of $10,000 was made, and in 1967 bonds were issued for $14,000. In connection with the acquisition of the Meade Photo Company for $24,000, $7,000 was borrowed from the Harrisburg Fidelity and Trust Company and the seller was given a chattel mortgage for $17,000, payable $180 a week. In addition Meade receives a payment of 10% of the net sales, which are transacted from their former customers for a period of 5 years. During the year more equipment was purchased with money obtained in the form of notes from the bank. The amount due the bank is made up of five installment notes, secured by various pieces of equipment. Other notes payable consist of $5,500 payable to a large film manufacturer; $8,500 payable to Meade Photo; and the balance to others. Notes payable after 1 year are due to Meade Photo. Mr. Morse, the president, estimates that sales during the fiscal year 1968 will be $320,000.

**EXHIBIT 2**

Morse Photo Company, Balance Sheets, 1966–1967

|  | *April 30, 1966* | *April 30, 1967* |
|---|---|---|
| Cash | $    320 | $    439 |
| Accounts receivable, net | 11,503 | 16,201 |
| Inventory at cost | 12,712 | 12,681 |
| Current assets | 24,535 | 29,321 |
| Fixed assets |  |  |
| Cost | 58,331 | 93,574 |
| Depreciation | 12,573 | 21,492 |
| Net | 45,758 | 72,082 |
| Other assets | 2,839 | 9,641 |
| Total assets | $ 73,132 | $111,044 |
| Accounts payable | $   9,953 | $ 22,311 |
| Note payable, bank | 5,136 | 9,360 |
| Notes payable, other | 9,127 | 15,158 |
| Income tax | 198 | 373 |
| Other tax | 3,123 | 2,546 |
| Interest payable | – | 96 |
| Payroll payable | – | 1,514 |
| Current liabilities | 27,537 | 51,358 |
| Notes payable, officers | 2,648 | 2,648 |
| Notes payable, bank | 764 | – |
| Notes payable, other | – | 810 |
| Bond payable | – | 14,000 |
| Total liabilities | 30,949 | 68,816 |
| Preferred stock | 10,000 | 10,000 |
| Common stock | 32,100 | 32,100 |
| Earned surplus | 83 | 128 |
| Net worth | 42,183 | 42,228 |
| Total liabilities and net worth | $ 73,132 | $111,044 |

**EXHIBIT 3**

Morse Photo Company, Income Statements, 1966–1967

|  | April 30, 1966 | April 30, 1967 |
|---|---|---|
| Net sales | $162,898 | $269,461 |
| Cost of goods sold | | |
| Material | 58,453 | 88,079 |
| Wages | 33,963 | 65,263 |
| Other | 28,841 | 44,049 |
| Total cost of goods sold | 121,257 | 197,391 |
| Gross profit | 41,641 | 72,070 |
| Administrative and selling expenses | | |
| Officers' salaries | 12,000 | 22,000 |
| Office salaries | 5,733 | 10,000 |
| Sales commissions | – | 3,568 |
| Depreciation | 7,848 | 10,071 |
| Other | 15,779 | 25,613 |
| Total administrative and selling expenses | 41,360 | 71,252 |
| Net earnings before tax | 281 | 818 |
| Income tax | 198 | 373 |
| Earnings | 83 | 445 |
| Dividends | – | 400 |
| Earnings transferred to surplus | $ 83 | $ 45 |

**EXHIBIT 4**

Morse Photo Company, Credit Record as of May 15, 1967

| High Credit | Owes Currently | Past Due | Terms | Payments |
|---|---|---|---|---|
| $3,000 | $ 0 | $ 0 | Net 30 | Prompt |
| 2,693 | 0 | 0 | 2% 10 E.O.M. | Prompt |
| 2,740 | 245 | 127 | Net 30 | Slow 8 months |
| 582 | 0 | 0 | 2% 10 | Prompt to slow 60 days |
| 108 | 108 | 108 | Net 10 | Slow |
| 2,518 | 2,518 | 0 | Net 30 | Prompt |
| 582 | 61 | 0 | 2% 10 | Prompt |
| 9,308 | 8,854 | 4,601 | 2% 10, net 30 | Slow 30 to 60 days |
| 5,000 | 4,800 | 4,800 | 2% 10 E.O.M. | Slow 90 to 120 days |
| 4,492 | 3,452 | 3,452 | 2% 10 E.O.M. | Slow 90 to 120 days |
| 167 | 0 | 0 | Net 30 | Slow 60 days |
| 118 | 118 | 118 | Net 15 | Slow 60 to 90 days |

**EXHIBIT 5**
Morse Photo Company, Credit References

---

**Letter from the Harrisburg Fidelity and Trust Company**

Allen Distribution Company                                     June 6, 1967
Philadelphia, Pennsylvania

Attention: Credit Manager

GENTLEMEN:

Morse Photo Company has maintained a satisfactory account with us for a number of years and such accommodation as we have extended them is cared for as agreed. It is our feeling that they are entitled to their reasonable trade requirements.

> Yours very truly,
> *(Signed)* GEORGE GRUBB
> *Assistant Vice-President*
> *Harrisburg Fidelity and Trust Company*

**Letter from a Large Film Manufacturer**

Allen Distribution Company                                     June 5, 1967
Philadelphia, Pennsylvania

Attention: Credit Manager

GENTLEMEN:

   Re: Morse Photo Company

With reference to your inquiry regarding the above account, we wish to advise that we have been doing business with them since 1961.

Recently we have had a fair amount of trouble with them because of overexpansion in relation to their net worth. In the past, customer's promises for payment could not be depended upon, although there has been a decided improvement in the last six months. Around the first of the year we had to take notes totaling $7,500 for the past-due accounts. At the present time $2,500 is still outstanding, but the notes are not in default. In April, we extended them $2,700 worth of credit, $2,600 of which was under the term ⅓ payable every ten days. The last payment was not received until June 1, whereas it was due May 22. At the present time the concern owes us outside of the notes $115 of which $76.70 represents the April charge which is past due in our books.

To sum the whole thing up, we are willing to extend credit up to $5,000 but must watch the account carefully.

> Yours very truly,
> *(Signed)* ANNE WHITTIER
> *Credit Manager*

*(continued)*

**EXHIBIT 5** (*concluded*)

### Letter from a Large Chemical Company

Allen Distribution Company                                      June 7, 1967
Philadelphia, Pennsylvania

Attention: Credit Manager

GENTLEMEN:

The following summary is the information you requested with respect to Morse Photo Company:

How Long Sold—May, 1965
Last Sale June, 1967
Highest Credit—$700
Amount Owing—$700
Past Due—0
Terms—2% 10 days
Amount Secured—None
Manner of Payment—Previous sales C.O.D.

This is a trial order on restricted credit terms. Future policy will be determined by payment record.

Yours very truly,
*(Signed)* ARNOLD HEAD
*Credit Manager*

### Letter from Oliver Electric Company

Allen Distribution Company                                      June 9, 1967
Philadelphia, Pennsylvania

Attention: Credit Manager

GENTLEMEN:

Re: Morse Photo Company
How Long Sold—July, 1962
Date of Last Sale—April, 1967
High Credit—$1,600
Amount Owing—$630
Past Due—$630
Terms—2% 10 End of the Month

Other comments:

We would suggest watching this account carefully. It has been up to nine months slow with us.

Yours very truly,
*(Signed)* J. E. STEWART
*Credit Manager*

# The O. M. Scott & Sons Company

Between 1955 and 1961 management of the O. M. Scott & Sons Company launched a number of new programs aimed at maintaining and increasing the company's past success and growth. Largely in response to these activities, Scott's field sales force grew from 6 to 150, several entirely new and expanded production facilities went on stream, and the number of products in the company's product line tripled. Sales increased from about $10 million to $43 million. In late 1961 company officials were preparing to review the results of all these changes to ascertain how, if at all, Scott's plans and financial policies should be changed.

The O. M. Scott & Sons Company commenced operations in 1868, when it began processing the country's first clean, weed-free grass seed. Scott's early business came from a small but rapidly growing local market in central Ohio. Later, however, the company went through several stages in its growth. At about the turn of the century Scott began to sell grass and other farm seeds over a wider geographic area by mail. As its mail-order business became successful, the company began to advertise extensively and in 1927 added a free magazine called *Lawn Care,* which has been widely distributed ever since. In all these early promotional activities Scott sought to sell its name, its products, and the idea of improved care of lawns. In the 1920s a special lawn fertilizer developed for home use was added to the product line. During the 1930s the company began to distribute its products on a small scale through selected retail stores and garden centers. Sales and profits increased steadily throughout these years. Scott continued to grow along these same general lines until 1945, by which time sales had reached $2.7 million and net profits after taxes were about $30,000.

Over the decade immediately following the war, pioneering research by Scott led to the development and introduction of a wide range of new chemical weed and garden pest controls and special-purpose lawn fertilizers. In addition, the company's grass seed lines were upgraded and supplemented. Largely in response to the success of this research, sales increased to $11.4 million and profits to over $210,000 in fiscal 1955.

By 1955, however, despite the company's impressive postwar record of growth in sales and profits, management was convinced that neither Scott nor its competitors had begun to develop and tap the potential inherent in the national lawn care market. In Scott's own case this was attributed to the fact that Scott's customers could not buy its products easily where and when they expected to find them. The company's distribution system had not evolved adequately in response to developing market opportunities, and in many instances the company's dealers either were poorly stocked or were not the right kind of dealer for the company's products.

Thus began a new stage in Scott's development. Early in 1955 the company launched a program to build a national field sales organization with the objective of increasing the number, quality, and performance of its distributors so as to capitalize more fully on the success of its product research and development efforts. When this program started, the company had six field salespeople. By 1960, Scott had a field sales force of 150, serving almost 10,000 retail dealers across the country. These dealers were mainly department stores and small hardware stores and garden supply centers. Scott's salespeople spent most of their time training the dealers how to do a better selling job with Scott products, and they were paid a salary plus a bonus based on factory shipments to dealers.

Scott's product development program continued apace with the buildup in the direct selling force, so that by the end of the 1950s the company was engaged in the purchase, processing, and sale of grass seed, and the manufacture and sale of fertilizers, weed and pest control products, mechanical spreaders, and electric lawn mowers. In 1959 sales increased to $30.6 million and profits to $1.5 million. A large proportion of these sales comprised new products that had been developed and patented by the company within the past few years.

Reviewing the company's progress again in early 1959, management was still not satisfied that the company was marketing its products as effectively as possible. For one thing, it was estimated that an annual market potential of at least $100 million existed for Scott products. Another important consideration was that several nationally known chemical firms had either begun or were expected to begin competing against Scott in certain lines. These facts led management to conclude that the most effective way for Scott to preserve its preeminent market position would be to push for immediate further market penetration. If successful, such a strategy would enable Scott to eclipse competition as completely as possible before its competitors could establish a firm market position against the company.

In this context, an annual growth rate in sales and profits of up to 25% was thought to be a reasonable goal for the company over the next few years.

Apart from the need to continue strengthening the company's field sales force and dealer organization, management thought in early 1959 that the most important factor standing in the way of further rapid growth and market penetration was the inability of the typical Scott dealer to carry an adequate inventory of Scott products. Because of the highly seasonal character of sales at retail of the company's products, it was essential that dealers have enough inventory on hand to meet local sales peaks when they came. Experience showed that in many parts of the country a large percentage of dealer sales were made on a few weekends each season. Failure to supply this demand when it materialized most often resulted in a sale lost to a competitor, although sometimes a customer simply postponed buying anything. Ensuring adequate dealer inventories had become more of a problem in recent years. The effectiveness of Scott's product development program meant that dealers were expected to carry many more products than in the past. In addition, Scott had shifted its marketing emphasis from selling individual products to selling complete lawn and garden programs. And in order to sell a full lawn maintenance program it was necessary that the dealer carry the complete Scott line and have it on hand when needed by the consumer.

Because of their small size and often weak working capital position, most of Scott's dealers could not realistically be expected to increase their inventory investment in Scott products. This meant that any desired buildup in dealer inventory levels would have to be financed in some way by Scott itself. In the past the company had extended generous seasonal datings to its dealers, as was industry practice. As a normal pattern, winter and early spring shipments became due at the end of April or May, depending on the geographical area. Shipments during the summer months were due in October or November. The purpose of these seasonal datings was to enable and encourage as many dealers as possible to be well stocked in advance of seasonal sales peaks. Anticipation at the rate of .6% a month was offered on payments made in advance of these seasonal dates, although few dealers availed themselves of this opportunity. With purchases made outside the two main selling seasons, dealers were expected to pay on the 10th of the second month following shipment.

The company's past experience with seasonal datings suggested certain changes in the event Scott proceeded to finance a higher level of dealer inventories. Because of the seasonal nature of the business and the fact that most dealers were thinly capitalized, payment was not often received by Scott until the merchandise involved was sold, irrespective of the terms of sale. This meant that many dealers were continually asking for credit extensions. Another problem inherent in the seasonal dating policy was that Scott retained little or no effective security interest in the goods involved. A final problem was that in the past Scott had followed a policy of not selling to dealers that could not be relied upon to maintain prices at reasonable levels. It was thought that widespread selling at discount prices would undermine the company and the market image it was trying to project. Thus, in any decision to expand dealer inventories, management hoped to contrive a procedure whereby

Scott would retain the right to reclaim goods from third parties in the event any of its dealers began selling at wholesale to a discounter.

After considerable study it was decided to continue the traditional seasonal dating plan and to introduce a new trust receipt plan as well. This combination was thought to fulfill all the requirements outlined in the previous paragraph. As the particular trust receipt plan adopted by Scott worked, a trust receipt dealer was required to sign a trust receipt that provided for (1) immediate transfer to the dealer of title to any Scott products shipped in response to a dealer order, (2) retention of a security interest by Scott in merchandise so shipped until sold by the dealer acting in his capacity as a retailer, and (3) segregation of a sufficient proportion of the funds received from such sales to provide for payment to Scott as billed. Among other things, these provisions made it possible for Scott to move in and reclaim any inventory held by third parties that had been sold by a trust receipt dealer acting illegally as a wholesaler. Exhibit 5 shows the trust receipt form used by Scott. In addition to obtaining the trust receipt from its dealers, the company also was required to file a statement of trust receipt financing with the secretary of state in each state where a trust receipt plan dealer was domiciled. Such a statement is shown in Exhibit 6. Dealers using the trust receipt plan were charged an extra 3% on the cost of purchases from Scott. They also had to place all purchase orders directly through Scott's field sales force, inasmuch as these account executives were held responsible by the company for controlling dealer inventories in connection with the trust receipt plan.

This last-mentioned role of Scott's sales force was absolutely central to the proper functioning of the trust receipt plan. Apart from simply policing the level and character of dealer inventories, the account executives also periodically inventoried the trust receipt dealers so that Scott could bill the dealers for merchandise sold. During the two peak retail selling seasons these physical inventories were taken once a month, and even oftener in the case of large dealers. In the off seasons the inspections occurred much less frequently. In any event, the terms of payment associated with the trust receipt plan required that the dealer pay Scott within ten days of receipt of an invoice from the company for goods sold since the last physical inventory date.

After introduction of the two payment plans in 1960, about half of Scott's sales were by seasonal dating and half by trust receipt. The trust receipt dealers were for the most part local garden centers and hardware stores, whereas the seasonal dating dealers were the larger chain garden centers and department stores. The company's overall collection experience with both plans was that about 75% of receivables were collected in the month due, another 16% in the following month, an additional 6% in the next month after that, and the balance thereafter.

The rapid growth in outstanding receivables resulting from the trust receipt program was financed largely by a combination of subordinated notes, a revolving line of bank credit, and increased use of supplier credit arising out of special deferred payment terms extended by the company's chemical suppliers. The company also retained almost all its earnings each year as it had in the past.

At the end of fiscal 1961, Scott and its subsidiaries had $16.2 million of long-term debt outstanding, of which $12 million comprised renewable 5-year subordinated notes of the parent company held by four insurance companies and a trustee and $4.2 million was publicly held bonds owed by Scotts Chemical Plant, Inc., a wholly owned subsidiary. The key terms associated with the $12 million of subordinated notes are summarized in the notes following Exhibits 1 and 2. The governing loan indenture limited the unconsolidated parent company's maximum outstanding debt at any time to an amount not greater than three times what was termed the company's "equity working capital" as of the preceding March 31. What was meant by equity working capital and the calculation of maximum allowed debt are shown in Exhibit 7. The note indenture restricted outstanding subordinated notes to only 60% of maximum allowed debt as determined by the above equity working capital formula. The agreement also required that Scott be out of bank debt for 60 consecutive days each year and that the company earn before taxes 1½ times its fixed financial charges including interest on funded and unfunded debt, amortization of debt discount, and rentals on leased properties.

In addition to the long-term debt just described, Scott also had a $12.5 million line of credit at the end of fiscal 1961 with a group of seven commercial banks. The purpose of this line was to provide for seasonal funds needs, and in recent years the maximum line had been used each year. An informal understanding covering this seasonal financing arrangement required that Scott maintain average compensating balances with the banks of 15% of the line of credit.

As far as accounts payable were concerned, Scott had negotiated an arrangement with its principal chemical suppliers whereby the company settled with these suppliers just once or twice a year. It had been possible to negotiate these favorable terms because the suppliers were persuaded that it was in their best interests to help Scott develop and expand the home lawn market. Generally, no interest or other charges were levied on these amounts.

As fiscal 1961 drew to a close, management was generally pleased with what appeared to have been the results of the trust receipt program, although final figures for the year just ending were not yet available. Company sales had increased from $31 million in 1959 to over $43 million in 1961. At this level of operations the company's break-even point was estimated at $27.5–30 million.

By the end of 1961, when company officials were reviewing the results of fiscal 1961 and preparing plans for the 1962 selling season, the audited statements shown in Exhibits 1 and 2 were available, as well as the unaudited and unconsolidated quarterly statements in Exhibits 3 and 4. In addition, on the basis of a physical inventory taken by the company's sales force, combined standard and trust receipt plan dealer inventories were estimated to be at a level of about $28 million at the end of calendar 1961. This compared with roughly $17 million at the end of 1960. On the basis of these and other data, Scott's sales department estimated that in terms of cost of sales, dealer sales in fiscal 1961 reached an all-time high of over $30 million. The recent record of earnings, dividends, and market price range is shown in Exhibit 8.

It was against this background that company officials began their review and evaluation of recent operations and current financial position. They were particularly anxious to formulate any indicated changes in company plans and financial policies before the new production and selling seasons.

**EXHIBIT 1**
Consolidated Balance Sheets at September 30, 1957–1961 (thousands of dollars)

| | 1957 | 1958 | 1959 | 1960[a] | 1961[e] |
|---|---|---|---|---|---|
| Cash | $ 533.9 | $ 1,232.0 | $ 1,736.4 | $ 2,328.7 | $ 1,454.3 |
| Accounts receivable | 2,640.0 | 4,686.5 | 5,788.4 | 15,749.7 | 21,500.5[f] |
| Inventories | 2,340.3 | 3,379.8 | 6,993.2 | 3,914.3 | 5,590.5 |
| Current assets | 5,514.2 | 9,298.3 | 14,518.0 | 21,992.7 | 28,545.3 |
| Land, buildings, equipment | 2,253.5 | 2,439.5 | 7,364.6 | 8,003.4 | 8,370.2 |
| Less: Accumulated depreciation | 544.0 | 650.0 | 1,211.3 | 1,687.1 | 2,247.1 |
| Net fixed assets | 1,709.5 | 1,789.5 | 6,153.3 | 6,316.3 | 6,123.1 |
| Investment in and advances to affiliates | 1,165.6 | 28.9 | 232.3 | 462.0 | 133.6 |
| Other assets | 488.5 | 376.6 | 837.5 | 1,132.0 | 937.8 |
| Total assets | $8,877.8 | $11,493.3 | $21,741.1 | $29,903.0 | $35,739.8 |
| Accounts payable | $1,540.8 | $ 2,134.6 | $ 4,140.2 | $ 2,791.0 | $ 6,239.2 |
| Notes payable, banks | 300.0 | – | 1,000.0 | – | – |
| Accrued taxes, interest, and other expenses | 674.3 | 1,437.7 | 1,900.7 | 1,941.2 | 1,207.7 |
| Current sinking fund requirements | 77.0 | 173.9 | 324.3 | 382.5 | 512.5 |
| Current liabilities | 2,592.1 | 3,746.2 | 7,365.2 | 5,114.7 | 7,959.4 |
| Long-term debt | | | | | |
| Of parent company[c,h] | 2,186.7 | 2,059.7 | 1,777.2 | 9,000.0 | 12,000.0 |
| Of subsidiary[c,h] | – | – | 5,162.6 | 4,649.5 | 4,170.4 |
| Total liabilities[d] | 4,778.8 | 5,805.9 | 14,305.0 | 18,764.2 | 24,129.8 |
| Preferred stock[i] | 1,757.2 | 2,432.2 | 2,392.5 | 2,347.5 | 2,254.3 |
| Common stock and surplus | 2,341.8 | 3,255.2 | 5,043.6 | 8,791.3[b,g] | 9,355.7 |
| Net worth | 4,099.0 | 5,687.4 | 7,436.1 | 11,138.8 | 11,610.0 |
| Total liabilities and net worth | $8,877.8 | $11,493.3 | $21,741.1 | $29,903.0 | $35,739.8 |

Notes (a) to (i) refer to Notes to Financial Statements, following Exhibits 1 and 2.

**EXHIBIT 2**
Consolidated Income Statements for Years Ending September 30, 1957–1961 (thousands of dollars)

| | 1957 | 1958 | 1959 | 1960[a] | 1961[e] |
|---|---|---|---|---|---|
| Net sales[b,g] | $18,675.9 | $23,400.2 | $30,563.7 | $38,396.4 | $43,140.1 |
| Cost of products sold including processing, warehousing, delivery, and merchandising (incl. lease rentals) | 15,500.9 | 18,914.7 | 24,119.5 | 30,416.8[d] | 34,331.7 |
| General and administrative, research and development expenses | 1,817.2 | 2,134.1 | 2,499.3 | 2,853.6 | 3,850.7 |
| Depreciation and amortization | 263.2 | 185.9 | 377.6 | 584.2 | 589.6 |
| Interest charges | 199.8 | 212.7 | 410.6 | 881.6 | 1,131.5 |
| Total cost of sales | 17,781.1 | 21,447.4 | 27,407.0 | 34,736.2 | 39,903.5 |
| Earnings before taxes on income | 894.8 | 1,952.8 | 3,156.7 | 3,660.2 | 3,236.6 |
| Federal and state taxes on income | 443.5 | 1,051.6 | 1,671.2 | 1,875.2 | 1,665.9 |
| Net income after taxes | $ 451.3 | $ 901.2 | $ 1,485.5 | $ 1,785.0 | $ 1,570.7 |

Notes (a) to (g) refer to Notes to Financial Statements, following Exhibits 1 and 2.

Notes to Financial Statements (Exhibits 1 and 2)

---

### a. 1960 Auditor's Statement

The Board of Directors
The O. M. Scott & Sons Company
Marysville, Ohio

We have examined the statement of consolidated financial position of the O. M. Scott & Sons Company and its subsidiaries as of September 30, 1960, the related consolidated statements of operations, capital surplus and retained earnings for the fiscal year then ended, and accompanying notes to financial statements. Our examination was made in accordance with generally accepted auditing standards, and accordingly included such tests of the accounting records and such other auditing procedures as we considered necessary in the circumstances.

In our opinion, the accompanying statements, together with the explanatory notes, present fairly the consolidated financial position of the O. M. Scott & Sons Company and its subsidiaries at September 30, 1960, and the results of their operations for the year ended, in conformity with generally accepted accounting principles, except as described in note *(b)*, applied on a basis consistent with that of the preceding year.

Peat, Marwick, Mitchell & Co.

Columbus, Ohio
November 23, 1960

**b. Sales.** For several years the company has followed a prebilling system to obtain more efficient and economical control of production through the medium of unappropriated inventory. Under this system, the invoicing of customers predates shipment. Consequently, both fiscal 1960 and 1959 sales stated in the operating statement include firm orders received, billed, and costed out in late September which were shipped early in the immediately following October. Prior to September 30, 1960, the amounts involved were not significant, but toward the end of that month shipment was delayed by the company to facilitate the taking of physical inventories at storage warehouses as of the month end. The result of the foregoing is to include an additional amount of approximately $343,000 in net earnings for the year 1960. In management's opinion, the earnings on these sales are properly earnings of the year 1960.

**c. Long-Term Debt.** All long-term obligations of the parent company at September 30, 1959, were retired prior to December 31, 1959.

In fiscal 1960 the parent company sold 5-year subordinated promissory notes, principally to certain insurance companies, at the principal amount of $9 million, maturing October 13, 1964. The notes bear interest to October 10, 1960, at 6½% per annum and thereafter to maturity at (a) 6% per annum, or (b) the New York prime commercial rate plus 1½%, whichever is higher.

The loan agreement provides, among other things, that (a) payment of principal and interest on the notes is subordinated to repayment of bank loans due within one year, (b) new or additional notes may be sold on October 28th of each future year, and (c) any holder of the notes may, before October 15th of each year, require payment by October 10th of the immediately ensuing year of all or part of the notes held.[1]

All holders of the notes at September 30, 1960, surrendered the notes then held in exchange for new notes having exactly the same terms but maturing October 28, 1965, at an interest rate of 6% per annum to October 10, 1961. Interest after October 10, 1961, accrues at the rate determinable under the provisions of the loan agreement.

---

1. Such payments were to be made in four equal annual installments beginning on October 10 of the immediately ensuing year.

*(continued)*

Notes to Financial Statements (Exhibits 1 and 2) *(continued)*

Long-term obligations of subsidiary outstanding on September 30, 1960:

| | |
|---|---:|
| 20-year 5¾% first mortgage bonds due Mar. 15, 1977 . . . . . . . . . . | $1,026,000 |
| 18-year 6% secured sinking fund debentures due Feb. 1, 1977 . . . . . . . . | 2,840,500 |
| 10-year 6% sinking fund notes due Mar. 15, 1967 . . . . . . . . . | 178,000 |
| 10-year 6% subordinated debentures due Dec. 15, 1967 . . . . . . . . . | 950,000 |
| | $4,994,500 |
| Less: Current sinking fund provision . . . | 345,000 |
| | $4,649,500 |

The above obligations of a subsidiary are secured by property mortgages, and/or assignment of lease rentals payable by the parent company.

**d. Long-Term Leases.** The main production, warehousing, and office facilities used by the company are leased from affiliated interests not consolidated, namely, the company's Pension and Profit Sharing Trusts, and also from a consolidated subsidiary, Scotts Chemical Plant, Inc. These leases, all having over 10 years to run, required minimum annual rentals in fiscal 1960 of $872,577. This represented less than 17% of net taxable profit before deduction for rentals, depreciation, and expenses based on net profits. It is anticipated that in fiscal 1961, the fixed rentals under these leases will approximate the same amount.

**e. 1961 Auditor's Statement**

Board of Directors
The O. M. Scott & Sons Company
Marysville, Ohio

We have examined the statement of consolidated financial position of the O. M. Scott & Sons Company and its subsidiaries as of September 30, 1961, and the related statements of consolidated operations, capital surplus, and retained earnings for the year then ended. Our examination was made in accordance with generally accepted auditing standards, and accordingly included such tests of the accounting records and such other auditing procedures as we considered necessary in the circumstances.

In our opinion, the accompanying statements of financial position, operations, capital surplus, and retained earnings present fairly the consolidated financial position of the O. M. Scott & Sons Company and its subsidiaries at September 30, 1961, and the consolidated results of their operations for the year then ended, in conformity with generally accepted accounting principles which, except for the changes (in which we concur) referred to in notes *(f)* and *(g)*, have been applied on a basis consistent with that of the preceding year.

ERNST & ERNST

Dayton, Ohio
January 6, 1962

**f. Accounts Receivable.** Accounts receivable are stated net after reserve of $740,000 for dealer adjustments, allowances, and doubtful accounts.

In 1959 the company adopted a plan of deferred payments for certain retail dealers. Accounts receivable include $16,033,093 for shipments under this plan which are secured by trust receipts executed by the dealers. The trust receipt arrangements provide for (1) immediate transfer to the dealers of title to the merchandise shipped in response to the dealers' orders, (2) retention by the company of a security interest in the merchandise until sold by the dealers, and (3) payment by the dealers to the company as the merchandise is sold at retail. The

*(continued)*

Notes to Financial Statements (Exhibits 1 and 2) *(concluded)*

dealers, whether trust receipt or other, do not have the right to return any part of merchandise ordered by them and delivered in salable condition, but they may tender merchandise in full or part payment of their accounts in the event of termination by the company of their dealerships. To provide for possible adjustments and allowances in the liquidation of dealer accounts receivable, the company has provided an increase in reserve by a charge to net earnings of the current year of $150,000 and a charge to retained earnings at October 1, 1960, of $530,000.

**g. Sales.** In the financial statements for the year ended September 30, 1960, attention was directed to the company's policy of including in the operating statement firm orders received, billed, and costed out in late September which were shipped early in the immediately following October. During 1961 this policy was discontinued. In order to reflect this change in policy prebilled sales at September 30, 1960, together with related costs and expenses included in operations of the year then ended, have been carried forward and included in the operating statement for the year ended September 30, 1961, with a resulting charge to retained earnings at October 1, 1960, of $429,600. This change in accounting principle did not have a material effect on net earnings for the year ended September 30, 1961.

**h. Long-Term Debt: Five-Year Subordinated Promissory Notes.** The notes bear interest to October 10, 1961, at 6% per annum and thereafter to maturity at a rate which is the higher of (a) 6% per annum, or (b) the New York prime commercial rate plus 1½%. The loan agreement provides, among other things, that (a) payment of principal and interest on the notes is subordinated to repayment of bank loans due within one year, and (b) elections may be exercised annually by the holders to (1) exchange the notes currently held for new notes having a maturity extended by one year, (2) purchase additional notes if offered for sale by the company, or (3) require payment of all or part of the notes held, such payments to be made in four equal annual installments beginning on October 10 of the immediately ensuing year.

All holders of the notes at September 30, 1961, except for $1 million, surrendered the notes then held in exchange for new notes having exactly the same terms but maturing October 28, 1966, at an interest rate of 6% per annum to October 10, 1962. Subsequent to September 30, 1961, arrangements have been made for the note for $1 million not exchanged to mature September 1, 1962, and to issue a note for $1 million to another lender maturing October 28, 1966.

Obligations of Subsidiaries:

| | | |
|---|---:|---:|
| 5¾% first mortgage bonds, due Mar. 15, 1977 | $ 964,000 | |
| 6% sinking fund notes, due Mar. 15, 1967 | 147,500 | |
| 6% subordinated debentures, due Dec. 15, 1967 | 819,000 | |
| 6% secured sinking fund debentures due Feb. 1, 1977 | 2,620,500 | |
| | $4,551,000 | |
| Less: Classified as current liability | 414,000 | $4,137,000 |
| Real estate mortgage notes ($252 payable monthly for interest at 6% per annum and amortization of principal) | $ 34,383 | |
| Less: Classified as current liabilities | 1,000 | 33,383 |
| | | $4,170,383 |

The above long-term obligations of subsidiaries are secured by mortgages on property, plant, and equipment, and/or assignment of lease rentals payable by the parent company.

**i. Preferred Stock.** Preferred stock is 5% cumulative, $100 par value.

**EXHIBIT 3**

Unconsolidated Quarterly Balance Sheets of Parent Company for Fiscal 1961
(thousands of dollars)

| | 1960 | 1961 | | |
|---|---|---|---|---|
| | Dec. | Mar. | June | Sept. |
| Cash . . . . . . . . . . . . | $ 1,810 | $ 2,140 | $ 1,760 | $ 2,070 |
| Accounts receivable | | | | |
| Standard plan . . . . . . . | 1,500 | 6,540 | 3,110 | 4,400 |
| Trust receipt plan . . . . . . | 8,660 | 15,880 | 11,890 | 16,830 |
| Total receivables . . . . . . | 10,160 | 22,420 | 15,000 | 21,230 |
| Inventories | | | | |
| Finished goods . . . . . . . | 7,390 | 5,850 | 6,420 | 4,040 |
| Raw materials and supplies . . . . . | 2,380 | 2,520 | 1,890 | 1,460 |
| Total inventories . . . . . . | 9,770 | 8,370 | 8,310 | 5,500 |
| Current assets . . . . . . . | 21,740 | 32,930 | 25,070 | 28,800 |
| Land, buildings, equipment . . . . . | 2,130 | 2,190 | 2,270 | 2,290 |
| Less: Accumulated depreciation . . . . | 800 | 830 | 870 | 910 |
| Net fixed assets . . . . . . | 1,330 | 1,360 | 1,400 | 1,380 |
| Other assets . . . . . . | 1,990 | 1,730 | 1,720 | 1,240 |
| Total assets . . . . . . | $25,060 | $36,020 | $28,190 | $31,420 |
| Accounts payable . . . . . . | $ 1,390 | $ 3,680 | $ 3,150 | $ 7,040 |
| Notes payable, bank . . . . . . | 6,250 | 12,000 | 5,750 | – |
| Accrued taxes, interest, and other expenses . | (390) | 950 | 110 | 1,170 |
| Current liabilities . . . . . . | 7,250 | 16,630 | 9,010 | 8,210 |
| Subordinated promissory notes . . . . | 9,000 | 9,000 | 9,000 | 12,000 |
| Total liabilities . . . . . . | 16,250 | 25,630 | 18,010 | 20,210 |
| Preferred stock . . . . . . | 2,380 | 2,380 | 2,350 | 2,250 |
| Common stock and surplus . . . . . | 6,430 | 8,010 | 7,830 | 8,960 |
| Net worth . . . . . . | 8,810 | 10,390 | 10,180 | 11,210 |
| Total liabilities and net worth . . . . | $25,060 | $36,020 | $28,190 | $31,420 |

*Note:* Excludes items relating to certain nonoperating subsidiaries. Unaudited and unpublished. For these reasons Exhibit 3 does not correspond exactly with Exhibit 1. In particular, the cash account in Exhibit 3 is not consistent with that in Exhibit 1.

**EXHIBIT 4**

Unconsolidated Quarterly Income Statements of Parent Company for Year Ending September 30, 1961 (thousands of dollars)

| | Quarter Ending | | | | |
|---|---|---|---|---|---|
| | Dec. 60 | Mar. 61 | June 61 | Sept. 61 | Year |
| Net sales . . . . . . . . . . . | $ 1,300 | $15,780 | $9,570 | $14,740 | $41,390 |
| Cost of products sold including processing, depreciation, warehousing, delivery, and merchandising . . . . . . | 3,250 | 11,730 | 8,670 | 10,790 | 34,440 |
| General and admin., research and development expenses . . | 660 | 800 | 940 | 1,000 | 3,400 |
| Interest charges . . . . . . | 150 | 240 | 260 | 200 | 850 |
| Total cost of sales . . . . | 4,060 | 12,770 | 9,870 | 11,990 | 38,690 |
| Earnings before taxes on income | (2,760) | 3,010 | (300) | 2,750 | 2,700 |
| Federal taxes on income . . . | (1,440) | 1,570 | (160) | 1,390 | 1,360 |
| Net income after taxes . . . . | $(1,320) | $ 1,440 | $ (140) | $ 1,360 | $ 1,340 |

*Note:* Excludes items relating to certain nonoperating subsidiaries. Unaudited and unpublished.

**EXHIBIT 5**

Trust Receipt

---

The undersigned Dealer, as Trustee, and Entruster agree to engage in Trust Receipt financing of the acquisition by Trustees of seed, fertilizer, weed controls, pest controls, applicators, mowers and other lawn and garden products, all bearing the brands and trade marks of the O. M. Scott & Sons Company. Entruster will direct said company to deliver said products from time to time as ordered by Dealer.

*(a)* Dealer agrees to hold said products in trust for the sole purpose of making sales to consumers, functioning as a retailer and not as a wholesaler.

*(b)* Dealer agrees to hold a sufficient proportion of the funds received from such sales for payment to Entruster as billed.

*(c)* Either party may terminate this Trust Receipt on notice. In such event Dealer will surrender to Entruster his complete stock of the O. M. Scott & Sons Company products, proceeds thereof to be credited to Dealer.[a]

Official Business Name of Dealer as Trustee:

Accepted at Marysville, Ohio

_____

_____ , 19__

Street & No. _____

City _____ Zone ___ State _____

THE O. M. SCOTT & SONS COMPANY
(Entruster)

Authorized
Signature_____ .

Date _____ Title _____

President

---

a. This statement differs from the statement quoted in Notes to Financial Statements *(f),* following Exhibits 1 and 2. Presumably the statement in Exhibit 5 is correct.

**EXHIBIT 6**

Statement of Trust Receipt Financing

---

The Entruster, the O. M. Scott & Sons Company, whose chief place of business is at Marysville, Ohio, and who has no place of business within this state, is or expects to be engaged in financing under trust receipt transactions, the acquisition by the Trustee, whose name and chief place of business within this state is:

of seed, fertilizers, weed controls, pest controls, applicators, mowers and other lawn and garden products, all bearing the brands and trade marks of the O. M. Scott & Sons Company.

Entruster: The O. M. Scott & Sons Company

By: _____
                President

Date_____ , 19__
For the Trustee                                    (Dealer)
By: _____

---

**EXHIBIT 7**

Example Showing Calculation of Equity Working Capital and Maximum Allowed Debt of Parent Company for the 12 Months Following March 31, 1961 (millions of dollars)

---

*Calculation of Equity Working Capital*

| | | |
|---|---:|---:|
| Current assets | | $32.9 |
| Current liabilities | $16.6 | |
| Long-term debt | 9.0 | |
| Total debt | $25.6 | 25.6 |
| Equity working capital | | $ 7.3 |

*Calculation of Maximum Allowed Parent Company Debt*

| | |
|---|---:|
| 300% of equity working capital | $21.9 |
| Actual parent borrowings—March 31, 1961 | 21.0 |
| Available debt capacity | $ .9 |

*Calculation of Maximum Allowed Subordinated Debt of Parent*

| | |
|---|---:|
| 60% of maximum allowed total debt ($21.9 million × 60%) | $13.1 |

---

*Note:* Calculations based on figures taken from Exhibit 3.

**EXHIBIT 8**

Record of Earnings, Dividends, and Market Price Range, 1958–1961

---

| Fiscal Year | Earnings per Share | Dividends per Share | Market Price Range[a] |
|---|---|---|---|
| 1958 | $ .69 | 10% stk. | 6⅛–1½ |
| 1959 | 1.15 | 10% stk. | 32⅞–6⅛ |
| 1960 | 1.21 | 10% stk. | 51–31⅞ |
| 1961 | .99 | 10¢ + 5% stk. | 58¾–30 |

---

a. Calendar year; bid prices. Closing prices September 29 and December 29, 1961, were $49 and $32¼ respectively. Stock first sold publicly in 1958 and has traded over-the-counter since then. The company had about 4,100 common shareholders in 1961.

# Carrefour, S.A.

In mid-1972 the top management of Carrefour, S.A. faced several important policy decisions. They concerned the speed and direction of future growth and how that growth ought to be financed.

## Company Background

Carrefour began operations with a single 650-sq m supermarket in Annecy, France, in the summer of 1960. This store tested the response of retail-food customers to the idea of one-stop,[1] self-service shopping with discount prices. The store proved to be popular; after considerable study, the firm's founders decided to test their retailing formula with additional products such as clothing, sporting equipment, auto accessories, and consumer electronics. In 1963, Carrefour thus opened the first hypermarket[2] in France at a location just outside of Paris. The store covered 2,500 sq m, sold both food and nonfood products at discount prices, and provided parking for 450 cars.

---

1. In France, as in most of Europe, retail distribution in 1960 was a highly fragmented activity. Small shopkeepers accounted for almost all sales of both food and nonfood products, and product lines in individual stores were very narrow. Food shopping was essentially a daily activity, and visits to four entirely separate shops were required in order to purchase baked goods, dairy products, meat products, and vegetables.

2. A hypermarket was defined as a store with a selling area of 2,500 sq m or more. (One square meter equals approximately 10 sq ft.)

The Carrefour hypermarket was accepted enthusiastically by French consumers, and the company began to grow rapidly. Between 1965 and 1971, corporate assets grew rapidly (Exhibit 1), keeping pace with a sales growth in excess of 50% (Exhibit 2). Nonfood items accounted for about 40% of total volume.

As the company's revenues increased, so did the size of its stores. Starting in 1970 new stores, called commercial centers, were opened with selling areas as large as 25,000 sq m.

By the end of 1971, Carrefour had built and was operating 16 *wholly owned* stores; had an equity interest in 5 stores operated as *joint ventures;* and had *franchise* agreements with 7 additional stores. Plans were under way to open 15 new stores under one of these three operating arrangements in 1972 (Exhibit 3).

Carrefour's strategy was to build its stores outside of towns in locations where highways provided easy access and land could be acquired very inexpensively.[3] The company favored inexpensive construction in combination with low-cost land, which gave Carrefour a total investment per square meter of selling space in a fully equipped store equal to about one third that of traditional supermarkets and department stores.

Carrefour also followed a strategy of decentralized management. Each store manager was a profit center with almost complete freedom in decision making. One Carrefour store manager (paid F 12,000 per month versus F 2,500 two years earlier when he was a store manager in a smaller competing supermarket chain) made the following comments:

> My previous job was demoralizing. It took a month to get authorization to buy something for the store which cost 14 francs. Now I am free to make all of my own decisions. I can hire ten people, buy a new refrigeration unit, or hire a band for a parking lot festival.[4]

## Factors Favoring Growth

The high degree of consumer acceptance which fueled Carrefour's growth at 50% per year stemmed in large measure from factors like convenience and price. Almost any product purchased more than once a year could be bought at a Carrefour store. The company even operated discount gasoline outlets at many stores. Indeed, Carrefour operated five of the ten largest-volume gasoline stations in France.

While convenience was undoubtedly a strong factor in Carrefour's growth, so was price. Gross margins on food and nonfood items differed somewhat, but Carrefour operated on an average gross margin of about 15% (Exhibit 2). The gross margins (and, by implication, the prices) of retailers in traditional outlets averaged 5 to 10 percentage points more than Carrefour's.

---

3. In a few situations where large plots of land were not available for purchase within a market area, Carrefour leased land.

4. *Les Informations,* January 11, 1971, p. 25.

## Obstacles to Growth

Convenience and price favored the growth of discount retail stores in France. Nonetheless, these firms suffered from obstacles not met by most rapidly growing businesses. First, for many years the nation's distribution system had lagged behind most other sectors of the economy in adopting modern techniques. When an economic rationalization of this sector started to occur, its results were especially severe for many small shopkeepers. As shown in Table A, 40% or almost 80,000 of the 203,600 small retail shops in operation in 1961 had disappeared by 1971. These small shopkeepers represented a significant political force in France, and their problems could not be easily ignored.[5]

One way of addressing the problem of the small merchant was to slow down the growth of hypermarkets; another was to ease the financial burden of those merchants forced out of business. Each of these solutions was used to some extent to reduce the size of the problem caused by the growth of hypermarkets in France. In an effort to slow the growth of hypermarkets, national and local governments in almost every country in Europe made it difficult to obtain construction permits to build large new retail stores.[6] Local merchants would generally lobby vigorously against the issuance of new construction permits in their market areas. This prompted some discount retailers to offer plans for large commercial centers in which space could be leased to as many as 40 independent shopkeepers. This type of plan allowed small merchants to set up specialty stores and boutiques, and usually generated some measure of local merchant support for the issuance of permits.

While specialty stores in commercial centers eliminated financial hardships for a few small merchants, this idea hardly represented a complete solution. In an attempt to attack the problem more broadly, the French National Assembly

**TABLE A**
Number of Retail Stores in Operation, 1961–1971

|  | *1961* | *1967* | *1969* | *1971* |
|---|---|---|---|---|
| Grocery and dairy stores (selling area less than 400 sq m) | 149,100 | 111,900 | 96,480 | 85,090 |
| Chain stores and cooperatives (selling area less than 400 sq m) | 35,000 | 31,980 | 29,295 | 26,050 |
| Drug stores | 19,500 | 14,280 | 14,280 | 13,710 |
| Totals | 203,600 | 158,160 | 140,055 | 124,850 |

*Source: Points de Vente,* March 1972, p. 125.

---

5. Groups of shopkeepers often staged protest demonstrations at public appearances of high government officials and at new hypermarkets. In May 1970, Carrefour's largest store was totally destroyed by a fire which did not appear to be accidental.

6. Permits were usually issued for a store of a specific size to be built in a specific location for a specific firm or individual. Once a permit was issued, it could not be sold, but the building itself, once constructed, could be sold to another firm or individual.

passed legislation in mid-1972 to tax retail stores in order to provide pensions for small shopkeepers who were unable to continue in business. The tax was to be paid by all retail merchants; the heaviest burden was to be borne by operators of large stores built after 1962. For Carrefour, the tax (based on 1971 operations) would have amounted to roughly F 3 million.[7]

## Joint Ventures and Franchises

The ability to get construction permits had a major impact on corporate growth potential for a retail discount chain. Through the late 1960s and early 1970s, Carrefour's rapid growth was made possible by the fact that the firm had been able to get two new construction permits each year. As more firms entered the discount retail field, however, the competition for permits became more difficult as many firms and individuals vied for authorization to build in attractive locations. In the late 1960s, to achieve a more rapid pace of expansion than the firm could achieve if it were limited to two new stores per year, Carrefour offered to share its retailing know-how, trademark, and consumer goodwill with potential partners both in France and elsewhere in Europe. Carrefour offered its expertise in exchange for either an ownership interest in stores under construction or franchise fees. In joint ventures Carrefour purchased an ownership interest of 10–50% (Exhibit 3). Under franchising, Carrefour received a fee of .2% of total store sales, and Carrefour's central buying office for nonfood products (SAMOD) received a fee equal to 1% of the store's sales of nonfood items.[8]

Between 1969 and 1971, Carrefour was quite successful in adding selling area under the Carrefour name by means of joint ventures and franchises (Exhibit 4). Success in the area of joint ventures was evidenced by Carrefour's investments and advances to affiliates, which had grown to almost F 19 million (Exhibit 1). Joint venture stores that had been in operation long enough to permit evaluation of their profitability (e.g., SOGARA) were as profitable as wholly owned Carrefour stores (Exhibit 5).[9] However, they seemed to take a little longer than wholly owned stores to reach that position.

## Competition

Carrefour's early success in discount retail distribution naturally attracted considerable competition. While Carrefour was by far the hypermarket leader in France in terms of selling space, other firms were becoming important factors in the

---

7. An equivalent volume of sales generated in small shops built prior to 1962 would have generated a tax liability of about F 500,000.

8. SAMOD received a similar fee from the firm's wholly owned stores as well for performing the purchasing function on nonfood products.

9. Carrefour did not consolidate the results of joint ventures and other affiliates for financial reporting purposes. The only income from these ventures included in Exhibit 2, for example, arose from dividends as shown in Exhibit 5.

**TABLE B**
Leading French Hypermarket Chains, June 30, 1972

| Trade Name | Owner Group | Number of Stores Operated under Trade Name | Total Selling Area of Stores (000 sq m) |
|---|---|---|---|
| Carrefour . . . | Carrefour | 28 | 250 |
| Mammoth . . . | Paridoc | 28 | 153 |
| Escale[a] . . . . | Au Printemps | 13 | 83 |
| Radar . . . . | Docks Remois | 9 | 44 |
| Rond-Point . . . | | 8 | 27 |
| Euromarché[a] . . | G.S.R.P. | 7 | 32 |
| Auchan . . . . | | 5 | 47 |
| Record . . . | | 5 | 23 |
| Geant Casino . . | Casino | 4 | 36 |
| Delta . . . . . | | 4 | 24 |

*Source: Enterprise,* July 1972, p. 63; September 15, 1972, p. 78.

a. In mid-1972, Au Printemps and Euromarché concluded an agreement according to which all Au Printemps stores would be operated under the Euromarché trade name. This consolidation was believed to represent an effort by Au Printemps to compete more effectively in the future with Carrefour.

business (see Table B). By 1970 the combined building activity of all hypermarket operators was adding about 250,000 sq m per year of new selling space (Exhibit 6). Some industry analysts[10] suggested that consumer needs for stores of this size in France would be satisfied when total hypermarket selling area reached 2.2 million sq m. About one half this amount was in place by June 30, 1972.

Outside of France, Carrefour's management saw a need for hypermarkets as great as the need in France. However, existing large retailers outside of France appeared to be somewhat stronger financially than the competition that Carrefour had faced in France (Exhibit 7).

10. *Enterprise,* September 15, 1972, p. 75.

**EXHIBIT 1**

Carrefour, S.A. Balance Sheet Data, 1965–1971 (millions of French francs)

| | 1965 | 1966 | 1967 | 1968 | 1969 | 1970 | 1971 |
|---|---|---|---|---|---|---|---|
| 1. Intangible assets | – | – | – | – | F  4 | F  1 | F  1 |
| 2. Land | F  5 | F  8 | F  8 | F  14 | 20 | 25 | 28 |
| 3. Buildings and equipment | 11 | 22 | 26 | 50 | 82 | 136 | 202 |
| 4. Other fixed assets | 6 | 9 | 14 | 21 | 38 | 52 | 49 |
| 5. Total fixed assets | 22 | 39 | 48 | 85 | 140 | 213 | 279 |
| 6. Less: Depreciation | 5 | 8 | 12 | 10 | 22 | 35 | 63 |
| 7. Net fixed assets | 17 | 31 | 36 | 75 | 118 | 178 | 216 |
| 8. Investments and advances to affiliates | 2 | 3 | 4 | 5 | 10 | 12 | 19 |
| 9. Inventory | 6 | 14 | 17 | 30 | 65 | 72 | 107 |
| 10. Accounts receivable | – | – | 1 | 2 | 2 | 3 | 4 |
| 11. Other current assets | 1 | 9 | 19 | 58 | 50 | 75 | 124 |
| 12. Cash | 9 | 5 | 8 | 18 | 51 | 116 | 151 |
| 13. Current assets | 16 | 28 | 45 | 108 | 168 | 266 | 386 |
| 14. Total assets | F  35 | F  62 | F  85 | F 188 | F 300 | F 457 | F 622 |
| 15. Shareholders' equity | F  11 | F  14 | F  17 | F  39 | F  89 | F  98 | F 112 |
| 16. Special provisions | – | – | – | – | – | 1 | 1 |
| 17. Long-term debt | 3 | 9 | 14 | 26 | 25 | 64 | 64 |
| 18. Accounts payable | – | – | – | – | 48 | 61 | 77 |
| 19. Trade notes (non-interest bearing) | 16 | 33 | 39 | 100 | 79 | 147 | 244 |
| 20. Other current liabilities | 5 | 6 | 15 | 23 | 59 | 86 | 124 |
| 21. Current liabilities | 21 | 39 | 54 | 123 | 186 | 294 | 445 |
| 22. Total liabilities | F  35 | F  62 | F  85 | F 188 | F 300 | F 457 | F 622 |
| 23. Current ratio | .76 | .72 | .83 | .88 | .90 | .90 | .87 |
| 24. Total debt/shareholders' equity | 2.2 | 3.4 | 4.0 | 3.8 | 2.4 | 3.7 | 4.6 |
| 25. Net working capital (millions of francs) | (5) | (11) | (9) | (15) | (18) | (28) | (59) |
| 26. Number of shares outstanding (000s)[a] | 347 | 347 | 347 | 462 | 588 | 588 | 588 |

a. Over the course of its growth, Carrefour sold equity for the company's own account to groups outside the families of the founders on only two occasions. In early 1968 the firm sold approximately 75,000 shares at F 145 per share to 40 employees at all levels in the firm (including store floorwalkers). In late 1969, the firm sold privately approximately 120,000 shares at F 342 per share. About 50,000 of these shares were sold to the Banque Pour L'expansion Industrielle, which later offered them to the public (along with about 70,000 shares supplied by the founders), when Carrefour's stock was first introduced for trading on the Paris Bourse in June 1970. At 12/31/71 the company had granted employee stock options covering 4,880 shares to 244 employees. All case data adjusted for stock splits and stock dividends.

**EXHIBIT 2**
Carrefour, S.A. Income Statement Data, 1965–1971 (millions of French francs except per share data)

| | 1965 | 1966 | 1967 | 1968 | 1969 | 1970 | 1971 |
|---|---|---|---|---|---|---|---|
| 1. Revenues (all taxes included) . . . . . . | F 156 | F 220 | F 339 | F 524 | F 1,025 | F 1,445 | F 2,234 |
| 2. Less: Value added tax . . . . . . . | 3 | 5 | 7 | 11 | 147 | 195 | 298 |
| 3. Revenues (net of value added tax) . . . . . | 153 | 215 | 332 | 513 | 878 | 1,250 | 1,936 |
| 4. Starting inventory . . . . . | 6 | 6 | 14 | 17 | 34 | 65 | 72 |
| 5. Plus: Purchases . . . . . | 133 | 194 | 291 | 454 | 782 | 1,063 | 1,670 |
| 6. Less: Ending inventory . . . . . . . | 6 | 14 | 17 | 30 | 65 | 72 | 107 |
| 7. Cost of goods sold . . . . | 133 | 186 | 288 | 441 | 751 | 1,056 | 1,635 |
| 8. Gross margin . . . . . . | 20 | 29 | 44 | 72 | 127 | 194 | 301 |
| 9. Salaries . . . . . . . | 8 | 11 | 16 | 26 | 56 | 82 | 119 |
| 10. Depreciation and amortization . . . . . . | 2 | 5 | 4 | 8 | 15 | 19 | 32 |
| 11. Other expenses . . . . . | 3 | 7 | 11 | 17 | 26 | 41 | 61 |
| 12. Operating profit . . . . . | 7 | 6 | 13 | 21 | 30 | 52 | 89 |
| 13. Nonoperating gains (losses) . . . . . | (1) | 0 | 1 | 1 | 4 | (5) | 1 |
| 14. Investment provision . . . . . . . . | – | – | – | – | (4) | (7) | (10) |
| 15. Profit before tax . . . . . | 6 | 6 | 14 | 22 | 30 | 40 | 80 |
| 16. Income tax . . . . . . . | 3 | 3 | 7 | 12 | 14 | 17 | 36 |
| 17. Profit after tax . . . . . . | F 3 | F 3 | F 7 | F 10 | F 16 | F 23 | F 44 |

*Allocation of Profit after Tax*

| | | | | | | | |
|---|---|---|---|---|---|---|---|
| 18. To: Shareholders' equity . . | F 3 | F 2 | F 5 | F 3 | F 3 | F 3 | F 4 |
| 19. To: Employee profit sharing[a] . . . . . . . . | – | – | – | 4 | 7 | 10 | 20 |
| 20. To: Dividends . . . . . . | – | 1 | 2 | 3 | 6 | 10 | 20 |

*Selected Financial Statistics*

| | | | | | | | |
|---|---|---|---|---|---|---|---|
| 21. Gross profit margin . . . . | 13.1% | 13.5% | 13.3% | 14.0% | 14.4% | 15.5% | 15.5% |
| 22. Profit/sales (net of VAT) . . . . . . . . | 2.0% | 1.4% | 2.1% | 2.0% | 1.8% | 1.8% | 2.3% |
| 23. Profit/equity . . . . . . . | 27.0% | 22.0% | 43.0% | 26.0% | 18.0% | 23.0% | 39.0% |
| 24. Earnings per share (francs) . . . . . . | 8.6 | 8.6 | 20 | 22 | 27 | 39 | 75 |
| 25. Dividends per share (francs) . . . . . . | – | 2 | 4 | 7 | 11 | 18 | 34 |
| 26. Book value per share (francs) . . . . . . | 33 | 40 | 48 | 84 | 151 | 168 | 191 |
| 27. Market value per share (francs) . . . . . . | – | – | – | – | – | 1,040 | 1,980 |
| 28. Price-earnings ratio . . . . | – | – | – | – | – | 27 | 27 |
| 29. Dividend yield . . . . . . | – | – | – | – | – | 1.7% | 1.7% |
| 30. Dividend payout ratio . . . | 0% | 33.0% | 29.0% | 30.0% | 38.0% | 43.0% | 45.0% |

a. According to French law, large firms must share with employees a portion of profits after tax in excess of 5% of net worth. The amount shared is earned by employees in 1 year (line 19), becomes a tax-deductible expense to the firm in the second year (included in line 9), and becomes the basis for a duplicate tax deduction (line 14) in the second year if the firm continues to make fixed asset investments equal to the charge. This legislation makes it possible for a firm to share profits with employees, yet incur no real after-tax cost (except for a potential one-year lag between profit-sharing payments and tax recovery) since the burden falls entirely on the government via a reduction in corporate income taxes.

**EXHIBIT 3**
Carrefour New Store Opening Data, 1960–1972

| Country and City | Affiliate Name | Carrefour Ownership Interest (%) | Opening Date | Selling Surface (000 sq m) | Parking Spaces (000s) |
|---|---|---|---|---|---|
| *Wholly Owned Stores* | | | | | |
| France: Annecy . . . . . | | 100 | 6/60 | .7 | .1 |
| Annecy . . . . . | | 100 | 5/63 | .8 | .1 |
| Paris (region) . . . | | 100 | 6/63 | 5.5 | 1.0 |
| Lyon . . . . . . | | 100 | 3/64 | 2.5 | .2 |
| Chalon-sur-Saône . | | 100 | 5/65 | 1.0 | .2 |
| Lyon . . . . . | | 100 | 10/66 | 11.5 | 2.0 |
| Chartres . . . . . | | 100 | 10/67 | 5.5 | .7 |
| Annecy . . . . . | | 100 | 4/68 | 4.3 | .7 |
| Dijon . . . . . . | | 100 | 9/68 | 9.0 | 1.5 |
| Paris (region) . . . | | 100 | 10/68 | 9.1 | 2.4 |
| Chambéry . . . . | | 100 | 5/69 | 4.6 | .8 |
| Grenoble . . . . . | | 100 | 8/69 | 7.1 | 1.5 |
| Paris (region) . . . | | 100 | 3/70 | 7.6 | 1.8 |
| Marseille . . . . . | | 100 | 9/70 | 21.3 | 4.0 |
| Orléans . . . . . | | 100 | 4/71 | 14.0 | 1.5 |
| Melun . . . . . . | | 100 | 6/71 | 15.0 | 3.6 |
| Meaux . . . . . . | | 100 | 10/72 | 11.3 | 3.0 |
| Lyon . . . . . . | | 100 | 11/72 | 6.0 | 1.9 |
| | | | | 136.8 | 27.0 |
| *Joint Venture Stores* | | | | | |
| France: Bayonne . . . . . | SOGARA | 49.9 | 3/67 | 3.2 | .9 |
| Bordeaux . . . . . | SOGARA | 49.9 | 10/69 | 16.2 | 1.8 |
| Toulouse . . . . | SOGARA | 49.9 | 3/72 | 25.0 | 4.0 |
| LeMans . . . . . | SOGRAMO | na | 6/72 | 7.5 | 1.0 |
| Angers . . . . . | SOGRAMO | na | 6/72 | 8.2 | 1.1 |
| Nantes . . . . . | SOGRAMO | na | 11/72 | 13.8 | 1.4 |
| Charleville . . . . | Ardennais | 14.6 | 3/70 | 7.7 | 1.2 |
| Belgium: Mons . . . . . . | Ditrimas | 49.9 | 11/69 | 7.6 | 1.0 |
| Liège . . . . . . | Ditrimas | 49.9 | 9/72 | 17.3 | 2.0 |
| Switzerland: Lausanne . . . . | Hypermarche S.A. | 30 | 4/70 | 6.3 | 1.0 |
| Berne . . . . . . | Hypermarche S.A. | 30 | 3/72 | 9.2 | 1.1 |
| U.K.: Cardiff . . . . . | Hypermarket Ltd. | 10 | 9/72 | 5.5 | 1.0 |
| | | | | 127.5 | 17.5 |
| *Franchise Stores* | | | | | |
| France: Paris (region) . . . | Bouriez | 0 | 9/69 | 7.5 | 1.3 |
| Strasbourg . . . . | Bouriez | 0 | 11/70 | 12.7 | 1.5 |
| Lille . . . . . . | Bouriez | 0 | 5/71 | 9.4 | 1.3 |
| Nancy . . . . . | Bouriez | 0 | 10/71 | 8.7 | 1.5 |
| Béthune . . . . . | Bouriez | 0 | 5/72 | 8.4 | 1.2 |
| Lens . . . . . . | Bouriez | 0 | 9/72 | 8.2 | 2.0 |
| Colmar . . . . . | Bouriez | 0 | 12/72 | 6.6 | 1.0 |
| Caen . . . . . . | Promodes | 0 | 2/70 | 9.4 | 3.0 |
| Alençon . . . . . | Promodes | 0 | 8/72 | 3.8 | .9 |
| Paris (region) . . . | Promodes | 0 | 11/72 | 8.7 | 1.6 |
| Valenciennes . . . | Promodes | 0 | 10/72 | 8.6 | 1.4 |
| Bourges . . . . . | Dock de Nevers | 0 | 3/69 | 7.5 | 1.1 |
| Nevers . . . . . | Dock de Nevers | 0 | 10/69 | 7.1 | 1.2 |
| | | | | 106.6 | 19.0 |

na = not available.

**EXHIBIT 4**
Store Selling Area Operated under the Carrefour Name, 1960–1972

| | 1960–1963 | 1964 | 1965 | 1966 | 1967 | 1968 | 1969 | 1970 | 1971 | 1972 |
|---|---|---|---|---|---|---|---|---|---|---|
| | *New Selling Area Opened Each Year (000 sq m)* | | | | | | | | | |
| Wholly owned stores . | 6.9 | 2.5 | 1.0 | 11.5 | 5.5 | 22.4 | 11.7 | 28.9 | 29.0 | 17.3 |
| Joint venture stores . . | | | | | 3.2 | | 23.8 | 14.0 | | 86.5 |
| Franchise stores . . . | | | | | | | 22.1 | 22.1 | 18.1 | 44.3 |
| Total . . . . . | 6.9 | 2.5 | 1.0 | 11.5 | 8.7 | 22.4 | 57.6 | 65.0 | 47.1 | 148.1 |
| | *Cumulative Selling Area Operating under Carrefour Name (000 sq m)* | | | | | | | | | |
| Wholly owned stores . | 6.9 | 9.4 | 10.4 | 21.9 | 27.4 | 49.8 | 61.5 | 90.4 | 119.4 | 136.7 |
| Joint venture stores . . | | | | | 3.2 | 3.2 | 27.0 | 41.0 | 41.0 | 127.5 |
| Franchise stores . . . | | | | | | | 22.1 | 44.2 | 62.3 | 106.6 |
| Total . . . . . | 6.9 | 9.4 | 10.4 | 21.9 | 30.6 | 53.0 | 110.6 | 175.6 | 222.7 | 370.8 |
| | *Percent of Cumulative Selling Area under Each Form of Operation* | | | | | | | | | |
| Wholly owned stores . | 100 | 100 | 100 | 100 | 90 | 94 | 56 | 52 | 54 | 37 |
| Joint venture stores . . | | | | | 10 | 6 | 24 | 23 | 18 | 34 |
| Franchise stores . . . | | | | | | | 20 | 25 | 28 | 29 |
| Total . . . . . | 100 | 100 | 100 | 100 | 100 | 100 | 100 | 100 | 100 | 100 |

**EXHIBIT 5**
Ownership, Profitability, and Investment Data for Carrefour Affiliates, 1969–1971

| Affiliate Name | Year | Carrefour Ownership (%) | Revenues (million F) | Profit after Tax (000 F) | Dividends to Carrefour (000 F) | Investments and Advances (million F)[a] |
|---|---|---|---|---|---|---|
| SAMOD . . . . . | 1969 | 92 | F 5 | F 417 | F 174 | |
| | 1970 | 92 | 13 | 607 | 221 | |
| | 1971 | 90 | 17 | 1,089 | 221 | F 1.8 |
| SOGARA . . . . | 1969 | 49.9 | 97 | 219 | 0 | |
| | 1970 | 49.9 | 257 | 3,930 | 150 | |
| | 1971 | 49.9 | 304 | 7,710 | 500 | 5.0 |
| Ardennais . . . . | 1969 | | | | | |
| | 1970 | | | | | |
| | 1971 | 14.6 | 58 | 175 | 0 | .8 |
| Ditrimas . . . . . | 1970 | 49.9 | 42 | 8 | 0 | |
| | 1971 | 49.9 | 45 | 19 | 0 | 2.6 |
| Hypermarche S.A. . | 1969 | 30 | na | na | 0 | |
| | 1970 | 30 | na | na | 0 | |
| | 1971 | 30 | na | na | 0 | 4.8 |
| Italmare . . . . . | | 50 | | | | 2.2 |
| Hypermarket Ltd. . . | | 10 | | | | 1.3 |
| Pelaza . . . . . | | 68 | | | | |
| Other affiliates . . . | | — | | | | .2 |
| | | | | | | F 18.7 |

na = not available.

a. At cost; does not include equity in earnings retained in affiliate.

**EXHIBIT 6**

Number and Size of Hypermarkets Constructed in France, 1963–1972

| Store Type | 1963–1966 | 1967 | 1968 | 1969 | 1970 | 1971 | 6 mos. 1972 |
|---|---|---|---|---|---|---|---|
| *Number of Hypermarkets Constructed* | | | | | | | |
| Independent | 3 | 3 | 6 | 16 | 11 | 7 | 8 |
| Chain | 1 | 2 | 8 | 19 | 21 | 10 | 14 |
| Department stores | – | 2 | – | 7 | 5 | 4 | 5 |
| Cooperatives and others | – | 1 | 2 | 3 | 5 | 8 | 5 |
| Total for year | 4 | 8 | 16 | 45 | 42 | 29 | 32 |
| Cumulative total | 4 | 12 | 28 | 73 | 115 | 144 | 176 |
| *Hypermarket Selling Space Constructed (000 sq m)* | | | | | | | |
| Selling space constructed in year | 19 | 42 | 77 | 270 | 258 | 155 | 207 |
| Cumulative selling space constructed | 19 | 61 | 138 | 408 | 666 | 821 | 1,028 |
| *Carrefour Hypermarket Selling Space Constructed (000 sq m)* | | | | | | | |
| Wholly owned | 17 | 8 | 22 | 12 | 29 | 29 | 0 |
| Joint venture | – | 3 | 0 | 16 | 8 | 0 | 41 |
| Franchise | – | – | – | 22 | 22 | 18 | 8 |
| Total for year | 17 | 11 | 22 | 50 | 59 | 47 | 49 |
| Cumulative total | 17 | 28 | 50 | 100 | 159 | 206 | 255 |
| (Carrefour/industry) cumulative | .87 | .46 | .37 | .25 | .24 | .24 | .24 |

*Sources: Enterprise,* March 6, 1971, p. 10; September 15, 1972, p. 75; and *Carrefour Annual Report,* 1971, p. 21.

*Note:* Data in Exhibit 6 differ somewhat from data in Exhibit 4 because (1) not all stores operating under the Carrefour name were located in France, and (2) Carrefour constructed three stores prior to 1966 which were not large enough to be classified as hypermarkets.

**EXHIBIT 7**
Financial Data for Large Retail Firms in Europe, 1967–1971

| Country | Firm | Sales (million F) | | | | Net Worth (million F) | | | | Net Profit/Net Worth (percent) | | | |
|---|---|---|---|---|---|---|---|---|---|---|---|---|---|
| | | 1967–68 | 1968–69 | 1969–70 | 1970–71 | 1967–68 | 1968–69 | 1969–70 | 1970–71 | 1967–68 | 1968–69 | 1969–70 | 1970–71 |
| France | Au Printemps | F 5,151a | F 5,480a | F 6,120a | F 6,719a | F 372 | F 373 | F 378 | F 372 | 4.7% | 4.9% | 1.9% | .5% |
| | Carrefour | 524 | 1,025 | 1,445 | 2,234 | 39 | 89 | 98 | 112 | 26 | 18 | 23 | 39 |
| | Casino | 1,245 | 1,380 | 1,589 | 1,868 | 79 | 110 | 118 | 141 | 21 | 14 | 14 | 16 |
| | Docks Remois | 586 | 627 | 683 | 732 | 85 | 89 | 92 | 95 | 5.3 | 5.3 | 5.9 | 6.9 |
| | Galeries Lafayette | 556 | 484 | 545 | 582 | 275 | 267 | 243 | 160 | (1.9) | (1.5) | (9.9) | (52) |
| Belgium | G. B. Enterprises | 664 | 812 | 1,343 | 1,719 | 138 | 145 | 225 | 247 | 9.9 | 11 | 11 | 15 |
| | S. A. Innovation | 419 | 381 | 853 | 971 | 145 | 152 | 262 | 260 | 6.8 | 4.5 | 6.0 | 4.8 |
| Germany | Karstadt | 4,888 | 5,281 | 5,745 | 6,644 | 1,029 | 1,102 | 1,190 | 1,272 | 13 | 13 | 13 | 13 |
| | Kaufhof | 4,459 | 4,929 | 5,218 | 5,928 | 759 | 816 | 858 | 931 | 13 | 14 | 15 | 14 |
| | Nechermann | 2,048 | 2,190 | 2,348 | 2,697 | 210 | 216 | 209 | 222 | 10 | 11 | 5 | 7 |
| U.K. | Great Universal | 4,084 | 4,370 | 4,856 | 5,079 | 1,971 | 2,002 | 2,154 | 2,364 | 15 | 15 | 15 | 15 |
| | Marks and Spencer | 3,226 | 3,626 | 4,124 | 4,766 | 1,328 | 1,371 | 1,424 | 1,858 | 18 | 18 | 20 | 24 |
| Italy | La Rinascente | 1,366 | 1,426 | 1,564 | 1,744 | 298 | 306 | 324 | 314 | 8.2 | 8.1 | 7.8 | 8.3 |

| Country | Firm | Current Ratio | | | | Total Debt/Shareholders' Equity | | | |
|---|---|---|---|---|---|---|---|---|---|
| | | 1967–68 | 1968–69 | 1969–70 | 1970–71 | 1967–68 | 1968–69 | 1969–70 | 1970–71 |
| France | Au Printemps | 1.0 | 1.0 | 1.2 | .9 | .9 | 1.1 | 1.2 | 1.4 |
| | Carrefour | .9 | .9 | .9 | .9 | 3.8 | 2.4 | 3.7 | 4.6 |
| | Casino | 1.1 | 1.1 | 1.2 | 1.0 | 3.5 | 2.8 | 3.6 | 4.0 |
| | Docks Remois | 1.2 | 1.3 | 1.2 | 1.4 | 1.3 | 1.7 | 2.0 | 2.1 |
| | Galeries Lafayette | 1.2 | 1.0 | 1.1 | 1.0 | .8 | 1.0 | 1.2 | 1.6 |
| Belgium | G. B. Enterprises | 1.7 | 1.6 | 1.6 | 1.4 | 1.0 | 1.3 | 1.1 | 1.9 |
| | S. A. Innovation | 2.6 | 3.1 | 1.5 | 1.1 | .8 | .8 | 1.3 | 1.4 |
| Germany | Karstadt | 4.1 | 3.4 | 2.6 | 2.0 | .8 | .8 | .9 | .9 |
| | Kaufhof | 1.7 | 1.9 | 2.7 | 2.1 | 1.5 | 1.4 | 1.5 | 1.6 |
| | Nechermann | 1.6 | 2.0 | 2.0 | 1.6 | 2.2 | 2.6 | 2.8 | 3.3 |
| U.K. | Great Universal | 2.8 | 2.6 | 2.6 | 2.8 | .5 | .7 | .7 | .7 |
| | Marks and Spencer | 1.1 | 1.1 | 1.0 | 1.1 | .6 | .7 | .8 | .8 |
| Italy | La Rinascente | .9 | .8 | .8 | .7 | 1.5 | 1.6 | 1.8 | 2.0 |

a. Includes sales of affiliated stores.

# Part II

# Long-Term Financing

*Capital Structure Policy*

# Note on the Theory of Optimal Capital Structure

This note examines the interrelations between the objective of maximizing share-holder value and the objective of achieving an optimal capital structure. The problem of meeting these objectives will be approached from the standpoint of theory, since a basic understanding of the theory is important in dealing with the practical problems encountered in attempting to achieve an optimal capital structure for a specific firm.

In raising funds to finance operations, firms can utilize a number of alternatives, including issuing debt or equity. Exhibit 1 illustrates the capital structure choice in a highly simplified context. A firm has invested $500,000 in plant, equipment, and working capital. The investment generates earnings before interest and taxes (EBIT) of $120,000 in perpetuity. Annual depreciation charges exactly equal capital expenditures, and the firm pays out all of its earnings as dividends. The firm's sales do not grow but remain stable over time. The firm has the opportunity to select its capital structure from among the debt/total capital ratios presented in line 1 of Exhibit 1.

Locating the optimum capital structure for our hypothetical firm, given the data in Exhibit 1, is a trivial problem. Simply locating this optimum point is not our objective. The educational usefulness of Exhibit 1 comes from achieving an understanding of the logic behind the assumptions utilized in the exhibit and the interrelations among the variables presented in the exhibit. These assumptions and interrelations need to be explored in some detail.

## Impact of Leverage on Total Payments to Security Holders

Lines 1–8 of Exhibit 1 show the impact of leverage on the firm's income statement. The firm's earnings stream, EBIT, is unaffected by leverage. As debt is added to the capital structure, interest charges increase and profit after taxes falls. Total payments to security holders (i.e., interest plus profit after taxes) increase with leverage. This increase can be attributed entirely to tax savings resulting from the tax deductibility of interest payments. The increase in total payments to security holders is a key advantage flowing from the use of debt capital.

## Cost of Funds

Lines 9 and 10 of Exhibit 1 show the rates of return required to induce investors to acquire the debt and equity securities of our hypothetical firm. As leverage increases, both bondholders and shareholders are subjected to increased risk. This risk includes both the risk of bankruptcy and the risk of increased variability in annual returns. As the level of debt increases, investors require higher returns to compensate them for accepting increased risk. The required (expected) returns (lines 9 and 10) represent the critical assumptions in the optimal capital structure analysis which follows. These assumptions reflect a fundamental trade-off between risk and return. Since the returns must be paid to investors in order to allow the firm to raise funds, these returns represent capital costs. The required return on the firm's debt is the cost of debt capital, $k_D$ (line 9), and the required return on the firm's equity is the cost of equity capital, $k_E$ (line 10).

## Market Value of Securities

In theory, the market value of any security can be determined by calculating the present value of its expected cash flows. The discount rate employed in the present value calculation must be the investors' required return on a security of comparable risk (i.e., the rates in lines 9 and 10). The resulting present value is an estimate of the aggregate market value and price of the security. If investors purchase the security at this price, they expect to earn the required return on their investment. If the price were higher, investors would not purchase the security, since their expected return would be less than the return on other securities with comparable risk. If the price were lower, investors would promptly purchase the security, since it would offer a higher return than other securities of comparable risk. The actions of investors would bid up the price of the security until its value equaled the present value calculated as described.

The example in Exhibit 1 employs cash flows that are expected to continue in perpetuity. The present value *(V)* of a stream of cash payments *(CF)* that is expected to continue in perpetuity is calculated in the following way: $V = CF/r$, where $r$ is the appropriate discount rate. The market value of the firm's equity can be estimated as the present value of the future cash flows expected by shareholders (i.e., dividends) discounted at the cost of equity capital, or $V_E = \text{DIV}/k_E$ (line 12). Similarly, the market value of the firm's debt is $V_D = \text{Interest}/k_D$ (line 11).

The market value of the firm as a whole is simply the sum of the market value of its debt and equity, or $V_F = V_D + V_E$ (line 13). Note that as debt is added to the capital structure, the market value of the firm, $V_F$ (line 13), first rises and later falls. The reasons for this phenomenon will be explored later. The maximum value of the firm, $540,274, occurs with $150,000 of debt in the capital structure.

## Profitability and "Business" versus "Investor" Returns

Lines 14–18 of Exhibit 1 present book value and profitability data for the firm. The *market* values of both the firm's equity (line 12) and its total capital (line 13) are greater than the *book* values (lines 15 and 16) of the firm's equity and total capital. The use of leverage has created this incremental value. The entire value increase accrues to the shareholders, since they are the residual owners of the firm. This value increase is a one-time windfall gain to the shareholders. Thereafter the shareholders can expect to receive only their required rate of return (i.e., the firm's cost of equity capital).

The return on total capital (ROTC) is simply EBIT after tax divided by total invested capital. Total capital is measured at book values. Return on total capital is unaffected by leverage. Return on equity (ROE) is profit after taxes divided by the book value of equity: $ROE = PAT/BV_E$. With no debt, ROTC = ROE. However, the addition of debt "leverages" the return on equity, and ROE rises above ROTC. While ROE represents the return on the book value of equity, investors do not necessarily receive this same return. Investors instead receive the *market* return, which reflects dividends received plus any changes in the price of their shares. ROE is thus a measure of *business* return, not *investor* return. This is a critical distinction.

## Earnings per Share and Price-Earnings Ratio

Lines 19–22 of Exhibit 1 demonstrate the effects of changes in a firm's capital structure on its earnings per share (EPS) and on its price-earnings ratio. The calculations assume the firm has no debt initially. In adding a given amount of debt to the capital structure, it is assumed that the firm issues debt and repurchases shares of stock with the proceeds of the debt issue. Specifically, the following sequence of events is assumed: (1) the firm announces its intention to carry out an alteration in its long-run capital structure, (2) the price of its stock changes to reflect the new anticipated value of the firm (thereby producing a one-time windfall gain for shareholders), and then (3) the firm markets a debt issue and repurchases stock at the new price. Note that EPS increases with additional debt. However, this does not *necessarily* imply that shareholders are always better off with higher levels of debt. The price-earnings ratio of the stock falls with increased leverage, since EPS is riskier.[1] As debt increases, investors pay a smaller price per dollar

---

1. In this simple perpetuity example, the cost of equity capital is equal to the inverse of the price-earnings ratio (i.e., $k_E = EPS/P$). This is *not* true in general.

of expected earnings per share in order to reflect the increased risk (or lower "quality") of earnings. By definition $P = (P/EPS) \times (EPS)$. As leverage increases, EPS rises, and the stock's price-earnings ratio falls. The impact on stock price of leverage is determined by the trade-off of these two effects. Note that for low levels of leverage, the increase in EPS dominates the reduction in the price-earnings ratio, and the stock price rises with leverage. For high levels of debt, the opposite occurs; thus, the price of the stock first rises and then falls with leverage.

## Weighted Average Cost of Capital

The weighted average cost of capital is the percentage of debt in the capital structure multiplied by the after-tax cost of debt plus the percentage of equity in the capital structure multiplied by the after-tax cost of equity. Because of the tax deductibility of interest payments, the after-tax cost of debt to the firm, $k^t_D$, is less than the return paid to bondholders, $k_D$. With $t = .50$, the after-tax cost of debt is only one half its pre-tax cost. The cost of equity is already in after-tax terms. Thus, using market value weights, the weighted average cost of the firm's capital is

$$k = \left(\frac{V_D}{V_E + V_D}\right) k_D (1 - t) + \left(\frac{V_E}{V_E + V_D}\right) k_E = \left(\frac{V_D}{V_F}\right) k^t_D + \left(\frac{V_E}{V_F}\right) k_E$$

Most financial theorists recommend calculating a firm's cost of capital using *market* value weights rather than *book* value weights for debt and equity in the firm's capital structure. Although market values are used in the calculation of $k$ in line 25, the use of book values would have very little impact on the results. This is a particularly happy outcome, since financial managers, lenders, and rating agencies characterize a firm's capital structure, almost without exception, in terms of *book* value weights. It is important to note also that when a firm sells a new issue of common stock, the issue is sold at market prices. For this incremental equity addition the book value and the market value of the capital raised are equal. This equality removes the potential for any conflict in the use of market versus book value weights in setting hurdle rates for capital investments financed in part via new equity additions.

In lines 11–13, the value of the firm was calculated by adding the value of the firm's debt and equity securities. In a capital budgeting analysis, a comparable valuation is reached in a more direct manner. The technique involves calculating the firm's (or investment project's) free cash flow (FCF). Free cash flow is the after-tax cash flow generated by the firm's investments ignoring all payments to providers of capital (i.e., ignoring all financing charges such as interest and dividends and ignoring the tax savings attributable to the use of debt). In the example outlined in Exhibit 1, free cash flow is simply EBIT after tax. The value of the firm is the present value of FCF discounted at the weighted average cost of the capital invested in the firm. In our perpetuity example, $V_F = \text{FCF}/k$. The costs of financing are not deducted in the calculation of FCF. They are incorporated by discounting FCF at the weighted average cost of capital, which includes these capital costs.

Thus, using free cash flow and the weighted average cost of capital, the value of the firm (or the investment project) can be calculated directly. Note that the resulting values of $V_F$ in line 27 are the same as those in line 13, which are derived by valuing debt and equity separately.

## Implications

The most important results of the Exhibit 1 example are contained in lines 13, 20, and 25. In the simple world outlined in Exhibit 1, the firm's optimal capital structure *simultaneously* (a) maximizes the value of the firm and (b) its share price, and (c) minimizes the firm's weighted average cost of capital. Given the assumptions concerning the cost of debt and equity (lines 9 and 10), as debt is added to the capital structure, the weighted average cost of capital falls. This increases the value of the firm. Since this increase in the firm's value accrues to the owners of the firm, the price of the firm's stock rises. In this example, the firm's optimal (or target) book value debt ratio is in the range of 30–40%. The determination of the firm's optimal (or target) capital structure is also displayed in the graphs in Exhibit 2.

Exhibits 1 and 2 are based on very simple assumptions. They are designed to delineate the mechanics of the capital structure decision. The exhibits do not provide a detailed explanation of the economic rationale for the behavior portrayed. One common rationale is that as debt is added, $V_F$ rises ($P$ rises, $k$ falls) due to the tax savings provided by debt. Recall that these tax savings increase the total cash payments to security holders (line 8). The value of the firm is therefore increased by the present value of these tax savings. This is a major benefit of leverage. As leverage is increased, however, so is the probability of financial distress. Firms with very high debt ratios (and low bond ratings) may have difficulty raising funds in periods of tight money. This affects the firm's ability to make investments and remain competitive. Higher debt ratios also increase the chances that in periods of difficulty, management decisions will be constrained by creditors. Violation of debt covenants could restrict the freedom of managers to make decisions in the best interests of shareholders. The firm might be unable to undertake attractive investment opportunities or might be forced by creditors to sell assets or issue equity at extremely unattractive times. At worst, the firm could face bankruptcy or liquidation. Such decisions would probably not be in the long-term interests of shareholders.

The other side of the argument has also been advanced as an explanation of the limits to leverage, however. During a period of extreme financial distress, a management group might feel that it has little to lose by making operating or investment decisions with a very high potential payoff (i.e., high enough to save the firm from bankruptcy if the projects were successful) but with a very low probability that the projects would actually be successful. Such decisions could serve the interests of managers and equity shareholders but work to the detriment of creditors. To insure against this risk, the return required by bondholders, $k_D$ (the cost of debt), rises precipitously at high levels of debt.

There are many potential costs associated with financial distress. These costs are embedded implicitly in the costs of capital assumed in this example (lines 9 and 10). As a firm's debt ratio rises, the probability of financial distress increases, and the value of the firm is reduced by the present value of these expected costs. At low levels of debt, the disadvantages of leverage are outweighed by the advantages of leverage, and the value of the firm rises. At high debt ratios, the present value of the expected costs of financial distress is larger than the present value of the tax savings, and increased leverage reduces the value of the firm. An intermediate level of debt which represents the optimal trade-off between these two factors maximizes the value of the firm (and the price of the stock) and minimizes the cost of capital.

## Conclusions

The example outlined in this note is based on many simplifications; that is, perpetuity cash flows, 100% dividend payout, capital expenditures equal to depreciation, no sales growth, and so forth. However, the analysis in Exhibits 1 and 2 does provide a conceptual framework for the determination of optimal capital structure. Unfortunately, in practice it is not easy to apply these concepts in a straightforward manner. It is quite difficult to estimate accurately the cost of capital for a firm given its existing capital structure. It is no simpler to estimate the firm's capital cost given some proposed *new* capital structure. To further complicate the problem, in contrast to the Exhibit 1 example, firms' capital structures can include not only straight debt and common equity but also preferred stock and convertible securities.

While there are significant practical problems associated with determining a firm's optimal capital structure, some statistical tools and benchmarks are available to aid financial decision makers in their search for the best capital structure.[2]

---

2. For example, bond ratings and their determinants, interest rates by bond rating, statistics on the availability of debt in credit crunches by bond rating, interest coverage and cash flow coverage ratios as measures of leverage, statistical studies of similar firms with different debt ratios, statistical estimates of the cost of equity capital, and so forth. A statistical method for estimating the cost of equity capital for a firm can be found in "Diversification, the Capital Asset Pricing Model, and the Cost of Equity Capital" and "Financial Leverage, the Capital Asset Pricing Model, and the Cost of Equity Capital" notes in Part III.

# EXHIBIT 1
Hypothetical Calculation of the Impact of Capital Structure on Securities Valuation

| | 0% | 10% | 20% | 30% | 40% | 50% |
|---|---|---|---|---|---|---|
| 1. Debt in the capital structure[a] | 0% | 10% | 20% | 30% | 40% | 50% |
| 2. Earnings before interest and taxes (EBIT) | $120,000 | $120,000 | $120,000 | $120,000 | $120,000 | $120,000 |
| 3. Interest | 0 | 4,125 | 8,750 | 14,625 | 22,000 | 31,250 |
| 4. Profit before taxes (PBT) | 120,000 | 115,875 | 111,250 | 105,375 | 98,000 | 88,750 |
| 5. Taxes | 60,000 | 57,938 | 55,625 | 52,688 | 49,000 | 44,375 |
| 6. Profit after taxes (PAT) | $ 60,000 | $ 57,937 | $ 55,625 | $ 52,687 | $ 49,000 | $ 44,375 |
| 7. Dividends (DIV) | $ 60,000 | $ 57,937 | $ 55,625 | $ 52,687 | $ 49,000 | $ 44,375 |
| 8. Total payments to security holders: (line 3 + line 6) | $ 60,000 | $ 62,062 | $ 64,375 | $ 67,312 | $ 71,000 | $ 75,625 |
| 9. Required return on debt capital, $k_D$ (cost of debt capital) | 8.00% | 8.25% | 8.75% | 9.75% | 11.00% | 12.50% |
| 10. Required return on equity capital, $k_E$ (cost of equity capital) | 12.00% | 12.50% | 13.00% | 13.50% | 14.50% | 16.00% |
| 11. Market value of debt, $V_D$: (line 3 ÷ line 9) | $ 0 | $ 50,000 | $100,000 | $150,000 | $200,000 | $250,000 |
| 12. Market value of equity, $V_E$: (line 7 ÷ line 10) | 500,000 | 463,496 | 427,885 | 390,274 | 337,931 | 277,344 |
| 13. Market value of the firm, $V_F$: (line 11 + line 12) | $500,000 | $513,496 | $527,885 | $540,274 | $537,931 | $527,344 |
| 14. Book value of debt, $BV_D$ | $ 0 | $ 50,000 | $100,000 | $150,000 | $200,000 | $250,000 |
| 15. Book value of equity, $BV_E$ | 500,000 | 450,000 | 400,000 | 350,000 | 300,000 | 250,000 |
| 16. Book value of the firm, $BV_F$ (total capital) | $500,000 | $500,000 | $500,000 | $500,000 | $500,000 | $500,000 |
| 17. Return on total capital (ROTC): (EBIT(1-$t$) ÷ line 16) | 12.0% | 12.0% | 12.0% | 12.0% | 12.0% | 12.0% |
| 18. Return on equity (ROE): (line 6 ÷ line 15) | 12.0% | 12.9% | 13.9% | 15.1% | 16.3% | 17.8% |
| 19. Number of shares outstanding (N) | 5,000 | 4,513 | 4,053 | 3,612 | 3,141 | 2,630 |
| 20. Price per share of common stock (P): (line 12 ÷ line 19) | $ 100.0 | $ 102.7 | $ 105.6 | $ 108.1 | $ 107.6 | $ 105.5 |
| 21. Earnings per share of common stock (EPS): (line 6 ÷ line 19) | $ 12.00 | $ 12.84 | $ 13.72 | $ 14.59 | $ 15.60 | $ 16.87 |
| 22. Price-earnings ratio (P/EPS): (line 20 ÷ line 21 = line 12 ÷ line 6) | 8.3 | 8.0 | 7.7 | 7.4 | 6.9 | 6.3 |
| 23. Book value debt ratio: (line 14 ÷ line 16) | 0% | 10% | 20% | 30% | 40% | 50% |
| 24. Market value debt ratio, $V_D/V_F$: (line 11 ÷ line 13) | 0% | 9.7% | 18.9% | 27.8% | 37.2% | 47.7% |
| 25. Weighted average cost of capital, $k$ (using market values; see text) | 12.0% | 11.7% | 11.4% | 11.1% | 11.2% | 11.4% |
| 26. Free cash flow (FCF): (EBIT (1-t) = line 2 × .50) | $ 60,000 | $ 60,000 | $ 60,000 | $ 60,000 | $ 60,000 | $ 60,000 |
| 27. Market value of the firm, $V_F$: (line 26 ÷ line 25) | $500,000 | $513,496 | $527,885 | $540,274 | $537,931 | $527,344 |

a. Calculated using book value weights for debt and equity.

**EXHIBIT 2**
Determining Optimal Capital Structure

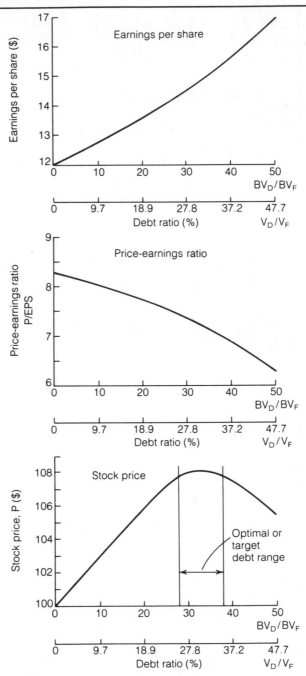

*(continued)*

**EXHIBIT 2** *(concluded)*

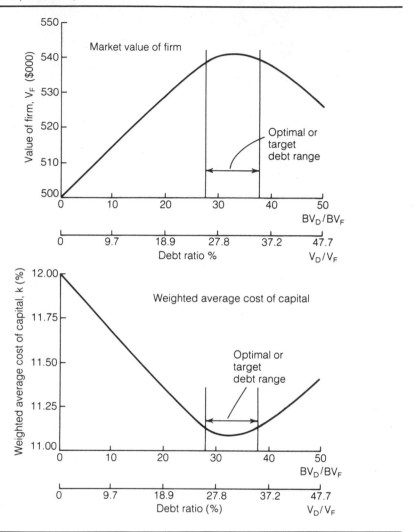

# Continental Carriers, Inc.

In May 1988, Elizabeth Thorp, treasurer of Continental Carriers, Inc. (CCI), was considering the advantages and disadvantages of several alternative methods of financing CCI's acquisition of Midland Freight, Inc. At a recent meeting of the board of directors, there had been substantial disagreement as to the best method of financing the acquisition. After the meeting Ms. Thorp had been asked by John Evans, president of CCI, to assess the arguments presented by the various directors and to outline a position to be taken by management at the June directors' meeting.

CCI was a regulated general commodities motor carrier whose routes ran the length of the Pacific Coast, from Oregon and California to the industrial Midwest, and from Chicago to several points in Texas. Founded in 1952 by three brothers, the firm had experienced little growth until the mid-1970s. At that point Mr. Evans joined the firm as president after many years as an executive of a major eastern carrier. Mr. Evans first concentrated his efforts on expanding CCI's revenues on existing routes through an intensive marketing effort and a renewed emphasis on improving service. In 1982, utilizing the proceeds of CCI's initial public offering of common stock, Mr. Evans began a program designed to reduce operating costs through a combination of extensive computerization of operations and improvement in terminal facilities. As a result of these changes, CCI had become a large and profitable concern, widely respected in the industry for its aggressive management.

By 1988, Mr. Evans and the directors of the firm had concluded that the key to continued expansion in revenues and income was a policy of selected acquisitions. After a study of potential candidates for acquisition, negotiations began with Midland

Freight, Inc., a common carrier serving Michigan and Indiana from Chicago. The owners of Midland agreed to sell the firm to CCI for $50 million in cash. Mr. Evans felt that Midland was an outstanding acquisition in that it would expand CCI's route system and seemed well suited for the type of marketing and cost reduction programs that had fostered CCI's growth. The board had unanimously approved the merger.

CCI's lawyers felt that no difficulty would be encountered in gaining the approval of the Interstate Commerce Commission for the merger, and the closing date for the acquisition was set for October 1, 1988. Mr. Evans realized that the funds for the Midland acquisition would have to be raised from outside sources. Given that Midland would add $8.4 million in earnings before interest and taxes (EBIT) to CCI on an annual basis, he felt that such external financing would not be difficult to obtain.

CCI's management had followed a consistent policy of avoiding long-term debt. The company had met its needs through use of retained earnings supplemented with the proceeds of the 1982 stock offering and infrequent short-term bank loans. As of 1988, CCI's capitalization consisted of common stock and surplus with no fixed debt of any kind. Most of the common stock was held by management. Ownership of the stock was widely distributed, and there was no real dominant interest other than management. The shares were traded infrequently in the over-the-counter market. Discussions with an investment banker led Ms. Thorp to believe that, barring a major market decline, new common stock could be sold to the public at $17.75 per share. After underwriting fees and expenses, the net proceeds to the company would be $16.75 per share. Thus, if common stock were used, the acquisition would require issuance of 3 million new shares.

For the past few years, Ms. Thorp and Mr. Evans had been disappointed in the market performance of CCI's common stock (see Exhibit 1). Thus, they decided to reconsider the firm's policy of avoiding long-term debt (see Exhibit 2). It was felt that such a change might be justified by the anticipated stability of CCI's future earnings. Ms. Thorp had determined that the firm could sell $50 million in bonds to a California insurance company. The interest rate on these bonds would be 10% and they would mature in 15 years. An annual sinking fund of $2.5 million would be required, leaving $12.5 million outstanding at maturity. Although the bond terms would create a sizable need for cash, Ms. Thorp felt that they were the best that could be obtained.

In addition, Ms. Thorp had calculated that, given the tax deductibility of bond interest and CCI's current marginal tax rate of 40% (34% federal corporate income tax; 9% deductible state and local corporate income taxes), the 10% rate was the equivalent of 6% on an after-tax basis. In contrast, she thought the stock at $16.75 per share and a dividend of $1.50 per share would cost CCI nearly 9%. This cost comparison made the debt alternative seem desirable to Ms. Thorp.

At the May directors' meeting, the Midland acquisition received enthusiastic approval. Ms. Thorp then decided to sound out the board's opinions regarding the possibility of financing the acquisition with long-term debt rather than with common stock. She presented the foregoing cost calculations. To her concern, an acrimonious debate broke out among the directors concerning financing policy.

Ms. Thorp was immediately questioned as to the cost of the debt issue, since her figures did not include the annual payment to the sinking fund. One director argued that this represented 8% of the average size of the bond issue over its 15-year life, and he felt that the stock issue had a smaller cost than the bonds. In addition, he emphasized the cash outlay required by the bond alternative and the $12.5 million maturity, especially in view of CCI's already existing lease commitments. He felt that the use of debt added considerable risk to the company, making the common stock more speculative and causing greater variation in market price.

Another director argued for the issuance of common stock because "simple arithmetic" showed that CCI would net 10% or $5 million, per year after taxes from the acquisition. Yet, if an additional 3 million shares of common stock were sold, the dividend requirements, at the current rate of $1.50 per share, would be only $4.5 million per year. Since management was not considering raising the dividend rate, she could not see how the sale of the common stock would hurt the interests of present stockholders. Further, if there were any immediate sacrifice by existing shareholders, she argued, it would be overcome as expansion of the firm continued. Under these circumstances, she argued, the bond issue should be rejected, given the cash demands it would place on the firm.

On the other hand, one director became very agitated in arguing that the stock was a "steal" at $17.75 per share. He pointed out that CCI's policy of retaining earnings had built the book value of the firm to $45.00 per share as of December 1987. In addition, he felt that the true value of the company was understated, since the book value of CCI's assets was considerably below current replacement cost. This director was also worried by the substantial dilution of management's voting control of CCI that was implicit in the 3 million share offering. Thus, he concluded, the sale of common stock at this time would be a "gift" to new shareholders of the substantial value held by current stockholders.

Two directors agreed that sale of stock would dilute the stock's value, but they measured this dilution in terms of earnings per share instead of book or replacement value. These directors anticipated that postacquisition earnings would equal $34 million before interest and taxes. If common stock were sold, earnings per share would be diluted to $2.72. In contrast, they argued, the sole use of debt would increase earnings per share to $3.87. The two directors felt that it was not important that the sinking fund equaled $.56 per share each year.

Finally, a director mentioned some personal observations he had made about financing in the trucking industry. First, he noted that CCI was one of the few major common carriers that had no long-term debt in their capital structures, while CCI's price-earnings ratio was among the lowest in the industry. Second, he wondered whether Ms. Thorp had given consideration to the possibility of issuing preferred stock. This director had determined that CCI could sell 500,000 shares of preferred stock bearing a dividend rate of $10.50 per share and a par value of $100. The director criticized Ms. Thorp for failing to deal with the issues he had raised.

This debate had caused the directors' meeting to run over its scheduled conclusion and no signs of agreement had developed. Ms. Thorp asked that the discussion of financing alternatives be held over until the June meeting to allow her time to prepare additional material. Now, as the date for the meeting approached, Ms. Thorp once again turned her attention to the issues raised at the board meeting. She realized that a considerable number of issues raised by the directors needed to be considered, and she designed a chart to aid in the comparison of the debt and stock alternatives (Exhibit 3).

## EXHIBIT 1

Selected Income and Dividend Data, 1982–1988 (thousands of dollars except per share data)

| | Operating Revenue | Income before Taxes | Income after Taxes | Income per Share | Dividends per Share | Market Prices per Share of Common Stock | |
|---|---|---|---|---|---|---|---|
| | | | | | | High | Low |
| 1982 . . . . . . . | $ 630,000 | $14,490 | $ 7,245 | $1.61 | $1.00 | 16¼ | 11¼ |
| 1983 . . . . . . . | 693,750 | 16,650 | 8,325 | 1.85 | 1.15 | 19 | 14¾ |
| 1984 . . . . . . . | 737,305 | 19,170 | 9,585 | 2.13 | 1.25 | 20⅛ | 15 |
| 1985 . . . . . . . | 858,460 | 22,320 | 11,160 | 2.48 | 1.25 | 23¾ | 17⅜ |
| 1986 . . . . . . . | 926,665 | 25,020 | 12,510 | 2.78 | 1.25 | 27⅝ | 22¼ |
| 1987 . . . . . . . | 1,028,570 | 28,800 | 15,725 | 3.49 | 1.50 | 25 | 18½ |
| 1988 est.[a] . . . . | 1,080,000 | 25,600 | 15,360 | 3.41 | 1.50[b] | 20[c] | 16⅜[c] |

a. Excluding the proposed acquisition and its financing.

b. Annual rate.

c. To May 1 (May 1 prices were 18⅞–19⅛).

## EXHIBIT 2

Summary Balance Sheet at December 31, 1987
(thousands of dollars)

| | |
|---|---|
| Cash . . . . . . . . . . . . . . . . . . . | $ 19,000 |
| Accounts receivable . . . . . . . . . . . . . . | 38,450 |
| Inventory . . . . . . . . . . . . . . . . | 8,100 |
| Prepaid expenses . . . . . . . . . . . . . . | 9,100 |
| Current assets . . . . . . . . . . . . . . | 74,650 |
| Carrier operating property (cost) . . . . . . . . . | 236,650 |
| Less: Accumulated depreciation . . . . . . . . . | 89,100 |
| Net carrier operating property . . . . . . . . . . | 147,550 |
| Other assets . . . . . . . . . . . . . . . | 30,900 |
| Total assets . . . . . . . . . . . . . . | $253,100 |
| Accounts payable . . . . . . . . . . . . . . | $ 25,300 |
| Miscellaneous payables and accruals . . . . . . . | 20,250 |
| Taxes payable . . . . . . . . . . . . . . . | 5,050 |
| Current liabilities . . . . . . . . . . . . | 50,600 |
| Common stock ($1 par) . . . . . . . . . . . . | 4,500 |
| Paid-in surplus . . . . . . . . . . . . . . | 40,000 |
| Retained earnings . . . . . . . . . . . . . . | 158,000 |
| Stockholders' equity . . . . . . . . . . . . | 202,500 |
| Total liabilities and stockholders' equity . . . . . . . . | $253,100 |

**EXHIBIT 3**
Analysis of Financial Alternatives

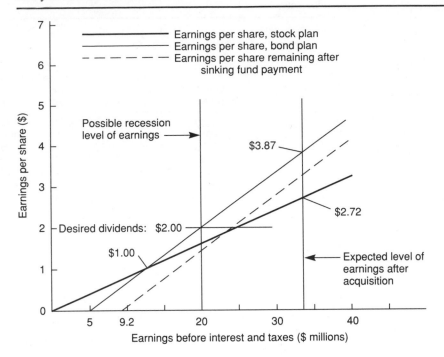

Calculation of Points to Determine Lines (thousands of dollars except per share data)

|  | Bonds | Stock | Bonds | Stock |
|---|---|---|---|---|
| EBIT . . . . . . . . . . . . . | $12,500 | $12,500 | $34,000 | $34,000 |
| Interest, 1st year . . . . . . . . | 5,000 | − | 5,000 | − |
| Taxable earnings . . . . . . | 7,500 | 12,500 | 29,000 | 34,000 |
| Tax at 40% . . . . . . . . . | 3,000 | 5,000 | 11,600 | 13,600 |
| After-tax earnings . . . . . . | 4,500 | 7,500 | 17,400 | 20,400 |
| Earnings per share |  |  |  |  |
| ÷ 4,500,000 . . . . . . . | $ 1.00 | − | $ 3.87 | − |
| ÷ 7,500,000 . . . . . . . | − | $ 1.00 | − | $ 2.72 |
| Annual sinking fund . . . . . . | $ 2,500 | − | $ 2,500 | − |

*Note:* The effects of leverage and dilution are indicated by the differing slopes of the lines, and can be expressed: "For each million dollar change of EBIT, the bond plan brings a change in earnings per share that is $.0535 greater than the stock plan. Leverage is favorable from EBIT of $12.5 million upward."

# E. I. du Pont de Nemours and Company (1983)

In early 1983 the management of E. I. du Pont de Nemours and Company (Du Pont) looked back on two decades of turbulence in the firm's operations. Difficulties in the 1970s and the mega-merger with Conoco had led the company to abandon its long-held policy of an all-equity capital structure. Following the Conoco acquisition in 1981, Du Pont's ratio of debt to total capital had peaked at 42%—the highest in the firm's history. The rapid escalation in financial leverage had cost Du Pont its cherished AAA bond rating. Du Pont had not regained the top rating despite a reduction in debt to 36% of capital by the end of 1982.

The operations of Du Pont had changed dramatically in the past 20 years. With the task of digesting Conoco underway, management faced an important financial policy decision—determining a capital structure policy appropriate for Du Pont in the 1980s. This decision would have implications for Du Pont's financial performance and possibly for its competitive position as well.

E. I. du Pont de Nemours and Company was founded in 1802 to manufacture gunpowder. By 1900, Du Pont had begun to expand rapidly through research and acquisitions. A technological leader in chemicals and fibers, the firm grew to be the largest U.S. chemical manufacturer. At the end of 1980 the firm ranked fifteenth on the Fortune 500 list of U.S. industrials. The 1981 merger with Conoco, Inc., a major oil company, elevated Du Pont to seventh place on the list of U.S. industrials.

## Capital Structure Policy, 1965 –1982

Historically Du Pont had been well known for its policy of extreme financial conservatism. The company's low debt ratio was feasible in part because of its success in its product markets. Du Pont's high level of profitability allowed it to finance its needs through internally generated funds (see Exhibits 1 and 2 for selected financial data). In fact, financial leverage was actually negative between 1965 and 1970, since Du Pont's cash balance exceeded its total debt. Du Pont's conservative use of debt combined with its profitability and technological leadership in the chemical industry had made the company one of the few AAA-rated manufacturers. Du Pont's low debt policy maximized its financial flexibility and insulated its operations from financing constraints.

In the late 1960s competitive conditions in Du Pont's fibers and plastics businesses began to exert pressure on the firm's financial policy. Between 1965 and 1970 increases in industry capacity outstripped demand growth, resulting in substantial price declines. As a result, Du Pont experienced decreases in gross margins and return on capital. Despite continued sales growth, net income fell by 19% between 1965 and 1970.

Three factors combined to intensify the pressure on Du Pont's financing policy in the mid-1970s. In response to competitive pressures Du Pont in the early 1970s embarked on a major capital spending program designed to restore its cost position. The escalation of inflation ballooned the cost of the program to more than 50% over budget by 1974. Since capital spending was critical to maintaining and improving its competitive position, Du Pont was reluctant to reduce or postpone these expenditures. Second, the rapid increase in oil prices in 1973 pushed up Du Pont's feedstock costs and increased required inventory investment, while oil shortages disrupted production. Du Pont experienced the full impact of the oil shock in 1974; its revenues rose by 16% and costs jumped by 30%, causing net income to fall by 31%. Finally, the recession in 1975 had a dramatic impact on Du Pont's fiber business. Between the second quarter of 1974 and the second quarter of 1975, Du Pont's fiber shipments dropped by 50% on a volume basis. Net income fell by 33% in 1975. Over the period 1973–1975 Du Pont's net income, return on total capital, and earnings per share all fell by more than 50%.

Severe financing pressures resulted from the combination of inflation's impact on needed capital expenditures, cost increases driven by the escalation in oil prices, and recessionary conditions in the fiber business. The required investment in working capital and capital expenditures increased dramatically at a time when internally generated funds were shrinking. Du Pont responded to the financing shortfall by cutting its dividend in 1974 and 1975 and slashing working capital investment.

Since these measures were insufficient to meet the entire financing requirement, Du Pont turned to debt financing. With no short-term debt outstanding in 1972, the firm's short-term debt rose to $540 million by the end of 1975. In addition, in 1974, Du Pont floated a $350 million 30-year bond issue and a $150 million issue of 7-year notes. The former was Du Pont's first public long-term debt issue in the U.S. since the 1920s. As a result, Du Pont's debt ratio rose from 7% in

1972 to 27% in 1975, while interest coverage collapsed from 38.4 to 4.6 over the same period. Despite concern that the rapid increase in the company's debt ratio might result in a downgrading, Du Pont retained its AAA bond rating during this period. Had Du Pont abandoned its policy of financial conservatism, or was this a temporary departure from that policy forced by extraordinary financing pressures? In December 1974, Du Pont CEO Irving Shapiro stated, "We expect to use prudent debt financing over the long term."

Nonetheless, Du Pont moved quickly to reduce its debt ratio. Between 1976 and 1979 financing pressures eased. Capital expenditures declined from their 1975 peak as the spending program initiated in the early 1970s neared completion. Net income more than tripled during the period 1975–1979, helped by relatively moderate energy price increases and the economywide recovery from the 1974–1975 recession. Du Pont reduced the dollar value of its total debt in 1977, 1978, and 1979. By the end of 1979, Du Pont's debt had been pared to about 20% of total capital and interest coverage had rebounded to 11.5 from 4.6 in 1975. Once again the firm was well within the AAA-rated range. However, it was not apparent that the firm would return to the zero debt policy of the past. In 1978, Richard Heckert, a Du Pont senior vice president, noted, "While we presently anticipate some further reduction in borrowings, we have considerable borrowing capacity and hence considerable flexibility."

An abrupt departure from maximum financial flexibility occurred in the summer of 1981. In July, Du Pont entered a bidding contest for Conoco, Inc., a major oil company and the fourteenth largest U.S. industrial. After a brief but frenetic battle, Du Pont succeeded in buying Conoco in August 1981. The price of almost $8 billion made the merger the largest in U.S. history and represented a premium of 77% above Conoco's preacquisition market value. With the acquisition, Du Pont virtually doubled its size and significantly increased its orientation toward undifferentiated commodity products. Both Du Pont's stock price and industry analysts responded negatively to the acquisition. Major concerns included the high price Du Pont had paid and the question of how Conoco would contribute to Du Pont's strategic objectives.

To finance the purchase of Conoco, Du Pont issued $3.9 billion in common stock and $3.85 billion in floating rate debt. In addition, Du Pont assumed $1.9 billion of outstanding Conoco debt. The acquisition propelled Du Pont's debt ratio to nearly 40% from slightly over 20% at the end of 1980. Du Pont's bond rating was downgraded to AA, marking the first time in its history that the firm had fallen below the top rating.

The first year after the merger was a difficult one for Du Pont. Conoco's performance was hampered by declining oil prices in 1982, while an economic recession plagued the chemical industry. Although Du Pont's 1982 revenues were 2½ times 1979 sales, net income in 1982 fell below 1979 results; return on total capital was cut in half during this period and earnings per share fell by 40%.

As Du Pont's management worked to frame and implement a coherent strategy for the merged company, they also got to work to repair the firm's extended financial condition. To reduce interest rate exposure, Du Pont refunded most of the firm's floating-rate debt with fixed-rate long-term debt issues. Plans to reduce debt with the proceeds from the sale of $2 billion in Conoco coal and oil assets were frustrated by depressed energy prices. One analyst complained, "Du Pont managed to acquire Conoco at the peak of the oil cycle, and now they are looking at a tremendous glut of coal assets for sale that is going to make it very difficult to sell coal properties." Nevertheless, by the end of 1982, Du Pont had pared its debt ratio to 36% from the postmerger peak of 42%. Poor earnings in 1982 held interest coverage down to a near record low of 4.8. The firm retained its AA bond rating.

The increase in debt ratio accompanying the Conoco merger marked the second time in 10 years that Du Pont departed from its traditional capital structure policy. This, plus the fundamental changes in Du Pont's businesses, mandated the determination of a capital structure policy that would be feasible and appropriate for the years ahead.

## Future Capital Structure Policy

Du Pont's financing policy had always been predicated on the notion of maximizing financial flexibility. This ensured that financing constraints did not interfere with the firm's competitive strategy. However, competitors differed widely from Du Pont and each other in their use of financial leverage (see Exhibit 3). Why should not Du Pont, like Dow Chemical and Celanese, reap the benefits of aggressive debt financing even if this resulted in a further reduction in its bond rating? (See Exhibit 4 for bond rating data.) Of course, electric utilities and telephone companies maintained high bond ratings despite aggressive use of debt (see Exhibit 4). While Du Pont's performance was more volatile than a company like AT&T, it was less volatile than many competitors and other industrial firms (see Exhibit 5).

In framing a debt policy, a key concern was how risky were Du Pont's businesses. The degree of business risk would help determine how much debt Du Pont could safely employ in its capital structure without unduly constraining its competitive strategy. The last 20 years had documented the increased volatility of Du Pont's basic businesses. Du Pont's competitive position and profitability had declined in many product lines. In many businesses, products were close to being undifferentiated commodities, and intense competition was common. Excess capacity and the economics of high-fixed-cost businesses pressured prices and profits. Moreover, Conoco competed in a volatile commodity business, a business in which Du Pont's management had little experience. The increased risk of Du Pont's operations argued for a relatively conservative capital structure.

Nonetheless, several factors suggested that the firm could pursue an aggressive debt policy. Du Pont was still the nation's largest chemical manufacturer, and large-scale economies were a common characteristic of chemical production processes. The firm remained the technological leader in the industry, and its success at R&D was second to none. Du Pont was pursuing capital spending programs designed to reduce costs in all business segments. The firm was widely diversified in terms of products and markets. In the past, Du Pont's economic muscle had often been constrained by aggressive antitrust policy, but the near-term future held some promise of a more benign regulatory environment. As for the impact of Conoco on Du Pont's business risk, some analysts thought the major diversification move would dampen the volatility of the firm's earnings. Edward Jefferson, who succeeded Irving Shapiro as Du Pont's chief executive officer, agreed, reasoning that the merger would "reduce the exposure of the combined companies to fluctuations in the price of energy."

Even with a recovery in gross margins, strong sales growth, and successful sales of Conoco assets, Du Pont would be forced to seek external financing each year from 1983 to 1987 (see Exhibit 6 for projections). The major reason was the need for a continued high level of capital expenditures. Capital spending was viewed as critical to Du Pont's future success because it was the key to minimizing the firm's cost position in existing products and launching new products swiftly and efficiently. In view of its importance, capital spending was essentially nondeferrable and often had to be increased rather than cut in bad times in order to redress the causes of poor performance.

Because of its large, nondeferrable financing needs, Du Pont was concerned about the cost and availability of financing (see Exhibit 7 for data on financing costs and volumes). Companies with high debt ratios and low bond ratings appeared to have some difficulty in obtaining debt financing in some years. However, firms rated A and above appeared to have little difficulty in raising funds. But compared with AAA-rated firms, the cost of debt financing was higher for A-rated firms, and the spread between A and AAA rates widened in high-interest-rate environments. In view of the importance and magnitude of Du Pont's projected financing needs, the firm was concerned about how the cost and availability of debt might affect its ability to pursue capital spending programs critical to its competitive position.

## Capital Structure Policy Alternatives

One alternative for Du Pont was to restore its historical financial strength and AAA rating. Given Du Pont's substantial projected capital spending requirements, a return to zero debt was infeasible. A target ratio of debt to capital of 25% should be sufficient to ensure a high degree of financial flexibility and insulate Du Pont's competitive strategy from capital market conditions. However, achieving this debt ratio would not be easy (see Exhibit 8 for data on policy alternatives). Reducing the debt ratio from 36% in 1982 to 25% by the end of 1986 would require large equity issues in each year. Maintaining the target of 25% debt in 1987 would require additional large equity infusions. As of the end of 1982, Du Pont's stock price had yet to recover from the market's negative reaction to the Conoco merger reinforced by the continuing recession. This raised questions concerning the terms and availability of the substantial new equity financing required to achieve a 25% debt ratio (see Exhibit 7 for equity issue data).

Although a conservative capital structure policy had the force of tradition, it was not clear that conservatism was appropriate for Du Pont in the 1980s. The cost of conservatism was clear (see Exhibit 8). Were Du Pont to abandon forever its historical conservatism and maintain a 40% target debt ratio, many measures of financial performance would benefit. For the recovery scenario projected in Exhibits 6 and 8, a high-debt policy generated higher projected earnings per share, dividends per share, and return on equity. No equity issues would be required through 1985. Equity issues in 1986 and 1987 would be much smaller than projected for the low-debt policy and thus might be more easily timed to take advantage of favorable market conditions. However, with higher financial leverage comes higher risk. In a pessimistic scenario (e.g., a recession), earnings per share and return on equity would suffer more severe declines with the high-debt policy. Other concerns were the availability of funds in all economic conditions with the high-debt alternative and the constraints limited availability might place on Du Pont's operations.

## The Decision

The two decades drawing to a close in 1982 brought fundamental changes in Du Pont's businesses, culminating in the historic acquisition of Conoco. This acquisition also forced a dramatic departure from Du Pont's long-held capital structure policy. These changes both mandated and provided the opportunity for a fundamental reassessment of Du Pont's financing policy. In view of the escalation in Du Pont's debt ratio, the downgrading of its bond rating, and the negative stock market response to the Conoco merger, there was a considerable degree of uncertainty concerning Du Pont's financial policy. This underscored the importance of determining, committing to, and communicating a capital structure policy in the near future.

Note: Exhibits 1 and 2 are on pp. 148–49.

**EXHIBIT 3**
Financial Data for Selected Chemical Companies, 1980 and 1982 (millions of dollars)

| | Du Pont | | Dow Chemical | | Monsanto | | Celanese | |
|---|---|---|---|---|---|---|---|---|
| | 1980 | 1982 | 1980 | 1982 | 1980 | 1982 | 1980 | 1982 |
| Sales | $13,652 | $33,331 | $10,626 | $10,618 | $6,574 | $6,325 | $3,348 | $3,062 |
| 10-year compound annual sales growth rate | 14.2% | 22.5% | 18.7% | 16.0% | 12.8% | 11.0% | 12.4% | 7.4% |
| 10-year compound annual EPS growth rate | 7.5% | 2.9% | 19.9% | 5.7% | 8.3% | 9.9% | 8.9% | 7.3%[a] |
| Net income | $ 744 | $ 894 | $ 805 | $ 399 | $ 149 | $ 352 | $ 122 | $ (34) |
| Net income/Sales | 5.4% | 2.7% | 7.6% | 3.8% | 2.3% | 5.6% | 3.6% | (1.1)% |
| Return on total capital | 10.9% | 6.6% | 7.2% | 7.9% | 5.3% | 8.3% | 9.3% | (.3)% |
| Return on equity | 13.1% | 8.2% | 18.1% | 9.6% | 5.5% | 10.1% | 11.2% | (1.2)% |
| Dividend payout | 58.1% | 64.0% | 36.2% | 101.7% | 86.6% | 45.2% | 42.7% | 42.7%[a] |
| Stock price/EPS[b] | 8.4 | 9.9 | 7.6 | 13.7 | 13.7 | 8.3 | 6.3 | 6.7[a] |
| Market value/Book value[b] | 109% | 82.9% | 138% | 93.4% | 72% | 84.7% | 67% | 75.7% |
| Debt/Total capital | 20.4% | 35.7% | 48.5% | 42.7% | 33.4% | 24.5% | 40.7% | 42.9% |
| Interest coverage | 10.9 | 4.8 | 2.2 | 1.6 | 2.8 | 7.1 | 4.5 | 3.8[a] |
| Bond rating (senior debt) | AAA | AA | A | A | AA | AA | A | BBB |

*Source:* Moody's Investors Service.

a. Celanese 10-year compound annual EPS growth rate, dividend payout ratio, stock price/EPS, and interest coverage use 1981 instead of 1982.

b. Market value/Book value and stock price/EPS are based on average of year's high and low stock prices.

147

## EXHIBIT 1
Selected Financial Data, 1965–1982 (millions of dollars except per share data)

| | 1965 | 1966 | 1967 | 1968 | 1969 | 1970 | 1971 | 1972 |
|---|---|---|---|---|---|---|---|---|
| 1. Sales . . . . . . | $2,999 | $3,159 | $3,079 | $3,455 | $3,632 | $3,618 | $3,848 | $4,366 |
| 2. EBIT . . . . . . | 767 | 727 | 574 | 764 | 709 | 590 | 644 | 768 |
| 3. Interest . . . . . | 2 | 4 | 7 | 7 | 10 | 11 | 15 | 20 |
| 4. Profit after taxes . . . | 407 | 389 | 314 | 372 | 356 | 329 | 356 | 414 |
| 5. Profit after taxes/Sales . | 13.6% | 12.3% | 10.2% | 10.8% | 9.8% | 9.1% | 9.3% | 9.5% |
| 6. After-tax return on total capital[a] . . . | 18.5% | 16.6% | 13.0% | 14.2% | 12.8% | 11.1% | 10.9% | 12.1% |
| 7. Return on equity . . . | 18.6% | 16.8% | 13.0% | 14.6% | 13.3% | 11.8% | 11.5% | 12.7% |
| 8. Earnings per share . . . | $ 2.96 | $ 2.83 | $ 2.24 | $ 2.66 | $ 2.54 | $ 2.29 | $ 2.44 | $ 2.83 |
| 9. Dividends per share . . | 2.00 | 1.92 | 1.67 | 1.83 | 1.75 | 1.68 | 1.67 | 1.82 |
| 10. Average stock price . | 81.04 | 80.88 | 54.42 | 54.25 | 44.46 | 38.29 | 47.92 | 54.77 |
| 11. Average stock price/ Earnings per share . . . | 27.4 | 28.6 | 24.3 | 20.4 | 17.5 | 16.7 | 19.6 | 19.4 |
| 12. Market value/ Book value . . . . . | 5.40 | 5.28 | 3.26 | 3.07 | 2.38 | 1.98 | 2.40 | 2.61 |
| 13. S&P 400 P/E . . . . . | 16.8 | 15.2 | 17.0 | 17.3 | 17.5 | 16.5 | 18.0 | 18.0 |
| 14. S&P 400 market value/ Book value . . . . . | 2.13 | 1.96 | 2.00 | 2.12 | 2.07 | 1.69 | 1.95 | 2.10 |

*Sources:* Du Pont annual reports; Standard and Poor's Corporation.

a. After-tax return on total capital = (EBIT) (1 − Tax rate)/(All debt + Equity). Average stock price is average of year's high and low values. Per share data restated to be comparable with number of shares outstanding at December 31, 1982.

## EXHIBIT 2
Selected Data Related to Funds Needs and Financial Strength, 1965–1982 (millions of dollars)

| | 1965 | 1966 | 1967 | 1968 | 1969 | 1970 | 1971 | 1972 |
|---|---|---|---|---|---|---|---|---|
| Capital expenditures . . . . . | $ 327 | $ 531 | $ 454 | $ 332 | $ 391 | $ 471 | $ 454 | $ 522 |
| Change in working capital[a] . . . . . . . | − | (163) | 121 | 102 | 154 | 135 | (39) | 63 |
| Capital structure Short-term debt . . . . . . | $ 0 0% | $ 0 0% | $ 31 1.2% | $ 57 2.1% | $ 45 1.6% | $ 56 1.9% | $ 0 0% | $ 0 0% |
| Long-term debt . . . . . . | $ 34 1.5% | $ 58 2.4% | $ 95 3.7% | $ 150 5.5% | $ 141 4.9% | $ 160 5.3% | $ 236 7.1% | $ 240 6.8% |
| Equity . . . . . . . . | $2,190 98.5% | $2,317 97.6% | $2,409 95.1% | $2,540 92.4% | $2,685 93.5% | $2,790 92.8% | $3,095 92.9% | $3,267 93.2% |
| Total capital . . . . . . | $2,224 100.0% | $2,375 100.0% | $2,535 100.0% | $2,747 100.0% | $2,871 100.0% | $3,006 100.0% | $3,331 100.0% | $3,507 100.0% |
| Interest coverage . . . . . | 383.5 | 181.8 | 82 | 109.1 | 70.9 | 53.6 | 42.9 | 38.4 |
| Bond rating (senior debt) . . . . . . . | AAA | AAA | AAA | AAA | AAA | AAA | AAA | AAA |

*Source:* Du Pont annual reports.

a. Working capital investment is defined here as net working capital excluding cash, marketable securities, and short-term debt.

**EXHIBIT 1** *(concluded)*

| 1973 | 1974 | 1975 | 1976 | 1977 | 1978 | 1979 | 1980 | 1981 | 1982 |
|---|---|---|---|---|---|---|---|---|---|
| $5,964 | $6,910 | $7,222 | $8,361 | $9,435 | $10,584 | $12,572 | $13,652 | $22,810 | $33,331 |
| 1,100 | 733 | 574 | 961 | 1,141 | 1,470 | 1,646 | 1,209 | 2,631 | 3,545 |
| 34 | 62 | 126 | 145 | 169 | 139 | 143 | 111 | 476 | 739 |
| 586 | 404 | 271 | 459 | 545 | 797 | 965 | 744 | 1,081 | 894 |
| 9.8% | 5.8% | 3.8% | 5.5% | 5.8% | 7.5% | 7.7% | 5.4% | 4.7% | 2.7% |
| 15.1% | 9.0% | 6.6% | 9.7% | 11.1% | 13.7% | 15.1% | 10.9% | 7.5% | 6.6% |
| 16.3% | 10.7% | 7.1% | 11.4% | 12.6% | 16.7% | 18.2% | 13.1% | 10.3% | 8.2% |
| $ 4.01 | $ 2.73 | $ 1.81 | $ 3.30 | $ 3.69 | $ 5.18 | $ 6.23 | $ 4.73 | $ 5.81 | $ 3.75 |
| 1.92 | 1.83 | 1.42 | 1.75 | 1.92 | 2.42 | 2.75 | 2.75 | 2.75 | 2.40 |
| 58.13 | 43.92 | 35.96 | 46.42 | 40.04 | 39.34 | 42.63 | 40.32 | 45.88 | 37.19 |
| 14.5 | 16.1 | 19.9 | 15.0 | 10.9 | 7.3 | 6.6 | 8.4 | 10.0 | 9.8 |
| 2.49 | 1.81 | 1.46 | 1.76 | 1.41 | 1.26 | 1.22 | 1.09 | 1.04 | .83 |
| 13.4 | 9.4 | 10.8 | 10.4 | 9.6 | 8.2 | 7.1 | 8.4 | 8.5 | 10.4 |
| 1.89 | 1.34 | 1.31 | 1.46 | 1.33 | 1.20 | 1.17 | 1.26 | 1.22 | 1.16 |

**EXHIBIT 2** *(concluded)*

| 1973 | 1974 | 1975 | 1976 | 1977 | 1978 | 1979 | 1980 | 1981 | 1982 |
|---|---|---|---|---|---|---|---|---|---|
| $ 727 | $1,008 | $1,036 | $ 876 | $ 704 | $ 714 | $ 864 | $1,297 | $ 2,389 | $ 3,195 |
| 278 | 561 | (122) | 20 | 243 | 341 | 438 | 17 | 2,046 | (987) |
| $ 169 | $ 320 | $ 540 | $ 259 | $ 229 | $ 258 | $ 230 | $ 393 | $ 445 | $ 319 |
| 4.2% | 6.5% | 10.3% | 4.6% | 4.0% | 4.2% | 3.5% | 5.5% | 2.6% | 1.9% |
| $ 250 | $ 793 | $ 889 | $1,282 | $1,236 | $1,058 | $1,067 | $1,068 | $ 6,403 | $ 5,702 |
| 6.2% | 16.2% | 16.9% | 23.0% | 21.4% | 17.4% | 16.1% | 14.9% | 37.0% | 33.8% |
| $3,593 | $3,782 | $3,835 | $4,032 | $4,315 | $4,761 | $5,312 | $5,690 | $10,458 | $10,850 |
| 89.6% | 77.3% | 72.8% | 72.4% | 74.6% | 78.4% | 80.4% | 79.6% | 60.4% | 64.3% |
| $4,012 | $4,895 | $5,264 | $5,573 | $5,780 | $ 6,077 | $6,609 | $7,151 | $17,306 | $16,871 |
| 100.0% | 100.0% | 100.0% | 100.0% | 100.0% | 100.0% | 100.0% | 100.0% | 100.0% | 100.0% |
| 32.4 | 11.8 | 4.6 | 6.6 | 6.8 | 10.6 | 11.5 | 10.9 | 5.5 | 4.8 |
| AAA | AAA | AAA | AAA | AAA | AAA | AAA | AAA | AA | AA |

**EXHIBIT 4**
Bond Rating Medians for 1979–1981

|  | *AAA* | *AA* | *A* | *BBB* | *BB* | *B* |
|---|---|---|---|---|---|---|
| *Industrial Corporations* | | | | | | |
| Interest coverage . . . . | 18.25 | 8.57 | 6.56 | 3.82 | 3.27 | 1.76 |
| Total debt/Capitalization . . | 17.04% | 23.70% | 30.41% | 38.62% | 48.07% | 58.77% |
| *Electric Utilities* | | | | | | |
| Interest coverage . . . . | >4.00 | 3.25–4.25 | 2.50–3.50 | <3.00 | – | – |
| Total debt/Capitalization . . | <45% | 42–47% | 45–55% | >55% | – | – |
| *Telephone Companies* | | | | | | |
| Interest coverage . . . . | >4.50 | 3.70–4.70 | 2.80–4.00 | <3.00 | – | – |
| Total debt/Capitalization . . | <40% | 40–48% | 48–58% | 58–64% | – | – |

*Source:* Standard and Poor's Corporation.

**EXHIBIT 5**
Return on Total Capital

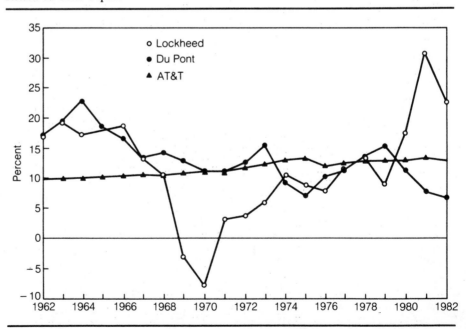

**EXHIBIT 6**

Financial Projections, 1983–1987 (millions of dollars)

|  | *1983* | *1984* | *1985* | *1986* | *1987* |
|---|---|---|---|---|---|
| *Sources of Funds* | | | | | |
| Net income | $1,009 | $1,196 | $1,444 | $1,591 | $1,753 |
| Depreciation | 2,101 | 2,111 | 2,212 | 2,396 | 2,667 |
| Funds from operations | 3,110 | 3,307 | 3,656 | 3,987 | 4,420 |
| Assets sold | 600 | 600 | 600 | 0 | 0 |
| Decrease in cash | 199 | (200) | (200) | (150) | (150) |
| Other sources | 74 | 135 | 135 | 135 | 135 |
| Sources before new financing | $3,983 | $3,842 | $4,191 | $3,972 | $4,405 |
| *Uses of Funds* | | | | | |
| Dividends | $ 571 | $ 658 | $ 794 | $ 896 | $ 964 |
| Capital expenditures | 2,767 | 3,386 | 4,039 | 4,202 | 4,667 |
| Increase in net working capital[a] | 973 | 414 | 594 | 587 | 650 |
| Other | 10 | 10 | 10 | 10 | 10 |
| Total uses | $4,321 | $4,468 | $5,437 | $5,695 | $6,291 |
| Net financing requirement | $ 338 | $ 626 | $1,246 | $1,723 | $1,886 |

*Sources:* Analysts' forecasts and casewriter's estimates.

*Note:* Assumptions are as follows: Sales are average of analysts' forecasts; average annual sales growth rate is 10%. EBIT recovers to 8.1% of sales by 1985. Net working capital (excluding cash) equals 13% of sales. Dividend payout ratio is 55%, and no dividend reductions are allowed. Net fixed assets equal 40% of sales. Depreciation is 15% of net fixed assets in the previous year.

a. Net working capital excludes cash, marketable securities, and short-term debt.

# EXHIBIT 7
Debt Financing Costs and Volumes, 1970–1982 (millions of dollars)

| | 1970 | 1971 | 1972 | 1973 | 1974 | 1975 | 1976 | 1977 | 1978 | 1979 | 1980 | 1981 | 1982 |
|---|---|---|---|---|---|---|---|---|---|---|---|---|---|
| **Gross New Bond Issues by Industrials** | | | | | | | | | | | | | |
| AAA debt | . . . | . . . | . . . | . . . | $1,650 | $ 2,875 | $ 700 | $ 800 | $ 275 | $ 1,550 | $ 1,750 | $ 1,852 | $ 543 |
| AA debt | . . . | . . . | . . . | . . . | 2,415 | 3,310 | 2,030 | 1,125 | 700 | 1,800 | 2,900 | 2,458 | 3,347 |
| A debt | . . . | . . . | . . . | . . . | 2,060 | 5,355 | 2,205 | 960 | 1,310 | 1,500 | 4,220 | 3,887 | 3,075 |
| BBB debt | . . . | . . . | . . . | . . . | 440 | 420 | 1,010 | 445 | 210 | 0 | 345 | 0 | 1,357 |
| **Common and Preferred Stock Issues** | | | | | | | | | | | | | |
| Cash offerings | $9,200 | $13,000 | $13,100 | $11,100 | $7,400 | $11,900 | $13,300 | $14,100 | $14,600 | $17,100 | $28,600 | $34,400 | $38,700 |
| Net[a] | 6,800 | 13,500 | 13,000 | 9,100 | 4,300 | 10,500 | 10,300 | 6,800 | (1,400) | (1,900) | 18,200 | 12,000 | 16,400 |
| Cash offerings by industrials | 3,500 | 3,200 | 3,100 | 1,500 | 1,000 | 2,400 | 2,800 | 2,300 | 2,900 | 3,600 | 10,400 | 11,900 | 9,600 |
| **Maturity Distribution of New Debt Issues** | | | | | | | | | | | | | |
| Medium-term | | | | | | 43% | 30% | 16% | 21% | 30% | 44% | 55% | 62% |
| Long-term | | | | | | 57 | 70 | 84 | 79 | 70 | 56 | 45 | 38 |
| **Interest Rates** | | | | | | | | | | | | | |
| 90-day commercial paper | 7.89% | 5.12% | 4.63% | 8.11% | 10.06% | 6.41% | 5.28% | 5.45% | 7.73% | 10.72% | 12.37% | 15.15% | 11.91% |
| New issue AAA debt | 8.39 | 7.39 | 7.10 | 7.42 | 8.57 | 8.70 | 8.15 | 7.88 | 8.63 | 9.39 | 11.74 | 14.30 | 14.14 |
| New issue AAA–AA spread | .26 | .12 | .10 | .10 | .20 | .27 | .17 | .09 | .14 | .22 | .44 | .50 | .38 |
| New issue AAA–BBB spread | 1.35 | 1.07 | .71 | .75 | 1.67 | 2.57 | 1.44 | .79 | .81 | 1.12 | 1.95 | 2.09 | 1.87 |
| S&P 500 price/earnings ratio | 16.5 | 18.0 | 18.0 | 13.4 | 9.4 | 10.8 | 10.4 | 9.6 | 8.2 | 7.1 | 8.4 | 8.5 | 10.4 |

Sources: Salomon Brothers Inc, Bankers Trust Company, and Standard and Poor's Corporation.

a. Stock offerings less stock repurchases.

**EXHIBIT 8**

Projected Financial Results under Two Financial Policy Alternatives, 1983–1987
(millions of dollars except per share data)

| | 1983 | 1984 | 1985 | 1986 | 1987 | 1987 with 20% Lower EBIT |
|---|---|---|---|---|---|---|
| **40% Debt Scenario** | | | | | | |
| Debt/Total capitalization | 36.0% | 37.1% | 39.7% | 40.0% | 40.0% | 40.0% |
| Interest coverage[a] | 3.67 | 3.88 | 3.95 | 3.89 | 3.86 | 3.09 |
| Earnings per share | $4.20 | $4.98 | $ 6.02 | $ 6.31 | $ 6.62 | $ 4.83 |
| Dividends per share | $2.38 | $2.74 | $ 3.31 | $ 3.56 | $ 3.64 | – |
| Return on total capital | 7.9% | 8.6% | 9.3% | 9.3% | 9.2% | 7.4% |
| Return on equity | 9.0% | 10.1% | 11.5% | 11.5% | 11.4% | 8.3% |
| New equity issues | $ 0 | $ 0 | $ 0 | $ 704 | $ 816 | $ 816 |
| Millions of shares sold[b] | 0 | 0 | 0 | 11.7 | 13.0 | 13.0 |
| **25% Debt Scenario** | | | | | | |
| Debt/Total capitalization | 33.8% | 31.4% | 28.2% | 25.0% | 25.0% | 25.0% |
| Interest coverage[a] | 3.91 | 4.60 | 5.57 | 6.23 | 6.17 | 4.94 |
| Earnings per share | $4.13 | $4.77 | $ 5.41 | $ 5.46 | $ 5.60 | $ 4.27 |
| Dividends per share | $2.29 | $2.49 | $ 2.71 | $ 2.72 | $ 2.72 | – |
| Return on total capital | 7.9% | 8.6% | 9.3% | 9.3% | 9.2% | 7.4% |
| Return on equity | 8.8% | 9.8% | 10.7% | 10.4% | 10.2% | 7.8% |
| New equity issues | $ 398 | $ 686 | $1,306 | $1,783 | $1,271 | $ 1,271 |
| Millions of shares sold[b] | 9.5 | 14.3 | 28.8 | 36.2 | 25.2 | 25.2 |

*Sources:* Analysts' forecasts and casewriter's estimates, based on assumptions of Exhibit 6.

a. Interest coverage is defined as EBIT/interest.

b. Assumes new shares sold at a price-earnings ratio of 10.

# American Home Products Corporation

"I just don't like to owe money," said William F. Laporte when asked about his company's almost debt-free balance sheet and growing cash reserves.[1] The exchange took place in 1968, 4 years after Mr. Laporte had taken over as chief executive of American Home Products (AHP). The 13 subsequent years did not improve his opinion of debt financing. During Mr. Laporte's tenure as chief executive, AHP's abstinence from debt continued, while the growth in its cash balance outpaced impressive growth in both sales and earnings. At the end of 1980, AHP had almost no debt and a cash balance equal to 40% of its net worth. In 1981, after 17 years as chief executive, Mr. Laporte was approaching retirement, and analysts speculated on the possibility of a more aggressive capital structure policy.

## Description of the Company

AHP's 1981 sales of more than $4 billion were produced by over 1,500 heavily marketed brands in four lines of business: prescription drugs, packaged (i.e., proprietary or over-the-counter) drugs, food products, and housewares and household products. Consumer products included a diversity of well-known brand names, such as Anacin, Preparation H, Sani-Flush, Chef Boy-Ar-Dee, Gulden's Mustard, Woolite, and the Ekco line of housewares. AHP's largest and most profitable business, prescription drugs, included sizable market shares in antihypertensives, tranquilizers, and oral contraceptives. AHP's success in these lines of business

---

1. *Forbes,* September 1, 1968, p. 87.

was built on marketing expertise. Whether the product was an oral contraceptive or a toilet bowl cleaner, "they sell the hell out of everything they've got," said one competitor.[2]

## AHP's Corporate Culture

AHP had a distinctive corporate culture which, in the view of many observers, emanated from its chief executive. This culture had several components. One was reticence. A poll of Wall Street analysts ranked AHP last in corporate communicability among 21 drug companies. A second element of AHP's managerial philosophy was frugality and tight financial control. Reportedly, all expenditures greater than $500 had to be personally approved by Mr. Laporte even if authorized in the corporate budget.

Another important component of AHP's culture was conservatism and risk aversion. AHP consistently avoided much of the risk of new product development and introduction in the volatile drug industry. Most of its new products were acquired or licensed after their development by other firms or were copies of new products introduced by competitors. A substantial portion of AHP's new products were clever extensions of existing products. AHP thus avoided risky gambles on R&D and new product introductions and used its marketing prowess to promote acquired products and product extensions. When truly innovative products were introduced by competitors, AHP responded with "me-too" products and relied on its marketing clout to erode competitors' head start.

Finally, an integral part of AHP's corporate philosophy was the firm's long-standing policy of centralizing complete authority in the chief executive. The current incumbent was described by a former colleague as a "brilliant marketer and tight-fisted spender."[3] Mr. Laporte's management style was characterized as management from the top, unparalleled in any firm of comparable size. Though reticent in discussing operations, Mr. Laporte was emphatic in stating the objective underlying his use of this authority: "We run the business for the shareholders."[4] The author of a *Business Week* article on the firm commented, "One of the most common business platitudes is that a corporation's primary mission is to make money for its stockholders and to maximize profits by minimizing costs. At American Home, these ideas are a dogmatic way of life."[5]

## AHP's Performance

This managerial philosophy produced impressive results. AHP's financial performance was characterized by stable, consistent growth and profitability. The firm

---

2. *The Wall Street Journal,* December 28, 1981, p. 1.

3. *The Wall Street Journal,* December 28, 1981, p. 6.

4. *HBS Bulletin,* January/February 1981, p. 123.

5. *Business Week,* March 21, 1970, p. 76.

had increased sales, earnings, and dividends for 29 consecutive years through 1981. This growth had been consistent and steady, ranging in recent years between 10% and 15% annually (see Exhibit 1 for a 10-year review of AHP's performance). Under Mr. Laporte's stewardship, AHP's return on equity had risen from about 25% in the 1960s to 30% in the 1980s. Because of its passion for parsimony, AHP had been able to finance this growth internally while paying out almost 60% of its annual earnings as dividends.

During Mr. Laporte's reign as chief executive, AHP's price-earnings ratio had fallen by about 60%, reflecting the marketwide collapse of price-earnings ratios of growth companies. Nonetheless, AHP's more than sixfold growth in earnings per share had pushed up the value of its stock by a factor of 3 during his tenure. AHP's stock was widely held by major institutional investors. Its popularity among investors reflected analysts' assessment of AHP's management. In the opinion of one analyst, "When you think of American Home Products, you think of the best-managed company in the whole pharmaceutical field."[6] Nevertheless, AHP's excess liquidity and low degree of leverage were criticized by many analysts. Others wondered whether it would be a good idea to tinker with success.

## Capital Structure Policy

Many drug firms were relatively unleveraged, but none matched AHP's conservative capital structure. Because of AHP's diversified operations it was difficult to find a truly comparable firm for comparative analysis. However, Warner-Lambert Company was about the same size as AHP and competed in roughly similar lines of business (see Exhibit 2 for a comparison of AHP and Warner-Lambert). Warner-Lambert had a debt ratio of 32% and its bond rating was on the borderline between AAA and AA in 1980.

For many years analysts had speculated on the impact of a more aggressive AHP capital structure policy. An example of a pro forma recapitalization analysis is presented in Exhibit 3. This exhibit shows actual 1981 performance plus pro forma restatements of the 1981 results under three alternative capital structures: 30% debt, 50% debt, and 70% debt. As described in Exhibit 3, these restatements assume that AHP issued debt and used the proceeds plus $233 million of excess cash to repurchase stock in early 1981 at the then prevailing stock price of $30 per share. Though this approach is only one of several ways to achieve a higher debt ratio, it illustrates, in approximate terms, the impact of higher debt on AHP's financial performance.

In view of AHP's firmly rooted financial conservatism, it was premature to consider the details of a realistic recapitalization plan. However, the likely imminent retirement of the firm's strong-willed chief executive fueled speculation concerning an appropriate capital structure policy for AHP and the magnitude of the payoff from such a policy.

---

6. David S. Saks, Wertheim & Co., quoted in *The Wall Street Journal,* January 7, 1981, p. 18.

# EXHIBIT 1
Selected Financial Data for American Home Products Corporation, 1972–1981 (millions of dollars except per share data)

| | 1972 | 1973 | 1974 | 1975 | 1976 | 1977 | 1978 | 1979 | 1980 | 1981 |
|---|---|---|---|---|---|---|---|---|---|---|
| Sales | $1,587.1 | $1,784.4 | $2,048.7 | $2,258.6 | $2,471.7 | $2,685.1 | $3,062.6 | $3,406.3 | $3,798.5 | $4,131.2 |
| Cash | — | — | — | — | 358.8 | 322.9 | 436.6 | 493.8 | 593.3 | 729.1 |
| Total debt | — | — | — | — | 7.8 | 10.3 | 13.7 | 10.3 | 13.9 | 16.6 |
| Net worth | — | — | — | — | 991.5 | 1,035.3 | 1,178.0 | 1,322.0 | 1,472.8 | 1,654.5 |
| Total assets | 1,042.0 | 1,126.0 | 1,241.6 | 1,390.7 | 1,510.9 | 1,611.3 | 1,862.2 | 2,090.7 | 2,370.3 | 2,588.5 |
| Net income | 172.7 | 199.2 | 225.6 | 250.7 | 277.9 | 306.2 | 348.4 | 396.0 | 445.9 | 497.3 |
| Earnings per share | $ 1.08 | $ 1.25 | $ 1.42 | $ 1.58 | $ 1.75 | $ 1.94 | $ 2.21 | $ 2.51 | $ 2.84 | $ 3.18 |
| Dividends per share | .59 | .625 | .777 | .90 | 1.00 | 1.15 | 1.325 | 1.50 | 1.70 | 1.90 |
| *Percentages* | | | | | | | | | | |
| Annual growth in sales | — | 12.4% | 14.8% | 10.2% | 9.4% | 8.6% | 14.1% | 11.1% | 11.7% | 8.8% |
| Annual growth in EPS | — | 15.7 | 13.6 | 11.3 | 10.8 | 10.9 | 13.9 | 13.6 | 13.1 | 12.0 |
| Dividend payout | 54.6% | 50.0 | 54.7 | 57.0 | 57.1 | 59.3 | 60.0 | 59.8 | 60.0 | 59.7 |
| After-tax profit margin | 10.9 | 11.2 | 11.0 | 11.1 | 11.2 | 11.4 | 11.4 | 11.6 | 11.7 | 12.0 |
| Return on equity | 25.9 | 28.2 | 28.2 | 27.9 | 28.0 | 29.5 | 29.6 | 30.0 | 30.3 | 30.1 |

**EXHIBIT 2**

1980 Data for American Home Products Corporation and Warner-Lambert Company
(millions of dollars except per share data)

| | American Home Products Corporation | Warner-Lambert Company |
|---|---|---|
| Sales | $3,798.5 | $3,479.2 |
| 5-year compound annual growth rate | 11.0% | 9.9% |
| Profit after taxes | $ 445.9 | $ 192.7 |
| 5-year compound annual growth rate | 12.2% | 3.3% |
| Cash and equivalents | $ 593.3 | $ 360.3 |
| Accounts receivable, net | 517.3 | 541.5 |
| Inventory | 557.3 | 645.8 |
| Net property, plant, and equipment | 450.5 | 827.1 |
| Other | 251.9 | 582.5 |
| Total assets | $2,370.3 | $2,957.2 |
| Total debt | $ 13.9 | $ 710.1 |
| Net worth | 1,472.8 | 1,482.7 |
| Earnings per share | $ 2.84 | $ 2.41 |
| 5-year compound annual growth rate | 12.4% | 3.0% |
| Dividends per share | $ 1.70 | $ 1.32 |
| 5-year compound annual growth rate | 13.6% | 8.0% |
| Stock price (end of 1980) | $ 30 | $ 20 |
| Price-earnings ratio | 10.6 | 8.3 |
| Profit margin (Profit after taxes/Sales) | 11.7% | 5.5% |
| Return on equity | 30.3% | 13.0% |
| Percentage of total debt to total capital | .9% | 32.4% |
| Interest coverage | 436.6 | 5.0 |
| Bond rating | AAA | AAA/AA[a] |

a. Warner-Lambert's debt was rated triple A, but analysts felt the firm was close to being downgraded to double A.

**EXHIBIT 3**

Pro Forma 1981 Results for Alternative Capital Structure (millions of dollars except per share data)

| | Actual 1981 | Pro Forma 1981 for Varying Percentages of Debt to Total Capital | | |
| --- | --- | --- | --- | --- |
| | | 30% | 50% | 70% |
| Sales | $4,131.2 | $4,131.2 | $4,131.2 | $4,131.2 |
| EBIT[a] | 954.8 | 922.2 | 922.2 | 922.2 |
| Interest | 2.3 | 52.7 | 87.8 | 122.9 |
| Profit before taxes | 952.5 | 869.5 | 834.4 | 799.3 |
| Taxes | 455.2 | 417.4 | 400.5 | 383.7 |
| Profit after taxes | 497.3 | 452.1 | 433.9 | 415.6 |
| Dividends on preferred stock | .4 | .4 | .4 | .4 |
| Earnings available to common shareholders | 496.9 | 451.7 | 433.5 | 415.2 |
| Dividends on common stock | 295.3 | 271.0 | 260.1 | 249.1 |
| Average common shares outstanding | 155.5 | 135.7 | 127.3 | 118.9 |
| Earnings per share | $ 3.18 | $ 3.33 | $ 3.41 | $ 3.49 |
| Dividends per share | 1.90 | 2.00 | 2.04 | 2.10 |
| **Beginning of Year after Recapitalization** | | | | |
| Cash and equivalents | $ 593.3 | $ 360.3 | $ 360.3 | $ 360.3 |
| Total debt | 13.9 | 376.1 | 626.8 | 877.6 |
| Net worth | 1,472.8 | 877.6 | 626.9 | 376.1 |
| Common stock price | $ 30 | – | – | – |
| Aggregate market value of common stock | $4,665.0 | – | – | – |

a. EBIT is reduced in pro forma results because of the loss of interest income from the $233 million in excess cash used to repurchase stock.

*(continued)*

**EXHIBIT 3** *(concluded)*
Detailed Assumptions for Pro Forma Recapitalizations

1. Debt is assumed to be added to the capital structure by issuing debt and using the proceeds to repurchase common stock. All repurchases are assumed to be executed in January 1981.
2. Stock is assumed to be repurchased at a price of $30 per share, which was the prevailing stock price in early January 1981.
3. The minimum cash balance is assumed to be $360.3 million (equal to Warner-Lambert's 1980 cash balance); thus $233 million in excess cash is available for use in repurchasing stock.
4. A tax rate of 48% is used.
5. The common dividend payout ratio is 60%.
6. Interest rate on all debt in all recapitalizations is assumed to be 14% before tax.
7. Interest foregone on excess cash is assumed to be at a rate of 14% before tax, so with recapitalization, EBIT falls by .14 times excess cash of $233 million or $32.6 million. Thus, pro forma EBIT is $922.2 million (actual EBIT of $954.8 million minus $32.6 reduction in interest from excess cash).

Details of Recapitalizations (millions of dollars)

|  | 30% Debt | 50% Debt | 70% Debt |
|---|---|---|---|
| Excess cash . . . . . . . . . . | $233.0 | $233.0 | $  233.0 |
| Additional debt . . . . . . . . . | 362.2 | 612.9 | 863.7 |
| Total repurchase . . . . . . . . | 595.2 | 845.9 | 1,096.7 |
| Reduction in common shares outstanding (million shares) . . . . | 19.8 | 28.2 | 36.6 |

# Colt Industries, Inc.

In July 1986, David Margolis, chairman and chief executive officer of Colt Industries, Inc. was weighing a recent proposal by the investment bank Morgan Stanley and Co. Morgan Stanley had suggested that Colt effect a leveraged recapitalization in order to ''unlock significant shareholder value.'' The plan called for public shareholders to receive a large one-time cash payment and one new share for each Colt share currently held. The cash payment would be in the $75–90 range, or substantially in excess of Colt's current market price of $66.75 per share. Financing the cash payout would require Colt to adopt over $1 billion of new debt.

Colt shares held on behalf of 5,000 Colt employees in a retirement savings plan (RSP) would not receive the cash distribution. These shares, currently representing about 7% of Colt's outstanding shares, would instead receive an equivalently valued package of new shares only. This asymmetric treatment would greatly increase the percentage of voting stock held by the RSP. (Exhibit 1 provides information on the structure and bylaws of the RSP.)

Such a leveraged recapitalization was not the only available option. Colt had also been approached by several firms specializing in financing leveraged buyouts, who had recommended consideration of a management-led leveraged buyout. Thus Mr. Margolis had to decide first if a leveraged recapitalization was the most desirable course of action. If it was, there remained questions about the exact structure of the deal: Just how much cash should be paid out to the public shareholders? What should be the mix of senior bank debt and subordinated debentures in the capital structure?

Copyright © 1988 by the President and Fellows of Harvard College.
Harvard Business School case 289–012.

This case was prepared by Professor Jeremy C. Stein.

## Overview of Current Business

Colt Industries was a conglomerate that manufactured and sold a diversified line of industrial products through its numerous consolidated subsidiaries. Its operations were reported in three broad industry groups: Aerospace/government, Automotive, and Industrial. Exhibit 2 shows Colt's balance sheet as of December 31, 1985. Exhibit 3 presents income statements broken down by industry group. Military sales were an important part of the company's business, representing 17% of sales from continuing operations in 1985.

### Aerospace/Government

The largest business in this group was Menasco, which manufactured landing gear assemblies. Landing gear accounted for 12.5% of Colt's 1985 sales. Menasco's commercial sales were concentrated among a limited number of purchasers, most notably Boeing. Military programs such as the F-16 and the B-1B aircraft also represented a significant portion of Menasco's business.

Other products in this group included aerospace controls, gas turbine products, jet engine components, aircraft instrumentation, and firearms such as the M-16 rifle and Colt handguns. Employees of the firearms division had been on strike since January 24, 1986. Some replacement workers had been hired, and further hiring was anticipated.

### Automotive

The most important products in the automotive group were carburetors and related components, which accounted for 19.6% of Colt's 1985 sales. The continuing trend toward fuel injection and away from carburetors was expected to increase over the next several years, resulting in declining sales. The company was attempting to compensate by developing fuel injection systems and components. Other products in this group included ignition systems, sealing systems, and parts for truck exhaust systems.

### Industrial

The largest business in this group was electrical distribution transformers. This was a highly competitive industry, in which General Electric and Westinghouse were the dominant players. Other products in this group were seals, packing and gasketing materials, weighing equipment, and machine tools.

## Recent Developments

Although Colt had achieved rapid growth in sales and earnings in earlier years via successful acquisitions, management felt that attractive opportunities were rapidly becoming scarce. According to Mr. Margolis, "The fundamentals in the market place had changed, and the prices for the companies we might be interested in were getting to the point where they didn't make sense for us.'' Hence Colt's management had begun to focus upon restructuring its existing businesses.

On November 6, 1985, Colt announced an agreement for the sale of its wholly owned Crucible Metals Corporation and Crusteel Limited subsidiaries. The historical income data in Exhibit 3 have been adjusted to reflect the discontinuation of these operations. These divestitures completed a move out of the steel business, which had accounted for about 60% of Colt's sales and earnings 10 years earlier, in 1975.

Also in November 1985, Colt acquired Walbar, Inc., a leading producer of precision-machined jet engine blades. The purchase price was $196 million. Walbar's net income was $9.2 million in 1984, compared to $7.6 million in 1983.

In addition to the operational restructuring, Colt had in recent years also been changing the structure of its balance sheet. Between 1979 and 1985, 10.7 million shares (about one third of outstanding shares) were repurchased at an average cost of $38 per share. In December 1985, $300 million of debt securities were issued, consisting of $150 million 10⅛% notes due December 1, 1995, and $150 million 11¼% debentures due December 1, 2015. The debt was rated A+/A1.

Exhibit 4 shows Colt's recent stock price performance compared to the S&P 400 index. As can be seen, Colt stock had fallen sharply in recent months after having reached a high of $75 in April 1986. Analysts attributed the decline to the recent earnings disappointments stemming from the automotive group and the strike in the firearms division.

More generally, during this period the stocks of most aerospace and other military contractors had not been doing well; and since the Crucible divestiture, Colt was becoming more clearly identified with this group. Exhibit 5 gives some data on price-earnings multiples for Colt, the S&P 400 index, and selected aerospace /defense stocks. The exhibit makes it clear that Colt was not alone in its underpricing relative to the S&P 400.

## Future Projections

Exhibit 6 shows earnings and cash flow projections for the years 1986–1991 made by Colt management in April 1986. In spite of the problems in the automotive group and the firearms division, Mr. Margolis was optimistic about the future. He considered Colt to be a very disciplined, tightly run company with an excellent management team.

## The Recapitalization Plan

### Basic Structure

Morgan Stanley's plan called for public shareholders to receive a one-time cash distribution in the $75–$90 range plus a new share, or ''stub,'' in exchange for each share currently held. At the same time, the RSP would receive an equivalently valued package of new shares only in exchange for its holdings.

This equivalence was to be achieved through the use of a floating exchange ratio that embodied a market valuation of the new shares, based on their median closing price during the first 15 days of trading on the New York Stock Exchange. For example, suppose that the cash distribution to public shareholders was $80 and that the stub traded at a median price of $15 during the first 15 days of trading. The package received by the public shareholders would be deemed to be worth $95. In order to obtain equal treatment, the RSP would receive 6.33 new shares (6.33 = $95 ÷ $15) for each old share.

The plan would increase the concentration of voting power in the hands of the RSP. Continuing with the above example, if the RSP did receive 6.33 new Colt shares per old Colt share, its voting interest in Colt would rise from 7% to slightly over 32%. Colt's 15 executive officers owned beneficially 9% of the RSP stock. The remaining 91% was owned beneficially by approximately 5,000 salaried employees. The RSP's trustees, who were four Colt executive officers, normally voted the RSP stock. However, the trust agreement did allow individual RSP participants to direct the trustees as to the voting of shares in connection with a corporate control transaction. (Colt's corporate charter specified that 80% of all outstanding shares must be voted in favor to approve a takeover of the company.)

The asymmetric treatment of the RSP shareholders relative to public shareholders had important tax consequences. In order for the cash payout to public shareholders to be treated as a capital gain rather than as a dividend, the IRS required that the percentage of the company owned by each public shareholder must decline by at least 20% in the recapitalization. In other words, public shareholders could own no more than 74.4% of the company after the transaction (74.4% = 93% × 80%). Therefore, it was important that RSP participants be in favor of the recapitalization and not transfer or withdraw their shares beforehand. If they did so to any notable extent, the RSP might not wind up with the 25.6% minimum ownership required for favorable tax treatment. Exhibit 7 goes into further detail on certain legal and tax issues associated with the recapitalization. This exhibit also notes some differences in the treatment accorded to leveraged buyouts.

Colt's executive officers also owned 646,000 shares (about 3% of the company) that they held directly rather than through the RSP. Because of unfavorable tax consequences to the officers that might result if they received the cash payout, these shares would be sold in the open market before the effective date of the recapitalization. However, Colt executive officers would continue to hold their options on Colt stock. These options would be converted to options on new shares at the same exchange ratio used for RSP participants. Thus, if the exchange ratio were 6.33, every existing option would be converted to an option on 6.33 shares. Exhibit 8 provides a breakdown of Colt's stock and option ownership.

## Financing the Transaction

Almost all the money for the cash payout to shareholders as well as for the estimated $60 million in fees and expenses relating to the transaction would have to come from new borrowing. Two bank credit facilities were available through a syndicate

**TABLE A**
Principal Repayments, 1987–1994 (millions of dollars)

|  | *Principal Repayment* | *Maximum Outstanding Balance* |
|---|---|---|
| 1987 . . . . . . . . . . | $ 50 | $650 |
| 1988 . . . . . . . . . . | 50 | 600 |
| 1989 . . . . . . . . . . | 50 | 550 |
| 1990 . . . . . . . . . . | 100 | 450 |
| 1991 . . . . . . . . . . | 100 | 350 |
| 1992 . . . . . . . . . . | 100 | 250 |
| 1993 . . . . . . . . . . | 125 | 125 |
| 1994 . . . . . . . . . . | 125 | 0 |

of commercial banks, with Bankers Trust Company as the agent. The syndicate was willing to extend up to $700 million as a term loan and $300 million in a revolving credit facility. The balance of funds required would come from the sale of 15-year senior subordinated debentures or from Colt's cash reserves.

Colt would have three options in terms of interest payments under the term loan: (1) LIBOR plus 2.5%; (2) Banker's Trust prime plus 1.5%; (3) New York dealer certificate-of-deposit rate plus 2.625%. These margins were subject to increase or decrease based on a leverage ratio test described in the loan agreement. The term loan also would require mandatory principal repayments as shown in Table A.

The revolving credit facility would be secured by Colt's accounts receivable and inventories and would also offer three interest rate options: (1) LIBOR plus 2%; (2) Bankers Trust prime plus 1%; (3) certificate-of-deposit rate plus 2.125%. Again, these margins would be subject to increase or decrease based on a leverage ratio test. Both bank facilities would have a variety of restrictive covenants covering the supply of information, subsidiary debt, mergers, capital expenditures, and three ratio tests related to the current ratio, interest coverage, and leverage. Also, Colt would be required to enter into an interest rate swap to convert at least $375 million of the bank debt into an effectively fixed-rate obligation.[1]

The debentures would not require any principal repayment until 1997, at which time a sinking fund provision would take effect. Unlike the bank debt, they would feature a fixed rate of interest. Their covenants would be generally less restrictive than those on the bank debt. Colt's investment bankers believed that they could finance the transaction with debentures yielding 12.5%.

Exhibit 9 summarizes some relevant interest rate information.

---

1. An interest rate swap is an agreement with another party to exchange a variable stream of cash flows (indexed to the LIBOR rate, for example) for a fixed stream. It can be used to eliminate the interest rate exposure associated with a variable-rate loan, albeit at a cost. Exhibit 9 shows how to calculate the cost of swapped funds.

### An Earlier Comparable Deal—FMC Corporation

Exhibit 10 presents some statistics for the recapitalization of FMC Corporation, consummated in May 1986. FMC, like Colt, was a broadly diversified company, engaged in the production of chemicals (approximately 47% of sales); defense systems (32% of sales); and machinery (21% of sales).

## EXHIBIT 1
The Colt Retirement Savings Plan (RSP)

Employees could elect to contribute between 2% and 6% of their salaries to the RSP. Colt made matching contributions, depending on a corporate earnings requirement. In 1981 through 1985, Colt matched employee contributions fully, except in the last nine months of 1983, when the rate of matching was only 50%. Approximately 5,000 out of 6,000 eligible employees participated in the RSP.

Contributions from employees could be invested in a fixed-income fund, an equity fund consisting of stock of companies other than Colt, or a money market fund, according to the employee's choice. Company contributions, on the other hand, were invested only in Colt shares. The Colt shares were held in Fund C of the RSP. Participants in Fund C could direct the trustees as to the voting of their shares with respect to the recapitalization plan, a merger, or consolidation of the company, or to tender their shares in connection with a tender offer for Colt.

While a participant in the RSP could instruct the trustees to transfer investments among the fixed-income, stock, and money market funds on a periodic basis, no such provision was made to permit such transfers of the company stock contribution except that a participant who was eligible for early retirement could instruct the trustees to sell all the Colt stock credited to such participant's account and to invest the proceeds in one or more of the other funds of the RSP. However, under the proposed terms of the recapitalization, an amendment to the RSP would allow any participant to sell his or her new shares without penalty for a period of 12 months after the effective date of the transaction. The proceeds of such a sale would be reinvested in other funds of the RSP.

At January 1, 1985, for continuing operations, the actuarially computed present value of vested benefits in *all* Colt pension and retirement plans was $163.4 million. The value of nonvested benefits was $14.4 million, and the plan's total net assets and book accruals available for benefits were $239.2 million.

## EXHIBIT 2
Consolidated Balance Sheet at December 31, 1985 (millions of dollars)

| | | | | |
|---|---|---|---|---|
| Cash and marketable securities | $ 215.6 | Notes payable to banks | $ 4.1 |
| Accounts receivable | 179.9 | Current maturities of long-term debt | 4.5 |
| Inventories | 277.2 | Accounts payable | 85.8 |
| Deferred taxes | 17.3 | Accrued expenses | 184.6 |
| Other | 5.5 | Current portion of liabilities | |
| Current assets | 695.5 | of discontinued operations | 7.0 |
| | | Current liabilities | 286.0 |
| Property, plant, and equipment | 564.7 | Long-term debt | 342.4 |
| Less: Accumulated depreciation | | Deferred taxes | 5.6 |
| and amortization | 262.8 | Minority interest in subsidiaries | 4.0 |
| | 301.9 | Other liabilities | 106.4 |
| | | Liabilities of discontinued operations | 91.8 |
| Costs in excess of net assets | | Total liabilities | 836.2 |
| acquired, net of amortization | 167.5 | | |
| Other assets | 85.6 | Common stock, $1 par value, | |
| Total assets | $1,250.5 | 27,616,918 shares issued, | |
| | | including 8,243,763 in treasury | 27.6 |
| | | Capital in excess of par value | 143.5 |
| | | Retained earnings | 593.2 |
| | | Foreign currency translation adjustments | (10.7) |
| | | Less: Cost of shares in treasury | 339.3 |
| | | Shareholders' equity | 414.3 |
| | | Total liabilities and shareholders' equity | $1,250.5 |

**EXHIBIT 3**
Income Statements for Years Ending December 31, 1981–1985 (millions of dollars except per share data)

|  | 1981 | 1982 | 1983 | 1984 | 1985 |
|---|---|---|---|---|---|
| **Sales** | | | | | |
| Aerospace/government | $ 461 | $ 424 | $ 441 | $ 497 | $ 539 |
| Automotive | 441 | 405 | 478 | 580 | 542 |
| Industrial | 560 | 458 | 427 | 506 | 501 |
| Elimination | (10) | (9) | (3) | (1) | (3) |
| Total | 1,452 | 1,278 | 1,343 | 1,582 | 1,579 |
| **Operating income from continuing operations** | | | | | |
| Aerospace/government | 81.8 | 74.4 | 78.3 | 91.8 | 91.8 |
| Automotive | 59.0 | 45.3 | 81.6 | 106.4 | 97.8 |
| Industrial | 65.2 | 31.7 | 40.3 | 57.6 | 61.9 |
| Corporate and other | (1.9) | (16.9) | (32.4) | (37.4) | (19.1) |
| Total | 204.1 | 134.6 | 167.9 | 218.4 | 232.4 |
| Net interest income (expense) | 4.3 | (2.0) | 7.3 | 1.4 | (5.6) |
| Earnings before taxes from continuing operations | 208.5 | 132.6 | 175.2 | 219.8 | 226.8 |
| Earnings from continuing operations | 122.7 | 81.9 | 97.4 | 120.0 | 129.3 |
| Discontinued operations | (13.2) | (243.2) | 1.9 | 12.3 | 8.7 |
| Net earnings | $109.6 | $(161.4) | $ 99.3 | $132.2 | $138.0 |
| **Earnings per share** | | | | | |
| Continuing operations | $ 4.43 | $ 3.21 | $ 3.93 | $ 5.43 | $ 6.47 |
| Discontinued operations | (.48) | (9.54) | .08 | .56 | .44 |
| Net | $ 3.95 | $ (6.33) | $ 4.01 | $ 5.99 | $ 6.91 |
| Depreciation and amortization | $ 24.7 | $ 27.3 | $ 29.4 | $ 33.2 | $ 31.6 |
| Capital expenditures | 40.4 | 27.5 | 27.5 | 41.0 | 41.3 |

*Note:* Discontinued operations include the divested Crucible Metals Corporation and Crusteel subsidiaries. These statements do not include the newly acquired Walbar division. Walbar's net income was $6.7 million in 1982, $7.6 million in 1983, and $9.2 million in 1984.

Figures may not add exactly because of rounding.

**EXHIBIT 4**
Indexed Closing Prices, 1985–1986

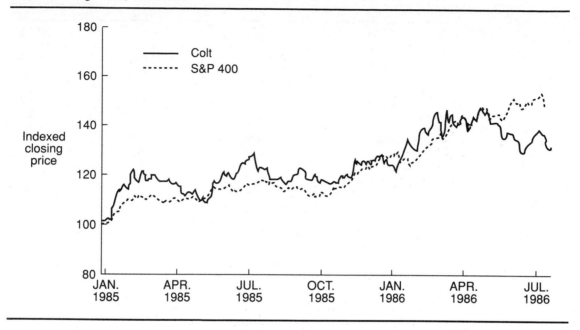

**EXHIBIT 5**
Price-Earnings Ratios of Selected Aerospace/Defense Stocks,
July 18, 1986

| Company | Stock Price | Earnings per share[a] | Price-Earnings Ratio |
|---|---|---|---|
| Colt | $ 66.75 | $ 5.83 | 11.4 |
| Boeing | 61.25 | 4.11 | 14.9 |
| General Dynamics | 73.38 | 8.58 | 8.6 |
| Grumman | 27.00 | 2.14 | 12.6 |
| Lockheed | 47.25 | 6.28 | 7.5 |
| McDonnell Douglas | 80.25 | 7.69 | 10.4 |
| Northrop | 49.25 | 3.00 | 16.4 |
| Rockwell | 42.68 | 3.95 | 10.8 |
| S&P 400 index | 261.47 | 17.73 | 14.7 |

a. Earnings per share are for last 12 months (July 1, 1985, to June 30, 1986) except for S&P 400 index, where the earnings are the current estimates for the calendar year 1986 made by Standard and Poor's Corporation. Alternatively, one could look at the actual 1985 earnings of $15.34, which implies a price-earnings ratio of 17.1.

**EXHIBIT 6**
Management Projections for Years Ending December 31, 1986–1991 (millions of dollars)

| | Actual 1985 | Pro forma | | | | | |
|---|---|---|---|---|---|---|---|
| | | 1986 | 1987 | 1988 | 1989 | 1990 | 1991 |
| Sales | | | | | | | |
| Aerospace/government | $ 539.0 | $ 647.0 | $ 740.6 | $ 769.9 | $ 815.0 | $ 874.2 | $ 926.7 |
| Automotive | 542.0 | 531.0 | 485.6 | 497.1 | 552.3 | 610.6 | 649.8 |
| Industrial | 501.0 | 490.1 | 523.3 | 557.9 | 592.5 | 626.4 | 659.7 |
| Elimination | (3.0) | (4.0) | (7.0) | (6.0) | (6.0) | (7.0) | (7.8) |
| Total | 1,579.0 | 1,664.1 | 1,742.5 | 1,818.9 | 1,953.8 | 2,104.2 | 2,228.4 |
| EBIT | | | | | | | |
| Aerospace/government | 91.8 | 89.6 | 126.2 | 132.1 | 138.8 | 150.5 | 158.0 |
| Automotive | 97.8 | 85.9 | 80.9 | 82.5 | 91.8 | 101.5 | 107.3 |
| Industrial | 61.9 | 65.4 | 79.8 | 84.3 | 89.3 | 93.7 | 98.1 |
| Corporate and other | (19.1) | (23.0) | (27.5) | (25.0) | (26.0) | (27.0) | (28.0) |
| Total | 232.4 | 217.9 | 259.4 | 273.9 | 293.9 | 318.7 | 335.4 |
| Depreciation and amortization | 31.6 | 42.4 | 43.3 | 46.9 | 50.7 | 54.7 | 57.1 |
| Capital expenditures | 41.3 | 53.0 | 62.0 | 61.0 | 59.5 | 51.7 | 51.9 |
| Investment in working capital | 136.7 | 39.0 | 22.1 | 7.6 | 10.2 | 14.2 | 5.5 |

*Note:* These projections were made in April 1986. While presented with numerical specificity, they are based upon a variety of assumptions relating to the businesses of the company, which though considered reasonable by the company, may not be realized and are subject to a number of uncertainties, many of which are beyond the company's control. There can be no assurance that the projections will be realized, and actual results may vary materially from those shown.

**EXHIBIT 7**
Some Legal and Tax Implications of the Proposed Colt Transaction

The transaction would constitute a recapitalization of the company within the meaning of Section 368(a)(1)(E) of the IRS Code. Accordingly, it would not be a taxable transaction to the company but would be taxable to the public shareholders.

Section 302 of the IRS Code provided that any distribution would be a capital gain rather than a dividend if the following "safe harbor" test were met: a shareholder's percentage ownership of total outstanding new shares immediately after the recapitalization must be less than 80% of his or her percentage ownership of total outstanding old shares immediately prior to the transaction.

Since the transaction did not constitute a sale of the company, the General Utilities doctrine did not apply. Under the General Utilities rule, an acquiring company could step up the tax basis of the assets of an acquired company (and hence increase depreciation tax shields) without recognizing a gain or loss for federal income tax purposes other than for certain items of recapture income. In contrast, the General Utilities rule *would* apply in a leveraged buyout, which *was* considered a sale of the company.

(It should be noted that while this distinction was of importance at the time of the case, the 1986 tax law has repealed the General Utilities rule. As a result, some of the tax benefits previously associated with acquisitions are no longer available.)

**EXHIBIT 8**
Distribution of Stock and Option Ownership

| | Number of Shares (000s) | Percent of Total Outstanding Shares | Percent of Total Outstanding Shares and Common Stock Equivalents[a] |
|---|---|---|---|
| Public shareholders (institutions, individuals) . . . . | 17,397 | 89.7% | 87.3% |
| Retirement savings plan | | | |
| Executive officers . . . . . . . | 121 | .6 | .6 |
| Other participants . . . . . . . | 1,226 | 6.4 | 6.2 |
| Total . . . . . . . . . . | 1,347 | 7.0 | 6.8 |
| Executive officers | 646 | 3.3 | 3.2 |
| Total outstanding shares . . . . | 19,390 | 100.0% | 97.3 |
| Options | | | |
| Executive officers . . . . . . | 413 | | 2.1 |
| Other employees . . . . . . | 114 | | .6 |
| Total . . . . . . . . . . | 527 | | 2.7 |
| Total outstanding shares and common stock equivalents . . . | 19,917 | | 100.0% |

a. Reflects maximum possible dilution from outstanding options.

**EXHIBIT 9**
Interest Rate Information

As of July 21, 1986:

| | |
|---|---|
| 3-month LIBOR . . . | 6.65% |
| 3-month CD . . . . | 6.37% |
| Prime rate . . . . . | 8.11% |

Swap quote: A fixed payer receiving 3-month LIBOR for 5 years must pay a rate of 8.04%. Consequently, the cost of swapped funds to someone who can borrow at, say, LIBOR plus 2.5%, is 10.54%. (The borrower pays the counterparty 8.04%, in return for which the borrower receives from the counterparty the prevailing LIBOR rate. The borrower then takes this LIBOR payment, adds 2.5%, and meets the bank debt interest obligation at a total cost of 8.04% + 2.5% = 10.54%.)

Historical data (annual and monthly averages):

| | 3-Month LIBOR | 3-Month CD | Prime Rate |
|---|---|---|---|
| 1980 . . . . | 14.06% | 12.97% | 15.27% |
| 1981 . . . . | 16.83 | 15.90 | 18.87 |
| 1982 . . . . | 13.38 | 12.41 | 14.86 |
| 1983 . . . . | 9.60 | 8.98 | 10.79 |
| 1984 . . . . | 10.88 | 10.40 | 12.04 |
| 1985 . . . . | 8.42 | 8.07 | 9.93 |
| 1986 | | | |
| January . . | 8.00 | 7.70 | 9.50 |
| February . . | 8.06 | 7.74 | 9.50 |
| March . . . | 7.88 | 7.65 | 9.25 |
| April . . . | 7.44 | 7.10 | 8.75 |
| May . . . | 6.88 | 6.58 | 8.50 |
| June . . . | 7.19 | 6.82 | 8.50 |

**EXHIBIT 10**
FMC Corporation Recapitalization, May 1986

Preannouncement price per share: $70 (represents a price-earnings ratio of 9.4).
Public shareholders: Receive $80 in cash plus one new share.
Management and ESOP: Receive 5.67 new shares (no floating exchange ratio).
Employee thrift plan: Receive $25 plus 4.21 new shares.

Market value of package: Stub traded at $20 initially, so total value to public shareholders = $100, a 43% premium over the preannouncement price.

| Capitalization | Pre-Recapitalization | Post-Recapitalization |
|---|---|---|
| Total debt . . . . . . . . . . . . | $ 398.7 | $2,228.8 |
| Equity . . . . . . . . . . . . | 1,138.7 | (665.9) |
| Total capitalization . . . . . . | $1,537.4 | $1,572.9 |
| Interest coverage . . . . . . . | 8.5 | 1.1 |
| Moody's/S&P debt rating . . . . . . | A2/A | B1/B+ |

# Massey-Ferguson Ltd. (1980)

Massey-Ferguson Ltd. was a multinational producer of farm machinery, industrial machinery, and diesel engines. The company was founded in 1847; by 1980 it had manufacturing and assembly operations in 31 countries throughout the world. Massey-Ferguson was then the West's largest producer of farm tractors and the world's largest supplier of diesel engines to original equipment manufacturers.

In 1978, however, Massey reported an unprecedented year-end loss of U.S.$262.2 million. (Recent and historical financial data are provided in Exhibits 1–4.) The new president, Victor A. Rice, pledged to restore Massey to profitability by the end of its 1979 fiscal year. Massey did show a profit of U.S.$37.0 million in 1979 but reported a loss on continuing operations of U.S.$35.4 million (see Exhibit 2). Sales in the first half of fiscal 1980 were up, but earnings remained severely depressed.

In April 1980 a preferred share issue of Can.$300–500 million was postponed indefinitely.[1] The postponement was attributed to Massey's operating problems and to the fact that Argus Corporation, Massey's largest shareholder, refused to take a block of the preferreds as a vote of confidence in Massey.

As 1980 progressed, it became apparent that without an equity infusion Massey would be in default on several loan covenants before the end of the fiscal year (October 31, 1980). Cross-default provisions made substantially all long- and short-term debts callable if any single default occurred. If Massey's lenders then cut off credit and moved to secure their loans, company operations would quickly

---

1. At the time of this case, the Canadian dollar was trading in the range of U.S.$.80–$.85.

come to a halt. Plant shutdowns, further worker layoffs, and a liquidation of corporate assets would follow. Creditors and customers around the world wondered if Massey would make it through the looming financial crisis.

## Background

Massey-Ferguson had been called "the one true multinational." Its products—farm equipment, industrial machinery, and diesel engines—were sold throughout the world by dealers, distributors, and company retail outlets. Exhibit 5 shows a breakdown of 1980 sales by national markets. Table A summarizes Massey-Ferguson's sales by product line and geographical area.

Massey's production facilities were also dispersed around the world. Exhibit 5 shows the distribution of M-F capacity by country. Massey's largest facilities were located in Canada (Brantford and Toronto), France (Marquette), England (Coventry), and Australia (Melbourne). Diesel engine production was concentrated in England (Peterborough).

In certain markets, primarily North America, Massey financed retail sales of farm and industrial machinery through wholly owned finance subsidiaries. In Europe and Australia, Massey's finance subsidiaries were primarily involved in financing sales to distributors, but they sometimes financed dealer receivables in their home markets. In October 1980, Massey's finance subsidiaries had assets totaling U.S.$1,130.6 million and outstanding debts of U.S.$825.6 million. (Massey's finance subsidiaries are not consolidated in the financial statements of Exhibits 1–4.)

### Farm and Industrial Machinery

Massey's farm machinery line consisted of tractors, combine harvesters, balers, forage harvesters, cane harvesters, agricultural implements, farmstead equipment, and other equipment for agricultural use. The industrial machinery line consisted of industrial tractors, tractor loaders, tractor-loader-backhoes, rough terrain fork lifts, skid steer loaders, utility loaders, and log skidders. In 1980, Massey held 17% of the worldwide market for tractors, 14% of the market for combines, and 13% of the market for industrial machinery.

Massey's competition in farm and industrial machinery included both large multinational companies with full product lines and medium to small companies conducting business locally with a limited range of products. In the large North American farm equipment market, Massey had traditionally ranked third in sales of farm equipment behind Deere & Co. and International Harvester. However, in 1980 it held first or second position in markets for small (30–90 HP) tractors and combine harvesters. Exhibit 6 compares Massey's sales, operating, and financial data with Deere and Harvester for the years 1976–1980.

Historically, Massey's strength had been in markets outside North America and Western Europe. In less developed countries Massey had success in dealing directly with governments or public institutions. During the 1970s, Massey entered

**TABLE A**
Breakdown of Massey-Ferguson's Sales

|  | Farm and Industrial Equipment | | Diesel Engines |
|---|---|---|---|
| 1980 sales ($ millions) . . . . | $2,533 | | $599 |
| Percent North America | | | |
| (U.S., Canada, Mexico) . . . | | 33.2% | |
| Percent Western Europe . . . | | 35.6 | |
| Percent rest of world . . . . | | 31.2 | |
| | | 100.0% | |

*Source:* Massey-Ferguson annual report.

into agreements to supply farm equipment or construct manufacturing facilities in Peru, Pakistan, Egypt, Iran, Libya, Mozambique, Turkey, Saudi Arabia, Sri Lanka, and the Sudan. In 1974, Massey obtained a $360-million contract to modernize and expand Poland's tractor and diesel engine industry.

## Diesel Engines

Diesel engines were produced in England by the Perkins Engine Group. Perkins produced 60 basic models of multicylinder diesel engines in the 30–300-brake horse-power range. Perkins' engines were used in Massey-Ferguson's equipment and were also sold to manufacturers of a wide variety of agricultural, industrial, and construction equipment. In 1980, Perkins exported 86% of its product: over 50% of its exports were to Massey-Ferguson's subsidiaries and affiliates.

Because of rising gasoline prices, many auto and equipment manufacturers were expanding research and development in diesel engines. The emerging market for small, high-powered engines used in automobiles and light trucks was particularly promising. Perkins' long-range business plan called for it to maintain and increase its market share in areas such as agriculture vehicles, industrial and construction equipment, and marine craft. Perkins also was engaged in research on the dieseliza-tion of gasoline engines and the development of engines capable of operating on a variety of fuels.

## Massey's Financial Difficulties

During the 1960s and 1970s, Massey-Ferguson was involved in an ambitious program of acquiring assets and expanding operations. The 1970s were a decade of dramatic growth, which was financed by debt, much of it short-term. By 1978, Massey's debt-to-equity ratio was 2.1 (see Exhibit 4). In that year, Massey lost U.S.$262 million. Management attributed the massive loss to the imposition of credit and monetary restrictions in Argentina and Brazil, which caused sharp declines in farm machinery sales; the decline in North American farm prices and incomes; poor weather in Western Europe; and high interest rates, which raised the cost of carrying excess inventory.

Between 1978 and 1980, Massey reacted to the loss by cutting its labor force from 68,000 to 47,000 and its manufacturing space from 30 million sq ft to 20 million sq ft. The company reduced inventories from U.S.$1,083.2 million to U.S.$988.9 million. Unprofitable operations in the manufacture of office furniture, garden tractors, and construction machinery were eliminated. Twenty-four plants were closed. The divestment program initiated in 1978 resulted in the sale of more than U.S.$300 million in assets by 1980.

Despite these efforts, in fiscal 1979, Massey's loss on continuing operations was U.S.$35.4 million, or U.S.$2.38 per share; losses from discontinued operations amounted to another U.S.$23.0 million. The company showed a positive net income in 1979 only as a result of an extraordinary item reflecting the recovery of previous years' taxes.

In the first three quarters of fiscal 1980, Massey's financial condition deteriorated even further. At the end of the third quarter, year-to-date losses totaled U.S.$62 million, including an unfavorable currency adjustment of $37 million. Preliminary reports indicated that Massey's fourth quarter losses would be as high as those of the three previous quarters combined.

Massey's continuing problems were caused by high interest rates, low demand, lack of alignment between products and markets, and failure to penetrate the North American market.

### Interest Rates

The high interest rates of 1979–1980 had a doubly negative impact on Massey's performance. First, the cost of Massey's short-term debt rose dramatically. Second, high interest rates depressed markets for farm and industrial machinery and thus hurt company sales.

### Demand

The North American market for farm machinery crashed in the fall of 1980. The decline in demand was attributed to high interest rates, an economic recession, the Soviet grain embargo, and a severe drought during the summer of 1980. Because of the recession, European and Third World markets were also severely depressed.

The recession made 1980 a difficult year for all farm equipment manufacturers. In North America, both Deere and Harvester experienced reduced sales and profits and showed sharp increases in short- and long-term debt. By the end of 1980, International Harvester was in technical violation of debt covenants and was in the process of negotiating a refinancing plan with its bankers.

### Product-Market Alignment

Massey's farm equipment production was in rough regional alignment with its sales. At the margin North America and the United Kingdom were net suppliers to the rest of the world (see Table A and Exhibit 5). Engine production, however, was heavily concentrated in the United Kingdom. In 1980, with the influx of North Sea oil, the pound rose dramatically relative to currencies in which Massey sold its products. The high price of the pound increased Massey's cost of goods sold, reducing margins and thus hurting the competitiveness of Massey's products.

Lack of alignment between production sites and markets meant that currency fluctuations were a recurring problem for Massey-Ferguson. For example, in 1974, Massey purchased Hanomag, a West German construction equipment manufacturer. The venture was unprofitable, in part because the strong German mark made its exports too costly in world markets. In 1980 the Hanomag subsidiary was sold to IBH Holdings for an undisclosed amount.

Massey-Ferguson's product-market alignment would continue to have an unfavorable impact on profits as long as the British pound was strong and the company's operations concentrated in the United Kingdom. However, political risk argued against matching production and sales on a country-by-country basis. Although successful in negotiating directly with Third World and East Bloc governments, Massey was vulnerable to changing political conditions in these countries. During the 1970s several governments with whom Massey had dealings, including Iran, Pakistan, Libya, and Poland, were overthrown as a result of coups or civil unrest.

Economies of scale in engine production also made it advisable to concentrate facilities at a few sites. One possibility discussed within Massey was to relocate capacity at the margin in Canada. Concentration of assets in Canada would bring the company closer to North American markets and make its costs similar to those of Deere and Harvester. Massey already had two large Canadian facilities, forming a base on which it could expand.

## North American Efforts

In the 1960s, Massey concentrated its marketing and product development efforts overseas. As a result, the company lagged in its development of the high horsepower tractors and combines desired by farmers in the Canadian and U.S. farm belts.

In 1975, Massey turned its attention to the North American market, introducing a new range of 34–81 HP tractors as well as an improved baler line. In 1978, Massey introduced large, high-horsepower tractors in Europe and North America. Management claimed:[2]

> These new products will make Massey-Ferguson fully competitive in North American and European markets and will demonstrate the company's ability to design, produce, and market large tractors as successfully as tractors in the 40–90 horsepower range.

Unfortunately, Massey's drive into North America coincided with a depressed market and the beginnings of its own financial difficulties. Doubts about the future of the company eroded sales and weakened the distribution network. During 1980 the number of Massey's dealerships in North America fell by 50%, from 3,600 to 1,800.

---

2. Massey-Ferguson annual report (1978).

## The Future

Despite these problems, and even though in the fall of 1980 worldwide demand for farm equipment stood at depression levels, management continued to be optimistic about the future. In the 1980 annual report Mr. Rice reaffirmed that the cost-cutting efforts initiated in 1978 had made Massey a viable company. As evidence, he pointed to a 1% increase in Massey's worldwide tractor sales over the first nine months of 1980, an increase achieved in spite of the collapse of the North American market (see Exhibit 2).

However, in order to take advantage of its long-run opportunities, Massey had to raise capital to finance its investment programs. New funds were needed for: (1) ongoing R&D for new product development; (2) repair and replacement of existing facilities; (3) reallocation of facilities from the United Kingdom to Canada; (4) penetration of the North American market; (5) defense of markets in Europe and the rest of the world; (6) further growth in the Third World; and (7) Perkins' prospective entry into the market for small diesel engines. It was not known for sure how much would be needed for each of these programs, but in aggregate they might require U.S. $500–700 million over the next 5 years.

A major unresolved question was the future of the Perkins Engine subsidiary. Perkins was Massey's most valuable salable asset, but at the same time, diesel engines were the company's best hope for profitable future growth. Some thought Massey should seek to cut its currency exchange losses while concurrently pleasing the governments of Canada and Ontario by setting up diesel engine production in Canada. The possibility of selling Perkins to a third party was also discussed; however, some felt that Perkins' future depended on the existence of a healthy Massey-Ferguson that was able to buy Perkins products.

The most immediate problem, however, was to engineer Massey's survival. By mid-1980 all expenditures except those necessary to continued operations had been suspended in an effort to conserve cash. Despite these efforts, the cash continued to flow out; by September, bank lines were nearly exhausted and the company's position became daily more precarious.

A major restructuring of claims on Massey-Ferguson was necessary. However, to achieve a restructuring, Massey's lenders and major shareholders had to consent to a refinancing plan. By September 1980 top management knew that a default on Massey's existing debt was practically inevitable at the fiscal year-end. Once Massey defaulted, any lender could potentially trigger a worldwide scramble for assets that would bring company operation to a halt. For this reason, the economic interest of each category of claimant had to be carefully considered to be sure that any refinancing plan proposed would be acceptable to all.

## The Players

### The Banks

As of late fiscal 1980, Massey-Ferguson had total debt of U.S.$1.6 billion outstanding with more than 100 banks around the world. Exhibits 7 and 8 provide a breakdown of Massey's short-term lines of credit and long-term debt. Most of the borrowing was unsecured. In addition, Massey's finance company subsidiaries owed another U.S.$825 million worldwide. Finance company debt usually was not guaranteed, but Massey had agreed to maintain assets in the subsidiaries in certain specified relations to their indebtedness.

As Exhibits 7 and 8 show, Massey's borrowings were dispersed among lenders in Canada, Great Britain, West Germany, France, Italy, and the United States. Except for a consortium of U.S. banks, which had issued a revolving credit, most lenders operated independently of one another. The numerous covenants related to these loans hampered Massey's free access to the capital markets. For example, before Massey could issue new preferred shares (as it had proposed in April 1980) it had to pay accumulated preferred dividends, which were U.S.$14 million in arrears as of December 1979. But since March 1978, when Massey announced first losses, covenants on certain U.S. loans had caused dividends to both preferred and common shares to be suspended.

The Canadian Imperial Bank of Commerce was Massey's largest lender, with an aggregate exposure estimated at between Can.$200 and Can.$300 million. Commerce had ties not only to Massey-Ferguson but to Massey's largest shareholder, Argus Corporation. Conrad Black, Massey's chairman from 1978–1980 and president of Argus from 1978, was made a director of the bank in 1980.

## Argus Corporation

Since the 1960s, Argus Corporation, a Canadian holding company, had owned a controlling interest in Massey-Ferguson. Argus' philosophy was to make major investments in a small number of promising enterprises. In 1956, shortly after Massey Harris merged with the Ferguson Company to become Massey-Ferguson, several Argus directors had played a major role in saving the newly formed company from bankruptcy by forcing it to liquidate certain assets and cut its prices on farm equipment. In 1980, Argus held 16.5% of the outstanding shares. Six of the 18 board members were Argus appointees.

In 1978, Conrad Black, age 34, son of one of the founders of Argus, took over as president of Argus and, as a result, became chairman of the board of Massey-Ferguson. Black picked Victor Rice to succeed Albert Thornburgh as Massey's president; 2 years later, in 1980, Mr. Black relinquished the chairmanship of Massey to Mr. Rice.

Argus was considered by the financial community to be a potential source of equity capital for Massey, but Mr. Black's public comments on the company were highly equivocal. In a 1979 interview he indicated that Argus was "not interested in putting up a lot of money and staying at 16%." He expressed surprise that Massey's lenders kept approaching him for advice when Argus held only 16% of the stock and was therefore much less exposed than the major lenders. There were also perennial rumors that "Conrad Black has been trying to peddle Massey-Ferguson's stock."

In April 1980 a preferred stock issue was postponed, in part because Argus was reluctant to take a block of shares. Chairman Black was quoted as saying:

"We could finance the company tomorrow. I'm not going to get panicky. We're good for another year." Mr. Black also maintained that he was willing to contribute Can.$100–500 million to Massey-Ferguson "on the right terms."

### Other Preferred and Common Shareholders

Massey had two issues of preferred stock outstanding, Series A and B. Each had a liquidation value of $25 per share and was entitled to annual cumulative dividends of $2.50 per share. A total of 1,526,300 shares of Series A preferred had been issued in April 1975, followed by 2,298,500 shares of Series B in March 1976. The purpose of each issue was "to reduce (Massey's) short-term debt." Dividends on the preferred shares were suspended in 1978. Indentures provided that after a failure to pay dividends for eight quarters, each class of preferred stock would have the right to elect two members to Massey's board of directors. Board representation was attained by Series B shareholders in March 1980 and by Series A shareholders in April 1980.

Massey's 18,250,000 shares of common stock were listed on the New York, London, Toronto, Montreal, and Vancouver stock exchanges. From January 1976 through July 31, 1980, Massey lost 16⅞ points per share, or 69% of market value (see Exhibit 9). Over the same period, the New York Stock Exchange composite index gained 30%.

### The Governments of Canada, Ontario, and the United Kingdom

Finally, Mr. Rice and Mr. Black had for some time been trying to convince the governments of Canada, Ontario, and the United Kingdom to intervene on Massey's behalf. Massey had approached the Trudeau and Thatcher governments for aid as early as June 1980. The governments were anxious to avoid a loss of jobs (6,700 in Ontario and 17,000 in the combined Massey and Perkins operations in the United Kingdom); but in both Canada and the United Kingdom there was strong resistance to bailing out a privately owned multinational. Talks with the governments were continuing, but very little progress had been made and time was rapidly running out.

## The Situation in the Fourth Quarter of 1980

In August 1980 the international financial press reported that the Canadian governments were considering some form of financial assistance for Massey. It was said that Mr. Rice hoped to make a positive announcement when Massey released its third quarter results in September. Mr. Black was quoted:

> It's fair to assume that if there isn't any indication of possibility of some equity when third quarter results are released, the situation could become quite hairy. . . . Either Massey is going to go right under or the company will be restored, not only to its former position, but to a position of strength it hasn't known before.

In September, Massey postponed publication of its third quarter results as talks continued with the Canadian governments. By October, Massey and its finance subsidiaries had debt of U.S.$2.5 billion outstanding to 150 banks worldwide, and speculation on the probability of Massey's survival was rampant.

Only a few weeks remained before the November 1 deadline when Massey would be technically in default on several loans. Cross-default provisions made substantially all outstanding loans callable if any single default occurred. Suddenly, on October 2, 1980, Argus donated its 16.5% controlling interest to Massey-Ferguson's two pension funds. This move made Massey the world's largest employee-controlled corporation and resulted in a Can.$23-million tax write-off for Argus. On the same day, the government of Canada announced it would "work closely" with Massey to achieve a refinancing.

Two weeks later, on October 20, 1980, the governments of Canada and Ontario announced they had reached an agreement in principle with Massey and its major lenders:

> The governments are prepared to guarantee the capital risk of a portion of the new equity investment in Massey, providing various conditions are met, including a satisfactory degree of cooperation from the existing lenders.

The press attributed the governments' actions to the upcoming Ontario provincial election and the need to protect jobs. According to the *Economist:*

> While the federal government is Liberal, Ontario is still Conservative. . . . It needs both the Massey jobs and Mr. Black, a Conservative supporter, who is in favor of more Massey investment in Canada. . . . Meanwhile, the Trudeau government is trying to use Massey to help its constitutional plans.[3]

However, other press reports indicated that the governments had been forced to act, and "in effect [they are] still supplying only inexpensive moral support for the company at this time."

On October 31, Massey-Ferguson closed its books on fiscal year 1980. The loss for the year (subsequently reported) amounted to U.S.$225.2 million, or $12.79 per share. Scheduled principal repayments were suspended in October; interest payments were suspended on December 1, 1980.

Massey-Ferguson began fiscal year 1981 in default on its U.S.$2.5 billion of outstanding debt. The company's future depended on the ability of lenders, the governments of Canada and Ontario, and management to agree on a feasible refinancing plan. In the course of the continuing negotiations, serious questions were raised about Massey's long-term ability to compete in its industry. Persons close to the situation wondered what sort of restructuring would allow the company to survive, and whether Massey would ever regain its status as a self-sufficient corporation.

---

3. The repatriation of the Constitution was a major political issue in Canada in 1980–1981.

**EXHIBIT 1**
Consolidated Balance Sheets at October 31, 1978–1980 (millions of U.S. dollars)

|  | 1978 | 1979 | 1980 |
|---|---|---|---|
| Cash | $ 23.4 | $ 17.2 | $ 56.2 |
| Receivables | 531.3 | 731.1 | 968.2 |
| Inventories | 1,083.8 | 1,097.6 | 988.9 |
| Prepaid expenses, other | 63.8 | 89.8 | 93.0 |
| Current assets | 1,702.3 | 1,935.7 | 2,106.3 |
| Investments | 213.3 | 217.1 | 205.8 |
| Fixed assets, net | 602.2 | 568.7 | 488.2 |
| Other assets and deferred charges | 29.3 | 24.0 | 27.3 |
| Total assets | $2,547.1 | $2,745.5 | $2,827.6 |
| Bank borrowings | $ 362.3 | $ 511.7 | $1,015.1 |
| Long-term debt, current portion | 115.0 | 59.3 | 60.2 |
| Accounts payable and accrued charges | 778.7 | 907.4 | 793.8 |
| Other | 16.1 | 31.1 | 24.5 |
| Current liabilities | 1,272.1 | 1,509.5 | 1,893.6 |
| Deferred income tax | 64.3 | 13.8 | 14.3 |
| Long-term debt (less current portion) | 651.8 | 624.8 | 562.1 |
| Minority interest in subsidiaries | 18.4 | 19.1 | 4.5 |
| Total liabilities | 2,006.6 | 2,167.2 | 2,474.5 |
| Redeemable preferred shares | 95.8 | 95.8 | 95.8 |
| Common (18,250,350 shares) | 176.9 | 176.9 | 176.9 |
| Retained earnings | 267.8 | 305.6 | 80.4 |
| Shareholders' equity | 540.5 | 578.3 | 353.1 |
| Total liabilities and shareholders' equity | $2,547.1 | $2,745.5 | $2,827.6 |

**EXHIBIT 2**
Consolidated Income Statements for Years Ending October 31, 1978–1980
(millions of U.S. dollars)

| | 1978 | 1979 | 1980 |
|---|---|---|---|
| Net sales | $2,925.5 | $2,973.0 | $3,132.1 |
| Cost of goods sold, at average exchange rates for year | $2,371.2 | $2,381.8 | $2,568.5 |
| Effect of foreign currency exchange rate changes[a] | – | 18.6 | 7.7 |
| | 2,371.2 | 2,400.4 | 2,576.2 |
| Marketing, general, and administrative | 372.0 | 351.9 | 404.7 |
| Engineering and product development | 66.0 | 58.2 | 59.7 |
| Interest on long-term debt | 78.6 | 75.7 | 71.0 |
| Other interest expenses | 108.0[b] | 128.8 | 229.9 |
| Interest income | – | (40.3) | (42.0) |
| Exchange adjustments | 90.9 | (24.9) | 49.9 |
| Minority interest | (.8) | 1.4 | .2 |
| Miscellaneous income | (10.6) | (10.3) | (13.5) |
| Total costs and expenses | $3,075.3 | $2,940.9 | $3,336.1 |
| Profit (loss) before items shown below | $ (149.8) | $ 32.1 | $ (204.0) |
| Provision for reorganization expense | (116.0) | (95.0) | (28.5) |
| Income tax recovery | (11.8) | 6.3 | 10.1 |
| Equity in net income of finance subsidiaries | 16.3 | 16.6 | 22.7 |
| Equity in net income of associate companies | 4.6 | 4.6 | – |
| Income (loss) from continuing operations | (256.7) | (35.4) | (199.7) |
| Loss from discontinued operations | – | (23.0) | (25.5) |
| Extraordinary item | – | 95.4 | – |
| Net income (loss) | $ (256.7) | $ 37.0 | $ (225.2) |
| Unfavorable (favorable) impact on continuing operations of exchange adjustments and foreign currency exchange rate changes in cost of goods sold | – | $ (6.3) | $ 57.6 |

a. This item is the difference between costs of goods sold translated to U.S. dollars at average exchange rates and such costs translated at historical rates.

b. Amounts shown are net of interest income.

**EXHIBIT 3**

Consolidated Statement of Changes in Financial Position for Years Ending October 31, 1978–1980 (millions of U.S. dollars)

|  | 1978 | 1979 | 1980 |
|---|---|---|---|
| *Sources of Funds* | | | |
| Disposal of investments in associate companies and changes in long-term advances to finance subsidiaries | – | $ 29.1 | $ 41.3 |
| Proceeds on disposal of fixed assets | $ 11.3 | 31.1 | 34.1 |
| Extraordinary item (less $31.4 in 1979 not affecting working capital) | – | 64.0 | – |
| Proceeds from long-term debt issues | 169.0 | 35.8 | – |
| Total sources | $ 180.3 | $ 160.0 | $ 75.4 |
| *Uses of Funds* | | | |
| Funds used in operations | $ 176.2 | $ 30.0 | $168.4 |
| Reductions in long-term debt | 158.6 | 59.0 | 67.1 |
| Additions in fixed assets | 99.3 | 76.6 | 46.2 |
| Other (net) | 18.2 | (.7) | 7.2 |
| Total uses | $ 452.3 | $ 164.9 | $ 288.9 |
| *Working Capital* | | | |
| Decrease in working capital | $(272.0) | $ (4.9) | $(213.5) |
| At beginning of year | 703.1 | 431.1 | 426.2 |
| At end of year | 431.1 | 426.2 | 212.7 |
| *Changes in Elements of Working Capital* | | | |
| Cash | $ 10.8 | $ (6.3) | $ 39.0 |
| Receivables | (19.9) | 174.4 | 237.1 |
| Inventories | (52.1) | 13.8 | (108.7) |
| Prepaid expenses, other | (8.4) | 26.0 | 3.2) |
| Current assets | $ (69.6) | $ 207.9 | $ 170.6 |
| Bank borrowing and current portion of long-term debt | (132.2) | (93.8) | (504.3) |
| Accounts payable and accrued charges | 55.1 | (156.0) | (54.3) |
| Accrued charges | – | – | 59.3 |
| Income, sales, and other taxes payable | (5.4) | 33.4 | 6.0 |
| Advance payments from customers | (9.7) | 3.6 | .6 |
| Current liabilities | $(202.4) | $(212.8) | $(384.1) |
| Decrease in working capital | $(272.0) | $ (4.9) | $(213.5) |

**EXHIBIT 4**

Selected Operating Data and Balance Sheets, 1971–1980 (millions of U.S. dollars and percentage of sales or total assets)

| | 1971 | | 1972 | | 1973 | | 1974 | | 1975 | | 1976 | | 1977 | | 1978 | | 1979 | | 1980 | |
|---|---|---|---|---|---|---|---|---|---|---|---|---|---|---|---|---|---|---|---|---|
| **Selected Operating Data** | | | | | | | | | | | | | | | | | | | | |
| Sales | $1,029 | 100% | $1,190 | 100% | $1,497 | 100% | $1,791 | 100% | $2,554 | 100% | $2,772 | 100% | $2,805 | 100% | $2,631 | 100% | $2,973 | 100% | $3,132 | 100% |
| Operating profit[a] | — | — | — | — | — | — | — | — | 111 | 4 | 126 | 5 | 77 | 3 | (133) | (5) | (30) | (1) | (139) | (4) |
| Net income[b] | — | — | — | — | — | — | — | — | 100 | 4 | 118 | 4 | 32 | 1 | (262) | (10) | 37 | 1 | (225) | (7) |
| **Balance Sheets** | | | | | | | | | | | | | | | | | | | | |
| Cash | $ 33 | 3% | $ 10 | 1% | $ 8 | 1% | $ 13 | 1% | $ 20 | 1% | $ 7 | — | $ 13 | — | $ 23 | 1% | $ 17 | 1% | $ 56 | 2% |
| Receivables | 339 | 33 | 368 | 35 | 417 | 33 | 433 | 27 | 485 | 24 | 558 | 24% | 542 | 21% | 531 | 21 | 731 | 27 | 968 | 34 |
| Inventory | 335 | 33 | 362 | 34 | 461 | 37 | 711 | 44 | 878 | 44 | 967 | 42 | 1,136 | 44 | 1,084 | 43 | 1,098 | 40 | 989 | 35 |
| Other | 31 | 3 | 33 | 3 | 53 | 4 | 66 | 4 | 72 | 4 | 83 | 4 | 81 | 3 | 64 | 2 | 90 | 3 | 93 | 3 |
| Current assets | 738 | 72 | 773 | 73 | 939 | 75 | 1,223 | 76 | 1,455 | 73 | 1,615 | 70 | 1,772 | 68 | 1,702 | 67 | 1,936 | 71 | 2,106 | 74 |
| Net P.P.&E | 186 | 19 | 180 | 17 | 205 | 16 | 278 | 17 | 401 | 20 | 519 | 23 | 594 | 23 | 602 | 24 | 569 | 21 | 488 | 17 |
| Other (investment) | 87 | 9 | 104 | 10 | 105 | 9 | 113 | 7 | 141 | 7 | 171 | 7 | 228 | 9 | 243 | 9 | 241 | 8 | 234 | 9 |
| Total assets | $1,011 | 100% | $1,057 | 100% | $1,249 | 100% | $1,614 | 100% | $1,997 | 100% | $2,305 | 100% | $2,594 | 100% | $2,547 | 100% | $2,746 | 100% | $2,828 | 100% |
| Bank borrowings | $ 168 | 17% | $ 139 | 13% | $ 81 | 6% | $ 163 | 10% | $ 170 | 9% | $ 113 | 5% | $ 249 | 10% | $ 362 | 14% | $ 512 | 19% | $1,015 | 36% |
| L-T debt, due 1 yr | 10 | 1 | 11 | 1 | 13 | 1 | 16 | 1 | 47 | 2 | 66 | 3 | 96 | 4 | 115 | 5 | 59 | 2 | 60 | 2 |
| Other | 224 | 22 | 251 | 24 | 406 | 32 | 542 | 34 | 613 | 31 | 704 | 30 | 730 | 28 | 795 | 31 | 938 | 34 | 819 | 29 |
| Current liabilities | 402 | 40 | 401 | 38 | 500 | 39 | 721 | 45 | 830 | 42 | 883 | 38 | 1,075 | 42 | 1,272 | 50 | 1,509 | 55 | 1,894 | 67 |
| Long-term debt | 187 | 18 | 196 | 18 | 244 | 20 | 325 | 20 | 452 | 23 | 529 | 23 | 616 | 24 | 652 | 26 | 625 | 23 | 562 | 20 |
| Other | 18 | 2 | 16 | 1 | 35 | 3 | 44 | 3 | 63 | 3 | 90 | 4 | 96 | 3 | 82 | 3 | 33 | 1 | 19 | 1 |
| Owners' equity | 404 | 40 | 444 | 43 | 470 | 38 | 524 | 32 | 652 | 32 | 803 | 35 | 807 | 31 | 541 | 21 | 579 | 21 | 353 | 12 |
| Tot. liabilities, equity | $1,011 | 100% | $1,057 | 100% | $1,249 | 100% | $1,614 | 100% | $1,997 | 100% | $2,305 | 100% | $2,594 | 100% | $2,547 | 100% | $2,746 | 100% | $2,828 | 100% |

*Note:* Operating data are shown as percentage of sales, and balance sheet data as percentage of total assets.

a. Operating profit (loss) is defined as total revenue less those recurring expenses that are controllable by management. It excludes extraordinary items, net exchange adjustments, and reorganization expense pertaining to continuing operations.

b. Prior to 1978 results reflect sales and income from construction machinery businesses. After 1978 construction machinery is treated as a discontinued operation.

**EXHIBIT 5**

Worldwide Sales and Distribution of Capacity by Country

| | 1980 Sales | | Percent Capacity | |
|---|---|---|---|---|
| | U.S. $ millions | Percent | Farm Equipment | Diesel Engines |
| **North America** | | | | |
| Canada . . . . . . . | $ 219 | 7.0% | 27.4% | – |
| United States . . . . . | 819 | 26.1 | 14.6 | 3.4% |
| Mexico . . . . . . . . | 75 | 2.4 | – | – |
| | 1,113 | 35.5 | 42.0 | 3.4 |
| **Western Europe** | | | | |
| United Kingdom . . . . . | 297 | 9.5 | 15.6 | 76.7 |
| France . . . . . . . . | 227 | 7.2 | 10.2 | 1.0 |
| Italy . . . . . . . . . | 211 | 6.7 | 8.0 | – |
| West Germany . . . . . | 157 | 5.0 | 5.5 | – |
| Spain . . . . . . . . | 8 | .3 | – | – |
| Benelux . . . . . . . | 28 | .9 | – | – |
| | 928 | 29.6 | 39.3 | 77.7 |
| **South America** | | | | |
| Brazil . . . . . . . . | 306 | 9.8 | 6.4 | 17.9 |
| Argentina . . . . . . . | 44 | 1.4 | 1.8 | – |
| | 350 | 11.2 | 8.2 | 17.9 |
| Australia . . . . . . . | 131 | 4.2 | 10.5 | 1.0 |
| Scandinavia . . . . . . | 114 | 3.6 | – | – |
| South Africa . . . . . . | 66 | 2.1 | – | – |
| Iran . . . . . . . . . | 31 | 1.0 | – | – |
| Pakistan . . . . . . . | 29 | .9 | – | – |
| Japan . . . . . . . . | 25 | .8 | – | – |
| Turkey . . . . . . . . | 14 | .4 | – | – |
| All others . . . . . . . | 331 | 10.6 | – | – |
| Totals . . . . . . . | $3,132 | 100.0% | 100.0% | 100.0% |

*Note:* Percentages may not total to 100% because of rounding.

**EXHIBIT 6**
Comparative Data on Farm Equipment Producers, 1976–1980 (millions of dollars)

| Company | 1976 | 1977 | 1978 | 1979 | 1980 |
|---|---|---|---|---|---|
| *Massey-Ferguson Limited* | | | | | |
| Sales | $2,772 | $2,805 | $2,631 | $2,973 | $3,132 |
| Operating profit[a] | 126 | 77 | −133 | −30 | −139 |
| Net income | 118 | 32 | −262 | 37 | −225 |
| Assets | 2,305 | 2,594 | 2,547 | 2,746 | 2,828 |
| Short-term debt[b] | 180 | 345 | 477 | 571 | 1,075 |
| Long-term debt | 529 | 469 | 505 | 478 | 415 |
| Equity | 803 | 807 | 541 | 578 | 353 |
| Capital expenditures | 175 | 147 | 99 | 77 | 46 |
| Operating profit/Sales | 4.55% | 2.74% | −4.55% | −1.01% | −4.44% |
| Net income/Sales | 4.25% | 1.17% | −8.77% | 1.24% | −7.19% |
| Short-term debt/Capital[c] | 11.89% | 21.29% | 31.35% | 35.09% | 58.33% |
| Total debt/Capital | 46.90% | 50.24% | 64.50% | 64.46% | 80.85% |
| Sales/Assets | 1.20 | 1.08 | 1.15 | 1.08 | 1.11 |
| Coverage[d] | 2.10 | 1.42 | .14 | .82 | .46 |
| Market share[e] | 33.94% | 32.08% | 31.03% | 27.09% | 28.19% |
| Capital exp. share[f] | 47.80% | 33.10% | 24.69% | 17.22% | 7.43% |
| *International Harvester* | | | | | |
| Sales | $5,488 | $5,975 | $6,664 | $8,392 | $6,312 |
| Agricultural sales | 2,262 | 2,334 | 2,348 | 3,069 | 2,507 |
| Operating profit, firm[a] | 473 | 531 | 610 | 827 | −262 |
| Operating profit, ag. | 0 | 0 | 288 | 442 | −1 |
| Net income | 173 | 204 | 187 | 370 | −397 |
| Assets | 3,575 | 3,788 | 4,316 | 5,247 | 5,843 |
| Agricultural assets | 0 | 0 | 1,385 | 1,548 | 1,739 |
| Short-term debt[b] | 302 | 292 | 380 | 442 | 860 |
| Long-term debt | 923 | 926 | 933 | 948 | 1,327 |
| Equity | 1,564 | 1,734 | 1,876 | 2,199 | 1,896 |
| Capital expenditures | 158 | 164 | 210 | 285 | 384 |
| Operating profit/Sales | 8.61% | 8.89% | 9.15% | 9.85% | −4.15% |
| Ag. oper. profit/Ag. sales | − | − | 12.25% | 14.40% | −.04% |
| Net income/Sales | 3.15% | 3.41% | 2.80% | 4.40% | −6.29% |
| Short-term debt/Capital[c] | 10.84% | 9.90% | 11.91% | 12.31% | 21.07% |
| Total debt/Capital | 43.93% | 41.28% | 41.16% | 38.73% | 53.56% |
| Sales/Assets | 1.54 | 1.58 | 1.54 | 1.60 | 1.08 |
| Ag. sales/Ag. assets | − | − | 1.70 | 1.98 | 1.44 |
| Coverage[d] | 3.66 | 4.11 | 4.21 | 4.92 | .24 |
| Market share[e] | 27.70% | 26.70% | 24.90% | 27.96% | 22.57% |
| Capital exp. share[f] | 17.79% | 14.43% | 18.45% | 23.30% | 24.62% |

*(continued)*

## EXHIBIT 6 *(concluded)*

| Company | 1976 | 1977 | 1978 | 1979 | 1980 |
|---|---|---|---|---|---|
| *Deere & Company* | | | | | |
| Sales . . . . . . . . | $3,134 | $3,604 | $4,155 | $4,933 | $5,470 |
| Operating profit[a] . . . . | 438 | 483 | 537 | 564 | 470 |
| Net income . . . . . . | 242 | 256 | 265 | 311 | 228 |
| Assets . . . . . . . | 2,944 | 3,429 | 3,892 | 4,179 | 5,202 |
| Short-term debt[b] . . . . | 134 | 242 | 137 | 202 | 742 |
| Long-term debt . . . . | 494 | 482 | 637 | 619 | 702 |
| Equity . . . . . . . | 1,379 | 1,571 | 1,756 | 1,974 | 2,141 |
| Capital expenditures . . . | 126 | 233 | 228 | 266 | 421 |
| Operating profit/Sales . . | 13.98% | 13.40% | 12.92% | 11.43% | 8.59% |
| Net income/Sales . . . . | 7.71% | 7.09% | 6.37% | 6.30% | 4.17% |
| Short-term debt/Capital[c] . | 6.69% | 10.55% | 5.43% | 7.22% | 20.69% |
| Total debt/Capital . . . . | 31.31% | 31.55% | 30.61% | 29.36% | 40.28% |
| Sales/Assets . . . . . | 1.06 | 1.05 | 1.07 | 1.18 | 1.05 |
| Coverage[d] . . . . . . | 6.15 | 6.32 | 6.38 | 6.32 | 3.19 |
| Market share[e] . . . . . | 38.37% | 41.22% | 44.07% | 44.95% | 49.24% |
| Capital exp. share[f] . . . | 34.41% | 52.47% | 56.86% | 59.48% | 67.96% |

a. Casewriter's estimates. Operating profit excludes extraordinary items, foreign exchange gains or losses, and reorganization expense on continuing operations.

b. Short-term debt equals bank borrowing plus long-term debt due in 1 year.

c. Capital equals long- and short-term debt plus equity.

d. Coverage is here defined as operating profit plus interest and lease rental expense divided by interest and lease rental expense plus preferred dividends. No adjustment for taxes was made because of the unstable tax status of these companies in this period. As a result, Deere's actual coverage is understated relative to Massey's in all years and Harvester's in 1980.

e. For each company, market share is calculated as own sales (agricultural only for Harvester) divided by total (three company) agricultural sales.

f. For each company, capital expenditure share is calculated as own capital expenditures divided by total (three company) capital expenditures. Harvester's total capital expenditures are adjusted by the ratio of its agricultural sales to total sales.

**EXHIBIT 7**
Summary of Long-Term Debt Outstanding at October 31, 1979–1980
(millions of U.S. dollars)

| | 1979 | 1980 |
|---|---|---|
| *Bonds, Debentures, Notes, and Loans*[a] | | |
| Massey-Ferguson Perkins S.A. (Brazil): Bank loans maturing 1981–1984 repayable in U.S. dollars bearing interest at ¾% to 2½% above Eurodollar interbank rate | $ 30.9 | $ 14.3 |
| Massey-Ferguson S.A. (France): Bank loans maturing 1981–1985 bearing interest at 1.95% above base rate | 24.4 | 23.4 |
| Massey-Ferguson S.p.A. (Italy): Bank loans maturing 1981–1982 repayable in U.S. dollars bearing interest at 1.3% above Eurodollar interbank rate | 10.0 | 10.0 |
| Massey-Ferguson Holding Limited (United Kingdom): 7½% loan stock maturing 1986–1992 | 16.6 | 19.4 |
| Bank loans maturing 1981–1984 bearing interest at various London bank market rates | 38.6 | 34.5 |
| Massey-Ferguson Inc. (USA): 8.55% promissory notes maturing 1981–1984 | 26.3 | 21.6 |
| 5⅞% subordinated notes maturing 1981–1984 | 12.0 | 10.4 |
| Massey-Ferguson (Delaware) Inc. (USA): 9% senior notes maturing 1983–1997 | 150.0 | 150.0 |
| Perkins Diesel Corporation (USA): Capitalized value of property and equipment lease terminating 1993 discounted at 10% | 25.5 | 24.5 |
| General-purpose loans (repayable in U.S. dollars): 9½% debentures maturing 1991[b] | 66.0 | 61.5 |
| 9¾% sinking fund debentures maturing 1981–1982 | 32.0 | 30.0 |
| Other long-term debt[c] | 104.8 | 75.7 |
| Total unsubordinated long-term debt | $537.1 | $475.3 |
| *Convertible Subordinated Notes*[d] | | |
| Massey-Ferguson (Delaware) Inc. (USA): 10% convertible subordinated notes maturing 1988–1992 | 147.0 | 147.0 |
| Total long-term debt | $684.1 | $622.3 |

a. Debts are repayable in currency of country indicated unless otherwise shown. Current maturities are included in this summary; maturity dates are for fiscal years ending October 31. As of September 1980 the company had met all contractual sinking fund requirements. An additional $800,000 in sinking fund payments was due in October 1980. Sinking fund requirements and debt maturities during the next 5 years were as follows: 1981—$60.2 million; 1982—$78.5 million; 1983—$46.3 million; 1984—$54.3 million; 1985—$25.9 million.

b. The company is obligated to purchase for cancellation up to $4.5 million of these debentures each year to 1986 if the market price is below par value during the period March 1 to May 31.

c. Other long-term debt includes long-term loans, each of which is less than $10.0 million.

d. These notes are convertible into common shares of Massey-Ferguson Ltd. at an initial price of U.S.$45.00 per share rising to U.S.$55.00 per share in 1982. There is no dilution of 1980 or 1979 annual results per common share as a result of this convertible feature.

**EXHIBIT 8**
Short-Term Credit Lines by Bank at June 30, 1980 (millions of U.S. dollars)

| | Canada | U.S. | Finance Companies Australia | Germany | Italy | UK | Finag | Total |
|---|---|---|---|---|---|---|---|---|
| CIBC | 37.8 | | | | | 27.1 | | 64.9 |
| Barclays | | | | | | 42.5 | | 42.5 |
| Midland | | | | | | 54.3 | | 54.3 |
| Lloyds | | | | | | 42.5 | | 42.5 |
| Citibank | | 17.5 | | | | | | 17.5 |
| Société Générale | | | | | | 9.0 | | 9.0 |
| Deutsche Bank | | | | 3.3 | | | | 3.3 |
| Chase Manhattan | | 15.0 | | | | | | 15.0 |
| Crédit Lyonnais | | | | | | 9.0 | | 9.0 |
| Banque National de Paris | | | 7.8 | | | 11.3 | | 19.1 |
| Continental Illinois | | 21.0 | | | 3.8 | 4.5 | | 29.3 |
| Bank of America | | 17.5 | | | | | | 17.5 |
| Dresdner | | | | 3.3 | | | | 3.3 |
| Commerzbank | | | | 3.3 | | | | 3.3 |
| Bankers Trust | | 13.0 | | | | | | 13.0 |
| FNB Chicago | | 15.0 | | | | | | 15.0 |
| Chemical | | 13.0 | | | | | | 13.0 |
| Allied & Associates | | | | | | 18.5 | 45.0 | 63.5 |
| Banque Francais du Commerce Extérieur | | | | | | | | – |
| Royal Bank of Canada | | | | | | 11.3 | | 11.3 |
| Toronto Dominion | | | | | | 6.8 | | 6.8 |
| Others | | 78.1 | 23.4 | 7.8 | 81.2 | 50.8 | | 241.3 |
| Total | $37.8 | $190.1 | $31.2 | $17.7 | $85.0 | $287.6 | $45.0 | $694.4 |

*Note:* Because of sales seasonality, the maximum use of credit lines usually occurs in June or July.
By September 1980 borrowing by manufacturing companies had decreased to approximately
U.S. $1.0 billion. Borrowing by finance subsidiaries was down to between U.S. $.8 and $.9 billion.

a. Includes Perkins UK.

b. Includes MF AG, Agrotrac, MF International, and MF Nederland.

**EXHIBIT 8** *(concluded)*

| | | | | | Manufacturing Companies | | | | | | | | | | |
|---|---|---|---|---|---|---|---|---|---|---|---|---|---|---|---|
| Brazil | Argentina | Canada | U.S. | Australia | France | Eicher | GabH | Italy | UK Total[a] | Corporate Companies[b] | France | Brazil | Other | Total | Grand Total |
| | | 222.9 | | | 3.6 | | | | 3.4 | | | | | 229.9 | 294.8 |
| | | | | | | | | | 133.4 | | | | | 133.4 | 175.9 |
| | | | | | | | | | 36.2 | | | | | 36.2 | 90.5 |
| | | | | | | | | | 36.2 | | | | | 36.2 | 78.7 |
| | .5 | | 17.5 | | | | | 3.0 | 1.1 | | | | | 22.1 | 39.6 |
| | | | | | 50.1 | | | | | | | | | 50.1 | 59.1 |
| | | | | | | 5.6 | 26.6 | | | | | | | 32.2 | 35.5 |
| | | | 15.0 | | | | | | | | | | | 15.0 | 30.0 |
| | | | 3.0 | | 33.0 | | | | | | 3.3 | | | 39.3 | 48.3 |
| | | 15.0 | | | 34.6 | | | | | | 3.8 | | | 53.4 | 72.5 |
| | | | 21.0 | | | | | | | | | | | 21.0 | 50.3 |
| | | | 17.5 | 3.3 | | | | | | | | | | 20.8 | 38.3 |
| | | | | | | 3.3 | 33.3 | | | | | | | 36.6 | 39.9 |
| | | | | | | 3.9 | 27.8 | | | | | | | 31.7 | 35.0 |
| | | | 13.0 | | | | | | | | | | | 13.0 | 26.0 |
| | | | 15.0 | | | | | | | | | | | 15.0 | 30.0 |
| | | | 13.0 | | | | | 1.2 | | | | | | 14.2 | 27.2 |
| | | | | | | | | | | 5.0 | | | | 5.0 | 68.5 |
| | | | | | 18.3 | | | | | 12.2 | 3.3 | | | 33.8 | 33.8 |
| | | | 15.0 | | | | | | | 5.0 | | | | 20.0 | 31.3 |
| | | | 15.0 | | | | | | | | | | | 15.0 | 21.8 |
| 31.2 | 40.1 | | 48.2 | 25.5 | 16.1 | 15.4 | 28.9 | 56.3 | 19.2 | 51.8 | 1.0 | 7.7 | 7.0 | 348.4 | 589.7 |
| $31.2 | $40.6 | $237.9 | $193.2 | $28.8 | $155.7 | $28.2 | $116.6 | $60.5 | $229.5 | $74.0 | $11.4 | $7.7 | $7.0 | $1,222.3 | $1,916.7 |

**EXHIBIT 9**

Common Stock Price Data: Massey-Ferguson and NYSE Composite Price Index, by Quarters, 1976–1980

| | Massey-Ferguson Common Stock | | NYSE Composite Price Index |
|---|---|---|---|
| | Quarterly Dividend | Market Price | |
| 1976: March | $.25 | $27¾ | 54.80 |
| June | .25 | 28¾ | 55.71 |
| September | .25 | 22¾ | 56.23 |
| December | .33 | 21¾ | 57.88 |
| 1977: March | .25 | 19⅜ | 53.53 |
| June | .25 | 19⅞ | 55.10 |
| September | .25 | 17 | 52.81 |
| December | .25ᵃ | 14½ | 52.50 |
| 1978: March | | 9 | 49.85 |
| June | | 10½ | 53.66 |
| September | | 11 | 57.78 |
| December | | 8¾ | 53.62 |
| 1979: March | | 11¾ | 57.13 |
| June | | 12⅝ | 58.38 |
| September | | 10½ | 62.24 |
| December | | 10¼ | 61.95 |
| 1980: March | | 8⅜ | 57.65 |
| June | | 6¾ | 65.34 |
| September | | 6½ | 72.38 |
| October | | 5½ | 73.53 |

*Note:* Prices as of the last trading day in the month.

a. Dividends were discontinued after December 1977.

# *Hospital Corporation of America (A)*

In January 1982, Hospital Corporation of America (HCA) faced a complex financial situation. Following a major acquisition in 1981, HCA's ratio of debt to total capital was approaching 70%, well in excess of its well-established target ratio of 60%. Interest coverage had dropped below its target of 3.0 to 2.4, the lowest level experienced since HCA was founded in 1968. Although some investors justified, even welcomed, HCA's more aggressive use of leverage, others were concerned. HCA's capital structure could cost the company its single-A bond rating. Mounting interest expense on the debt could also result in a decline in HCA's first-quarter earnings per share relative to that for a year ago. If it did, it would be the first such quarter-to-quarter decline in earnings per share in HCA's 13-year history. In light of these developments, HCA's management had to decide what, if anything, should be done about its capital structure and what specific steps should be taken in the near future to achieve the desired mix of debt and equity.

## Early Development

Hospital Corporation of America is a proprietary hospital management company. It was founded in Nashville, Tennessee, by two physicians, Thomas F. Frist, Sr., and Thomas F. Frist, Jr., and by Jack C. Massey, a former pharmacist and former owner of Kentucky Fried Chicken. Beginning with only a single 150-bed hospital in 1968, HCA grew to become the nation's largest hospital management company. By 1981, HCA owned or managed 349 hospitals in the United States and overseas and had net operating revenues of $2.1 billion. Since its founding, revenues and earnings had grown at an annual rate of 32.2% and 32.6%, respectively. Pre-tax profit margins, averaging 9%, were the highest and most consistent among the major proprietary hospital chains. Recent financial statements and a 10-year summary of HCA's operations are presented in Exhibits 1–4.

## The Proprietary Hospital Industry

Proprietary hospital management companies—that is, corporations that own and manage chains of hospitals on a for-profit basis—were a relatively new phenomenon in the $118 billion U.S. hospital care business. The enactment of entitlement programs such as Medicare and Medicaid in 1965 stimulated demand for hospital services and virtually eliminated the tremendous bad-debt burden (i.e., weak accounts receivable) that had traditionally plagued the hospital industry. This created a valuable opportunity for private investors to build or acquire hospitals and operate them profitably. Tight control over costs and efficiencies in such areas as staffing, purchasing, and hospital design enabled hospital management companies to offer high-quality services at reasonable cost while achieving attractive profit margins.

With the ability to sell equity and other financial securities not generally available to nonprofit hospitals, proprietary hospital management companies expanded rapidly in the 1970s. While the number of hospitals operating in the United States actually declined steadily between 1975 and 1980 from a high of 7,200, the proprietary hospital chains expanded the number of hospitals under their control at a 12.5% annual rate. By 1980, 38 proprietary hospital chains owned or operated 12.4% of the 6,965 hospitals and 7.9% of the 1.37 million licensed hospital beds in the United States. The five largest hospital chains controlled 632 hospitals and 87,502 beds in 1981. A comparison of the major hospital chains is provided in Exhibit 5.

It was expected that revenue growth of the hospital management companies as a group would be approximately 13–14% annually throughout the 1980s. The five major chains, however, were expected to grow at an annual rate of 25% during the first half of the decade. Although still rapid, this expected rate of growth was less than the 35% annual rate they experienced between 1975 and 1980. Shrinkage in the number of attractive acquisitions, along with high costs for construction and acquisition, accounted for the expected slowdown.

## Past Growth

HCA's growth during the 1970s was achieved both through acquisition of existing hospitals and construction of new units. Between 1968 and 1981, HCA constructed 70 new and replacement facilities and acquired or leased the rest of its hospitals. Each year HCA evaluated many potential acquisitions and areas for construction and was rather selective in the facilities it acquired. Criteria for selection included the target community's need for health care services, the quality of the target hospital's medical staff and personnel, the population growth pattern in the area served, the facility's suitability for future expansion, and the hospital's overall financial position. Most of HCA's domestic hospitals were located in the Southeast and in the rapidly expanding ''sunbelt'' area of the United States (see Exhibit 6). This geographic preference reflected, in part, a more favorable regulatory environment in these parts of the United States and, in part, more favorable demographic trends. Roughly 40% of HCA's U.S. facilities were the only hospitals in their areas.

Some of HCA's unit growth had been achieved through the acquisition of other proprietary hospital management companies. A run on other proprietary chains was triggered in 1978 when Humana, Inc. merged with American Medicorp, then the third largest chain. Following that acquisition, ten other hospital management companies were acquired by the five majors by 1981. HCA accounted for four of these acquisitions. Its most recent one occurred on August 26, 1981, when it purchased Hospital Affiliates International from INA Corporation, an insurance company, for $425 million cash and common stock valued at $190 million. This acquisition provided HCA with 57 additional owned hospitals and 78 more hospitals under management contract.[1] With revenues of $704 million and earnings of $29 million in 1980, Hospital Affiliates had been the nation's fifth largest hospital management chain.

## Sources of Capital

HCA's operations generated substantial cash that could be used for reinvestment. However, its ambitious construction and acquisition program also required substantial financing from external sources.

Generally, external financing during HCA's early growth period followed a simple pattern: Revolving bank credits were used to fund hospitals under construction, while industrial revenue bonds and privately placed long-term mortgage loans from insurance companies were used to fund completed hospitals and acquisitions. Other sources of capital were difficult to tap at first because of the newness of the proprietary hospital industry, the small size and short track record of HCA itself, and the generally poor image that many investors had of hospital management companies at that time.

However, as the hospital management industry matured and HCA's strong performance became recognized, other types of financing were used beginning in the mid-1970s. In 1975, HCA issued $33 million of 15-year first-mortgage bonds, the first public bond offering undertaken by a hospital management company.

---

1. Proprietary hospital management companies frequently managed hospitals for others on a contractual fee basis. Such management contracts did not require much in the way of capital investment, but neither did they provide as much revenue as owned and operated facilities. They were valuable, however, as a source of potential acquisition candidates and as a means for scouting potential new areas for expansion. In 1981, HCA operated hospitals under management contracts in 38 states throughout the United States.

Standard and Poor's initially rated the bonds BBB and later upgraded them to A.[2] In an effort to tap sources of funds overseas, HCA also issued $25 million of Eurodollar notes in 1978. In another first for the industry, the company sold $47 million of commercial paper in 1980. The issue was rated A-2 by Standard and Poor's and P-2 by Moody's.

In 1981, HCA added $891 million of debt to its balance sheet. Most of this debt was to mature in less than 7 years, and a substantial portion of it bore fluctuating interest rates that were tied to the prime rate or the London Interbank Offered Rate[3] (a complete schedule of HCA's debt is shown in Exhibit 7). Of this, $425 million was in the form of a revolving bank credit that was used to finance the purchase of Hospital Affiliates. This sudden increase in the level of debt on HCA's books made HCA the highest leveraged company in the United States with a single-A bond rating.

HCA had also issued common stock on a number of occasions. It had a public offering of new equity each year from 1969 to 1971 as it built its capital base. Since 1971, HCA had only two public offerings of stock: one in 1976 and the other in 1979, when it sold 2.2 million common shares, receiving net proceeds of $85.8 million, the largest stock deal done that year by an industrial company. HCA also issued new common shares in connection with some of its acquisitions.

HCA's management hoped not to have to issue new equity any more frequently than every other year. Nonetheless, they were very careful to maintain close contact with the equity market. They did so through frequent presentations to security analysts and clear and complete disclosure of information in HCA's financial reports.

## Future Growth

One of HCA's principal objectives was to realize at least 13% annual growth in earnings per share after removing the effects of inflation. As a practical matter, however, HCA sought annual growth in the 25–30% range (including the effects of inflation) for the foreseeable future. This aggressive rate was sought for several reasons. One was competition from other management companies in the acquisition of hospitals. As Bill McInnes, vice president of finance for HCA, noted:

> There is a feeling here that we must be prepared to strike while the iron is hot. There are only 7,000 hospitals out there and we can't expect to have them all. With, perhaps, three to five good years [of growth by acquisition] left, we will have to move along in an expeditious manner to get our fair share.

---

2. Moody's refused to rate the bonds, claiming that HCA's substantial investment in hospital construction meant that it was actually a real estate company. Because enterprises such as real estate investment trusts (REITs) and hotel chains were performing so poorly at this time, Moody's chose not to rate real estate companies at all. The rating agency eventually changed its mind and gave an A to HCA's $23 million industrial revenue bond issue in 1979.

3. The London Interbank Offered Rate is the interest rate offered for dollar deposits in the London market. It serves as a benchmark interest rate for dollar loans in Europe much as the prime rate serves as a benchmark for some loans in the United States.

Management also recognized that HCA's expected growth rate was a major factor influencing the price of the company's equity. "This is a company in which people check the stock price two or three times a day," Mr. McInnes said.[4] "No one wants to see what will happen [to the stock price] if the growth rate starts to unwind." Management's attention to growth and its impact on equity prices was undoubtedly heightened by security analyst reports on HCA, many of which were predicting 1982 earnings per share of $3.00—a 35% increase over 1981.

Management expected growth to continue in the same basic directions that it had taken since the company's founding—through acquisition, construction of new hospitals, expansion of services, and the signing of new management contracts. Some indication had been given that the company was likely to expand into new areas, but only into other health services such as home health care and outpatient surgery.

As far as future growth by acquisition was concerned, it seemed likely that a somewhat different tack would be taken. Partly for antitrust reasons, many analysts and industry participants believed that the acquisition of other hospital management companies had nearly run its course as a major source of new growth for the large chains in the 1980s. Thereafter, it was believed, growth by acquisition would have to occur primarily through the purchase of nonprofit county, municipal, and religious order hospitals. Many such hospitals had old buildings in need of renovation, obsolete equipment, and unsophisticated management systems. Because of the unwillingness or inability of their present owners to raise taxes or issue new debt to continue operations, it was likely that many of these units would be put up for sale.

HCA appeared to be well positioned to make inroads into this market. Interestingly, this position had as much to do with HCA's quality image as its financial strength. Among the major hospital management companies, HCA was considered one of the most attractive by which to be acquired because of its industry leadership position, its decentralized management style, and the high quality of its corporate management. Its list of directors read like a page from *Who's Who in Finance and Industry*. The board was chaired by Donald MacNaughton, former chairman and chief executive officer of Prudential Insurance Co. of America, and included other prominent business leaders such as Robert Anderson, chairman and CEO of Rockwell International Corp; Frank Borman, chairman, president, and CEO of Eastern Air Lines; Owen Butler, chairman of Procter & Gamble Co.; John de Butts, retired chairman and CEO of American Telephone and Telegraph; and Irving Shapiro, chairman of the finance committee of E. I. du Pont de Nemours and Co.

HCA's quality image was important when approaching nonprofit hospitals because of the misgivings that some of their owners often had about selling to a profit-oriented management company. Many nonprofit hospitals were directed by

---

4. Officers and directors of HCA as a group owned 3.6 million shares of HCA's common stock and 1.8 million options on HCA's common shares.

politicians, public agents, and other public figures who sometimes balked at the thought of profits being earned on the care of sick people or who incorrectly believed that past abuses associated with nursing home companies also characterized the proprietary hospital management business. HCA's quality image was often the critical factor in overcoming the doubts of such trustees and convincing them to sell to HCA.

## Other Goals

Besides its growth objective, HCA had several other explicitly stated goals and guidelines. A very important one was its 60% target ratio of debt to total capital. This target was in line with the degree of leverage more or less expected by the rating agencies for an A-rated hospital management company. Its origin, however, was somewhat informal. Typically, debt was used to finance real estate development projects on a 75% loan-to-value basis. In HCA's early years management reasoned that, since 15% of their expenditures on hospital projects were for equipment rather than property or plant, they would be conservative and use only 60% debt financing for their hospital construction. Ultimately, this ratio became the standard for the entire proprietary hospital management industry. However, insofar as many hospitals in the 1980s were built and operated on a stand-alone basis with as much as 90% debt financing, a case could be made on comparative grounds for a higher debt ratio for a healthy hospital management company. In fact, several of HCA's managers expressed the belief that HCA could comfortably accommodate as much as 75–85% debt in its capital structure if it so desired.

Return on total capital was expected to be a minimum of 11% after taxes, and return on equity was expected to be at least 17% after taxes. Although very important goals, these target rates of return could be difficult to maintain during periods of rapid growth, especially if that growth were achieved largely through acquisition. The reason was that growth by acquisition often meant the takeover of hospitals that needed to be turned around. This process could take several years and result in the squeezing of profit margins in the meantime.

HCA's other goals included a dividend payout of 15% of net income and the maintenance or improvement of net profit margins as a percent of operating revenues. Sam Brooks, senior vice president of finance and chief financial officer of HCA, had also expressed his desire to keep the average interest cost for all HCA's debt at 15% or lower in the foreseeable future.

## Regulatory Change and the Outlook for the Future

The future of the hospital management industry appeared bright in several respects. In the near term, continued growth in revenues and earnings seemed assured as nonprofit hospitals became available for acquisition. In the long run, as growth by acquisition and new construction subsided, the natural expansion and aging of the population could be relied upon to increase occupancy rates, thus providing still further growth. Moreover, because of the high *operating* leverage created by hospitals' fixed costs, much of the growth in revenues due to higher occupancy rates could be expected to translate directly into higher earnings. The provision of additional services and a concentration on further cost containment rather than on geographic expansion could further add to growth in earnings in the long run.

The future was not without its risks, however. The federal government had been exploring ways to reduce hospital and medical costs in order to cut federal expenses for Medicare, VA hospitals, and other government-backed health care programs. Various types of industry deregulation tended to be favored in the political climate of the early 1980s as a means of improving production efficiency and increasing consumer welfare.

Regulatory reform of health care could have potentially far-reaching implications for the hospital management companies. For example, under the present regulatory system, hospital expansion was controlled by local health planning agencies through "certificates of need." New hospital projects would be granted such a certificate only if it could be demonstrated that there existed a genuine need for the new services or expanded capacity being contemplated. Although a bureaucratic headache, this requirement restricted new hospital construction and in the process tended to provide existing hospitals with protected franchises. Were certificates of need eliminated, as had been proposed, this form of protection would be removed. This might stimulate rapid expansion by competing hospitals, possibly resulting in the duplication of services, excess bed capacity, and lower occupancy rates than might otherwise be expected. The average occupancy rate for all U.S. hospitals was only 75% in 1979, down from 83% in 1969.

Of equal concern were various proposals to reform the nation's system of health care insurance so that consumers would become more price-sensitive and hospitals more cost-conscious. Because 90% of all Americans were covered by some form of health insurance, the bulk of hospital revenues came from third-party payers. Consequently, the demand for hospital services by the ultimate consumer was relatively price-insensitive. It had been estimated that hospitals could vary prices by as much as 20% up or down without a material effect on patient utilization.[5]

Similarly, because most hospitals received a substantial part of their reimbursements from government-backed programs such as Medicare and Medicaid, incentives to control costs were diminished. The reason was that such reimbursement programs were "cost-based." That is, hospitals were reimbursed for their costs of providing services to covered patients. Costs allowable under Medicare/Medicaid programs included depreciation and interest, but excluded costs of research, losses on bad debts, and expenses for charitable cases. In addition, Medicare allowed a return on equity (excluding nonpatient related assets and liabilities) at a rate equal to 150% of the average annual interest rate on certain debt obligations of the Federal Hospital Insurance Trust Fund. The pre-tax return on equity allowed was 12.3% in 1978, 13.7% in 1979, 16.5% in 1980, and 20.0% in 1981.

---

5. Todd B. Richter, "The Hospital Management Industry: Survival of the Fittest," *Industry Trend Analysis* (Morgan Stanley & Co., Inc., Investment Research), September 30, 1982, p. 11.

One of the effects of this system of insurance in the United States was to provide hospitals with relatively stable revenue streams that were largely insulated from economic cycles, inflation, and other economywide risks. Another was that hospitals tended to compete with one another on the basis of quality and breadth of services, reputation of medical staffs, and advertising rather than on the basis of low prices. Proposals to make consumers bear a greater proportion of their hospital expenses out of their own pockets and to change Medicare and Medicaid to something other than cost-based reimbursement systems could change these characteristics significantly. Some of the proposals being considered included treating health insurance premiums paid by employers as taxable income to employees, increasing the level of out-of-pocket expenses borne by Medicare/Medicaid patients, turning the Medicare program into a voucher system that provided fixed benefits independent of costs, eliminating return on equity provisions in Medicare and Medicaid reimbursements, and revising the Medicare/Medicaid programs so that they were *prospective* reimbursement systems. Under a system of prospective reimbursement, hospitals would be paid on the basis of "prospectively" set rates rather than actually realized costs. If a hospital provided services at a lower cost than the established rates, it could earn a profit; if not, it would realize a loss.

Most industry analysts predicted that some form of prospective reimbursement would be implemented some time in the 1980s. What was unclear was the exact composition of hospital costs that would be covered by such a system. One possibility would be a system in which capital costs would be prospectively set along with other costs of providing services. If this were to occur, hospitals would no longer be able to count on recouping the full amount of their allowable interest expense from the federal government. Another possibility was that interest expenses would continue to be paid retrospectively, but the return on equity provisions would be dropped altogether. This outcome would place even greater pressure on the private-patient side of a hospital's business to provide an adequate return on capital. Whatever type of prospective reimbursement system was adopted, it seemed probable that the virtual elimination of losses and the subsidizing of capital costs heretofore provided by the cost-based reimbursement system would be reduced. This would instill greater volatility in hospital revenues and earnings.

## Financial Decisions

HCA's growth objective implied capital expenditure outlays of $575 million in 1982. This level could be expected to expand by 20% a year for the next several years. Given these increasing capital requirements, its debt repayment schedule (see Exhibit 7), the future prospects of the hospital care industry, and HCA's other goals, senior management had to determine how best to prepare financially for HCA's future.

The first issue that had to be addressed in this process was HCA's target capital structure. Was its long-standing 60% target ratio of debt to total capital too high, too low, or about right? The rating agencies had made it clear that HCA would have to return to its 60–40 capital structure if it were to retain its A bond rating. In a meeting with the rating agencies, prearranged for the day after the acquisition of Hospital Affiliates was announced, Sam Brooks was "given the distinct impression that we had roughly until the end of the summer of 1982 to do something about our debt ratio." Loss of its A bond rating could make access to the debt markets more difficult for HCA. Historical data on debt issued with various credit ratings are presented in Exhibit 8.

Others, however, saw HCA's high level of debt in a more positive light. One Wall Street analyst was quoted as saying that the acquisition of Hospital Affiliates and the debt burden that accompanied the transaction "removes the stigma, if it is one, that Hospital Corp. is too conservative. It said for a long time that it would stick to a 60–40 ratio of debt to equity. . . . [This] shows they're willing to be flexible when the right move comes along."[6] Although maintaining its high degree of leverage would cost HCA its A bond rating, the loss might not be all that damaging. Du Pont, for example, lost its long-standing AAA bond rating with its acquisition of Conoco in 1981 without a dramatic rise in its cost of debt or a loss of access to the debt market.

Still others argued that even a 60% ratio of debt to total capital could be too high in light of potential changes in the regulatory environment. By increasing the risk surrounding the cash flows of the hospital management companies, such changes might necessitate a capital structure with only 50% debt or less. Reducing leverage to such a level would take time to accomplish and would require corrective action well in advance of the anticipated changes even if one were beginning at a 60% debt level. As Bill McInnes said, "A $2½ billion capital structure can't be turned around on a dime."

## EXHIBIT 1
Consolidated Income Statements, 1979–1981 (millions of dollars except per share data)

|  | 1979 | 1980 | 1981 |
|---|---|---|---|
| Operating revenues | $1,043 | $1,429 | $2,406 |
| Contractual adj. and doubtful accounts | 143 | 197 | 343 |
| Net revenues | 901 | 1,232 | 2,064 |
| Operating expenses | 726 | 998 | 1,682 |
| Depreciation and amortization | 41 | 53 | 88 |
| Interest expense | 38 | 50 | 131 |
| Income from operations | 95 | 130 | 162 |
| Other income | 1 | 6 | 22 |
| Income before income taxes | 96 | 136 | 184 |
| Provision for income taxes |  |  |  |
| Current | 28 | 44 | 49 |
| Deferred | 14 | 11 | 24 |
| Net income | $ 54 | $ 81 | $ 111 |
| Average number of common and common equivalent shares (millions) | 41 | 47 | 50 |
| Earnings per share | $ 1.34 | $ 1.73 | $ 2.23 |

*Note:* Figures may not add exactly because of rounding.

---

6. "Hospital Corp. to Buy INA Unit for $650 Million," *The Wall Street Journal,* April 21, 1981, p. 27.

**EXHIBIT 2**
Consolidated Balance Sheets at December 31, 1979–1981 (millions of dollars)

| | 1979 | 1980 | 1981 |
|---|---|---|---|
| Cash and cash equivalents . . . . . . . . . . . . . . . | $    30 | $    29 | $    50 |
| Accounts receivable, net   . . . . . . . . . . . . . . | 149 | 214 | 363 |
| Supplies   . . . . . . . . . . . . . . . . . . . . . | 29 | 44 | 65 |
| Other current assets   . . . . . . . . . . . . . . . | 10 | 15 | 18 |
| Current assets   . . . . . . . . . . . . . . . | 218 | 303 | 498 |
| Net property, plant, and equipment   . . . . . . . . . | 802 | 1,187 | 2,066 |
| Investments and other assets   . . . . . . . . . . . | 40 | 81 | 188 |
| Intangible assets   . . . . . . . . . . . . . . . . | 18 | 38 | 207 |
| Total assets   . . . . . . . . . . . . . . . | $1,078 | $1,610 | $2,958 |
| | | | |
| Accounts payable   . . . . . . . . . . . . . . . . | $    38 | $    58 | $    93 |
| Dividends payable   . . . . . . . . . . . . . . . . | 2 | 3 | 4 |
| Accrued liabilities   . . . . . . . . . . . . . . . . | 45 | 80 | 166 |
| Income taxes payable   . . . . . . . . . . . . . . | 56 | 71 | 61 |
| Current maturities of long-term debt   . . . . . . . . | 19 | 26 | 43 |
| Current liabilities   . . . . . . . . . . . . . . | 160 | 238 | 367 |
| Long-term debt   . . . . . . . . . . . . . . . . . | 427 | 775 | 1,649 |
| Deferred income taxes   . . . . . . . . . . . . . . | 74 | 85 | 117 |
| Other liabilities   . . . . . . . . . . . . . . . . | 30 | 43 | 58 |
| Total liabilities   . . . . . . . . . . . . . . | 691 | 1,141 | 2,191 |
| Common stock (issued 52,210,645 shares in 1981; 45,378,375 shares in 1980; 19,456,634 shares in 1979)   . . . . . . . . . . . . . . . . . | 19 | 45 | 52 |
| Additional paid-in capital   . . . . . . . . . . . . . | 157 | 144 | 342 |
| Retained earnings   . . . . . . . . . . . . . . . | 210 | 279 | 374 |
| Shareholders' equity   . . . . . . . . . . . . . | 387 | 469 | 768 |
| Total liabilities and shareholders' equity   . . . . . . . | $1,078 | $1,610 | $2,958 |

*Note:* Figures may not add exactly because of rounding.

**EXHIBIT 3**
Ten-Year Historical Summary, 1972–1981 (millions of dollars except per share data)

| | 1972 | 1973 | 1974 | 1975 | 1976 | 1977 | 1978 | 1979 | 1980 | 1981 |
|---|---|---|---|---|---|---|---|---|---|---|
| *Summary of Operations* | | | | | | | | | | |
| Operating revenues | $ 173 | $ 223 | $ 298 | $ 393 | $ 506 | $ 627 | $ 797 | $1,043 | $1,429 | $2,406 |
| Interest expense | 6 | 9 | 13 | 17 | 21 | 24 | 32 | 38 | 50 | 131 |
| Income before income taxes | 18 | 23 | 30 | 36 | 47 | 59 | 74 | 96 | 136 | 184 |
| Net income | 10 | 12 | 16 | 21 | 27 | 33 | 42 | 54 | 81 | 111 |
| Average shares | | | | | | | | | | |
| outstanding (millions)[a] | 35 | 34 | 34 | 35 | 38 | 39 | 40 | 41 | 47 | 50 |
| Earnings per share[a] | $ .30 | $ .35 | $ .45 | $ .59 | $ .71 | $ .86 | $ 1.05 | $ 1.34 | $ 1.73 | $ 2.23 |
| Cash dividends per share[a] | .02 | .04 | .05 | .06 | .09 | .12 | .17 | .22 | .27 | .34 |
| Dividend payout | 6.7% | 11.4% | 11.1% | 10.2% | 12.7% | 14.0% | 16.2% | 16.4% | 15.6% | 15.2% |
| *Financial Position* | | | | | | | | | | |
| Total assets | $ 275 | $ 321 | $ 417 | $ 508 | $ 602 | $ 709 | $ 857 | $1,078 | $1,610 | $2,958 |
| Total debt | 155 | 175 | 240 | 298 | 327 | 363 | 427 | 446 | 801 | 1,692 |
| Shareholders' equity | 91 | 107 | 121 | 142 | 186 | 215 | 252 | 387 | 469 | 768 |
| Book value per share (year-end) | $ 2.69 | $ 3.12 | $ 3.53 | $ 4.09 | $ 4.89 | $ 5.65 | $ 6.57 | $ 8.84 | $ 10.33 | $ 14.70 |
| Average price-earnings ratio | 33.7 | 18.1 | 7.3 | 8.0 | 9.2 | 8.6 | 10.9 | 11.8 | 15.9 | 18.5 |
| *Stock Performance* | | | | | | | | | | |
| High | $12.10 | $9.90 | $5.10 | $7.10 | $7.60 | $9.00 | $15.30 | $19.90 | $37.00 | $50.70 |
| Low | 8.10 | 2.80 | 1.50 | 2.30 | 5.40 | 5.80 | 7.50 | 11.60 | 17.90 | 31.70 |
| *Selected Ratios* | | | | | | | | | | |
| Current ratio | 1.3 | 1.4 | 1.2 | 1.5 | 1.5 | 1.4 | 1.4 | 1.4 | 1.3 | 1.4 |
| Net profit margin | 6.0% | 5.5% | 5.2% | 5.3% | 5.3% | 5.3% | 5.2% | 5.2% | 5.7% | 4.6% |
| Return on beginning assets | 5.3% | 4.4% | 4.9% | 5.0% | 5.3% | 5.5% | 5.9% | 6.3% | 7.5% | 6.9% |
| Return on beginning equity | 14.3% | 13.4% | 14.5% | 17.0% | 19.0% | 17.9% | 19.3% | 21.5% | 20.9% | 23.7% |
| Asset turnover | .89 | .81 | .93 | .94 | 1.00 | 1.04 | 1.12 | 1.22 | 1.33 | 1.50 |
| Total debt/Total capital | 63.1% | 62.0% | 66.4% | 67.8% | 63.7% | 62.7% | 62.9% | 53.5% | 63.1% | 68.8% |

a. Average share figures include unexercised options. Per share earnings and dividends were computed based on average shares outstanding.

**EXHIBIT 4**
Key Statistics for HCA's Hospitals, 1972–1981

| | 1972 | 1973 | 1974 | 1975 | 1976 | 1977 | 1978 | 1979 | 1980 | 1981 |
|---|---|---|---|---|---|---|---|---|---|---|
| *Hospitals in Operation* | | | | | | | | | | |
| Owned and leased, U.S. | 46 | 53 | 56 | 62 | 68 | 72 | 81 | 88 | 144 | 188 |
| Managed, U.S. | 2 | 4 | 6 | 8 | 15 | 21 | 26 | 45 | 56 | 146 |
| Owned and managed, international | — | — | — | 2 | 2 | 2 | 5 | 15 | 18 | 15 |
| Total | 48 | 57 | 62 | 72 | 85 | 95 | 112 | 148 | 188 | 349 |
| Bed capacity | 7,304 | 8,507 | 9,280 | 11,648 | 13,458 | 14,465 | 18,036 | 22,543 | 28,204 | 49,866 |
| Occupancy rate (U.S.-owned only) | na | na | 70% | 66% | 66% | 66% | 65% | 68% | 69% | 68% |
| *Sources of Revenues by Payer* | | | | | | | | | | |
| Cost-based | | | | | | | | | | |
| Medicare | 27% | 27% | 29% | 30% | 32% | 33% | 35% | 36% | 37% | 38% |
| Medicaid | 4 | 3 | 3 | 4 | 4 | 4 | 4 | 3 | 3 | 5 |
| Blue Cross | 8 | 9 | 8 | 7 | 5 | 5 | 5 | 4 | 4 | 3 |
| Total cost-based | 39% | 39% | 40% | 41% | 41% | 42% | 44% | 43% | 44% | 46% |
| Charge-based | 61 | 61 | 60 | 59 | 59 | 58 | 56 | 57 | 56 | 54 |
| Total | 100% | 100% | 100% | 100% | 100% | 100% | 100% | 100% | 100% | 100% |

na = not available.

**EXHIBIT 5**

Comparative Data on Selected Publicly Held Hospital Management Companies, 1980–1981 (millions of dollars except per share data)

| | Hospital Corporation of America | | Humana, Inc. | | American Medical International, Inc. | | National Medical Enterprises, Inc. | | Lifemark | |
|---|---|---|---|---|---|---|---|---|---|---|
| | 1980 | 1981 | 1980 | 1981 | 1980 | 1981 | 1980 | 1981 | 1980 | 1981 |
| *Summary of Operations* | | | | | | | | | | |
| Operating revenues | $1,429 | $2,406 | $1,392 | $1,704 | $ 766 | $1,117 | $ 723 | $1,044 | $ 203 | $ 323 |
| Interest expense | 50 | 131 | 76 | 60 | 25 | 41 | 26 | 33 | 6 | 12 |
| Income before income taxes | 136 | 184 | 120 | 177 | 66 | 97 | 54 | 96 | 16 | 31 |
| Net income | 81 | 111 | 65 | 93 | 33 | 51 | 29 | 52 | 14 | 18 |
| Earnings per share, primary | $ 1.73 | $ 2.23 | $ 1.53 | $ 2.33 | $ 1.23 | $ 1.60 | $ .91 | $ 1.24 | $ 1.77 | $ 1.80 |
| Cash dividends per share | .27 | .34 | .35 | .54 | .38 | .45 | .20 | .30 | .33 | .42 |
| Dividend payout | 15.6% | 15.2% | 22.9% | 23.2% | 30.9% | 28.1% | 22.0% | 24.2% | 18.6% | 23.3% |
| *Financial Position* | | | | | | | | | | |
| Total assets | $1,610 | $2,958 | $1,327 | $1,502 | $ 663 | $ 984 | $ 596 | $ 867 | $ 211 | $ 387 |
| Total debt | 801 | 1,692 | 757 | 776 | 312 | 396 | 274 | 299 | 102 | 171 |
| Preferred stock | – | – | 66 | 64 | – | – | 5 | 5 | – | – |
| Shareholders' equity | 469 | 768 | 216 | 297 | 201 | 327 | 200 | 376 | 61 | 135 |
| Book value per share | $10.33 | $14.70 | $ 5.97 | $ 8.01 | $ 7.36 | $10.20 | $ 5.47 | $ 8.39 | $ 7.56 | $13.18 |
| Average price-earnings ratio | 15.9 | 18.5 | 11.9 | 16.3 | 18.3 | 16.9 | 8.2 | 15.6 | 16.1 | 10.3 |
| *Stock Performance* | | | | | | | | | | |
| High | $37.00 | $50.70 | $26.20 | $46.38 | $22.50 | $32.50 | $10.50 | $27.25 | $35.80 | $28.10 |
| Low | 17.90 | 31.70 | 10.25 | 29.75 | 9.88 | 21.50 | 4.38 | 11.50 | 21.20 | 9.10 |
| Bond rating[a] | A | A | NR | B+ | Ba | NR | Ba | B+ | Ba | BB+ |
| *Selected Ratios* | | | | | | | | | | |
| Current ratio | 1.3 | 1.4 | 1.4 | 1.4 | 1.6 | 1.5 | 1.8 | 2.0 | 1.7 | 1.2 |
| Net profit margin | 5.7% | 4.6% | 4.6% | 5.5% | 4.3% | 4.5% | 4.1% | 5.0% | 6.9% | 5.7% |
| Return on beginning assets | 7.5% | 6.9% | 5.4% | 7.0% | 6.5% | 7.7% | 9.2% | 8.7% | 11.1% | 8.7% |
| Return on beginning equity | 20.9% | 23.7% | 38.1% | 43.1% | 21.3% | 25.2% | 27.0% | 25.9% | 40.3% | 30.3% |
| Asset turnover | 1.3 | 1.5 | 1.2 | 1.3 | 1.5 | 1.7 | 2.3 | 1.8 | 1.6 | 1.5 |
| Total debt/Total capital | 63.1% | 68.8% | 72.8% | 68.2% | 60.8% | 54.8% | 57.2% | 44.0% | 62.7% | 55.9% |
| *Hospitals in Operation* | | | | | | | | | | |
| Owned/managed | 188 | 349 | 90 | 89 | 61 | 102 | 54[c] | 57[c] | 30 | 35 |
| Bed capacity | 28,204 | 49,866 | 16,765 | 16,431 | 6,117[b] | 9,713[b] | 6,593[c] | 6,929[c] | 3,546 | 4,563 |
| Occupancy rate | 69%[d] | 68%[d] | 58.9% | 61.3% | 60.6%[b] | na | na | na | na | na |

*(continued)*

**EXHIBIT 5** (*concluded*)

| | Hospital Corporation of America | | Humana, Inc. | | American Medical International, Inc. | | National Medical Enterprises, Inc. | | Lifemark | |
|---|---|---|---|---|---|---|---|---|---|---|
| | 1980 | 1981 | 1980 | 1981 | 1980 | 1981 | 1980 | 1981 | 1980 | 1981 |
| *Sources of Revenues by Payer* | | | | | | | | | | |
| Cost-based | | | | | | | | | | |
| Medicare | 37% | 38% | 39% | 40% | 45% | 45% | 42.1% | 42.0% | – | – |
| Medicaid | 3 | 5 | 5 | 5 | 7 | 7 | 12.6 | 12.7 | – | – |
| Blue Cross | 4 | 3 | 5 | 5 | 3 | 2 | 4.1 | 4.5 | – | – |
| Total cost-based | 44% | 46% | 49% | 50% | 55% | 54% | 58.8% | 59.2% | 44% | 42% |
| Charge-based | 56 | 54 | 51 | 50 | 45 | 46 | 41.2 | 40.8 | 56 | 58 |
| Total | 100% | 100% | 100% | 100% | 100% | 100% | 100.0% | 100.0% | 100% | 100% |
| *Growth Rates, 1976–1981* | | | | | | | | | | |
| Revenues | | 35.3% | | 41.1% | | 31.2% | | 47.0% | | 31.0% |
| Net income | | 32.4 | | 54.6 | | 46.1 | | 52.7 | | 40.9 |
| Total assets | | 34.2 | | 30.0 | | 22.7 | | 34.3 | | 39.7 |
| Hospitals in operation | | 30.1 | | 6.8 | | 13.4 | | 18.7 | | 11.7 |

*Note:* Fiscal year ends August 31 for Humana and American Medical International; December 31 for HCA and Lifemark; May 31 for National Medical Enterprises. NR = not rated; na = not available.

a. Excludes convertibles.

b. For owned hospitals only.

c. Excludes long-term care facilities (i.e., nursing homes).

d. U.S.-owned only.

**EXHIBIT 6**
HCA's Hospital Locations in the United States

**EXHIBIT 7**
Schedule of Outstanding Long-Term Debt, 1979–1981 (millions of dollars)

| | *1979* | *1980* | *1981* |
|---|---|---|---|
| Mortgage notes and bonds, | | | |
| 6%–16½%, due through 1998 . . . . . . . . . . | $288 | $153 | $ 176 |
| Revenue bonds, 6¼%–13½%, due through 2011 . . . . | 63 | 102 | 134 |
| Notes, debentures, and capitalized leases, | | | |
| 7%–16½%, due through 1999 . . . . . . . . . . | 75 | 227 | 281 |
| Revolving credit and term loan agreements at | | | |
| prime or LIBOR, plus ½%–⅝% . . . . . . . . . | – | 168 | 515 |
| Commercial paper and bank financing, 13¼% | | | |
| composite effective rate | | | |
| at December 31, 1981[a] . . . . . . . . . . . | – | 125 | 208 |
| Convertible subordinated debentures: | | | |
| 8¾%, due 1996, convertible at $43.50 per share . . . | – | – | 80 |
| 8¾%, due 2006, convertible at $41.17 per share . . . | – | – | 125 |
| 12%, due 1996, convertible at $62.30 per share . . . | – | – | 81 |
| Guaranteed notes, 15½%, due 1988 . . . . . . . . | – | – | 50 |
| Total . . . . . . . . . . . . . . . . . . | $427 | $775 | $1,649 |

Debt maturing in the next 5 years ($ millions):
| | |
|---|---|
| 1982 | $ 34 |
| 1983 | 70 |
| 1984 | 71 |
| 1985 | 117 |
| 1986 | 163 |

a. In 1980 and 1981 the company entered into revolving credit agreements with a group of banks, aggregating $160 million and $278 million, respectively. The lines were used to support commercial paper and other bank financing during these 2 years. Because of the availability of long-term financing under these agreements, the company classified the commercial paper issue under long-term debt.

**EXHIBIT 8**
Debt Issued in the U.S. Public Market by Industrial Corporations with Varying Credit Ratings, 1974–1981 (millions of dollars)

| Credit Rating | 1974 | | 1975 | | 1976 | | 1977 | | 1978 | | 1979 | | 1980 | | 1981 | |
|---|---|---|---|---|---|---|---|---|---|---|---|---|---|---|---|---|
| Aaa | $1,650 | 25.1% | $2,875 | 24.0% | $700 | 11.7% | $800 | 20.5% | $275 | 8.6% | $1,550 | 27.4% | $1,750 | 17.9% | $1,852 | 20.8% |
| Aa | 2,415 | 36.7 | 3,310 | 27.7 | 2,030 | 33.8 | 1,125 | 28.9 | 700 | 21.8 | 1,800 | 31.8 | 2,900 | 29.7 | 2,458 | 27.7 |
| A | 2,060 | 31.3 | 5,355 | 44.7 | 2,205 | 36.8 | 960 | 24.6 | 1,310 | 40.8 | 1,500 | 26.5 | 4,220 | 43.2 | 3,887 | 43.7 |
| Baa | 440 | 6.7 | 420 | 3.5 | 1,010 | 16.8 | 445 | 11.4 | 210 | 6.5 | 0 | 0 | 345 | 3.6 | 0 | 0 |
| Other | 15 | .2 | 9 | .1 | 53 | .9 | 567 | 14.6 | 713 | 22.3 | 809 | 14.3 | 549 | 5.6 | 690 | 7.8 |
| | $6,580 | 100.0% | $11,969 | 100.0% | $5,998 | 100.0% | $3,897 | 100.0% | $3,208 | 100.0% | $5,659 | 100.0% | $9,764 | 100.0% | $8,887 | 100.0% |

*Source:* Salomon Brothers Inc.

# Crown Corporation

In February 1969, Walter Bennett, treasurer of Crown Corporation, was considering several financing alternatives. Crown's decision to integrate backward into the production of primary aluminum ingot had resulted in very heavy capital expenditures. Its need for funds for working capital and for completion of a large aluminum plant now outstripped the company's internal cash generation, and it would be necessary to raise $30 million within the next six months to cover capital needs for 1969. Mr. Bennett hoped to develop a financing program that would meet the immediate and the longer-term needs without jeopardizing Crown's 70-cent dividend rate.

## Company Description

A series of acquisitions and divestitures during the 1960s had totally transformed Crown Corporation from a mining company into a manufacturer of superalloy castings for aircraft and industrial uses and aluminum products for the building, packaging, and aircraft industries. Sales were evenly divided between castings and aluminum products.

Crown's castings were for the most part designed for operation in the "hot part" of the gas turbine engine. The company worked from designs prepared chiefly by aircraft engine manufacturers. These manufacturers, in their endeavor to obtain greater thrust, designed parts that would function at engine operating temperatures ranging to 2,150 degrees Fahrenheit. The high temperatures required

Copyright © 1973 by the President and Fellows of Harvard College.
Harvard Business School case 273–086.

**TABLE A**
Consumption, Production, and Sales of Aluminum, 1965–1973

| | **Actual** (millions of pounds) | | | | **Estimates** (millions of pounds) | | |
|---|---|---|---|---|---|---|---|
| | *1965* | *1966* | *1967* | *1968* | *1969* | *1970* | *1973* |
| Consumption of primary aluminum by Crown's fabricating divisions . . | 94 | 107 | 116 | 135 | 160 | 185 | 290 |
| Production of primary aluminum | | | | | | | |
| Intalco . . . . . . . . . . . . | 0 | 16 | 69 | 88 | 130 | 130 | 130 |
| Eastalco . . . . . . . . . . | 0 | 0 | 0 | 0 | 0 | 85 | 170 |
| Purchases (sales) of primary aluminum by Crown . . . . . . | 94 | 91 | 47 | 47 | 30 | (30) | (10) |

the use of precision castings for blades and vanes. The techniques and know-how involved in casting operations were important, and the commercial success of such an operation was in large measure dependent upon achieving a low ratio of rejects. Crown's constant emphasis on quality and technical excellence had established a high level of confidence among its customers. For adherence to a rigid standard of performance and quality, it had been selected to participate in the majority of United States jet engine programs in the past 10 years. (Exhibit 1 provides information on jet engine production in the United States.)

The other half of Crown's sales comprised aluminum products, including a broad product line for the building and construction industry (see Table A). Major efforts had been made to increase the company's captive source of primary aluminum ingot for consumption by its fabricating operations. To ensure a steady and economical source, Crown had become a producer of primary aluminum in 1966 through participation with American Metal Climax, Inc. in a project known as Intalco. Crown's share of Intalco's output was 130 million pounds, roughly 81% of its total need.

In 1967 the decision was made to build a second aluminum ingot plant, named Eastalco, at a cost of $50 million. Eastalco was expected to start operations in mid-1970, providing Crown with additional primary aluminum capacity of 85 million pounds a year and increased net income of $3–4 million. A planned addition of 85 million pounds in 1972 would raise Eastalco's capacity to 170 million pounds and would meet the company's objective to be a fully integrated producer (see Table A).

## Company Performance

Crown's sales had risen sharply from $60 million in 1958 to $230 million in 1968 on the strength of 23 acquisitions, strong internal growth, and a firming of aluminum prices.[1] The company's earnings had been considerably more erratic,

---

1. The history of the aluminum industry is drawn in large part from Y. Levy, *Aluminum: Past and Future* (San Francisco: Federal Reserve Bank of San Francisco, 1971).

however, with the volatility the result largely of instability in its aluminum business. After reaching a peak of $1.13 in 1959, earnings per share fell to $.34 in 1963 as overcapacity developed in the aluminum business and prices of fabricated products were eroded. (Crown's operating results are shown in Exhibit 2.) The "great growth potential" of aluminum had encouraged major capacity additions by established producers and entry by new producers during the 1950s. Domestic industry capacity rose by 79% between 1954 and 1960. American producers were also faced with a tremendous buildup in capacity elsewhere in the world. After a decade of generally rising prices, excess capacity began to take its toll in 1958. In April of that year, the producer price for American ingot was lowered from 26 to 24 cents per pound to match a similar reduction initiated by Canadian firms in the world market. By December 1962 the quotation had dropped to 22.5 cents per pound.

In the fabricated products market, where the relative ease of entry had brought in many small- and medium-sized independent concerns, competition for the available business was even keener and price erosion more severe. List prices of fabricated products dropped on the average about 20% between late 1961 and late 1963. (Exhibit 3 provides data on aluminum shipments and prices.) The decline in actual market prices undoubtedly was even sharper because of a method of discounting—called commodity pricing—that was undertaken in order to penetrate new markets. This method, most prevalent in sheet, strip, coil, and plate products, involved selling a product for a specific application at a price lower than the published price. The seller then attempted to confine the lower price to specific product areas so as not to reduce revenues. However, in the late 1950s, the whole price structure came tumbling down and profits came tumbling after. Profits of the three major aluminum companies collapsed from $175 million in 1956 to a low of $88 million in 1960.

Demand-supply conditions in the industry finally improved in the early 1960s and with the improvement came sharply higher earnings for Crown and other aluminum producers. Over the 1961–1966 period, industry shipments of aluminum increased by 14% annually. Despite increases in supply, the price of ingot went up four times between October 1963 and November 1964, from a low of 22.5 to 24.5 cents per pound. But price weakness continued at the fabricating level during this period. The hundreds of small fabricators lowered prices to obtain business for their idle machinery, while consumers increasingly came to disregard published mill prices.

Prices of fabricated products remained weak until 1965, when strike-anticipation hedge buying bolstered demand and pushed up operating rates. Producers raised prices several times early in the year, and then again after a new 3-year labor contract was signed in June. For the next 3 years shipments of aluminum products continued to rise 8–10% annually and prices firmed further. Shortly after a new 3-year labor contract was signed in 1968, producers raised the price of ingot by 4%, to 26 cents per pound, and the price of fabricated products by a comparable amount. After a brief period of discounting in the wake of the labor settlement, the new list prices apparently took hold. In January 1969, producers raised the price of ingot from 26 to 27 cents per pound and prices on a wide range of mill products by an average of 5%, and further price increases were anticipated.

The strong price situation improved industry profitability dramatically. Profits of the three major aluminum firms rebounded from the 1960 low of $88 million to $230 million in 1966 (see Exhibit 4). Crown's record was no less dramatic. Rising from a low of $.34 per share in 1963, Crown's earnings reached $2.03 per share in 1967. Its stock, which had sold at less than $5 per share in 1963, reached a high of $51 in mid-1968 on the strength of record earnings and an increased dividend rate.

## Surpluses of the Seventies?

The improved industry price structure in the late 1960s encouraged aluminum producers to move forward to meet the demands and the opportunities of the 1970s. Throughout the world, producers began to build new smelters and enlarge older ones. In the United States the expansion in capacity contemplated over the next 3 years seemed moderate in terms of past trends in demand. American producers were scheduled to boost their primary production potential from almost 4.2 million tons in 1970 to 5 million tons by 1973, or at a 6.4% annual rate. This rate of expansion, although substantial, was below the 10% rate of growth of domestic aluminum consumption during the 1960s.

In reducing their rate of expansion, U.S. producers recognized that they were facing the strongest counterattack from other materials in their history. Aluminum's success in penetrating the territory staked out by other metals had been phenomenal. Shipments of aluminum ingot and mill products grew at more than twice the rate of durable goods output and construction activity over the 1960s. The industry was successful, through research and development and aggressive marketing techniques, in creating new uses for the metal and in displacing traditional materials in older applications.

The steel industry, the giant of the metal field with 1968 ingot production of 130 million tons as against aluminum's 3 million tons, had initiated a strong fight to ward off the lightweight metal's further advances. In particular, steel was fighting hard to protect its position in the $3.5 billion can market and in the rapid transit market, which could evolve into a $10 billion outlet over the 1970s. The copper industry was also fighting to protect its markets, and the plastics industry was challenging aluminum in each of aluminum's principal markets— construction, transportation, and packaging.

However, the most effective dampening influence on the domestic industry was the huge increase in aluminum capacity abroad. Plans in 1969 called for capacity elsewhere in the non-Communist world to rise at well over double the U.S. rate between 1970 and 1973, as major European and Asian nations built up their own production in an effort to reduce their dependence on imports. With almost 4.4 million tons of new capacity—3.5 million tons overseas plus .9 million tons in the United States—scheduled to come on stream in the 1970–1973 period, world capacity could rise from about 9.4 million to 13.7 million tons, or at a 14% annual rate.

This expansion in capacity would exceed the anticipated growth in demand, since most industry analysts expected that world aluminum consumption would not exceed the 9% rate of growth registered during the 1960–1968 period. If all the capacity programmed was brought in on schedule, growth in consumption at the 9% level over the next several years could result in as much as 2 million tons of excess capacity by 1973, representing about 15% of the industry's total production capability.

Before jumping to the conclusion that the industry's price structure was in danger of weakening, however, Mr. Bennett realized that the major aluminum producers might stretch out their expansion projects over a longer period, especially where expansion was scheduled through incremental additions to existing plants. Projects not yet started might be postponed or canceled. Furthermore, he did not underestimate the ability of the industry to boost consumption above anticipated levels by imaginative research and development and marketing programs.

## Crown's Expected Growth

Mr. Bennett expected that Crown's sales would increase at 6–8% annually, exclusive of acquisitions, over the foreseeable future. No growth was forecast through 1974 in the precision castings business as sharp reductions in defense procurement needs would offset the 15% per year increase in commercial sales. However, sales of aluminum products were expected to rise by 15–20% annually as the company broadened its penetration of major aluminum consuming markets. This sales growth would necessitate heavy spending on aluminum reduction facilities and fabricating capacity. Total capital expenditures, including the Eastalco project, were forecast at $39 million in 1969, $32 million in 1970, $7 million in 1971, and $50 million in 1972. The heavy capital spending would require that Crown raise $30 million in 1969, $22 million in 1970, and $30 million in 1972.

## Financing Alternatives

Several alternatives were open to Crown to meet its financing needs in 1969 (see the balance sheets for 1965–1968 shown in Exhibit 5). The company's investment bankers believed that a $30-million common stock issue was possible and pointed to the future financing flexibility afforded by the use of equity financing. On the other hand, the dilution of earnings per share that would result from sale of additional stock was a matter of concern to Mr. Bennett. Crown stock had fallen from $51 per share in May 1968 to a level of $30 per share as investors reacted to disappointing earnings in 1968. (Comparative industry stock price data are provided in Exhibit 6.) Further near-term price weakness seemed likely as earnings per share remained depressed as Crown absorbed heavy start-up costs for the production of the main landing gear for the McDonnell Douglas DC-10 in 1969. Under these conditions, announcement of a large equity issue would drive the stock price down to the low twenties, at which price it would be necessary to sell 1.4 million shares to raise the $30 million net to the company. Mr. Bennett wondered whether equity financing should be deferred until the company resumed its pattern of earnings gains.

As an alternative to equity financing, a consortium of commercial banks had agreed to lend the company up to $30 million at 7¼% interest. The term loan would be repayable at an annual rate of $5 million beginning in 1970 and ending in 1975. Under the provisions of the loan agreement, net working capital must exceed $55 million, dividend payments were restricted to earnings accumulated after the date of the loan agreement, and additional funded debt was limited to $20 million.

It would also be possible to place a $30 million subordinated convertible debenture issue privately with the Northern Life Insurance Company. The debentures would carry a coupon of 6% with annual debt retirement of $2 million in years 6 through 20. The issue would not be callable for 10 years, except at par for mandatory debt retirement, and would be convertible into common stock at $31.50.

Mr. Bennett was interested in the debt alternatives. Although the company's use of debt had increased sharply and coverage ratios had narrowed, its coverage of interest costs was still considered adequate. On the other hand, the flexibility afforded by use of equity financing could be valuable in future years.

**EXHIBIT 1**

Aircraft Engine Production, 1946–1968 (number of engines)

| | Total | Military | | | Civil | | |
|---|---|---|---|---|---|---|---|
| | | Total Military | Recip-rocal | Jet | Total Civil | Recip-rocal | Jet |
| 1946 . . | 43,407 | 2,585 | 1,680 | 905 | 40,822 | 40,822 | – |
| 1947 . . | 20,912 | 4,561 | 2,683 | 1,878 | 16,351 | 16,351 | – |
| 1948 . . | 14,027 | 4,988 | 2,495 | 2,493 | 9,039 | 9,039 | – |
| 1949 . . | 11,972 | 7,990 | 2,981 | 5,009 | 3,982 | 3,982 | – |
| 1950 . . | 13,675 | 9,361 | 3,122 | 6,239 | 4,314 | 4,314 | – |
| 1951 . . | 20,867 | 16,287 | 6,471 | 9,816 | 4,580 | 4,580 | – |
| 1952 . . | 31,041 | 25,659 | 8,731 | 16,928 | 5,382 | 5,382 | – |
| 1953 . . | 40,263 | 33,616 | 13,365 | 20,251 | 6,647 | 6,647 | – |
| 1954 . . | 26,959 | 21,440 | 7,868 | 13,572 | 5,519 | 5,519 | – |
| 1955 . . | 21,108 | 13,469 | 3,875 | 9,594 | 7,639 | 7,639 | – |
| 1956 . . | 21,348 | 9,849 | 2,663 | 7,186 | 11,499 | 11,499 | – |
| 1957 . . | 21,984 | 11,087 | 2,429 | 8,658 | 10,897 | 10,859 | 38 |
| 1958 . . | 18,869 | 8,121 | 1,452 | 6,669 | 10,748 | 10,233 | 515 |
| 1959 . . | 17,162 | 4,626 | 661 | 3,965 | 12,536 | 11,152 | 1,384 |
| 1960 . . | 16,189 | 3,673 | 756 | 2,917 | 12,516 | 10,891 | 1,625 |
| 1961 . . | 15,832 | 5,172 | 417 | 4,755 | 10,660 | 9,669 | 991 |
| 1962 . . | 15,919 | 5,441 | 241 | 5,200 | 10,478 | 9,921 | 557 |
| 1963 . . | 17,185 | 5,390 | 155 | 5,235 | 11,795 | 11,322 | 473 |
| 1964 . . | 19,585 | 5,380 | 175 | 5,205 | 14,205 | 13,346 | 859 |
| 1965 . . | 23,378 | 5,191 | 92 | 5,099 | 18,187 | 17,018 | 1,169 |
| 1966 . . | 30,810 | 7,548 | 45 | 7,503 | 23,262 | 21,324 | 1,938 |
| 1967 . . | 28,858 | 8,046 | – | 8,046 | 20,812 | 18,324 | 2,488 |
| 1968 . . | 29,761 | 8,542 | – | 8,542 | 21,219 | 17,806 | 3,413 |

*Source: Aerospace Facts and Figures 1973/1974* (New York: Aerospace Industries Association of America, Inc., 1973), p. 48.

**EXHIBIT 2**

Selected Operating Data, 1963–1968 (millions of dollars except per share data)

| | 1962 | 1963 | 1964 | 1965 | 1966 | 1967 | 1968 |
|---|---|---|---|---|---|---|---|
| Net sales . . . | $ 110 | $ 122 | $ 122 | $ 141 | $ 176 | $ 213 | $ 230 |
| Operating profit[a] . | $ 8.3 | $ 4.6 | $ 5.5 | $ 9.1 | $ 18.5 | $ 27.8 | $ 28.5 |
| Other income (expense)[b] . . | (.4) | (.6) | (.3) | (.8) | (.1) | (.7) | (1.0) |
| Income before taxes | 7.9 | 4.0 | 5.2 | 8.3 | 18.4 | 27.1 | 27.5 |
| Federal income taxes . . . . | 3.7 | 1.5 | 2.3 | 3.6 | 7.6 | 12.3 | 13.8 |
| Net income . . . | $ 4.2 | $ 2.5 | $ 2.9 | $ 4.7 | $ 10.8 | $ 14.8 | $ 13.7 |
| Earnings per share | $ .57 | $ .34 | $ .42 | $ .66 | $ 1.50 | $ 2.03 | $ 1.87 |
| Dividends per share | 0 | .20 | .20 | .23 | .40 | .60 | .70 |
| Market price | | | | | | | |
| High . . . . | 9 | 7 | 7 | 11 | 27 | 51 | 51 |
| Low . . . . . | 5 | 5 | 5 | 6 | 10 | 22 | 32 |
| Price-earnings ratio | | | | | | | |
| High . . . . | 16 | 21 | 17 | 17 | 18 | 25 | 27 |
| Low . . . . . | 9 | 15 | 12 | 9 | 7 | 11 | 17 |

a. After deduction of depreciation expense ($5 million in 1968).

b. Other income and other expenses including interest expense are offset against each other.

**EXHIBIT 3**
Price Chronology

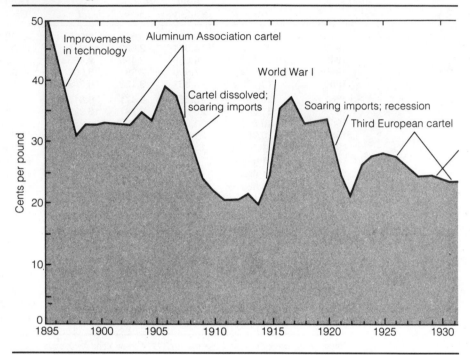

Little over a century ago, aluminum was still a rare metal, costing $545 per pound in 1852. Yet after several decades of technological advance, the price dropped to $8 per pound in 1885. Then, with the development of the electrolytic process for producing aluminum, the metal began to come within the reach of the average consumer. On the eve of World War I, aluminum was selling for 19½ cents per pound, thanks to the growth of a technologically advanced industry in Europe and North America—and despite the efforts of producers' cartels to maintain a high price structure for the metal. As a consequence of this price decline, aluminum markets were no longer confined to specialty items in the cooking, military, and surgical fields but had spread also to tonnage items in the fast-growing electrical and automotive industries. During World War I prices practically doubled despite the rapid expansion of production facilities. But by the end of 1921 prices were back to prewar levels as producers here and abroad fought to find peacetime markets for wartime-swollen supplies. During the next several decades, aluminum prices trended downwards. In the 1920s and 1930s industry cartels set prices and

**EXHIBIT 3** *(continued)*

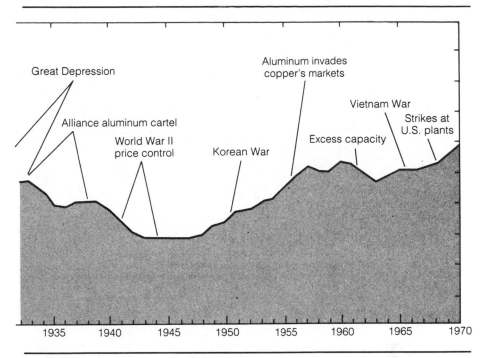

imposed output restrictions worldwide in an attempt to manage markets that had been unsettled by lagging demand and increasing capacity. In the 1940s, as the domestic industry expanded rapidly to meet insatiable wartime demands, the government held the price line by setting the ingot price at 14 cents per pound. Prices have generally moved upward since World War II. The surprisingly high level of civilian reconversion demand, plus the heavy Korean War and strategic-stock-pile demand, helped push prices from 14 to 25½ cents per pound between 1947 and 1957. But then prices slumped, reaching 22½ cents per pound in 1963, as military and civilian demand turned sluggish in the face of a tremendous buildup in capacity throughout the world. Finally, with the industrial expansion and the war boom of the late 1960s, prices increased again.

*Source:* Y. Levy, *Aluminum: Past and Future* (San Francisco: Federal Reserve Bank of San Francisco, 1971).

**EXHIBIT 3** *(concluded)*

Statistics on Industry Shipments and Prices: total Aluminum Industry Shipments, 1942–1969 (millions of pounds, net shipments)

| | Total | Ingot | Domestic Mill Products | Imported Mill Products |
|---|---|---|---|---|
| 1942 . . . . . . . . . | 1,452.7 | 507.4 | 933.6 | 11.7 |
| 1943 . . . . . . . . . | 2,217.2 | 724.6 | 1,492.4 | .2 |
| 1944 . . . . . . . . . | 2,566.4 | 952.0 | 1,613.0 | 1.4 |
| 1945 . . . . . . . . . | 1,886.4 | 549.2 | 1,329.8 | 7.4 |
| 1946 . . . . . . . . . | 1,672.4 | 529.2 | 1,140.8 | 2.4 |
| 1947 . . . . . . . . . | 2,040.1 | 631.8 | 1,408.2 | .1 |
| 1948 . . . . . . . . . | 2,282.0 | 629.8 | 1,640.2 | 12.0 |
| 1949 . . . . . . . . . | 1,654.1 | 479.9 | 1,158.1 | 16.1 |
| 1950 . . . . . . . . . | 2,460.6 | 724.6 | 1,713.4 | 22.6 |
| 1951 . . . . . . . . . | 2,506.6 | 709.8 | 1,756.2 | 40.6 |
| 1952 . . . . . . . . . | 2,694.5 | 811.2 | 1,850.4 | 32.9 |
| 1953 . . . . . . . . . | 3,276.8 | 982.9 | 2,228.2 | 65.7 |
| 1954 . . . . . . . . . | 3,036.0 | 920.2 | 2,086.6 | 29.2 |
| 1955 . . . . . . . . . | 4,035.1 | 1,205.4 | 2,791.8 | 37.9 |
| 1956 . . . . . . . . . | 4,154.6 | 1,223.5 | 2,885.8 | 45.3 |
| 1957 . . . . . . . . . | 3,880.1 | 1,161.6 | 2,677.6 | 40.9 |
| 1958 . . . . . . . . . | 3,631.2 | 974.0 | 2,597.1 | 60.1 |
| 1959 . . . . . . . . . | 5,061.0 | 1,575.0 | 3,386.1 | 100.1 |
| 1960 . . . . . . . . . | 4,732.5 | 1,608.6 | 3,049.1 | 74.8 |
| 1961 . . . . . . . . . | 4,970.1 | 1,536.6 | 3,345.1 | 88.4 |
| 1962 . . . . . . . . . | 5,772.5 | 1,858.6 | 3,811.3 | 102.7 |
| 1963 . . . . . . . . . | 6,377.0 | 2,032.6 | 4,257.2 | 87.2 |
| 1964 . . . . . . . . . | 7,171.3 | 2,228.6 | 4,834.9 | 107.8 |
| 1965 . . . . . . . . . | 8,150.2 | 2,337.3 | 5,679.4 | 133.5 |
| 1966 . . . . . . . . . | 9,031.6 | 2,340.1 | 6,457.5 | 234.1 |
| 1967 . . . . . . . . . | 8,946.4 | 2,486.4 | 6,350.6 | 109.5 |
| 1968 . . . . . . . . . | 9,977.4 | 2,694.8 | 7,167.0 | 115.6 |
| 1969[a] . . . . . . . . . | 10,825.0 | 3,050.0 | 7,660.0 | 115.0 |

*Sources:* Ingot and mill products, domestic: 1942–1945—Aluminum and Magnesium Division, War Production Board; 1946 to date—U.S. Department of Commerce, Bureau of the Census, Industry Division, and Bureau of Domestic Commerce, Aluminum and Magnesium Industries Operations, Facts for Industry 1946–1959, and Current Industrial Report Series M33–2, 1960 to date.

Mill products, imported: U.S. Department of Commerce, Bureau of the Census, Foreign Trade Division, and CIR Series M33-2.

*Note:* Details may not add to totals because of rounding.

a. Forecast.

**EXHIBIT 4**

Charts Showing Improvement in Profits of the Three Major Aluminum Firms in the Late 1960s along with Rising Prices

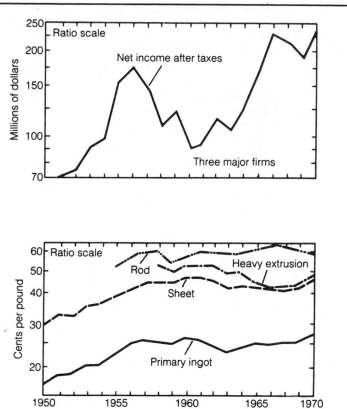

*Source:* Y. Levy, *Aluminum: Past and Future* (San Francisco: Federal Reserve Bank of San Francisco, 1971).

**EXHIBIT 5**
Balance Sheets at December 31, 1965–1968 (millions of dollars)

|  | 1965 | 1966 | 1967 | 1968 |
|---|---|---|---|---|
| Cash | $ 3 | $ 3 | $ 5 | $ 4 |
| Marketable securities | 7 | 10 | 23 | 6 |
| Accounts receivable | 20 | 23 | 35 | 42 |
| Inventories | 28 | 38 | 45 | 50 |
| Other | 0 | 0 | 1 | 1 |
| Current assets | 58 | 74 | 109 | 103 |
| Investments in aluminum plants | | | | |
| Intalco | 32 | 29 | 34 | 36 |
| Eastalco | 0 | 0 | 0 | 4 |
| Other net property, plant and equipment | 28 | 31 | 34 | 42 |
| Other | 3 | 4 | 4 | 4 |
| Total assets | $121 | $138 | $181 | $189 |
| | | | | |
| Accounts payable | $ 8 | $ 10 | $ 13 | $ 14 |
| Accrued liabilities | 6 | 7 | 7 | 10 |
| Accrued taxes | 4 | 8 | 8 | 6 |
| Dividends payable | 1 | 1 | 1 | 1 |
| Current maturities—long-term debt | 2 | 2 | 2 | 4 |
| Current liabilities | 21 | 28 | 31 | 35 |
| Long-term debt[a] | 30 | 28 | 56 | 52 |
| Deferred federal taxes | 1 | 2 | 3 | 3 |
| Stockholders' equity (7,273,000 shares outstanding at year-end 1968) | 69 | 80 | 91 | 99 |
| Total liabilities and net worth | $121 | $138 | $181 | $189 |

a. Crown Corporation placed a $56 million debt issue directly with several life insurance companies in 1967. Of the proceeds, $26 million represented a refinancing of existing debt and the balance of $30 million represented new money to the company. The debentures have a coupon of 6% with debt retirement of $4 million annually beginning in 1968 and ending in 1981.

**EXHIBIT 6**
Comparative Data on Aluminum Companies

| | Alcan | Alcoa | Harvey | Crown | Braun[a] | S&P 425 Industrials |
|---|---|---|---|---|---|---|
| **Earnings per share** | | | | | | |
| 1962 | $1.14 | $2.52 | $1.19 | $.57 | $1.74 | $3.87 |
| 1963 | 1.01 | 2.27 | .90 | .34 | 1.23 | 4.24 |
| 1964 | 1.57 | 2.72 | .77 | .42 | 1.55 | 4.83 |
| 1965 | 1.93 | 3.41 | .53 | .66 | 2.14 | 5.51 |
| 1966 | 2.41 | 4.83 | 2.24 | 1.50 | 3.30 | 5.89 |
| 1967 | 1.94 | 4.93 | 2.36 | 2.03 | 3.00 | 5.66 |
| 1968 | 2.14 | 4.75 | 2.16 | 1.87 | 2.81 | 6.15 |
| 1969 est. | 2.30 | 5.40 | 1.75 | 1.85[b] | 3.00 | 6.25 |
| **Price-earnings ratio** | | | | | | |
| 1962 | 15–25 | 18–27 | 13–25 | 9–16 | 14–21 | 17 |
| 1963 | 20–28 | 23–31 | 20–27 | 15–21 | 25–34 | 18 |
| 1964 | 17–21 | 22–30 | 22–29 | 12–19 | 18–27 | 18 |
| 1965 | 13–17 | 18–23 | 34–44 | 9–17 | 13–19 | 17 |
| 1966 | 10–18 | 14–20 | 9–13 | 7–18 | 9–16 | 15 |
| 1967 | 12–17 | 14–19 | 11–25 | 11–25 | 13–20 | 18 |
| 1968 | 10–13 | 13–17 | 15–25 | 17–27 | 15–17 | 18 |
| Feb. 1969 | 13 | 14 | 20 | 16 | 13 | 18 |
| 1968 sales ($ millions) | $1,081 | $1,353 | $ 177 | $230 | $ 850 | – |
| Book value per share (1968) | $  23 | $  49 | $ 20 | $ 13 | $ 25 | – |
| Current dividend rate | 1.10 | 1.80 | 1.20 | .70 | 1.00 | 3.21 |
| Long-term debt as percent of total capital | 46% | 39% | 41% | 34% | 55% | – |
| Times interest earned | 5.2 | 6.6 | 6.7 | 9.1 | 4.8 | – |
| **Debt rating** | | | | | | |
| Senior debt | A | A | – | NR | NR | – |
| Convertible subordinated debt | – | BBB | BBB | – | – | – |

NR = not rated.

a. Affiliated with Braun Industries.

b. Before any new financing.

*Financing Decisions and Tactics*

# American Telephone and Telegraph Company (1983)

On the evening of January 8, 1982, AT&T announced that it had agreed to a settlement of the Justice Department's antitrust suit against the company. The settlement provided that AT&T would divest itself of its 22 local telephone operating companies by January 1984. The scope of this reorganization (referred to as divestiture) would require a major rearrangement of AT&T's capital structure. AT&T's treasurer had begun the process in 1982 by the public sale of more than $1.5 billion in new stock and a sharp reduction in the sale of new debt. At the beginning of 1983 the treasurer had to decide what further steps would be necessary in the final year before divestiture.

## Company Background

Founded in 1876 on the basis of Alexander Graham Bell's original telephone patent, the American Telephone and Telegraph Company (commonly called the Bell System) had provided telephone service in the United States for more than a century. Prior to divestiture, AT&T supplied telecommunications services to over 80% of U.S. telephone users. This was done primarily through 22 local telephone operating subsidiaries, each of which offered local telephone service, customer telephone equipment (e.g., telephone sets and switchboards), intrastate long-distance service, Yellow Pages directory advertising, and other communications services (e.g., data and TV program transmission) within specified geographic areas. AT&T also included the Long Lines Department, which provided interstate long-distance services; Western Electric, an equipment manufacturing subsidiary; and Bell Laboratories, which performed all R&D for both Western Electric and the telephone operating companies.

In 1981, AT&T as a whole was the largest private enterprise in the world. Total assets at the end of 1981 were $137.7 billion, and AT&T employed 1,060,378 workers (798,000 in the local operating companies). Revenues in 1981 were $58.2 billion (see Exhibit 1). AT&T was also the most widely held company in the United States. At the end of 1981 it had 3,055,495 shareholders, 95.3% of whom held less than 600 shares. AT&T was regarded as the archetypical "widows and orphans" stock, having neither missed nor lowered its dividend payment since 1885.

## Divestiture and Settlement of the Antitrust Suit

The principal provision of the antitrust settlement was that AT&T's local operating companies would be spun off into seven completely independent regional corporations. These seven companies would be NYNEX (N.Y. Telephone and New England Telephone); Bell Atlantic (N.J. Bell, Bell of Pennsylvania, Diamond State Telephone, and four Chesapeake and Potomac Telephone companies); Bell South (South Central Bell and Southern Bell); Ameritech (Indiana Bell, Michigan Bell, Illinois Bell, Wisconsin Bell, and Ohio Bell); U.S. West (Mountain Bell, Pacific Northwest Bell, and Northwestern Bell); Southwestern Bell (Southwestern Bell); and Pacific Telesis (Pacific Telephone, Nevada Bell). Each regional company would continue to provide local telephone service, Yellow Pages directory advertising, and other local telecommunications services (e.g., mobile radio telephone service) within its designated geographic area. In addition, the regional companies would be allowed to sell (but not manufacture) customer telephone equipment and to undertake any other ventures as long as these did not violate existing antitrust laws.

## The "New" AT&T

Postdivestiture, the remaining AT&T company would consist of AT&T Communications, Western Electric, Bell Labs, AT&T Information Systems (ATTIS), AT&T International, and minority holdings in Cincinnati Bell and the Southern New England Telephone Company (see Exhibit 2). The major parts of this organization would have the following characteristics.

### AT&T Communications

This subsidiary, established as a direct result of divestiture, would be responsible for providing both interstate and intrastate long-distance communications services. It would be a public utility in the traditional sense of having its prices determined by regulatory oversight bodies (state public utility commissions for intrastate phone rates and the Federal Communications Commission for interstate rates). However, in the years prior to 1983 a variety of companies had begun to offer competing long-distance services, most notably MCI, GTE (through its recently acquired

Sprint System), and ITT. Thus, in contrast to a traditional utility, AT&T would not enjoy an exclusive monopoly franchise. Moreover, although AT&T held more than 95% of the long-distance market in 1982, competition in this market was likely to intensify. Prior to the antitrust settlement, customers of AT&T's long-distance competitors usually had to dial up to 20 digits in order to make a long-distance call. The antitrust settlement directed that by 1989 local operating companies were to offer customers "equal access" to all competing long-distance providers. This stipulation, together with prior deregulation of the market for specialized business communications services, promised to draw many strong new competitors (like IBM through its Satellite Business Systems affiliate) into the long-distance market. At the same time the rapid development of new telecommunications technologies was making it increasingly easy for large business customers (perhaps AT&T's most lucrative market) to develop their own private long-distance networks. Advancing technology was also making much of AT&T's existing plant obsolete.

The initial assets, revenues, and labor force of AT&T Communications were established as part of the antitrust settlement and, by the beginning of 1983, could be predicted relatively accurately. Forecasts of future operating results could also be estimated (see Exhibit 3). The long-distance market as a whole was expected to grow at about a 10% annual rate, but AT&T's share was expected to decline from 95% to 60–65% in the first 5 years following divestiture. Operating profit margins were expected to be below those earned in the past, both because of intensifying competition and regulatory pressure to reduce long-distance prices. Any compensating reductions in the share of long-distance revenues passed on to the local operating companies would depend on government decisions whose outcomes were difficult to predict. Thus, the operating margins contained in Exhibit 3 could be in error by as much as 10% (i.e., margins could range from 20% to 0%).

## Western Electric (WE)

In the predivestiture Bell System, Western Electric provided telecommunications equipment supplies and service support to the local telephone operating companies. Western Electric was almost fully integrated, sold little of its output to the world outside AT&T, and controlled almost the entire market for sales of equipment to the 22 Bell operating companies. The antitrust settlement would change this situation in two important ways. First, WE's share of the telecommunications equipment market would obviously erode as the newly independent regional companies began to look to other potential equipment suppliers. Both existing U.S. manufacturers (Motorola, Northern Telecom, etc.) and foreign suppliers (from Japan and Europe) would be serious competitors. Second, the 1981 antitrust settlement vacated conditions of an earlier 1956 settlement which prohibited WE from either selling equipment to non-Bell telephone companies or entering a broad range of telecommunications-related fields such as data processing. Since one of AT&T's principal aims in settling the antitrust suit was to be able to compete in these markets, WE would be entering a variety of new competitive markets. For this purpose, WE had organized two new divisions, one to sell computers and other data-processing equipment and one actively to pursue defense and other government contracts. WE had also reoriented its components division to begin selling high-technology semiconductors in general commercial markets.

Several serious questions about Western Electric's future profitability (see Exhibit 3) were raised by these changes. First and foremost, it was not clear whether WE could acquire the necessary marketing and product development skills to operate in competitive (as opposed to captive) markets. Second, many WE plants were old, and its manufacturing labor force was almost fully unionized. Thus, despite its generally effective record in cost management, WE might have great difficulty matching the costs of highly automated competitors with nonunion or offshore facilities. Third, even when it had substantial control over prices, WE's business was highly cyclical. Competitive price responses in the new environment were likely to exacerbate these cyclical fluctuations, and WE would have to learn to cope with a highly unstable environment. Consequently, the pre-tax earnings forecasts in Exhibit 3 might be off by as much as $1 billion in any given year.

## AT&T Information Systems (ATTIS)

ATTIS was established in response to a 1980 FCC decision which required that AT&T provide customer telecommunications equipment through an "arm's-length" subsidiary. ATTIS was scheduled to begin operations, selling equipment to businesses and households, on January 1, 1983. The divestiture agreement required that by January 1984 the local telephone operating companies transfer their existing base of leased equipment (e.g., leased home telephones) to ATTIS. This lease base had a book value of about $9 billion and would produce revenues of between $5 billion and $7 billion in 1983. Altogether ATTIS in its postdivestiture form would have had assets of about $10 billion and revenues of about $8 billion in 1983 (see Exhibit 3).

Earnings prospects for ATTIS (see Exhibit 3), like those for the rest of the company, were highly uncertain. Although traditionally customers had leased their telephone equipment from the local operating companies, they had recently begun to buy instead. This trend, which had been steadily eroding AT&T's lease base, was likely to accelerate. After divestiture AT&T would no longer be able to provide one-stop shopping for both telephone equipment and access lines. In addition, the new regional companies would be offering their own equipment in direct competition with AT&T. Finally, it was not clear how successfully AT&T, with its regulated experience, could operate in the newly competitive market for selling telecommunications equipment. AT&T's share of the rapidly expanding market for new business equipment had fallen from 80% in 1970 to about 40% in 1982 (where it appeared to stabilize), as companies like Rolm and Northern Telecom captured the greater part of the emerging demand. A similar AT&T share decline had occurred in the market for sales of home telephones. To succeed in these markets AT&T had to acquire skills in marketing and rapid product development which were largely alien to its traditional way of doing business. Taking all these factors into account, the pre-tax earnings forecasts in Exhibit 3 might be off by as much as $2 billion in any given year.

## Bell Laboratories

Bell Laboratories would continue to perform research and development activities after divestiture. However, this was expected to occur at a reduced level and ultimately the development parts of the laboratories would be integrated into the WE divisions responsible for particular product lines.

## AT&T International

Established in 1980 primarily as a vehicle for selling and servicing overseas telecommunications systems, AT&T International had obtained important contracts in Korea and Egypt. However, revenues and earnings were both expected to be relatively minor before the very late 1980s.

## Historical Financial Policies

AT&T's financial policy had historically been determined by its continuing need for large amounts of capital (see Exhibit 4) and the perception of management that the company was a preeminent "widows and orphans" stock. Both dividend and debt policy placed a premium on stability and maintaining financial integrity. Dividends were never reduced. Overall financial policy was also designed to maintain a relatively low level of volatility for the share price. Target debt ratios and interest coverage were designed in order to maintain AAA ratings for both AT&T and Western Electric (see Exhibit 5). Maintaining a top-level credit rating was intended both to reduce AT&T's borrowing cost and to ensure that funds would be available to AT&T even in periods of severe financial dislocation. In 1982 yields on seasoned corporate bonds averaged 13.5%, 14.2%, 15.0%, and 15.7%, for AAA, AA, A, and BBB rated bonds, respectively. An increase in average interest costs of .1% (10 basis points) would have increased AT&T's borrowing cost in 1982 by $47.9 million.

Until the late 1950s the company's target ratio of debt to total capital (debt plus book value of equity plus unamortized investment tax credits) had been between 30 and 40%. In the 1960s it became generally recognized that large pre-World War II fluctuations in economic activity had been mitigated and therefore companies could safely carry larger debt ratios (i.e., ratios of debt to total capital). At the same time, a generally depressed stock market in the 1970s and an apparent decline in real interest rates (the difference between nominal interest rates and the rate of inflation) favored the issue of debt over equity. In response to these forces, AT&T allowed its debt ratio to rise steadily from 32% in 1965 to 46.7% in 1980 (see Exhibit 1). The target level of the debt ratio increased to about 45%. Pre-tax interest coverage changed in a way consistent with the increasing debt ratio. Coverage fell steeply from more than 10 times in 1965 and to below 4 times in the early 1970s (see Exhibit 1).

Public underwritten equity offerings by AT&T were relatively rare (see Exhibit 6). Between 1970 and 1980 there were just two offerings of 12 million shares each in 1976 and 1977. AT&T's financial managers were reluctant to issue equity during a period when AT&T's market value was below its book value per share. Issuing equity under these circumstances would have reduced book value per share. Yet AT&T issued substantial amounts of new equity through conversion of preferred stock, a dividend reinvestment plan (which allowed investors to purchase new stock with their dividends at 95% of the current market price), and employee investment programs.

Dividend policy was also relatively conservative for a utility. The target payout ratio was 60%, with actual payouts fluctuating between 58 and 67% (see Exhibit 1). The relatively low payout ratio for a utility was determined by the company's large capital requirements and by the desire to provide some protection for maintaining the stability of dividends. Approximately one third of dividends were reinvested by stockholders (see Exhibit 6).

In 1981, in response to increased competition and a far more volatile regulatory climate, AT&T began to return to a more conservative financial policy. In June 1981, AT&T raised $1,006 million through the public sale of 18.15 million shares of common stock (see Exhibit 7). And total debt outstanding increased in 1981 by only $2,352 million, down from increases of $4,398 million in 1980 and $3,331 million in 1979.

## The Impact of Divestiture

Investor reactions to the planned divestiture were generally positive. On the Monday following the late Friday announcement of the antitrust settlement, AT&T's stock rose 1⅞ points (see Exhibit 7), indicating an increase in expected earnings. However, the uncertainty created by such a massive reorganization greatly increased the perceived risks associated with AT&T securities. On the same Monday the prices of bonds (whose contractual return was fixed) of both AT&T and its subsidiaries fell by between 1½% and 2% in light trading. On Tuesday ( January 12, 1982), Standard and Poor's announced that AT&T and its subsidiaries were being added to its list of candidates for possible rating changes. The same day Moody's Investors Service expressed concern that the restructuring could hurt the credit quality of some Bell system units (although by January 1, 1983, no official rating changes had occurred). According to one independent investment analyst, ''Nobody really knows what the devil is going to happen eventually to each individual company.''

The extent of this uncertainty was such that, in February 1982, AT&T's chief financial officer admitted, ''All of a sudden I have a situation where it probably isn't likely for some time that the subsidiaries will be able to go to the debt market.'' And AT&T's treasurer added that no new debt issues by the operating companies could be expected before divestiture. Moreover, as a leading telecommunications analyst had previously noted, ''AT&T sees its terminal (customer equipment) and long-distance business . . . becoming competitive. It may be appropriate for a utility to have a 45% debt ratio and still maintain its AAA rating. But the proper capital ratio for an industrial concern is about 25%." Thus, as *Value Line* summarized the matter in August 1982, the postdivestiture AT&T might "no longer be a haven for widows and orphans."

## Postsettlement Financial Policy

In 1982, AT&T's shift to a more conservative financial posture was helped along by an increase in the availability of internal funds due to changes in the tax laws and liberalization of regulatory depreciation schedules (more rapid depreciation meant higher regulated prices and increased cash flow). At the same time, a deep recession reduced the need for new telecommunications capacity. In January 1982, AT&T's projected 1982 construction budget was $18.9 billion. Actual construction expenditures for 1982 eventually came to only $16.8 billion. AT&T also conserved funds by maintaining the dividend at $5.40 per share despite widespread expectations that some increase was due (see Exhibit 8). Sales of securities by AT&T during 1982 consisted of 27.7 million shares of common stock, raising $1,670 million, and $400 million in 7-year Eurobonds at a coupon rate of 14¼% (see Exhibits 6 and 7). Thus, on a consolidated basis, AT&T was able to reduce its total outstanding debt by $725 million in 1982. At year-end AT&T's debt ratio stood at 42.3%, down from 46.7% in 1980 (see Exhibit 1).

## Conditions in 1983

On January 17, 1983, AT&T common stock closed at $68.50 per share on the NYSE, a 17-year high. Moreover, the continuing impact of the recession on demand for new telephone service and improvements in internal fund flows meant that AT&T's 1983 need for external funds for normal operations would be minimal. In December 1982, the 1983 construction budget was estimated to be $16.8 billion. Assuming that there would be no increase in the dividend, no change in total debt outstanding (i.e., new issues would exactly balance repayments), and no public offerings of equity in 1983, internal funds plus continuing investment programs (e.g., the dividend reinvestment program) would both cover the construction budget and add about $1 billion to net cash holding (see Exhibits 3 and 9). Furthermore, the antitrust settlement provided that much of AT&T's existing debt would be assumed by the divested regional operating companies. Consequently, the balance sheet of the "new" AT&T on January 1, 1984, would be characterized by a sharply reduced debt ratio (see Exhibit 9).

The critical issue in formulating financial policy for 1983 was not, therefore, the need to raise funds to finance investment. Rather, as in 1982, it was whether the balance sheet in Exhibit 9 would be appropriate for a company like the "new" AT&T. For comparison purposes, Exhibit 10 presents financial data for companies in areas of business similar to that of the "new" AT&T. However, these companies do not necessarily have the same financial and strategic goals as AT&T nor do they face exactly the same markets or uncertainties.

**EXHIBIT 1**
Selected AT&T Financial and Operating Information, 1973–1982 (billions of dollars except per share data)

| | 1973 | 1974 | 1975 | 1976 | 1977 | 1978 | 1979 | 1980 | 1981 | 1982 |
|---|---|---|---|---|---|---|---|---|---|---|
| *Operating Data* | | | | | | | | | | |
| Revenues | $ 23.5 | $ 26.2 | $ 29.0 | $ 32.8 | $ 36.5 | $ 41.0 | $ 45.4 | $ 50.8 | $ 58.2 | $ 65.1 |
| Operating earnings (EBIT) | 6.3 | 7.0 | 7.5 | 8.8 | 9.7 | 11.0 | 11.6 | 12.4 | 14.3 | 15.2 |
| Interest expense | 1.73 | 2.06 | 2.30 | 2.40 | 2.44 | 2.69 | 3.08 | 3.77 | 4.36 | 3.93 |
| Net income (PAT)[a] | 2.95 | 3.17 | 3.15 | 3.83 | 4.54 | 5.27 | 5.67 | 6.08 | 6.89 | 6.99 |
| *Balance Sheet Data* | | | | | | | | | | |
| Cash, cash equivalents | $ 1.06 | $ 1.12 | $ 1.12 | $ 1.49 | $ 1.28 | $ 1.42 | $ .86 | $ 1.01 | $ 1.26 | $ 2.45 |
| Adjusted working capital[b] | (.73) | (.70) | (.43) | (.75) | (1.26) | (2.07) | (2.13) | (1.88) | (1.98) | (.91) |
| Plant, equipment | 58.6 | 64.9 | 70.4 | 75.9 | 82.4 | 90.4 | 99.9 | 110.0 | 120.0 | 128.1 |
| Total assets | 67.1 | 74.1 | 80.2 | 86.7 | 94.0 | 103.0 | 113.4 | 125.6 | 137.7 | 148.2 |
| Total debt | 28.4 | 32.3 | 34.0 | 35.0 | 35.7 | 37.9 | 41.2 | 45.6 | 47.9 | 47.1 |
| Total equity | 31.2 | 32.6 | 34.6 | 37.2 | 40.9 | 42.6 | 46.4 | 51.2 | 56.8 | 63.8 |
| *Profitability Data* | | | | | | | | | | |
| Return on sales, after-tax | 12.6% | 12.1% | 10.9% | 11.7% | 12.5% | 12.9% | 12.5% | 12.0% | 11.8% | 10.7% |
| Return on capital,[c] pre-tax | 8.2 | 8.3 | 7.9 | 8.3 | 8.7 | 9.8 | 9.3 | 9.4 | 9.7 | 8.6 |
| Return on common equity, after-tax | 10.5 | 10.5 | 9.8 | 11.2 | 12.3 | 13.1 | 13.0 | 12.6 | 12.9 | 12.2 |
| *Per Share Data* | | | | | | | | | | |
| Earnings per share | $ 4.98 | $ 5.27 | $ 5.13 | $ 6.05 | $ 6.97 | $ 7.74 | $ 8.04 | $ 8.19 | $ 8.55 | $ 8.06 |
| Dividends per share | 2.87 | 3.24 | 3.40 | 3.80 | 4.20 | 4.60 | 5.00 | 5.00 | 5.40 | 5.40 |
| Price range per common share | 45–55 | 39–53 | 44–52 | 51–65 | 58–66 | 57–65 | 51–65 | 45–56 | 47–62 | 50–65 |
| Book value per common share | 49.40 | 51.40 | 52.86 | 55.08 | 57.78 | 60.67 | 63.67 | 65.51 | 67.52 | 69.07 |
| *Other Financial Relations* | | | | | | | | | | |
| Debt ratio | 46.8% | 48.7% | 48.1% | 46.7% | 44.6% | 46.3% | 46.2% | 46.7% | 45.3% | 42.3% |
| Interest coverage | 3.65 | 3.40 | 3.26 | 3.67 | 3.99 | 4.11 | 3.77 | 3.30 | 3.28 | 3.86 |
| Dividend payout | 58% | 61% | 66% | 63% | 60% | 59% | 62% | 61% | 63% | 67% |

*Source:* AT&T annual reports.

a. Before special items.

b. Working capital excluding cash, cash equivalents, and short-term debt.

c. Income before interest charges and income taxes divided by debt plus equity plus deferred tax credits.

**EXHIBIT 2**
AT&T Organizational Structures

Predivestiture

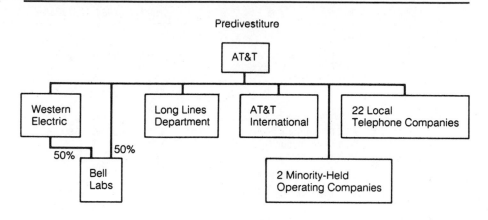

Postdivestiture

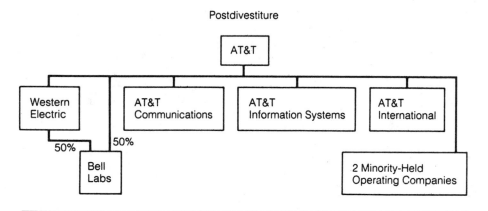

*Source:* Published reports.

**EXHIBIT 3**

Operating Projections for the "New" AT&T, 1983–1988 (billions of dollars)

| | 1983 | 1984 | 1985 | 1986 | 1987 | 1988 |
|---|---|---|---|---|---|---|
| *Revenues* | | | | | | |
| AT&T Communications . . . . . | $35.0 | $35.0 | $35.0 | $36.0 | $37.5 | $39.0 |
| AT&T Information Systems . . . | 8.0 | 8.0 | 7.5 | 7.0 | 7.0 | 7.5 |
| Western Electric . . . . . . . | 11.5 | 11.0 | 11.0 | 12.0 | 13.0 | 14.0 |
| Total . . . . . . . . . . | $54.5 | $54.0 | $53.5 | $55.0 | $57.5 | $60.5 |
| *Operating Earnings (EBIT)[a]* | | | | | | |
| AT&T Communications . . . . . | $ 3.5 | $ 3.5 | $ 3.5 | $ 3.6 | $ 3.8 | $ 3.9 |
| AT&T Information Systems . . . . | .5 | .5 | .5 | .5 | .6 | .8 |
| Western Electric . . . . . . . | .9 | 1.0 | 1.1 | 1.2 | 1.3 | 1.4 |
| Total . . . . . . . . . . | $ 4.9 | $ 5.0 | $ 5.1 | $ 5.3 | $ 5.7 | $ 6.1 |
| *Net Plant and Equipment (Year-End)* | | | | | | |
| AT&T Communications . . . . . | $22.0 | $24.0 | $26.3 | $28.0 | $29.0 | $30.0 |
| AT&T Information Systems . . . | 10.0 | 9.0 | 8.0 | 7.0 | 6.5 | 6.0 |
| Western Electric . . . . . . . | 3.0 | 3.0 | 3.0 | 3.2 | 3.4 | 3.6 |
| Total . . . . . . . . . . | $35.0 | $36.0 | $37.3 | $38.2 | $38.9 | $39.6 |
| Total interest[b] . . . . . . . | $ .8 | $ .9 | $ .9 | $ 1.0 | $ 1.0 | $ 1.0 |
| Total after-tax earnings[c] . . . . | 2.84 | 2.87 | 2.94 | 3.01 | 3.26 | 3.54 |
| Total dividends[d] . . . . . . | 1.70 | 1.72 | 1.76 | 1.81 | 1.96 | 2.12 |

*Source:* Casewriter's estimates based on published reports.

a. Operating earnings are calculated including Bell Labs expenditures and depreciation as costs.

b. Assumes no net change in debt outstanding after January 1, 1983, but gradual increase in average interest rate to 11%.

c. After-tax earnings here represent earnings after taxes *actually paid*. Historically, AT&T calculated earnings after taxes by using a figure for taxes that represented the taxes AT&T would have paid in the absence of investment tax credits and accelerated depreciation. In the past, the difference between taxes *actually paid* and these "taxes" used in calculating earnings appeared as increases in "deferred taxes and tax credits" on the AT&T balance sheet. Also, the use of taxes *actually paid* in these projections accounts for the low average tax rate; marginal tax rates are 45–50% throughout the period.

d. Assumes 60% payout ratio.

**EXHIBIT 4**
Sources and Uses of Funds, 1978–1982 (billions of dollars)

|  | 1978 | 1979 | 1980 | 1981 | 1982 |
|---|---|---|---|---|---|
| *Sources* | | | | | |
| Funds from operations | | | | | |
| Net income | $ 5.3 | $ 5.7 | $ 6.0 | $ 6.8 | $ 7.3 |
| Depreciation | 5.5 | 6.1 | 7.0 | 7.9 | 8.7 |
| Deferred taxes, tax credits, other | 2.2 | 2.5 | 2.6 | 2.8 | 4.9 |
|  | 13.0 | 14.3 | 15.6 | 17.5 | 20.9 |
| External sources | | | | | |
| Continuing equity investments[a] | 1.2 | 1.7 | 2.6 | 2.2 | 2.8 |
| Underwritten equity offerings | – | – | – | 1.0 | 1.7 |
| Net increase in debt | 2.5 | 3.3 | 4.4 | 2.4 | (.8) |
|  | 3.7 | 5.0 | 7.0 | 5.6 | 3.7 |
| Total sources | $16.7 | $19.3 | $22.6 | $23.1 | $24.6 |
| *Uses* | | | | | |
| Dividends | $ 3.2 | $ 3.6 | $ 3.8 | $ 4.4 | $ 4.7 |
| Gross plant, equipment investment | 13.7 | 15.8 | 17.3 | 18.1 | 16.8 |
| Increase in noncash working capital[b] | (.8) | .1 | .2 | (.1) | 1.1 |
| Increase in cash holdings | .1 | (.6) | .1 | .3 | 1.2 |
| Other | .5 | .4 | 1.2 | .4 | .8 |
| Total uses | $16.7 | $19.3 | $22.6 | $23.1 | $24.6 |

*Source:* AT&T annual reports.

a. Dividend reinvestment, employee stock plans, other.

b. Working capital excluding cash holdings and short-term debt.

**EXHIBIT 5**
Bond Rating Guidelines for Industry Groups

|  | *AAA* | *AA* | *A* | *BBB* |
|---|---|---|---|---|
| *Telephone (Senior)* | | | | |
| Debt ratio | 40% | 44% | 53% | >58% |
| Pre-tax interest coverage | 4.5 | 3.7–4.7 | 2.8–4.0 | < 3 |
| *Electric Utility (Senior)* | | | | |
| Debt ratio | 45% | 47% | 55% | >55% |
| Pre-tax interest coverage | 4.0 | 3.25–4.0 | 2.5–3.5 | < 3 |
| *Industrial (Sinking Fund Debentures)* | | | | |
| Debt ratio | 20% | 25% | 35% | >40% |
| Pre-tax fixed payment coverage[a] | 12 | 8 | 6 | 3.5 |

*Source:* Adapted from Standard and Poor's rating guidelines.

a. Fixed charges consist of interest plus preferred dividends.

**EXHIBIT 6**
AT&T Common Stock Issues, 1978–1982 (millions)

|  | 1978 | 1979 | 1980 | 1981 | 1982 |
|---|---|---|---|---|---|
| *Shares Issued* | | | | | |
| Underwritten offerings | – | – | – | 18.2 | 27.7 |
| Dividend reinvestment[a] | 13.5 | 17.3 | 22.6 | 24.3 | 28.3 |
| Employee stock plans | 6.5 | 13.1 | 16.2 | 16.8 | 17.9 |
| Other[b] | 1.9 | 1.4 | 14.6 | 1.0 | 7.4 |
| Total shares issued | 21.9 | 31.8 | 53.4 | 60.3 | 81.3 |
| Year-end shares outstanding | 669.5 | 701.4 | 754.8 | 815.1 | 896.4 |
| *Proceeds* | | | | | |
| Underwritten offerings | – | – | – | $1,006 | $1,670 |
| Dividend reinvestment | $ 786 | $ 967 | $1,107 | 1,234 | 1,493 |
| Employee stock plans, other | 371 | 737 | 1,485 | 929 | 1,300 |
| Total proceeds | $1,157 | $1,704 | $2,592 | $3,169 | $4,463 |

*Source:* AT&T annual reports.

a. Dividends could be automatically reinvested to purchase common stock at 95% of the current market price.

b. Conversion of preferred stock, purchase of minority holdings in Pacific Telephone, etc.

**EXHIBIT 7**
Recent Events Concerning AT&T

| Date | Event | Closing Stock Price | Change from Previous Close | S&P 500 Index Closing Level | Percentage Change from Previous Close |
|------|-------|---------------------|---------------------------|------------------------------|----------------------------------------|
| June 1, 1981 | Sale of 16.5 million shares announced | $56½ | $(1⅜) | $132.41 | −.14% |
| June 10, 1981 | Syndicate sells 18.15 million shares | 57 | 0 | 132.32 | +.26 |
| Jan. 11, 1982 (Monday) | Reaction to antitrust settlement announced Jan. 8 | 60½ | 1⅞ | 116.78 | −2.32 |
| Feb. 1, 1982 | Authorized common stock increased from 900 million to 1.2 billion shares | 59 | (⅞) | 117.78 | −2.22 |
| Mar. 2, 1982 | Financing requirements reduced | 54⅞ | ¼ | 112.68 | −.50 |
| Mar. 5, 1982 | $400 million Eurobond issue announced | 56⅜ | 1 | 109.34 | −.49 |
| Apr. 26, 1982 | 10 million share shelf registration announced | 55⅝ | (⅝) | 119.26 | +.52 |
| May 6, 1982 | 2 million shares sold to Morgan Stanley | 55¼ | ½ | 118.68 | +.85 |
| Aug. 11, 1982 | Court accepts antitrust settlement subject to modification | 50½ | ⅜ | 102.60 | −.23 |
| Aug. 25, 1982 | 8 million shares sold to syndicate | 56¾ | (⅜) | 117.58 | +1.91 |
| Nov. 17, 1982 | $1 billion equity offer announced | 61⅝ | (¼) | 137.93 | +1.82 |
| Dec. 2, 1982 | $1.062 billion raised by equity sale | 60¼ | ¼ | 138.82 | +.07 |

*Sources: The Wall Street Journal; New York Times.*

**EXHIBIT 8**

Quarterly Earnings, Dividend Announcements, 1982

| | Earnings | | | | |
|---|---|---|---|---|---|
| Date | Earnings per Share | Percent Change[a] | Closing Stock Price | Change in Stock Price | Daily Percent Change in S&P 500 Index |
| Mar. 17, 1982 . . | $2.40 | +28% | $56⅞ | $(¼) | −.18% |
| June 16, 1982 . | 1.96[b] | +1 | 51¼ | (¾) | −.75 |
| Sept. 15, 1982 . | 2.27 | −1 | 56 | (½) | +.96 |
| Dec. 15, 1982 . . | 2.05 | −13 | 60½ | (1⅜) | −1.59 |

| | Dividends (Increased to $1.35/Share in Feb. 1981) | | | | |
|---|---|---|---|---|---|
| Date | Dividend | Percent Change | Closing Stock Price | Change in Stock Price | Daily Percent Change in S&P 500 Index |
| Feb. 17, 1982 . . | $1.35 | 0% | $57 | $(1⅛) | −.33% |
| May 19, 1982 . . | 1.35 | 0 | 54⅛ | (¼) | −.83 |
| Aug. 18, 1982 . . | 1.35 | 0 | 54¼ | (¾) | −.47 |
| Nov. 17, 1982 . . | 1.35 | 0 | 61⅝ | (¼) | +1.82 |

*Source: The Wall Street Journal.*

a. From four quarters past.

b. Subsequently restated to $1.68 per share.

**EXHIBIT 9**

Projected Balance Sheets for the "New" AT&T, 1983–1988 (billions of dollars)

| | 1983[a] | 1984 | 1985 | 1986 | 1987 | 1988 |
|---|---|---|---|---|---|---|
| Cash, cash equivalents[b] . . . . | $ 2.6 | $ 2.6 | $ 2.6 | $ 2.6 | $ 2.6 | $ 2.6 |
| Other current assets . . . . . . | 5.1 | 5.1 | 5.0 | 5.1 | 5.4 | 5.7 |
| Current assets . . . . . . | 7.7 | 7.7 | 7.6 | 7.7 | 8.0 | 8.3 |
| Plant, equipment (net) . . . . . | 35.0 | 36.0 | 37.3 | 38.2 | 38.4 | 39.6 |
| Other . . . . . . . . . . . | 1.9 | 1.9 | 2.0 | 2.0 | 2.1 | 2.1 |
| Total assets . . . . . . | $44.6 | $45.6 | $46.9 | $47.9 | $48.5 | $50.0 |
| Current liabilities[c] . . . . . . . | $ 5.0 | $ 5.0 | $ 4.9 | $ 5.0 | $ 5.3 | $ 5.6 |
| Total debt[d] . . . . . . . . . | 9.3 | 9.3 | 9.3 | 9.3 | 9.3 | 9.3 |
| Deferred tax credits[e] . . . . . . | 8.2 | 8.2 | 8.2 | 8.2 | 8.2 | 8.2 |
| Equity[f] . . . . . . . . . . . . | 22.1 | 24.3 | 26.6 | 28.9 | 31.4 | 34.0 |
| Total liabilities . . . . . . | $44.6 | $46.8 | $49.0 | $51.4 | $54.2 | $57.1 |

*Source: Casewriter's estimates based on published reports.*

a. Figures are for year-end.

b. 1983 figure is estimated cash on hand; subsequent figures represent "base case" of no change in cash on hand. Cash needs for operating purposes are roughly 2% of sales. Absent any change in other assumptions, the gap separating total assets from total liabilities after 1983 would be eliminated by changes in the cash account.

c. Excludes short-term debt, which is included in total debt.

d. 1983 figure is estimated debt; subsequent figures represent "base case" of no change.

e. 1983 figure is estimated tax credits; subsequent figures use earnings estimates from Exhibit 3, which include increases in tax credits and deferred taxes as part of earnings (see Exhibit 3, note c), hence the constant level of deferred tax credits.

f. Increases in equity are due to retained earnings at 60% payout ratio, dividend reinvestment of an assumed one third of dividends, and employee stock purchases of about $500 million per year.

**EXHIBIT 10**
Comparison of Companies, 1982 (billions of dollars)

|  | AT&T | MCI | GTE | IBM | ITT | Northern Telecom | Burroughs | Rolm | Motorola |
|---|---|---|---|---|---|---|---|---|---|
| Revenues | $ 65.1 | $1.1 | $12.1 | $34.4 | $16.0 | $2.5 | $4.1 | $.38 | $3.8 |
| Net income | 6.99 | .17 | .90 | 4.41 | .70 | .12 | .09 | .03 | .17 |
| Assets | 148.2 | 2.1 | 21.9 | 32.5 | 14.1 | 2.0 | 4.1 | .27 | 2.8 |
| Return on |  |  |  |  |  |  |  |  |  |
| Sales, after-tax | 10.7% | 15.9% | 7.4% | 12.8% | 4.4% | 5.0% | 2.2% | 7.8% | 17.0% |
| Assets, pre-tax | 8.6 | 11.0 | 4.1 | 14.1 | 4.8 | 6.4 | 2.1 | 12.5 | 5.9 |
| Equity, after-tax | 12.2 | 32.4 | 15.6 | 22.9 | 12.7 | 15.9 | 4.3 | 21.0 | 10.4 |
| Payout ratio | 67 | 0 | 61 | 47 | 54 | 23 | 120 | 0 | 36 |
| Debt ratio[a] | 43 | 55 | 57 | 14 | 38 | 21 | 28 | 18 | 18 |
| Current ratio | .9 | 2.2 | 1.0 | 1.6 | 1.3 | 1.9 | 2.1 | 2.2 | 2.6 |
| Interest coverage | 3.6 | 4.2 | 2.4 | 18 | 2.5 | 5.9 | 1.4 | 21 | 5.4 |
| Bond rating | AAA | NR | BBB | AAA | A | A | A | NR | AA |
| Price-earnings range | 6–8 | 8–27 | 6–10 | 8–13 | 5–7 | 9–21 | 14–23 | 22–44 | 11–20 |

*Sources:* Standard and Poor's Reports; Moody's *Industrial Manual.*

NR = no rated debt outstanding.

a. Debt/Total capital.

# MCI Communications Corporation (1983)

In April 1983, Wayne English, chief financial officer of MCI Communications Corporation, faced the problem of setting financial policy in an environment characterized by a large potential demand for external funding and great uncertainty concerning MCI's future. MCI, which provided long-distance telecommunications services in competition with AT&T, had seen its revenues grow from almost nothing in FY1974 (ending March 31, 1974) to more than $1 billion in FY1983. During that period, the company climbed from a loss of $38.7 million in FY1975 to a profit of $170.8 million in FY1983. In the last 2 years, its stock price had increased more than fivefold.

Nevertheless, the antitrust settlement between AT&T and the U.S. Department of Justice in January 1982 had significantly altered the economic landscape for MCI. The settlement, providing for the breakup of AT&T by early 1984, would affect MCI in two important ways. On the one hand, it offered the opportunity for greatly increased growth, since AT&T would be required, for the first time, to compete on equal quality-of-service terms with MCI. On the other hand, the settlement posed new uncertainties, since it promised to eliminate certain MCI cost advantages and to increase AT&T's competitive flexibility.

Even in the face of intensifying competition from AT&T, however, MCI was committed to extending the reach and capacity of its network. According to Brian Thompson, senior vice president for corporate development: "Economies of scale and scope are everything in this business. In the long term, the strategic high ground lies in owning your own facilities for basic call services and then leveraging off this to provide value-added services."

## Company Background

MCI was organized in August 1968 under the leadership of William McGowan as the Federal Communications Commission (FCC) appeared willing to allow increased competition with AT&T in the long-distance market. In June 1971 the FCC formally adopted a policy of allowing qualified new companies to enter the market for specialized long-distance services, which consisted chiefly of *private line* (i.e., dedicated telephone line) services for large telephone users. By June 1972, MCI was ready to begin construction of its telecommunications network.

To provide the necessary funds, MCI sold 6 million shares of common stock to the public at $5 per share.[1] Net proceeds after expenses and commissions were $27.1 million. MCI also obtained a $64 million line of credit from a group of four banks headed by the First National Bank of Chicago and further loan promises of $6.45 million from private investors in the form of 7½% subordinated notes (with attached warrants) of up to 5-year maturities. The bank loans carried an interest rate of 3¾% above prime, plus a commitment fee of ½% per annum on the unborrowed balance.

By March 31, 1974, the MCI communications system had grown to 2,280 route-miles of transmission circuits, linking 15 major metropolitan areas. Still, this was far short of the 11,600 route-mile system originally planned in 1972. MCI had to rely on AT&T facilities to carry calls from its subscribers to MCI transmission centers in each metropolitan area. Since AT&T had successfully resisted providing a full range of these interconnection services, MCI was unable to generate significant subscriber revenues. Late in 1973, MCI suspended all construction activity as it pursued legal and regulatory remedies. As part of this process, it filed an antitrust suit against AT&T in March 1974 (Exhibit 1 presents this sequence of events schematically). The FCC ordered AT&T to provide MCI with the full range of interconnection facilities as of May 1974; MCI then resumed construction of its network.

In FY1975, MCI had revenues of $6.8 million but losses of $38.7 million. By September 1975, despite a network consisting of 5,100 route-miles connecting 30 major metropolitan areas, MCI had a negative net worth of $27.5 million, an accumulated operating deficit of $87.3 million, and a stock market price just below $1 per share (see Exhibit 2 for MCI's financial and operating history). MCI had exhausted its line of credit from the banks, had been forced to renegotiate the previous credit agreement to defer interest payments, and was in technical default of many provisions of the revised credit agreement. In the midst of this crisis, MCI managed a public sale of 9.6 million shares of common stock in December 1975, each share having an associated 5-year warrant with an exercise price of $1.25. The net proceeds of this offering, which amounted to $8.2 million (or about $.85 per share-plus-warrant, compared with a then prevailing market price of $.875 per share), enabled MCI to survive.

---

1. This and subsequent prices and numbers of shares have been adjusted for all stock splits on or before April 1, 1983.

MCI reached a turning point in 1976. "Execunet" service, which had been introduced in the winter of 1974, began to yield substantial revenues and changed the nature of the company. Execunet provided a service comparable to standard long-distance calling, with customers having random access to MCI's transmission lines. This enabled MCI to attract small business subscribers who could not afford the expense of dedicated private lines between particular cities (private line customers tended to be large corporations with large call volumes). Partly as a result, revenues increased to $28.4 million in FY1976 and $62.8 million in FY1977 (about half of which came from Execunet). Interest payments to the consortium of lending banks, which had been previously suspended, were resumed in August 1976. Just as MCI made its first profit of $100,000 in September 1976, the FCC won a court order that restricted Execunet to existing subscribers; this order was not lifted completely until May 1978.

The order restricting Execunet slowed, but did not halt, MCI's progress. Revenue growth slowed to 18% between FY1977 and FY1978 but quickly returned to annual rates of more than 50% once the order was lifted. The number of employees tripled from 605 in March 1977 to 1,980 in March 1981; plant grew from $136.6 million to $410.0 million over the same period. More important, MCI's profitability improved rapidly. After-tax earnings from continuing operations rose from a loss of $1.7 million for FY1977 to a profit of $21.1 million in FY1981 (see Exhibit 2). As a result, MCI had exhausted its tax loss carry-forward by the end of FY1981, and stockholders' equity was a positive $148 million.

This record paled, however, in comparison to MCI's growth in subsequent years. In March 1980, MCI offered Execunet service to residential customers (hitherto it had been available exclusively to businesses) on a trial basis in Denver, Colorado. The results were so striking that within a week plans were made to offer Execunet to households nationwide. MCI's growth was then constrained only by a lack of investment capital, which soon became available in substantial quantities (see Exhibit 3). Revenues more than doubled to $506 million in FY1982 and, with the acquisition of Western Union International from Xerox for $195.1 million in June 1982, revenues doubled again to $1,073 million in FY1983. Income from operations was $295.1 million, with net earnings of $170.8 million. A range of new products such as MCI Mail (an electronic mail service) and the results of AT&T's settlement with the Department of Justice offered dramatic opportunities for further growth. (Income statements and balance sheets for MCI for 1981–1983 are presented in Exhibits 4 and 5.)

## Financial Policy

Until 1976 the need to obtain funds to continue operations dominated MCI's financial policy. The court's 1976 order preventing the extension of Execunet service to new customers restricted opportunities for growth and consequently reduced the need for investment funds. At the same time, restrictive covenants associated with the bank loans from the syndicate headed by the First National Bank of Chicago severely limited MCI's ability to raise new capital for expansion. Between

1976 and the summer of 1978, lease financing of new fixed investment was the only substantial source of funds available. This went largely into expanding capacity in MCI's existing markets.

Withdrawal of the court's Execunet order in May 1978 opened the way for accelerated growth if the required investment funds could be obtained. Wayne English, who had arrived as chief financial officer in February 1976, spent the summer of 1978 preparing to do this. First, he obtained agreement from the majority of the lending banks to a public offering of securities whose proceeds would retire their loans. Second, he arranged for the loans of those banks that refused this accommodation to be bought out by private investors. Finally, he bought up or converted a number of outstanding warrants and loans held by earlier investors. Consequently, in December 1978, MCI was able to enter the public capital markets for the first time since the equity issue of December 1975, with an offering of convertible preferred stock which raised $25.8 million—net of all issue expenses (see Exhibit 6). A second convertible preferred offering in September 1979 raised $63.1 million and a third in October 1980 netted $46.7 million.

The choice of convertible preferred stock was dictated on the one hand by the need for some form of equity capital, and on the other hand by the fact, as expressed by Mr. English, that "it was always our conviction that issuing more common would knock the props out from under the stock." As it was, the conversion price on the preferred stock rose with each offering, from $2.1875 in December 1978 to $5 in September 1979 to $9 in October 1980. In addition, the dividend on the preferred stock would be 85% tax-deductible to corporate purchasers without costing MCI a significant loss of tax benefits, since MCI's earnings were still sheltered by the carry-forward of past losses.

An additional feature of these preferred issues was a *call* provision that enabled MCI to force investors to convert to common stock, thus eliminating the drain of preferred dividends on cash flow. This provision typically specified that if the market price of MCI's common stock exceeded the conversion price by more than a stated margin (e.g., 25%) for 30 consecutive trading days, MCI could call the unconverted preferred shares in question for redemption at 110% of their issue value. Owners of preferred stock would, of course, voluntarily exchange their shares for common at the conversion price rather than allow them to be repurchased. A steadily rising stock price enabled MCI to use this mechanism to convert all three preferred issues to common stock by November 1981.

Proceeds from these preferred offerings allowed MCI to retire its short-to-intermediate term bank debt and to issue longer-term debt. Leasing activity decreased and, in July 1980, MCI raised $50.5 million through the public sale of 20-year subordinated debentures.

In FY1981, as the demand for investment funds intensified, the direction of MCI's financial policy shifted slightly from offerings of convertible preferreds to convertible debt. After obtaining $102.1 million in April 1981 through a straight subordinated debenture issue, MCI raised $98.2 million in August 1981 and $245.9 million in May 1982 with convertible debentures.

These convertible debentures carried forced conversion (i.e., *call*) provisions

· similar to those of the earlier preferred stock issues. As a result, MCI was able to force conversion of the May 1982 issue in December 1982 and of the August 1981 issue in February 1983. The consequent additions to common equity enabled MCI to take on a still greater debt burden. Thus, a straight debenture issue in September 1982 yielded $209.9 million and a further convertible debenture in March 1983 produced almost $400 million.

In all, MCI raised about $1,050 million from the public sale of securities in FY1982 and FY1983. As with all MCI offerings, the initial issues were oversubscribed. Interest costs were relatively high (see Exhibit 7), but in the words of Mr. English, ''Availability of funds [was] the paramount consideration''; cost was ''secondary.'' Moreover, since profitability was increasing more rapidly than interest expense, interest coverage actually increased during this time. Considering the situation in 1975, and in comparison to other companies (see Exhibit 8), this was a remarkable achievement.

However, as details of the FCC's response to the AT&T antitrust settlement began to emerge, the resulting uncertainty cast doubt on MCI's continued ability to raise funds in these amounts. MCI would have to proceed with care, agility, and imagination.

## The AT&T Antitrust Settlement and Other Developments

Historically, AT&T provided a necessary part of the MCI system—and its most serious competition. One part of AT&T—the local telephone operating companies (e.g., Illinois Bell, New England Telephone)—supplied MCI with connections to subscribers through their local telephone networks. MCI paid for these services at a rate negotiated in 1978, under the FCC's supervision, between MCI and the local telephone companies (predominantly AT&T subsidiaries). This charge was about $230 per month per access line, or $172.7 million a year by FY1983. MCI also used AT&T and other long-distance facilities to enable its customers to reach areas not already served by the MCI network. In FY1983, MCI paid at the standard commercial rate $137.2 million for these services.

MCI's principal competitor in the market for interstate long-distance services was AT&T's Long Lines division, with about 95% of the market in March 1983. AT&T Long Lines also reimbursed local operating companies for access lines, but at a rate about three times that charged MCI and the other competing carriers, such as GTE Sprint and ITT. This discrepancy was justified by the fact that MCI customers usually had to dial 20 digits to reach a long-distance number, compared with 11 digits (1, plus area code, plus 7-digit number) for an AT&T customer. Thus, AT&T Long Lines was expected to pay more for ''superior access.''

The settlement of the antitrust suit between AT&T and the Justice Department in January 1982 would separate AT&T from its local operating subsidiaries. AT&T would retain the Long Lines division and the intrastate long-distance facilities of the local companies. After separation occurred in January 1984, the long-distance operations would be consolidated in a new AT&T subsidiary named AT&T Communications. AT&T Communications would eventually compete on a more or less equal basis with MCI and the other long-distance companies (GTE, ITT, and so on). To ensure this result, the settlement required that by 1986 the newly independent local telephone companies provide *equal* quality of *access* to all competing long-distance providers. To implement equal access, a series of elections would be held in communities nationwide in which consumers would be asked to select a long-distance provider. Simultaneously, an FCC plan would phase out the differential in access charges between AT&T and its competitors by increasing the fees paid by MCI and others. Although equal access would be phased in over 2 to 3 years, the FCC plan in its original form called for an initial increase of about 80% in MCI access charges in 1984. Thus, on the one hand, MCI would eventually gain by acquiring equal access but, on the other hand, would immediately lose much of its existing cost advantage over AT&T.

The value of equal access to MCI was difficult to measure precisely. Some customers already enjoyed effectively equal access, since electronic switchboards had features that would automatically route calls via MCI lines whenever the usual 10- or 11-digit long-distance number was dialed. However, these tended to be large business customers who made up only a small fraction of MCI's revenue. A trial of equal access in part of Iowa led to an almost immediate increase in MCI's share of the long-distance market, from less than 5% to about 20%. In this case, however, competition from MCI's non-AT&T competitors was not severe, and AT&T still paid more in access fees.

The impact of equalized access charges on market share was also difficult to judge. Under the FCC plan, AT&T's access pricing flexibility was expected to increase as deregulation of the long-distance market—the FCC's ultimate goal—proceeded. In principle, therefore, AT&T would be able to reduce its prices to prevent further erosion of its market share. In practice, however, it would make little economic sense for AT&T, with 95% of the market, to cut prices for the sake of preventing anything less than massive losses of market share to MCI and its other competitors. The outcome would depend on the direction taken by AT&T's management, which had been surprisingly aggressive in the past.

In the face of these uncertainties, it was difficult to predict MCI's growth in revenues and earnings in FY1984 and beyond. Forecasting the need for fixed and working capital was equally difficult; nevertheless a consensus forecast is presented in Exhibit 9. Against these contingencies, MCI held about $550 million in cash in the spring of 1983. At the beginning of April 1983, its stock price stood at $47, and long-term interest rates had declined dramatically.

**EXHIBIT 1**
Chronology of Significant Events, 1971–1984

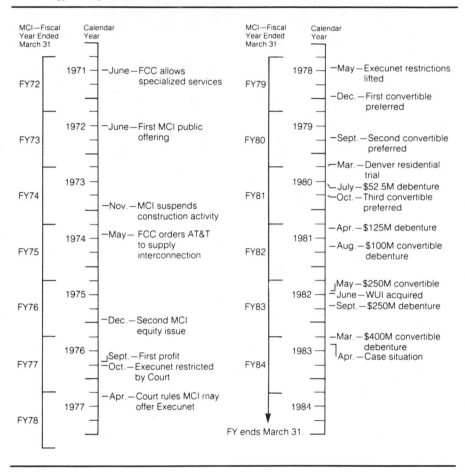

| MCI—Fiscal Year Ended March 31 | Calendar Year | |
|---|---|---|
| FY72 | 1971 | —June—FCC allows specialized services |
| FY73 | 1972 | —June—First MCI public offering |
| FY74 | 1973 | |
| | | —Nov.—MCI suspends construction activity |
| FY75 | 1974 | —May—FCC orders AT&T to supply interconnection |
| FY76 | 1975 | |
| | | —Dec.—Second MCI equity issue |
| FY77 | 1976 | ⌐Sept.—First profit / ⌐Oct.—Execunet restricted by Court |
| FY78 | 1977 | —Apr.—Court rules MCI may offer Execunet |

| MCI—Fiscal Year Ended March 31 | Calendar Year | |
|---|---|---|
| FY79 | 1978 | —May—Execunet restrictions lifted |
| | | —Dec.—First convertible preferred |
| FY80 | 1979 | |
| | | —Sept.—Second convertible preferred |
| FY81 | 1980 | —Mar.—Denver residential trial / ⌐July—$52.5M debenture / ⌐Oct.—Third convertible preferred |
| FY82 | 1981 | —Apr.—$125M debenture / —Aug.—$100M convertible debenture |
| FY83 | 1982 | ⌐May—$250M convertible / ⌐June—WUI acquired / —Sept.—$250M debenture |
| FY84 | 1983 | —Mar.—$400M convertible debenture / ⌐Apr.—Case situation |
| | 1984 | |

FY ends March 31

**EXHIBIT 2**
MCI Operating History for Years Ending March 31, 1974–1983 (millions of dollars except per share data)

| | 1974 | 1975 | 1976 | 1977 | 1978 | 1979 | 1980 | 1981 | 1982 | 1983 |
|---|---|---|---|---|---|---|---|---|---|---|
| Revenues | $ .7 | $ 6.8 | $ 28.4 | $ 62.8 | $ 74.0 | $ 95.2 | $144.3 | $ 234.2 | $ 506.4 | $ 1,073.2 |
| Operating income | (15.0) | (17.3) | (10.6) | 17.7 | 25.0 | 30.6 | 37.2 | 51.3 | 167.0 | 295.1 |
| Net interest | 3.8 | 11.6 | 15.5 | 18.4 | 20.5 | 23.1 | 24.1 | 27.4 | 35.1 | 54.1 |
| Net after-tax earnings | (20.1) | (38.7) | (27.2) | (1.7) | 5.2 | 7.1 | 13.3 | 21.1 | 86.5 | 170.8 |
| Cash, cash equivalents | 1.2 | 1.4 | 3.7 | 2.8 | 4.3 | 10.3 | 7.9 | 12.7 | 144.8 | 542.0 |
| Working capital[a] | .3 | (7.4) | (12.7) | (18.3) | (21.7) | (26.9) | (34.1) | (24.8) | 42.5 | 391.8 |
| Plant, equipment | 60.0 | 81.0 | 120.8 | 136.6 | 148.9 | 188.9 | 282.0 | 410.0 | 619.5 | 1,324.2 |
| Total assets | 71.8 | 90.1 | 131.2 | 147.7 | 161.2 | 209.5 | 309.8 | 466.9 | 860.4 | 2,070.5 |
| Short-term debt[b] | 1.2 | 4.0 | 9.8 | 17.0 | 20.2 | 25.8 | 31.6 | 39.9 | 40.3 | 48.0 |
| Long-term debt | 48.4 | 95.2 | 144.3 | 149.7 | 152.8 | 153.3 | 172.9 | 242.7 | 400.0 | 895.9 |
| Stockholders' equity | 19.1 | (14.4) | (29.1) | (32.2) | (22.7) | 11.5 | 78.8 | 148.0 | 240.8 | 765.6 |
| Million shares outstanding[c] | 27 | 30.6 | 41 | 40.2 | 40.6 | 43.4 | 65.8 | 75.6 | 97.4 | 117.2 |
| Earnings per share[d] | $ (.74) | $ (1.42) | $ (.81) | $ (.06) | $ .05 | $ .04 | $ (.01) | $ .09 | $ .91 | $ 1.69 |
| Price range—common stock | 1½–4½ | ½–2½ | ½–2½ | 1–2 | 1–2½ | 1½–3½ | 2–4½ | 2½–7 | 7–18 | 16–47 |

*Sources:* MCI annual reports, 10-K reports, and prospectuses.

a. Current assets less current liabilities (current assets include cash, cash equivalents).
b. Includes long-term debt payable within 1 year.
c. At year-end. MCI has never paid any dividend on its common stock.
d. Earnings per common share after preferred dividends, before extraordinary items.

**EXHIBIT 3**
Sources and Uses of Funds for Years Ending March 31, 1978–1983 (millions of dollars)

|  | *1978* | *1979* | *1980* | *1981* | *1982* | *1983* |
|---|---|---|---|---|---|---|
| *Sources of Funds* | | | | | | |
| Funds from operations | | | | | | |
| Retained earnings[a] | $ 2.5 | $ 1.6 | $ (1.1) | $ 7.2 | $ 83.1 | $ 170.8 |
| Depreciation | 11.2 | 13.6 | 18.3 | 27.2 | 60.8 | 108.6 |
| Other[b] | 2.7 | 3.5 | 7.0 | 6.1 | 35.2 | 57.1 |
| Total | 16.4 | 18.7 | 24.2 | 40.5 | 179.1 | 336.5 |
| Funds from external financing | | | | | | |
| Net increase in lease obligations | 10.2 | 35.0 | 65.4 | 47.7 | (5.0) | (18.3) |
| Other net borrowing, sale of securities | (4.6) | (.8) | 19.3 | 85.1 | 158.8 | 842.2 |
| Total | 5.6 | 34.2 | 84.7 | 132.8 | 163.8 | 823.9 |
| Total sources | $22.0 | $52.9 | $108.9 | $173.3 | $342.9 | $1,160.4 |
| *Uses of Funds* | | | | | | |
| Investment in plant, equipment | $22.2 | $52.5 | $110.3 | $155.7 | $271.5 | $ 623.0 |
| Acquisitions | — | — | — | — | — | 195.1 |
| Increase in adjusted working capital[c] | (1.7) | (5.6) | 1.0 | 12.8 | (60.4) | (55.2)[d] |
| Change in cash holdings | 1.5 | 6.0 | (2.4) | 4.8 | 131.8 | 397.5 |
| Total uses | $22.0 | $52.9 | $108.9 | $173.3 | $342.9 | $1,160.4 |

*Sources:* MCI annual reports, 10-K reports.

*Note:* Numbers may not add exactly because of rounding.

a. Net income less preferred dividends.

b. Deferred taxes, employee stock purchase plan.

c. Working capital excluding cash and short-term debt.

d. Not including working capital of WUI.

**EXHIBIT 4**
MCI Income Statements for Years Ending March 31, 1981–1983 (millions of dollars)

|  | *1981* | *1982* | *1983* |
|---|---|---|---|
| Revenues | $234 | $506 | $1,073 |
| Operating expenses (excluding depreciation) | 157 | 283 | 674 |
| Depreciation | 26 | 56 | 104 |
|  | 183 | 339 | 778 |
| Operating income | 51 | 167 | 295 |
| Interest expense | 28 | 54 | 75 |
| Interest income (less other expense) | 1 | 16 | 21 |
|  | 27 | 38 | 54 |
| Profit before taxes | 24 | 129 | 241 |
| Provision for income taxes | 5 | 43 | 70 |
| Net income | 19 | 86 | 171 |
| Extraordinary item | 2 | 0 | 0 |
| Adjusted net income | 21 | 86 | 171 |
| Preferred dividends | 11 | 3 | 0 |
| Income available for common stock | $ 10 | $ 83 | $ 171 |

**EXHIBIT 5**

MCI Balance Sheets at March 31, 1981–1983 (millions of dollars)

|  | *1981* | *1982* | *1983* |
|---|---:|---:|---:|
| Cash, cash equivalents | $ 13 | $144 | $ 542 |
| Accounts receivable | 32 | 79 | 162 |
| Other | 4 | 5 | 9 |
| Current assets | 49 | 228 | 713 |
| Plant, equipment (net) | 410 | 619 | 1,324 |
| Other | 8 | 13 | 33 |
| Total assets | $467 | $860 | $2,070 |
| Accounts payable, accrued liabilities | $ 34 | $137 | $ 251 |
| Accrued taxes | 0 | 8 | 22 |
| Debt due within 1 year | 40 | 40 | 48 |
| Current liabilities | 74 | 185 | 321 |
| Long-term debt | 243 | 400 | 896 |
| Deferred income taxes | 2 | 34 | 88 |
| Total liabilities | 319 | 619 | 1,305 |
| Preferred stock (par value) | 1 | 0 | 0 |
| Common stock (par value) | 4 | 5 | 12 |
| Surplus capital paid in | 220 | 230 | 576 |
| Retained earnings (deficit) | (77) | 6 | 177 |
| Total liabilities and net worth | $467 | $860 | $2,070 |

**EXHIBIT 6**
Public Sales of Securities by MCI, 1972–1983

| Date | Instrument | MCI Price on Issue Date | Amount/Price | Net Proceeds | Date Called for Conversion |
|---|---|---|---|---|---|
| June 1972 | Common stock | IPO | 6,000,000 shares @$5 | $ 27,070,000 | na |
| Nov. 1975 | Common stock plus 5-year warrant attached (exercise price—$1.25) | $ 7/8 | 9,600,000 units @$1 | $ 8,165,000 | na |
| Dec. 1978 | $2.64 convertible cumulative preferred stock (conversion price—$2.1875 per share of common) | $ 1 7/8 | 1,120,000 shares @$25 | $ 25,760,000 | Mar. 1980 |
| Sept. 1979 | $1.80 senior convertible cumulative preferred stock (conversion price—$5 per share of common) | $ 3 1/4 | 4,500,000 shares @$15 | $ 63,125,000 | May 1981 |
| July 1980 | 15% subordinated debentures due August 1, 2000 | — | $52,500,000 @100% of face value | $ 50,545,000 | na |
| Oct. 1980 | $1.84 cumulative convertible preferred stock (conversion price—$9 per share of common) | $ 6 1/16 | 3,300,000 shares @$15 | $ 46,725,000 | Nov. 1981 |
| Apr. 1981 | 14 1/8% subordinated debenture due April 1, 2001 | — | $125,000,000 @84.71% of face value | $102,055,000 | na |
| Aug. 1981 | 10 1/4% convertible subordinated debenture due August 15, 2001 (conversion price—$12.825 per share of common) | $10 7/8 | $100,000,000 @100% of face value | $ 98,200,000 | Feb. 1983 |
| May 1982 | 10% convertible subordinated debenture due May 15, 2002 (conversion price—$22.50 per share of common) | $18 5/8 | $250,000,000 @100% of face value | $245,925,000 | Dec. 1982 |
| Sept. 1982 | 12 7/8% subordinated debenture due October 1, 2002 | — | $250,000,000 @85.625% of face value | $209,922,500 | na |
| Mar. 1983 | 7 3/4% convertible subordinated debenture due March 15, 2003 (conversion price—$52.125 per share) | $43 3/8 | $400,000,000 @100% | $393,675,000 | — |

*Source:* MCI prospectuses.

*Note:* All prices and share figures adjusted for subsequent stock split. Amounts are initial offering levels. In each case, the offerings were oversubscribed and additional funds were raised.

na = not available.

**EXHIBIT 7**
Comparative Interest Rates, 1978–1983

| | Industrials | | | | Utilities | | | MCI[c] |
| | Bonds[a] | | Preferred Stock[b] | | Bonds[a] | | Preferred Stock[b] | Bonds, Preferred |
| Issue Date | A | BBB | Medium | Speculative | A | BBB | Medium | Stock at Issue |
|---|---|---|---|---|---|---|---|---|
| Dec. 1978 . . | 9.17% | 9.76% | 9.45% | 10.34% | 9.50% | 9.78% | 10.48% | PS 10.56% |
| Sept. 1979 . . | 9.74 | 10.41 | 9.76 | 11.53 | 10.05 | 10.51 | 10.97 | PS 12.00 |
| July 1980 . . | 11.35 | 11.74 | 10.56 | 10.91 | 11.54 | 12.60 | 12.32 | D 15.00 |
| Oct. 1980 . . | 12.92 | 13.03 | 11.43 | 11.98 | 12.79 | 14.14 | 14.32 | PS 12.27 |
| Apr. 1981 . . | 13.29 | 14.18 | 13.19 | 13.65 | 14.01 | 15.17 | 15.12 | D 16.80 |
| Aug. 1981 . . | 16.25 | 17.25 | 13.46 | 14.99 | 17.50 | 18.00 | 15.85 | CD 10.25 |
| May 1982 . . | 15.50 | 16.50 | 13.16 | 14.62 | 16.25 | 17.00 | 14.93 | CD 10.00 |
| Sept. 1982 . . | 13.75 | 14.63 | 13.21 | 14.49 | 14.00 | 15.13 | 14.11 | D 15.17 |
| Mar. 1983 . . | 12.50 | 13.00 | 11.36 | 12.67 | 12.75 | 13.25 | 12.51 | CD 7.75 |

PS = convertible preferred stock; D = straight debenture; CD = convertible debenture.

a. Standard and Poor's rating.

b. Rates are for nonconvertible preferred stock.

c. MCI bonds are nonrated for most of this period.

**EXHIBIT 8**
Comparison of Companies, 1983 (billions of dollars)

| | MCI[a] | AT&T | GTE | IBM | ITT |
|---|---|---|---|---|---|
| Revenues . . . . . . . . . | $ 1.1 | $ 65.1 | $12.1 | $34.4 | $16.0 |
| Net income . . . . . . . | .17 | 6.99 | .90 | 4.41 | .70 |
| Assets . . . . . . . . . | 2.1 | 148.2 | 21.9 | 32.5 | 14.1 |
| Return on | | | | | |
|   Sales . . . . . . . . . | 15.9% | 10.7% | 7.4% | 12.8% | 4.4% |
|   Assets . . . . . . . . | 11.0 | 8.6 | 4.1 | 14.1 | 4.8 |
|   Equity . . . . . . . . | 32.4 | 12.2 | 15.6 | 22.9 | 12.7 |
| Payout ratio . . . . . . . | 0 | 67 | 61 | 47 | 54 |
| Debt ratio[b] . . . . . . . . | 55 | 43 | 57 | 14 | 38 |
| Current ratio . . . . . . . | 2.2 | .9 | 1.0 | 1.6 | 1.3 |
| Interest coverage . . . . . . | 4.2 | 3.6 | 2.4 | 18 | 2.5 |
| Bond rating . . . . . . . | NR | Aaa | Baa | Aaa | A |
| Price-earnings range . . . . . | 8–27 | 6–8 | 6–10 | 8–13 | 5–7 |

*Source:* Standard and Poor's reports; Moody's.

NR = not rated.

a. Fiscal year ending March 31.

b. Total debt to capital.

**EXHIBIT 9**

Baseline Forecast of Anticipated MCI Operating Characteristics for Years Ending March 31, 1983–1990 (millions of dollars)

| | 1983 | 1984 | 1985 | 1986 | 1987 | 1988 | 1989 | 1990 |
|---|---|---|---|---|---|---|---|---|
| 1. Interstate long-distance market | $27,000 | $29,800 | $32,800 | $36,000 | $39,700 | $43,600 | $48,000 | $52,800 |
| 2. MCI market share[a] | 4.0% | 6.2% | 9.6% | 13.5% | 18.6% | 19.8% | 20.0% | 20.0% |
| 3. MCI revenues [(1) × (2)] | $ 1,073 | $ 1,850 | $ 3,160 | $ 4,870 | $ 7,380 | $ 8,660 | $ 9,600 | $10,560 |
| 4. Access charges (% of sales) | 16% | 23% | 29.5% | 29.5% | 29.5% | 28.5% | 27.5% | 26.5% |
| 5. Operating margin[b] | 27.5% | 20.5% | 12.0% | 12.0% | 12.0% | 13.0% | 14.0% | 15.0% |
| 6. Operating earnings (EBIT) [(3) × (5)] | $ 295 | $ 380 | $ 390 | $ 590 | $ 890 | $ 1,125 | $ 1,345 | $ 1,580 |
| 7. Interest paid | $ 75 | $ 100 | $ 100 | $ 100 | $ 100 | $ 100 | $ 100 | $ 100 |
| 8. Other income | $ 21 | $ 13 | $ 3 | $ 4 | $ 4 | $ 5 | $ 5 | $ 5 |
| 9. Provision for taxes | $ 70 | $ 83 | $ 58 | $ 123 | $ 206 | $ 299 | $ 400 | $ 475 |
| 10. After-tax net income [(6) − (7) + (8) − (9)] | $ 171 | $ 210 | $ 235 | $ 371 | $ 588 | $ 731 | $ 850 | $ 1,010 |
| 11. Increase in deferred taxes | $ 53 | $ 65 | $ 88 | $ 106 | $ 120 | $ 140 | $ 146 | $ 140 |
| 12. Incremental investment factor | 1.15 | 1.15 | 1.12 | 1.10 | 1.08 | 1.06 | 1.04 | 1.0 |
| 13. Capital expenditures for new capacity [Change in (3) × (12)] | $ 623 | $ 890 | $ 1,467 | $ 1,881 | $ 2,710 | $ 1,357 | $ 980 | $ 960 |
| 14. Capital expenditures for replacement | — | — | — | $ 50 | $ 50 | $ 100 | $ 100 | $ 100 |
| 15. Total capital expenditures [(13) + (14)] | $ 623 | $ 890 | $ 1,467 | $ 1,931 | $ 2,760 | $ 1,457 | $ 1,080 | $ 1,060 |
| 16. Depreciation | $ 104 | $ 173 | $ 272 | $ 412 | $ 601 | $ 749 | $ 800 | $ 826 |
| 17. Net plant, equipment (end of year) | $ 1,324 | $ 2,041 | $ 3,236 | $ 4,755 | $ 6,914 | $ 7,622 | $ 7,902 | $ 8,136 |
| 18. Additional working capital required | 0 | 0 | 0 | 0 | 0 | 0 | 0 | 0 |

*Source:* Casewriter's estimates based on security analysts' forecasts.

a. This is total MCI revenue as a fraction of long-distance revenues and includes non-long-distance revenues. MCI's actual share of the interstate long-distance market would be slighty lower.

b. Includes depreciation as a cost.

*(continued)*

**EXHIBIT 9** *(concluded)*
Assumptions Underlying the Forecasts

1. The interstate long-distance market, which amounted to about $27 billion in FY1983, would grow at 10% per year through FY1990.

2. MCI's revenues would increase from 4% of total long-distance revenues in FY1983 to 20% in FY1990. The increase would be rapid in the years immediately following the advent of *equal access,* but would subsequently slow down as AT&T began to defend its reduced share of the market, other competitors developed their networks, and the market itself adapted to the shock of competition. This pattern is shown on line 2. In each year, 10% of MCI revenues would come from other than long-distance growth. Thus, in FY1990, MCI was projected to hold 18% of the long-distance market. MCI's management was believed to be committed to a growth program of the dimensions shown on line 3 and would, if necessary, sacrifice profit margins to achieve it.

3. Access charges paid by MCI would almost double between FY1983 and FY1985. They would then taper off to about 26.5% of total revenues in FY1990. This was consistent with announced FCC intentions at the end of March 1983. However, there was a great deal of uncertainty in this area. AT&T currently paid access charges amounting to more than 50% of revenues, and reductions to the levels on line 4 would depend on the imposition of *direct access* charges on households and businesses. Legislation in Congress with a reasonable chance of passage forbade the imposition of such direct access charges.

4. MCI's operating margin (operating earnings as a fraction of revenues) would shrink under the dual pressure of higher access charges and increased competition from both AT&T and other long-distance suppliers. Ultimately, however, as access charges fell and the market stabilized, margins were expected to recover to a level of about 15%. Anticipated yearly margins are shown on line 5. However, as noted, these were subject to substantial uncertainty. In the best case, favorable regulatory and legislative action, coupled with restrained competitor behavior, might increase margins by as much as 7% (up to 22% of sales) from these levels. In an unfavorable situation, severe competition and high access charges could reduce margins by an equal amount.

5. Interest payments on MCI's outstanding debt were running at an annual rate of about $100 million at the end of FY1983 (for the year as a whole, interest payments were only $75 million because the debt level increased during the year) and, with no net change in indebtedness, would remain stable at this level through FY1990.

6. Other income, shown on line 8, represents interest on holdings of cash equivalents. As *excess* cash is used up, this figure is expected to decline to $3 million and then grow roughly with sales. This projection does not include interest on the proceeds of any future security offerings that are added temporarily to cash.

7. Provision for taxes, shown on line 9, amounts in 1984 to 25% of net income, which is below the 46% base rate because of investment tax credits and other special credits. As growth and investment slow in later years and reduce the available credits, taxes as a percentage of net income should increase.

8. Increases in deferred taxes, shown on line 11, accumulate at a rate related to present and past capital expenditures. As growth slows, so does the rate of accumulation of deferred tax credits.

9. In March 1983 each extra dollar of revenue required about $1.15 worth of investment in fixed plant and equipment. This factor was expected to fall to about $1.00 by FY1990, as improved electronic technology reduced equipment costs. The expected yearly pattern is shown on line 12. It was possible, however, that in the latter part of the period (post-FY1987) this factor would fall substantially below $1.00.

10. Replacement of older equipment would require the investments described on line 13.

11. Depreciation would be charged at an annual rate equal to 9.8% of the value of plant and equipment in place at the beginning of each year plus 4.9% of the value of total new investment.

12. No additions to working capital would be required throughout the period and any cash on hand at the end of FY1983 could be devoted to investment programs.

13. MCI would not penetrate intrastate toll market.

# Union Tank Car Company

In the winter of 1980 the top management of Union Tank Car Company was grappling with the problem of restructuring the company's leasing contracts for tank cars. Growing evidence indicated that a recent regulatory change was going to have a dramatic and lasting impact on the fundamental economics underlying the use of tank cars. It would also affect shippers' lease versus buy/borrow decisions. If Union Tank Car was to remain profitable in this business, it would have to tailor its leasing contracts to fit shippers' interests in the new environment. However, the leasing terms would also have to be competitive with those offered by other leasing companies.

## Company Background

Union Tank Car Company (UTC) engaged in the manufacture and leasing of railway tank cars and other rail vehicles to North American shippers of bulk liquids; compressed gas; and powdered, pelletized, or dry bulk products. At the end of 1979 its fleet of vehicles comprised 55,920 cars. Approximately 83% of that fleet consisted of tank cars and represented the second largest fleet of privately held tank cars in the world. Revenues in 1979 totaled $404 million and had grown at a 15% compounded annual rate over the previous 5 years. Profit after taxes in 1979 was $45.2 million. Financial statements for UTC are presented in Exhibits 1 and 2.

Most of UTC's tank cars were leased directly to several hundred manufacturers and other railroad shippers. In particular, UTC was a principal source of railway transportation equipment for the petroleum industry. Management of UTC estimated that cars carrying compressed gases accounted for the greatest portion of the company's leasing revenues, followed by refined petroleum products, chemicals and acids, food products, and liquid fertilizers.

UTC had been organized in 1891 and publicly owned from 1912 until June 1, 1969, when it became an operating subsidiary of Trans Union Corporation in a holding company reorganization. In 1980, Trans Union was the sole owner of UTC's common stock. Trans Union had total revenues of $923 million, taxable income of $100 million, net income of $58 million, and earnings per share of $4.81 in 1979. Cash dividends were paid at an annual rate of $2.36 per share. At the close of 1979, Trans Union's common stock traded at about $35 per share on the New York Stock Exchange (approximately 12 million shares were outstanding).

## The Tank Car Leasing Business

Ever since tank cars were developed, railroads have been reluctant to own and provide them to shippers using their lines. Tank cars were too specialized to be managed economically by the railroads because they required special maintenance and cleaning. Moreover, the operation of tank cars entailed higher use and regulatory risks than did the operation of other freight cars.

Because of this attitude on the part of railroads, shippers found it necessary to supply their own tank cars. However, given limited capital for purchasing tank cars; an aversion to the risks of ownership; and, for the average shipper, too small a fleet of tank cars to realize any economies of scale in maintenance (the typical shipper used only 200–300 tank cars), shippers did not find ownership particularly attractive. Thus an opportunity arose for leasing companies to intermediate the tank car market profitably. In a leasing arrangement shippers could finance their use of tank cars while passing the risks and obligations of ownership to the lessor. If priced correctly, a leasing arrangement could be mutually beneficial to both parties.

As the tank car leasing industry matured, four major competitors emerged to dominate the market. The largest were GATX Corporation and Union Tank Car Company (see Exhibit 3 for summary descriptions of the major competitors). The industry became fairly stable as far as the threat of new competition was concerned. Entry was difficult because of high capital requirements and the need to achieve economies of scale in maintenance. A minimum of 12,000 cars was needed to exploit maintenance economies fully, and a newly built tank car cost approximately $45,000 in 1980.

A potential new entrant also faced a number of significant risks. Since some tank cars were designed to carry a specific type of commodity, technological innovations in transportation or a permanent decline in demand for a particular commodity could render many tank cars obsolete. Health, safety, and environmental regulations could also influence how, or even whether, a particular commodity could be carried by rail. Tank car modifications to comply with regulatory changes in these areas could be substantial and costly.

Despite these risks and barriers to entry, two new companies, Richmond Tank Car Company and Trinity Industries, had managed to break into the tank car market in recent decades. However, these companies concentrated on selling tank cars rather than leasing them, thus minimizing their initial capital requirements. Both new companies were still struggling to establish themselves as of 1980.

Competition among established companies in the leasing industry focused on quick delivery time, quality of vehicles provided, price, and service. Servicing cars quickly and returning them for use was particularly important. Lessees placed a premium on avoiding shipping disruptions due to the loss of cars for repair.

## Types of Leases

If a tank car was purchased, the shipper assumed all the costs (e.g., maintenance, repair, insurance, property taxes) and benefits (e.g., depreciation tax shields, investment tax credits) of ownership, including those associated with the financing of the vehicle. Under a leasing arrangement, these costs and benefits could be unbundled and redistributed between the owner/lessor and the user/lessee, often to their mutual benefit. Precisely how this redistribution was made depended upon the type of lease.

Most leases can be roughly classified into one of four groups according to the length of time covered by the lease and the party assuming ownership costs (see Table A).

**TABLE A**
Major Categories of Leasing Contracts

Net: Lessee assumes ownership costs
1. Full payout—long-term
2. Operating—short-term

Full service: Lessor assumes ownership costs
3. Full payout—long-term
4. Operating—short-term

1. A *net full-payout lease,* often called a net financing lease or a net capital lease, is a long-term lease through which the lessee has use of the equipment for most of its useful life. The lessee also assumes all nonfinancial costs associated with the asset while under the lease (e.g., maintenance and administrative expenses) and generally assumes ownership of the asset at the end of the lease term. The lessor usually recovers the acquisition cost of the leased equipment and earns a profit; hence, the lessor's role is primarily one of providing financing.

2. A *net operating lease* is a short-term lease through which the lessee assumes nonfinancial ownership costs. Such leases are rare in the case of railroad

cars because lessors are reluctant to relinquish control of maintenance for cars that might be returned to them before the end of their useful lives.

3. A *full-service full-payout lease* is a long-term lease through which all ownership and operating costs are assumed by the lessor. All acquisition costs, nonfinancial costs, and a profit are returned to the lessor by the end of the lease life through rental payments. Shippers and short-line railroads are most likely to select this type of lease when they are unwilling to manage their own equipment but wish to retain it for most of its useful life.

4. A *full-service operating lease* has a term much shorter than the life of the asset and may often be canceled at the option of the lessee. All ownership costs are assumed by the lessor.

The full-service operating lease and the net full-payout lease are the most widely used forms of leases in the railroad industry. UTC offered all types of leases, but most were full-service operating leases. As with other tank car lessors, these leases generally had terms of 10–12 years and could not be canceled.

## Establishing Renewal Rates on Short-Term Leases

Because tank cars have useful lives of 20 years or more, the relatively short duration of their leases presents some investment risk to tank car lessors. At the end of a typical leasing period shippers who still require the use of a tank car would have the option of leasing a brand new tank car at the prevailing rental rate for new cars or renewing the expired lease on the old tank car at some rate appropriate for older cars. If a large number of shippers choose not to renew their leases, a lessor could find itself saddled with a substantial number of unleased vehicles in its fleet.

To avoid this contingency, lessors attempt to set renewal rates on older vehicles at a level that will promote rapid redeployment while still allowing the lessor to earn a profit. As a practical matter, the prevailing rental rate on a new vehicle establishes a ceiling on the renewal rate of an older vehicle. No shipper would renew a lease on an old tank car at a higher rental rate than that for a new car if new cars were available. Similarly, a floor on the renewal rate is determined by the lessor's anticipated costs of ownership and the scrap value of the car. Lessors would renew a lease only if the rental payments are expected to cover costs and if the present value of the lease's net cash flow exceeds that which could be obtained by scrapping the car immediately. Between these two bounds, the precise level of the renewal rate in any given year is ultimately determined by the forces of supply and demand, the relative bargaining strengths of lessees and lessors, and competition within the leasing industry. Generally, renewal rates on tank car leases remain very close to the upper bound.

The cash flows involved in a typical lease versus buy/borrow decision for a tank car in 1980 are shown in Exhibit 4. For simplicity, a 10-year leasing term and a 20-year car life have been assumed. A shipper purchasing a tank car is assumed to be able to borrow up to 75% of the cost of the car. The loan would be repaid over 20 years and would bear an interest rate of 15%. Other assumptions are specified in Exhibit 4. As is evident from the final two columns of Exhibit 4, the lease renewal rate after year 10 represents an unknown quantity facing lessee and lessor alike at the inception of the new lease.

Because of high rates of inflation in the 1970s and a stable competitive environment, tank car lessors benefited from rising lease renewal rates on their older vehicles. Both tank car construction costs and other costs of ownership had inflated at a 6–7% annual rate during the previous decade. This inflation helped to push up leasing rates on new vehicles, which in turn allowed renewal rates on old vehicles to rise. In 1980 car construction and other costs were expected to continue rising at an annual rate of approximately 6%.

## Ex Parte 328

Because shippers themselves provided tank cars when transporting by rail, railroads compensated them for ownership in the form of a mileage allowance. A shipper earned mileage credits for each loaded mile traveled. The allowance was calculated using a complicated formula that included such variables as an interest rate factor, loaded miles traveled, and the value of the tank car at the time of its construction. Tank car lessors usually passed this mileage allowance straight to the shippers leasing their cars. Thus, there was essentially no difference between leasing and owning a tank car as far as mileage allowance was concerned.

In 1979 the prevailing mileage allowance formula was changed through a negotiated agreement among railroad representatives, tank car leasing interests, and shipper interests, all under the auspices of the U.S. Interstate Commerce Commission (ICC). The purpose of the change was to update the formula to reflect rising tank car costs and other effects of inflation. Under the old formula, the mileage allowance could increase with the original value of the tank car only up to a value of $20,000. Newer, more costly cars would not be compensated above that value.

On June 14, 1979, the ICC approved the negotiated agreement in a proceeding known in the industry as Ex Parte 328.[1] Under the new formula, the mileage allowance for a vehicle would increase steadily with its value at the time it was placed in service. A graphic illustration of the old mileage allowance system, implemented in 1976, and the new one is given in Exhibit 5.

Although the continued pass-through of the mileage allowance would not alter the economics of leasing a *given* car, the new formula clearly would affect shippers' choices for the type of car used. Specifically, shippers would prefer to use newer, higher-valued cars under Ex Parte 328 in order to earn the greatest possible mileage allowance.

The new preferences of shippers presented a problem to lessors as far as renewal of leases was concerned. The maximum renewal rate that lessors could

---

1. This term represents the ICC docket number for this particular rule-making case.

expect to charge without causing shippers to switch to newer cars would no longer be just the leasing rate on new vehicles. Under Ex Parte 328 the new ceiling for renewal rates would be those rates that equated out-of-pocket leasing costs (i.e., total leasing rate less mileage allowance) of old and new vehicles. Assuming continued inflation, the ceiling for renewal rates could be expected to be lower under Ex Parte 328.

An illustration of this effect for a tank car built in 1980 is shown in Table B. The table assumes that new car values and leasing rates inflate at 6% per year. Mileage allowance is calculated by extrapolating the line shown in Exhibit 5 and assuming that the vehicles in question travel 6,000 loaded miles per year.

**TABLE B**
Maximum Lease Renewal Rates in 1990 under Ex Parte 328

| (1)<br>Tank Car<br>Value | (2)<br>Mileage<br>Allowance | (3)<br>Annual Mileage<br>Earnings | (4)<br>Annual Leasing<br>Rate | (5)<br>Out-of-Pocket<br>Cost of Lease<br>(col. 4 − col. 5) |
|---|---|---|---|---|
| $45,000<br>(built 1980) | $.61 per<br>loaded mile | $3,660 ──── | $4,425 | $ 765 |
| $80,588<br>(built 1990) | $.97 per<br>loaded mile | $5,820 | $7,925 | $2,105<br>+ 3,660 |
| | | Maximum renewal rate for 1980-built car: | | $5,765 |

## Responding to Ex Parte 328

The lower renewal rates that could be expected under Ex Parte 328 would dramatically reduce the residual value of tank cars held under short-term leases. Estimates of that reduction ranged from 25% to 50% of the value of the existing fleet. For UTC this might mean a loss in value of $100–200 million.

The size of this potential loss prompted UTC's management to consider various responses that might allow the company to preserve value under Ex Parte 328. One possibility was to continue offering full-service operating leases but to increase the rental rate in the first 10 years *before* renewal. Another possibility was to shift emphasis to another type of leasing contract, for example, a full-service full-payout lease or a net full-payout lease. A final alternative was to switch from leasing tank cars to selling them. The choice among these alternatives had to be made in the context of the economics underlying the lease versus buy/borrow decision and the competitive environment of the tank car leasing industry.

**EXHIBIT 1**
Consolidated Income Statements for Years Ending December 31, 1977–1979
(thousands of dollars)

| | 1977 | 1978 | 1979 |
|---|---|---|---|
| Revenues | $297,900 | $355,585 | $404,043 |
| Cost of sales and services | 136,468 | 173,648 | 183,899 |
| Depreciation | 36,566 | 38,790 | 42,480 |
| Selling, general, and administrative expenses | 31,611 | 37,279 | 40,910 |
| Interest expense | 40,634 | 43,362 | 52,109 |
| Income before taxes | 52,621 | 62,506 | 84,645 |
| Provision for taxes | | | |
| Current | 8,000 | 10,660 | 18,010 |
| Deferred | 15,100 | 14,550 | 11,930 |
| Deferred investment tax credit | 1,350 | 4,570 | 9,460 |
| Total | 24,450 | 29,780 | 39,400 |
| Net income | $ 28,171 | $ 32,726 | $ 45,245 |

**EXHIBIT 2**
Consolidated Balance Sheets at December 31, 1978–1979
(thousands of dollars)

| | 1978 | 1979 |
|---|---|---|
| Cash and marketable securities | $ 7,256 | $ 8,134 |
| Accounts receivable, net | 47,641 | 53,169 |
| Inventories | 49,730 | 65,412 |
| Prepaid expenses, deferred charges | 9,632 | 8,208 |
| Other | 9,954 | 16,869 |
| Current assets | 124,213 | 151,792 |
| Railcar lease fleet | | |
| Cost | 992,037 | 1,157,415 |
| Accumulated depreciation | 291,082 | 318,250 |
| | 700,955 | 839,165 |
| Other fixed assets | 96,498 | 115,177 |
| Other investments | 112,917 | 65,479 |
| Total assets | $1,034,583 | $1,171,613 |
| Accounts payable | $ 18,255 | $ 15,043 |
| Accrued expenses | 36,990 | 43,702 |
| Federal income tax payable | 3,902 | 6,590 |
| Other | 644 | 1,567 |
| Current liabilities | 59,791 | 66,902 |
| Long-term debt | 530,442 | 619,245 |
| Deferred taxes | 244,710 | 244,770 |
| Total liabilities | 814,943 | 930,917 |
| Stockholders' equity | 219,640 | 240,696 |
| Total liabilities and stockholders' equity | $1,034,583 | $1,171,613 |

**EXHIBIT 3**
Selected Data on Tank Car Leasing Companies, 1979 (millions of dollars except per share data)

| | Union Tank Car Co. | ACF Industries | GATX Corp. | North American Car Corp. | Richmond Tank Car Co. | Trinity Industries |
|---|---|---|---|---|---|---|
| Tank car fleet (no. of cars) | 46,240 | 20,489 | 53,295 | 16,540 | 2,879 | na |
| Total revenues | $ 404.0 | $1,000.6 | $ 912.3 | $ 322.6 | $ 108.9 | $ 277.2 |
| Total net income | 45.2 | 47.8 | 71.0 | 36.2 | 6.4 | 9.4 |
| Total assets | 1,171.6 | 1,016.8 | 2,257.7 | 1,109.8 | 99.5 | 151.3 |
| Total debt | 619.2 | 364.3 | 732.5 | 565.7 | 20.1 | 29.6 |
| Shareholders' equity | 240.7 | 348.4 | 487.5 | 232.2 | 47.2 | 79.4 |
| Leasing revenues | 277.7 | 118.9 | 209.7 | 303.7 | 10.4 | na |
| Pre-tax leasing profits | 63.9 | 38.0 | 43.9 | 38.8[c] | 2.8 | na |
| Common stock price, 1979 | | | | | | |
| High | [a] | $ 39¾ | $ 46 | [b] | $ 15¾ | $ 25⅝ |
| Low | [a] | 29⅛ | 23⅞ | [b] | 11¾ | 16⅛ |
| Closing | [a] | 34¼ | 36¾ | [b] | 15 | 24⅜ |
| Number of common shares outstanding (000s) | [a] | 8,787.5 | 12,095.0 | [b] | 5,143.5 | 3,862.2 |
| Selected ratios | | | | | | |
| Net profit margin | 11.2% | 4.8% | 7.8% | 11.2% | 5.9% | 3.4% |
| Return on equity | 18.8% | 13.7% | 14.6% | 15.6% | 13.6% | 11.8% |
| Total debt/Total capital | 72.0% | 51.1% | 60.0% | 70.9% | 27.9% | 27.2% |
| Asset turnover | .3 | 1.0 | .4 | .3 | 1.1 | 1.8 |
| Current ratio | 1.6 | 2.0 | 2.6 | 2.6 | 2.6 | 2.5 |
| Annual growth rate, 1974–1979 | | | | | | |
| Total revenues | 15.3% | 13.1% | 11.8% | 25.4% | 36.6% | 7.6% |
| Total net income | 5.7% | 10.7% | 4.3% | 16.6% | 40.2% | 10.1% |

na = not available.

a. The common equity of Union Tank Car Company is owned by Trans Union Corporation.

b. The common equity of North American Car Corporation is owned by Tiger International, Inc.

c. Casewriter's estimate.

# EXHIBIT 4
Cash Flows Associated with a Shipper's Ownership, Use, and Financing of a Tank Car

| | Ownership Cash Flows | | | | Operating Cash Flows[a] | | Financing Cash Flows | | | | |
| | | | | | | | Debt | | | Lease | |
| Year | Sale Price of Tank Car | Investment Tax Credit | Depreciation Tax Shield | Scrap Value | After-Tax Maintenance Expense | After-Tax Administration Expense | Loan | Principal Repayment | After-Tax Interest Expense | Lease Payment | After-Tax Lease Payment |
|---|---|---|---|---|---|---|---|---|---|---|---|
| 0 | $(45,000) | — | — | | — | — | $33,750 | — | — | $(4,425) | $(2,390) |
| 1 | | $4,500 | $ 3,185 | | $ (196) | $ (141) | | $ (329) | $ (2,734) | | |
| 2 | | | 2,919 | | (207) | (149) | | (379) | (2,707) | | |
| 3 | | | 2,654 | | (220) | (158) | | (436) | (2,676) | | |
| 4 | | | 2,389 | | (233) | (167) | | (501) | (2,641) | | |
| 5 | | | 2,123 | | (247) | (178) | | (576) | (2,601) | | |
| 6 | | | 1,858 | | (262) | (188) | | (663) | (2,554) | | |
| 7 | | | 1,592 | | (278) | (199) | | (762) | (2,500) | | |
| 8 | | | 1,327 | | (294) | (212) | | (876) | (2,439) | | |
| 9 | | | 1,061 | | (312) | (224) | | (1,008) | (2,367) | | |
| 10 | | | 796 | | (330) | (238) | | (1,159) | (2,286) | | |
| 11 | | | 531 | | (350) | (252) | | (1,333) | (2,192) | | |
| 12 | | | 264 | | (372) | (267) | | (1,533) | (2,084) | | |
| 13 | | | | | (394) | (283) | | (1,763) | (1,960) | | |
| 14 | | | | | (417) | (300) | | (2,027) | (1,817) | | |
| 15 | | | | | (442) | (318) | | (2,331) | (1,653) | | |
| 16 | | | | | (469) | (337) | | (2,681) | (1,464) | (4,425) Renewal Rate | (2,390) Renewal Rate After Tax |
| 17 | | | | | (497) | (357) | | (3,083) | (1,247) | | |
| 18 | | | | | (527) | (379) | | (3,545) | (997) | | |
| 19 | | | | | (558) | (401) | | (4,077) | (710) | | |
| 20 | | | | $4,860 | (592) | (426) | | (4,688) | (380) | | |
| **Present value using various discount rates** | | | | | | | | | | | |
| After-tax cost of debt, 8.1% | $(45,000) | $4,163 | $14,753 | $1,024 | $(3,024) | $(2,174) | $33,750 | $(11,684) | $(22,067) | | |
| Pre-tax cost of debt, 15% | (45,000) | 3,913 | 11,641 | 297 | (1,748) | (1,257) | 33,750 | (5,730) | (15,131) | | |
| Cost of equity, 20% | (45,000) | 3,750 | 10,033 | 127 | (1,281) | (921) | 33,750 | (3,776) | (12,140) | | |
| Weighted avg cost of capital, 11.1% | (45,000) | 4,050 | 13,242 | 592 | (2,338) | (1,680) | 33,750 | (8,395) | (18,503) | | |

*Note:* Assumptions are as follows: investment tax credit 10%; depreciation 12-year, sum-of-years digits; scrap value 20% of original sale price less tax on gain; tax rate 46%; loans 75% of sale price at interest rate of 15%, repayable in equal annual installments over 20 years; rate of inflation 6% per year; weighted average cost of capital .75(15%) (1 − .46) + .25(20%) = 11.1%.

a. It had been estimated that Union Tank Car Company had at least a 25% cost advantage over shippers in maintenance and administrative expenses.

**EXHIBIT 5**
Mileage Allowance by Value: Ex Parte 328 (1979) versus Previous System (1976)

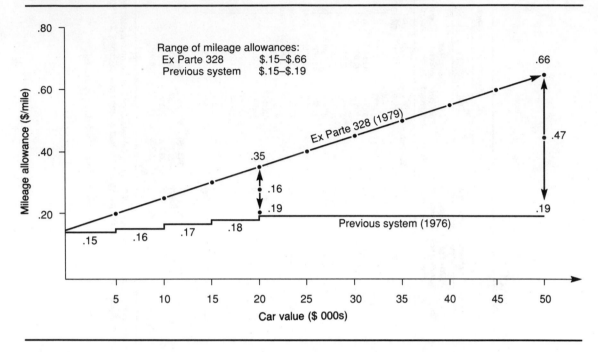

# Novo Industri A/S (1981)

In January 1981, the management of Novo Industri A/S was considering how best to fund the expansion planned for the next several years. Projections in the company's budget revealed a deficit of DK (Danish kroner) 220 million in 1981 and DK 127 million in 1982. After financing opportunities inside and outside Denmark had been explored, three major alternatives had been chosen for further evaluation. These alternatives were convertible debt to be issued in the Eurobond market or in the United States; a preemptive rights offering at par to current shareholders; or a general public offering of new shares to overseas investors in London and the United States. As its largest external financing to date, it was important that Novo's choice be consistent with its overall corporate strategy and financial policies, and that it reflect management's concern for shareholder interests.

## Company and Industry Background

Novo Industri A/S, founded in Denmark in 1925 by Harald and Horvald Pedersen, was a leader in the manufacture and sale of insulin, enzymes, and other pharmaceutical and biochemical products. It was incorporated in 1940, a time during which it exported insulin to over 30 countries. Since then, Novo had developed two major product segments through its strength in research and process technologies: enzymes and pharmaceuticals (primarily insulin).

---

A major source of background information for this case was Arthur I. Stonehill and Kare B. Dullum, *Internationalizing the Cost of Capital* (New York: Wiley, 1982).

Enzymes, which are proteins that act as catalysts in biochemical processes, have a variety of industrial uses. They are produced by extraction from animal or vegetable tissues or by fermentation of micro-organisms. Firmly established as the world leader in industrial enzyme production, Novo made an operating profit of DK 135 million on enzymes in 1980, compared with DK 96 million for pharmaceuticals. The majority of its clients were in the detergent and starch industries. Although many large companies produced their own enzymes, Novo held about 50% of the noncaptive market, estimated at DK 1.6 billion in 1980.

Novo's pharmaceuticals manufacturing was based on the process of extraction, although fermentation and synthesis processes were also used. Its most important products from this division were insulin preparations. In 1980, Novo ranked as the second largest producer of insulin after Eli Lilly and Company. It was estimated that Eli Lilly captured 85–90% of the U.S. insulin market in 1980 and that Novo controlled 60% of the European market. Most of Novo's pharmaceutical products were sold by prescription only. Their introduction, pricing, and marketing were subject to control by the public authorities in the various international markets in which they were sold.

Novo's corporate goal was "to remain a highly specialized basic manufacturer within a well-defined biological and biochemical area, primarily based on its own research and development." It pursued this objective through a strategy of international expansion. In 1980, an estimated 97% of Novo's business originated outside Denmark. The company operated production plants in Denmark, France, Switzerland, and South Africa and established two subsidiaries in the United States. The development of a production plant in Japan was also under way. A summary of Novo's consolidated operations is shown in Exhibit 1.

Research, development, and quality control were cornerstones of Novo's strategy. About one-fourth of Novo's employees in Denmark worked in the laboratories, and approximately 10% of annual sales was devoted to research and development. Additional research and technical support were conducted in the United States, Switzerland, and Japan.

By 1981, Novo had become locked in one of the first great battles for a genetically engineered product. Both Novo and Eli Lilly were spending millions to develop a less expensive human insulin to replace the animal insulin that was then most prevalent in world markets. Each intended to use the product to spearhead a push in the other's home market, hoping to break their competitor's dominant position there. Comparative data for Novo and several of its major competitors are given in Exhibit 2.

## Financial History

Two classes of common stock were established when Novo was founded. The A shares (par value DK 100), which were nontransferable and granted ten votes per share, were issued to the Novo Foundation, a nonprofit organization composed of scientists, academicians, and business executives who distributed income from the stock for humanitarian, scientific, and cultural purposes. The B shares (par value DK 100), each granted one vote, were given to the founders and their families.

families. Although the Novo Foundation initially controlled more than 75% of voting rights, it did not involve itself directly in the management of Novo. Nevertheless, it did make clear its intention of preserving at least a two-thirds voting majority.

In 1974 the company was taken public, primarily to enable family members to trade their stock and also to provide access to additional equity funding. Initially, only the required minimum of 10% of transferable shares was listed on the Danish After Market (Efterbøren) and later on the Main Copenhagen Stock Exchange (Copenhagen Fondsboers).[1] The stock was offered at the public price of DK 150 per share, although the book value was DK 241 per share.

Prior to 1981, Novo conducted four major financing efforts in the open market (see Exhibit 3). The first was a rights offering in December 1975, a time when Novo's stock price was at an all-time high of DK 275. This rights issue increased the number of outstanding shares by 50.6%, raised net proceeds of DK 46.8 million, and added DK 6 million to Novo's dividend payments.[2]

A second rights issue, offered in December 1977, included both A and B shares. Novo's share price at this point was around DK 300. This offering represented a 39.7% increase in the shares outstanding and netted Novo DK 56.5 million. Overall, this issue improved the group's capital base, with total liabilities as a percentage of total assets decreasing from 53% in 1976 to 47% in 1977.

In 1977, Novo's management became concerned about the company's ability to obtain the funds necessary for continued expansion, especially given future growth predictions showing a large and continued demand for capital. In Denmark domestic capital was scarce and expensive. In fact, the prior Novo rights issue had been regarded as a large issue for the Danish market and had represented 25% of the total new equity funds raised in Denmark that year. Novo's future needs were expected to exceed that issue.

Furthermore, with 95% of its sales outside Denmark, Novo was planning to invest actively abroad. However, the Bank of Denmark insisted that all foreign investment be financed abroad to conserve the bank's low foreign currency reserves. To resolve this problem, Novo explored various financing alternatives with its principal overseas bank, Morgan Guaranty. Two potential foreign sources of capital were identified: a private placement of straight debt in the United States, and a convertible bond issue in either the United States or the Eurobond market.

Private placement was eventually ruled out because Novo was not well known

---

1. Although the Main Exchange is a stock exchange, relatively little trading in shares takes place there; it is largely a secondary market for mortgage bonds. Most stock trading takes place in the After Market, which is subject to the same fundamental rules as the Main Exchange even though it is an unofficial market. Two important exceptions are that securities can be traded in the After Market by telephone between banks rather than by specialized stock brokers and that the After Market is open from 8 A.M. to 6 P.M. rather than just the few hours to which the Main Exchange is limited.

2. A preemptive rights offering is a method by which new shares are offered to existing shareholders first. This technique is based on the notion that shareholders are entitled to anything of value that the company may distribute and therefore that they should have a preemptive right to subscribe to new offerings. Existing shareholders have the option to exercise, sell, or disregard these rights.

in the U.S. financial community and would therefore have difficulty achieving a successful offering. Convertible bonds issued in the Eurobond market were believed to be a better alternative, although this too would require Novo to heighten its visibility abroad.

The first step in making Novo better known occurred when the British stockbroker Grieveson, Grant and Company decided to add Novo Industri to its research portfolio. Its reports in 1977 were optimistic; Novo was classified as a "buy." Morgan Grenfell in London was called in as Novo's main adviser, and it was decided that the firm would manage a convertible bond issue denominated in U.S. dollars. Novo's management also took steps to convert the company's B stock from registered shares to bearer shares and to obtain a listing of the B shares on the London Stock Exchange.

Finally, in October 1978, Novo asked its shareholders to give up their preemptive rights and authorize a $20 million issue of bonds convertible into B shares at a 10% premium over the Copenhagen Stock Exchange listed price at the time of the offering. Other details of the bond issue are provided in Exhibit 3.

Although the convertible bond was well received by both investors and the financial press, it did little to lift Novo's stock price. In fact, Novo's stock price, which had been declining slowly since mid-1977, continued its fall, dipping to a low of DK 200 by early 1979 (see Exhibit 1). Some analysts viewed this as an undervaluation, while others argued that it was a natural response to the eventual dilutive impact of the convertible issue.

Whatever the cause, European investors' interest in the convertible bond encouraged management to begin promoting Novo's stock abroad. During 1979 presentations to investors were made throughout Europe. Numerous banks, underwriters, and financial publishers were also invited to visit the company. Some promotional literature was published in English, and in the spring of 1980 a special seminar was held in New York City for journalists and financial analysts. The seminar discussed the development of the biotechnology industry in general and Novo's position in that industry in particular. The upshot of this public relations effort appeared to be several encouraging "buy" recommendations and substantial foreign buying of Novo's shares through the London market. The price per share rose to a high of DK 300 by the end of June 1980.

Finally, in the fall of 1980, Novo announced another rights offering that was expected to raise DK 125.2 million. It was structured in two parts (see Exhibit 3). The first would raise the number of A and B shares by 20% at a price of DK 105 per new share. The second would increase the B shares by yet another 10% at a price of DK 250 per share, a 15% discount from market value. Concurrent with the rights offering, the company also announced a dividend increase. The dividend on the A shares was increased from 0.5% of par value to 6%, and on B shares from 12% to 13% of par value. Copenhagen Handelsbank and Gudme Raaschou & Co. underwrote the rights offering. A rising stock price during the offering period helped ensure that the entire issue was sold. Since much of the subscription took place in London, it was estimated that about 50% of Novo's shares were now held abroad, primarily in the United Kingdom and the United States.

# Current Dilemmas Facing Management

Early in January 1981 members of Novo's top management met in Copenhagen with financial advisers from the Copenhagen Handelsbank, Morgan Grenfell (London), and Goldman, Sachs & Co. (United States). The agenda for the meeting was Novo's 1981 funds needs and a plan to execute the financing that would be necessary. Three alternatives were developed, each involving equity or an equity-linked security:

1. A second U.S. dollar convertible bond to be issued either in the Eurobond market or in the United States.
2. A preemptive rights offering to existing shareholders at a subscription price 10–15% below market.
3. A general public offering of B common shares to overseas investors in London or the United States.[3]

Novo's stock price had continued climbing during the fall of 1980, lifted in part by a general rise in the Copenhagen and London stock markets (see Exhibit 4). It reached DK 700 by January 1981. At this level, many analysts believed a near-term high had been attained, although others remained generally bullish (see Exhibit 5 for a selection of comments and recommendations).

The convertible bond alternative seemed attractive in light of the success enjoyed by the first issue in 1978. Although that issue had not yet been fully called, investors had already converted roughly a quarter of the issue in 1980. At the current rate of conversion, one could expect that less than half the issue would remain outstanding by the end of 1981.

A second convertible could be offered with terms similar to the first, except that under current market conditions the conversion price would likely be set at DK 770 per DK 100 par value B shares at a fixed exchange rate of $1 = DK 5.3650. The coupon on the bond would probably be fixed at 8.00%.

A preemptive rights offering would present a means of raising new equity capital without diluting the ownership share of existing holders of B shares, assuming all such shareholders exercised their subscription privilege. This would allow current shareholders to reap the rewards of future growth entirely for themselves. The risk of a rights offering was that the issue might not be fully subscribed, thus yielding less capital than required by the company. Typically, this risk was covered by an oversubscription privilege that allows subscribing shareholders to purchase all unsubscribed rights on a pro rata basis or by entering into a purchase and standby agreement with an underwriter. Under such an agreement, an underwriter would stand ready to purchase all the unsubscribed shares at the subscription price less a take-up fee. For this service, underwriters were usually paid a standby fee of approximately 0.5% of the size of the issue and a take-up fee of another 0.5–1%.

---

3. Arthur I. Stonehill and Kare B. Dullum, *Internationalizing the Cost of Capital* (New York: Wiley, 1982), p. 56.

A general public offering of B common shares represented the surest way of raising equity capital immediately at current market prices. The question was how best to do so. One possible approach was to issue shares directly in London, where the stock was already listed. However, London Stock Exchange rules restricted general public offers without preemptive rights for existing shareholders to no more than 5% of total shares outstanding. This rule would effectively limit the size of Novo's equity offering to 152,626 B shares.

Should Novo choose to offer equity in the United States, it would have to consider setting up an American Depository Receipt system as a prerequisite to listing on one of the exchanges. This was usually accomplished by having a U.S. bank or trust company hold the newly issued shares, against which American depository receipts (ADRs) would then be issued. By using ADRs, U.S. residents wishing to buy shares of foreign companies could execute all transactions, including the receipt of dividends, in U.S. dollars.[4]

Of perhaps greater concern regarding a general public offering in the United States was the fact that a host of initial public offerings by biotechnology companies was hitting the market at the same time. Genentech had gone public in late 1980 with annual revenues of $9 million and operating cash flow of only 6¢ per share. Its stock sold for $35 per share at the time of the issue, a level quickly surpassed in the immediate after-market despite the lack of a commercially viable product or an established operating record. Cetus Corporation, another biotechnology company with virtually no earnings, was also planning a public offering early in 1981. A number of other such companies were rumored to be preparing initial public offerings as well. With this rush of new companies coming to market, there was a threat that U.S. equity investors would become saturated with biotechnology stocks, thus diminishing their incentive to add Novo to their portfolios. Furthermore, from a public relations viewpoint, it was questionable whether Novo should allow itself to be linked to such companies in the public's mind by issuing equity at the same time. Misperceptions about Novo's current businesses and future prospects could set the stage for investors' disenchantment later if unrealistically high expectations were not met.

In choosing among these financing alternatives, a number of considerations seemed pertinent. Novo's present and future needs for funds, the cost of the capital raised, the likelihood of a successful offering and its effect on Novo's reputation, and current shareholder control of the company were issues meriting careful thought in the decision-making process. This, the biggest financing effort of Novo's history, would be a milestone in the company's development and could set a precedent that would influence future financing decisions.

---

4. In 1981 dividends paid by Danish companies to U.S. residents were subject to a withholding tax of 30%. Dividends paid to Danish shareholders would be taxed as ordinary income at marginal rates up to 75%. Capital gains were taxed domestically at a rate of 50% for shares held more than 2 years and at personal tax rates for shares held less than 2 years.

**EXHIBIT 1**
Consolidated Financial Statements and Ratios, 1977–1980 (millions of Danish kroner except per share data)

| | 1977 | 1978 | 1979 | 1980 |
|---|---|---|---|---|
| Sales | DK 864 | DK 939 | DK 1,275 | DK 1,579 |
| Pre-tax income | 103 | 97 | 138 | 239 |
| Net income | 73 | 75 | 103 | 176 |
| Sales abroad as percent of total sales | 96% | 96% | 96% | 97% |
| Capital expenditures | DK 75 | DK 160 | DK 126 | DK 201 |
| Total assets | DK 1,027 | DK 1,391 | DK 1,498 | DK 1,994 |
| Long-term debt | na | na | 387 | 418 |
| Net worth | 545 | 590 | 667 | 959 |
| Return on assets | 7% | 5.3% | 6.8% | 8.8% |
| Return on net worth | 13.3% | 12.7% | 15.4% | 18.3% |
| Debt-to-net-worth ratio | na | na | 58% | 44% |
| Earnings per 100 kroner nominal amount of A and B shares, primary | DK 22.33 | DK 22.28 | DK 30.54 | DK 50.01 |
| Fully diluted earnings per 100 kroner nominal amount of A and B shares | 22.33 | 20.98 | 28.88 | 47.02 |
| Stock price | | | | |
| High | 362.50 | 266.50 | 227.50 | 684.00 |
| Low | 241.25 | 215.50 | 199.75 | 207.00 |
| Dividends per share | | | | |
| A shares | .50 | .50 | .50 | 6.00 |
| B shares | 8.00 | 10.00 | 12.00 | 13.00 |

na = not available.

**EXHIBIT 2**
Comparative Data on Selected Competitors, 1980 (currencies in millions)

| | Novo Industri | | Gist Brocades | | Eli Lilly | Miles Labs |
|---|---|---|---|---|---|---|
| Revenues | DK 1,579.0 | $280.2 | f 1,415.4[a] | $711.9 | $2,558.6 | $686.1 |
| Net income | 175.8 | 31.2 | 24.2 | 12.2 | 342.0 | 7.4 |
| Total assets | 1,993.9 | 331.5 | 1,074.8 | 504.7 | 2,607.5 | 635.9 |
| Total debt | 655.1 | 108.9 | 300.0 | 140.9 | 217.6 | 108.1 |
| Total equity | 959.0 | 159.4 | 350.3 | 164.5 | 1,736.7 | 318.3 |
| Growth rates | | | | | | |
| Revenues | 23.9% | | 12.2% | | 13.7% | 15.3% |
| Earnings | 70.1% | | 5.2% | | 2.5% | 208.4% |
| Return on sales | 11.1% | | 1.7% | | 13.4% | 1.1% |
| Return on equity | 18.3% | | 6.9% | | 19.7% | 2.3% |
| Debt/Capital | 40.6% | | 46.1% | | 11.1% | 25.3% |
| Current ratio | 1.8 | | 1.4 | | 2.1 | 1.7 |
| Interest coverage | 4.7 | | 2.2 | | 30.7 | na |

na = not available.

a. Dutch Guilders.

**EXHIBIT 3**

Major Financing, 1974–1980

1974
  Novo goes public on the Copenhagen Stock Exchange with a secondary offering of 90,000 B shares. At the time, a total of 450,000 A shares and 900,000 B shares were outstanding.

December 4, 1975. Rights issue.
  One new B share at DK 105 for every three A or three B shares held. B shares increased by 450,000. Net proceeds: DK 46.8 million. Bonus issue: one new B share for every six A or six B shares held. 8,470 new B shares issued to employees.

December 1, 1977. Rights issue.
  One new A share at DK 105 for every four A shares held; one new B share at DK 105 for every four B shares held. A shares increased by 112,500, and B shares increased by 395,860. Net proceeds: DK 56.5 million. Bonus issue: one new A share for every eight A shares held; one new B share for every eight B shares held. 45,030 new B shares issued to employees.

October 3, 1978. Convertible Eurodollar bond.
  7% convertible bonds due 1989; par value $20 million. Convertible from April 15, 1979, through December 30, 1988, into fully paid B shares. Conversion ratio: 20.631 B shares per $1,000 face value (effective conversion price of DK 259 per B share at a fixed exchange rate of DK 5.3435 per dollar). Bonds are callable in whole or in part at the option of the company at premiums declining from 2.5% to 0.5% starting in 1980.

October 1, 1980. Rights issue.
  One new A share at DK 105 for every five A shares held; one new B share at DK 105 for every five B shares held; one new B share at DK 250 for every ten A or ten B shares held. A shares increased by 123,750, and B shares increased by 732,150. Net proceeds: DK 125.2 million.

1980. Conversion of U.S. dollar convertible bond.
  Conversion of $580,000 into 11,966 B shares; conversion of $3,675,000 into 77,819 B shares.

**EXHIBIT 4**

End-of-Year Stock Market Indices and Exchange Rates, 1974–1980

| | Stock Exchange Indices | | | Exchange Rates | |
|---|---|---|---|---|---|
| | New York[a] | London[b] | Copenhagen | DK/$ | DK/£ |
| 1974 . . . . . . . . . . | 68.56 | 66.89 | 75.63 | 6.0550 | 14.4957 |
| 1975 . . . . . . . . . . | 90.19 | 158.08 | 100.41 | 5.7462 | 12.7669 |
| 1976 . . . . . . . . . . | 106.88 | 151.96 | 100.18 | 6.0450 | 10.9185 |
| 1977 . . . . . . . . . . | 95.10 | 214.53 | 96.42 | 6.0032 | 10.4786 |
| 1978 . . . . . . . . . . | 96.11 | 220.22 | 88.96 | 5.5146 | 10.5853 |
| 1979 . . . . . . . . . . | 107.94 | 229.79 | 87.37 | 5.2610 | 11.1617 |
| 1980 . . . . . . . . . . | 135.78 | 292.22 | 95.61 | 5.6359 | 13.1108 |

*Source: Financial Times, London, various issues.*

a. Standard and Poor Corporation's composite index.

b. *Financial Times,* actuaries' all-shares index.

**EXHIBIT 5**
Sample Comments from Analysts' Reports, 1980–1981

*Danish Boersinformation*

September 5, 1980. Novo's price-earnings ratio is at 10. Novo [stock] passed 400 last week, and the increase must be regarded as fantastic. We are inclined to regard the rights offering as negative, but the stock price movements and international stock ownership may negate this tendency.

November 5, 1980. An increasing international portfolio interest in Novo's stock is an important determinant when explaining the relatively rapid appreciation of the stock price. This is partly due to the fact that Novo has received a valuation as an expansionary research-based biochemical firm. Stock price will depend on foreign exchanges. At the present time, we do not recommend the stock for short-term investment.

*Grieveson, Grant and Co., U.K.*

September 2, 1980. Recommendation: strong hold. The share price has risen sharply this week as selling by Danish holders dried up in anticipation of the statement. While we believe that existing holders should maintain their stakes, we suggest that intending buyers wait to see how the market develops.

January 6, 1981. We rated the shares a hold at 610 at the end of October 1980. We now feel that in the short view they are high enough and that intending investors in what we still regard as a first-class growth company can wait until later in 1981.

*Cazenove & Co., U.K.*

September 8, 1980. The recent rise in Novo's share price recognizes the strength of the company's current earnings and its technical and commercial position in the field of biotechnology. These appear to us to merit at least the current rating [price], which is not excessive for an international specialist in a growth phase.

*Quilter, Goodison & Co., U.K.*

September 1, 1980. Recommendation: buy. We continue to think that the shares are substantially undervalued despite the rise in price from 217 at the beginning of 1979.

*Source:* Arthur I. Stonehill and Kare B. Dullum, *Internationalizing the Cost of Capital* (New York: Wiley, 1982).

# *Distribution Policy*

# Tandy Corporation (A)

Between the summer of 1976 and the spring of 1977 the citizens band (CB) radio market began a slide that would cause two firms to go bankrupt and others to sustain large losses. Excessive inventory positions, leading to massive price cuts, loomed large on the horizon. Many large consumer electronics companies, including General Electric and RCA, which had entered the market swiftly over the past year, left just as quickly. The boom that no one had predicted had become the bust that no one was prepared for.

In the face of this, Tandy Corporation, parent company of over 6,000 Radio Shack stores[1] and a major force in the CB market, made a series of moves that would leverage the firm to where debt constituted over 50% of capitalization. The moves culminated in June 1977 with the company's announcement that it would tender for 3.5 million shares of its common stock. The shares would be paid for with $100 million of short-term bank debt, to be refinanced as a 52-month bank loan. This tender followed by just eight months an exchange of 2.4 million shares of outstanding common stock for $100 million of subordinated debentures. In the 1977 annual report, Charles D. Tandy, president and chairman of the board, commented:

> The management of your company has been sometimes called unorthodox in recent years because our actions do not always conform to the conventional wisdom of the professional investment community.

Copyright © 1979 by the President and Fellows of Harvard College.
Harvard Business School case 280–020.

This case was prepared by Steven J. Zorowitz.

1. Includes dealers, franchisees, and foreign stores.

## Company Background

Tandy Corporation was founded in 1899 as American Hide and Leather. In 1956 its name was changed to General American and in 1960 to Tandy Corporation. In the 1950s the company was a hybrid mail-order retail store operation. It comprised hobby craft stores and factories; a manufacturer of leather goods called Tex Tan; and a division specializing in sportswear. However, Tandy wanted to expand into new fields, those that appealed to consumers' do-it-yourself desires. In 1963, with the assistance of the First National Bank of Boston, Tandy acquired Radio Shack Corporation, a Boston area consumer electronics company with nine stores and $12 million in sales.

Despite early financial difficulties with Radio Shack, Tandy grew and made acquisitions until in 1973 the corporation was composed of the following divisions:

1. Consumer electronics: 1,900 Radio Shack stores, and manufacturing operations for some products
2. Hobbies and crafts: 730 retail outlets specializing in leather crafts, handicrafts, colored floor tile, and tree nurseries
3. Manufacturing and distribution: fine leather accessories, saddlery and riding equipment, mineral and vitamin feed supplements for the livestock industry
4. General retailing: servicing of vending machines, auto service centers, and Leonard's and Mitchell's department stores

Two events occurred in 1974 that would set the pattern for Tandy Corporation for the next few years. First, Tandy divested itself of the general retailing segment, selling its department stores. The divestitures continued until October 1975, when Tandy spun off all nonelectronics operations into separate corporations, TandyBrands and TandyCrafts. What had once been a leather crafts company was now solely a major retailer in the field of consumer electronics.

The second event of 1974 that aroused the interest of the investment community was an offer by Tandy to exchange up to 2 million shares of its outstanding common stock, then selling for $23.50 per share,[2] for $29 principal amount of 10% subordinated debentures maturing in 1994. The company explained this move as follows:

> Management believes that the common stock is at present undervalued and that the purchase of shares of common stock in exchange for $29 principal amount of debentures per share is a sound investment by the company. The interest expense resulting from the increase in debt will have the effect of decreasing the company's net earnings. However, the decrease in the number of shares of common stock outstanding will have the effect of increasing earnings per share at the present level of operations.

Tandy Corporation thus ended its 1975 fiscal year (ending June 30) in the financial condition presented in Exhibits 1 and 2. The company was now preparing for an unprecedented market explosion—in the CB radio market.

---

2. Subsequent to the exchange offer, in December 1975, the stock was split 2–1.

# Radio Shack

At June 30, 1975, there were 3,865 Radio Shack stores operating worldwide
(see Table A). Each store carried a wide range of consumer electronics products
ranging from expensive stereo components and radios to inexpensive electronics
parts and accessories. Exhibit 3 lists sample Radio Shack products and indicates
how companywide sales could be characterized. The various classes of products
and their percentages of total dollar sales are shown in Table B. While most of
the products were purchased from Japanese manufacturers, self-manufacturing,
particularly fabrication and assembly, increased to 36% of the products sold. Tandy's
major product has changed over time, from radios and phonographs, to calculators,
and then to video games. In fact, Radio Shack had promoted one item aggressively
each month in order to build store traffic. As one company official commented,
"The store is a distribution channel in which the product mix changes over time."

The nearest competition in size to Radio Shack was Lafayette Radio Electronics,
only one-eighth the size of Tandy. Tandy was proud to claim that there were
only four national retailers—Sears, J. C. Penney, McDonald's, and Radio Shack.

One major factor in Radio Shack's success was its use of advertising. The
advertising budget was set at 8–9% of the sales dollar, compared to the traditional
retail expenditure of 3–4% of sales. More than 100 million direct mail fliers and
over 250 million newspaper inserts were distributed each year. The company kept
mailing lists of repeat purchasers, segmented by dollar volume of purchases.

Expansion plans called for Radio Shack stores to open at the rate of two or

**TABLE A**
Radio Shack Stores, June 30, 1975

|  | U.S. | Canada | Overseas | Total |
|---|---|---|---|---|
| Company-owned | 2,118 | 246 | 287 | 2,651 |
| Dealers | 944 | 92 | – | 1,036 |
| Franchises | 126 | – | 52 | 178 |
| Total | 3,188 | 338 | 339 | 3,865 |

*Source:* Company 10-K report.

**TABLE B**
Sales of Radio Shack Products, 1974–1975

| | Percent of Sales | |
|---|---|---|
| Product Class | 1974 | 1975 |
|---|---|---|
| Radios, tape recorders, and phonographs | 25.2% | 22.8% |
| Citizens band radios, walkie-talkies, scanners | 10.9 | 16.8 |
| Speakers, receivers, changers, turntables | 23.9 | 20.9 |
| Microphones, headphones, test equipment, toys, intercoms, telephones, other special merchandise | 14.3 | 14.7 |
| Electronic parts, antennas, tapes, batteries, other parts and accessories | 25.7 | 24.8 |

*Source:* Company 10-K report.

three per business day, a growth rate that no other retailing chain ever achieved. In July 1975 ground-breaking ceremonies were held for the first phase of Tandy Center in downtown Fort Worth, Texas, which would include a 19-floor office tower for the international Tandy headquarters, a public ice-skating rink, a three-floor galleria of shops, and banking facilities.

## CB Radios—The Boom

The boom in the CB radio market could be traced to two factors. First, the 1974 oil crisis and the resulting 55-mile-per-hour speed limit on the nation's highways served to spotlight the life of long-haul independent truckers and their use of CB radios as warning devices against radar traps and unfriendly "smokeys." The truckers then expanded their use of CBs to exchange information about emergencies, dangerous road conditions, and general conversation. This growing CB popularity among truckers quickly spread to the general public, who viewed CBs as a status symbol that *had* to be purchased.

The second factor was regulatory in nature. Effective September 15, 1975, the Federal Communications Commission rescinded two bans that had severely curtailed the CB radio market: one had made illegal the use of the citizens band (23 broadcast channels from 26.965 to 27.225 MHz) for hobby purposes, and the other had outlawed CB radio use for interstate communications.

The CB market took off at a rate much faster than anyone could have anticipated. Estimates of future sales were revised frequently, as market events made old forecasts obsolete (see Table C). Optimism over the prospects in the CB market was widespread. Ray Gates, vice president of the consumer electronics group of Panasonic, said, "By the year 2000 every automobile will be equipped with communication capabilities." In January 1976, General Electric and RCA announced that they would enter the CB market with Japanese-built units. Motorola and Panasonic were to follow them soon thereafter. This optimism was not unfounded: from 1973 to 1975 the CB market grew by a factor of almost 10, easily outstripping all estimates, and all firms in the industry increased their CB sales dramatically (Exhibit 4).

During this period Tandy Corporation played a major part in the CB market. CB sales went from 8% of total sales of North American Radio Shack stores in

**TABLE C**
CB Retail Sales Volume Predicted (millions of dollars)

| Date of Estimate | 1975 | 1976 | 1980 |
|---|---|---|---|
| May 5, 1975 . . . . . . . . . | $468 | – | – |
| Oct. 27, 1975 . . . . . . . . | – | – | $  500 |
| Feb. 9, 1976 . . . . . . . . | – | $  825 | 2,250 |
| Mar. 12, 1976 . . . . . . . . | – | 1,000 | – |
| Mar. 26, 1976 . . . . . . . . | – | 1,650 | – |

*Sources: Merchandising Week, Advertising Age, Merchandising Month, Electronic News, Mart Magazine.*

**TABLE D**
Comparative Profit Margin Data for Manufacturers, Retailers, and Combined
Manufacturers/Retailers of CB Radios

| | Manufacturer | Retailer | Combined |
|---|---|---|---|
| Price of CB | $100 | $145 | $ 145 |
| Cost of goods sold | 67 | 100 | 67 |
| Transportation cost | 0 | 2 | 2 |
| Gross margin | 33% | 30% | 48% |
| Selling and administrative expenses, labor | $ 25 | $ 33 | $ 58 |
| Other | 2 | 1 | 3 |
| Total expenses | $ 94 | $136 | $ 130 |
| Pre-tax profit | $ 6.0 | $ 9.0 | $15.0 |
| Pre-tax margin | 6.0% | 6.2% | 10.3% |

1974 to 13% in fiscal 1975 and 23% in fiscal 1976. Its many retail outlets, aggressive merchandising techniques, and low-cost products helped make Radio Shack the leading retailer of CB radios in the world. Self-manufacture of the CB radios gave Tandy a cost advantage over the individual manufacturer or retailer, which translated into higher than normal margins, as shown in the hypothetical example in Table D.

Riding on the CB boom, Tandy recorded the financial results for fiscal year 1976 presented in Exhibit 2. Sales increased 40%, and net income rose 95%. The stock market reflected this enormous growth as the price of Tandy's common stock rose from a low of 5 in 1974 to a high of 45 in February 1976 (see Exhibit 5 for Tandy's stock price history).

## Problems on the Horizon

The rapid growth of the CB radio market had created some problems for the FCC. Use of the 23 channels allocated to CBs was increasing at an enormous pace, resulting in clogged airwaves, TV interference, and the logging of a large number of complaints with the FCC. Faced with these problems, the FCC announced in July 1976 that it would expand the number of CB channels from 23 to 40. However, the commission would not allow the new 40-channel CBs to be marketed until January 1, 1977. This meant that CB manufacturers could only offer the soon-to-be obsolete 23-channel sets to consumers for the next six months. Consumers, on the other hand, began to hold off from purchasing the 23-channel sets in anticipation of the new expanded units. Thus, retail sales of CBs started to sag from their high levels, and inventory was accumulated in distribution channels.

## The Exchange Offer

On October 13, 1976, Tandy Corporation announced an offer to exchange its outstanding common stock, then selling at $32.625, for $40 face value of 10% subordinated debentures due in 1991. As in the exchange offer of 1974, management

**TABLE E**
Pro Forma Effect of Exchange Offer on Tandy's June 30, 1976, Financial Data
(thousands of dollars except per share data)

| | Actual June 30, 1976 | Adjusted for 1 Million Share Exchange | Adjusted for 1.5 Million Share Exchange |
|---|---|---|---|
| Total long-term debt . . . . . . . | $ 56,099 | $ 96,099 | $116,099 |
| Stockholders' equity . . . . . . . | 205,882 | 163,798 | 142,758 |
| Interest expense, net . . . . . . | 7,282 | 11,282 | 13,282 |
| Net income . . . . . . . . . | 67,524 | 65,444 | 64,404 |
| Net income per share . . . . . . | $ 3.73 | $ 3.83 | $ 3.88 |
| Average common shares outstanding . . . . . . . . . | 18,103 | 17,103 | 16,603 |

*Source:* Company prospectus.

stated that the reason for the offer was that the common stock was undervalued and that earnings per share would increase. The pro forma effects of the share exchange on Tandy's fiscal year 1976 balance sheet and income statement are shown in Table E. A total of 5.4 million shares were tendered, of which Tandy accepted 2.4 million. Tandy Corporation now had the highest debt ratio of any player in the CB radio market.

## CB Radios—The Bust of 1977

In 1976 manufacturers shipped 13 million CB units to dealers, up from 5.3 million units in 1975. Retail sales were 11.3 million units in 1976, up from 4.5 million in 1975. Manufacturers were estimated to be holding approximately 1.5 million units in inventory by the end of 1976. The excess inventory situation led to price wars over the 23-channel sets and to many inventory write-downs. These lower prices also carried over to the new 40-channel sets, as the CB fad seemed to be wearing off. Many of the competitors in the field saw the CB profits of 1975 and 1976 turn into losses in 1977. In April 1977, HyGain declared bankruptcy, and Gladding followed a few months later. In May projections of 1977 CB sales indicated an 8% decline from 1976 levels. In June that decline was projected at 27%. RCA indicated that it was "pruning" its CB product line, and Regency was teetering on the brink of bankruptcy.

Tandy, using the economies of its retailing-distribution-manufacturing operation and heavy advertising, followed the price cuts while, according to the company, never selling a CB radio at a loss. In fact, during the entire first half of 1977, the company bought the CB sets of other squeezed-out manufacturers at distress-sale prices and moved them out through their Radio Shack stores.

Still, the market predictions for the summer of 1977 were for more price cutting on both the 23- and 40-channel sets. Regulation came into play again as the FCC put a deadline on the sale of 23-channel hand-held CB radio units, putting more price pressure on the manufacturers and retailers of those sets. A new issue was also arising—cheap foreign imports. Domestic manufacturers petitioned the U.S. government to launch a probe of possible dumping of Japanese CB imports and asked it to raise tariffs on those imports from 6% to 56%. Tandy, self-manufacturing in Korea and a major purchaser of Japanese CBs, would have been particularly hurt by such a move.

While there was still a great deal of uncertainty over the future of the CB radio market, by mid-1977 a few facts were clear. Industry sales were at no more than 8 million units for 1977 and declining compared to the 11.3 million units sold in 1976 (see Exhibit 6 for measures of industry performance). The CB market was never going to return to the sales levels of 1975 and 1976, and the dramatic bust had made its mark on the financial performance of the industry participants (Exhibit 7).

## The Cash Offer

On June 20, 1977, Tandy Corporation surprised the investment community by offering to purchase up to 3.5 million shares of its outstanding common stock for cash at $29 per share. At that time, the stock was selling at $24.375. The 3.5 million shares represented 23% of the common shares outstanding at the date of the announcement. The company would be required to accept *all* tendered shares up to the 3.5 million limit.

As stated in the tender prospectus, the funding for the transaction was to be accomplished by internally generated cash flow and by a temporary $100 million line of credit with the First National Bank (FNB) of Boston and Continental Illinois. The short-term note payable would be refinanced as a 52-month revolving credit by the FNB of Boston and 12 other banks, with an additional $50 million of backup credit to be available for working capital purposes.

The pro forma effects of the tender offer on Tandy's March 31, 1977, balance sheet and income statement are presented in Table F. This third stock repurchase

**TABLE F**
Pro Forma Effect of Tender Offer on Tandy's March 31, 1977, Financial Data
(thousands of dollars except per share data)

|  | Actual March 31, 1977 | Adjusted for 2.5 Million Share Tender | Adjusted for 3.5 Million Share Tender |
|---|---|---|---|
| Total long-term debt | $152,412 | $224,912 | $253,912 |
| Stockholders' equity | 158,642 | 83,704 | 53,750 |
| Interest and debt expense | 11,508 | 16,096 | 17,931 |
| Net income | 56,206 | 53,768 | 52,814 |
| Book value per share | $ 10.26 | $ 6.46 | $ 4.49 |
| Net income per share | 3.32 | 3.72 | 3.92 |
| Average common shares outstanding | 16,954 | 14,454 | 13,454 |
| Common shares outstanding as of March 31, 1977 | 15,465 | 12,965 | 11,965 |

in 3 years would reduce the number of shares outstanding to 12 million and increase the debt-to-capitalization ratio to 82.5%.

One reason presented by management for leveraging the firm was that the CB problems the company was facing were going to cause a reduction in profitability, all the more reason to boost earnings per share. This argument was predicated on the belief that the company's price-earnings ratio would not get any lower. Charles Tandy commented, "When you sleep on the floor, you never fall out of bed." The company expanded on this point a few months later.

## The 1977 Annual Report

In its 1977 annual report, Tandy Corporation included two unique sections: one compared Tandy in various categories with other major retailers (see Exhibit 8); the other, entitled "A Statement of Financial Philosophy," explained the reasons for all the stock repurchases and why the company refused to pay a dividend. Some excerpts from the 1977 annual report follow.

> What is the rationale behind the decision to repurchase shares? Tandy management and directors believe the shares represent an attractive investment for the company and its stockholders. At prices prevailing in recent years, which have been quite modest multiples of current earnings relative to historical norms, the purchase of shares with borrowed funds will enhance the future return on equity and earnings per share growth because the profit margins of the company are in excess of the interest costs of the funds borrowed. The explanation lies in the interrelation between the operating variables of an ongoing enterprise and its financial structure. . . . The interrelation is expressed in the following classic investment formula:

$$\frac{\text{Asset}}{\text{turnover}} \times \frac{\text{Return}}{\text{on sales}} = \frac{\text{Return}}{\text{on assets}} \times \frac{\text{Financial}}{\text{leverage}} = \frac{\text{Return}}{\text{on equity}}$$

$$\frac{\text{Sales}}{\text{Avg assets}} \times \frac{\text{Net income}}{\text{Sales}} = \frac{\text{Net income}}{\text{Avg assets}} \times \frac{\text{Avg assets}}{\text{Avg equity}} = \frac{\text{Net income}}{\text{Avg equity}}$$

Tandy's performance in accordance with this equation is presented in Table G.

**TABLE G**
Key Financial Ratios Driving Tandy's Profitability

| At June 30 | Asset Turnover | × | Return on Sales | = | Return on Assets | × | Financial Leverage | = | Return on Equity |
|---|---|---|---|---|---|---|---|---|---|
| 1972 | 1.39 | × | 3.9% | = | 5.4% | × | 1.61 | = | 8.7% |
| 1973 | 1.34 | × | 4.4 | = | 5.9 | × | 2.06 | = | 12.1 |
| 1974 | 1.47 | × | 3.6 | = | 5.3 | × | 2.41 | = | 12.8 |
| 1975 | 1.71 | × | 5.1 | = | 8.7 | × | 2.53 | = | 22.0 |
| 1976 | 2.04 | × | 8.7 | = | 17.7 | × | 2.18 | = | 38.7 |
| 1977 | 2.16 | × | 7.3 | = | 15.7 | × | 2.37 | = | 37.2 |

The statement continued:

> In relating the above discussion to the original question—"Why does management consider the repurchase of outstanding stock an attractive investment?"—two reasons emerge: (1) The current net profit margin is considerably in excess of the interest cost of the funds borrowed to effect the transactions. The effective cost of our debt is less than 5% in after-tax dollars, while our net profit margin in fiscal 1977 was 7.3%. (2) Asset turnover or operating leverage should show gradual further improvement in future years.
>
> If asset turnover continues to improve and profit margins do not significantly deteriorate, return on assets should remain at a high level and possibly show further improvement as well. By modestly increasing the financial leverage through substitution of long-term debt for a portion of outstanding stock, a further substantial gain in the percentage return on equity and growth in earnings per share should be achievable in the short-term future. If this occurs, the attractiveness of Tandy stock as an investment for its stockholders should be enhanced over the longer term.

The statement went on to address the financial risk of increasing leverage:

> Investors equate increased financial leverage on a balance sheet with increased levels of risk and tend to pay less (or discount the investment) for stocks of highly leveraged companies. Thus, if the course of action discussed above were achieved only through permanent deterioration of the balance sheet of Tandy Corporation, management would be accomplishing little for the stockholders, even if the return on equity rises, because the higher return would tend to be offset by the higher risk.
>
> This has not been the case with Tandy [see stock price performance, Exhibit 5] in the two prior exchange offers, as witnessed by the fact that the financial leverage factor has been relatively flat since fiscal 1974. Further, management does not expect that the recently completed cash tender offer will have a lasting negative effect on our financial structure, even though $100 million of revolving debt was assumed to buy the 3.5 million shares. While balance sheet leverage has increased temporarily each time we have repurchased shares, our growing retained earnings and internal cash flow have permitted rapid rebuilding of the stockholders' equity account and the timely repayment of debt.
>
> In summary, the program discussed here has been embarked upon after carefully considering the potential benefits to be achieved, the temporary impact the program will have on the balance sheet, and the cash flow necessary to quickly return the balance sheet of the company to its normal strength.

The company next discussed its dividend philosophy:

> The accumulation of the capital required to pursue the business opportunities available to the company has been a priority item for many years. Because of that continuing attention, our growth has been essentially self-financed and a sound financial position has been maintained. Consistent with the rationale that the potential benefits to the stockholders of the stock repurchase program will be maximized by quickly restoring the stockholders' equity account and reducing the revolving debt, a cash dividend is unlikely in the immediate future.
>
> A "token" dividend has been suggested as an "entrance requirement" to certain institutional portfolios for Tandy Corporation common stock. Since the real objective of an equity investment is capital appreciation and since its total return in a competitive

sense must rely entirely on that appreciation, a "token" dividend would in fact be little more than a gesture and would bring little real benefit to the taxable shareholder.

A caveat and a summary followed:

None of the discussion relating to the stock repurchase transactions or the dividend policy of Tandy Corporation should be construed as a projection that such programs will necessarily persist in the future. . . . There may be a time when the capital requirements of the company, dividend tax policy, and money market patterns will point to the adoption of a dividend program for the common stock. Until then, however, it appears the most effective service to shareholders will be the continued effort to provide capital appreciation through continued growth of our company.

Tandy management does not view itself as merely custodians of our shareholders' investment in the typical sense. We are an aggressive growth company, and we feel our shareholders want us to attempt to maximize the long-term return on their investment, consistent with prudent risk. We remain convinced that our long-term approach both in the conduct of our merchandising operations and in our financial planning will yield the greatest benefits.

**EXHIBIT 1**

Balance Sheets at June 30, 1975–1977 (thousands of dollars)

| | 1975 | 1976 | 1977 |
|---|---|---|---|
| Cash and marketable securities | $ 32,659 | $ 44,284 | $ 20,930 |
| Accounts receivable, net | 10,537 | 9,442 | 7,082 |
| Inventories | 183,034 | 233,384 | 300,279 |
| Other | 4,692 | 7,534 | 16,552 |
| Current assets | 230,992 | 294,644 | 344,843 |
| Property and equipment | | | |
| Consumer electronics | 49,053 | 59,724 | 70,624 |
| Tandy Center | 11,711 | 19,589 | 39,547 |
| | 60,764 | 79,313 | 110,171 |
| Other | 101,967 | 29,765 | 19,661 |
| Total assets | $393,653 | $403,722 | $474,675 |
| Notes payable, current | $ 27,426 | $ 42,669 | $ 62,670 |
| Accounts payable | 21,898 | 33,243 | 47,968 |
| Other | 31,518 | 65,829 | 42,769 |
| Current liabilities | 80,842 | 141,741 | 153,407 |
| Notes payable, noncurrent | 72,688 | 10,487 | 8,565 |
| Subordinated debentures | | | |
| 6½%, 1978 | 2,492 | 2,208 | – |
| 10%, 1994 | 25,541 | 23,563 | 23,682 |
| 10%, 1991 | – | – | 98,039 |
| Other | 13,491 | 19,841 | 26,645 |
| Noncurrent liabilities | 114,212 | 56,099 | 156,931 |
| Capital account | 84,186 | 62,203 | 40,268 |
| Retained earnings | 114,413 | 143,679 | 124,069 |
| Stockholders' equity | 198,599 | 205,882 | 164,337 |
| Total liabilities and stockholders' equity | $393,653 | $403,722 | $474,675 |

**EXHIBIT 2**

Income Statements for Years Ending June 30, 1975–1977
(thousands of dollars except per share data)

| | 1975 | 1976 | 1977 |
|---|---|---|---|
| Net sales and other income | $532,249 | $744,371 | $953,030 |
| Costs and expenses | | | |
| Cost of products sold | 249,006 | 331,400 | 434,031 |
| Selling and administrative | 204,107 | 270,308 | 350,878 |
| Depreciation and amortization | 7,392 | 8,034 | 11,140 |
| Interest expense, net | 14,044 | 7,282 | 15,192 |
| | 474,549 | 617,024 | 811,241 |
| Income from continuing operations | 57,700 | 127,347 | 141,789 |
| Provision for income taxes | 29,078 | 63,066 | 69,970 |
| | 28,622 | 64,281 | 71,819 |
| Loss from discontinued operations | (1,820) | – | (2,777) |
| Income from spun-off operations | 7,794 | 3,243 | – |
| Net income | $ 34,596 | $ 67,524 | $ 69,042 |
| Income per share[a] | | | |
| Continuing operations | $    1.57 | $    3.55 | $    4.34 |
| Discontinued operations | (.10) | – | (.17) |
| Spun-off operations | .43 | .18 | – |
| Net income per share | $    1.90 | $    3.73 | $    4.17 |
| Average common shares outstanding | 18,176 | 18,103 | 16,542[b] |

a. Adjusted for 2–1 stock split in December 1975.

b. Does not reflect June 1977 tender offer.

**EXHIBIT 3**
Radio Shack Products and Sales Data

### Sample Products

| | |
|---|---|
| Stereo systems | LEDs |
| Stereo components | Electronics books |
| Headphones | Digital testers |
| Audio cables | Smoke alarms |
| Records, cassettes, 8-track tapes | Security devices |
| Car stereos | Metal detectors |
| Tape recorders | Hobby tools, chemicals |
| Cassette radios | Batteries, rechargers |
| Microphones | Calculators |
| Intercom systems | Electronic project kits |
| Telephones | Walkie-talkies |
| Wires and cables | TV antennas |
| Switches | Scanners |
| Solid state devices | CB radios |
| Printed circuit boards | AM/FM radios |
| Transistors | Digital clock radios |

| Retail Price of Items | Percent of Dollar Sales | Percent of Items Stocked |
|---|---|---|
| $    .01–$   5.00  . . . | 23% | 72% |
| 5.01–   . . . | 19 | 17 |
| 20.01– 20.00  . . . | 17 | 6 |
| 50.01– 50.00  . . . | 13 | 3 |
| 100.01 +100.00  . . . . | 28 | 2 |

*Source:* Tandy Corporation 1976 annual report.

**EXHIBIT 4**
CB Radio Sales of Leading U.S. Manufacturers and Suppliers, 1973–1976
(millions of dollars)

| | 1973 | 1974 | 1975 | 1976 |
|---|---|---|---|---|
| Midland International . . . . . . . . . . . | $10.0 | $ 25.0 | $ 56.0 | $  169.0 |
| Radio Shack . . . . . . . . . . . . . | 10.0 | 25.0 | 52.0 | 116.0 |
| Dynascan . . . . . . . . . . . . . . | 3.0 | 8.5 | 34.0 | 82.6 |
| Masco (Royce) . . . . . . . . . . . . | .9 | 9.5 | 40.0 | 80.0 |
| Pathcom . . . . . . . . . . . . . . | 3.0 | 13.0 | 48.0 | 75.0 |
| E. F. Johnson . . . . . . . . . . . . | 10.0 | 24.0 | 51.0 | 54.0 |
| HyGain . . . . . . . . . . . . . . | – | 4.0 | 14.0 | 45.0 |
| Gladding . . . . . . . . . . . . . . | 5.0 | 12.0 | 25.0 | – |
| SBE . . . . . . . . . . . . . . . | 3.0 | 5.5 | 14.0 | 28.0 |
| Lafayette Radio . . . . . . . . . . . | 3.0 | 7.0 | 11.0 | 15.0 |
| Total market . . . . . . . . . . . . | 55.7 | 146.8 | 500.0 | 1,144.0 |

*Source:* Frost & Sullivan.

**EXHIBIT 5**

Tandy Corporation Stock Price Data, 1974–1977

|  | High | Low | Closing | Price-Earnings Ratio (P/E)[a] | Closing P/E |
|---|---|---|---|---|---|
| **1974** | | | | | |
| 3rd quarter . . . . | $10.125 | $ 6.375 | $ 7.125 | – | 7.4 |
| 4th . . . . . . | 8.125 | 4.875 | 5.75 | – | 5.2 |
| **1975** | | | | | |
| 1st quarter . . . . | 17 | 5.125 | 16.1875 | – | 11.6 |
| 2nd . . . . . . | 24.5 | 15.3125 | 24.5 | 15.6 | 14.0 |
| 3rd . . . . . . | 25.1875 | 17.5 | 19.6875 | 10.5 | 10.4 |
| 4th . . . . . . | 26.375 | 18.875 | 26 | 9.9 | 12.0 |
| **1976** | | | | | |
| 1st quarter . . . . | 28.125 | 27.9375 | 43 | 13.7 | 15.6 |
| 2nd . . . . . . | 45 | 32.25 | 35.25 | 9.2 | 11.2 |
| 3rd . . . . . . | 37.375 | 28.875 | 32.75 | 8.2 | 8.8 |
| 4th . . . . . . | 42.375 | 31.25 | 42.125 | 9.8 | 10.6 |
| **1977** | | | | | |
| January . . . . . | 42.875 | 38.50 | 38.75 | 9.0 | 9.1 |
| February . . . . | 40 | 36 | 36.25 | 8.4 | 8.5 |
| March . . . . . | 39.25 | 36 | 36.375 | 8.5 | 8.5 |
| April . . . . . . | 36.375 | 27.75 | 28.375 | 6.9 | 6.6 |
| May . . . . . . | 30.50 | 26.625 | 27.875 | 6.7 | 6.5 |
| June . . . . . . | 28.375 | 21 | 27.875 | 6.7 | 6.5 |

*Note:* Stock prices are adjusted for 2–1 split in December 1975.

a. Computed using last four quarters' earnings.

**EXHIBIT 6**

CB Industry Performance Measures, 1974–1977

| CB Industry Sales (millions) | 1974 | 1975 | 1976 | 6 Months 1977[a] |
|---|---|---|---|---|
| Units shipped . . . . . . | 2.00 | 5.3 | 13.0 | – |
| Units sold . . . . . . | 1.75 | 4.5 | 11.3 | 4.1 |
| Wholesale sales . . . . . | $150 | $500 | $1,100 | – |
| Retail sales . . . . . . | – | $780 | $1,580 | – |

| Japanese CB Exports to U.S. (000 units) | 1976 | 1977 | FCC CB License Applications, 1977 (000s) | |
|---|---|---|---|---|
| January . . . . . . . | 641 | 584 | January . . | 980 |
| February . . . . . . | 696 | 727 | February . . | 504 |
| March . . . . . . . | 1,060 | 747 | March . . . | 561 |
| April . . . . . . . | 1,169 | | April . . . . | 426 |
| May . . . . . . . | 1,273 | | | |
| June . . . . . . . | 1,473 | | | |
| July . . . . . . . | 1,664 | | | |
| August . . . . . . | 1,290 | | | |
| September . . . . . | 1,350 | | | |
| October . . . . . . | 877 | | | |
| November . . . . . | 762 | | | |
| December . . . . . | 862 | | | |

*Sources: Electronics, 1977; Mart Magazine, 1977.*

a. Estimated.

**EXHIBIT 7**

Financial Performance of CB Industry Participants, 1974–1977 (millions of dollars)

| | 1974 | 1975 | 1976 | 1977 |
|---|---|---|---|---|
| **Tandy Corporation** | | | | |
| CB revenues | $ 33.0 | $ 59.3 | $ 157.0 | $ 200.1 |
| Total revenues | 413.4 | 532.2 | 744.4 | 953.0 |
| Net income | 20.4 | 34.6 | 67.5 | 69.0 |
| Debt/Capitalization | 36.1% | 36.5% | 21.4% | 48.8% |
| **Dynascan** | | | | |
| CB revenues | $ 8.5 | $ 33.8 | $ 82.6 | $ 62.3 |
| Total revenues | – | 48.6 | 102.5 | 84.1 |
| Net income | – | – | 19.1 | 4.8 |
| Debt/Capitalization | 0% | 0% | 0% | 0% |
| **Midland International (Beneficial Corp.)** | | | | |
| CB revenues | $ 25.0 | $ 56.0 | $ 169.0 | $ 65.3 |
| Total revenues | – | 1,481.0 | 1,740.0 | 1,819.0 |
| Net income | – | 78.4 | 100.4 | 85.6 |
| Debt/Capitalization | – | 43.8% | 42.2% | 41.0% |
| **Masco (Royce)** | | | | |
| CB revenues | $ 9.5 | $ 40.0 | $ 80.0 | – |
| Total revenues | – | 310.9 | 423.2 | $ 450.7 |
| Net income | – | 33.7 | 47.1 | 49.7 |
| Debt/Capitalization | 45.2% | 40.2% | 47.2% | 42.2% |
| **Pathcom** | | | | |
| CB revenues | $ 13.0 | $ 48.0 | $ 75.0 | – |
| Total revenues | – | 52.2 | 82.3 | $ 21.6 |
| Net income | – | 5.3 | (3.0) | (6.3) |
| Debt/Capitalization | 0% | 0% | 0% | 0% |
| **E. F. Johnson** | | | | |
| CB revenues | $ 24.0 | $ 51.0 | $ 54.0 | $ 22.1 |
| Total revenues | – | 72.1 | 82.0 | 53.3 |
| Net income | – | 5.0 | 0.3 | (19.0) |
| Debt/Capitalization | 52.3% | 1.9% | 9.0% | 22.8% |
| **SBE** | | | | |
| CB revenues | $ 5.5 | $ 14.0 | $ 28.0 | $ 11.8 |
| Total revenues | – | 14.3 | 31.8 | 14.9 |
| Net income | – | 1.2 | 2.3 | (4.0) |
| Debt/Capitalization | 23.5% | 16.1% | 5.1% | 12.5% |
| **HyGain[a]** | | | | |
| CB revenues | $ 4.0 | $ 14.0 | $ 45.0 | – |
| Total revenues | – | 34.6 | 96.9 | $ 50.3 |
| Net income | – | 3.7 | 17.3 | (24.6) |
| Debt/Capitalization | 47.2% | 29.3% | 4.9% | 1.6% |
| **Gladding[a]** | | | | |
| CB revenues | $ 12.0 | $ 27.7 | – | – |
| Total revenues | – | 64.1 | – | – |
| Net income | – | (8.0) | – | – |
| Debt/Capitalization | – | – | – | – |

*Sources:* Company annual reports and 10-K reports.

a. HyGain declared bankruptcy in April 1977. Gladding followed a few months later.

**EXHIBIT 8**  Performance Comparisons

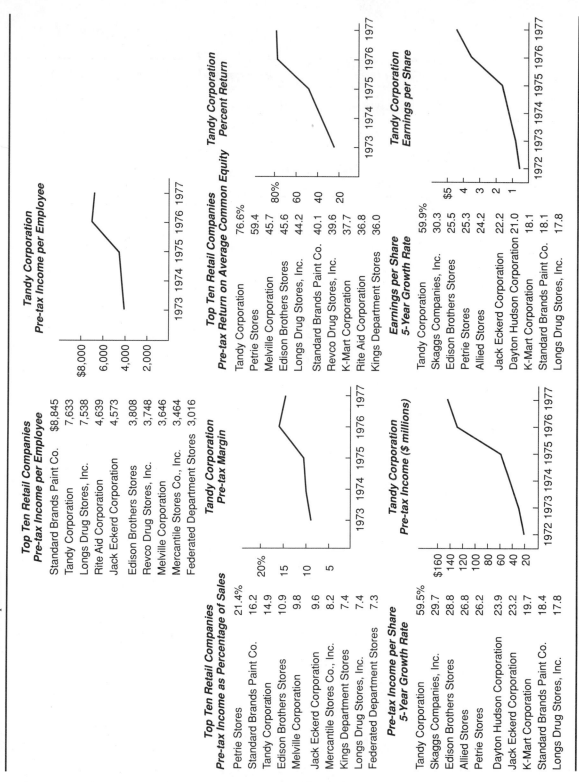

**Top Ten Retail Companies**
**Pre-tax Income per Employee**

| | |
|---|---|
| Standard Brands Paint Co. | $8,845 |
| Tandy Corporation | 7,633 |
| Longs Drug Stores, Inc. | 7,538 |
| Rite Aid Corporation | 4,639 |
| Jack Eckerd Corporation | 4,573 |
| Edison Brothers Stores | 3,808 |
| Revco Drug Stores, Inc. | 3,748 |
| Melville Corporation | 3,646 |
| Mercantile Stores Co., Inc. | 3,464 |
| Federated Department Stores | 3,016 |

**Tandy Corporation**
**Pre-tax Income per Employee**

**Top Ten Retail Companies**
**Pre-tax Return on Average Common Equity**

| | |
|---|---|
| Tandy Corporation | 76.6% |
| Petrie Stores | 59.4 |
| Melville Corporation | 45.7 |
| Edison Brothers Stores | 45.6 |
| Longs Drug Stores, Inc. | 44.2 |
| Standard Brands Paint Co. | 40.1 |
| Revco Drug Stores, Inc. | 39.6 |
| K-Mart Corporation | 37.7 |
| Rite Aid Corporation | 36.8 |
| Kings Department Stores | 36.0 |

**Tandy Corporation**
**Percent Return**

**Earnings per Share**
**5-Year Growth Rate**

| | |
|---|---|
| Tandy Corporation | 59.9% |
| Skaggs Companies, Inc. | 30.3 |
| Edison Brothers Stores | 25.5 |
| Petrie Stores | 25.3 |
| Allied Stores | 24.2 |
| Jack Eckerd Corporation | 22.2 |
| Dayton Hudson Corporation | 21.0 |
| K-Mart Corporation | 18.1 |
| Standard Brands Paint Co. | 18.1 |
| Longs Drug Stores, Inc. | 17.8 |

**Tandy Corporation**
**Earnings per Share**

**Top Ten Retail Companies**
**Pre-tax Income as Percentage of Sales**

| | |
|---|---|
| Petrie Stores | 21.4% |
| Standard Brands Paint Co. | 16.2 |
| Tandy Corporation | 14.9 |
| Edison Brothers Stores | 10.9 |
| Melville Corporation | 9.8 |
| Jack Eckerd Corporation | 9.6 |
| Mercantile Stores Co., Inc. | 8.2 |
| Kings Department Stores | 7.4 |
| Longs Drug Stores, Inc. | 7.4 |
| Federated Department Stores | 7.3 |

**Tandy Corporation**
**Pre-tax Margin**

**Tandy Corporation**
**Pre-tax Income ($ millions)**

**Pre-tax Income per Share**
**5-Year Growth Rate**

| | |
|---|---|
| Tandy Corporation | 59.5% |
| Skaggs Companies, Inc. | 29.7 |
| Edison Brothers Stores | 28.8 |
| Allied Stores | 26.8 |
| Petrie Stores | 26.2 |
| Dayton Hudson Corporation | 23.9 |
| Jack Eckerd Corporation | 23.2 |
| K-Mart Corporation | 19.7 |
| Standard Brands Paint Co. | 18.4 |
| Longs Drug Stores, Inc. | 17.8 |

*Source:* Standard and Poor's Corporation Compustat Service.

**289**

# Appendix

# Supplementary Data from Tandy Corporation's 1982 Annual Report

**EXHIBIT A1**
Sales of Self-Manufactured Products as a Percent of Total Sales (unaudited), 1978–1982 (millions of dollars)

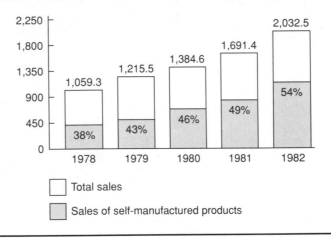

**EXHIBIT A2**
Selected Financial Data, 1972–1982 (millions of dollars)

|  | Sales | Assets | Borrowed Money | Net Worth | Borrowed Money as Percent of Total Capital |
|---|---|---|---|---|---|
| 1972 . . | $ 426 | $ 282 | $ 63 | $169 | 27% |
| 1973 . . | 515 | 350 | 107 | 186 | 36 |
| 1974 . . | 579 | 393 | 120 | 195 | 38 |
| 1975 . . | 724 | 415 | 157 | 199 | 44 |
| 1976[a] . . | 744 | 404 | 79 | 206 | 28 |
| 1977 . . | 953 | 475 | 193 | 164 | 54 |
| 1978 . . | 1,065 | 554 | 290 | 139 | 68 |
| 1979 . . | 1,227 | 610 | 268 | 208 | 56 |
| 1980 . . | 1,396 | 710 | 255 | 283 | 47 |
| 1981 . . | 1,707 | 937 | 161 | 572 | 28 |
| 1982 . . | 2,033 | 1,228 | 169 | 813 | 21 |

a. Spin-off of TandyBrands and TandyCrafts.

# EXHIBIT A3
Financial Objectives

For a number of years the management of Tandy Corporation has expressed its philosophies on investing in assets, measuring how efficiently a company employs its assets, financing the acquisition and carrying of those assets, and our attitudes about shareholder returns. The investment equation has been the framework for these discussions.

**Asset turnover** (sometimes called operating leverage) is the ratio of sales per dollar of assets employed during the year. Inventory is Tandy's largest single operating asset, accounting for more than half of total assets. The majority of our other asset investments have been made to enhance the return on our inventory investment. We are willing to accept lower asset turnover for a higher gross margin. Our continuing investment in self-manufacturing and vertical integration is indicative of this approach. Future investments or acquisitions that increase technological manufacturing integration are and will continue to be a high priority, even though such investment may temporarily impede asset turnover. The acquisition of the Consumer Products Division of Memorex in the fourth quarter of fiscal 1982 is an example of this approach. This acquisition gives Tandy Corporation manufacturing capabilities in magnetic media and a competitive, ongoing source of private label videotape for our Radio Shack stores. While the short-term effect depresses asset turnover, the long-term prognosis for an enhanced gross margin and return on investment is excellent.

Another factor that lowered asset turnover in fiscal 1982 to 1.88 from 2.06 in the prior year has been a substantial buildup in cash and short-term marketable securities. Because of the uncertainties in the economy recently and the accompanying high interest rates, Tandy has maintained a relatively large cash position (averaging more than $155 million for the twelve months ended June 30, 1982) during the year. While this temporarily lowers asset turnover and return on assets, it allows the company maximum flexibility to capitalize on emerging reinvestment opportunities.

**Return on sales** (or net profit margin) is the percentage of profit earned on sales. From a management perspective, it is important to break down this component between the operating profit margin and interest costs so that the impact of changes in financial leverage can be quantified. On the operating side, we believe gross margin is the biggest factor in determining the net profit margin. Operating expenses (payroll, advertising, rent, etc.) can only be controlled to a certain degree before sales are impacted.

Fiscal 1982 was the fourth consecutive year that Tandy improved gross margins, despite a growing competitive environment for computers in particular and consumer electronics overall. This enhanced gross profit performance, combined with significantly lower interest expense (because of interest income earned on invested cash), enabled Tandy to achieve an 11.0% *after-tax* return on sales.

**Return on assets,** the percentage of net profits earned on average assets, exceeded 20% for the second consecutive year. Since cash is considered a temporary investment, management also addresses the more narrowly defined return on noncash assets. The after-tax return on noncash assets improved in fiscal 1982 to 24.2%, up from 23.4% in fiscal 1981 and 18.3% in fiscal 1980. The acquisition of the Consumer Products Division of Memorex and the high cash balances maintained during the year retarded return on total assets in the current year, but a slight increase was achieved nevertheless.

**Financial leverage** is the ratio of a company's asset base to its equity investment. Tandy reduced its financial leverage in fiscal 1982 because high interest rates persisted during the year and our cash flow was rising. At June 30, 1982, Tandy had no substantial senior indebtedness. As a result, our financial leverage ratio in fiscal 1982 was 1.56—the lowest in more than a decade.

**Return on equity** is net income expressed as a percentage of the stockholders' investment. The reduction of indebtedness, combined with an increase in stockholders' equity from retained earnings, lowered Tandy's after-tax return on equity to 32.3%, compared with 39.7% in fiscal 1981. However, this return, achieved with little financial leverage, is still the highest of any major retailer.

Changes in asset turnover or return on sales can change the return on assets. For example, a rise in operating leverage could increase the return on assets and ultimately the return on equity, but not if the increase in asset turnover is achieved by reducing net margin. Similarly, changing the financial leverage has a direct impact on the return on stockholders' equity but also affects net margin. Increasing financial leverage through more borrowings to finance assets could increase the return on equity, but not if the added interest costs seriously erode the net profit margin earned on sales. The point is that management must look at all the components

*(continued)*

291

---

### EXHIBIT A3 *(concluded)*

of the investment equation, within the context of the whole, to earn the highest *long-term* return for stockholders. In the latest *Fortune* magazine survey of the 50 largest retailers, Tandy showed the greatest 10-year total return to its shareholders—a 32.5% average per annum. Tandy management believes giving the shareholder this return through capital appreciation and letting him/her take a dividend as desired by selling shares is preferable under existing tax laws.

Tandy Corporation has reduced financial leverage, lowered interest costs, and raised return on sales for the last 4 years. In the high-inflation, high-interest rate environment that has persisted through most of this period, we believe this has been the prudent course to follow. If the recent downward trend in interest rates persists and our cash flow continues to accelerate, a change in our financial structure may be appropriate.

Investment Equation

| At June 30 | Asset Turnover Sales / Avg Assets | × | Return on Sales Net Income / Sales | = | Return on Assets Net Income / Avg Assets | × | Financial Leverage Avg Assets / Avg Equity | = | Return on Equity Net Income / Avg Equity |
|---|---|---|---|---|---|---|---|---|---|
| 1973 | 1.34 | × | 4.4% | = | 5.9% | × | 2.06 | = | 12.1% |
| 1974 | 1.47 | × | 3.6 | = | 5.3 | × | 2.41 | = | 12.8 |
| 1975 | 1.71 | × | 5.1 | = | 8.7 | × | 2.53 | = | 22.0 |
| 1976 | 2.04 | × | 8.7 | = | 17.7 | × | 2.18 | = | 38.7 |
| 1977 | 2.16 | × | 7.3 | = | 15.7 | × | 2.37 | = | 37.2 |
| 1978 | 2.06 | × | 6.2 | = | 12.8 | × | 3.39 | = | 43.6 |
| 1979 | 2.09 | × | 6.9 | = | 14.3 | × | 3.35 | = | 47.9 |
| 1980 | 2.10 | × | 8.1 | = | 17.0 | × | 2.69 | = | 45.7 |
| 1981 | 2.06 | × | 10.0 | = | 20.6 | × | 1.93 | = | 39.7 |
| 1982 | 1.88 | × | 11.0 | = | 20.7 | × | 1.56 | = | 32.3 |

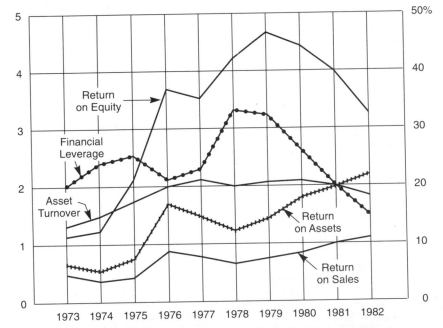

# Avon Products, Inc.

On June 1, 1988, Hicks B. Waldron, chairman and chief executive officer of Avon Products, Inc., was reviewing a package of proposals that he and his financial advisers were to present to the Avon board of directors for final approval the following day. These proposals included (1) a public announcement that Avon would explore plans to divest two of its businesses, probably at a considerable book loss; (2) a reduction of the dividend on Avon's common stock; and (3) an exchange offer under which Avon would issue an unusual preferred stock in exchange for up to 25% of its common shares.

## Background

Avon Products, Inc., founded in 1886, was one of the world's largest manufacturers and marketers of beauty products. The company was famous for its direct selling beauty business, in which a sales force of independent contractors purchased products from Avon and then resold them door-to-door, largely to their friends and neighbors. In addition, by the mid-1980s, the company was an important national provider of sub-acute health care services.

Avon's Beauty Group produced and sold cosmetics, fragrances, toiletries, and fashion jewelry and accessories; it also sold gift and decorative products. While it sold several fragrances through retail establishments, most of the Beauty Group's revenues were from its direct sales operations. In 1988, Avon had 1.4 million active sales representatives worldwide, including 400,000 in the United

This case was prepared by Professor Jonathan Tiemann.

Copyright © 1989 by the President and Fellows of Harvard College.
Harvard Business School case 289–049.

States. Avon's other principal business group was its Health Care Group, which comprised Foster Medical Corporation, the Mediplex Group, and Retirement Inns of America. They provided home health care, operated retirement living facilities, and provided certain sub-acute health care services. Exhibit 1 gives a 10-year review of Avon's financial performance, and Exhibit 2 gives data by lines of business for the period 1982–1987. Exhibit 3 shows balance sheets for 1986 and 1987, and Exhibit 4 gives a historical perspective on Avon's stock price.

## Recent Company History

As a result of its strong cash flow, Avon was able to increase its dividend regularly in the late 1970s while aggressively seeking acquisitions. By 1981, Avon had raised the dividend on its common stock to $3.00, up from $2.55 in 1978. But more important, in the early 1980s, Avon made a major strategic decision to diversify its business by entering the health care field. Its first acquisition in that field was made in January 1982, when Avon acquired Mallinckrodt, Inc., a specialty chemical company whose sales were largely to the health care industry.

However, during this same period, an important demographic shift was beginning to threaten Avon's Beauty Group. The majority of Avon's sales representatives and their customers had traditionally been women who spent much of the day at home. But increasingly these women were entering occupations that required them to be away from home during the day. Therefore Avon was losing both its sales force and its customers. From 1979 to 1981, Avon's margins on beauty product sales declined as the company broadened its direct sales product line and offered increasingly generous sales incentives, and by 1982 beauty product sales began to decline as well.

By mid-1982, Avon suddenly found itself in a weakened cash flow position as a result of the declining beauty business and the $710 million Mallinckrodt acquisition. Strapped for cash, the company reduced its dividend in August 1982 from $3.00 to $2.00 per share per year. Avon's stock price hardly moved when the company made the dividend announcement, but *The Wall Street Journal* reported at the time that observers had expected the dividend reduction. In any event, Avon's stock price had dropped from $30 per share at the end of 1981 to $20.375 per share immediately before the dividend announcement.

In 1984, having just become Avon's CEO, Mr. Waldron began to reshape the company's beauty operations. Instead of remaining primarily a direct sales company, he decided, Avon would broaden its approach to the beauty business by developing additional distribution channels. The company also continued to look for acquisitions in the health care area so that Avon could remain viable in the event the changes it was making to its beauty business failed.

In May 1984, Avon acquired Foster Medical Corporation in a share exchange. Foster Medical seemed a particularly attractive acquisition because of the possibility that public health care policy would change to encourage a shift from expensive hospital-based care to the less expensive home care, which was a major part of Foster's business. Avon also acquired Retirement Inns of America in November

1985 and the Mediplex Group in April 1986. Mediplex operated sub-acute health care facilities such as alcohol and drug abuse treatment centers, nursing homes, and psychiatric hospitals. Mediplex and Retirement Inns both managed retirement living centers of various types. Consistent with this increasing focus on the provision of health care, Avon sold Mallinckrodt in 1986 for $675 million.

Although Mediplex and Retirement Inns served patients who paid for care themselves or through private insurers, Foster Medical's revenues came primarily from Medicare, the largest public health insurance program in the United States. A change in Medicare in 1986 effectively cut Foster Medical's charges for Medicare patients by 18%. Foster Medical was not able to respond successfully to this change, and in 1987, Avon's management recommended to the board that it review Avon's commitment to the health care industry. The board concluded that Foster Medical, Mediplex, and Retirement Inns could no longer grow at an attractive rate and still show acceptable profits. In addition, by 1987 the performance of the Beauty Group had begun to improve markedly. The board decided that the Beauty Group's strength permitted Avon to shed the Health Care Group companies. It started by selling Foster Medical Supply, a distribution company, in November 1987. Early in 1988, Avon also began the process of selling the entire Foster Medical Corporation. Avon anticipated an after-tax loss of $125 million on the sale.

Also in 1987, Avon acquired Giorgio, Inc. for $165 million in cash and Parfums Stern, Inc. for $160 million. These acquisitions not only added prestige fragrances, sold through retail stores, to Avon's beauty line but also continued Avon's transition away from the direct sales approach to the beauty business.

## The Exchange Offer

Mr. Waldron felt that at the same time that Avon was reorganizing its business, it should also reconsider its financial policies, including its dividend policy. The company was about to begin the last phase of its exit from the health care business with the sale of Mediplex and Retirement Inns. In addition, Waldron and the board agreed that Avon should redouble its commitment to its core beauty products business, whose recent results were encouraging. Among other things, this implied that Avon would continue to invest significant additional capital in that business.

In December 1987, Avon raised additional capital by selling 40% of the common stock of its wholly owned Japanese subsidiary, Avon Products Company Limited, in a public offering in Japan that raised $218 million. The price was over six times book value and around 50 times earnings. Avon booked an after-tax gain of $121.1 million, or $1.72 per share, on the sale.

The board also felt that Avon should conserve cash flow by reducing its dividend from $2.00 to $1.00 per share, but Mr. Waldron worried about the consequences of simply cutting Avon's dividend. Avon had maintained its dividend at $2.00 per share per year since the dividend cut in August 1982. Although the reduction had not resulted in any sudden drop in Avon's stock price, Avon's stock had been falling for some time in advance of the cut. This time might be different. Avon's 1987 annual report had stated that the firm expected to maintain the current annual $2.00 dividend, and Avon's stock price had remained fairly steady during 1988.

Exhibit 5 lists the 25 largest institutional holders of Avon stock. Many of those investors might sell their Avon shares quickly if Avon simply reduced its dividend. As Mr. Waldron put it, "For five years I had been telling them that we weren't going to cut the dividend, and for five years they had been telling me they didn't believe me." Some investors had stated that they held Avon stock because it paid a high dividend. Avon's board asked its financial adviser, Morgan Stanley and Co., what steps the company could take to avoid having the dividend reduction drive down the stock price. The exchange offer was one element of the solution.

Morgan Stanley proposed that Avon offer to exchange one share of a new $2.00 preferred equity-redemption cumulative stock (PERCS) for each of up to 18 million of Avon's 71.7 million outstanding common shares. The new preferred would pay cumulative quarterly dividends of 50 cents ($2.00 per year) accrued from June 1, 1988, to September 1, 1991. Although the company would be able to redeem the preferred shares at any time before September 1, 1991, according to a declining schedule,[1] the important provisions concerned mandatory redemption of the PERCS shares on September 1, 1991.

On that date the PERCS shares would expire. Their holders would receive one common share for every PERCS share if the price of the common stock was less than or equal to $31.50, or $31.50 worth of common stock per PERCS share if the common stock was above that price.

As was usual with preferred stock, Avon would not be able to pay its common dividend at any time its preferred dividend was in arrears. In addition, this preferred stock included a restriction providing that Avon could never pay a common dividend of $1.50 or more per share per year unless it first redeemed the preferred.

Mr. Waldron felt confident that the financial markets would understand the new security. Third-party issuers had successfully marketed at least one product similar to the PERCS, Americus Trust PRIME units. An Americus Trust was a corporation whose sole asset was common stock of a particular company. The basic idea was that shareholders of that company placed their shares in the trust, which issued two units, called a PRIME and a SCORE, against each share. The PRIME units received all the dividends the stock earned; the SCORE units received no dividends. At a predetermined terminal date, the trust would liquidate the shares it held. The PRIME holders would receive the value of the shares up to a certain predetermined level, and the SCORE holders would receive any excess. The PERCS might appeal to investors who would buy PRIMEs.

---

1. The redemption price would be $34.75 per share, plus accrued dividends, for the quarter starting June 1, 1988. It would decline by 25 cents per share for each quarter thereafter through the quarter beginning March 1, 1991. The redemption price would fall to $31.75 per share on June 1, 1991, and then to $31.50 per share on July 1, 1991. The company would have the option of redeeming the preferred for either cash or common shares.

Mr. Waldron realized that he would need to convince his colleagues on the board that the terms of the offer would be fair to all the company's shareholders but especially appealing to those who desired high dividends. Avon's stock closed at $24.125 per share on June 1, 1988. Exhibit 6 gives the June 1 closing prices of options on Avon's stock, which were listed on the Chicago Board Options Exchange.

**EXHIBIT 1**
Ten-Year Financial Summary, 1978–1987 (millions of dollars except per share data)

| | 1978 | 1979 | 1980 | 1981 | 1982 | 1983 | 1984 | 1985 | 1986 | 1987 |
|---|---|---|---|---|---|---|---|---|---|---|
| Net sales | $2,014.7 | $2,377.5 | $2,569.1 | $2,613.8 | $3,000.8 | $3,000.1 | $3,141.3 | $2,470.1 | $2,883.1 | $2,762.5 |
| Cost of sales | 721.0 | 899.7 | 959.9 | 1,018.1 | 1,278.7 | 1,290.1 | 1,330.4 | 959.5 | 1,034.0 | 980.3 |
| Marketing, distribution, administrative expenses | 859.5 | 1,034.8 | 1,169.4 | 1,199.2 | 1,306.8 | 1,368.7 | 1,435.0 | 1,256.3 | 1,530.4 | 1,495.3 |
| Provision for restructure | — | — | — | — | — | — | — | — | — | 50.0 |
| Interest expense, net | (24.5) | (33.4) | (39.8) | (49.3) | (7.2) | 4.3 | 19.3 | 16.9 | 38.6 | 46.2 |
| Loss (gain) on stock offering | — | — | — | — | — | — | — | — | — | (191.0) |
| Other (income) expense, net | 2.7 | (3.8) | 7.3 | .1 | 30.5 | 26.8 | 20.4 | 13.1 | 6.5 | (2.8) |
| Total expenses | 1,558.7 | 1,897.3 | 2,096.8 | 2,168.1 | 2,608.8 | 2,689.9 | 2,805.1 | 2,245.8 | 2,609.5 | 2,378.0 |
| Pre-tax earnings from continuing operations | 456.0 | 480.2 | 472.3 | 445.7 | 392.0 | 310.2 | 336.2 | 224.3 | 273.6 | 384.5 |
| Income taxes | 228.1 | 229.5 | 231.0 | 225.8 | 195.4 | 145.8 | 154.5 | 96.1 | 114.9 | 146.3 |
| Net earnings from continuing operations | 227.9 | 250.7 | 241.3 | 219.9 | 196.6 | 164.4 | 181.7 | 128.2 | 158.7 | 238.2 |
| Discontinued operations | | | | | | | | | | |
| Net earnings (loss) | — | — | — | — | — | — | — | 34.9 | — | (55.4) |
| (Loss) on sale, net | — | — | — | — | — | — | — | (223.0) | — | (23.7) |
| Net earnings (loss) | $ 227.9 | $ 250.7 | $ 241.3 | $ 219.9 | $ 196.6 | $ 164.4 | $ 181.7 | $ (59.9) | $ 158.7 | $ 159.1 |
| No. of common shares | 58.16 | 60.14 | 60.15 | 60.15 | 71.46 | 74.49 | 83.84 | 79.35 | 71.65 | 71.65 |
| Earnings per common share | | | | | | | | | | |
| Continuing operations | $ 3.92 | $ 4.17 | $ 4.01 | $ 3.66 | $ 2.75 | $ 2.21 | $ 2.16 | $ 1.61 | $ 2.23 | $ 3.38 |
| Discontinued operations | — | — | — | — | — | — | — | (2.37) | — | (1.12) |
| Net earnings per share | 3.92 | 4.17 | 4.01 | 3.66 | 2.75 | 2.21 | 2.16 | (.76) | 2.23 | 2.26 |
| Cash dividend per share | 2.55 | 2.75 | 2.95 | 3.00 | 2.50 | 2.00 | 2.00 | 2.00 | 2.00 | 2.00 |
| Cash, short-term investments | $ 339.6 | $ 307.0 | $ 308.4 | $ 257.8 | $ 161.2 | $ 183.7 | $ 124.5 | $ 86.1 | $ 80.2 | $ 73.8 |
| Net property and equipment | 285.7 | 382.2 | 465.8 | 518.3 | 729.6 | 760.4 | 807.7 | 666.4 | 743.2 | 637.5 |
| Capital expenditures | 74.8 | 116.3 | 117.7 | 114.2 | 128.9 | 128.3 | 140.5 | 91.2 | 120.5 | 90.8 |
| Total assets | 1,226.1 | 1,406.0 | 1,571.4 | 1,567.8 | 2,233.2 | 2,285.8 | 2,437.7 | 2,289.0 | 2,296.3 | 2,559.2 |
| Long-term debt | 3.1 | 4.1 | 2.6 | 4.8 | 297.3 | 318.4 | 440.5 | 617.8 | 709.2 | 816.4 |
| Shareholders' equity | 738.4 | 857.2 | 921.2 | 933.0 | 1,219.4 | 1,204.2 | 1,157.1 | 926.4 | 681.3 | 758.6 |
| Per share | $ 12.70 | $ 14.25 | $ 15.32 | $ 15.51 | $ 17.06 | $ 16.17 | $ 14.47 | $ 11.69 | $ 9.76 | $ 10.66 |
| Return on equity | 30.9% | 29.2% | 26.2% | 23.6% | 16.1% | 13.7% | 15.7% | — | 23.3% | 21.0% |

**EXHIBIT 2**
Line-of-Business Data, 1982–1987 (millions of dollars)

*1982*

| | Net Sales | Pre-Tax Earnings | Identifiable Assets |
|---|---|---|---|
| Cosmetics, fragrances, toiletries | $1,998.0 | $279.8 | $  969.9 |
| Fashion jewelry, accessories | 338.3 | 61.9 | 185.0 |
| Health care | 340.6 | 52.7 | 713.3 |
| Direct response | 124.3 | 17.1 | 32.4 |
| Fine jewelry, tableware | 114.6 | 6.7 | 111.2 |
| Other | 86.9 | 7.5 | 87.3 |
| Corporate, eliminations | (1.9) | (10.4) | 134.1 |
| Consolidated | $3,000.8 | $415.3 | $2,233.2 |

*1984*

| | Net Sales | Pre-Tax Earnings | Identifiable Assets |
|---|---|---|---|
| Cosmetics, fragrances, toiletries | $1,832.3 | $237.2 | $  932.9 |
| Fashion jewelry, accessories | 350.9 | 55.0 | 201.3 |
| Health care | 542.9 | 91.7 | 961.3 |
| Direct response | 186.0 | 2.9 | 100.2 |
| Other | 234.3 | 11.7 | 142.5 |
| Corporate, eliminations | (5.1) | (22.6) | 99.5 |
| Consolidated | $3,141.3 | $375.9 | $2,437.7 |

*1986*

| | Net Sales | Pre-Tax Earnings | Identifiable Assets |
|---|---|---|---|
| Cosmetics, fragrances, toiletries | $1,923.8 | $236.8 | $1,089.1 |
| Fashion jewelry, accessories | 310.0 | 45.0 | 204.1 |
| Health care | 431.8 | 65.0 | 731.9 |
| Direct response | 216.2 | 11.6 | 139.7 |
| Other | 1.3 | — | .7 |
| Corporate, eliminations | — | (39.7) | 130.8 |
| Consolidated | $2,883.1 | $318.7 | $2,296.3 |

*1983*

| | Net Sales | Pre-Tax Earnings | Identifiable Assets |
|---|---|---|---|
| Cosmetics, fragrances, toiletries | $1,884.3 | $219.8 | $  945.7 |
| Fashion jewelry, accessories | 330.2 | 43.5 | 166.7 |
| Health care | 402.2 | 63.6 | 747.6 |
| Direct response | 144.0 | 11.7 | 55.7 |
| Fine jewelry, tableware | 124.6 | 8.1 | 127.8 |
| Other | 119.7 | 14.2 | 87.8 |
| Corporate, eliminations | (4.9) | (19.6) | 154.5 |
| Consolidated | $3,000.1 | $341.3 | $2,285.8 |

*1985*

| | Net Sales | Pre-Tax Earnings | Identifiable Assets |
|---|---|---|---|
| Cosmetics, fragrances, toiletries | $1,609.6 | $192.3 | $  963.2 |
| Fashion jewelry, accessories | 394.2 | 42.3 | 244.2 |
| Health care | 260.3 | 51.2 | 315.6 |
| Direct response | 205.2 | 8.8 | 128.8 |
| Discontinued operations | — | — | 524.9 |
| Corporate, eliminations | .8 | (40.3) | 112.3 |
| Consolidated | $2,470.1 | $254.3 | $2,289.0 |

*1987*

| | Net Sales | Pre-Tax Earnings | Identifiable Assets |
|---|---|---|---|
| Cosmetics, fragrances, toiletries | $1,807.9 | $251.3 | $1,385.5 |
| Gift and decorative | 412.3 | 54.6 | 157.0 |
| Fashion jewelry, accessories | 375.2 | 45.7 | 237.3 |
| Health care | 167.1 | 10.1 | 396.5 |
| Discontinued operations | — | — | 253.4 |
| Corporate, eliminations | — | 22.8 | 129.5 |
| Consolidated | $2,762.5 | $384.5 | $2,559.2 |

**EXHIBIT 3**

Balance Sheets, 1986 and 1987 (millions of dollars)

|  | 1986 | 1987 |
|---|---|---|
| Cash and equivalents | $ 80.2 | $ 73.8 |
| Accounts receivable (less allowance) | 371.6 | 310.5 |
| Inventories | 410.1 | 398.6 |
| Prepaid expense and other current | 184.8 | 144.1 |
| Current assets | 1,046.7 | 927.0 |
| Total property and equipment | 1,132.4 | 1,046.4 |
| Less: Accumulated depreciation | 389.2 | 408.9 |
| Net property and equipment | 743.2 | 637.5 |
| Net assets of discounted operations | — | 253.4 |
| Other assets | 506.4 | 741.3 |
| Total assets | $2,296.3 | $2,559.2 |
| Short-term debt | $ 110.2 | $ 62.4 |
| Accounts payable | 169.0 | 196.1 |
| Accruals | 211.0 | 277.7 |
| Taxes payable | 182.7 | 222.6 |
| Current liabilities | 672.9 | 758.8 |
| Long-term debt | 709.2 | 816.4 |
| Other liabilities | 66.2 | 117.3 |
| Deferred income taxes | 166.7 | 108.1 |
| Net worth | 681.3 | 758.6 |
| Total liabilities and net worth | $2,296.3 | $2,559.2 |

**EXHIBIT 4**

Stock Price Performance, 1978–1988

|  | Price | | | Average Weekly Volume (000 shares) | S&P 500 |
|---|---|---|---|---|---|
|  | High | Low | Closing |  |  |
| 1978 | $63 | $43⅞ | $50¾ | 373.5 | 96.11 |
| 1979 | 56 | 37¼ | 39⅜ | 420.3 | 107.94 |
| 1980 | 40¾ | 31⅛ | 34⅛ | 570.0 | 136.76 |
| 1981 | 42⅜ | 29⅛ | 30 | 491.4 | 122.55 |
| 1982 | 30½ | 19⅜ | 26¾ | 992.7 | 140.64 |
| 1983 | 36⅞ | 21¼ | 25⅛ | 1,277.2 | 164.93 |
| 1984 | 26 | 19¼ | 21⅞ | 1,229.2 | 167.24 |
| 1985 | 29 | 17⅞ | 27⅝ | 1,572.4 | 211.28 |
| 1986 |  |  |  |  |  |
| First quarter | 34 | 25¾ | 33½ | 1,319.6 | 238.90 |
| Second | 36⅜ | 30¾ | 35¾ | 1,217.6 | 250.84 |
| Third | 36⅛ | 31¼ | 32⅞ | 1,026.2 | 231.22 |
| Fourth | 34⅝ | 27 | 27 | 1,296.7 | 242.17 |
| 1987 |  |  |  |  |  |
| First | 32½ | 26¼ | 31⅛ | 1,769.3 | 291.70 |
| Second | 35 | 28¾ | 33¾ | 1,577.2 | 304.00 |
| Third | 35⅝ | 32⅞ | 35⅛ | 1,503.6 | 321.83 |
| Fourth | 35 | 19¼ | 25¾ | 1,345.8 | 247.08 |
| 1988 |  |  |  |  |  |
| First | 28⅜ | 22⅝ | 24⅛ | 1,369.1 | 258.89 |
| Second (through June 1) | 26¼ | 22⅝ | 24⅛ | 1,310.9 | 266.69 |

**EXHIBIT 5**
Twenty-Five Largest Institutional Shareholders

| | Shares Purchased or Sold Jan 1–Mar. 31, 1988 | Shares Held Mar. 31, 1988 | Percent of Total Avon Shares Outstanding | Primary Investment Objective of Owner |
|---|---|---|---|---|
| Delaware Management Co. | −1,489,400 | 4,467,900 | 6.3% | Yield |
| United Banks of Colorado | 0 | 3,603,425 | 5.1 | Turnaround |
| Lazard Frères & Co. | 0 | 3,515,800 | 4.9 | Yield |
| Barrow Hanley Mewhinney | 1,665,500 | 3,487,300 | 4.9 | Yield |
| PNC Financial Corp. | 0 | 1,618,037 | 2.3 | Mixed |
| Wells Fargo Bank N.A. | 0 | 1,479,546 | 2.1 | Index |
| Scudder, Stevens & Clark | 0 | 1,443,733 | 2.0 | Mixed |
| New York St. Common Ret. | 0 | 1,202,200 | 1.7 | Index |
| Irving Trust Company | 0 | 1,136,781 | 1.6 | Mixed |
| Lord Abbett & Company | 0 | 1,090,200 | 1.5 | Yield |
| Bankers Trust NY Corp. | 211,025 | 934,856 | 1.3 | Index |
| Dreyfus Corporation | 0 | 884,700 | 1.2 | Mixed |
| Capital Research & Mgmt. | 0 | 800,000 | 1.1 | Mixed |
| Center Bancorporation | 0 | 770,783 | 1.1 | Mixed |
| Amsouth Bancorporation | 0 | 764,343 | 1.1 | Mixed |
| College Retire. Equities | −165,700 | 712,000 | 1.0 | Index |
| Dean Witter Reynolds Int. | 0 | 700,090 | 1.0 | Mixed |
| Mellon Bank Corporation | 0 | 699,693 | 1.0 | Index |
| Eaton Vance Management | 0 | 650,000 | .9 | Mixed |
| E. I. du Pont de Nemours | 382,600 | 598,760 | .8 | Mixed |
| General Electric Master Ret. | 0 | 596,800 | .8 | Mixed |
| Hagler Mastrovita & Hewitt | −175,600 | 520,300 | .7 | Mixed |
| California Public Empl. Ret. | 0 | 499,000 | .7 | Index |
| American National B&T | 0 | 494,275 | .7 | Index |
| Chase Manhattan Corp. | 12,400 | 489,695 | .7 | Mixed |
| Total | +440,825 | 33,160,217 | 46.5% | |
| | | Yield | 17.6% | |
| | | Turnaround | 5.1 | |
| | | Mixed | 15.3 | |
| | | Index | 8.5 | |
| | | | 46.5% | |

*Source:* 13-F filings with the Securities and Exchange Commission.

**EXHIBIT 6**
Chicago Board Options Exchange, Listed Options Trading, Closing Prices, June 1, 1988

| Strike Price | Calls | | | Strike Price | Puts | | |
|---|---|---|---|---|---|---|---|
| | June | July | October | | June | July | October |
| $22½ | $2 | r | $3⅛ | $22½ | $3⁄16 | r | $1 1⁄16 |
| $25 | $7⁄16 | $⅞ | $1 13⁄16 | $25 | r | $1⅞ | $2½ |
| $30 | r | $¼ | $9⁄16 | $30 | r | r | r |

r = not traded that day.
The closing price for Avon Products common stock on June 1, 1988 was $24⅛.

*Note:* An option is a contract giving the holder the right, but not the obligation, to buy or sell a given asset at a specified price (the *exercise price* or *strike price*) on or before a given date (the *exercise date* or *expiration date*). A *call* option gives the holder the right to buy, while a *put* option gives the holder the right to sell. This right is valuable, and options on many stocks are traded on organized exchanges. Exchange-listed options like these expire on the Saturday after the third Friday of the month indicated. A contract represents an option on 100 shares. The entries in the table give the prices (sometimes called option *premia*) of the options themselves, per share of Avon stock. Thus, one June 25 call option contract gives the holder the right to buy 100 shares of Avon stock for $25 per share on or before Saturday, June 18, 1988. Such a contract traded on June 1 for $43.75, which is $7⁄16 × 100. Tables like this one for most exchange-listed options appear daily in financial publications, including *The Wall Street Journal* and the business section of the *New York Times*.

# Consolidated Edison Company (Abridged)

Charles F. Luce, chairman of the board of Consolidated Edison Company (Con Ed), faced a difficult decision on April 22, 1974. The board of trustees was scheduled to meet on the next day to decide whether Con Ed should pay a cash dividend in the second quarter; and if so, how much the dividend should be. The company had paid a dividend every year since 1885, and many of its stockholders counted on this regular source of income. However, Con Ed desperately needed to conserve funds as sale of equity at the currently depressed stock price was painful.

## Background

When Charles F. Luce became chief executive of Con Ed in 1967, the giant utility was already a favorite target for criticism from customers, public officials, the press, and even some business consultants. After citing the company's difficulties with customers, *Fortune* magazine labeled it "the company you love to hate." *The Wall Street Journal* noted that Con Ed "seems to have a unique capacity for alienating its 4.2 million customers, including the biggest customer of all, the city."

The article in the *Journal* presented a list of complaints that had become standard for Con Ed critics: "Con Ed charges the highest electric rates of any big-city utility, contributes a major share of New York's air pollution, noisily chops 40,000 holes in the streets each year, inefficiently operates an aging system that produces nearly 1,900 neighborhood power failures annually—and is rude in the bargain."

Management conceded that its rates were high and that service needed improvement but pointed out in defense that the problems of doing business in New York City were without parallel. Con Ed's bill of $193 million for state and local taxes in 1967 was several times that of other large utilities, and the city requirement that most of its transmission lines be placed underground added considerably to the costs of construction and maintenance.

## Continuing Difficulties

Mr. Luce attempted a variety of reforms to rejuvenate Con Ed. He began a huge construction program to replace more than 2 million kilowatts of obsolete capacity and to add 2.8 million kilowatts of new generating capacity by 1972. (Total system generating capacity was 7.5 million kilowatts in 1967.) He tried diligently to introduce modern business techniques throughout an organization deemed "hidebound" by *Fortune* in 1966. He instituted a formal budgeting system, put procurement on a competitive basis, and dismissed personnel who had received favors from contractors doing business with Con Ed. He was instrumental in the installation of a modern computer-based billing and customer service system to expedite the handling of customer complaints.

Progress was slow and results were not always apparent. Between 1968 and 1973 many of the problems Mr. Luce had first encountered seemed to worsen. Brownouts increased during the summer months through 1970, and there were three network failures—two in 1972 and one in 1973. Breakdowns of equipment already on line were the direct cause of these difficulties, but the more basic cause was the inability of Con Ed to meet power plant construction deadlines.

However, by September 1973, Con Ed appeared to be coming out of its difficulties: the generating and transmission systems had performed well during the hottest summer in 15 years; 3 million kilowatts of new generating capacity was near completion; the Public Service Commission[1] had recently granted a 13.8% permanent rate increase; earnings were on the rise; and the new customer service system was showing impressive results. Then, without warning, the energy crisis struck.

## The Energy Crisis

The Arab oil embargo and the "energy crisis" placed Con Ed in an extremely tight, almost helpless, situation. The company had been forced by the city council in 1971 to burn only low-sulfur oil—oil that was available principally from OPEC member countries. At best, Con Ed seemed to be confronted with sharply higher fuel prices; oil priced at $172 million in 1972 was $293 million in 1973, and on

---

1. The Public Service Commission is the New York State agency authorized to regulate public utilities. Its powers include approving rate schedules for gas, steam, and electricity, and approving utility stock and bond offerings.

the basis of prices quoted in early 1974, Con Ed's bill for that year was estimated at $800 million. At worst, the company ran the risk of absolute shortages of fuel.

Con Ed responded to the crisis by appealing for reduced energy consumption. Total electric sendout was reduced in the first quarter of 1974 by 10%—this in spite of a "normal" growth of 3½–4%. As fuel was conserved, however, finances deteriorated. Many of the utility's costs—taxes, maintenance, labor, interest charges—were high and increasing and largely unrelated to sendout. Lower revenues and higher costs meant drastically lower earnings. Had it not been for an accounting change (approved by the Public Service Commission), Con Ed would have reported a loss in both November and December of 1973. (See Exhibit 1 for a financial summary.)

## Need for Rate Relief

Con Ed needed a massive rate increase to cover sharply higher fuel and interest costs as well as the adverse impact of lower volume. The full amount of the increase in fuel costs was automatically passed through to the consumers under a fuel adjustment clause. In addition, a $315 million electric rate increase request was submitted to the Public Service Commission. The company also requested a $108 million "conservation adjustment" rate increase, arguing that, since decreased energy sendout could not be matched by decreased costs, a higher rate per unit of energy sold was necessary to maintain the same corporate rate of return. The total rate request of $423 million represented a 30% increase over a 2-year period (1974–1975). Approval of the entire increase, coupled with the automatic fuel adjustment pass-throughs, would increase the typical customer's monthly bill from $15.59 to $26.

The Public Service Commission was not wholly sympathetic. There had been a series of rate hikes since 1958, and the City of New York had grown increasingly vehement in its opposition to them. The city itself was a huge consumer of power; it felt an obligation to represent the interests of millions of its residents, many of them poor; and it claimed that high electricity costs were to the detriment "not only of the ordinary user of electric current but also of commerce and industry and the general economy of the city." If the rate increase were approved, the utility's residential customers would pay the highest electric rates in the U.S.—8 cents per kilowatt hour for the average residential customers, nearly double the rate in other major cities. High rates for satisfactory service were bad enough, critics charged, but high rates from a utility as negligent as Con Ed were intolerable. (Some observers added that it was good politics for elected officials to take a stand against Con Ed and in "the public interest.")

The Public Service Commission granted a temporary increase of $175 million in February 1974, substantially less than the minimum felt necessary by Con Ed. It was announced concurrently that a final decision on a permanent rate increase would not be rendered for months.

## Financial Needs and Plans

The commission's decision introduced substantial uncertainty into the company's financing plans. A planned January offering of $50 million of preferred stock and $50 million of bonds was postponed. In March, a $150 million offering of 9⅛% bonds was finally issued. Almost immediately they were bid down to a market yield of 10.45%, the highest in the utility industry. Investor confidence in the company was obviously quite low.

The situation was extremely serious. Con Ed's construction program was enormous, swollen in recent years by inflation. Management planned to spend $3.5 billion on new plant and equipment during 1974–1978, and any major delays would increase the likelihood of brownouts and system breakdowns. An additional $1.5 billion would be needed for repayment of existing debt and for cash dividends on the preferred and common stock (see Exhibit 2).

Of the $5.0 billion funds needs, $2.2 billion would be generated by operations. It was planned to raise the remaining $2.8 billion in a mix consistent with management's policy that debt, preferred stock, and common stock represent 51%, 13%, and 35% of total capital, respectively. Con Ed's senior debt had been downgraded recently to BBB by Standard and Poor's, reflecting a substantial deterioration in interest coverage (see Exhibit 1). Furthermore, the $150 million bond issue in March 1974 had dropped the company's interest coverage to a level only slightly above the minimum set in its existing bond indentures. Management felt it essential to limit debt to no more than 51% of total capital.

## Financing Alternatives

Con Ed's "cash crisis" demanded total external financing of $610 million in 1974 (see Exhibit 2). An alternative to issuing additional equity, long-term debt, and preferred stock in the proportions set by management debt structure policy was to use short-term bank loans. Con Ed had total bank lines of $300 million, of which only $64 million was in use at year-end 1973. An increase of $236 million in the company's bank loans, combined with the $150 million debt issue in March, represented a large percentage of Con Ed's total external financing need in 1974 (see Exhibit 2). It would still be necessary, however, to raise an additional $224 million somehow during 1974.

Management was hesitant to sell large amounts of new equity. The company's stock had suffered along with those of most electric utilities and was selling at $18, a 10-year low and substantially below book value. Investors were increasingly attracted to historically high bond yields and the prices of utility stocks had found little support in recent months (see Exhibits 3 and 4). Large new issues of common stock seemed likely to dilute per share results excessively.

As an alternative, Mr. Luce was considering the sale of two Con Ed power plants to the State of New York. It was proposed that the New York State Power Authority pay Con Ed $500 million for two partly completed generating plants. The state would need to spend an additional $300 million to complete the two plants and might then lease the plants back to Con Ed.

A bill had been submitted to the state legislature in early April. The outcome of the legislative debate was uncertain, however, at the time of the board meeting. Constituents of many New York City and Westchester County Democrats and Republicans had complained bitterly about Con Ed's higher rates. These legislators were also concerned that city and county tax revenues would be lost if the tax-exempt New York State Power Authority took over the plants as proposed in the legislation. Furthermore, they were reluctant to believe that Con Ed was really in as bad shape as it claimed. The problem was complicated by the apparent lack of interest of some upstate Republican legislators in the difficulties of Democrat-controlled New York City.

Mr. Luce was thus faced with the dividend question. On the one hand, the cash shortage was quite critical and would deteriorate further in the months ahead. Customer complaints about rate increases had risen sharply. There was reason to suppose that some legislators would vote against the plant purchase if any money were to be used for dividend payments.

On the other hand, a regular quarterly or semiannual dividend had been paid faithfully by Con Ed and its predecessors since 1885. Although the dividend had not been increased in 7 years, Con Ed stock was still acquired for income purposes. For many stockholders, especially older ones on social security, the average $360 of annual dividends was extremely important. Any cut in the dividend would inflict widespread personal hardship and possibly damage Con Ed's reputation in the capital markets.

**EXHIBIT 1**
Summary of Financial Results, 1969–1974 (millions of dollars except per share data)

| | | | | | | 1st Quarter | |
|---|---|---|---|---|---|---|---|
| | *1969* | *1970* | *1971* | *1972* | *1973* | *1973* | *1974* |
| Operating revenues . . . . . | $1,027 | $1,128 | $1,314 | $1,480 | $1,736 | $425 | $553 |
| Net income . . . . . . . . | 135 | 128 | 145 | 148 | 182 | 55 | 41 |
| Preferred stock dividends . . . . | 34 | 34 | 38 | 40 | 44 | 11 | 11 |
| Net income for common stock . . | $ 101 | $ 94 | $ 107 | $ 108 | $ 138 | $ 44 | $ 30 |
| *Per Share of Common* | | | | | | | |
| Earnings per share . . . . . . | $ 2.68 | $ 2.30 | $ 2.35 | $ 2.06 | $ 2.32 | $ .80 | $ .49 |
| Dividends per share . . . . . | 1.80 | 1.80 | 1.80 | 1.80 | 1.80 | .45 | .45 |
| Market price . . . . . . . | 30 | 25 | 27 | 26 | 22 | 25 | 20 |
| Price-earnings ratio . . . . . . | 11 | 11 | 11 | 13 | 9 | – | – |
| Dividend yield . . . . . . . | 6.0% | 7.2% | 6.7% | 6.9% | 8.2% | – | – |
| *Debt Position* | | | | | | | |
| Interest coverage . . . . . . | 2.6 | 2.2 | 2.2 | 2.1 | 2.2 | 2.2 | 1.8 |
| Debt as percent of total capital . . | 52% | 53% | 52% | 51% | 52% | – | – |
| Bond rating . . . . . . . . | A | A | A | A | BBB | – | – |
| *Operating Statistics* | | | | | | | |
| Capital expenditures . . . . . | $ 305 | $ 401 | $ 430 | $ 519 | $ 686 | – | – |
| Percent earned on capital . . . | 5.4% | 5.5% | 5.6% | 5.6% | 6.1% | – | – |
| Percent earned on book equity . . | 8.6% | 7.5% | 7.5% | 6.7% | 7.6% | – | – |
| Percent earned on market equity . | 8.9% | 9.1% | 8.9% | 8.0% | 10.7% | – | – |
| Number of customers (000s) . . | 2,903 | 2,895 | 2,866 | 2,842 | 2,847 | – | – |
| Sales kwh (000,000s) . . . . . | 30,296 | 32,399 | 32,997 | 33,144 | 34,733 | – | – |

**EXIIIBIT 2**

Future Sources and Uses of Funds, 1974–1978 (millions of dollars)

| | 1974 | 1975 | 1976 | 1977 | 1978 | Total |
|---|---|---|---|---|---|---|
| **Sources** | | | | | | |
| Cash flow from operations | | | | | | |
| Net income | $ 210 | $ 250 | $ 280 | $ 310 | $ 340 | $1,390 |
| Noncash charges | 140 | 155 | 170 | 190 | 205 | 860 |
| External sources[a] | | | | | | |
| Bond issues | 330 | 338 | 280 | 410 | 374 | 1,732 |
| Preferred stock issues | 100 | 67 | 72 | 88 | 72 | 399 |
| Common stock issues | 180 | 123 | 127 | 145 | 113 | 688 |
| Total sources | $ 960 | $ 933 | $ 929 | $1,143 | $1,104 | $5,069 |
| | | | | | | |
| **Uses** | | | | | | |
| Construction expenditures | $ 625 | $ 650 | $ 700 | $ 800 | $ 725 | $3,500 |
| Preferred dividends | 55 | 58 | 65 | 73 | 82 | 333 |
| Common dividends | 122 | 139 | 155 | 170 | 188 | 774 |
| Repayment of debt | 80 | 86 | 9 | 100 | 109 | 384 |
| Repayment of current liability | 78 | – | – | – | – | 78 |
| Total uses | $ 960 | $ 933 | $ 929 | $1,143 | $1,104 | $5,069 |
| | | | | | | |
| **Memoranda** | | | | | | |
| Common dividend | $1.80 | $1.80 | $1.80 | $ 1.80 | $ 1.80 | |
| Millions of common shares outstanding | 73 | 81 | 88 | 98 | 105 | |
| Assumed net issue price | $ 16 | $ 16 | $ 17 | $ 16 | $ 16 | |
| Long-term debt as percent of capital | 51% | 51% | 51% | 51% | 51% | |
| Times interest earned | 2.22 | 2.20 | 2.17 | 2.12 | 2.08 | |
| Rate increases (excluding fuel adjustment increases) | 15% | 15% | 10% | 10% | 10% | |
| Earnings per share (average shares outstanding) | $2.33 | $2.49 | $2.54 | $ 2.55 | $ 2.54 | |

*Source:* Casewriter's estimates.

a. External financing raised in proportions demanded by management policy.

**EXHIBIT 3**

Historical Comparison of Stock Prices and Interest Rates, 1965–1973

| | 1965 | 1966 | 1967 | 1968 | 1969 | 1970 | 1971 | 1972 | 1973 |
|---|---|---|---|---|---|---|---|---|---|
| **Moody's Utilities Index** | | | | | | | | | |
| Market price | $117 | $103 | $102 | $98 | $95 | $79 | $84 | $80 | $71 |
| Earnings per share | 5.92 | 6.30 | 6.67 | 6.67 | 6.92 | 6.89 | 7.14 | 7.73 | 7.55 |
| Dividends per share | 3.86 | 4.11 | 4.34 | 4.50 | 4.61 | 4.70 | 4.77 | 4.87 | 5.01 |
| Price-earnings ratio | 20 | 16 | 15 | 15 | 14 | 11 | 12 | 10 | 9 |
| Dividend yield | 3.3% | 4.0% | 4.3% | 4.6% | 4.9% | 5.9% | 5.7% | 6.1% | 7.0% |
| **Consolidated Edison** | | | | | | | | | |
| Market price | $ 45 | $ 37 | $ 33 | $ 33 | $ 30 | $ 25 | $ 27 | $ 26 | $ 22 |
| Earnings per share | 2.42 | 2.31 | 2.58 | 2.57 | 2.68 | 2.30 | 2.35 | 2.06 | 2.32 |
| Dividends per share | 1.80 | 1.80 | 1.80 | 1.80 | 1.80 | 1.80 | 1.80 | 1.80 | 1.80 |
| Price-earnings ratio | 19 | 17 | 13 | 13 | 11 | 11 | 11 | 13 | 9 |
| Dividend yield | 4.0% | 4.9% | 5.5% | 5.5% | 6.0% | 7.2% | 6.7% | 6.9% | 8.2% |
| Book value per share | 28 | 29 | 30 | 30 | 31 | 31 | 31 | 31 | 31 |
| **Cost of Money** | | | | | | | | | |
| BBB utility bonds | 5.0% | 6.1% | 6.9% | 7.2% | 8.9% | 9.0% | 8.4% | 7.8% | 8.5% |
| Medium-grade utility preferred stocks | 4.9% | 5.7% | 6.5% | 6.5% | 7.8% | 7.6% | 7.4% | 7.6% | 8.4% |

310

**EXHIBIT 4**   Standard and Poor's Bond Information

### Rising Yields Enhance Bonds' Appeal

This is an unusually good time for investors who need income—as well as for those who are apprehensive about the stock market—to look into what the bond market has to offer. The basic attractions of bonds now are largely self-evident: yields are exceptionally high—in most areas close to the record levels of 1970.

*Buying bonds now with a view to long-term holding can lock in the high returns currently available. When yields peak out, a process that may not be too far off, prices of most bonds, which move inversely to yields, should begin to rise.* Finally, the bond market normally offers in some degree a refuge against the generally volatile price action of stocks.

It must be recognized, however, that the bond market, except for convertible issues, does not provide protection against the long-term erosion of buying power that continued inflation—even at a pace slower than in recent months—will exact on the dollars invested.

The immensity of the credit markets and the diversity of choices they offer may be somewhat surprising even to experienced investors accustomed to dealing mainly in stocks. One recent study placed the total amount of credit outstanding in the U.S. at the end of 1973 at almost $1.9 trillion, or more than 2½ times the market value of all New York Stock Exchange issues.

Including private placements, corporate financing in 1973 totaled $33.4 billion, of which two-thirds ($22.3 billion) consisted of bonds and notes, with preferred ($3.4 billion) and common stock ($7.7 billion) accounting for the remainder. In addition, the U.S. Government offered over $19 billion and state and local governments sold over $22 billion in various debt issues.

### Three Major Bond Areas

There are three major areas of bond investment for the individual: corporate, U.S. Government, and tax-exempt. Bonds range in maturity from a few months (for some Governments and municipals) to over 30 years.

Yields, currently at or near all-time peaks, are close to 9% for new AA-rated corporates, 8.5% for 90-day Treasury bills and 5.60% for recent New York State (AA) bonds.

Most brokers dealing in stocks also trade in bonds. In general, bonds are bought and sold in units of $1,000, with a minimum commission of $2.50 per bond by New York Stock Exchange firms; on small orders, the charge is frequently higher.

Many factors play a part in determining the amounts of debt financing and the yield at which new offerings can be brought to market, but the key determinants are the demand for

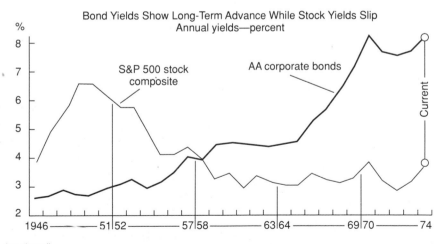

Bond Yields Show Long-Term Advance While Stock Yields Slip
Annual yields—percent

*(continued)*

**EXHIBIT 4** *(continued)*

and supply of funds. In general, when economic factors are favorable, the need to borrow tends to rise, and lenders get a better price.

Inflation and inflationary expectations, particularly in recent years, have also had a profound effect on yields. This is so because lenders tend to demand compensation, in the form of higher yields, for the reduced value of the dollars in which the bonds will eventually be paid off. The chart showing "real" yields illustrates this—the real rate of return on AA-rated corporate bonds, adjusted for inflation, has traditionally tended to run at 2% to 4%. The difference between this and the yields shown by the upper line represents allowance for the effects of inflation.

Short-term rates are also basically determined by supply-demand factors, and these in turn can be strongly influenced by Federal Reserve policy. The Fed has these main tools: (1) It can buy or sell Government securities in the open market, raising or lowering the amount of lendable funds in the banking system. (2) It can alter reserve requirements for member banks, tightening them when it considers credit to be too freely available, and vice versa. (3) It can raise or lower the discount rate to help accomplish similar objectives. Finally—as it has done frequently in recent years—it can resort to moral suasion, or jawboning, to affect banks' lending policies.

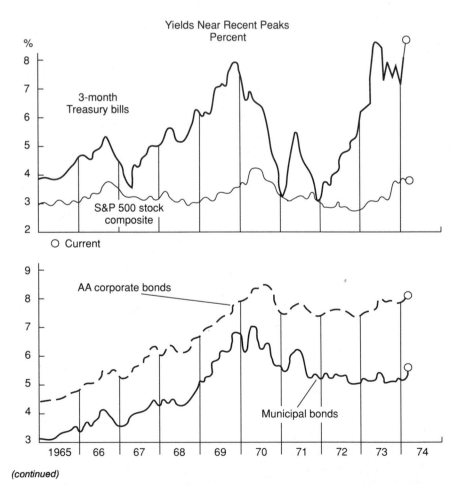

*(continued)*

**EXHIBIT 4** *(continued)*

### Short-Term Yields Rise

Traditionally, short-term yields have been lower than those available from long-term obligations. But in recent years heavy demand for short-term funds and the assumption that present rates of inflation will moderate have reversed the pattern. As charted, interest rates for short-term credit now generally equal or exceed those for long-term credit. For example, three-month negotiable certificates of deposit are now at about 10%, while new issues of 20-year high-grade utilities are selling to yield just under 9%.

There has also been a marked shift in the relation of bond to stock yields. Typical yields on high-quality bonds are now well over twice that of the S&P 500 stock price index, whereas prior to the mid-1950s stock yields consistently exceeded bond yields (see chart).

Two considerations help to explain the shift. First, a rather steady rise in price/earnings multiples of stocks in the years following World War II had the effect of bringing stock yields down. Second, surging inflation has augmented the yield compensation demanded by bond investors.

### Where Matters Stand

In the past two months, with demand for funds still exceedingly heavy, short-term rates have swung dramatically upward and bond prices have deteriorated. But special factors have entered into this bulge in rates, and it may even now be not too far from cresting, including the bank prime lending rate, which has now returned to its 10% record.

As for inflationary pressures, the worst may be behind for at least the time being. If, as we foresee, there is some easing in inflation over the next several months, existing yield levels would look attractive in retrospect.

### Attractive Areas of the Bond Market

Representative top-quality seasoned corporate bonds now yield over 8%, and still higher returns are available from new issues, which tend to reflect current money-market trends. Top-grade utilities, for example, are now being offered on close to a 9% basis with five-year call protection.

The relative safety of individual issues of bonds is identifiable by the quality ratings assigned by S&P. Issues rated AAA are of highest grade, but AA bonds differ from them in only a small degree. A-rated issues are regarded as upper-medium grade. The BBB rating is borderline between definitely sound obligations and those in which the speculative element begins to predominate. The BBB group is the lowest qualifying for commercial bank investment; most individual investors probably will not want to buy bonds that are more speculative than this.

### Discount Bonds

While the bond market should not be regarded as a trading area except for professional investors, there is much to be said for the capital-gain potentials of discount bonds, particularly for high-bracket taxpayers. Consider for example the AT&T 2¾s, maturing in October, 1975, and now selling around 94. When they are paid off at par, the holder will have realized $60 per $1,000 bond as a long-term capital gain, in addition to the annual interest of $27.50. The yield to maturity works out at about 5.35%, with well over half the total in the form of capital gain taxable at a lower rate.

### Municipals Afford Tax Exemption

Investors requiring a degree of tax protection should not overlook municipal bonds, the interest on which is free from Federal income taxes and sometimes also from state and city income taxes. They are payable from taxes imposed by the issuer, or in the case of revenue bonds, from revenues received from the users of the facilities financed thereby.

Municipal bond yields, rising steeply recently, are still somewhat below record highs. For example, an A-rated 20-year bond yielding 6.00% to maturity can be purchased in today's market. An investor in the 36% tax bracket (taxable income of $24,000 to $28,000) filing a

*(continued)*

**EXHIBIT 4** *(continued)*

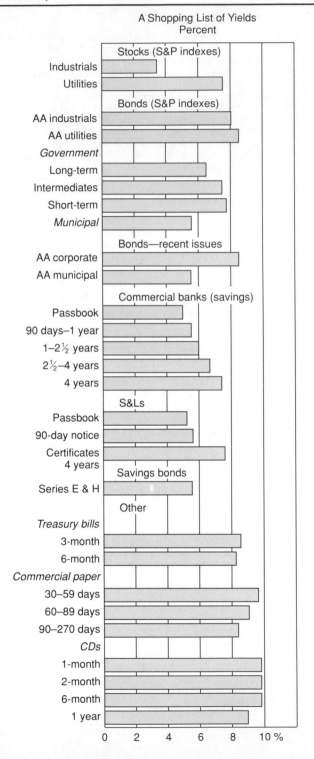

A Shopping List of Yields
Percent

## EXHIBIT 4 *(continued)*

joint return would have to purchase a taxable bond with an equivalent 9.3% yield to match this return. Profits from the sale of municipal bonds are not exempt from capital gains taxes.

### Shorter Governments Preferable

In the Government sector, long-term Treasury bonds, typically yielding about 7.8%, fully taxable, appear comparatively unattractive relative to shorter maturities—three-month bills, for example, which are currently around an 8.5% basis.

So-called "flower bonds" fit a special need. These are U.S. Treasury bonds that can be bought at discounts but applied at par value against estate taxes. Issuance of this type of obligation was halted by law a few years ago, so the list is shrinking. However, a number of

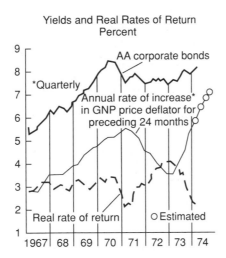

Yields and Real Rates of Return
Percent

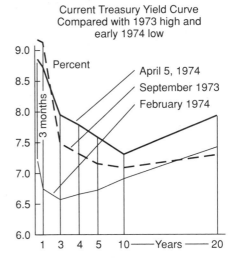

Current Treasury Yield Curve
Compared with 1973 high and
early 1974 low

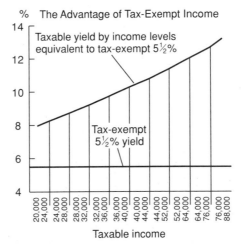

% The Advantage of Tax-Exempt Income

Taxable income

*(continued)*

**EXHIBIT 4** *(concluded)*

bonds are still available at prices in the 70s and 80s, bearing current returns of between 4% and close to 6%.

### Convertibles as a Middle Ground

Convertible bonds, most of which may be converted into a stated number of shares of common stock, offer an interesting middle ground for investing in fixed-income securities that may also, in strong stock markets, show rewarding appreciation.

The basic features of attraction of convertible securities are that (1) those selling at no more than moderate premiums over their values in common stock tend to participate in any sizable price appreciation in the stock, (2) their yields as bonds are almost always higher than the returns on the commons, and (3) they are in some degree protected by their interest-rate "floors."

In the tables [on the previous page] we list a number of bonds in each of five categories, to fit various needs.

### Who Should Buy Bonds

Are bonds suitable for you? A categorical yes or no answer would be hard to defend, for requirements differ widely. Those whose primary concerns are income and safety of principal would in almost all cases be well advised to have adequate bond representation. Even young married people, for whom estate building may be vital, should not overlook convertibles. Others whose current income suffices for their needs and who may have considerable capital committed in other ways—such as bank deposits, stocks, or real estate—may wish to sweeten over-all yields by buying some bonds.

In general, bonds are not an appropriate vehicle for those willing to accept stock market risks in order to obtain long-run growth of capital. In today's circumstances, however, it is possible to nail down yields that are not too far from average total-return performance of stocks historically. Thus the average investor may find some participation in bonds worthwhile, with a view to maintaining reasonable portfolio balance.

*Source: The Outlook,* April 15, 1974; Standard and Poor's Corp. Reprinted with permission.

# The Corporation in the Capital Markets

# *Valuation and Discounted Cash Flows*

1. The Bane & Company pension fund manager has projected a large outflow of funds to pension plan beneficiaries 15 years in the future. To fund this future liability he has decided to invest in a Guaranteed Investment Contract (GIC) with one of two insurance companies. Bane will make a single $10 million up-front payment in exchange for a GIC that promises a single (larger) maturity payment to Bane in 15 years at a promised interest rate. The GIC options offered to the Bane fund manager are

- Pru-Johntower Life Insurance Company's GIC, promising an annual rate of interest of 10%
- Tom Paine Mutual Life Insurance Company's GIC, promising a rate of interest of 9.72% per year, compounded monthly

*Compare the effective annual rates of the two GICs; also, compare the future promised payment that Bane will receive in 15 years under each option.*

2. Mr. and Mrs. Spirit purchased a $35,000 house 20 years ago. They took a 30-year mortgage for $30,000 at a 3% annual interest rate. They have just made their twentieth annual payment. Their bank, the First Amityville National Bank, has recently offered the Spirits two alternatives by which they could prepay their mortgage:

This case was prepared by Professor Michael E. Edleson.

Copyright © 1991 by the President and Fellows of Harvard College. Harvard Business School case 291–028.

- The Spirits could prepay their mortgage at a 30% discount from the current principal outstanding. Current 10-year mortgage rates are 12%. Ignore taxes, and assume payments are made at the end of each year (instead of monthly).
- The Spirits' existing mortgage would be replaced with a 5-year zero-interest loan in the amount of their current mortgage's principal outstanding. This new loan would be repaid in five equal annual payments. The banker pointed out that this option would "save them well over $2,000 in interest."

*Which alternative, if either, should the Spirits pursue?*

3. You are considering buying a new $25,000 car. The car dealer offers you a 13.6% loan with 30 equal monthly payments. Upon questioning the dealer, you find that this unusual loan has "add-on" interest, so that an interest charge of $8,500 (13.6% × $25,000 × 2.5 years) is added on to the $25,000 for a total amount to be repaid of $33,500. The payments are $1,116.67 each month ($33,500 ÷ 30).

*What is the approximate effective annual interest rate of this loan?*

4. Ms. Alumm is the portfolio manager for a large insurance company. She is considering investing $1 million to purchase the bonds of Patriot Enterprises, Inc.

a. All of Patriot's bonds have market prices that imply a yield to maturity of 8% bond-equivalent yield (that is, 4% every six-month period).[1] Each Patriot bond is described here, based on a $1,000 face value (par value), which is the promised payment at maturity.

- Bond A has 5 years until maturity and pays a 9% coupon yield ($45 every six months on a $1,000 face value bond).
- Bond B has 10 years until maturity, pays an 8% coupon yield ($40 semiannual payments), and is being offered in a private placement at par.
- Bond C is a zero coupon bond that pays no explicit interest but will pay the face amount of $1,000 per bond at maturity in 10 years.

*At what price should each bond sell currently?*

---

1. Most domestic U.S. bonds pay interest of half the coupon rate semiannually. The bond-equivalent yield to maturity is generally stated in terms of twice the semiannual yield, ignoring the compounding of the midyear coupon payment. Thus the yield to maturity as commonly stated for semiannual bonds actually understates the true annual effective yield. For additional information, see page 225, E. Brigham and L. Gapenski, *Financial Management, Theory and Practice*, 6th ed. (Troy, Mo.: Dryden Press, 1991), including the footnote on that page.

b. Ms. Alumm realizes that in addition to determining the current prices of these bonds, she would also like to know how these prices might respond to changing interest rates once her company has purchased them.

If the bonds are purchased at an 8% bond-equivalent yield, *what would happen to the price of each bond, and how much money would the company make, if market yields on Patriot bonds fell to 6%? rose to 10%?*

c. As an alternative, Ms. Alumm has been invited to invest $1 million in a private placement of a 10-year Eurobond[2] of a second firm, Nationaliste, S.A. Nationaliste bonds are similar in risk to Bond B—they promise an 8% coupon yield for 10 years—but coupons are paid annually, not semiannually. The Nationaliste bonds are priced at a 1% discount from par, or $990 per $1,000 face value.

*What yield to maturity is implied by the Nationaliste Eurobond? Compare this yield to the 8% bond-equivalent yield of the Patriot semiannual coupon bond (Bond B). What should Ms. Alumm do?*

d. Ms. Alumm receives a call from a Japanese bond dealer who offers to sell her the same Nationaliste bonds, priced at the "Japanese yield to maturity" of 8.16%. In calculating the yield to maturity of a coupon-bearing bond, it is Japanese practice to use the following formula:[3]

$$\text{Yield} = \frac{\text{Annual coupon} + (\text{Par value} - \text{Price})/\text{Years to maturity}}{\text{Price}} \times 100\%$$

*Should Ms. Alumm purchase the Nationaliste bonds from the Japanese dealer or in the private placement?*

5. You are the chief financial officer of the firm Ponce de Leon Foods. The board has decided to offer an early retirement plan whereby the typical 55-year-old worker can retire now with a small cash severance and draw a pension of $10,000 per year, expected to last for 30 years (the first payment would be made 1 year from now). You plan to set aside sufficient money now to fund the plan, and you have secured guarantees from your insurance company promising you

---

2. See the definition of Eurobond in Barron's *Dictionary of Finance and Investment Terms.* One key point is that Eurobonds generally pay *annual* coupon payments, as opposed to the semiannual convention for typical bonds. If you calculate the yield to maturity based on these annual payments, you will get an effective annual rate—this differs from the semiannual-based bond-equivalent yield that is the convention for bond yield quotes in the United States.

3. Basically, this Japanese yield to maturity formula takes the *current yield* (coupon ÷ price) of the bond and adds to it a simple annual proration of the premium (price over par) or discount (price under par) of the bond.

an 8% annual return on all funds deposited by you, to meet these projected payments based on the stated terms and to bear any risk (such as interest rate surprises or greater-than-expected life spans). You expect 100 workers to take advantage of the plan, so you must fund expected pension payouts of $1 million per year for 30 years.

The Amalgamated Paper-or-Plastic Workers have objected to the plan, since the pension payments "lose purchasing power" over time because of inflation. They propose an alternative plan of an $8,000 pension (also beginning in a year) that grows each year at a fixed rate of 5%. They claim that this plan should be attractive to the company, since it needs to pay less money to pensioners ($8,000 versus $10,000) during today's difficult economic times.

*How much will it cost you in terms of an up-front payment to fund each plan?*[4]

———

4. While you could easily solve this on a spreadsheet, you may instead choose to use the following formula for the present value *(V)* of an initial end-of-year annuity payout of $C (growing at $g\%$) per period, with an interest rate of $r\%$, for $T$ periods.

$$V = \frac{C}{r - g} [1 - \left(\frac{1 + g}{1 + r}\right)^T]$$

# Tom Paine Mutual Life Insurance Company (Abridged)

In December 1990, Jack Fuller, an assistant portfolio manager in the Investment and Pension Group (IPG) of Tom Paine Mutual Life Insurance Company, was mulling over what recommendations to make concerning the investment of funds from the sale of a new Guaranteed Investment Contract (GIC) to a large corporate retirement plan. Under the terms of the contract, Tom Paine would receive $109 million on January 15, 1991; it would have to pay $198.5 million on January 15, 1998, that is, $109 million plus accumulated interest calculated at a semiannually compounded rate of 8.75%. Mr. Fuller had been asked to review public and private debt instruments currently available to Tom Paine and to recommend to IPG purchases for the new GIC.

In connection with the assignment, Mr. Fuller had been informed that IPG had already purchased or committed to purchase assets that would absorb $89 million of the January 15 funds inflow. He had also been told that IPG's asset/liability management unit had determined that the remaining assets selected for the new GIC ought to mature approximately 7 years from January 15, 1991.

GIC management involved a number of challenges. Competition for GIC business was intense and focused on price, that is, the yield to maturity guaranteed by the insurer. This, in turn, forced GIC writers to attempt to realize high rates of return on invested assets. To achieve its profitability objectives for the GIC business, Tom Paine needed to invest funds at a gross rate of return approximately 100 basis points above the one guaranteed to the GIC purchaser, while holding credit losses to a minimum.[1]

This case was prepared by Professor Ronald W. Moore.

Copyright © 1991 by the President and Fellows of Harvard College.
Harvard Business School case 291–030.

1. A basis point is 1/100 of 1%.

If badly managed, the GIC business could result in serious direct and indirect losses. In the past 5 years, for example, one of the largest life insurance companies had incurred operating losses of more than $1 billion in the GIC business through overly aggressive guaranteed rate levels, mismanagement of its asset/liability structure, and credit losses on invested assets. That company's ratings had been reduced from AAA to A, a level that effectively precluded continued participation in the GIC business and seriously hindered efforts to sell other insurance products.

Nevertheless, the GIC business was important for Tom Paine, accounting for 27% of total assets and a rapidly growing proportion of profits.

## Background

Tom Paine, headquartered in Boston, Massachusetts, was the thirteenth largest life insurance company in the country. As of December 31, 1989, it had total assets of $26 billion, surplus of $1 billion, and insurance in force of $158 billion.[2] As a mutual company, Tom Paine was owned by its policyholders. Policyholders participated in profits through dividends, which had been paid without interruption since 1878. Exhibits 1 and 2 present recent balance sheets and income statements.

Tom Paine conducted most of its business through three major operating units, Retail Financial Services, Group Benefits, and IPG. Retail Financial Services marketed nationwide a broad array of individual life and health insurance products, mainly through more than 12,000 career agents (company-employed, commission salespeople). Tom Paine sold traditional insurance such as term life, whole life, and annuities, and newer, investment-oriented products such as universal life, variable life, and variable annuities.[3] Group Benefits, as the name implies, sold group life and health insurance as well as benefits administration services to employers of all sizes.

IPG invested Tom Paine's investable funds and marketed investment products and services to pension funds and other institutional accounts. In addition to its three main lines of business, Tom Paine was engaged through subsidiaries in a variety of related businesses, among them property and casualty insurance, mutual funds, credit cards, mortgage banking, and consumer finance.

For some time, IPG had taken an increasingly prominent role in Tom Paine's business mix. This reflected, on the one hand, the ongoing decline in the profitability

---

2. Surplus in a mutual insurance company is roughly equivalent to equity in an industrial corporation.

3. Term life is pure insurance coverage; premiums go to investment for future death benefits plus administrative expenses, sales commissions, and profits. Traditional whole life combines insurance coverage with a long-term, tax-deferred savings contract. Premiums, typically a multiple of term premiums, go to the same uses and to the policyholder's cash value account, where they earn a contractually fixed rate of return. In addition to pure insurance profits, the insurer earns the spread between its investment returns and the rate paid to the policyholder. Traditional annuities are, in effect, the savings contract component of traditional whole life. In the newer, investment-oriented products the policyholder earns on the savings component of the premium the full net returns achieved by mutual fund–like pools made available by the insurer. The insurer earns only a competitive management fee on the savings contract, not a spread.

of traditional individual life insurance products and, on the other hand, the rapid expansion of the GIC business. Throughout most of Tom Paine's long history, traditional whole life insurance had been the cornerstone of the company's growth and profitability. Since the mid-1970s, however, many factors, among them high inflation, volatile interest rates, the proliferation of retail investment vehicles, and the growth of employer-sponsored retirement plans, had combined to erode the profitability and salability of traditional whole life. In 1990, Tom Paine would earn on its traditional life insurance business a pre-tax return on assigned surplus of only about 8–8.5%.

Faced with these problems, senior management had been striving since the mid-1980s to redefine the company, seeking to convert it from a traditional marketer and servicer of insurance products to an institutional investor that gathered funds from a variety of sources including the sale of traditional and nontraditional insurance products. Toward this end, a number of programs had been initiated to reduce processing and distribution costs and to expand retail and institutional marketing of products emphasizing Tom Paine's investment skills. To date, the one unqualified success had come in guaranteed investment products, particularly GICs.

## GICs

The GIC market was large and rapidly growing. Tom Paine management estimated its size at $220 billion and anticipated annual growth of 20–25%. Most defined contribution retirement plans as well as employee thrift and profit-sharing plans included a GIC among the investment options available to plan participants, and 60–70% of the funds in such plans went into GICs.[4] Such plans had grown rapidly during the 1980s and were expected to continue to do so.

A GIC is a contract between a life insurance company and a plan sponsor. Pursuant to this contract, the insurer makes a commitment, fully backed by its general account, to pay on a future date an amount comprising up-front funds received from the plan plus interest thereon at a specified rate. GICs vary greatly in detail but generally take the form of a "bullet" or "window" arrangement. In a bullet contract the insurer is committed to pay a specified amount on a specified future date in return for one lump sum, up-front payment. In a typical window deal the insurer agrees to accept funds up to a specified maximum amount over a specified period (say, three, six, or twelve months) and to permit, without penalty, withdrawal of the accumulated balance by plan participants during the life of the contract. In return for providing such flexibility, Tom Paine generally guaranteed a rate 10–20 basis points lower than on a bullet of the same maturity.

The popularity of GICs is easy to understand. They typically yield more than AA corporate bonds (see Exhibit 3) yet are fully guaranteed by an AA or

---

4. High-grade corporate bonds are those assigned ratings of AAA or AA by the principal credit-rating agencies, Moody's Investors Service and Standard and Poor's Corporation. At the time of the case, high-grade, newly issued intermediate-term industrials were yielding about 40–70 basis points over Treasuries.

AAA life insurance company. And (as is not the case with direct investment in corporate bonds) the insurer, not the plan beneficiaries, bears all the risk of interest rate changes, early redemptions, bond rating downgrades, and credit losses.

The GIC market was dominated by the largest and most creditworthy life insurers (see Exhibit 4). While price remained a critical factor in getting GIC business, the credit quality of the insurer was also important. Not having an AA rating from at least one rating agency effectively barred an insurer from the GIC business, and an increasing number of sponsors were restricting their business to AAA-rated life insurance companies. In 1990 the many signs of distress in the financial system, for instance, the recent collapse of the junk bond market and the savings and loan system bailout, suggested that concern about the credit quality of GIC writers would continue and probably intensify.

Tom Paine enjoyed the highest claims-paying ability ratings, and senior management considered their maintenance essential to continued success in selling GICs and other guaranteed investment products. This perception strongly influenced Tom Paine's policies concerning the investment of GIC funds.

## Tom Paine's Investment Approach

The profitability of Tom Paine's GIC business depended primarily on the extent to which the company could invest GIC monies at higher rates of return than it contracted to pay. Top management of Tom Paine had mandated a relatively conservative approach to GIC investment. Thus, Tom Paine pursued a spread approach: it sought to lock in a spread, or gross margin, over the cost of its AAA-rated GIC obligations by investing the proceeds in lower-quality assets of similar maturity.

This approach minimized exposure to interest rate movements, which otherwise might significantly enhance or erode GIC returns. Exhibit 5, which shows historical annual returns on a variety of fixed-income instruments, suggests the possible rewards and risks of mismatching the maturities of assets and liabilities.

As to asset quality, senior management had severely limited investment in credit-rated BB or lower, namely, junk bonds. This reflected their assessment of the value of Tom Paine's credit ratings. After profitability, asset quality and surplus adequacy are the most important factors in the determination of these ratings, and significant investment in junk bonds would adversely affect both.

Senior management believed it was possible to earn adequate GIC returns with a non-mismatch, non-junk investment approach because of Tom Paine's expertise in credit analysis and in the valuation of debt instruments together with its access, as a sizable and active buyer, to most offerings in the private debt markets. These attributes, it was believed, enabled Tom Paine to book relatively high-yielding assets without necessarily bearing commensurate credit risk.

Top management had established a profitability objective for the GIC business of a pre-tax return on surplus of 15%. The amount of surplus allocated to the GIC business was 2.5% of assets, that is, $2.50 for every $100 of GIC assets. Estimated operating expenses associated with the GIC business currently amounted to about .5–.6% of GIC assets.

In addition, pursuant to regulatory requirements, GIC assets, like all general account debt securities, had to be charged on a current basis for potential credit losses. Tom Paine charged to securities valuation reserves over a 10-year period a total of 1% of the cost of A or better and equivalent unrated credits; 2% of BBB and equivalent credits; and 5% of BB and equivalent credits. With respect to lower-rated securities, 10% of B and equivalent credits had to be charged off over a 5-year period, as did 20% of lower-rated credits. Defaulted securities had to be carried at the lower of cost or estimated net realizable value. Although mortgages were not governed by regulation, Tom Paine charged 2% of mortgages to valuation reserves over a 10-year period. Tom Paine's actual credit experience in recent years had been considerably better than that implied by regulatory requirements.

## The Public Debt Market

Mr. Fuller had begun his investigation of public market investment possibilities by preparing a matrix of current new issue interest rate levels. These are shown in Exhibit 6.

Public debt is distinguished from privately placed debt in having been registered with the Securities and Exchange Commission (SEC) prior to issuance.[5] Securities so registered and cleared for sale by the SEC become freely salable to all investors, both upon initial distribution and in subsequent secondary market trading.

Late in December 1990 the domestic public market for nonconvertible corporate debt comprised over 3,500 rated issues with an aggregate principal amount in excess of $1,500 billion.[6] New issue volume in 1990 was $106.6 billion and over the preceding 5 years had averaged $125.8 billion.

The public market is almost always the most attractive domestic market for large, creditworthy issuers needing to raise debt of $100 million or more in one transaction. Because public issues are freely tradable and relatively liquid, this market usually affords the lowest all-in borrowing costs, the most flexible redemption and refunding provisions, the least restrictive covenants, and to the extent desired, the longest maturities and average lives.[7]

Based on the data in Exhibit 6 versus the yield requirements of the new GIC, Mr. Fuller had turned his attention to the secondary market. In the secondary market limited liquidity frequently poses a problem for a buyer seeking to accumulate more than 5–10% of an issue: such purchases can sharply push up prices from quoted levels, and in some instances sizable amounts are simply unobtainable. On the other hand, Mr. Fuller reasoned, limited liquidity could result in bargain purchase opportunities.

---

5. Registration entails filing with the SEC and making available to the public a number of documents, including a registration statement describing the issue and prescribed business and financial information on the issuer; it also obligates the issuer to file and make public on an ongoing basis annual and quarterly financial reports and other information.

6. Securities Data Company, Inc.

7. All-in borrowing costs take into account costs of issuance as well as the interest rate.

Mr. Fuller had developed a list of outstanding publicly traded bonds that might qualify for purchase. This list contained all non-bank and non-insurance bonds with ratings of A or BBB, $50 million or more of outstanding principal amount, and final maturities within three months of January 15, 1998 (the maturity date of the GIC). Data on these bonds are shown in Exhibit 7.

In connection with his review of secondary market bonds, Mr. Fuller had also examined restrictive covenants contained in a number of indentures. He had concluded that, unlike covenants in private placement note agreements, public issue covenants afforded little or no substantive protection to debtholders.

## The Private Placement Market

Privately placed corporate debt securities are not registered and therefore by law are salable only to large, sophisticated investors, those presumed not to need the protection of SEC-regulated disclosure documents. Accordingly, after-market liquidity is minimal. New issue volume in 1990 was approximately $113.6 billion; in 1989, $168.1 billion; in 1988, $171.2 billion; in 1987, $119.5 billion; in 1986, $105.8 billion.[8]

Large life insurance companies like Tom Paine dominate the buy side of the market. These institutions maintain sizable staffs of private placement specialists, who are trained and experienced in in-depth credit analysis, in structuring complex financing arrangements, and in tailoring and negotiating terms to meet the needs of both issuer and investor.

The main incentive for a financial institution to participate in the private placement market is the availability of higher yields. Private placement yields generally range from 25 to 35 basis points or more over public levels. This premium represents compensation to the investor for illiquidity and, in many instances, for a superior bargaining position vis-à-vis the borrower. Exhibit 8 sets forth a survey of private placement new issue rate levels as of late December 1990.

On the issuer side, a wide variety of companies make use of the private placement market. Most important, perhaps, are issuers whose requirements are too small for the public market minimum of $100 million. Such issues, if attempted in the public market, would incur a significant price penalty for illiquidity as well as substantially higher fixed costs of issuance (see Exhibit 9). Other users of the market are borrowers who could not or would not comply with SEC disclosure and reporting requirements (e.g., nonpublic companies, U.S. subsidiaries of foreign companies) and companies with especially complex operations or financing requirements.

Mr. Fuller's review of private placement offerings currently in-house at Tom Paine revealed two possibilities for investment by the new GIC: one was a proposed $40 million, 7-year, senior subordinated debt financing for Sam Adams Financial Corporation, the other a $25 million refinancing of bank debt for Ginne Enterprises, a family-owned publishing and broadcasting company.

---

8. Securities Data Company, Inc.

Sam Adams Financial Corporation, a wholly owned subsidiary of a *Fortune 50* corporation, was a major consumer and commercial finance company with related insurance operations. It was a frequent borrower in the public market, raising well over $1 billion annually. Occasionally, it raised in the private placement market relatively small amounts of subordinated debt to comply with certain covenants in the indenture for its 6⅛% senior debentures. Sam Adams' senior ratings were A2 by Moody's, A+ by S&P; its senior subordinated ratings Baa1 and A, respectively.

Tom Paine already enjoyed an existing credit relationship with Sam Adams Financial Corporation, having bought half ($7.5 million principal amount) of the company's last privately placed senior subordinated debt issue in 1988. The current investment opportunity had resulted from direct discussions between Sam Adams and Tom Paine. Exhibit 10 presents a summary term sheet prepared by Tom Paine. Exhibits 11 and 12 present summary operating and balance sheet data.

The proposed $25 million senior debt financing was for Ginne Enterprises, Inc., a family-owned print and broadcast communications firm based in Stamford, Connecticut. It was run by Jimmy and Sarah Ginne, who had a reputation in their industry as knowledgeable, shrewd, and cautious operators with a knack for acquiring cheap and turning around ailing properties. The purpose of the proposed financing was to refund $25 million of bank debt incurred to acquire a community newspaper in the third quarter of 1990. The proposed financing had been presented to Tom Paine by Ginne's investment banker. Ginne did not have rated debt.

With the acquisition of *The Daily Clarion* in Lakeville, Connecticut, Ginne published daily newspapers in ten communities in Connecticut, Massachusetts, upstate New York, New Hampshire, and Vermont. Eight of the ten enjoyed monopoly positions in their markets and commensurate profitability. Ginne also owned and operated two FM stations, located in western Connecticut and western Massachusetts. Although *The Daily Clarion* had not in recent years shown the kind of profitability to which the Ginnes were accustomed, they were confident they could restore circulation and advertising levels and effect significant operating economies by printing at their new state-of-the-art plant in Massachusetts.

Exhibit 13 presents a summary term sheet, prepared by Ginne's investment banker, for the proposed transaction. Exhibits 14 and 15 present summary operating and balance sheet data.

## Commercial Mortgage Debt

The commercial mortgage market supplies permanent financing (intermediate- and long-term fixed-rate debt) for office buildings, multifamily housing, shopping centers, hotels and other commercial real estate projects. Financing volume in 1989 was approximately $620 billion; in the preceding 3 years, it had averaged $533 billion.[9]

---

9. Board of Governors of the Federal Reserve System, Flow-of-Funds Accounts.

This market is based on the premise that well-managed, well-located, nonspecialized real property retains its value and, in most instances, appreciates over time. Thus, most financing is nonrecourse: that is, for asset protection and repayment, investors looked to the value and cash flow of the specific property financed rather than to the overall assets and cash flow of the underlying borrower. In addition to a note, the investor takes a lien (mortgage) on the property, which permits foreclosure in the event of a default. In other respects, the market is broadly similar to that for privately placed corporate debt. Large institutions, mainly life insurance companies, dominate; and after-market liquidity is minimal.[10]

Yields, reflecting the undiversified, nonrecourse nature of the credits, are generally somewhat higher than in the private corporate market. A matrix of current interest rates in the commercial mortgage market is presented as Exhibit 16.

At the time of the case, Tom Paine was approaching the mortgage market with particular caution and selectivity. Overbuilding in the 1980s, coupled with the 1990 recession, had resulted in falling property values and a sharp rise in commercial vacancy rates. Certain regional markets were experiencing vacancy rates as high as 27%. At the same time, commercial mortgage delinquencies in life insurance company portfolios were estimated at 3.9% and expected to rise.[11]

In spite of this unpropitious environment, Mr. Fuller had identified one offering that he considered a possibility. This was a $5.5 million, 7-year first mortgage to provide permanent financing on Pali Palms Plaza, a small office complex in the suburbs of Honolulu.

The borrower was Kailua Bay Investors, a California general partnership formed to buy Pali Palms Plaza and owned 50/50 by Tim and Glenda Hurley and Herb Newman. For many years, the Hurleys and Newman had made a success of jointly buying distressed properties at deep discounts from replacement cost, turning them around through a combination of management expertise and financial strength, then operating them as long-term investment properties. Among them, the partners had over 65 years of experience in real estate and an aggregate net worth of more than $100 million.

Kailua Bay Investors had bought Pali Palms Plaza from Bank of America for $4.2 million in cash in November 1988, following the bank's foreclosure on an $8.8 million construction loan to the original developer. Since that time, the partners had incurred additional costs of $1.3 million for extensive tenant improvements, leasing commissions, and operating deficits.

The property, completed in 1987, consisted of two three-story office buildings and a free-standing restaurant. It contained 58,390 sq ft of net rentable office space, 6,016 ft of restaurant space, and surface and under-building parking for 287 cars. Engineering consultants acceptable to Tom Paine had termed construction

---

10. Liquidity increased in the late 1980s with the development of securitization techniques, whereby diversified packages of mortgages are publicly or privately sold, generally with a limited guarantee by the seller.

11. *Barron's,* December 21, 1990.

sound and free of structural or other discernible defects, and environmental experts had certified the structure as being free of asbestos and other environmental hazards.

Pali Palms Plaza was located 12 miles north of Honolulu in the highly affluent residential suburb of Kailua. It was situated at a major intersection two miles northwest of the town center, directly across the street from a large shopping center and half a mile north of the Kaneohe Marine Corps Air Station.

Vacancy rates in suburban office space varied widely with location, building age and design, and rental levels. The range was zero to as much as 30%, with an overall rate of approximately 8% and a lower rate in the northern and western suburbs. Office vacancy in downtown Honolulu was approximately 11%.

Suburban rents ranged from $1.50 to $2.00 per square foot per month with operating expense stops, typically, of $.50 per square foot per month.[12] In downtown Honolulu rental rates for newer space ranged from $1.75 to $2.30 with expense stops of $.65 to $.75 and parking fees of $75 to $115 per month per space.

An appraiser satisfactory to Tom Paine had valued Pali Palms Plaza at $8.9 million. Summary operating data are shown in Exhibit 17. Currently, the property was 89% leased, with 49 tenants paying an average rental of $1.49 per square foot per month. Three leases had been signed in the last quarter at an average rental of $1.60 per square foot per month, and the partners expected to achieve 95% occupancy by mid-1991 on the basis of active discussions with several prospective lessees.

Exhibit 18 presents a summary term sheet for the proposed financing, and Exhibit 19 shows a comparison of the proposed transaction to Tom Paine's internal standards for commercial mortgage loans.

## Conclusion

As Mr. Fuller reflected on the options he had identified, he was mindful that the date for the scheduled cash inflow was nearing, and Tom Paine would want to get it fully invested with minimum delay. He was also mindful that Sam Adams had access to many sources of financing and that Ginne Enterprises and Pali Palms Plaza had been offered simultaneously to a number of major private market investors on a first-come, first-served basis. Finally, he was very much aware that as a result of credit problems besetting banks and thrift institutions Tom Paine, like all the major life insurers, was under increasing scrutiny from regulators and the rating agencies, particularly with respect to asset quality.

---

12. An operating expense stop obligates lessees to bear, on a pro rata square footage or other predetermined basis, operating expenses in excess of the stop.

## EXHIBIT 1

Consolidated Balance Sheets, Tom Paine Mutual Life Insurance Company, at December 31, 1988 and 1989 (millions of dollars)

|  | 1988 | 1989 |
|---|---|---|
| Bonds[a] | $ 8,053.8 | $ 8,769.6 |
| Stocks |  |  |
| Preferred[b] | 85.0 | 81.4 |
| Common[b] | 36.7 | 39.0 |
| Investments in affiliates | 351.5 | 458.7 |
|  | 473.2 | 579.1 |
| Mortgage loans on real estate[a] | 7,615.4 | 8,483.5 |
| Real estate[c] |  |  |
| Company-occupied | 154.1 | 165.8 |
| Investments | 1,059.0 | 971.6 |
|  | 1,213.1 | 1,137.4 |
| Policy loans | 1,727.7 | 1,669.2 |
| Cash items |  |  |
| In banks and offices | 80.9 | 131.9 |
| Temporary investments | 352.8 | 219.9 |
|  | 433.7 | 351.8 |
| Premiums due and deferred | 308.6 | 304.7 |
| Investment income accrued | 389.2 | 391.4 |
| Other assets | 709.3 | 793.1 |
| Separate accounts[d] | 2,644.6 | 3,395.4 |
| Total assets | $23,568.6 | $25,875.2 |
| Policy reserves | $11,085.2 | $11,512.6 |
| Policyholders' and beneficiaries' funds | 7,683.2 | 8,617.4 |
| Dividends payable | 317.0 | 330.8 |
| Policy benefits in process of payment | 188.1 | 171.8 |
| Other policy liabilities | 175.6 | 170.3 |
| Mandatory securities and other asset |  |  |
| valuation reserves[e] | 326.2 | 381.2 |
| Accrued taxes | 134.1 | 144.4 |
| Other liabilities | 89.0 | 134.2 |
| Separate accounts[f] | 2,623.1 | 3,371.1 |
| Total liabilities | 22,621.4 | 24,833.8 |
| Special surplus | 101.1 | 105.1 |
| Unassigned surplus | 846.1 | 936.3 |
| Total surplus | 947.2 | 1,041.4 |
| Total liabilities and surplus | $23,568.6 | $25,875.2 |

*Note:* Includes the accounts of U.S.-domiciled life insurance operations. Investments in other affiliates are included on the equity method.

a. Generally carried at amortized cost.

b. Sinking fund preferred stocks generally carried at cost; other stocks carried at market.

c. Carried at depreciated cost, less encumbrances.

d. Refers to third-party assets under management, mainly related to variable life and annuity and similar products and mainly comprising stock, bond, and real estate commingled funds. These funds are carried at market and also appear on the liability side of the balance sheet.

e. A reserve to cover the potential for default risk on debt securities.

f. See note (d). These funds are carried at market and also appear on the asset side of the balance sheet.

**EXHIBIT 2**

Consolidated Summary of Operations and Changes in Surplus, Tom Paine Mutual Life Insurance Company, for Years Ending December 31, 1988 and 1989 (millions of dollars)

| | *1988* | *1989* |
|---|---|---|
| Premiums, annuity considerations, and pension fund contributions | $4,243.5 | $5,094.1 |
| Investment income | 1,932.4 | 2,093.8 |
| Separate account capital gains | 147.0 | 304.6 |
| Other, net | 32.8 | 68.1 |
| Total income | 6,355.7 | 7,560.6 |
| Death benefits | 565.8 | 546.1 |
| Accident and health benefits | 443.1 | 412.5 |
| Annuity benefits | 599.5 | 642.9 |
| Surrender benefits and annuity fund withdrawals | 2,736.1 | 2,702.6 |
| Matured endowments | 18.2 | 16.6 |
| Payments to policyholders, beneficiaries | 4,362.7 | 4,320.7 |
| Additions to reserves | 952.3 | 2,141.2 |
| General and administrative expenses | | |
| Field sales | 248.8 | 247.8 |
| Home office and general | 289.8 | 317.8 |
| State premiums, payroll and misc. taxes | 57.5 | 58.6 |
| Total benefits and expenses | 5,911.1 | 7,086.1 |
| Gain from operations | 444.6 | 474.5 |
| Dividends paid to policyholders | 293.5 | 313.4 |
| Federal income taxes | 19.0 | 1.4 |
| Gain from operations before net realized capital gains | 132.1 | 159.7 |
| Net realized capital gains | 4.6 | 25.8 |
| Net income | 136.7 | 185.5 |
| Other changes in surplus | | |
| Net unrealized capital losses, other adjustments | (56.7) | (66.7) |
| Valuation reserve changes | (5.8) | 13.9 |
| Prior years' federal income taxes | 6.5 | (16.8) |
| Other adjustments | (15.3) | (2.6) |
| Net increase in surplus | $ 65.4 | $ 113.3 |

**EXHIBIT 3**

Representative GIC Rates, December 1990

| *Rates* | *3 Years* | *5 Years* | *7 Years* |
|---|---|---|---|
| High | 8.41% | 8.93% | 9.25% |
| Average | 7.98 | 8.52 | 8.82 |
| Low | 7.60 | 8.12 | 8.25 |
| Treasury notes | 7.48 | 7.84 | 8.08 |
| Number of GIC vendors | 34 | 36 | 30 |

*Source: Barron's,* December 21, 1990.

**EXHIBIT 4**
Largest GIC Providers as of January 1, 1990 (billions of dollars)

| | GIC Amounts | Total Assets | Claims-Paying Ability Ratings | | |
|---|---|---|---|---|---|
| | | | Best's[a] | Moody's[b] | S&P[c] |
| Prudential Insurance . . . | $21.2 | $164.0 | A+ | Aaa | AAA |
| Metropolitan Life . . . . | 17.1 | 98.9 | A+ | Aaa | AAA |
| Aetna Life & Casualty . . | 13.2 | 87.1 | A+ | Aaa | AAA |
| Equitable Life . . . . . | 11.1 | 61.7 | A | A1 | A |
| Travelers . . . . . . . | 9.2 | 56.5 | A+ | A1 | A+[d] |
| John Hancock . . . . . | 8.4 | 32.3 | A+ | Aaa | AAA |
| New York Life . . . . . | 7.9 | 46.7 | A+ | Aaa | AAA |
| Tom Paine . . . . . . | 7.0 | 25.9 | A+ | Aaa | AAA |
| Principal Financial . . . | 6.9 | 25.3 | A+ | Aaa | AAA |
| Provident National . . . | 5.7 | 11.9 | A+ | Aa1 | A+ |
| Massachusetts Mutual . . | 4.2 | 24.8 | A | Aaa | AAA |
| Continental Assurance . . | 3.7 | 8.9 | A+ | Aa1 | A+ |
| Connecticut Mutual . . . | 2.8 | 11.2 | A+ | Aa2 | AA− |
| State Mutual . . . . . | 2.7 | 7.2 | A+ | Aa1 | AAA |
| Crown Life . . . . . . | 2.6 | 7.2 | A+ | A1 | AA |
| Pacific Mutual . . . . . | 2.6 | 8.6 | A+ | Aa2 | AAA |

*Source: Pension and Investment Age.*

a. Ratings range from A+ to C−.

b. Ratings range from Aaa to C.

c. Ratings range from AAA to D.

d. On "credit watch" with negative implications.

**EXHIBIT 5**
Historical Annual Returns on Selected Fixed-Income Instruments, 1975–1989

| | Long-Term Corporate Bonds | U.S. Treasury Securities | | |
|---|---|---|---|---|
| | | Bills | Intermediate-Term Bonds | Long-Term Bonds |
| 1975 . . . . . | 14.64% | 5.80% | 7.83% | 9.19% |
| 1976 . . . . . | 18.65 | 5.08 | 12.87 | 16.75 |
| 1977 . . . . . | 1.71 | 5.12 | 1.40 | (.67) |
| 1978 . . . . . | (.70) | 7.18 | 3.48 | (1.16) |
| 1979 . . . . . | (4.18) | 10.38 | 4.09 | (1.22) |
| 1980 . . . . . | (2.62) | 11.24 | 3.91 | (3.95) |
| 1981 . . . . . | (.96) | 14.71 | 9.45 | 1.85 |
| 1982 . . . . . | 43.79 | 10.54 | 29.10 | 40.35 |
| 1983 . . . . . | 4.70 | 8.80 | 7.41 | .68 |
| 1984 . . . . . | 16.39 | 9.85 | 14.02 | 15.43 |
| 1985 . . . . . | 30.90 | 7.72 | 20.33 | 30.97 |
| 1986 . . . . . | 19.85 | 6.16 | 15.14 | 24.44 |
| 1987 . . . . . | (.27) | 5.47 | 2.90 | (2.69) |
| 1988 . . . . . | 10.70 | 6.35 | 6.10 | 9.67 |
| 1989 . . . . . | 16.23 | 8.37 | 13.29 | 18.10 |

*Source: Ibbotson Associates.*

*Note:* Returns represent interest income plus change in market value.

**EXHIBIT 6**

Indicative New Issue Levels for Publicly Offered Debt Securities: Reoffering Spreads over Treasury Securities, December 1990 (basis points)

| Issuer | Ratings Moody's/S&P | Years to Final Maturity | | | | | |
|---|---|---|---|---|---|---|---|
| | | 2 | 3 | 5 | 7 | 10 | 30 |
| U.S. agencies | | | | | | | |
| FNMA . . . . . . . . | NR/NR | 17 | 19 | 27 | 30 | 35 | 120[a] |
| TVA . . . . . . . | Aaa/AAA | 20 | 20 | 25 | 35 | 41 | 109[a] |
| Industrials | | | | | | | |
| IBM . . . . . . . . . | Aaa/AAA | 25 | 30 | 35 | 40 | 45 | 65 |
| Du Pont . . . . . . . | Aa2/AA | 40 | 50 | 60 | 70 | 75 | 100 |
| Pepsico . . . . . . | A1/A | 60 | 65 | 70 | 80 | 90 | 110 |
| ConAgra . . . . . . | Baa1/BBB | 110 | 120 | 130 | 140 | 150 | 165 |
| Utilities | | | | | | | |
| SoCal Edison . . . . | Aa2/AA | 60 | 70 | 75 | 80 | 85 | 135[b] |
| Alabama Power . . . | A1/A | 75 | 85 | 90 | 95 | 100 | 150[b] |
| Cincinnati Gas & Electric . | Baa1/BBB+ | 90 | 100 | 105 | 115 | 125 | 190[b] |
| Finance | | | | | | | |
| IBM Credit . . . . . | Aaa/AAA | 35 | 45 | 50 | 55 | 60 | na |
| Amex Credit . . . . . | Aa2/AA | 90 | 100 | 110 | 120 | 130 | na |
| CIT . . . . . . . . | A1/A+ | 135 | 155 | 165 | 175 | 190 | na |
| Banks[c] | | | | | | | |
| Morgan Guaranty Trust . . | Aaa/AAA | 60 | 60 | 65 | 75 | 85 | na |
| Bankers Trust . . . . | Aa2/AA | 70 | 85 | 105 | 125 | 140 | na |
| Bank of America . . . | Aa3/A | 80 | 95 | 115 | 135 | 155 | na |
| U.S. Treasury Securities . . | | 7.28% | 7.48% | 7.84% | 8.08% | 8.18% | 8.30% |

*Note:* All indications for noncall life instruments unless otherwise indicated.

NR = not rated; na = not available.

a. Nonredeemable for 5 years, thereafter redeemable at declining premiums over par.

b. Nonrefundable for 5 years, thereafter refundable at declining premiums over par.

c. For issuance of bank level, not holding company.

d. Actual prevailing yields, not new issue indications.

**EXHIBIT 7**
Price Data Relating to Selected Publicly Traded Debt Securities

| Issuer | Ratings Moody's/S&P | Issue Date | Outstand. Amount ($ mills.) | Coupon | Maturity | Sinking Fund Begins | Sinking Fund Retires[a] | Approx. Avg Life (years) | Call Begins | Call Price | Current Price |
|---|---|---|---|---|---|---|---|---|---|---|---|
| Cabot Corp. | Baa1/BBB+ | 1987 | $ 100 | 10¼% | 12/15/97 | – | – | 7.0 | – | – | $101½ |
| Capital Cities/ABC | A1/A+ | 1985 | 200 | 10½ | 9/1/97 | – | – | 6.8 | 9/1/92 | $100.00 | 104⅜ |
| Commercial Credit | A2/A | 1988 | 100 | 8½ | 2/15/98 | – | – | 7.2 | – | – | 98⅜ |
| Commonwealth Edison[b] | Baa1/BBB+ | 1968 | 50 | 6¼ | 2/1/98 | – | – | 7.2 | Current | 101.67 | 84¾ |
| Consumers Power[b] | Baa3/BBB– | 1988 | 250 | 8¾ | 2/15/98 | – | – | 7.2 | – | – | 98 |
| Dillard Dept. Stores | A2/A | 1988 | 50 | 9½ | 1/15/98 | – | – | 7.0 | – | – | 101 |
| Eastman Kodak | A2/A– | 1988 | 1,100 | 9⅛ | 3/1/98 | – | – | 7.2 | 3/1/95 | 100.00 | 98⅝ |
| Hertz Corp. | A3/BBB | 1988 | 75 | 9.70 | 9/15/97 | – | – | 6.7 | – | – | 99⅜ |
| Household Finance | A2/A+ | 1989 | 100 | 8¼ | 3/1/98 | – | – | 7.2 | 3/1/94 | 100.00 | 93⅜ |
| ITT Financial | A1/A+ | 1988 | 100 | 8½ | 1/15/98 | – | – | 7.0 | – | – | 98⅞ |
| Marriott Corp. | Baa2/BBB | 1987 | 150 | 9⅞ | 11/1/97 | – | – | 6.9 | 11/1/94 | 100.00 | 89¼ |
| Morgan Stanley | A1/A+ | 1988 | 100 | 9.80 | 1/15/98 | – | – | 7.0 | 6/15/95 | 100.00 | 103⅛ |
| New York Telephone | A1/A | 1960 | 60 | 4⅝ | 10/1/97 | – | – | 6.8 | Current | 100.33 | 79½ |
| Ohio Power[b] | A2/A– | 1988 | 100 | 9⅞ | 1/1/98 | Current | 1% | 6.8 | 5/31/93[e] | 102.83 | 103⅛ |
| Penn Central[c] | Baa1/BBB– | 1987 | 134 | 11 | 12/15/97 | – | – | 7.0 | Current | 102.00 | 101⅝ |
| J. C. Penney | A1/A+ | 1990 | 250 | 10 | 10/1/97 | – | – | 6.8 | – | – | 101⅜ |
| J. C. Penney | A1/A+ | 1988 | 200 | 9⅜ | 2/1/98 | – | – | 7.2 | 2/1/95 | 100.00 | 98⅝ |
| Pennsylvania Power & Light[b] | A2/A– | 1988 | 125 | 9¼ | 3/1/98 | Current | 1 | 7.1 | 2/28/93 | 102.56 | 99⅞ |
| Philadelphia Electric[b] | Baa3/BBB | 1967 | 75 | 6⅛ | 10/1/97 | – | – | 6.8 | Current | 101.40 | 83½ |
| Phillips Petroleum | Baa1/BBB | 1990 | 300 | 9½ | 11/1/97 | – | – | 7.0 | – | – | 99⅞ |
| Ryder System | A3/A– | 1988 | 100 | 9⅜ | 1/15/98 | – | – | 7.0 | 1/15/95 | 100.00 | 97 |
| Scott Paper | A3/BBB+ | 1990 | 200 | 9¾ | 10/1/97 | – | – | 6.8 | – | – | 101¼ |
| Southern California Gas[b] | A1/A+ | 1988 | 100 | 9⅜ | 1/15/98 | Current | 1 | 6.8 | 6/14/93 | 102.45 | 101¼ |
| Stanley Works | A2/A | 1988 | 50 | 9 | 2/1/98 | – | – | 7.2 | – | – | 99⅜ |
| Texas Eastern Corp.[d] | Ba1/BBB– | 1987 | 100 | 10½ | 12/15/97 | – | – | 7.0 | 12/15/94 | 100.00 | 100⅝ |
| Union Pacific Corp. | A2/A | 1988 | 200 | 8⅞ | 3/1/98 | – | – | 7.2 | 3/1/95 | 100.00 | 100⅛ |

a. Indicates amount to be retired annually.

b. Debt secured by a first mortgage on certain properties.

c. Subordinated debt.

d. Issuer has first mortgage debt outstanding.

e. Bonds are nonrefundable prior to this date; i.e., issuer is prohibited from redeeming the bonds directly or indirectly with money borrowed at a lower cost than the effective interest rate incurred on these bonds at date of issuance.

**EXHIBIT 8**

Indicative New Issue Levels for Privately Placed Debt Securities: Purchase Spreads over Treasury Securities, December 1990 (basis points)

| Ratings[a] | No. of Investors[b] | Average Life | | | | | | | | | |
|---|---|---|---|---|---|---|---|---|---|---|---|
| | | 3 Years | | 5 Years | | 7 Years | | 10 Years | | 15 Years | |
| | | Low | High | Low | High | Low | High | Low | High | Low | High |
| A+ . . . . . . . | 1 | 110 | – | 115 | – | 120 | – | 130 | – | – | – |
| A . . . . . . . . | 9 | 100 | 130 | 105 | 145 | 110 | 245 | 120 | 175 | 130 | 200 |
| A– . . . . . . . | 3 | 100 | 115 | 105 | 125 | 105 | 135 | 115 | 160 | 150 | – |
| BBB+ . . . . . . | 6 | 100 | 175 | 110 | 175 | 130 | 180 | 150 | 195 | 190 | 200 |
| BBB . . . . . . . | 10 | 100 | 180 | 100 | 185 | 125 | 195 | 145 | 200 | 150 | 240 |
| BBB– . . . . . . | 15 | 150 | 260 | 165 | 300 | 180 | 340 | 195 | 385 | 250 | 255 |
| BB+ . . . . . . . | 3 | 200 | 375 | 205 | 425 | 215 | 455 | 220 | 485 | 370 | 380 |

*Note:* Indications given by major insurance companies to a major investment banking firm between November 12, 1990, and December 12, 1990.

a. Investors not distinguishing within the A or BBB categories are shown here as indicating A or BBB.

b. Number of investors indicating interest in private placement purchases in the rating and maturity categories shown. Ratings shown are those indicated by such investors.

**EXHIBIT 9**

Comparison of Approximate Estimated Public and Private Issuance Costs for a $100 Million Intermediate-Term Debt Issue (thousands of dollars)

| | Public | Private |
|---|---|---|
| Accounting fees[a] . . . . . . . . . . . . . . . . . . . . . . . . . | $ 50 | – |
| Legal fees[a] . . . . . . . . . . . . . . . . . . . . . . . . . | 150 | $ 50 |
| New York Stock Exchange listing fee[b] . . . . . . . . . . . . . . . | 23 | – |
| Printing[a] . . . . . . . . . . . . . . . . . . . . . . . . . | 100 | – |
| Rating agency fees[b] . . . . . . . . . . . . . . . . . . . . . | 60 | – |
| SEC registration fee[b] . . . . . . . . . . . . . . . . . . . . | 25 | – |
| Trustee[a] . . . . . . . . . . . . . . . . . . . . . . . . . | 50 | – |
| Underwriting or agent commission[b] . . . . . . . . . . . . . . . | 625 | 375 |
| Other (engraving and printing of certificates, postage, etc.)[a] . . . . . . . . . . . . . . . . . . . . . . . . . | 25 | – |
| Total . . . . . . . . . . . . . . . . . . . . . . . . . | $1,108 | $425 |
| Approximate cost in basis points . . . . . . . . . . . . . . . | 23 | 9 |

a. Wholly or largely independent of issue size.

b. Wholly or largely dependent on issue size.

**EXHIBIT 10**
Summary of Proposed Terms of Senior Subordinated Notes, Sam Adams Financial Corporation

---

*Issuer:*   Sam Adams Financial Corporation.

*Amount:*   $40 million.

*Maturity:*   Seven years from date of closing.

*Interest rate:*   9.7%, payable semiannually in arrears.

*Issue price:*   100%.

*Closing:*   The legal documents will be executed and delivered as soon as practicable.

*Takedown:*   At closing.

*Mandatory prepayments:*   None.

*Optional prepayments:*   None.

*Seniority:*   These notes will be junior in right of payment to all indebtedness for borrowed money that is not expressly by its terms *parri passu* with or junior in right of payment to these notes.

*All other terms:*   To be identical to those contained in the company's note agreement, dated June 30, 1988, relating to the 9.2% senior subordinated notes due June 15, 1998. (This agreement limits the company's ability to engage in businesses other than consumer finance and commercial finance, to create liens against finance receivables without equally and ratably securing these notes, and to merge or sell all or substantially all of its assets without assumption of these notes by the successor entity. It provides for modification of nonmoney terms and acceleration by vote of 51% of holders of the notes.)

---

**EXHIBIT 11**

Summary Operating Data, Sam Adams Financial Corporation, for Years Ending December 31, 1985–1989 (millions of dollars)

*Operating Revenues*

| | |
|---|---|
| 1985 | $1,164.1 |
| 1986 | 1,285.5 |
| 1987 | 1,283.3 |
| 1988 | 1,461.9 |
| 1989 | 1,780.0 |

*Interest Expense*[a]

| | |
|---|---|
| 1985 | $467.5 |
| 1986 | 492.9 |
| 1987 | 489.3 |
| 1988 | 586.6 |
| 1989 | 761.7 |

*Provision for Credit Losses*

| | |
|---|---|
| 1985 | $133.8 |
| 1986 | 185.6 |
| 1987 | 248.3 |
| 1988 | 190.3 |
| 1989 | 288.7 |

*Pre-Tax Income and Margins*

| | | |
|---|---|---|
| 1985 | $140.5 | 12.1% |
| 1986 | 152.6 | 11.9 |
| 1987 | 118.2 | 9.2 |
| 1988 | 182.8 | 12.5 |
| 1989 | 184.3 | 10.4 |

*Net Income and Margins*

| | | |
|---|---|---|
| 1985 | $111.2 | 9.6% |
| 1986 | 134.8 | 10.5 |
| 1987 | 101.4 | 7.9 |
| 1988 | 138.9 | 9.5 |
| 1989 | 155.9 | 8.8 |

*Net Charge-Offs (Percent of Average Net Receivables)*[b]

| | |
|---|---|
| 1985 | 2.10% |
| 1986 | 2.79 |
| 1987 | 3.89 |
| 1988 | 2.31 |
| 1989 | 3.23 |

*Delinquencies (Year-End Net Receivables)*[c]

| | |
|---|---|
| 1985 | 5.16% |
| 1986 | 4.99 |
| 1987 | 3.58 |
| 1988 | 4.62 |
| 1989 | 5.69 |

a. Includes interest factor attributable to rentals.

b. Earlier of when account is deemed uncollectible or is 181 days past due.

c. 61 days or more past due.

**EXHIBIT 12**

Summary Balance Sheet Data, Sam Adams Financial Corporation, at December 31, 1989

| | |
|---|---:|
| Finance receivables, net | $ 8,563.8 |
| Investment securities[a] | 1,709.4 |
| Other assets | 316.0 |
| Total assets | $10,589.2 |
| | |
| Commercial paper and other short-term debt[b] | $ 4,587.4 |
| Deposits and certificates[c] | 390.7 |
| Insurance reserves | 407.5 |
| Funded debt | |
| Senior | 2,763.3 |
| Senior subordinated | 394.3 |
| Junior subordinated | 197.2 |
| | 3,354.8 |
| Other liabilities | 665.8 |
| Total liabilities | 4,020.6 |
| Common equity | 1,183.0 |
| Total liabilities and net worth | $10,589.2 |

a. Related to insurance subsidiaries; carried at amortized cost.

b. Includes $467.3 million in current maturities of funded debt.

c. Related to Newport Beach Savings and Loan Association, a wholly owned subsidiary.

**Exhibit 13**
Summary of Proposed Terms of Privately Placed Senior Notes, Ginne Enterprises, Inc.

*Issuer:* Ginne Enterprises, Inc.

*Amount:* $25 million.

*Maturity:* Eight years from date of closing.

*Interest rate:* 9.90%, payable semiannually in arrears.

*Issue price:* 100%.

*Closing:* The legal documents will be executed and delivered as soon as practicable.

*Takedown:* At Closing.

*Mandatory prepayments:* Beginning at the end of the sixth year, the company will make two equal annual payments of 33⅓% of the initial principal amount, leaving 33⅓% due at maturity. The resulting average life will be 7.0 years.

*Optional prepayments:* None.

*Use of proceeds:* The company will use the proceeds from the sale of the notes to retire existing short-term bank indebtedness.

*Restriction on incurrence of additional funded debt:* None permitted.

*Limitation on short-term debt:* Short-term debt not permitted for at least 30 consecutive days in every calendar year.

*Limitation on liens:* With certain exceptions, e.g., liens relating to performance bonds, governmental contracts and the like, none permitted without equally and ratably securing these notes.

*Limitation on sale and leasebacks:* Not permitted unless the net proceeds of such sales are applied to the retirement of funded debt.

*Restricted payments:* The company and its subsidiaries will not (a) pay dividends other than stock dividends; (b) purchase or otherwise acquire for value any shares of the company's capital stock; or (c) make loans or advances to, or investments, in the securities of entities other than subsidiaries, unless, after giving effect to such action, the aggregate of (a), (b), and (c) will not thereby exceed 50% of consolidated net income accumulated after closing plus $2.5 million.

*Merger and sale of substantially all assets:* Not permitted, unless the company is the survivor or the successor corporation is a U.S. corporation, assumes all obligations under the note agreement. There would be no default, and the company could incur $1.00 of additional funded debt.

*Sale of a substantial part of assets:* Except as provided under "Merger and Sale of Substantially All Assets," not permitted to exceed in any one fiscal year 10% of consolidated net tangible assets.

*Restriction on subsidiary debt:* None permitted.

*Modification:* Terms may be amended, modified, or waived with the consent of holders of not less than 66⅔% of the principal amount of the notes, except that no change may be made in the payment terms, e.g., coupon, principal amount, interest, and principal payment dates, without the consent of all holders.

*Events of default:* (a) Default for more than five days in payment of interest when due; (b) default in payment of principal when due; (c) default for more than 30 days in compliance with any other covenant in the note agreement.

*Acceleration:* In case of an event of default under this note agreement or under any other loan agreement, note agreement, indenture, or other evidence of indebtedness under which the company or any subsidiary is obligated, holders of not less than 25% of the principal amount of the notes may declare the principal and all accrued and unpaid interest to be due and payable.

**EXHIBIT 14**
Summary Operating Data, Ginne Enterprises, Inc., 1980–1990 (thousands of dollars)

*Operating Revenues*

| | |
|---|---|
| 1980 | $ 68,479 |
| 1983 | 86,279 |
| 1986 | 103,319 |
| 1987 | 110,462 |
| 1988 | 118,628 |
| 1989 | 126,269 |
| 1990 | 134,732 |

*Operating Income and Margins*[a]

| | | |
|---|---|---|
| 1980 | $18,275 | 26.7% |
| 1983 | 20,549 | 23.8 |
| 1986 | 23,560 | 22.8 |
| 1987 | 25,772 | 23.3 |
| 1988 | 25,586 | 21.6 |
| 1989 | 25,254 | 20.0 |
| 1990 | 27,290 | 20.3 |

*Interest Expense*

| | |
|---|---|
| 1980 | $4,633 |
| 1983 | 1,208 |
| 1986 | 1,231 |
| 1987 | 2,717 |
| 1988 | 3,747 |
| 1989 | 6,924 |
| 1990 | 7,866 |

*Pre-tax Income and Margins*[a]

| | | |
|---|---|---|
| 1980 | $13,642 | 19.9% |
| 1983 | 19,341 | 22.4 |
| 1986 | 22,329 | 21.6 |
| 1987 | 23,055 | 20.9 |
| 1988 | 21,839 | 18.4 |
| 1989 | 18,330 | 14.5 |
| 1990 | 19,424 | 14.4 |

*Net Income and Margins*[a]

| | | |
|---|---|---|
| 1980 | $ 7,452 | 10.9% |
| 1983 | 10,108 | 11.7 |
| 1986 | 12,098 | 11.7 |
| 1987 | 12,612 | 11.4 |
| 1988 | 12,386 | 10.4 |
| 1989 | 12,407 | 9.8 |
| 1990 | 13,148 | 9.8 |

*Operating Cash Flow*[a]

| | |
|---|---|
| 1980 | $ 9,315 |
| 1983 | 12,533 |
| 1986 | 15,243 |
| 1987 | 16,017 |
| 1988 | 15,359 |
| 1989 | 15,903 |
| 1990 | 16,435 |

a. Excludes gains on sales of properties as follows: 1980, $4.7 million; 1986, $7.3 million; 1988, $9.1 million.

**EXHIBIT 15**

Summary Balance Sheet Data, Ginne Enterprises, Inc., at September 30, 1990 (thousands of dollars)

| | |
|---|---:|
| Current assets | $ 64,688 |
| Less: Short-term debt | 30,888 |
| Less: Other current liabilities | 29,008 |
| Net working capital | 4,792 |
| Property, net | 131,223 |
| Other tangible assets[a] | 25,191 |
| Net tangible assets | $161,206 |
| | |
| Funded debt[b] | $ 71,014 |
| Deferred items[c] | 14,706 |
| Common equity | 141,524 |
| Less: Intangibles | 66,038 |
| Net tangible liabilities | $161,206 |

a. Primarily equity investments in associated companies.

b. Average interest rate of 9.75% with annual maturities as follows: 1991, $3.6 million; 1992, $7.3 million; 1993, $6.5 million; 1994, $18.5 million.

c. Primarily related to retirement and deferred compensation plans.

**EXHIBIT 16**

Indicative Rates for Immediate Takedown Fixed-Rate Commercial Mortgages

| Maturity | Amortization | Rate[a,b] Low | High | Number of Investors[c] | U.S. Treasury Securities |
|---|---|---|---|---|---|
| First mortgages | | | | | |
| 3 years | — | 9.25% | 9.85% | 9 | 7.48% |
| 5 years | — | 9.50 | 10.25 | 18 | 7.84 |
| 7 years | — | 9.75 | 10.50 | 18 | 8.08 |
| 10 years | 25–30 years | 10.05 | 11.05 | 20 | 8.18 |
| 30 years | 30 years | 10.40 | 10.85 | 2 | 8.30 |
| Second mortgages | | | | | |
| 3 years | — | 9.70 | — | 1 | 7.48 |
| 5 years | — | 10.75 | — | 1 | 7.84 |
| 7 years | — | 11.50 | — | 1 | 8.08 |
| 10 years | — | 11.75 | — | 1 | 8.81 |

*Note:* Commercial and industrial properties only. Does not include apartment buildings, for instance.

a. Semiannual equivalent of monthly pay interest rates.

b. Includes the effect of front-end fees where applicable.

c. Number of investors indicating interest in each maturity. Rates shown are those indicated by such investors.

**EXHIBIT 17**

Summary Operating Data for Pali Palms Plaza, Kailua Bay Investors (thousands of dollars)

| | Operating Results | |
|---|---|---|
| | Latest 12 Months | Projected |
| Base rent | | |
| Office[a] | $ 929.2[a] | $ 996.5 |
| Restaurant | 108.7 | 108.7 |
| Percentage rent, restaurant | 53.7 | 55.0 |
| C.A.M. recoveries[b] | 53.5 | 55.0 |
| Other income | 4.2 | 5.0 |
| Total income | 1,149.3 | 1,220.2 |
| Operating expenses | 329.3 | 350.0 |
| Miscellaneous | 11.5 | 12.5 |
| Total expenses | 340.8 | 362.5 |
| Net operating income | $ 808.5 | $ 857.7 |

**Lease Expirations (percent of space)**

| | |
|---|---|
| *1991* | *10%* |
| *1992* | *6* |
| *1993* | *15* |
| *1994* | *12* |
| *1995* | *20* |
| *After* | *12* |

a. Current vacancy rate is 11%. Projected results assume reduction in vacancies from 11% to 5% with new rentals at $1.60 per square foot per month.

b. Common area maintenance expenses, e.g., lobbies, elevators, passed through to tenants.

**EXHIBIT 18**

Summary of Proposed Terms of First Mortgage Loan, Kailua Bay Investors

*Issuer:* Kailua Bay Investors, a California general partnership whose sole operating asset is Pali Palms Plaza.

*Amount:* $5.5 million.

*Maturity:* Seven years from date of closing.

*Interest rate:* 10.50% (semiannual equivalent), payable monthly in arrears.

*Issue price:* 100%.

*Closing:* The legal documents will be executed and delivered as soon as practicable.

*Takedown:* At closing.

*Mandatory prepayments:* None. The resulting average life will be 7 years.

*Optional prepayments:* None, except in the event of sale of the property. In that event, the investor must prepay the notes at a price equal to the greater of (a) par plus accrued interest, or (b) the present value of all remaining interest and principal payments, such present value to be determined using a discount rate equal to .25% plus the yield on U.S. Treasury obligations having a maturity date corresponding with the remaining average life of the notes.

*Use of proceeds:* Permanent financing of earlier acquired property, which will serve as security for this loan.

*Security:* These notes will be secured by a first mortgage against the land and buildings of Pali Palms Plaza, located at 970 North Kalaheo Avenue, Kailua, Hawaii.

*Recourse:* None.

*Second Mortgage financing:* None permitted.

*Other restrictive covenants:* None.

*Undertakings:* Issuer will pay all property and other taxes when due, maintain adequate insurance, etc.

*Events of default:* (a) Default in payment of interest when due plus five days; (b) default in payment of principal when due; (c) failure to perform for 30 days any other terms of provisions of these notes.

**EXHIBIT 19**

Summary Comparison of Proposed Kailua Bay Investors Financing to Tom Paine's Commercial Mortgage Investment Standards

|  | Standard | Pali Palms Plaza |
|---|---|---|
| Debt service coverage[a] | 1.25 | 1.40 |
| Loan to appraised value | 75% | 61.8% |
| Interest rate (semiannual equivalent minimum rate for 7 years) | 10.25% | 10.50% |
| Amortization | 30 years | None |
| Break-even occupancy | 85% | 76.6% |
| Put or maturity | 10 years or less | 7 years |
| Elevators: up to a three-story building with 15,000 sq ft per floor or less | Minimum of 1 | Yes |
| Parking ratio (cars per 1,000 sq ft) | 3 | 4.2 |
| Efficiency minimum[b] | 80% | 83% |
| Lavatories | 1 set per floor | Yes |
| Net rentable space on leases of 3 years or more | 80% | 73% |
| Full expense stop or CPI adjustment | Required | Expense stop |

a. Annual net operating income divided by pro forma annual interest and principal payments.

b. Usable square feet as a percent of gross square feet.

# Metromedia Broadcasting Corporation

"Good luck, Tom—you're going to need it!"

As Tom Forsyth put down the phone, he began to question his plan to recommend a significant expansion in high-yield, or junk, bond investments to the board of directors of Anchor Savings and Loan. Mr. Forsyth had called David Willis, chairman and chief executive officer of Anchor, to request that his high-yield investment proposal be added to the agenda of the board's November 24th meeting. Upon hearing the subject of Mr. Forsyth's presentation, the chairman had warned him to expect a lively debate on the prudence of Anchor's investing in high-yield securities.

Anchor first purchased high-yield bonds in 1982, following the passage of legislation empowering federally insured thrifts to make commercial loans in amounts equal to 10% of their assets.[1] Like many thrifts, Anchor had suffered substantial losses on its portfolio of fixed-rate mortgages in the early 1980s. When its lending powers were broadened in 1982, Anchor aggressively sought high-yield investments to rebuild its diminished capital base. High-yield corporate bonds, which were debt issues rated below investment grade by the bond-rating agencies (Ba1 or lower by Moody's Investors Service, BB+ or lower by Standard and Poor's, or unrated), had seemed a particularly attractive diversification opportunity

This case was prepared by Fellow Sally E. Durdan under the supervision of Associate Professor Scott P. Mason.

Copyright © 1985 by the President and Fellows of Harvard College.
Harvard Business School case 286–044.

1. Although there was no formal ruling on the matter from the Federal Home Loan Bank Board (FHLBB), federally insured thrifts were generally allowed to classify investments in high-yield securities as commercial loans.

for Anchor. Publicly issued high-yield bonds offered investors liquidity as well as rich yields, which ranged 250–550 basis points over comparable maturity Treasuries over the period 1980–1984 (see Exhibit 1). Mr. Forsyth, who was responsible for Anchor's investment activities, had initiated the thrift's move into high-yield corporate bonds.

Early in November 1984, Mr. Forsyth had become concerned that Anchor's $9 million portfolio of 14 high-yield issues was inadequately diversified. In conversations with analysts at Drexel Burnham Lambert Inc., an investment bank active in the high-yield market, he had learned that 20–30 issues were required to properly diversify a portfolio of high-yield bonds. Because significant liquidity existed only in large blocks (positions of $1 million or more), he planned to recommend that Anchor increase its investment in high-yield securities to $25–30 million. As a first step, he would recommend the purchase of one or several pieces of a forthcoming issue of Metromedia Broadcasting Corporation (MBC) debt securities.

Unfortunately, David Willis had indicated, the board was unlikely to be receptive to Mr. Forsyth's investment proposal. Although Anchor's high-yield portfolio had performed well the previous year, several board members were alarmed by thrift regulators' recent criticisms of thrifts' investments in high-yield securities. Eric I. Hemel, director of the Federal Home Loan Bank Board's office of policy and economic research, had warned member thrifts that "the rapidly growing high-yield market opened a relatively new, high-risk investment strategy to savings institutions." The FHLBB, which regulated federally insured thrifts, and the Federal Savings and Loan Insurance Corporation (FSLIC), which insured thrift deposits of up to $100,000, were considering imposing stringent diversification requirements on thrifts' investments in low-grade corporate securities. In addition, members of both houses of Congress had introduced legislation prohibiting federally insured thrifts from holding any securities rated below investment grade.

## High-Yield Securities Market

Moody's Investors Service and Standard and Poor's Corporation provided investors with estimates of the default risk of corporate bonds. Moody's used a set of nine rating symbols to represent groups of bonds with broadly similar credit characteristics. The first four categories (Aaa, Aa, A, and Baa) were investment-grade ratings, with Aaa representing the highest investment quality and Baa medium investment quality. The remaining five categories (Ba, B, Caa, Ca, and C) covered more speculative issues, including securities that were near or in default. Standard and Poor's issued similar ratings, using the symbols AAA, AA, A, and BBB to denote investment-grade securities and BB, B, CCC, CC, C, and D to denote more speculative bonds.

In rating corporate bonds Moody's and Standard and Poor's relied heavily on measures of historical financial performance, including ratios of book debt to total capitalization, cash flow to debt, and before-tax fixed-charge coverage. Exhibit 2 shows suggested values for these and other ratios of industrial bond issuers of varying credit quality. Bond ratings appeared to be related to company size in that only *Fortune* 500 firms were awarded AAA and AA ratings. Although rating agencies considered such qualitative factors as a company's industry, market share, relative cost position, accounting policies, and quality of management in assigning credit ratings, financial measures tended to dominate their analyses. It was estimated that 85% of all U.S. public corporations would be rated below investment grade.

Historically, investor interest in low-rated debt had been weak because of legal or self-imposed quality restrictions on institutional investors' purchases of corporate bonds. Most state and local government pension funds were prohibited by law from investing in bonds rated below single A. Trust funds and corporate pension funds were generally subject to "prudent investor" tests, which authorized fiduciaries to "invest in such securities as would be acquired by prudent men of discretion and intelligence in such matters who are seeking a reasonable income and preservation of their capital." The vague wording of such tests prompted most fiduciaries to adopt conservative investment policies.

Because many institutions were unable or unwilling to buy securities rated below investment grade, the public corporate debt market was dominated by investment-grade issuers through 1977. The $25 billion high-yield bond market consisted primarily of the outstanding debt of large, troubled companies whose credit quality had fallen from investment grade. Reflecting the lack of investor interest in the high-yield sector, yield spreads between high-grade and low-grade corporate securities were inefficiently wide, providing investors with yield premiums in excess of those required to offset losses from default (see Exhibit 3).

In the mid-1970s, Drexel Burnham Lambert developed techniques for analyzing the credit quality of low-grade issuers. Focusing on market-adjusted leverage ratios, projected cash flows, business fundamentals, and management quality rather than on historical financial data, Drexel identified mature, downgraded issuers likely to achieve rating upgrades. In addition, Drexel noted that many small- and medium-sized "emerging growth" companies possessed sound financial prospects, although they would likely be rated below investment grade in view of their small size and brief credit histories. In 1977, Drexel pioneered the underwriting of high-yield securities for these unseasoned or highly leveraged companies, which had traditionally relied on commercial bank lending, private placements of debt, or equity issues for capital to finance their growth.

The issuance of public debt offered low-rated issuers several advantages over their traditional sources of funding:

1. Access to permanent, fixed-rate capital without the restrictive covenants imposed by institutional purchasers of private placements
2. Call features, enabling issuers to refund debt in the event of a decline in interest rates
3. Visibility in the public markets, which occasionally enhanced investor interest in a high-yield issuer's equity as well as debt securities
4. An alternative to equity issuance, enabling companies to increase financial leverage above historical levels

Over the period 1977–1984 the high-yield debt market tripled in size as over 350 low-rated companies issued $36.1 billion of original issue high-yield debt (see Exhibits 4 and 5). The volume of high-yield securities outstanding (including bonds of utilities and municipalities, preferred stocks, high-premium convertible bonds, and private placements of debt with registration rights) was expected to total $100 billion by year-end 1984. The largest public components of the high-yield bond market, straight industrial and finance issues ($48 billion face value) and straight utility issues ($11 billion face value), had grown to represent 14% of all public straight corporate debt outstanding in 1984.

Some $14 billion of public high-yield debt was placed in 1984, representing 35% of all public straight corporate debt issued in that year. Growth in the high-yield market was expected to continue at a rapid pace as new issuers entered the market. At year-end 1984 investment bankers had identified 2,000 potential high-yield issuers who had yet to tap the public debt markets. In addition, high-yield debt was being used with increasing frequency to finance merger and acquisition transactions, including leveraged buyouts and highly publicized hostile tender offers by corporate "raiders" like Boone Pickens and Carl Icahn. Some observers believed the development of the original issue high-yield debt market had increased the level of acquisition activity by providing small acquirers with the capital necessary to acquire large corporations. Approximately 12% of the public high-yield debt issued in 1984 was used to finance leveraged buyouts or acquisitions.

By educating the investment community about the exceptional returns realized historically on high-yield investments and maintaining a secondary market in high-yield issues, Drexel Burnham Lambert and other underwriters (see Exhibit 6) persuaded a broad range of institutions to invest in the high-yield sector. By 1984 high-yield mutual funds, insurance companies, bank trust departments, 200 of the *Fortune* 500 pension funds, commercial banks, and thrifts were active in the high-yield market. However, yield spreads between low-grade and investment-grade corporate bonds remained high. Market observers attributed the persistence of excessive yields on low-grade securities to a surge in new issue volume in the second half of 1984. Among the largest issues brought to market during this period was a $1.3 billion offering of senior and subordinated debt securities by the Metromedia Broadcasting Corporation (MBC).

## MBC Offering

In 1984 the principal business of Metromedia, Inc. (Metromedia) was the ownership and operation of seven television and nine radio stations. The company's television stations included six independents and one network affiliate located in seven of the country's ten largest media markets. The television group, whose size was limited to a maximum of seven stations under Federal Communications Commission (FCC) licensing rules, reached approximately 24% of all U.S. television homes, representing the largest audience coverage of any commonly owned television station group. Metromedia also produced television programming and was active in telecommunications, outdoor advertising, and other entertainment businesses.

On June 21, 1984, Metromedia was taken private by its management in a leveraged buyout transaction. John W. Kluge, chairman of the company and owner of 26% of Metromedia's equity prior to the leveraged buyout, joined three Metromedia managers in offering shareholders a package of cash, debentures, and debenture-purchase warrants valued at $41.50 per share in exchange for their stock. The offer represented an 85% premium over Metromedia's April 1984 stock price of $22 per share. The buyout was financed with $1.2 billion in bank debt, $125 million of preferred stock purchased by the Prudential Insurance Company, and $10 million of nonvoting common stock purchased by venture investors. The proceeds of this financing were used to make cash payments to Metromedia shareholders and to provide working capital for operations. The buyout increased John Kluge's ownership interest in Metromedia to 75.5% of total equity and raised Metromedia's total debt from 75% to over 90% of total capital.

The bank debt used to finance Metromedia's buyout carried an 8-year maturity and interest pegged to the prime rate. Upon entering into this credit agreement Metromedia paid lenders origination fees equal to 1% of its total borrowings. The terms of the agreement, which included a $100 million minimum net worth requirement, would have required Metromedia to sell a significant broadcasting asset by June 1985 in order to make a mandatory principal prepayment of $200 million.

In September 1984, Metromedia's management investigated a variety of alternatives for avoiding the asset sale required under the terms of its bank facility. Management was anxious to avoid the significant tax liability that would have resulted from such a sale and, more important, it believed that a reduction in the television group's audience coverage would adversely affect its competitive position. In October, Metromedia announced that it planned to refinance its bank indebtedness by raising approximately $1.3 billion in a public offering of senior and subordinated debt securities. The debt securities were to be issued by MBC, a wholly owned subsidiary of Metromedia, to which substantially all of Metromedia's broadcasting assets were to be transferred.

The MBC offering consisted of a series of four securities designed by Drexel Burnham Lambert (see Exhibit 7). All the securities had been approved for listing on the American Stock Exchange and were to be underwritten by Drexel Burnham Lambert and Bear, Stearns.

All but $50 million of the net proceeds of the offering were to be advanced to Metromedia to repay the senior bank indebtedness it had incurred in connection with its June 1984 leveraged buyout. The remaining $50 million were to be added to MBC's working capital and, if certain financial ratios were met during a period of 2 years, were to be advanced to Metromedia. Metromedia was not an obligor on the debt securities and had no responsibility to provide financial support to MBC. (See Exhibit 8 and the notes following it.)

In anticipation of the refinancing, Metromedia entered into a management agreement with MBC, pursuant to which Metromedia was to provide MBC with legal, accounting, cash management, and strategic and major financial planning services. In compensation, MBC was to pay Metromedia's out-of-pocket expenses and a monthly fee equal to 1.5% of MBC's gross revenues. This management fee was to be deferred until the end of the first 12-month period during which

MBC achieved a ratio of operating cash flow (before deduction of the management fee) to cash interest expense of 1.25 to 1. Upon achieving this ratio, MBC could pay Metromedia up to 1 year's deferred management fees.

The serial zero coupon senior notes consisted of six series of discount notes priced at the following yields:

| Series | Maturity | Yield to Maturity[a] |
|---|---|---|
| 1 | Dec. 1, 1988 | 13¾% |
| 2 | Dec. 1, 1989 | 14 |
| 3 | Dec. 1, 1990 | 14⅜ |
| 4 | Dec. 1, 1991 | 14¾ |
| 5 | Dec. 1, 1992 | 15 |
| 6 | Dec. 1, 1993 | 15¼ |

a. Assumes semiannual compounding of interest.

The notes were to rank equally in right of payment with other senior indebtedness of MBC, including the senior exchangeable variable-rate debentures due 1996, and were to be senior to the 15⅝% senior subordinated debentures due 1999 and the adjustable-rate participating subordinated debentures due 2002. The notes were redeemable at the option of the company at any time at par.

Interest on the senior exchangeable variable-rate debentures was to be paid quarterly at a rate equal to the greatest of (1) the three-month Treasury rate plus 375 basis points, (2) LIBOR plus 250 basis points, or (3) 107% of the 10-year Treasury rate, in each case adjusted quarterly, except that until June 1, 1985, a minimum rate of 15% per year was to be paid. The variable-rate debentures were redeemable at the option of the company at any time after December 1, 1987, in whole or in part, at the following prices (percent of par) together with accrued interest:

| 12 months beginning | |
|---|---|
| Dec. 1, 1987 | 105% |
| Dec. 1, 1988 | 103 |

On any quarterly interest payment date on or after December 1, 1985, and before December 1, 1989, the company could exchange all, or a portion equal to $50 million or any multiple thereof, of the variable-rate debentures for fixed-rate debentures maturing December 1, 1996. Any variable-rate debentures outstanding on December 1, 1989, were to be automatically exchanged. The fixed-rate debentures were to pay interest quarterly at a rate equal to 131% of the 10-year Treasury rate determined as of the exchange date. They were subject to redemption at the company's option at any time on or after the third anniversary of the final exchange of the variable-rate debentures at the following prices (percent of par) together with accrued interest:

| 12-month period from date of final exchange | |
| --- | --- |
| Fourth | 105% |
| Fifth | 103 |
| Sixth | 101 |
| Seventh | 100 |

The fixed-rate debentures carried sinking fund provisions requiring the retirement of debentures in the aggregate principal amount of $110 million on December 1, 1994, and December 1, 1995.[2]

The 15⅝% senior subordinated debentures were to rank senior in right of payment to the adjustable-rate participating subordinated debentures but junior to MBC's senior indebtedness. The debentures were to bear interest at an annual rate of 15⅝%, payable semiannually, and were to mature on December 1, 1999. They were redeemable in whole or in part at the company's option at any time after December 1, 1987, at 111.025% of par plus accrued interest, and thereafter at prices declining annually to 100% of par plus accrued interest on or after December 1, 1994. No redemption was to be made prior to December 1, 1989, using funds borrowed at an effective cost of less than 15¾%. A sinking fund requiring annual payments of $56,250,000 beginning December 1, 1996, was to retire 75% of the debentures prior to maturity.

The adjustable-rate participating subordinated debentures were to bear interest at annual rates of 13⅛% prior to December 1, 1989, and 17% thereafter, in each case payable semiannually. Commencing in 1988 holders of the debentures were to be entitled to additional interest based on increases in the company's participating operating cash flow, which was defined as net income before taxes and interest income, plus depreciation, amortization, and interest expense.

| *Average Percent Increase in Participating Operating Cash Flow over 3 Previous Fiscal Years* | *Additional Interest as Percent of Principal* |
| --- | --- |
| 0–10% | 0 % |
| 10–14 | 1.5 |
| 14–17 | 2.5 |
| 17+ | 4.0 |

---

2. Under the terms of the several bond indentures, MBC could fulfill its sinking fund obligations either by redeeming the specified principal amount of fixed-rate debentures or senior subordinated debentures at par or by purchasing an equivalent principal amount of the securities in the open market.

The debentures were to be subordinate to $1,520 million principal amount of senior and senior subordinated debt. The debentures were not to be redeemable by the company unless separate certificates representing the right to receive payments of additional interest had been distributed to the debenture holders. Once such a distribution had been made, the debentures were to be redeemable at the company's option in whole or in part at any time after December 1, 1987, except that no redemption was to be made prior to December 1, 1994, using funds borrowed at an effective cost of less than 17%. The debentures were to be redeemable at the following prices (percent of par) together with accrued interest:

| 12 months beginning | |
| --- | --- |
| Dec. 1, 1987 | 104% |
| Dec. 1, 1988 | 103 |
| Dec. 1, 1989 | 102 |
| Dec. 1, 1990 | 101 |
| Dec. 1, 1991 and thereafter | 100 |

A sinking fund requiring annual payments of $66 million beginning December 1, 1997, was to retire 83% of the debentures prior to maturity.[3]

The covenants of the debt securities prohibited MBC from incurring additional senior debt and limited its ability to make payments to affiliated companies. The covenants also prohibited MBC from entering into mergers outside the broadcasting industry or liquidating substantial portions of its assets unless the proceeds of such transactions were used to repay the principal of the notes, the senior variable-rate debentures, or the senior subordinated debentures (except that no more than 50% of such proceeds could be used to repay the senior subordinated debentures). All the senior and senior subordinated securities carried defeasance clauses enabling the company to discharge substantially all its obligations under the bond indentures by depositing in trust for the bondholders funds or U.S. government obligations sufficient to provide for all payments of the notes and debentures.

The prospectus for the offering clearly outlined Metromedia's reasons for refinancing its bank debt. First, Metromedia's cash interest expense over the succeeding 4 years was to equal 10.3% of the net proceeds of the offering, a reduction from the 14.9% rate paid on its bank debt. At the same time, tax-deductible interest expense was to increase from a rate of 14.9% to an average 15.4% of borrowings. The refinancing would defer all principal repayments, which would have totaled $290 million through 1988 under the terms of the bank debt, until the first series of senior notes matured in 1988 (see Exhibit 9). Under the refinancing Metromedia would be released from numerous affirmative and negative covenants, including those necessitating the sale of a broadcasting asset in 1985. Because

---

3. Under the terms of the bond indenture, MBC could fulfill its sinking fund obligations either by redeeming the specified principal amount of adjustable-rate participating subordinated debentures at par or by purchasing an equivalent principal amount of the securities in the open market.

the broadcasting assets were to be segregated from Metromedia's other operations, Metromedia would be free to borrow additional funds for use in its telecommunications and other activities.

Pro forma financial statements for MBC (see Exhibit 10) indicated that interest coverage subsequent to the refinancing would be less than 1:1 and a deficit of $53 million would be recorded in MBC's stockholders' equity account. Principally because of large goodwill amortization charges, MBC was expected to continue to report substantial accounting losses following the offering. The MBC prospectus described the risks to investors in the debt securities as follows:

> Based on current levels of operations (assuming no growth in revenues), the company's cash flow would be insufficient to make interest payments on the debt securities (other than the serial senior notes) and it would have to use other funds, to the extent available, to make such interest payments. However, the company has historically experienced significant rates of growth in broadcast revenues and cash flow . . . and expects continued growth which, if attained, would generate sufficient cash flow to enable it to make interest payments on the debt securities. Such payments would consume all or substantially all of such cash flow. . . .
>
> Based on current levels of operations and anticipated growth, the company does not expect to be able to generate sufficient cash flow to make all of the principal payments due on the serial senior notes, which commence on December 1, 1988, without taking action to refinance a portion of its indebtedness. No assurance can be given that such refinancing can be successfully accomplished.

Standard and Poor's rated the debt securities "highly speculative," noting that "this is an enormous amount of debt, even for [Metromedia's] good cash-generating properties" to support. However, Tom Forsyth had learned in a road show presentation preceding the offering that cash flow coverage of current interest expense would exceed 1:1, assuming cash flow growth of only 8% per year, a conservative estimate compared to Metromedia's historical growth rates of 15–20%. In addition, he had learned that industry experts considered Metromedia's broadcasting assets to be highly marketable, estimating their market value at the time of the offering at $1.8 billion.

## Investment Characteristics of High-Yield Bonds

As he prepared his presentation on high-yield bond investments for Anchor's board of directors, Mr. Forsyth reviewed several recent academic studies documenting the performance of high-yield securities since the mid-1970s. He was searching for statistics on default rates, return volatility, and secondary market liquidity of low-rated debt to help him respond to the board's questions concerning the riskiness of high-yield investments.

A study of default rates on low-rated debt by Professor Edward Altman of New York University provided overwhelming evidence that yields on low-rated bonds had historically been sufficient to compensate investors for losses from defaults. He found that an average of 1.6% of the par value of low-rated debt outstanding defaulted annually over the years 1974–1984, a period that included two recessions (see Exhibit 11). Because securities in default continued to trade at an average of 41% of par, actual losses from default were only 100 to 106 basis points per year. Although these default rates were substantially higher than those for the total straight corporate debt market, which averaged 8 basis points per year over the same period, Professor Altman noted that yields on low-rated debt had provided investors with adequate compensation for the increased risk of default. He estimated that returns on low-rated debt (net of losses from default) had averaged 490 to 580 basis points above the long-term government bond index over the period 1978–1983. (Exhibit 12 gives selected bond yields for November 1984.)

Professors Marshall Blume and Donald Keim of the Wharton School compared the volatility of returns (as measured by the standard deviation of monthly returns) on an index of lower-quality bonds with those of corporate bonds rated A and AAA and the S&P 500 from January 1982 through May 1984. The Blume-Keim study confirmed the Altman findings, estimating average annual returns on low-grade bonds, net of losses from default, at 20.3% per year versus 16.6% for A-rated bonds and 15% for AAA-rated bonds. The study also indicated that a diversified portfolio of lower-quality bonds experienced less volatility, or risk, than higher-grade corporates or equities over the period studied (see Exhibit 13). The Blume-Keim study noted that "this result was somewhat surprising" and suggested that much of the risk in low-grade corporate securities may be firm-specific and thus diversifiable.

Although few statistics on the secondary market for low-rated debt were publicly available, Mr. Forsyth was aware that Drexel Burnham Lambert, with a trading inventory of over $1 billion, handled approximately two thirds of all trading volume in high-yield securities (see Exhibit 14). Drexel estimated average daily trading volumes in high-yield bonds at 10% of the New York Stock Exchange volume, or $300 million per day. However, many high-yield issues were lightly traded, and trading spreads ranged as high as 100 basis points.

While Mr. Forsyth was relieved that academic research had confirmed his belief that high-yield bond investments had historically provided superior returns to investors, he remained uncertain of his recommendation to Anchor's board. He was troubled by speculation in the press that future performance in the high-yield market might not mirror the outstanding results of the previous 10 years:

> About $24 billion, or 80%, of outstanding new issue junk was floated in the past 3 years and was buoyed by an expanding economy and generally declining interest rates. Many of these companies are so laden with debt that even a modest shortfall in cash flow could have dire consequences. "The next time we have a recession, there's going to be a fallout," predicts Warren Greene, president of American Investors Income Fund, a 10-year-old junk mutual fund. "You've got to be careful you don't end up with three or four old maids at the end of the game."[4]

Mr. Forsyth realized that the task of convincing the board to triple its investment in the high-yield market would be a difficult one, particularly since the risk-return

---

4. "The Growing Respectability of the Junk Heap," *Business Week*, April 22, 1985.

performance of high-yield investments was not readily explicable. Why was the volatility of returns on high-yield bonds lower than that of investment-grade corporates? Why hadn't lower-grade spreads been arbitraged away as the high-yield market developed? How much liquidity could a small investor like Anchor expect in the secondary market? Given Anchor's weak capital position (see Exhibit 15), was the risk of default on high-yield securities, including the Metromedia issue, too great for Anchor to bear?

**EXHIBIT 1**
DBL 100 Yield versus Treasuries, 1980–1985

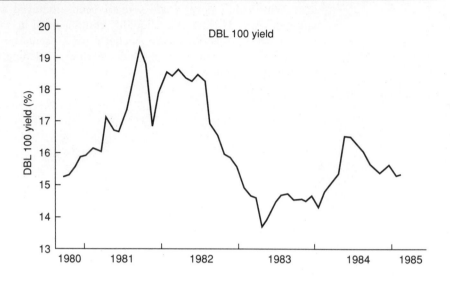

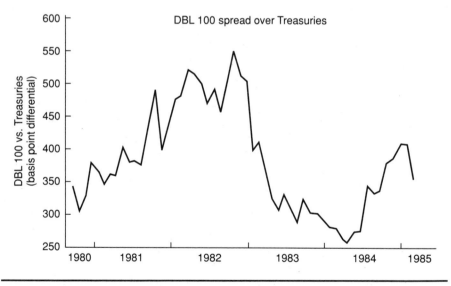

*Source:* Drexel Burnham Lambert.

*Note:* The DBL 100 indexed the 100 largest fixed-coupon, nonutility, high-yield issues outstanding over the period 1980–1985. In November 1984 the average coupon of the index was 13.2%, the average maturity November 2000, and the average quality slightly higher than single B.

**EXHIBIT 2**
Median Financial Ratios for Standard and Poor's Rated Industrial Issues, 1982–1984

| | Standard and Poor's Rating | | | | | |
|---|---|---|---|---|---|---|
| | **AAA** | **AA** | **A** | **BBB** | **BB** | **B** |
| Fixed-charge coverage[a] . . . . . . | 7.90 | 3.96 | 2.85 | 2.25 | 1.77 | 1.34 |
| Funds from operations/Long-term debt . | 308.72% | 111.02% | 68.89% | 43.31% | 22.78% | 14.19% |
| Funds from operations/Total debt . . . | 161.48 | 77.16 | 58.39 | 38.07 | 21.23 | 12.35 |
| Long-term debt/Capitalization . . . . . | 8.50 | 19.67 | 25.08 | 31.31 | 48.36 | 59.78 |
| Total debt/Capitalization, including short-term debt . . . . . . . . . . | 15.25 | 24.80 | 28.94 | 34.81 | 50.33 | 63.38 |
| Total liabilities/Tangible shareholders' equity and minority interest . . . . . | 69.56 | 99.34 | 112.37 | 127.26 | 197.78 | 294.65 |

*Source:* "Key Industrial Financial Ratios," *Standard and Poor's Creditweek,* August 19, 1985, p. 12.

a. Fixed-charge coverage is the ratio of pre-tax income to interest and rental expenses.

**EXHIBIT 3**
Low-Rated Bond Returns versus Treasuries, 1977–1984

| Initial S&P Rating | Annual Rate of Return versus Comparable Maturity Treasuries[a] (percentage points) |
|---|---|
| BBB . . . . . . . . . . . . . . . . . . . . . . . . . | +3.02 |
| BB . . . . . . . . . . . . . . . . . . . . . . . . . | +4.43 |
| B . . . . . . . . . . . . . . . . . . . . . . . . . | +3.87 |
| CCC . . . . . . . . . . . . . . . . . . . . . . . . . | +5.49 |

*Source:* Drexel Burnham Lambert.

a. Return comparisons are based on a study of the 391 original issue high-yield bonds underwritten over the period 1977–1984. Returns represent compound average annual returns from equal dollar investments in high-yield bonds and comparable maturity U.S. Treasury securities, assuming coupons are reinvested in each high-yield or Treasury issue. Results are time-weighted such that issues outstanding 4 years are given twice the weight of issues outstanding 2 years, and so on.

**EXHIBIT 4**
High-Yield Bond Issuance, 1977–1984 (billions of dollars)

| | *1977* | *1978* | *1979* | *1980* | *1981* | *1982* | *1983* | *1984* | *Total* |
|---|---|---|---|---|---|---|---|---|---|
| New issues . . . . . . . . | $ .55 | $1.45 | $1.30 | $1.27 | $1.38 | $2.51 | $7.52 | $14.21 | $30.19 |
| Exchange offers . . . . . . | .50 | .68 | .30 | .68 | .32 | .53 | .49 | .70 | 4.20 |
| Utilities . . . . . . . . . | .01 | .00 | .09 | .11 | .04 | .14 | .48 | .87 | 1.74 |
| Total . . . . . . . . . | $1.06 | $2.13 | $1.69 | $2.06 | $1.74 | $3.18 | $8.49 | $15.78 | $36.13 |

*Source: The Case for High-Yield Bonds* (Drexel Burnham Lambert, March 1985), p. 3.

*Note:* These figures include public, straight industrial, finance, transportation, and utility new issues of $10 million or more. Bonds issued below 70% are counted at issue price. All others are included at face value.

**EXHIBIT 5**
Recent Issuers of High-Yield Securities

| | |
|---|---|
| Beverly Enterprises | Lifemark (AMI) |
| Caesars World | Lorimar |
| Charter Medical Corporation | MCI Communications |
| Circus Circus | MGM Grand Hotels |
| Coastal Corporation | National Medical Enterprises |
| Comdisco | Occidental Petroleum |
| Eastern Airlines | People Express Airlines |
| Fairfield Communities | Resorts International |
| Golden Nugget | Southmark Corporation |
| Humana, Inc. | Sunshine Mining |
| Integrated Resources | Texas International |
| Kinder-Care | Universal Health |

**EXHIBIT 6**
Leading Underwriters of High-Yield Debt Offerings, 1982–1984 (millions of dollars)

| | 1984 | | | | 1983 | | | | 1982 | | | |
|---|---|---|---|---|---|---|---|---|---|---|---|---|
| | Rank | Amount | % | No. of Issues | Rank | Amount | % | No. of Issues | Rank | Amount | % | No. of Issues |
| Drexel Burnham Lambert | 1 | $ 9,555.2 | 67.6 | 68 | 1 | $4,380.9 | 58.1 | 48 | 1 | $1,380.8 | 55.3 | 25 |
| Prudential-Bache | 2 | 979.6 | 6.9 | 15 | 5 | 251.6 | 3.3 | 6 | 8 | 37.0 | 1.5 | 1 |
| Salomon Brothers | 3 | 850.7 | 6.0 | 9 | 3 | 443.4 | 5.9 | 5 | — | — | — | — |
| Merrill Lynch Capital Markets | 4 | 709.4 | 5.0 | 6 | 2 | 688.7 | 9.1 | 8 | 2 | 597.2 | 23.9 | 7 |
| Shearson Lehman Brothers | 5 | 484.5 | 3.4 | 7 | 6 | 202.4 | 2.7 | 1 | 10 | 21.2 | .8 | 1 |
| First Boston | 6 | 368.6 | 2.6 | 5 | 9 | 149.1 | 2.0 | 2 | — | — | — | — |
| Bear Stearns | 7 | 345.1 | 2.4 | 4 | 4 | 354.8 | 4.7 | 5 | 9 | 31.2 | 1.3 | 1 |
| Morgan Stanley | 8 | 306.3 | 2.2 | 5 | 13 | 80.0 | 1.1 | 1 | — | — | — | — |
| E. F. Hutton | 9 | 143.4 | 1.0 | 3 | 8 | 190.0 | 2.5 | 2 | 4 | 72.0 | 2.9 | 2 |
| Goldman, Sachs | 10 | 98.8 | .7 | 1 | 11 | 112.8 | 1.5 | 1 | — | — | — | — |
| Paine Webber | 11 | 73.4 | .5 | 2 | 7 | 196.3 | 2.6 | 2 | 3 | 177.0 | 7.1 | 4 |
| L. F. Rothschild, Unterberg, Towbin | 12 | 54.5 | .4 | 2 | 12 | 96.5 | 1.3 | 2 | — | — | — | — |
| Donaldson, Lufkin & Jenrette | 13 | 47.9 | .3 | 1 | — | — | — | — | — | — | — | — |
| Kidder, Peabody | 14 | 40.0 | .3 | 1 | 10 | 134.6 | 1.8 | 2 | — | — | — | — |
| Rooney, Pace | 15 | 24.7 | .2 | 1 | — | — | — | — | — | — | — | — |
| Dean Witter Reynolds | 16 | 15.0 | .1 | 1 | — | — | — | — | — | — | — | — |
| Advest | 17 | 12.0 | .1 | 1 | — | — | — | — | — | — | — | — |
| Werbel-Roth Securities | 18 | 2.3 | 0 | 1 | — | — | — | — | — | — | — | — |
| Total other banks | | — | | — | | 253.3 | 3.7 | 13 | | 182.6 | 7.3 | 15 |
| Total | | $14,111.4 | | 133 | | $7,534.4 | | 98 | | $2,499.0 | | 56 |

*Source:* IDD Information Services.

*Note:* High-yield nonconvertible debt offerings only. Debt at offering price. Full credit is given to book manager.

# EXHIBIT 7
Description of Securities Issued by MBC, November 29, 1984

| Security | Principal Amount ($ millions) | Maturity | Price to Public | Aggregate Price | Underwriting Commissions | Proceeds to Company |
|---|---|---|---|---|---|---|
| Zero coupon senior notes[a] | | | | | | |
| Series 1 | $ 160 | 12/1/88 | 58.834% | $ 94,134,400 | $ 2,353,360 | $ 91,781,040 |
| 2 | 160 | 12/1/89 | 50.911 | 81,457,600 | 2,036,440 | 79,421,160 |
| 3 | 160 | 12/1/90 | 43.545 | 69,672,000 | 1,741,800 | 67,930,200 |
| 4 | 160 | 12/1/91 | 39.986 | 59,177,600 | 1,479,440 | 57,698,160 |
| 5 | 160 | 12/1/92 | 31.489 | 50,382,400 | 1,259,560 | 49,122,840 |
| 6 | 160 | 12/1/93 | 26.685 | 42,696,000 | 1,067,400 | 41,628,600 |
| | | | | 397,520,000 | 9,938,000 | 387,582,000 |
| Senior exchangeable variable-rate debentures[a] | 335 | 12/1/96 | 99.000 | 331,650,000 | 7,463,800 | 324,186,200 |
| 15⅝% senior subordinated debentures[b] | 225 | 12/1/99 | 99.250 | 223,312,500 | 5,861,250 | 217,451,250 |
| Adjustable-rate participating subordinated debentures[b] | 400 | 12/1/02 | 87.299 | 349,196,000 | 9,888,000 | 339,308,000 |
| Total | $1,920 | | | $1,301,678,500 | $33,151,050 (2.55%) | $1,268,527,450 |

a. The senior debt securities were rated B+ by Standard and Poor's, B1 by Moody's.
b. The subordinated debt securities were rated B− by Standard and Poor's, B3 by Moody's.

**EXHIBIT 8**

Pro Forma Consolidated Condensed Balance Sheet for Metromedia, Inc. and Subsidiary Companies at September 30, 1984 (thousands of dollars)

| | Historical September 30, 1984 | Adjustments Increase/ Decrease Bond Transaction | Pro Forma |
|---|---|---|---|
| Cash and marketable securities at cost, which approximates market | $ 11,093 | $ 50,000[b] | $ 61,093 |
| Accounts receivable, less provisions for doubtful accounts of $943 | 129,132 | – | 129,132 |
| Film rights | 87,872 | – | 87,872 |
| Refundable income taxes | 39,794 | – | 39,794 |
| Other current assets | 32,488 | – | 32,488 |
| Current assets | 300,379 | 50,000 | 350,379 |
| Property, plant, equipment, at cost | 284,485 | – | 284,485 |
| Less: Accumulated depreciation | 7,776 | – | 7,776 |
| Film rights, noncurrent | 136,081 | – | 136,081 |
| Investment in tax leases | 8,181 | – | 8,181 |
| Intangible assets | 1,277,736 | – | 1,277,736 |
| Other noncurrent assets | 139,081 | 35,740[b] | 174,821 |
| Total assets | $2,138,167 | $ 85,740 | $2,223,907 |
| Current portion of long-term debt | $ 191,385 | $ (95,973)[b] | $ 95,412 |
| Film rights payable | 87,592 | – | 87,592 |
| Accounts payable | 80,739 | – | 80,739 |
| Accrued interest | 68,558 | (66,966)[b] | 1,592 |
| Other current liabilities | 39,774 | – | 39,774 |
| Current liabilities | 468,048 | (162,939) | 305,109 |
| Long-term debt | 1,165,248 | (1,053,000)[b] | 112,248 |
| Serial zero coupon senior notes, net of estimated discount of $562,480 | – | 397,520[b] | 397,520 |
| Senior exchangeable variable-rate debentures, net of estimated discount of $3,350 | – | 331,650[b] | 331,650 |
| 15⅝% senior subordinated debentures, net of estimated discount of $1,687 | – | 223,313[b] | 223,313 |
| Adjustable-rate participating subordinated debentures, net of estimated discount of $50,804 | – | 349,196[b] | 349,196 |
| Discount debentures, net of discount | 196,605 | – | 196,605 |
| Film rights payable, noncurrent | 86,750 | – | 86,750 |
| Deferred income taxes | 25,357 | – | 25,357 |
| Other noncurrent liabilities | 42,172 | – | 42,172 |
| Deferred credit, warrants | 9,325 | – | 9,325 |
| Total liabilities | 1,993,505 | 85,740 | 2,079,245 |
| Redeemable preferred stock | 128,125 | – | 128,125 |
| Class A nonvoting common stock | 10,000 | – | 10,000 |
| Common stock, authorized 6,300,000 shares, $.01 par value, issued 4,858,000 | 49 | – | 49 |
| Paid-in capital | 50,304 | – | 50,304 |
| Accumulated deficit | (37,216) | – | (37,216) |
| Less: Notes receivable, management group | 6,600 | – | 6,600 |
| Voting common stockholders' equity | 6,537 | | 6,537 |
| Total liabilities and net worth | $2,138,167 | $ 85,740 | $2,223,907 |

Source: Metromedia Broadcasting Corporation prospectus, November 29, 1984.

Notes (a) and (b) refer to Notes to Pro Forma Balance Sheet on the next page.

*(continued)*

**EXHIBIT 8** *(concluded)*
Notes to Pro Forma Balance Sheet

a. Historical consolidated condensed balance sheet of Metromedia, Inc. at September 30, 1984.

b. Adjustments related to the issuance by MBC of the debt securities and the use of all but $50 million of the net aggregate proceeds of the offerings to repay senior bank indebtedness and accrued interest related to such debt. Net proceeds from the issuance of the debt securities total $1,265,939,000 as follows (thousands of dollars):

| | |
|---|---:|
| Serial zero coupon senior notes, net of estimated discount of $562,480 . . . . . . . . . . . . | $ 397,520 |
| Senior exchangeable variable-rate debentures, net of estimated discount of $3,350 . . . . . . | 331,650 |
| 15⅝% senior subordinated debentures, net of estimated discount of $1,687 . . . . . . . . . | 223,313 |
| Adjustable-rate participating subordinated debentures, net of estimated discount of $50,804 . . . . . . . . . . . . . . . . . . . . . . . . . . | 349,196 |
| | 1,301,679 |
| Less: Debt expenses . . . . . . . . . . . . . . . . . . . . . . . . | 35,740 |
| Net proceeds . . . . . . . . . . . . . . . . . . . . . . . . . . . . | $1,265,939 |

MBC will transfer all but $50 million of the aggregate net proceeds of the offerings of the debt securities to Metromedia, including a $1,141 million dividend, and a $75 million advance in the form of a note receivable. It is contemplated that if at the end of 1985 (or at the end of any consecutive 12-month period thereafter) MBC has achieved a ratio of operating cash flow (before deduction of the proposed management fee payable to Metromedia) to cash interest expense of 1.10 to 1, $25 million may be advanced to Metromedia and the note referred to above shall be increased by such amount. If at the end of 1986 (or at the end of any consecutive 12-month period thereafter) MBC has achieved a ratio of operating cash flow to cash interest expense (as determined above) of 1.25 to 1, an additional $25 million may be advanced to Metromedia and the note referred to above shall be further increased by such amount.

Metromedia will use the $1,141 million dividend and the $75 million advance to repay senior bank indebtedness of $1,149 million and accrued interest of $67 million.

**EXHIBIT 9**
Schedule of Principal Payments on the Debt Securities (millions of dollars)

| | Serial Senior Notes | Senior Variable-Rate Debentures | Senior Subordinated Debentures | Participating Subordinated Debentures | Total |
|---|---|---|---|---|---|
| 1988 . . . . . . | $160 | | | | $160 |
| 1989 . . . . . . | 160 | | | | 160 |
| 1990 . . . . . . | 160 | | | | 160 |
| 1991 . . . . . . | 160 | | | | 160 |
| 1992 . . . . . . | 160 | | | | 160 |
| 1993 . . . . . . | 160 | | | | 160 |
| 1994 . . . . . . | | $110 | | | 110 |
| 1995 . . . . . . | | 110 | | | 110 |
| 1996 . . . . . . | | 115 | $56 | | 171 |
| 1997 . . . . . . | | | 56 | $66 | 122 |
| 1998 . . . . . . | | | 56 | 66 | 122 |
| 1999 . . . . . . | | | 57 | 66 | 123 |
| 2000 . . . . . . | | | | 66 | 66 |
| 2001 . . . . . . | | | | 66 | 66 |
| 2002 . . . . . . | | | | 70 | 70 |

*Source:* Metromedia Broadcasting Corporation prospectus, November 29, 1984.

## EXHIBIT 10

Selected Historical and Pro Forma Consolidated Financial Statements for MBC, 1979–1984 (thousands of dollars)

### Historical Financial Data[a]

#### Predecessor Operations[b]

| | Fiscal Year[c] | | | | | Jan. 2–<br>July 3,<br>1983 | Jan. 1–<br>June 20,<br>1984 | June 21–<br>Aug. 5,<br>1984 | Aug. 6–<br>Sept. 30,<br>1984 |
|---|---|---|---|---|---|---|---|---|---|
| | 1979 | 1980 | 1981 | 1982 | 1983 | | | | |
| Net revenues | $138,816 | $172,468 | $207,323 | $270,799 | $343,742 | $154,351 | $175,429 | $38,476 | $58,748 |
| Depreciation and amortization | 3,947 | 4,282 | 5,119 | 9,365 | 14,970 | 6,526 | 8,877 | 3,676 | 4,771 |
| Operating income[d] | 51,354 | 54,101 | 68,490 | 88,839 | 97,467 | 40,202 | 46,864 | 6,183 | 12,087 |
| Allocated interest expense[e] | 7,093 | 7,057 | 7,580 | 24,238 | 28,172 | 11,930 | 14,382 | 17,043 | 20,544 |
| Net income (loss) | 22,155 | 23,683 | 30,048 | 30,771 | 30,625 | 12,493 | 14,684 | (10,860) | (8,457) |
| Ratio of earnings to fixed changes[f,g] | | | | | | | | | |

### Pro Forma Financial Data—MBC and Subsidiaries[h]

| | Fiscal<br>Year<br>1983 | Jan. 2–<br>Oct. 2,<br>1983 | Jan. 1–<br>Sept. 30,<br>1984 | At<br>Sept. 30,<br>1984 |
|---|---|---|---|---|
| **Income Statement Data** | | | | |
| Net revenues | $354,998 | $251,842 | $272,653 | |
| Depreciation and amortization | 32,232 | 24,020 | 25,132 | |
| Operating income | 81,676 | 51,806 | 55,713 | |
| Interest expense (excl. amortization of debt discount and expenses) | 133,719 | 100,289 | 100,289 | |
| Amortization of debt discount and expenses | 70,341 | 52,756 | 52,756 | |
| Net loss | (122,384) | (101,239) | (97,332) | |
| Ratio of earnings to fixed charges [f,i] | | | | |
| **Balance Sheet Data** | | | | |
| Working capital[j,k] | | | | $ 97,022 |
| Total assets[j,k] | | | | 1,452,736 |
| Intangible assets, net of amortization | | | | 997,686 |
| Serial zero coupon senior notes | | | | 397,520 |
| Senior exchangeable variable-rate debentures | | | | 331,650 |
| 15 5/8% senior subordinated debentures | | | | 223,313 |
| Adjustable-rate participating subordinated debentures | | | | 349,196 |
| Stockholders' equity (deficiency)[j,k] | | | | (52,900) |

*Source:* Metromedia Broadcasting Corporation prospectus, November 29, 1984.

Notes (a) to (k) refer to Notes to Financial Statements on the next page.

*(continued)*

**EXHIBIT 10** *(concluded)*
Notes to Financial Statements

---

a. Prior to management's leveraged buyout of Metromedia.

b. WCVB-TV (Boston) was acquired in May 1982; WFLD-TV (Chicago) was acquired in April 1983; KRLD-TV (Dallas) was acquired in December 1983. The historical financial statements include the results of operations of such stations since their respective dates of acquisition.

c. The company's fiscal year approximates a calendar year.

d. A restatement of the historical financial statements gives effect to the management agreement, pursuant to which Metromedia will provide certain administrative, tax, legal, cash management, and financial advisory services for a fee.

e. The historical financial statements include an allocation of interest expense from Metromedia based on (1) specific borrowings identifiable with the acquisition of the broadcasting properties, and (2) a general allocation based on the ratio of total assets of the broadcasting properties to total consolidated Metromedia assets (exclusive of specific borrowings identifiable with assets other than the broadcasting properties).

f. Earnings used in computing the historical and pro forma ratios of earnings to fixed charges consist of earnings before fixed charges and taxes based on income. Historical fixed charges consist of allocated interest [see note (e)] and one third of rental expense, which is deemed to be representative of the interest factor of rental payments. Pro forma fixed charges consist of interest expense, amortization of debt discount and expenses, and one third of rental expense.

g. The amounts of earnings coverage deficiency for the period June 21, 1984, to August 5, 1984, and August 6, 1984, to September 30, 1984, were $10,860,000 and $8,457,000, respectively. In view of significant changes in capital structure, the ratio of earnings to fixed charges for predecessor operations has not been included.

h. The pro forma financial data are based on the historical financial statements of the company, giving effect to the acquisitions of WFLD-TV (Chicago) and KRLD-TV (Dallas) consummated during 1983; a real estate sale–leaseback transaction completed in November 1983; the merger on June 21, 1984, pursuant to which Metromedia became a privately held company; the contribution by Metromedia to MBC of the stock of two of its subsidiaries that own the broadcasting properties; the issuance of the debt securities; and the dividend or advance of all but $50 million of the net proceeds of the offerings of the debt securities. The pro forma income data for the periods January 2, 1983, to October 2, 1983, and January 1, 1984, to September 30, 1984, and for the fiscal year ended December 31, 1983, assume that the issuance of the debt securities and the other transactions described above took place at the beginning of each of such fiscal periods. The pro forma balance sheet data assume that Metromedia contributed the stock of its two subsidiaries that own the broadcasting properties to MBC on September 30, 1984, and that the issuance of the debt securities and the dividend or advance of all but $50 million of the net proceeds of the offerings of the debt securities took place on September 30, 1984 [see note (k)].

i. The amount of earnings coverage deficiency on a pro forma basis for the fiscal year ended December 31, 1983, was $122,384,000. The amounts of earnings coverage deficiency on a pro forma basis for the periods January 1, 1984, to September 30, 1984, and January 2, 1983, to October 2, 1983, were $97,332,000 and $101,239,000, respectively.

j. All but $125 million of the aggregate net proceeds of the offerings of the debt securities will be dividended to Metromedia. Of such $125 million, $75 million will be advanced to Metromedia and $50 million will be added to the company's working capital [see note (k)].

k. It is contemplated that if at the end of 1985 (or at the end of any consecutive 12-month period thereafter) MBC has achieved a ratio of operating cash flow (before deduction of the management fee) to cash interest expense of 1.15 to 1, $25 million may be advanced to Metromedia. If at the end of 1986 (or at the end of any consecutive 12-month period thereafter) MBC has achieved a ratio of operating cash flow (as determined above) to cash interest expense of 1.30 to 1, an additional $25 million may be advanced to Metromedia. If the $50 million referred to above was advanced to Metromedia simultaneously with the $75 million advance, pro forma total assets would be approximately $1,403 million, working capital would be approximately $47 million, and stockholders' deficiency would be approximately $103 million as of September 30, 1984.

---

**EXHIBIT 11**
Public Straight Debt Default Rate as Percent of High-Yield Debt Outstanding, 1974–1984

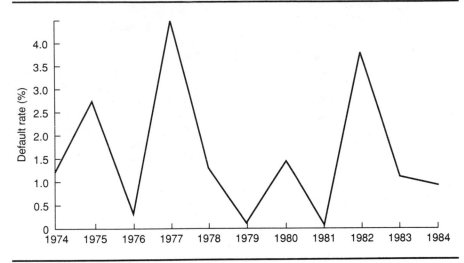

*Source:* Edward I. Altman and Scott A. Nammacher, *The Default Rate Experience on High Yield Corporate Debt* (New York: Morgan Stanley, 1985), p. 15.

Yield on 20-Year U.S. Treasuries, 1974–1984

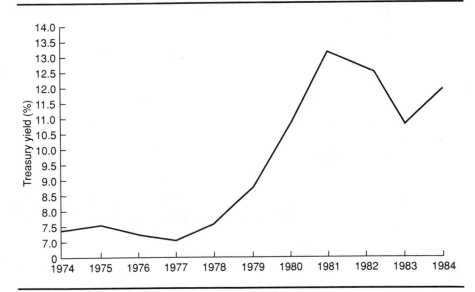

*Source:* Salomon Brothers Inc.

**EXHIBIT 12**

Selected Bond Yields, November 23, 1984

| Maturity | Instrument | Yield to Maturity |
|---|---|---|
| 1-year | Treasury bills | 8.65% |
| 3-year | Government bonds | 10.63 |
| | Zero coupon government bonds | 10.90 |
| 5-year | Government bonds | 10.99 |
| 7-year | Government bonds | 11.21 |
| | Zero coupon government bonds | 11.53 |
| 10-year | Government bonds | 11.27 |
| | New industrials (Aaa) | 11.50 |
| | New industrials (A) | 11.75 |
| 15-year | Government bonds | 11.36 |
| 25-year | Government bonds | 11.43 |
| | New industrials (Aaa) | 11.88 |
| | New industrials (A) | 12.25 |

**EXHIBIT 13**

Summary Statistics of Monthly Returns on Low-Quality Bonds versus Other Securities, January 1982–May 1984

| | Profile of Indices at Jan. 1, 1984 | | Average Returns | | Standard Deviation of Monthly Returns[a] (%) |
|---|---|---|---|---|---|
| Index | Average Coupon (%) | Average Maturity (years) | Monthly (%) | Annualized (%) | |
| Low-quality bonds . . . . | 12.72 | 17 | 1.55 | 20.3 | 2.74 |
| Corporate bonds | | | | | |
| A rating . . . . . . . | 9.58 | 22 | 1.29 | 16.6 | 3.49 |
| AAA rating . . . . . . | 9.09 | 24 | 1.17 | 15.0 | 3.59 |
| Salomon Long Government Bond | | | | | |
| Index . . . . . . . . | 10.67 | 23 | 1.02 | 13.0 | 3.55 |
| S&P 500 . . . . . . . . | na | na | 1.12 | 14.3 | 4.15 |

*Source:* Marshall E. Blume and Donald B. Keim, *Risk and Return Characteristics of Lower-Grade Bonds* (Rodney L. White Center for Financial Research, Wharton School, University of Pennsylvania, 1984), appendix table 1.

na = not available.

a. Standard deviation is a statistical measure of the dispersion of actual returns around their average, or expected, value. In general, the probability is 67% that the actual return on a portfolio will lie within one standard deviation of its expected value and 95% that the return will lie within two standard deviations of the expected value.

**EXHIBIT 14**

News Profile, *Inc. Magazine,* November 1983

### Making the Market

No man is a market. But in the highly specialized world of low-rated debt, Drexel Burnham Lambert Inc.'s Michael Milken comes awfully close. In the late 1960s, Milken, now a 37-year-old senior vice-president, demonstrated in his MBA thesis for the University of Pennsylvania's Wharton School that companies with debt rated B or less were far less prone to bankruptcy than most people had assumed. Upon joining Drexel in 1968, the enterprising analyst/salesman began introducing his new employer to an unexploited corner of the corporate underwriting market—one that has become the envy of Wall Street.

Drexel's strong franchise in low-rated debt didn't materialize overnight. In the early days, Milken worked long and hard out of Philadelphia and, later, New York, as a bond analyst, researching more than 2,000 issues—many of them the downgraded bonds of ailing conglomerates. But, as he and the firm's credit analysts began learning more about the high-yield, or "junk," bond universe than anyone else on Wall Street, Milken proposed—and got approval—to take the next step. "We started making markets in these securities," he says.

Once Drexel's knowledge of buyers and sellers took hold, the firm's investment bankers, headed by Frederick Joseph, began underwriting new debt issues in 1977 for younger and smaller companies. In doing so, however, they have drawn heavily on Milken's talents for both structuring deals and selling them. Says one investor: "It's no exaggeration to say he knows nearly all the buyers and what they want. He's the one who's sold them on junk bonds."

Five years ago, in recognition of Milken's unique market grasp, Drexel management signed off on his unusual request to move the entire high-yield and convertible-bond department from Wall Street to Los Angeles. The three-hour difference in time zones enables Milken, a workaholic of legendary proportions, to stay in touch with buyers and sellers on both coasts. On a typical day, he commutes 20 minutes from his San Fernando Valley home (once the residence of Clark Gable) to be in Drexel's Beverly Hills trading room by 5 A.M. For the next 14 hours or so, he quarterbacks a team of more than 50 analysts, traders, and salespeople from the center of a large, X-shaped trading desk. Competitors estimate that Drexel's Los Angeles operation accounts for 60% to 70% of the trading volume of a booming over-the-counter market that, Milken claims, never closes. "If a guy called me at home and wanted to sell, I'd buy on a Sunday morning," he says. At a price, he notes, "there's always a market."

Even with some of Wall Street's biggest guns angling to become more influential in low-rated bond trading and underwriting, Milken claims he doesn't feel the pressure. "We've worked hard for many years and brought in lots of capable people." With confidence, he shrugs and says, "Others have always been interested in the market. But time is the greatest competitor. You have only so much time in a day."

*Source:* Reprinted with permission from *Inc. Magazine,* November 1983. Copyright © 1983 by Goldhirsh Group, Inc., 38 Commercial Wharf, Boston, MA 02110.

**EXHIBIT 15**

Anchor Savings and Loan Consolidated Balance Sheet at June 30, 1984 (millions of dollars)

| | | | |
|---|---:|---|---:|
| Cash | $ 52 | Deposits | $ 870 |
| Loans receivable | 735 | Accounts payable and accruals | 21 |
| Investments | | Notes payable | 49 |
| Government and agency | | Federal Home Loan Bank | |
| securities | 105 | advances | 52 |
| Corporate bonds (investment- | | Other liabilities | 10 |
| grade) | 96 | Total liabilities | $1,002 |
| Commercial loans | 9 | Stockholders' equity | 45 |
| Federal Home Loan Bank stock | 21 | Total liabilities and | |
| Real estate held for sale or | | stockholders' equity | $1.047 |
| investment | 16 | | |
| Other assets | 13 | | |
| Total assets | $1,047 | | |

*Note:* Anchor Savings and Loan was a federally chartered thrift insured by the Federal Savings and Loan Insurance Corporation.

# Anheuser-Busch Company and Campbell Taggart Inc.

In mid-May 1984, Walter Suhre put a yellowing newspaper clipping (see Exhibit 1) back into a folder and closed his case file. The vice president and general counsel of St. Louis-based Anheuser-Busch Company, he believed his company may have suffered losses through insider trading during its acquisition of Campbell Taggart Inc. in 1982. As far as Mr. Suhre could tell, Paul Thayer, who in 1982 was a director of Anheuser-Busch, had leaked confidential information to friends about the impending Campbell Taggart acquisition. Mr. Thayer's friends and others had then purchased shares of Campbell Taggart in the open market (see Exhibits 2, 3, and 4).[1] Mr. Suhre had learned about the details of this insider trading in January 1984, from a legal complaint filed by the Securities and Exchange Commission (SEC) against Mr. Thayer and his friends.

Now, five months later, the SEC complaint was delayed in court. For the moment, Anheuser-Busch and Mr. Thayer had reached a stand-still agreement under which Anheuser-Busch would not sue Mr. Thayer as long as the SEC complaint remained unsettled. This agreement benefited both parties and was terminable by either Anheuser-Busch or Mr. Thayer. Anheuser-Busch gained more time to sue, because the statute of limitations was suspended for the duration of the stand-still. In addition, the company could use any evidence that emerged from the SEC proceedings against Mr. Thayer. Mr. Thayer gained the ability to defend himself against one set of charges at a time. As soon as the stand-still agreement

This case was prepared by Professor Erik R. Sirri.

Copyright © 1991 by the President and Fellows of Harvard College.
Harvard Business School case 291–020.

1. In all, 38 insiders and "tippees" purchased a total of 265,600 shares of Campbell Taggart. The figures reported in Exhibit 2 aggregate the trades of all 38 insiders and tippees.

lapsed, the statute of limitations would go back into effect and Anheuser-Busch would have to file suit within a short time period.

Mr. Suhre realized that he might have to present his recommendations on this matter to Anheuser-Busch senior management. But before he could make a proposal, he wanted to assure himself that the company could demonstrate in court that it had been damaged by the insider trading. On a more basic level, he needed both to confirm the company's stated intention to sue Mr. Thayer and to decide if the company should sue any parties other than Mr. Thayer.

## Reasons for the Acquisition

At the time of the acquisition, popular Anheuser-Busch brands such as Budweiser had allowed the company to achieve a dominant 32% share of the market for beer (see Exhibits 5 and 6 for financial statements). Anheuser-Busch's market strength was reflected in its stock performance, which remained good despite a traditionally low dividend yield.[2] Management believed this performance was due to the company's successful growth-based strategy, which stock analysts appreciated and rewarded with consistent "buy" recommendations. However, because management also believed that breweries had little room for continued growth, it was searching for routes to diversify.

The first such effort led to the internal development of Eagle brand snack foods, which were sold through bars, airports, and other distribution channels originally set up for beer sales. By 1982, Anheuser-Busch was considering acquisitions such as Campbell Taggert as well. During this period, Campbell Taggart was regarded as the bakery industry's low-cost producer. Its market share was second only to that of the ITT Continental Baking Company (see Exhibits 5 and 6 for financial statements). Sales were strongest in the rapidly growing southern and southwestern states, where Campbell Taggart breads, rolls, and cakes could be found in most supermarkets. Company stock had performed particularly well in the weeks preceding the merger announcement. In light of the rapid increase in Campbell Taggart's price, Anheuser-Busch made a public statement on August 2, 1982, about its interest in Campbell Taggart.

When the merger proposal was first announced publicly, industry analysts noted that by acquiring a bakery company externally, Anheuser-Busch was taking a new approach to its diversification goals, which previously had been met internally. To justify this shift, Anheuser-Busch looked to the benefits of a distribution network that Campbell Taggart had established at restaurants and supermarkets, where the brewer had been weak.

## The Acquisition Process

Anheuser-Busch decided to acquire Campbell Taggart through a negotiated merger. In this type of transaction, also known as a friendly takeover, the acquiring company negotiates a set of merger terms with the target company's board of directors. These terms usually specify the price to be paid for the acquired company and

---

2. The average dividend yield on an S&P 500 stock in 1981 was about 5.1%.

often address operating, employment, and seniority concerns as well. If the negotiations succeed, the board then asks its shareholders to approve the merger in a proxy vote.

An acquiring firm generally offers to pay a premium, or greater-than-market price, for the target's shares. One explanation for this premium is that the bidder must offer existing shareholders an incentive to induce them to sell shares they would normally retain. Another possible explanation is that investors believe the target company will have an intrinsically higher value when and if it falls under control of the new owner. Thus their reservation price, or indifference price, rises in anticipation. In either case, the prospect of receiving a premium for their shares usually causes target shareholders to support merger proposals. It is generally believed that without a reasonable premium, a merger proposal would fail.

The takeover premium that a bidder typically offers ranges from 20% to 40% over the target's premerger stock price.[3] The premium is defined as the percentage increase that the final negotiated offer price represents over the target stock price one month before the merger announcement. Curiously, the price of a target firm often begins to rise before any official announcement of a takeover attempt is made. During the weeks before a merger announcement, the target's price rises an average of 40% of the takeover premium.[4] Although the existence of a takeover premium is fairly consistent for a target stock, a bidding company's stock price tends to remain unchanged or to fall slightly.[5]

## Paul Thayer

Throughout his life, Paul Thayer enjoyed being a daredevil and adventurer. In World War II, he was a successful Air Force fighter pilot. After the war he continued flying, first as a commercial pilot for TWA and later as a test pilot for Chance Vought Aircraft. Not only did he survive this risky career, he advanced rapidly. By 1955 he had become a director of Vought, and after Vought merged with Ling-Temco to become LTV Aerospace, Mr. Thayer was elected chairman, CEO, and president of the new conglomerate. Mr. Thayer's stellar career and personal investments made him a multimillionaire. He began taking positions of civic leadership and sitting on corporate boards, including the Anheuser-Busch board, which he joined in January 1982. In April 1982, he became chairman of the U.S. Chamber of Commerce, where he caused bitter divisions by supporting a controversial tax increase proposed by President Reagan. Later in 1982, President Reagan appointed him Deputy Secretary of Defense, causing Mr. Thayer to resign his position on the Anheuser-Busch board. Once again, Mr. Thayer showed his strong will, this time by spearheading a major campaign to reduce military waste. In his spare time, though he was 62 years old, he continued to scuba dive, ride

3. Michael Jensen and Richard Ruback, "The Market for Corporate Control," *Journal of Financial Economics* 2 (1983): 5–50.

4. G. Jarrell and A. Poulson, "Stock Trading Before the Announcement of Tender Offers," *Journal of Law, Economics, and Organization* (1989, no. 5): 225–248.

5. Jensen and Ruback, "The Market for Corporate Control."

motorcycles through the Rocky Mountains, and perform death-defying stunts in a vintage World War II fighter plane.[6]

## The SEC Complaint

Apparently, Paul Thayer took this taste for adventure too far. According to an SEC complaint filed in January 1984, Mr. Thayer illegally disclosed stock-related information to friends, repeatedly tipping them off about the planned acquisitions, profits, and dividends of the three companies of which he was a director. One of these companies was Anheuser-Busch.

The SEC cited eight friends, the "tippees," in its complaint and claimed that they profited by purchasing shares of stock after hearing the inside information that Mr. Thayer had provided. Later, his friends sold the shares when public announcement of the merger made share prices rise. One tippee, Billy Bob Harris, was the highest paid stockbroker for A. G. Edwards, Inc., a St. Louis-based broker. A second, William Mathis, was a broker for Bear Stearns Companies, Inc., in Atlanta. A third tippee, Sandra Ryno, was a former LTV receptionist who allegedly maintained a "close personal relationship" with Mr. Thayer. The fourth, Julie Williams, an aerobic dance instructor in Dallas was alleged to have had a similar relationship with Mr. Harris. These four, along with four others, made up what *Time* magazine described as "a small circle of high-living Southerners."[7]

In an example cited by the SEC, Mr. Thayer spent the weekend of June 25, 1982, in Houston with Ms. Ryno, Mr. Harris, and Ms. Williams (see Exhibit 7). On the Monday following the weekend Mr. Harris "contacted a research analyst at A. G. Edwards and suggested to the analyst that Anheuser-Busch was interested in acquiring Campbell Taggart."[8] That same week Ms. Ryno purchased 2,000 shares of Campbell Taggart stock at $25\frac{3}{4}$ and $26\frac{3}{8}$ per share (see Exhibit 8). She sold her shares on August 10, after news had come out that Campbell Taggart was targeted in a takeover attempt and the stock price had risen. In its complaint the SEC accused the defendants of violating rules 10b-5 and 14e-3 of the Securities Exchange Act and stated that the tippees as a group made illegal profits of over $1.9 million from the information that Mr. Thayer had supplied.[9] Mr. Thayer himself did not share in these profits.

Although allegations of insider trading were relatively rare at the time, equivalent SEC charges were often settled out of court with a consent decree, which saved time and money for both sides. In a typical settlement the defendant would neither deny nor admit guilt but agree instead not to break securities laws in the

---

6. Grover Heiman, "The Flier Who Kept a Company from Crashing," *National Business,* June 1982, pp. 54–59.

7. Evan Thomas, "Life with Paul and Billy Bob," *Time,* January 16, 1984, p. 21.

8. SEC *v.* Thayer et al., U.S.D.C. S.D.N.Y. (January 5, 1984), p. 20.

9. SEC *v.* Thayer et al., p. 8.

future. If the defendant was later tried and convicted on a set of charges, the punishment would be more severe because of the violation of the consent decree. However, during negotiations in late 1983, Mr. Thayer refused such a settlement, possibly because it would be tantamount to an admission of guilt.[10] Given his high-profile position, the political embarrassment would be large. In January 1984, Mr. Thayer resigned from the Defense Department in order to avoid further damaging the Reagan Administration and to concentrate fully on defending himself against the SEC charges.

Mr. Thayer claimed that the charges were "entirely without merit." Billy Bob Harris, who gave regular stock reports on Dallas television, said that he had proven his innocence by passing a lie-detector test.

## Mr. Suhre's Decision

Mr. Suhre realized that Anheuser-Busch faced a sticky decision. Filing suit against Mr. Thayer or some other party might cost several million dollars in legal expenses with no guarantee of winning. And even if the company could recover part of the damages, press coverage of the suit could be embarrassing to both sides. To sue a former board director was virtually unprecedented, and Anheuser-Busch had no way to gauge how the rest of corporate America would react. To sue some other party—for example, Mr. Harris, Mr. Mathis, or their employers— had the advantage of increasing the potential size of the final settlement. However, Mr. Suhre wondered whether there would be any fallout from suing a major Wall Street firm.

Legal action had drawbacks, but so did inaction. Mr. Suhre felt that Anheuser-Busch had a corporate responsibility to initiate proceedings against Paul Thayer. Also, management was keenly aware of company losses from the merger, resulting both from the insider trading and from disappointing performance of the Campbell Taggart subsidiary during the 2 years following the merger. The SEC had a very strong case against Mr. Thayer. Mr. Suhre was worried that if Anheuser-Busch management did not sue, shareholders might file a derivative action[11] suit against Mr. Thayer or some other party. In any case, not to sue might be seen as tacit forgiveness for the incident.

----

10. Ibid.

11. If a corporation sustains significant losses that can be recovered through legal action and management fails to take this action, shareholders have the right to file a derivative suit on behalf of, and over the objections of, the corporation. Management may become a co-plaintiff along with the shareholders. The success of such a suit is often interpreted as a failure on the part of management.

**EXHIBIT 1**

News Article, *The Wall Street Journal*, August 10, 1982.

---

### ANHEUSER-BUSCH TO BUY CAMPBELL TAGGART INC.

#### Cash–Stock Offer Is Valued at $570 Million

Sᴛ. Lᴏᴜɪs—Anheuser-Busch Co. said it agreed in principle to acquire Campbell Taggart Inc., a Dallas-based baked-goods concern, for roughly $570 million in cash and stock.

The brewer, which had disclosed preliminary merger talks last week, said it would pay $36 each for about half of Campbell Taggart's 15 million shares. It would convert the rest into shares of a new Anheuser-Busch convertible preferred stock. Each new share would have a redemption value of $40, bear dividends at a rate of 9% a year, be noncallable for the first 5 years, and be convertible into .645 share of Anheuser-Busch common stock. The value of the new preferred stock is uncertain, but the acquisition would total about $570 million if the stock is assigned its redemption value. . . .

Under terms of the acquisition, Campbell Taggart shareholders may choose cash or stock for each share held, subject to proration if required. Anheuser-Busch said the stock swap is intended to be tax-free.

The acquisition requires a definitive agreement and approval of Campbell Taggart shareholders.

Anheuser-Busch said that Campbell Taggart will continue to operate under current management and that its chairman, Bill O. Mead, is expected to be asked to join the Anheuser-Busch board. . . .

Stock market response to the plan has been steady, with Campbell Taggart rising to $30.625, up $1, after the announcement last week and closing $1.75 higher yesterday at $31.75 in New York Stock Exchange composite trading. Anheuser-Busch dropped to $49.625 a share, down $4.375, after talks were disclosed and it closed yesterday on the Big Board at $47.50, down 50 cents. . . .

Emanuel Goldman of Sanford C. Bernstein & Co. said that the acquisition price was reasonable and that it would lead to a 10% decrease in per-share earnings unless Anheuser-Busch could raise the price of its beer.

---

**EXHIBIT 2**
Selected Daily Stock Data, June 1–September 1, 1982

| | Campbell Taggart | | | | Anheuser-Busch | | | |
| --- | --- | --- | --- | --- | --- | --- | --- | --- |
| Date | Closing Price | Volume (000s) | No. of Insider Trades | Insider Volume (000s) | Closing Price | Volume (000s) | S&P 500 Closing Level | NYSE Volume (millions) |
| 6/01 | $23.250 | 10.3 | 0 | 0 | $48.750 | 126.4 | 111.68 | 41.65 |
| 6/02 | 23.500 | 6.9 | 0 | 0 | 49.250 | 45.0 | 112.04 | 49.22 |
| 6/03 | 23.625 | 4.2 | 0 | 0 | 50.250 | 89.3 | 111.86 | 48.45 |
| 6/04 | 23.250 | 1.3 | 0 | 0 | 48.750 | 132.3 | 110.09 | 44.11 |
| 6/07 | 23.750 | 5.1 | 0 | 0 | 49.125 | 57.1 | 110.12 | 44.63 |
| 6/08 | 23.625 | 1.8 | 0 | 0 | 49.000 | 124.4 | 109.63 | 46.82 |
| 6/09 | 23.000 | 18.9 | 0 | 0 | 49.000 | 76.0 | 108.99 | 55.77 |
| 6/10 | 23.000 | 1.4 | 0 | 0 | 49.625 | 63.6 | 109.61 | 50.95 |
| 6/11 | 23.625 | 3.9 | 0 | 0 | 51.125 | 101.5 | 111.24 | 68.61 |
| 6/14 | 23.875 | 2.5 | 0 | 0 | 49.875 | 58.4 | 109.96 | 40.10 |
| 6/15 | 23.875 | 21.3 | 0 | 0 | 50.500 | 18.4 | 109.69 | 44.97 |
| 6/16 | 24.000 | 16.2 | 0 | 0 | 49.875 | 48.9 | 108.87 | 56.28 |
| 6/17 | 24.500 | 28.7 | 0 | 0 | 49.875 | 50.5 | 107.60 | 49.23 |
| 6/18 | 24.500 | 2.2 | 0 | 0 | 50.250 | 65.7 | 107.28 | 53.80 |
| 6/21 | 24.125 | 1.7 | 0 | 0 | 50.250 | 31.3 | 107.20 | 50.37 |
| 6/22 | 24.375 | 1.5 | 0 | 0 | 50.375 | 27.0 | 108.30 | 55.29 |
| 6/23 | 24.375 | 7.4 | 0 | 0 | 51.000 | 114.3 | 110.14 | 62.71 |
| 6/24 | 24.750 | 38.6 | 0 | 0 | 51.125 | 127.6 | 109.83 | 55.86 |
| 6/25 | 24.625 | 21.4 | 0 | 0 | 51.375 | 46.9 | 109.14 | 38.74 |
| 6/28 | 24.750 | 1.0 | 0 | 0 | 52.500 | 40.6 | 110.26 | 40.70 |
| 6/29 | 24.875 | 6.3 | 0 | 0 | 51.750 | 59.2 | 110.21 | 46.99 |
| 6/30 | 25.750 | 38.2 | 1 | .1 | 51.750 | 46.3 | 109.61 | 65.28 |
| 7/01 | 27.000 | 65.6 | 9 | 10.0 | 51.750 | 27.4 | 108.71 | 47.90 |
| 7/02 | 25.750 | 46.5 | 0 | 0 | 51.375 | 27.4 | 107.65 | 43.76 |
| 7/06 | 25.875 | 3.8 | 0 | 0 | 51.125 | 60.2 | 107.29 | 44.35 |
| 7/07 | 25.750 | 35.2 | 1 | 1.5 | 51.250 | 17.5 | 107.22 | 46.92 |
| 7/08 | 26.000 | 1.8 | 0 | 0 | 51.125 | 125.5 | 107.53 | 63.27 |
| 7/09 | 25.500 | 4.7 | 0 | 0 | 52.125 | 41.6 | 108.83 | 65.87 |
| 7/12 | 26.250 | 28.4 | 2 | 1.8 | 53.625 | 98.2 | 109.57 | 74.69 |
| 7/13 | 26.250 | 12.2 | 7 | 6.9 | 53.375 | 50.9 | 109.45 | 66.17 |
| 7/14 | 27.000 | 30.2 | 3 | 8.1 | 53.750 | 15.6 | 110.44 | 58.16 |
| 7/15 | 27.000 | 10.5 | 0 | 0 | 54.625 | 94.1 | 110.47 | 61.09 |
| 7/16 | 26.750 | 46.9 | 0 | 0 | 55.750 | 111.8 | 111.07 | 58.74 |
| 7/19 | 26.625 | 5.2 | 1 | .3 | 55.125 | 35.5 | 110.73 | 53.03 |
| 7/20 | 26.375 | 1.8 | 0 | 0 | 55.000 | 44.8 | 111.54 | 61.06 |
| 7/21 | 26.125 | 18.1 | 2 | 5.0 | 53.625 | 81.3 | 111.42 | 66.77 |
| 7/22 | 26.750 | 9.1 | 8 | 4.8 | 53.625 | 40.7 | 111.47 | 53.87 |
| 7/23 | 27.000 | 32.1 | 8 | 12.3 | 53.125 | 44.5 | 111.17 | 47.28 |
| 7/26 | 27.750 | 25.2 | 13 | 17.4 | 53.500 | 12.4 | 110.36 | 37.74 |
| 7/27 | 28.250 | 64.0 | 10 | 31.7 | 53.250 | 43.7 | 109.43 | 45.74 |
| 7/28 | 29.125 | 90.0 | 13 | 20.9 | 53.000 | 65.8 | 107.73 | 53.83 |
| 7/29 | 28.500 | 154.1 | 3 | 8.7 | 52.875 | 83.8 | 107.72 | 55.68 |
| 7/30 | 29.000 | 63.9 | 7 | 11.3 | 53.125 | 39.6 | 107.09 | 39.27 |
| 8/02 | 29.625 | 128.6 | 5 | 29.4 | 54.500 | 71.3 | 108.98 | 53.46 |
| 8/03 | 30.625 | 219.0 | 0 | 0 | 49.625 | 394.6 | 107.83 | 60.48 |
| 8/04 | 29.500 | 215.4 | 0 | 0 | 50.000 | 197.6 | 106.14 | 53.44 |

*(continued)*

**EXHIBIT 2** *(concluded)*
Selected Daily Stock Data, June 1–September 1, 1982

| Date | Campbell Taggart | | | | Anheuser-Busch | | S&P 500 Closing Level | NYSE Volume (millions) |
|---|---|---|---|---|---|---|---|---|
| | Closing Price | Volume (000s) | No. of Insider Trades | Insider Volume (000s) | Closing Price | Volume (000s) | | |
| 8/05 | $30.000 | 195.7 | 0 | 0 | $49.500 | 156.5 | 105.16 | 54.70 |
| 8/06 | 30.000 | 134.6 | 0 | 0 | 48.000 | 93.0 | 103.71 | 48.66 |
| 8/09 | 31.750 | 360.7 | 0 | 0 | 47.500 | 215.7 | 103.08 | 54.56 |
| 8/10 | 31.625 | 204.1 | 0 | 0 | 46.500 | 126.0 | 102.84 | 52.68 |
| 8/11 | 31.625 | 142.7 | 0 | 0 | 45.500 | 307.1 | 102.60 | 49.04 |
| 8/12 | 31.750 | 119.8 | 0 | 0 | 46.375 | 216.5 | 102.42 | 50.08 |
| 8/13 | 32.625 | 132.9 | 0 | 0 | 47.500 | 93.2 | 103.85 | 44.72 |
| 8/16 | 32.750 | 94.8 | 0 | 0 | 47.750 | 175.0 | 104.09 | 55.42 |
| 8/17 | 33.375 | 140.2 | 0 | 0 | 49.750 | 181.5 | 109.04 | 92.86 |
| 8/18 | 34.000 | 238.1 | 0 | 0 | 49.875 | 300.8 | 108.53 | 132.71 |
| 8/19 | 34.000 | 128.6 | 0 | 0 | 50.000 | 113.9 | 109.16 | 78.27 |
| 8/20 | 34.875 | 185.9 | 0 | 0 | 52.000 | 211.0 | 113.02 | 95.89 |
| 8/23 | 34.750 | 34.0 | 0 | 0 | 51.625 | 115.9 | 116.11 | 110.32 |
| 8/24 | 35.125 | 91.8 | 0 | 0 | 52.750 | 226.8 | 115.34 | 121.76 |
| 8/25 | 35.500 | 85.2 | 0 | 0 | 54.125 | 105.4 | 117.58 | 106.28 |
| 8/26 | 35.000 | 262.6 | 0 | 0 | 54.750 | 155.6 | 118.55 | 137.32 |
| 8/27 | 34.625 | 65.0 | 0 | 0 | 53.500 | 119.9 | 117.11 | 74.41 |
| 8/30 | 35.250 | 72.8 | 0 | 0 | 54.000 | 129.4 | 117.66 | 59.56 |
| 8/31 | 35.750 | 89.9 | 0 | 0 | 55.000 | 106.1 | 119.51 | 86.36 |
| 9/01 | 35.000 | 120.9 | 0 | 0 | 54.875 | 66.1 | 118.25 | 82.83 |

*Note:* Short interest is the number of shares investors have "sold short," that is, borrowed and then resold. The mid-month short interest in Campbell Taggart for June, July, August, and September 1982 was 255,969 shares; 255,405 shares; 6,300 shares; and 100 shares, respectively. The mid-month short interest in Anheuser-Busch for June, July, and August 1982 was 78,522 shares; 118,203 shares; and 88,097 shares, respectively.

**EXHIBIT 3**
Anheuser-Busch, Price and Volume

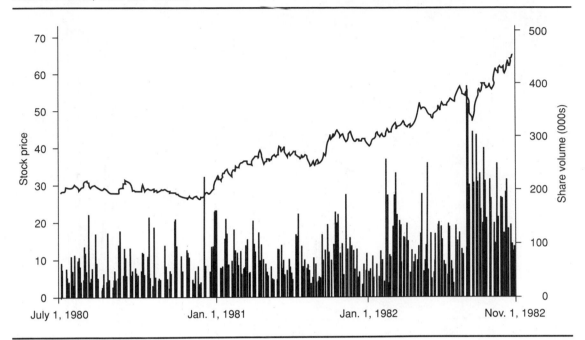

*Note:* The price data are plotted as a continuous line and should be read off the left-hand axis. The daily volume data are shown as vertical lines rising from the bottom of the plot and should be read off the right-hand axis.

**EXHIBIT 4**

Campbell Taggart, Price and Volume

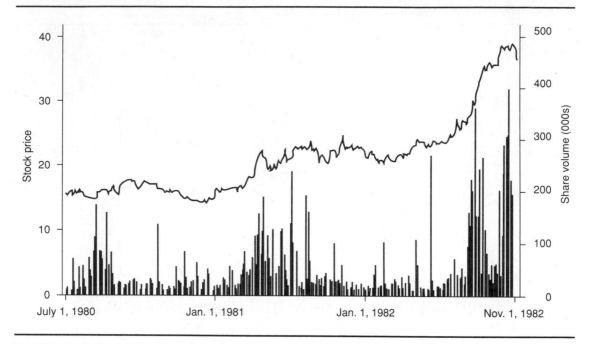

*Note:* The price data are plotted as a continuous line and should be read off the left-hand axis. The daily volume data are shown as vertical lines rising from the bottom of the plot and should be read off the right-hand axis.

**EXHIBIT 5**

Consolidated Balance Sheets at December 31, 1981 (millions of dollars)

| | Anheuser-Busch | Campbell Taggart |
|---|---|---|
| Cash and securities | $ 93.6 | $ 20.8 |
| Receivables and inventory | 376.1 | 147.1 |
| Other | 69.6 | 12.7 |
| Current assets | 539.3 | 180.6 |
| Investments and other assets | 78.3 | 42.0 |
| Plant and equipment | 2,257.6 | 292.2 |
| Total assets | $2,875.2 | $514.8 |
| Short-term debt | $ 29.5 | $ 11.6 |
| Accounts payable | 209.8 | 65.9 |
| Accruals and other | 254.1 | 42.3 |
| Current liabilities | 493.4 | 119.8 |
| Long-term borrowing | 817.3 | 125.5 |
| Deferred taxes | 357.7 | 21.8 |
| Minority interests | .0 | 22.7 |
| Shareholders' equity (issued 45,612,716 shares and 15,974,687 shares, respectively) | 1,206.8 | 225.0 |
| Total liabilities and equity | $2,875.2 | $514.8 |

**EXHIBIT 6**

Consolidated Income Statements for Year Ending December 31, 1981 (millions of dollars except per share data)

| | Anheuser-Busch | Campbell Taggart |
|---|---|---|
| Net sales | $3,847.2 | $1,257.5 |
| Net cost of goods sold | 2,975.5 | 657.6 |
| Marketing and research | 515.0 | 512.5 |
| Operating income | 356.7 | 87.4 |
| Other income | .0 | 1.6 |
| Total income | 356.7 | 89.0 |
| Net interest expense | 31.5 | 10.7 |
| Taxes | 107.8 | 36.6 |
| Net income | $ 217.4 | $ 41.7 |
| Earnings per share | $ 4.77 | $ 2.61 |
| Dividends per share | 1.38 | .90 |
| Rank in S&P 500 in 1981 | 139 | 334 |

**EXHIBIT 7**

Chronology of Events

| | |
|---|---|
| Jan. 5, 1982 | Paul Thayer is elected a director of Anheuser-Busch. |
| June 8, 1982 | Anheuser-Busch informs its investment banking firm that it is considering the acquisition of Campbell Taggart. |
| June 23, 1982 | Mr. Thayer attends Anheuser-Busch board meeting at which Campbell Taggart acquisition is considered. |
| June 25, 1982 | Mr. Thayer travels from Dallas to Houston with friends, returning the next day. |
| June 28, 1982 | Mr. Thayer allegedly tells Billy Bob Harris and others about the impending acquisition. |
| June 28, 1982 | Purchases of Campbell Taggart stock by defendants begin. |
| July 6, 1982 | Mr. Thayer telephones chairman of Anheuser-Busch's board of directors, then immediately phones Mr. Harris. |
| July 28, 1982 | Mr. Thayer attends Anheuser-Busch board meeting and telephones Sandra Ryno afterwards. |
| Aug. 2, 1982 | Anheuser-Busch announces merger talks with Campbell Taggart. |
| Aug. 9, 1982 | Anheuser-Busch announces agreement in principle to acquire Campbell Taggart. |
| Aug. 17, 1982 | Boards of both companies approve definitive merger agreement. |
| Oct. 27, 1982 | Campbell Taggart shareholders approve merger agreement. |
| Nov. 2, 1982 | Campbell Taggart becomes a wholly owned subsidiary of Anheuser-Busch. |
| Dec. 3, 1982 | SEC notifies Anheuser-Busch that it is investigating "unusual activity" in Campbell Taggart stock. Anheuser-Busch later cooperates with investigation. |
| Dec. 6, 1982 | President Reagan nominates Mr. Thayer to be Deputy Secretary of Defense. The Senate later confirms the nomination. |
| Dec. 31, 1982 | Mr. Thayer resigns his position on the Anheuser-Busch board. |
| Jan. 4, 1984 | Mr. Thayer resigns as Deputy Secretary of Defense. |
| Jan. 5, 1984 | SEC files a civil complaint against Mr. Thayer, claiming that he leaked corporate takeover plans to eight friends, who made $1.9 million in illegal profits from the information. |

**EXHIBIT 8**
Select Purchases and Sales of Campbell Taggart Stock by Insiders, 1982

| Defendant | Purchase Date | No. of Shares | Total Price Paid | Sales Date |
|---|---|---|---|---|
| Ms. Ryno . . . . . . | June 30 | 100 | $ 2,625 | Aug. 10 |
| | July 1 | 1,900 | 50,450 | |
| | July 27 | 4,000 | 113,827 | |
| Mr. Harris . . . . . | July 1 | 3,100[a] | 88,200 | Aug. 4 |
| | July 27 | 10,000 | 284,068 | |
| Mr. Mathis . . . . | July 7 | 1,500 | 38,745 | Aug. 4, Aug. 11, Aug. 24 |
| | July 14 | 6,200 | 168,144 | |
| | July 15 | 3,800 | 103,094 | |
| | July 21 | 5,000 | 130,788 | |
| | July 27 | 2,000 | 56,800 | |
| | July 30 | 2,300 | 65,895 | |
| | Aug. 2 | 10,000 | 300,075 | |
| Ms. Williams . . . . | July 28 | 2,000 | 57,251 | Aug. 3 |
| Tippee A . . . . . | July 28 | 2,000 | 57,251 | Aug. 3 |
| Tippee B . . . . . | July 28 | 13,000 | 383,195 | Aug. 3 |
| | July 30 | 2,000 | 58,506 | |
| Other tippees . . . | July 28 and later | 31,000 | Various | Various |

*Note:* This exhibit describes a subset of the insider trades documented in Exhibit 2.

a. This block of 3,100 shares was purchased for the account of his father and stepmother.

# Part III

# Investment Decisions, Mergers, and Acquisitions

# Cost of Capital

# Communications Satellite Corporation

In January 1975, the Federal Communications Commission (FCC) concluded an 11-year investigation of the appropriate economic regulation of the Communications Satellite Corporation (Comsat). In the coming months, the commissioners would deliver a decision that would address the full range of regulatory issues. One of the most important of these was the determination of a fair rate of return on Comsat's capital. The company had requested a 12% rate of return for the period 1964–1974 and 15% thereafter. However, the FCC's trial staff[1] had recommended setting Comsat's allowable return at 7% for the years between 1964 and 1971 and at 8.33% for 1972 with annual increases to 9.42% by 1975 (Exhibit 1). If the FCC rejected Comsat's request for 1975 in favor of the staff's recommendation, the company's revenues in that year might be reduced by as much as 30%, its net operating income could decline by 45%, and earnings per share could drop by 35%.

## History and Role of Comsat

The Communications Satellite Act of 1962 (the Satellite Act) set forth a national policy mandating the establishment of a worldwide communications satellite system in cooperation with other nations. This act authorized the formation of a new

1. In the FCC proceeding, representatives of the Common Carrier Bureau's trial staff took the role of public advocate. To fulfill this role, they were segregated from the commission's decision-making personnel.

private company to represent the United States in the proposed satellite system. Comsat was incorporated on February 1, 1963, to fulfill this role. Under the Satellite Act it was charged with establishing "as expeditiously as practicable" a commercial communications satellite system as part of an improved global communications network. The act specifically required the inclusion of economically less-developed countries in the development of this system. Although Comsat was incorporated as a private company, it was obliged under the Satellite Act to offer its customers the benefits of the new communications technology in terms both of improved quality and of reduced charges.

Comsat, under the provisions of the Satellite Act and as a U.S. communications carrier, was subject to regulation by the FCC. Other elements of the government were also involved in Comsat's operations. The National Aeronautics and Space Administration (NASA) was authorized to assist Comsat with satellite launchings and other such technical activities. The assistance of the State Department was authorized to facilitate the negotiation and maintenance of international agreements necessary to implement a global system. The president of the United States was also given certain supervisory powers over Comsat.

In August 1964 the International Telecommunications Satellite Corporation (INTELSAT) was created as an international partnership for the purposes of owning and developing the global satellite system. Comsat was designated the manager of INTELSAT and was accordingly responsible for the research, design, development, construction, establishment, and operation of the space segment of the system. By 1972, INTELSAT's initial 18-nation membership had increased to more than 84. These nations owned both the satellites and their related ground-control facilities. Voting rights and ownership interests in the partnership were based on the proportion a nation's usage of the system bore to total usage. Although Comsat still held the largest ownership interest in INTELSAT, its share had declined from about 52% in 1972 to 40% in 1973 and was expected to drop even lower as other nations increased their use of the system.

## Establishment and Growth of the Worldwide Communications System

Comsat's founders had a number of important technological and business decisions to make. One of the most important was choosing a satellite technology from among several alternatives, each of which had different technological and economic characteristics. Comsat's selection of a geostationary (or synchronous orbit) satellite system was, to a large extent, responsible for its rapid and successful development. A synchronous satellite is placed in circular orbit in the plane of the earth's equator and revolves about the polar axis in the same direction and with the same period as the earth's rotation. Such a geostationary orbit satellite system requires fewer satellites than alternative lower-altitude, nongeostationary orbit systems.

In April 1965, Early Bird, the world's first commercial communications satellite, was launched from Cape Kennedy by a Comsat-NASA team. Commercial service was established in June 1965, two years ahead of schedule. Although

Early Bird's capacity was limited by comparison with later-generation satellites, it increased trans-Atlantic telephone capacity by nearly two thirds, and it was the only transmitter of live transoceanic television.

Early Bird (later designated INTELSAT I) was the first of four generations of Comsat communications satellites. In 1966 the INTELSAT II series was designed by Hughes Aircraft in order to provide the expanded communications services required by early Apollo missions and by commercial users. Three of the four INTELSAT II satellites launched achieved synchronous orbit—one over the Atlantic and two over the Pacific.

In 1966, TRW, Inc. began work for Comsat on the INTELSAT III series. These satellites, the first designed expressly for global service, provided five times the power of the previous generation. Although the program was delayed by TRW's inability to meet delivery dates, it was eventually successful in placing five of eight satellites launched (between September 1968 and February 1969) in regular commercial service.

In late 1968, Comsat contracted with Hughes to develop the INTELSAT IV series. These satellites were designed to provide five times the capacity of the third generation, hopefully sufficient to meet global requirements through 1975. INTELSAT IV provided great flexibility in permitting simultaneous use for different types of services. The reliability of the system was enhanced by increased on-board redundancy (reserve capacity to be used when problems developed in the system). Five INTELSAT IVs were successfully placed in orbit by August 1973, providing complete global coverage.

In September 1975 the first INTELSAT IV-A, a modified version of the fourth-generation series, was placed into orbit. These satellites had twice the capacity of the INTELSAT IV and were developed to meet traffic demands in the latter half of the 1970s.

Comsat's early operations were very successful. It had experienced fewer launch failures in its start-up years than anticipated, and most satellites had achieved their design lives. The company's ability to maintain service was excellent, with only a single instance of a satellite outage causing a revenue loss (for one month in 1969). Beginning in 1972, Comsat had at least one spare satellite over each ocean basin for the purpose of restoring traffic during an outage. In addition to its redundancy in space, Comsat always maintained spares on the ground.

The earth stations that were part of the communications satellite system had also been technologically improved. Seven of the 68 earth stations existing in 1974 were located in the United States. Over a span of less than a decade, these stations had evolved through four distinct generations. Each successive generation was characterized by lower unit costs, greater and more diverse capabilities, increased reliability, and simpler operation and maintenance. By 1975, Comsat was approaching full earth station redundancy.

By 1975, Comsat had established a reliable global satellite system that exceeded all expectations. Its network, accessible to even the most remote areas of the earth, provided much of the world's transoceanic telephone, facsimile, teletype, telex, and television communications.

## Commercial and Financial Performance

In 1964, Comsat's managers estimated the development costs for its satellite system to be between $190 and $230 million. They considered it impractical and undesirable to issue debt to meet these needs in view of the company's lack of mortgageable property, the absence of established earning power, and the unforeseeable risks of the satellite project. Therefore, they decided to fund the entire capital requirement with an equity offering. In June 1964, Comsat sold half of its $200 million initial stock offering to 163 U.S. communication carriers and the other half to the public through a syndicate of 385 underwriting firms. Priced at $20 per share, the issue was oversubscribed, with over 130,000 individuals and institutions eventually acquiring shares. The price quickly rose to $27 in hectic over-the-counter trading. Three months later, the stock was listed on the New York, Midwest, and Pacific Coast Stock Exchanges.[2] The net proceeds of the issue were invested in a portfolio of marketable securities, which was drawn down as needed over the following 10 years to finance the communications satellite program.

Comsat's operating revenue was generated by the leasing of satellite half-circuits, transmitting channels between U.S. earth stations and INTELSAT satellites. Comsat leased half the channel; the other half-circuit was the responsibility of a foreign entity. Although half-circuit leases accounted for only 20% of 1965 revenues, they had increased to over 90% of 1971 revenues. Income from investment in marketable securities provided the balance of Comsat's revenues.

Comsat's customers were U.S. communications carriers that provided international interconnecting facilities and leased service directly to their customers. Comsat provided these carriers with television, telephone, data, and message services. Although telephone service accounted for the greatest volume by far of traffic in Comsat's first decade, data transmission and television revenues were small but growing. The advantages of Comsat's mature global system included its low cost (due to economies of scale), flexibility, reliability, and high-quality transmission.

Although Comsat's network represented the only technology capable of transmitting color television signals, most of the other services it provided were also offered by other carriers. Comsat's system received a large portion of its business from these carriers during cable outages and periods of excessive demand. Thus, Comsat's customers were also its chief competitors. Such competition among international carriers was regulated by the FCC.

Comsat's managers believed that the high start-up costs and the low operating revenues that characterized the company's development period justified its charging higher rates than its competition.[3] Thus, it adopted a "market-oriented" (versus

---

2. Reflecting investor interest, the NYSE waived its stringent listing requirements concerning the duration of a firm's earnings history.

3. Rates had been reduced substantially for some services (e.g., television) that were thought to be demand-elastic. Rates had also been reduced somewhat to reflect lower costs due to technological advances and greater system use (i.e., economies of scale). For instance, a voice grade half-circuit for service from the United States to Europe cost $2,850 per month in 1972, down from $4,200 per month in 1965.

a cost-plus-profit) approach to pricing. Ignoring the fact that the costs of providing satellite transmission were not sensitive to transmitting distance, they added a premium to the rates charged for competing undersea cable services. In certain instances, the market bore this premium based on Comsat's superior service; in others (such as television), it was borne only as the result of Comsat's monopolistic position. In the FCC hearings, Comsat's witnesses admitted that they had set "the highest possible rate we felt our customers would accept."[4]

Comsat's financial growth during its formative years was dramatic (Exhibits 2, 3, and 4). From 1965 to 1974, its revenues had grown at a 40% annual rate. In its early years, earnings consisted primarily of interest earned on marketable securities. However, in the fourth quarter of 1967, Comsat realized its first net operating profit on satellite operations. Net income had increased almost tenfold, from $4.6 million in 1967 to $44.9 million in 1974. In October 1970, Comsat had declared its first quarterly dividend (12½ cents per share), and by 1973 dividends had been increased to $1 per share. However, Comsat's stock, which had traded as high as $84 in 1971 (Exhibit 5), was trading in the mid-30s early in 1975, reflecting investors' uncertainty about the outcome of the FCC investigation.

Comsat's pioneering efforts in communications technology represented the major commercial benefit of the U.S. space program. The company's financial performance had been as dramatic as the operating performance of the satellite system it managed. However, the pending FCC proceeding could have a far-reaching impact on its future.

## The FCC Proceeding

The FCC proceeding was initiated in 1965 when the commission tentatively approved Comsat's first rate request. In approving the request, the commission authorized an investigation to consider the economic regulation of Comsat. However, the commission did not initiate a full investigation immediately, because of the national policy, outlined in the Satellite Act, of "expeditiously" establishing the satellite system and because of Comsat's lack of operating history. After several years of proposals and rulings, formal hearings commenced in March 1972 and continued intermittently through the summer of 1974. A major issue to be settled in the hearings was the determination of Comsat's fair rate of return. The rate case proceeding concerned the regulation of Comsat since its formation. Although Comsat argued that retroactive reductions of rates were unwarranted, the commission claimed the general authority to order refunds. Even if refunds were not ordered, the determination of Comsat's cost of capital and its rate base for past years was considered important as precedent for future regulatory decisions. The FCC delineated its guiding principles in a decision concerning American Telephone and Telegraph Company (AT&T):[5]

---

4. FCC Docket 16070, FCC 75–1304, 38249 at 331. The trial staff argued that Comsat's rates were excessive. It took the position that the rates should be based on Comsat's costs.

5. American Telephone and Telegraph Company, 9 FCC 2d at 51–52.

Generally, the rate of return to be set should be sufficient to enable a utility to maintain its credit and cover the cost of capital already committed to the enterprise as well as to attract additional capital, as needed, in competitive money markets at reasonable costs. . . . *In its simplest terms, rate of return is a percentage expression of the cost of capital.* It is just as real a cost as that paid for labor, material, supplies, or any other item necessary for the conduct of business. A return which is too low could impair the ability of a utility to raise additional needed capital, thus imperiling the integrity of existing investment, with adverse effects on the quality of service. A return which is set too high results in charges to the ratepayer above the just and reasonable level. [Emphasis supplied.]

The legal standards for determining the fair rate of return were articulated in several landmark cases, among them the *Federal Power Commission* v. *Hope Natural Gas Company,* 320 U.S., 591 (1944). The court opined (at 603):

The fixing of "just and reasonable" rates involves a balancing of the investor and the consumer interests. Thus, we stated in the *Natural Pipeline Co.* case that "regulation does not insure that the business shall produce net revenues" . . . the investor interest has a legitimate concern with the financial integrity of the company whose rates are being regulated. From the investor or company point of view it is important that there be enough revenue not only for operating expenses but also for capital costs of the business. These include service on debt and dividends on stock. *By that standard the return to the equity owner should be commensurate with returns on investments in other enterprises having corresponding risks.* That return, moreover, should be sufficient to assure confidence in the financial integrity of the enterprise, so as to maintain its credit and to attract capital. [Emphasis supplied.]

## Evaluation of Comsat's Operating Risk

The *Hope* case emphasized the need to consider the returns of "enterprises having corresponding risks" in setting a company's fair rate of return. Consistent with this standard, several parties to the proceeding attempted to compare Comsat's risk with that of other regulated carriers. AT&T was chosen as a benchmark because of its prominent position in the telecommunications industry and its long regulatory history. The trial staff took the position that Comsat was no more risky (and probably somewhat less risky) than AT&T in 1964, and that by 1974, Comsat was certainly less risky. The staff asserted that in Comsat's earlier days, its operating risks had been minimized owing to its government mandate and assistance. Furthermore, the nature of its risks had been fully disclosed to investors in Comsat's prospectus. The staff claimed that by 1974, the company (which still enjoyed government support) was a mature enterprise facing technical and business risks similar to those confronting AT&T. It argued further that Comsat's shareholders bore less risk than did AT&T shareholders as a result of Comsat's much more conservative financial policies. Comsat argued that it was subject to unique risks, substantially greater than those of a large established firm providing a proven technology. It contended that the international telecommunications market which it served was fundamentally riskier than the domestic telecommunications market, AT&T's primary revenue base. It believed that this higher level of risk justified a higher return to its shareholders. Lengthy debates ensued over the evaluation of Comsat's specific operating and financial risks. The company presented evidence concerning significant technological, business, demand, competitive, regulatory, and political risks.

Comsat's witnesses asserted that the company's *technological risk* was substantial, utilizing as it did a new and relatively untried technology. Among the early uncertainties were the risk of launch failures and the risk that satellites' operating lives might be significantly shorter than anticipated. The trial staff took the position that Comsat exaggerated these risks. It argued that in hindsight, Comsat's overstatement of risk was obvious: the satellite network's orderly technological evolution and relatively trouble-free operation demonstrated that Comsat's fears were unfounded. It was further argued that "only risks which can be foreseen are entitled to consideration in the formulation of an appropriate risk premium."[6]

In examining the company's *business risk,* Comsat's witnesses noted that in 1964 the company had had no demonstrated earnings capability and no historical record of earnings. They stated that investors' consequent uncertainty as to the level and timing of future earnings and dividends had exerted upward pressure on Comsat's cost of capital. Trial staff witnesses rebutted this argument, claiming that Comsat's prospectus, the Satellite Act of 1962, and various investment analysts' reports had pre-empted significant investor uncertainty: these documents had made it clear that although there was no government guarantee, there was a very strong mandate to provide Comsat the opportunity to earn a fair return.

Although Comsat's witnesses conceded that *demand risk* had abated somewhat by 1972, they testified that "in 1964 Comsat [had] faced substantial risks related to the demand for international telecommunications services."[7] Dr. Eugene F. Brigham asserted that the company still encountered "a great deal of difficulty in forecasting demand because its customers are a few large public utilities and because there have been only a relatively few years of dynamic growth."[8] The company characterized the international telecommunications market as highly variable. Trial staff witnesses countered that the demand risk was negligible based on a high average historic rate of growth and the forecast for continued rapid growth: they presented evidence demonstrating that the annual rate of growth for overseas telephone message services (expected to be Comsat's major source of revenues in its early years) between 1964 and 1972 varied between 19% and 35%.[9] They believed that this record and the expected continuing rapid growth in demand nearly eliminated the demand risk of operating in the international telecommunications market. They believed that Comsat's demand risk was no greater than that faced by AT&T and other international carriers.

Comsat asserted that it had also faced significant *competitive risks* in 1964 in

---

6. FCC Docket 16070, FCC 75–1304, 38249, at 217.

7. Ibid., at 226.

8. Ibid., at 227.

9. FCC Docket 16070, Trial Staff Exhibit No. 170.

the form of planned and existing cable system, high-frequency radio facilities, and the possible emergence of regional or domestic satellite systems. Moreover, company witnesses noted that an unusual competitive threat existed in the fact that Comsat's principal customers were also its principal competitors (as owners of alternative communications facilities such as cables). The trial staff argued that Comsat had faced only nominal risks regarding market share in 1964 and that by 1972 it faced no appreciable risk. They contended that Comsat would clearly benefit from the strong national policy recommendation that the satellite system should share in the growing international telecommunications traffic. They cited many FCC rulings which manifested the Commission's desire to maintain a reasonable balance between cable and satellite circuits on international routes. In their opinion these decisions constituted strong assurance to Comsat of a reasonable market share.

Comsat's witnesses testified that the company faced substantial *regulatory uncertainty* because of the undefined nature of Comsat's prospective regulation. They felt this uncertainty was greater than that facing well-established regulated enterprises, and that this should be reflected by an upward adjustment in its authorized rate of return. Comsat supported this claim by introducing as evidence investment brokers' reports. The trial staff rebutted Comsat's claims by again falling back on the significance of the national policy mandate for a global satellite system: presumably such policy support precluded unfair regulation. The staff argued that allowing Comsat "an additional risk premium based on the speculation that the commission might not grant all the regulatory benefits a utility desires, constitutes a grant of those benefits in another form."[10] Furthermore, it was noted that the brokers' reports introduced suggested that the investment community believed that the regulatory agencies would not allow large, speculative rewards. Rather, they expected the FCC to regulate Comsat on a common carrier basis with a rate of return in the range of 8–10%.[11]

Comsat's witnesses also claimed that the company faced substantial *political or international risk* in that its commercial success depended heavily on the cooperation and the participation of foreign entities. The trial staff responded that such operating uncertainties were minimized by the assistance received from the State Department and by the ratification of various relevant international agreements.

## Evaluation of Comsat's Financial Risk

The trial staff took the offensive in the discussion of Comsat's financial risk. Throughout its history, Comsat, a public utility, had maintained a 100% equity capital structure. The staff claimed that this policy reflected a degree of financial security unparalleled in the field of telecommunications common carriage: AT&T's 1973 debt-to-capitalization ratio was about 50%; the average debt ratios of 87

---

10. FCC Docket 16070, FCC 75–1304, 38249, at 238.

11. FCC Docket 16070, Comsat's Exhibits 47B and 48.

telephone and 7 telegraph carriers were 49% and 40%, respectively;[12] and the average debt ratio for all utilities was 61%.[13] The staff asserted that since debt is less costly than equity, Comsat's capital structure was unreasonably conservative and as such, it adversely affected both ratepayers and stockholders. The staff cited precedents demonstrating that ratepayers should not be penalized by managerial conservatism and that debt may be imputed in the determination of fair rates. Thus, it recommended that the commission impute debt at 45% of total capital in the determination of Comsat's rate of return from 1972 to the present.[14] The staff contended that such a level of imputed debt would not create appreciable financial risk and therefore would not warrant an increase in Comsat's allowable cost of equity. In determining Comsat's cost of debt, the staff reasoned that the company's all-equity capital structure and its recent operating performance would allow it to sell debt at Aa or Aaa utility rates. Thus, the trial staff recommended imputing a 45% debt level at the Aa rate in computing Comsat's cost of capital.

Comsat's witnesses maintained that the firm could not have raised debt before 1972. It supported this by recalling its operating risks and by noting that in 1964 Comsat had had no security to offer creditors and no demonstrated earnings power. (The staff pointed out that Western Union International, operating without monopoly power or government backing, had raised large amounts of debt in its first few years of operation while competing with other international carriers.) After the 1964 equity issue, the firm's capital requirements had not been sufficiently large to require another issue of either debt or equity. However, Comsat's managers did agree that "in the long run it would be desirable . . . to include some debt in its capital structure. . . ."[15]

Another subject under discussion was the appropriate rate base to be used in determining a fair pricing structure for Comsat. Briefly, the FCC determines a firm's allowable revenues by multiplying its rate base (or revenue-producing plant) by the authorized rate of return and adding operating expenses to that product.[16]

---

12. From the FCC's 1974 compilation of *Statistics of Communications Common Carriers.*

13. FCC Docket 16070, testimony of E. F. Brigham.

14. The year 1972 was recognized as the date Comsat was considered a "mature" enterprise (i.e., had demonstrated operational success). Witnesses for the trial staff did not recommend imputing debt during Comsat's developmental stages (i.e., before 1972). They characterized not doing so as "generous."

15. FCC Docket 16070, Comsat's Summary of Reply and Brief.

16. Regulatory decisions interact to determine a firm's prices through the revenue requirements formula:

$$R = (R_B)\, r + E$$

where

$R$ = Total revenue (i.e., revenue requirement)
$R_B$ = Firm's rate base; its capital employed in rendering service
$r$ = Authorized or fair rate of return (i.e., cost of capital)
$E$ = Operating expenses (including taxes)

By setting $R_B$ and $r$, the regulators determine the firm's maximum allowable revenue (i.e., the revenue requirement). The firm must then set its prices accordingly.

In 1964, Comsat had decided to raise at the outset all capital necessary to establish the satellite system. This decision reflected the favorable stock market conditions at the time, the desire to minimize the substantial fixed transaction costs typical of equity issues, and the high degree of uncertainty associated with Comsat's early years. However, several fortuitous technical, political, and financial developments combined to reduce the capital investment required to establish the system.[17] Thus, Comsat had held a large portfolio of liquid assets for a longer period of time than anticipated. This portfolio had amounted to $193 million in 1964 (96% of total assets) but had been reduced to $35 million by 1974 (8.9% of total assets). Comsat argued that a portion of its portfolio of liquid assets should be included in the rate base. Comsat maintained that the rate base for 1964 and subsequent years should include (1) all funds that were ultimately used in establishing the satellite system and (2) all additional funds used as a contingency reserve against adversities. The company claimed that investors who had supplied these funds in 1964 were entitled to earn a full and fair return.

The trial staff's response cited the FCC's established practice of allowing a return on investors' capital only to the extent it was actually employed in rendering consumer service. The staff argued further that business interruption insurance and such alternative sources of capital as bank credit lines were available at reasonable costs to cover contingencies, making Comsat's large liquid holdings unnecessary. The trial staff believed that Comsat's sizable portfolio of cash and marketable securities was yet another example of its extreme fiscal conservatism. As a consumer advocate, it felt strongly that allowing liquid holdings as part of the rate base would unduly penalize ratepayers. The staff also noted that Comsat's large liquid portfolio reduced its financial risks. It believed that this fact should be reflected in a lower authorized rate of return. The Department of Defense, another party to the proceedings, suggested that if the FCC were to allow a return on Comsat's cash and marketable securities, it should be no more than that actually earned in the competitive investment marketplace.

## Evaluation of Comsat's Cost of Capital

The *Hope* standard for determining a fair rate of return implied that the appropriate return is actually that required (or expected) by a firm's investors. Thus, Comsat's cost of capital would be equivalent to its fair rate of return. Several expert witnesses applied various methodologies designed to determine the market's expected return.

Dr. Eugene F. Brigham, a Comsat witness, suggested a discounted cash flow (DCF) approach, which incorporated a dividend growth model. However, because of Comsat's short operating history, the difficulty in forecasting its cash flows,

---

17. For instance, when Comsat issued equity in 1964, it planned to initiate parallel development of both nongeostationary and synchronous satellites. This was not necessary, because of the advances in synchronous technology made by Hughes Aircraft and NASA in the successful SYNCOM program in the mid-1960s. Comsat's ability to exploit this technology reduced substantially both the cost and the time required to establish the global system.

and the fact that Comsat had only recently begun paying dividends (1970), Dr. Brigham was convinced that a direct application of the DCF method was not feasible. Therefore, he calculated the rates of return on common stock for a sample consisting of 602 industrial firms and 56 utilities listed on Standard and Poor's Compustat computer files. He found that the average return on his sample between 1946 and 1964 was 12.4%. He felt that "one could argue that investors might assume similar returns would be earned in the future on equity investments."[18] Dr. Brigham also cited a study (by Arthur Andersen and Company) of the equity returns authorized in four utility cases in 1964. The four cases had allowed equity returns of 9.26–11.7%. Because they were utilities, Dr. Brigham considered these firms as belonging to a "low-risk class." He relied on this "indirect" approach of using returns on other firms' equity as a "benchmark" for determining Comsat's cost of equity in 1964. Since he considered Comsat's risk roughly equivalent to that of the Compustat sample and higher than the utilities, his estimate of Comsat's cost of equity for 1964 was 12–14%.

Dr. Brigham estimated that Comsat's cost of equity in 1971 was between 11% and 13% with a midpoint of 12%. He felt that Comsat was less risky in 1971 than in 1964 but that this had been partly offset by the general increase in interest rates over this period. His estimate was based on another Arthur Andersen survey of rate cases in 1970, which showed that the authorized rate of return in 26 utility decisions was between 9.3% and 13.7% with an average of 11.1%.

Consistent with the testimony of Dr. Brigham and its other witnesses, Comsat asked for a 12% rate of return for the period 1964 to September 30, 1974, and 15% since October 1, 1974.

The trial staff agreed that there was insufficient company history to allow a direct DCF calculation. However, they criticized Dr. Brigham's results as not comparable with Comsat. They noted that his Compustat study included mostly industrial firms rather than utilities such as Comsat. Furthermore, Dr. Brigham's study did not reveal whether any of the sample firms were capitalized on a 100% equity basis as Comsat was. Since most firms have debt in their capital structures, the returns in the sample might contain premiums for risk attributable to leveraged capital structure. Thus, the staff argued that the sample firms were not "other enterprises having corresponding risks" as required by the *Hope* standard.

Furthermore, the staff felt that the holding period of 1946–1964 was too short, resulting in a long-term average equity return that was unjustifiably high. A witness testified that the average return on common equity from 1926 to 1970 was 9.3%.

Concerning Dr. Brigham's use of the four rate-case decisions in 1964, the staff argued that these firms were not relevant to Comsat's case because these firms were all highly leveraged. The staff questioned Dr. Brigham's belief that these utilities were "low risk" while Comsat, a public utility, was not. Furthermore, no evidence was presented to demonstrate that these results were representative of rate cases in 1964. Indeed, a fifth case was omitted from the study under the assumption that the authorized return, 4.6%, was a typographical error.

---

18. FCC Docket 16070, testimony of E. F. Brigham.

The same points were raised in objection to Dr. Brigham's study of authorized returns in 1970. Furthermore, his study did not state whether these authorized returns were the cost of equity or the overall cost of capital. In general, the staff's chief criticism of Dr. Brigham's studies was his assumption that Comsat was riskier than other utilities and should be compared with riskier industrial firms.

The trial staff's recommendation was based on the testimony of Dr. Willard T. Carleton. Dr. Carleton agreed with Dr. Brigham that Comsat's short operating history and the difficulty in projecting future earnings and dividends precluded the use of DCF formulas to determine investors' required return. His alternative methodology could be expressed by the relation:

$$k_E = R_F + \text{Risk premium}$$

where

$k_E$        = Cost of equity

$R_F$        = Return on the least-risk (or risk-free) security

Risk premium = Additional return investors require as compensation for bearing the business and financial risks of the firm's equity

Dr. Carleton used long-term U.S. government bond yields as the relevant least-risk rate. For example, to determine Comsat's cost of equity for 1964, Dr. Carlton added a risk premium of 2–4% to the U.S. Treasury bond interest rate in 1964 of 4%. Thus, his estimate for 1964 was 6–8% with a midpoint of 7%. The relatively small risk premium is consistent with the staff's position that Comsat's investors faced relatively little risk.

Based on Dr. Carleton's analysis, the trial staff computed Comsat's cost of capital, imputing a 45% debt ratio for the period 1972–1975. The resulting weighted average costs of capital, also Comsat's recommended fair return, were 7% for the period 1964–1971 and 8.33% for 1972 with increases to 9.42% for 1975. These recommendations were consistent with the trial staff's position that AT&T's cost of capital represented an appropriate benchmark for estimating Comsat's allowable return: using a dividend growth model Dr. Carleton estimated AT&T's 1964 cost of equity to be 8.1%. The staff's recommendations for other years were also consistent with its interpretation of Comsat's risk relative to that of AT&T.[19]

Following the presentation of the direct cases, Dr. Stewart C. Myers, a rebuttal witness for Comsat, testified in support of Comsat's request. He asserted that applying the methodology of modern portfolio theory would reveal the only direct evidence of the risk of Comsat's equity as perceived by investors in the market. Thus, Dr. Myers relied on the capital asset pricing model (CAPM) to make his

---

19. For instance, the staff's recommended 1972 cost of capital for Comsat was 8.33%. In a widely publicized rate-case decision announced in 1971, the FCC ruled that AT&T's authorized rate of return (i.e., its cost of capital) was 9.75%. In the same case, AT&T's cost of equity was set at 10.5%.

estimates of investors' required returns. This methodology involves the statistical estimation of a security's systematic, nondiversifiable (or market-related) risk as measured by its beta. The following formulation was used:

$$k_E = R_F + \beta(k_M - R_F)$$

where

$k_E$ = Cost of equity capital
$R_F$ = Return on the least-risk (or risk-free) security
$k_M$ = Cost of equity (or the expected return) for the market as a whole
$\beta$ = Beta of the firm's stock

Dr. Myers' study, conducted with Dr. Gerald A. Pogue, was not designed to yield a specific estimate of Comsat's cost of equity: it was intended both to determine whether Dr. Brigham's estimate of Comsat's cost of capital at 12% was too high and to determine whether Comsat's equity was riskier than that of AT&T. Dr. Myers also hoped that his work would shed some light on whether Comsat had become riskier over the period 1964–1972.

Dr. Myers estimated Comsat's beta at approximately 1.7 over the period 1964–1972, with only a 16% probability that the "true" beta was less than 1.4 (the standard error of the beta was .3). Drs. Myers and Pogue assumed an expected return on the market of 11.5% with a range of 10–13%. They arrived at several estimates of Comsat's cost of equity by varying their assumptions about market return and the risk-free (or least-risk) rate. Additional estimates were made to account for discrepancies that have been found in empirical tests of the model. All of Dr. Myers' estimates of Comsat's cost of equity ranged between 11.2% and 17.2% with a midpoint of 14%. (Exhibits 6 and 7 present the methodology for estimating the cost of equity using CAPM.)

Although Dr. Myers found Comsat's beta to be relatively stable over time, his evidence did reveal a gradual increase in this measure of risk between 1964 and 1973. Therefore, he argued that Comsat's risk as perceived by investors had been increasing rather than decreasing as the trial staff suggested. Dr. Myers suggested that this effect may have been caused by the decrease over time in Comsat's liquid holdings relative to plant investment.

In the 1971 AT&T rate case, Drs. Myers and Pogue (testifying for the trial staff) had prepared a study that estimated AT&T's beta at approximately .7 and its cost of equity at 10.5%. Based on his analyses, Dr. Myers stated that the odds that Comsat's risk as measured by beta was less than that of AT&T's were "miniscule." This was also true of Comsat's total risk (or total variability in return as measured by the standard deviation of return). Dr. Myers also compared Comsat's systematic and total risk to major firms in other industries (Exhibits 8 and 9). He found that Comsat's risk was more than twice that of electric utilities and natural gas pipelines and roughly the same as a typical major airline. Furthermore, of the 921 stocks in his sample of data, only 145 had estimated betas higher than Comsat's; only 184 had higher estimates of total risk (standard deviations).[20]

Dr. Myers concluded that "Comsat's cost of equity capital is at least as large as a typical industrial firm's and well in excess of AT&T's. Twelve percent (Dr. Brigham's estimate and Comsat's request) is a reasonable estimate of Comsat's cost of capital—if anything, it is conservative." He considered CAPM sufficiently valid to "warrant according independent significance to beta evidence. . . . If there were no other evidence . . . in this proceeding, I would not hesitate in recommending that the Commission rely on beta in determining relative risk."[21]

Dr. Myers acknowledged that CAPM ignores "unsystematic" reasons (those unrelated to the market) for observed stock price movement. However, if stock prices are determined by investors holding large portfolios, only systematic, market-related risk is relevant in determining a stock's risk premium. Dr. Carleton argued that the issue at hand was to determine a rate of return such that Comsat would be enabled to attract capital and maintain its financial integrity. He stated that the issue was not—as Dr. Myers contended it was—to determine the "extent to which Comsat's stock contributes to the risk of a diversified portfolio."[22]

## The Decision

In the spring of 1975 the FCC held the complete, 20,000-page record of the Comsat proceedings for evaluation. Its task was to act as a surrogate for market competition in prescribing Comsat's economic regulation under the Satellite Act of 1962. At issue were Comsat's appropriate rate base, its fair rate of return, and its price structure.

Perhaps the most important of these issues was that of determining Comsat's fair rate of return—its cost of capital. The decision reached would have a major impact on the thousands of shareholders who had invested in Comsat securities. It would also directly affect Comsat's customers, because the allowed return was an important variable in the company's pricing formula. Furthermore, the commissioners' ruling would inevitably influence Comsat's internal capital budgeting process: the cost of capital they set would represent the relevant hurdle rate to be applied to proposed new investments.

The commissioners' task was complicated by the need to consider Comsat's unique government mandate to supply a new and complex technology for commercial

---

20. Dr. Myers used the file of security returns compiled by the Center for Research in Security Prices at the University of Chicago. His version contained almost all stocks listed on the New York Stock Exchange.

21. FCC Docket 16070, testimony of S. C. Myers.

22. FCC Docket 16070, testimony of S. C. Myers. In the 1971 AT&T rate case, Dr. Myers' estimate of the cost of capital using CAPM was accepted, while other estimates were rejected. This was also true of beta estimates (by Dr. Robert Haugen and Dr. Howard Thompson) of the costs of capital of Armco Steel and Republic Steel in a landmark civil case, the Reserve Mining Case, involving Reserve Mining's dumping of wastes into Lake Superior.

use. Moreover, the tools ordinarily employed to measure empirically investors' required rate of return were of questionable value given Comsat's brief operating history. The role of the FCC, as stated in the *Hope* standard, was to consider all such factors in balancing investor and consumer interests, consistent with generally accepted judicial guidelines.

**EXHIBIT 1**
Proposed Fair Rates of Return, 1964–1975

|  | Comsat Proposal | FCC Proposal |
|---|---|---|
| 1964–1971 . . . . . . | 12% | 7.00% |
| 1972 . . . . . . . | 12 | 8.33 |
| 1973 . . . . . . . | 12 | 8.70 |
| 1974 . . . . . . . | 12 | 9.15 |
| 1975 . . . . . . . | 15 | 9.42 |

**EXHIBIT 2**
Balance Sheets, 1968 and 1972–1974 (millions of dollars)

|  | 1968 | 1972 | 1973 | 1974 |
|---|---|---|---|---|
| Cash . . . . . . . . . . . . . | $ .8 | $ .7 | $ 1.2 | $ .4 |
| Marketable securities . . . . . . . . . . | 133.3 | 94.3 | 129.9 | 49.7 |
| Accounts receivable . . . . . . . . | 11.5 | 14.4 | 14.9 | 30.6 |
| Accrued interest receivable . . . . . . . . | 1.9 | 1.1 | 3.0 | .6 |
| Other current assets . . . . . . . . . . | .8 | 1.8 | 1.0 | 3.4 |
| Current assets . . . . . . . . . . | 148.3 | 112.3 | 150.0 | 84.7 |
| Property, plant, and equipment |  |  |  |  |
| Satellites . . . . . . . . . . | 21.7 | 137.9 | 121.4 | 129.8 |
| Earth stations . . . . . . . . . | 24.6 | 47.5 | 41.8 | 41.9 |
| Headquarters and laboratory . . . . . . | 5.5 | 27.5 | 29.3 | 30.2 |
|  | 51.8 | 212.9 | 192.5 | 201.9 |
| Less: Accumulated depreciation . . . . . . . | 20.3 | 71.7 | 83.6 | 100.9 |
| Construction in progress . . . . . . . . | 47.1 | 35.7 | 99.5 | 206.5 |
| Satellite system development costs . . . . . . | 20.9 | 12.9 | 9.5 | 6.8 |
| Research and development costs . . . . . . | 3.6 | 20.6 | 21.7 | 21.0 |
| Net property, plant, and equipment . . . . . . | 103.1 | 210.4 | 239.6 | 335.3 |
| Investments, deferred charges, and other assets . . . . . . . . . . . | 1.8 | 6.5 | 6.0 | 10.2 |
| Total assets . . . . . . . . . . | $253.2 | $329.2 | $395.6 | $430.2 |
| Accounts payable and accrued liabilities . . . . | $ 17.1 | $ 14.0 | $ 36.0 | $ 36.5 |
| Income taxes payable . . . . . . . . . . | – | 2.0 | 14.8 | 9.1 |
| Current liabilities . . . . . . . . . . | 17.1 | 16.0 | 50.8 | 45.6 |
| Deferred taxes and investment credit . . . . . | 18.1 | 34.8 | 36.3 | 40.2 |
| Common stock . . . . . . . . . . | 195.2 | 195.2 | 195.2 | 195.2 |
| Retained earnings . . . . . . . . . . | 22.8 | 83.2 | 113.3 | 149.2 |
| Net worth. . . . . . . . . . . . | 218.0 | 278.4 | 308.5 | 344.4 |
| Total liabilities and net worth . . . . . . . . | $253.2 | $329.2 | $395.6 | $430.2 |

**EXHIBIT 3**
Income Statements, 1968 and 1972–1974 (millions of dollars)

|  | 1968 | 1972 | 1973 | 1974 |
|---|---|---|---|---|
| Operating revenues | $30.5 | $105.9 | $119.3 | $133.5 |
| Operating expenses |  |  |  |  |
|    Operations and maintenance | 18.8 | 30.5 | 28.5 | 29.9 |
|    Depreciation | 7.2 | 24.7 | 22.8 | 20.0 |
|    Amortization | 2.3 | 7.3 | 8.5 | 9.9 |
| Operating income | 2.2 | 43.4 | 59.5 | 73.7 |
| Interest income | 8.6 | 4.5 | 8.8 | 7.4 |
| Other income (expense) | 1.7 | (.3) | 2.1 | 5.1 |
| Income before taxes | 12.5 | 47.6 | 70.4 | 86.2 |
| Income taxes |  |  |  |  |
|    On operating income | 1.2 | 22.0 | 30.1 | 37.4 |
|    On net other income | 4.5 | .6 | 4.0 | 3.9 |
|  | 5.7 | 22.6 | 34.1 | 41.3 |
| Net income | 6.8 | 25.0 | 36.3 | 44.9 |
| Dividends | – | 5.5 | 6.2 | 9.0 |
| Retained earnings | $ 6.8 | $ 19.5 | $ 30.1 | $ 35.9 |

**EXHIBIT 4**
Operating and Financial Performance, 1967–1974 (millions of dollars except per share data)

| | 1967 | 1968 | 1969 | 1970 | 1971 | 1972 | 1973 | 1974 |
|---|---|---|---|---|---|---|---|---|
| Operating revenues | $ 18.5 | $ 30.5 | $ 47.0 | $ 69.6 | $ 88.4 | $105.9 | $119.3 | $133.5 |
| Net operating income (after tax) | (.6) | 1.0 | 1.8 | 10.5 | 16.4 | 21.4 | 29.4 | 36.3 |
| Interest income | 7.9 | 8.6 | 7.5 | 7.9 | 6.1 | 4.5 | 8.8 | 7.4 |
| Net income | 4.6 | 6.8 | 7.1 | 17.5 | 22.5 | 25.0 | 36.3 | 44.9 |
| Net operating income/average equity | — | .5% | .8% | 4.5% | 6.6% | 8.0% | 10.0% | 11.1% |
| Net income/average equity | 2.2% | 3.2% | 3.2% | 7.5% | 9.0% | 9.3% | 12.4% | 13.8% |
| Net property, plant, and equipment | $ 70.6 | $103.1 | $138.5 | $182.5 | $208.6 | $210.3 | $239.5 | $335.3 |
| Cash and marketable securities | 155.6 | 134.1 | 102.1 | 100.6 | 104.7 | 95.0 | 131.2 | 50.1 |
| Earnings per share | $ .46 | $ .68 | $ .71 | $ 1.75 | $ 2.25 | $ 2.50 | $ 3.63 | $ 4.49 |
| Dividends per share | — | — | — | .125 | .50 | .545 | .62 | .90 |
| Book value per share | 21.11 | 21.80 | 22.51 | 24.14 | 25.89 | 27.84 | 30.85 | 34.44 |
| No. of full-time leased half-circuits—Comsat | 717 | 951 | 1,433 | 2,139 | 2,537 | 2,971 | 3,583 | 3,942 |
| No. of full-time leased half-circuits—global | 1,050 | 1,525 | 2,984 | 4,388 | 5,834 | 7,527 | 9,837 | 10,969 |

**EXHIBIT 5**

Comparative Stock Market Data for Comsat and AT&T, 1967–1974

| | Comsat | | | AT&T[a] | | |
|---|---|---|---|---|---|---|
| | Price per Share | | Price-Earnings Ratio | Price per Share | | Price-Earnings Ratio |
| | High | Low | | High | Low | |
| 1967 . . . . . . . . . | $77⅞ | $41⅛ | 129.3 | $62 | $49 | 15 |
| 1968 . . . . . . . . . | 64¾ | 41½ | 78.1 | 58 | 48 | 14 |
| 1969 . . . . . . . . . | 60⅞ | 41¾ | 72.3 | 58 | 48 | 13 |
| 1970 . . . . . . . . . | 57¾ | 25 | 23.6 | 54 | 40 | 12 |
| 1971 . . . . . . . . . | 84½ | 49⅛ | 29.7 | 54 | 41 | 12 |
| 1972 . . . . . . . . . | 75⅜ | 52 | 25.5 | 54 | 41 | 11 |
| 1973 . . . . . . . . . | 64½ | 37⅛ | 14.0 | 55 | 45 | 10 |
| 1974 . . . . . . . . . | 40⅜ | 22¾ | 7.0 | 53 | 40 | 9 |

*Sources:* Comsat's annual reports and *The Wall Street Journal.*

a. Rounded figures.

**EXHIBIT 6**

Examples of Estimating Comsat's Cost of Equity Capital Using CAPM with Different Expected Market Returns

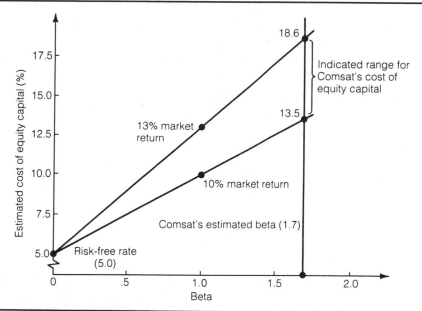

Security market line (SML): $k_E = R_F + \beta(k_M - R_F)$
  where   $R_F$ = Risk-free rate
          $\beta$  = Comsat's estimated beta
          $k_M = R_M$ = Expected return on the market as a whole
Assumptions: $R_F = .05$; $\beta = 1.7$
Comsat's estimated cost of equity capital:

| | |
|---|---|
| $k_M = .10$ . . . . . . . . . | $k_M = .13$ |
| $k_E = .05 + \beta(.05)$ . . . . . | $k_E = .05 + \beta(.08)$ |
| $= .05 + 1.7(.05)$ . . . . | $= .05 + 1.7(.08)$ |
| $= .135$ . . . . . . . | $= .186$ |
| $k_E = 13.5\%$ . . . . . . . | $k_E = 18.6\%$ |

**EXHIBIT 7**
Lower Bound Estimates of Comsat's Cost of Equity Capital Using CAPM

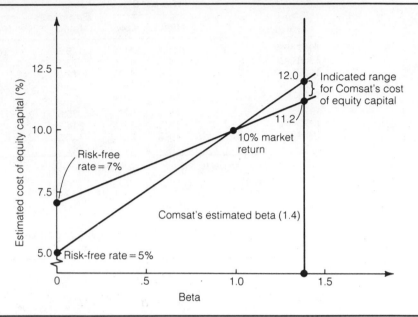

Security market line (SML): $k_E = R_F + \beta(k_M - R_F)$
Assumptions:
  $k_M = .10 =$ Low estimate of the return on the market
  $\beta \ \ = 1.4 =$ Low estimate of Comsat's beta
Comsat's estimated cost of equity capital:

| | |
|---|---|
| $R_F = .05$ . . . . . . . . . | $R_F = .07$ |
| $k_E = .05 + \beta(.05)$ . . . . . | $k_E = .07 + \beta(.03)$ |
| $\quad = .05 + 1.4(.05)$ . . . . | $\quad = .07 + 1.4(.03)$ |
| $\quad = .12$ . . . . . . . . . | $\quad = .112$ |
| $k_E = 12\%$ . . . . . . . . . | $k_E = 11.2\%$ |

**EXHIBIT 8**

Annual Market Returns on Selected Securities, 1967–1974

| | Comsat Common Stock | AT&T Common Stock | Moody's Industrials Common Stock Index | Baa Industrial Bonds | Aa Utility Bonds |
|---|---|---|---|---|---|
| 1967 . . . . . . . . | 17.51% | −.92% | 29.2% | 6.21% | 5.66% |
| 1968 . . . . . . . . | 9.60 | 8.28 | 8.7 | 6.90 | 6.35 |
| 1969 . . . . . . . . | 5.07 | −3.13 | −5.4 | 7.76 | 7.34 |
| 1970 . . . . . . . . | −12.06 | 4.00 | 3.0 | 9.00 | 8.52 |
| 1971 . . . . . . . . | 29.25 | −2.87 | 14.8 | 8.37 | 8.00 |
| 1972 . . . . . . . . | .65 | 25.03 | 19.7 | 7.99 | 7.60 |
| 1973 . . . . . . . . | −37.51 | −.71 | −14.3 | 8.07 | 7.72 |
| 1974 . . . . . . . . | −22.16 | −1.52 | −27.5 | 9.48 | 9.04 |
| Average . . . . . | −1.21 | 3.52 | 3.52 | 7.97 | 7.53 |

*Sources:* Comsat's annual reports; *The Wall Street Journal;* AT&T's annual reports; *Moody's Industrial Manual;* and *Moody's Public Utility Manual.*

**EXHIBIT 9**

Risk Measures for the Common Stock of Selected Firms and Industry Groups, October 1964–June 1970

| | | Systematic Risk | | Total Risk |
|---|---|---|---|---|
| Company | Time Period | Estimated Beta | Standard Error of Estimated Beta | Estimated Standard Deviations of Returns |
| Comsat . . . . . . . . | Oct. 1964–June 1970 | 1.69 | .30 | 11.2 |
| Comsat . . . . . . . . | Oct. 1964–July 1967 | 1.39 | .55 | 11.1 |
| Comsat . . . . . . . . | Aug. 1967–June 1970 | 1.79 | .34 | 10.9 |
| AT&T . . . . . . . . | Oct. 1967–June 1970 | .62 | .11 | 4.0 |
| AT&T . . . . . . . . | Oct. 1964–July 1967 | .54 | .18 | 3.7 |
| AT&T . . . . . . . . | Aug. 1967–June 1970 | .70 | .14 | 4.3 |
| Average of Moody's 24 utilities . . . . | Oct. 1964–June 1970 | .74 | | 5.3 |
| Average of 7 gas pipeline companies . . | Oct. 1964–June 1970 | .79 | | 6.4 |
| Average of 14 major grocery chains . . . | Oct. 1964–June 1970 | .83 | | 6.8 |
| Average of 33 major chemical companies . . | Oct. 1964–June 1970 | 1.19 | | 7.8 |
| Average of 20 major department stores . . | Oct. 1964–June 1970 | 1.36 | | 9.1 |
| Average of 21 office machine firms . . . . | Oct. 1964–June 1970 | 1.58 | | 11.5 |
| Average of 11 major airlines . . . | Oct. 1964–June 1970 | 1.69 | | 11.7 |

*Source:* FCC Docket 16070, Testimony of S. C. Meyers.

# Diversification, the Capital Asset Pricing Model, and the Cost of Equity Capital

## Risk as Variability in Return

The rate of return an investor receives from holding a stock for a given period of time is equal to the dividends received plus the capital gains in the period divided by the initial market value of the security:

$$R = \frac{\text{Dividends} + (\text{Ending price} - \text{Beginning price})}{\text{Beginning price}}$$

Alternatively, return can be viewed as the dividend yield plus the percentage capital appreciation:

$$R = \text{Dividend yield} + \text{Percentage capital appreciation}$$

Suppose an investor buys one common share of Du Pont for $100 on January 1. Over the year he or she receives $4 in dividends and sells the share for $108 on December 31. The return on this investment is 12%:

$$R_{\text{Du Pont}} = \frac{\$4 + (\$108 - \$100)}{\$100} = \frac{\$12}{\$100} = .12$$

or

$$R_{\text{Du Pont}} = 4\% \text{ dividend yield} + 8\% \text{ appreciation} = 12\%$$

If the ending price is $85, the return is $-11\%$.

The return on any security can be viewed as the cash the security holder

---

receives (including liquidation at the end of the period) divided by the initial investment. Investing in a savings account that offers a 5% interest rate results in an annual return of 5%:

$$R_{\text{Savings account}} = \frac{\$5 + (\$100 - \$100)}{\$100} = .05$$

There is an important difference, however, between investing in a savings account and investing in common stocks. The investor knows before committing

**FIGURE A**
Risk as Variability in Return

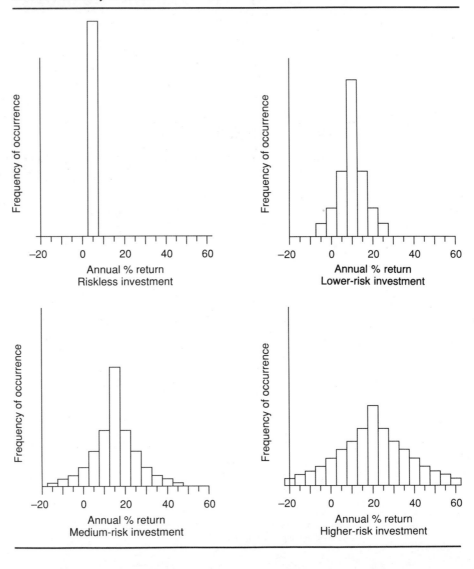

any funds that the savings account will earn a return of 5%. The actual return will not differ from the expected return of 5%. Thus, savings accounts are considered a safe or risk-free security.

On the other hand, an investor who expects a return of 12% on Du Pont's common shares may be disappointed or pleasantly surprised. The actual return on Du Pont may be less than or greater than 12%, since (1) Du Pont may change its dividend and, more important, (2) the market price at the end of the period may differ from the anticipated price. Actual returns on common stock vary widely from year to year. An investor committing funds at the beginning of any period cannot be confident of receiving the average or expected return.

In general, an investment with actual returns that are not likely to depart from the expected or average return is considered a low-risk investment. One with quite volatile returns from year to year is said to be risky. Thus, risk can be viewed as variability in return (see Figure A).

## Risk Reduction through Diversification

Risky stocks can be combined in such a way that the combination of securities, called a portfolio of securities, is less risky than any one of the component individual stocks. Consider the example outlined in Table A. Suppose we have two firms located on an isolated Caribbean island. The chief industry on the island is tourism. Company A manufactures and sells suntan lotion. Its sales, earnings, and cash

**TABLE A**
Example of Risk Reduction through Diversification

|  | Weather Conditions | Return on Stock $A = R_A$ |
|---|---|---|
| Company A: Suntan lotion manufacturer | Sunny year Normal year Rainy year | 33% 12 −9 |

|  | Weather Conditions | Return on Stock $B = R_B$ |
|---|---|---|
| Company B: Disposable umbrella manufacturer | Sunny year Normal year Rainy year | −9% 12 33 |

Returns on a Portfolio $(R_p)$ Consisting of 50% Invested in Stock A and 50% in Stock B: $R_p = .50 \ (R_A) + .50 \ (R_B)$

|  | Weather Conditions | Return on the Portfolio $= R_p$ |
|---|---|---|
| Portfolio containing A and B | Sunny year Normal year Rainy year | $.50 \ (33\%) + .50 \ (−9\%) = 12\%$ $.50 \ (12\%) + .50 \ (12\%) = 12\%$ $.50 \ (−9\%) + .50 \ (33\%) = 12\%$ |

flows are highest during sunny years. Thus, its stock does well in sunny years and poorly in rainy years. Company B manufactures and sells disposable umbrellas. Returns on its stock reflect its higher earnings in rainy years. In purchasing stock in either A or B, an investor is subject to considerable risk or variability in return. For instance, the investor's return on the stock of company B will vary from 33% to −9%, depending on weather conditions.

Suppose, however, that instead of buying only one security the investor puts half of his or her funds in stock A and half in stock B. The possible returns on this portfolio of securities are calculated in Table A. If a recession occurs, a $50 investment in stock A loses $4.50, while $50 invested in stock B returns $16.50. The total return on $100 invested in the portfolio is 12%:

$$\frac{-\$4.50 + \$16.50}{\$100}$$

Note that the return on this portfolio is 12% regardless of which weather condition prevails.

Combining these two risky securities yields a portfolio with a certain return. Since we are sure of earning 12% on the portfolio, it is a very low-risk investment comparable to a risk-free security such as a savings account. This example demonstrates risk reduction through diversification. By diversifying the investment over both firms, the investor creates a portfolio that is less risky than its two component stocks.

Total risk elimination is possible in this example because there is a perfect negative relation between the returns on stock A and B. In practice, such a perfect relation is very rare. Most firms' securities tend to move together, and therefore complete elimination of risk is not possible. However, as long as there is some lack of parallelism in the returns of securities, diversification will always reduce risk. Since companies' fortunes and therefore their stocks' returns do not move completely in parallel, investment in a diversified portfolio composed of many securities is less risky than investment in a few individual stocks.

## Systematic and Unsystematic Risk

Combining securities into portfolios reduces risk. When combined with other securities, a portion of a stock's variability in return is canceled by complementary variations in the returns of other securities. Some firms represented in the portfolio may experience unanticipated adverse conditions (e.g., a wildcat strike). However, this may well be offset by the unexpected good fortune of other firms in the portfolio. Nevertheless, since to some extent stock prices (and returns) tend to move in concert, not all variability can be eliminated through diversification. Even investors holding diversified portfolios are exposed to the risk inherent in the overall performance of the stock market (for instance, the stock market crash of October 1987). Thus, it is convenient to divide a security's total risk into that portion which is peculiar to a specific firm and can be diversified away (called

**FIGURE B**
Elimination of Unsystematic Risk through Diversification

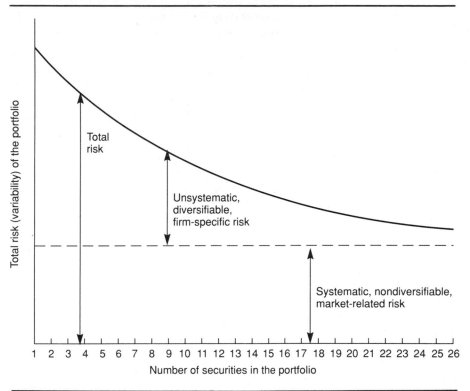

unsystematic risk) and that portion which is market-related and nondiversifiable (called systematic risk):

$$\text{Total risk} = \text{Unsystematic risk} + \text{Systematic risk}$$

Total risk = Unsystematic risk + Systematic risk
(diversifiable risk, (nondiversifiable risk,
firm-specific) market-related)

   Figure B illustrates the reduction of total risk as securities are added to a portfolio. Unsystematic risk is virtually eliminated in portfolios of 30 or 40 securities drawn from industries that are not closely related. Since the remaining, systematic risk is market-related, diversified portfolios tend to move in tandem with the market. The popular market indices (the Dow Jones Industrial Average, the S&P 500, and the New York Stock Exchange Index, for instance) are themselves diversified portfolios and tend to move in parallel. Thus, there is a close correspondence between swings in the returns of any diversified portfolio and in the returns on market indices such as the Dow. Examples of systematic and unsystematic risk factors are listed in Table B.

**TABLE B**
Systematic and Unsystematic Risk Factors

**Examples of Unsystematic Risk Factors**

A firm's technical wizard is killed in an auto accident.
A wildcat strike is declared.
A lower-cost foreign competitor unexpectedly enters a firm's product market.
Oil is discovered on a firm's property.

**Examples of Systematic Risk Factors**

Oil-producing countries institute a boycott.
Congress votes for a massive tax cut.
The Federal Reserve follows a restrictive monetary policy.
There is a precipitous rise in long-term interest rates.

## Risk, Return, and Market Equilibrium

Investors are risk-averse, and they must be compensated for taking risk. Thus, risky securities are priced by the market to yield a higher expected return than low-risk securities. This extra reward, called the risk premium, is necessary to induce risk-averse investors to hold risky securities. In a market dominated by risk-averse investors, there must be a positive relation between risk and expected return to achieve equilibrium. The expected return on a risk-free security (such as a Treasury bill) is the risk-free rate. The expected return on risky securities can be thought of as this risk-free rate plus a premium for risk:

$$R_S = R_F + \text{Risk premium}$$

The market's risk/return trade-off is illustrated in Figure C.

**FIGURE C**
Market's Risk/Expected Return Trade-Off in Equilibrium

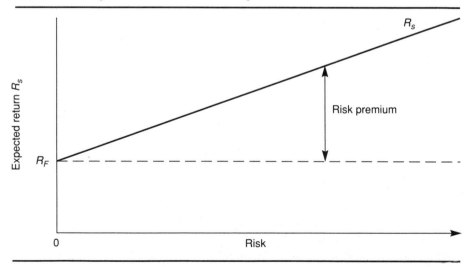

## The Capital Asset Pricing Model (CAPM)

The capital asset pricing model (CAPM) represents an idealized view of how the market prices securities and determines expected returns. It provides a measure of the risk premium and a method for estimating the market's risk/expected return curve.

In the CAPM, investors hold diversified portfolios to minimize risk. Since they hold portfolios consisting of many securities, events peculiar to specific firms (i.e., unsystematic risk) have a negligible impact on their overall return. Only a small fraction of an investor's funds are invested in each security. Furthermore, variations in returns from one security will, as likely as not, be canceled by complementary variations in the returns of other securities. Therefore, the only risk investors are sensitive to is systematic or market-related risk.

Since unsystematic risk can be eliminated simply by holding large portfolios, investors are not compensated for bearing unsystematic risk. Investors holding diversified portfolios are exposed only to systematic market-related risk. Therefore, the relevant risk in the market's risk/expected return trade-off is systematic risk, not total risk. The investor is rewarded with a higher expected return for bearing systematic, market-related risks. Only systematic risk is relevant in determining the premiums for bearing risk. Thus, the model predicts that a security's return is related to that portion of risk that cannot be eliminated by portfolio combination.

An individual investor who invests in only one stock is still exposed to both systematic and unsystematic risk. However, he or she is rewarded in terms of a higher expected return only for the systematic risk he or she bears. There is no reward for bearing unsystematic risk, since it can be eliminated by adequate diversification.

The CAPM provides a convenient measure of systematic risk. This measure, called beta ($\beta$), gauges the tendency of a security's return to move in parallel with the overall market's return (e.g., the return on the S&P 500). A stock with a beta of 1 tends to rise and fall the same percentage as the market (i.e., the S&P 500 index). Thus, $\beta = 1$ indicates an average level of systematic risk. Stocks with $\beta > 1$ tend to rise and fall by a greater percentage than the market. They have a high level of systematic risk and are very sensitive to market changes. Similarly, stocks with $\beta < 1$ have a low level of systematic risk and are less sensitive to market swings.

These results determine the risk/expected return trade-off under the CAPM. In general,

$$R_S = R_F + \text{Risk premium}$$

If the CAPM correctly describes market behavior,

$$R_S = R_F + \beta_S (R_M - R_F)$$

The expected return on a security $(R_S)$ is equal to the risk-free rate plus a risk premium. With the CAPM, the risk premium is $\beta$ multiplied by the return on the market $(R_M)$ minus the risk-free rate. Alternatively, the relation can be expressed in terms of the risk premium (i.e., the return over and above the risk-free rate):

$$R_S - R_F = \beta_S (R_M - R_F)$$

$$= \text{Risk premium for security } S$$

Thus, the risk premium on a stock (or portfolio or any security) varies directly with the level of systematic risk, $\beta$. This risk/expected return trade-off with the CAPM is called the security market line (SML) and is illustrated graphically in Figure D.

One perhaps counterintuitive aspect of the determination of expected returns with the CAPM can be illustrated with a simple example. Consider a firm engaged in oil exploration. The return (denoted $R_A$) to the shareholders in such a firm is very variable. If oil is found, the return is very high. If no oil is discovered, shareholders lose their entire investment and the return is negative. The stock's total risk level is very high. However, much of the variability in return is generated by factors independent of the returns on other stocks (i.e., the return on the market). This risk is unique to the firm and is therefore unsystematic risk. Since the stock's return is not closely related to the return on the market as a whole, it contributes little to the variability of a diversified portfolio. Its unsystematic risk can be diversified away by holding large portfolios. Nevertheless, the costs of exploration and the price of oil are related to the general level of economic activity. As a result, the stock does contain some systematic, market-related risk. Most of its total risk is unsystematic risk, however, associated with the chances of finding oil.

Although the firm's stock is very risky in terms of total risk, it has a low

**FIGURE D**
Security Market Line: The Risk/Expected Return Trade-Off with the CAPM

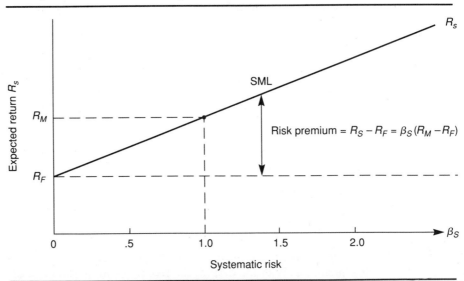

level of systematic risk. Its beta might be .8. The market will therefore price this stock to yield a relatively low expected return. From the viewpoint of investors holding large portfolios, it is a low-risk security. Its expected return is denoted $R_A$ in Figure E. Note that the return on this stock $(R_A)$ is less than the return on the average stock in the market $(R_M)$.

In contrast, consider a firm that manufactures computers. As a large stable firm, its total variability in return might be less than that of the oil exploration firm. However, its sales, earnings, and therefore stock returns are closely related to changes in overall economic activity. The return on its stock is very sensitive to changes in the return on the market as a whole. Therefore, its risk cannot be eliminated by diversification. When combined with other securities in a diversified portfolio, changes in its return tend to reinforce swings in the returns of the other securities. It has a relatively high level of systematic risk and a beta of perhaps 1.2. Viewed as an individual security, it appears less risky (in terms of total risk) than the oil exploration firm. Nevertheless, because of its high level of nondiversifiable risk, the market considers it the riskier security. Therefore, it is priced to yield a high expected return. Its return is labeled $R_B$ in Figure E. Such counterintuitive examples are rare, however. Most firms with high total risk also have high betas (and vice versa).

In summary, if the CAPM correctly describes market behavior, the relevant measure of a security's risk is its market-related or systematic risk (measured by beta). If a security's return has a strong positive relation with the return on the market (i.e., has a high beta), it will be priced to yield a high expected return (and vice versa). Since unsystematic risk can be easily eliminated through diversifica-

**FIGURE E**
Example of Determining Expected Returns with the CAPM

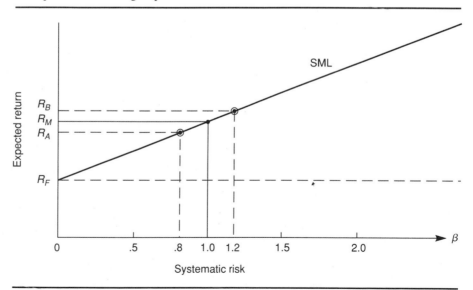

**TABLE C**
Summary of the Determination of Expected Returns with the CAPM

1. Total risk is defined as variability in return.
2. The investor can reduce risk by holding a diversified portfolio.
3. The total risk of a security can be divided into unsystematic and systematic risk.
    a. Risk that can be eliminated through diversification is called unsystematic risk. It is associated with events unique to the firm and independent of other firms.
    b. The risk remaining in a diversified portfolio is called systematic risk. It is associated with the movement of other securities and the market as a whole.
4. If the CAPM correctly describes market behavior, investors hold diversified portfolios to minimize risk.
5. Since investors hold diversified portfolios with the CAPM, they are exposed only to systematic risk. In such a market, investors are rewarded in terms of a higher expected return only for bearing systematic, market-related risk. There is no reward associated with unsystematic risk because it can be eliminated through diversification. Thus, relevant risk is systematic or market-related risk, and it is measured by beta.
6. The risk/expected return trade-off with the CAPM is called the security market line (SML). Securities are priced such that:

$$R_S = R_F + \text{Risk premium}, \quad \text{or} \quad R_S = R_F + \beta_S (R_M - R_F)$$

Thus, the SML gives us an estimate of the expected return on any security, $R_S$.

tion, it does not increase a security's expected return. The market cares only about systematic risk. These results are summarized in Table C.

## Application of the CAPM to Corporate Finance: Estimating the Cost of Equity Capital

The CAPM provides insight into the market's pricing of securities and the determination of expected returns. It has clear applications in investment management and in corporate finance. The cost of equity capital, $k_E$, is the expected (or required) return on a firm's common stock. The firm must be expected to earn $k_E$ on the equity-financed portion of investments to keep the price of its stock from falling. If the firm cannot expect to earn at least $k_E$, funds should be returned to the shareholders, who can earn $k_E$ on marketable securities of the same risk level. Since $k_E$ involves the market's expectations, it is difficult to measure. The CAPM can be used by financial managers to obtain an estimate of $k_E$.

The CAPM provides a conceptual framework for determining the expected return on common stocks, and it can be used to estimate firms' cost of capital. If the CAPM correctly describes market behavior, the market's expected return on a common stock is given by the security market line (SML):

$$R_S = R_F + \beta_S (R_M - R_F)$$

The expected return on a firm's stock is, by definition, its cost of equity capital. Therefore, in terms of cost of capital, the SML is

$$k_E = R_F + \beta_S (k_M - R_F)$$

where

$k_E = R_S$ = firm's cost of equity capital

$k_M = R_M$ = cost of equity for the market as a whole (or for an average firm in the market)

$\beta_S$ = beta of the firm's stock

Thus, to estimate $k_E$ we need estimates of $R_F$, the risk-free rate; $k_M = R_M$, the expected return on the market as a whole; and $\beta_S$, the level of systematic risk associated with the firm's stock.

$R_F$ can be estimated as the average or expected rate of return on Treasury bills in the future. In recent years, this rate has ranged between 5% and 10%. A reasonable estimate might be 9% per year.

The market risk premium is the difference between the return on the market, $k_M$, and the risk-free rate, $R_F$. The expected risk premium in the future is difficult to estimate. A common approach is to assume investors expect returns in the future to be about the same as returns in the past. The average annual market risk premium (equities versus Treasury bills) was 8.4% in the period 1926–1990.[1]

The stock's beta, $\beta_S$, can be estimated by linear regression.[2] Betas are also available from many brokerage firms and investment advisory services. Furthermore, one can get an intuitive estimate simply by observing the stock's reaction to swings in the market as a whole. Finally, a rough guess at beta can be made by noting the tendency of the firm's earnings and cash flows to move in parallel with the earnings and cash flows of other firms in the economy.

Betas for selected firms in four industries are presented in Table D. Despite relatively high degrees of operating and financial leverage, electric utilities have very stable earnings streams. Swings in the earnings and stock returns of utilities are modest relative to swings in the earnings and returns of most firms in the

**TABLE D**

Betas for Selected Firms in Four Industries

| Electric Utilities | | Airlines | | Computer Hardware | | Computer Software | |
|---|---|---|---|---|---|---|---|
| Company | β | Company | β | Company | β | Company | β |
| American Electric Power | .56 | AMR Corp. | 1.20 | Apple Comp. | 1.93 | Abode Systems | 2.11 |
| Baltimore Gas & Electric | .64 | Delta | .98 | Compaq | 1.25 | Aldus Corp. | 1.85 |
| Commonwealth Edison | .55 | Northwest | .91 | Digital Equip. | 1.22 | Ashton-Tate | 1.99 |
| Consolidated Edison | .60 | United | 1.18 | Hewlett-Packard | 1.31 | Borland International | 1.86 |
| Duke Power | .56 | USAir Group | 1.16 | IBM | 1.03 | Computer Assoc. | 1.35 |
| Niagara Mohawk | .61 | | | Tandy | 1.28 | Ingres Corp. | 1.49 |
| Ohio Edison | .53 | | | | | Lotus Development | 1.86 |
| Pacific Gas & Electric | .57 | | | | | Microsoft | 1.69 |
| Philadelphia Electric | .53 | | | | | Novell Inc. | 1.98 |

1. *Stocks, Bonds, Bills, and Inflation—1991 Yearbook: Market Results for 1926–1990* (Chicago: Ibbotson Associates, 1991).

2. The estimated regression equation is $R_S - R_F = \alpha + \beta_S (R_M - R_F) + e$. Given past values of $R_F$, $R_S$, and $R_M$, the regression yields estimates of alpha, $\alpha$ (which should be zero), and the stock's beta, $\beta_S$.

**TABLE E**
Examples of Estimating the Cost of Equity Capital Using the CAPM

| Assumptions | SML | | |
|---|---|---|---|
| $R_F = .09$ = risk-free rate | $k_E = R_F + \beta(k_M - R_F)$ | | |
| $R_M - R_F = .08$ | $= .09 + \beta(.08)$ | | |

| Commonwealth Edison | United Airlines | IBM | Lotus |
|---|---|---|---|
| $\beta_{Commonwealth} = .55$ | $\beta_{United} = 1.18$ | $\beta_{IBM} = 1.03$ | $\beta_{Lotus} = 1.86$ |
| $k_E \quad = .09 + .55(.08)$ $\quad = .13$ | $k_E \quad = .09 + 1.18(.08)$ $\quad = .18$ | $k_E \quad = .09 + 1.03(.08)$ $\quad = .17$ | $k_E \quad = .09 + 1.86(.08)$ $\quad = .24$ |

economy. Therefore, electric utilities have a low level of systematic risk and low betas.

At the other extreme, airline revenues are closely tied to passenger miles, which are in turn very sensitive to changes in economic activity. This basic variability in revenues is amplified by high operating and financial leverage. The result is earnings and returns that show wide variations relative to swings in the earnings and returns of most firms. Thus, airlines have high betas.

Estimates of the cost of equity capital for four firms are presented in Table E. Plugging the assumed values of $R_F$, $k_M$, and $\beta$ into the SML generates estimates of $k_E$. As expected, the low-risk utility has an estimated cost of equity below that of the other three firms.

The assumed value of $k_M$ represents a major potential source of error in these estimates. High and low estimates of $k_M$ can be used to generate a reasonable range of estimates of $k_E$. The estimation of $\beta$ also introduces error into the estimate of $k_E$.

## The CAPM and Risk-Adjusted Discount Rates

The CAPM provides a conceptual framework for determining the $k_E$ appropriate for a subsidiary's capital budgeting decisions. Assume that the holding company described in Figure F has no debt outstanding. The parent company owns all the equity in its subsidiaries, and the holding company's stock is publicly traded.[3] Such a firm can be viewed as a portfolio of assets. Its stock's beta is a weighted average of the betas associated with the riskiness of each subsidiary industry. Suppose that the parent company's beta is 1. However, the appropriate cost of equity capital for capital budgeting purposes is not the $k_E$ derived from the beta

---

3. The cost of equity is appropriate to evaluate capital investment only when the firm is all equity-financed. The note "Leveraged Betas and the Cost of Equity" explains how to estimate the cost of capital for firms that are financed with debt.

**FIGURE F**
Corporate Structure of a Holding Company with Three Subsidiaries

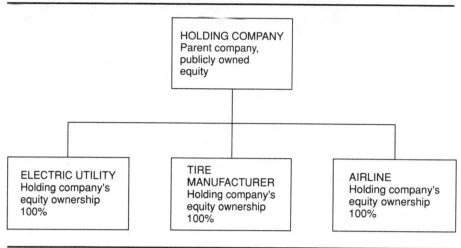

of the holding company's stock. The cost of equity capital used to evaluate investment proposals for a subsidiary should reflect the risk associated with the industry in which that subsidiary operates. Thus, while the holding company's beta of 1 yields a $k_E$ of 15%, investments in the utility subsidiary should be evaluated using a lower $k_E$, since the utility industry is less risky than the other subsidiary industries. Therefore, the market's expected (or required) return is lower for investments in the utility subsidiary. Since the airline industry is risky, a higher $k_E$ should be used in capital budgeting for an airline subsidiary.

Application of the firm's overall $k_E$ to the individual subsidiaries would result in poor decisions. Good projects in the utility subsidiary would be rejected while poor projects in the airline subsidiary would be accepted. When the cost of equity capital used in a subsidiary's capital budgeting decisions reflects the risk associated with that subsidiary's line of business, this ensures that project returns are measured against the returns shareholders would expect to receive on alternative investments of corresponding risk.

How can we estimate the beta appropriate for a subsidiary? An obvious approach is to use the beta on similar independent firms operating in the same industry. The resulting estimates of $k_E$ reflect the risk level of the industry and are therefore appropriate for investment decisions concerning a subsidiary operating in the same industry. If there are no independent firms in the industry, an intuitive estimate of beta can be made. This estimate would reflect the degree to which the subsidiary's earnings and cash flows tend to move in concert with other firms' earnings and cash flows.

## Conclusion and Caveats

The CAPM is widely applied in investment management and corporate financial management. Although some of the model's assumptions are clearly unrealistic, empirical tests demonstrate that there is a strong relation between returns and risk as measured by beta. However, the nature and stability of the relations predicted by the SML are not fully supported by these tests. Furthermore, application of the CAPM requires estimating $k_M - R_F$, the market risk premium, and $R_F$, the risk-free rate. The estimates of beta are also subject to error. Thus, the CAPM should not be relied upon as the sole answer to cost of capital determination.

Nevertheless, the model has much to say about the way returns are determined in the securities market. The cost of equity capital is inherently difficult to measure. The shortcomings of the CAPM appear less severe than those of alternative methods of estimating the cost of equity capital (for instance, the dividend growth model). Though imperfect, the CAPM represents an important approach to this difficult task. Using the CAPM in conjunction with more traditional approaches, corporate financial managers can develop realistic, useful estimates of the cost of equity capital.

# *Pioneer Petroleum Corporation*

One of the critical problems confronting management and the board of Pioneer Petroleum Corporation in July 1991 was the determination of a minimum acceptable rate of return on new capital investments. The company's basic capital budgeting approach was to accept all proposed investments with a positive net present value when discounted at the appropriate cost of capital. At issue was how the appropriate discount rate would be determined.

The company was weighing two alternative approaches for determining a minimum rate of return: (1) a single cutoff rate based on the company's overall weighted average cost of capital, and (2) a system of multiple cutoff rates that reflected the risk-profit characteristics of the several businesses or economic sectors in which the company's subsidiaries operated. The issue had assumed increased importance because of management's decision to extend the use of the cutoff rate to the evaluation of existing operations and investments. It was planned to evaluate divisional managers on the basis of their net profits after the deduction of a charge for capital employed by the division.

Pioneer Petroleum had been formed in 1924 through the merger of several formerly independent firms operating in the oil refining, pipeline transportation, and industrial chemicals fields. Over the next 60 years, the company integrated vertically into exploration and production of crude oil and marketing refined petroleum products, and horizontally into plastics, agricultural chemicals, and real estate development. It was restructured in 1985 as a hydrocarbons-based company, concentrating on oil, gas, coal, and petrochemicals. Pioneer was one of the primary producers of Alaskan crude, and in 1990, Alaska provided 60% of Pioneer's domestic petroleum liquids production. Pioneer was also one of the lowest-cost refiners on the West Coast and had an extensive West Coast marketing network. Pioneer's Alaskan crude production provided all the crude oil for its West Coast refining and marketing operations. This integration required collaboration and coordination among divisions to optimize overall performance and to decrease overall risk.

In 1990 total revenues exceeded $15.6 billion and net income was over $1.5 billion. (See Exhibit 1 for a financial summary of recent operations.) Volatile oil prices were a major concern for Pioneer. In 1990, for example, the price of West Texas Intermediate crude during the first quarter was $21.80 per barrel, and it reached a low of about $15.50 in mid-June. With the Iraqi invasion of Kuwait, crude prices rose to more than $40 per barrel, but they fell to about $25 per barrel as the year ended. The average price of West Texas Intermediate crude during 1990 was about $24.50 per barrel. The management of Pioneer emphasized the importance of operational and financial flexibility to respond to these price swings.

Pioneer spent about $3.1 billion on capital expenditures in 1990 and forecasted capital expenditures of almost $4.5 billion in 1991. Some of these expenditures, like the addition of a sulfur recovery facility and the improvement of a coker, allowed the refineries to more efficiently process the heavy Alaskan crude oil. These types of investments had provided good returns, and the light product yield in Pioneer's refineries was substantially higher than the industry average. Pioneer also invested in exploration and development, as it replaced all its 1990 production with new reserves. Most of this exploration was in the lower 48 states and the Gulf of Mexico. Investments were also directed to environmental projects, and Pioneer anticipated spending an additional $3 billion in the next 5 years to meet the new standards of the 1990 Clean Air Act amendments and the California Air Resources Board's regulations. These environmental regulations also provided opportunities for Pioneer to capitalize on its strengths. Pioneer's gasolines were among the cleanest-burning in the industry. And its chemical unit produced about one third of the world's supply of methyl tertiary butyl ether (MTBE), which was used to make cleaner-burning gasolines. The market for MTBE had been growing, and the new regulations were expected to lead to even higher growth. Also, Pioneer's SMOGMAN service centers specialized in state-required smog checks and related repairs.

## Weighted Average Cost of Capital

The company's weighted average cost of capital was calculated in three steps: first, the expected proportions of future funds sources were estimated; second, costs were assigned to each of these sources; third, a weighted average cost of capital was calculated on the basis of these proportions and costs (see Table A).

There was a general consensus in management on the mix of future funds sources. A firm policy had been adopted that funded debt should represent approximately 50% of total capital (defined as long-term debt plus book equity) to balance

**TABLE A**
1990 Weighted Average Cost of Capital Calculation

| Source | Estimated Proportion of Future Funds Sources | Estimated Future After-Tax Cost | Weighted Cost |
|--------|----------------------------------------------|---------------------------------|---------------|
| Debt | .50 | 7.9% | 4.0% |
| Equity | .50 | 10.0 | 5.0 |
|  |  |  | 9.0% |

the competing objectives of enhancing the returns to shareholders and maintaining financial flexibility. The company was committed to using its dividend and stock repurchase program to maintain appropriate financial leverage. Cash dividends increased by 10% in both 1990 and 1991. Its debt was A-rated.

Assigning an after-tax cost to debt was straightforward. Pioneer's investment bankers, Steven, Mitchell, O'Hara, forecasted early in 1990 that the company's future debt issues would require a coupon of 12%, assuming continuation of its debt policy and A rating. At a 34% tax rate, this represented a 7.9% after-tax cost.

The cost of equity had been more difficult to conceptualize or to estimate. After prolonged debate, Pioneer decided to use the current earnings yield on the stock as the cost of both new equity and retained earnings. Advocates pointed out that no dilution of earnings per share would occur if the company earned at least this return on new equity. With earnings per share estimated at $6.15 in 1990 and a market price of $63, cost of equity had been set at 10%.

## Divisional Costs of Capital

The alternative proposed by the supporters of multiple cutoff rates in lieu of a single companywide rate involved determining the cost of capital for each division. The divisional rate would reflect the risks inherent in each of the economic sectors or industries in which the company's principal operating subsidiaries worked. For example, the divisional cost of capital for production and exploration was 20%, and the divisional cost of capital for transportation was 10%. All the other divisional rates fell within this range. The suggestion was that these multiple cutoff rates determined the minimum acceptable rate of return on proposed capital investments in each of the main operating areas of the company and represented the rate charged to each of the various profit centers for capital employed. However, there were still areas of ambiguity. For example, it was unclear whether all environmental projects would have the same discount rate or the discount rate corresponding to the division.

The divisional cost of capital would be calculated using a weighted average cost of capital approach for each operating sector. The calculations would follow three steps: first, an estimate would be made of the usual debt and equity proportions of independently financed firms operating in each sector. Several such independents competed against each of the company's affiliates. Second, the costs of debt and equity given these proportions and sectors would be estimated in accordance with the concepts followed by the company in estimating its own cost of capital. Third, these costs and proportions would be combined to determine the weighted average cost of capital, or minimum acceptable rate of return, for net present value discounting purposes in each sector.

These multiple hurdle or discount rates had been calculated for several periods in the past, and it invariably turned out that their weighted average, when weighted according to the company's relative investment in each sector, exceeded the company's actual overall average cost of capital. The difference was attributed to the fact that the divisional cost of capital overlooked the risk diversification benefits of many investments undertaken by Pioneer Petroleum. As compared to nonintegrated enterprises operating in any given branch, a vertically and horizontally integrated firm such as Pioneer Petroleum enjoyed some built-in asset diversification and important captive markets between certain of its vertically integrated parts. For example, the risks associated with a refinery investment by an integrated company like Pioneer Petroleum were much less than for an identical investment made by an independent. It was proposed that this diversification premium be allocated back and deducted from the multiple subsidiary discount rates as calculated previously in proportion to the relation between the investment in each subsidiary and the company's total assets.

## The Management Discussion

As management and the board of Pioneer Petroleum began their latest review of the alternatives of using single or multiple minimum acceptable cutoff rates, the officers of the operating subsidiaries were asked to restate their positions.

Those supporting the use of a single target rate contended that the stockholders of Pioneer Petroleum expected the company to invest their funds in the highest return projects available. They suggested that without exception the affiliates backing multiple rates were those that were unable to compete effectively for new funds when measured against the corporate group's actual cost of capital. Furthermore, it was not obvious that the categories suggested by the advocates of multiple rates were very helpful in grouping projects according to their riskiness. For example, recent experience in tankers had been disastrous for many companies, and yet tanker investments would be initiated by the transportation division and would therefore be subjected to an unrealistically low hurdle rate.

The divisional costs of capital proponents argued that a single companywide cost of capital subsidized the higher-risk divisions at the expense of the lower-risk divisions. Because the cost of capital was too high for the low-risk divisions, too few low-risk investments were made. In the high-risk divisions too much investment occurred because the hurdle rate was too low. As evidence, proponents of multiple rates noted that Pioneer was the only major company that continued to invest heavily in exploration and development, and that it lagged behind its competitors in marketing and transportation investment. The proponents also argued that the companywide cost of capital was too low, and that investments should be required to earn at least as much as an investment in common stocks. The average return since 1980 on the S&P index of common stocks of 16.25% substantially exceeded the 9% companywide cost of capital (Exhibit 2). If Pioneer was serious about competing over the long run in industries with such disparate risk-profit characteristics, it was absolutely essential to relate internal target rates of return to the individual businesses.

**EXHIBIT 1**
Financial Summary, 1983–1990

|  | 1983 | 1984 | 1985 | 1986 | 1987 | 1988 | 1989 | 1990 |
|---|---|---|---|---|---|---|---|---|
| Sales ($ millions) | $20,397 | $20,268 | $18,594 | $12,687 | $14,182 | $15,259 | $13,417 | $15,646 |
| Net income ($ millions) | 1,133 | 326 | (297) | 428 | 923 | 1,211 | 1,542 | 1,555 |
| Earnings per share | $ 3.38 | $ 2.27 | $ .86 | $ 1.65 | $ 3.41 | $ 4.43 | $ 5.59 | $ 6.15 |
| Dividends per share | 1.75 | 1.50 | 1.20 | 2.00 | 2.00 | 2.00 | 2.20 | 2.45 |
| Return on book equity | 15.9% | 13% | 4.8% | 11.4% | 19.6% | 21.2% | 26.3% | 25% |
| Beta | | | | | | | | .8 |

**EXHIBIT 2**
Information on U.S. Capital Markets, 1980–1990

|  | 1980 | 1981 | 1982 | 1983 | 1984 | 1985 | 1986 | 1987 | 1988 | 1989 | 1990 |
|---|---|---|---|---|---|---|---|---|---|---|---|
| Yields on newly issued Aa industrials | 11.8% | 14.0% | 13.4% | 11.9% | 12.9% | 11.4% | 9.4% | 9.7% | 9.9% | 9.5% | 9.4% |
| Yields on 91-day T-bills | 11.2 | 14.7 | 10.5 | 8.8 | 9.9 | 7.7 | 6.2 | 5.5 | 6.4 | 3.4 | 7.8 |
| Realized returns on S&P 500 index of common stocks | 32.4 | −4.9 | 21.4 | 22.5 | 6.3 | 32.2 | 18.5 | 5.3 | 16.8 | 31.5 | −3.2 |

# Leveraged Betas and the Cost of Equity

A stock's expected return, its dividend yield plus expected price appreciation, is related to risk. Risk-averse investors must be compensated with higher expected returns for bearing risk. One source of risk is the financial risk incurred by shareholders in a firm that has debt in its capital structure. The objective of this note is to delineate a methodology for measuring the risk associated with financial leverage and estimating its impact on the cost of equity capital.

## Financial Leverage and Risk

The presence of debt in a firm's capital structure has an impact on the risk borne by its shareholders. In the absence of debt, shareholders are subjected only to basic business or operating risk. This business risk is determined by factors such as the volatility of a firm's sales and its level of operating leverage. As compensation for incurring business risk, investors require a premium in excess of the return they could earn on a riskless security such as a Treasury bill. Thus, in the absence of financial leverage, a stock's expected return can be thought of as the risk-free rate plus a premium for business risk.

The addition of debt to a firm's capital structure increases the risk borne by its shareholders. One source of additional risk is the increased risk of financial distress (e.g., bankruptcy). A second source is the effect of financial leverage on the volatility of shareholders' returns. The fixed obligations associated with debt amplify the variations in a firm's operating cash flows. The result is a more volatile stream of shareholders' returns. For investors to hold the shares of firms with debt in their capital structures, they must be compensated for the additional risk generated by financial leverage. The additional risk premium associated with the presence of debt in a firm's capital structure is the financial risk premium.

The expected return on a firm's stock is the risk-free rate plus a premium for risk:

$$\text{Expected return} = \text{Risk-free rate} + \text{Risk premium}$$

The risk premium consists of a premium for business risk and a premium for financial risk:

$$\text{Expected return} = \frac{\text{Risk-free}}{\text{rate}} + \frac{\text{Business risk}}{\text{premium}} + \frac{\text{Financial risk}}{\text{premium}}$$

This relation can be expressed in symbols:

$$R_S = R_F + BRP + FRP$$

Thus, the expected return on a firm's stock can be decomposed into three components. These components are (1) the return on a riskless security, $R_F$, (2) a premium reflecting the firm's basic business (or operating) risk in the absence of financial leverage, $BRP$, and (3) a premium for the additional risk created by the existence of debt in a firm's capital structure, $FRP$. This relation is illustrated graphically in Exhibit 1. The capital asset pricing model (CAPM) provides a methodology for measuring these risk premiums and estimating the impact of financial leverage on expected returns.

## The Effect of Financial Leverage on Beta

The CAPM is an idealized representation of the manner in which capital markets price securities and thereby determine expected returns.[1] Since the CAPM models the risk/expected return trade-off in the capital markets, it can be used to examine the impact of financial leverage on expected returns.

In the CAPM, systematic (or market-related) risk is the only risk relevant in the pricing of securities and the determination of expected returns. Systematic risk is measured by beta ($\beta$). The CAPM provides a measure of a stock's risk premium employing beta, which facilitates the estimation of the stock's expected return. In general,

$$R_S = R_F + \text{Risk premium}$$

If the CAPM correctly describes market behavior,

$$R_S = R_F + \beta(R_M - R_F)$$

---

1. For a more complete description of the CAPM, see the note "Diversification, the Capital Asset Pricing Model, and the Cost of Equity Capital."

A stock's expected return is equal to the risk-free rate, $R_F$, plus a premium for risk. With the CAPM the risk premium is beta times the expected return on the market, $R_M$, minus the risk-free rate. This basic CAPM expression is known as the security market line, the SML.

If a firm has no debt in its capital structure, the stock's risk premium consists solely of a business risk premium. The stock's beta therefore reflects the systematic risk inherent in the firm's basic business operations. With no financial leverage, this beta is the stock's unlevered beta, $\beta^U$. This unlevered beta is the beta the stock would have if the firm had no debt in its capital structure.

The presence of debt in a firm's capital structure results in additional risk. The systematic risk inherent in the firm's basic business operations is amplified by financial leverage. With financial leverage, the beta on a firm's stock reflects both business and financial risk. This beta is called a levered beta, $\beta^L$. Employing a levered beta in the CAPM expression, the SML measures both the business risk premium and the financial risk premium. The beta published by various investment advisory services reflects *both* the business and the financial risk experienced during the time period over which the beta was determined.

Under the assumptions of the CAPM there is a simple relation between levered and unlevered betas:

$$\beta^L = \beta^U(1 + D/E)$$

Alternatively,

$$\beta^U = \frac{\beta^L}{1 + D/E}$$

A stock's levered beta is equal to its unlevered beta multiplied by a factor that includes the firm's ratio of debt to equity, $D/E$. Therefore, a stock's beta (and its expected return) increases as its debt ratio increases. The increase in beta reflects the additional systematic risk generated by financial leverage. The resulting increase in expected return reflects the increase in the financial risk premium required by investors as compensation for additional risk.[2]

These results can be employed to estimate the impact on expected return of a change in a firm's capital structure. The approach is illustrated in Exhibit 2. Assuming the firm currently employs debt in its capital structure, its observed beta will be the levered beta associated with its current ratio of debt to equity. The beta the stock would have if the firm changed its debt ratio can be estimated by a two-step procedure. The first step involves unlevering the stock's beta. Given its current debt ratio, $D/E$, and its current beta, $\beta^L$, its unlevered beta, $\beta^U$, can be calculated from the foregoing equation. The second step consists of relevering

---

2. This relation is only valid when the firm's debt does not have any systematic risk. It would be inappropriate to use this approach when the firm has risky debt outstanding.

the stock's beta to reflect a change in capital structure. Given $\beta^U$ and the new hypothetical debt ratio, $D/E$, the other equation presented can be used to calculate the stock's new levered beta, $\beta^L$. This levered beta is an estimate of the beta the stock would have if the debt ratio changed to that employed in the second stage of the procedure. The resulting estimate of beta can then be plugged into the familiar CAPM expression presented earlier, the security market line, to estimate the stock's expected return associated with the proposed debt ratio.

An example of levering and unlevering beta and expected return is presented in Exhibit 3 for General Electric. A reduction in GE's ratio of debt to equity from approximately .33 to .11 would result in a decrease in its beta from 1.24 to 1.03. The reduction in financial risk would result in a reduction in the financial risk premium required by investors. Therefore, the estimated expected return on GE's stock falls from about 17% to roughly 15%. Similarly, an increase in GE's debt ratio would increase its beta and expected return.

## The Decomposition of Expected Return into the Risk-Free Rate, Business Risk Premium, and Financial Risk Premium

The CAPM can be employed to decompose a stock's expected return into its basic components. This can be accomplished by combining the equation relating levered and unlevered beta and the basic CAPM expression, the SML. The general and CAPM versions of this decomposition are

$$\text{Expected return} = \frac{\text{Risk-free}}{\text{rate}} + \frac{\text{Business risk}}{\text{premium}} + \frac{\text{Financial risk}}{\text{premium}}$$

$$R_S = R_F + \beta^U (R_M - R_F) + \beta^U (D/E)(R_M - R_F)$$

Alternatively,

$$R_S = R_F + \beta^U (R_M - R_F) + (\beta^L - \beta^U)(R_M - R_F)$$

Thus, the expected return on a stock can be decomposed into (1) the risk-free rate, (2) a business risk premium present with no debt in the firm's capital structure (i.e., $D/E = 0$), and (3) the additional risk premium created by the existence of debt in the capital structure. With no debt in a firm's capital structure, the expected return on its stock consists only of the first two components. The effects of financial leverage are captured entirely in the third component. With the CAPM this third component, the financial risk premium, is simply the increase in its beta, $\beta^L - \beta^U$, caused by financial leverage, multiplied by the risk premium on the market as a whole, $R_M - R_F$. Additional debt amplifies the systematic risk inherent in a firm's basic business operations and drives up the beta and expected return on its stock.

The example presented in Exhibit 4 demonstrates the use of these concepts to decompose the expected returns on two stocks, Procter & Gamble (P&G) and Colgate-Palmolive. Colgate's business (or operating) risk is substantially greater than Procter & Gamble's. Colgate's unlevered beta is .88 versus .72 for P&G, leading to a business risk premium of 7.04% for Colgate compared with 5.76% for P&G. Colgate's basic business risk is amplified by the higher level of debt in its capital structure, resulting in a financial risk premium which is roughly 1 percentage point more than P&G's. Thus, Colgate's overall risk premium, business risk premium plus financial risk premium, is substantially larger than P&G's. Consequently, Colgate's levered beta and the expected return on its stock reflect its higher level of business and financial risk relative to P&G.

An example of the decomposition of the expected return on GE's stock at different debt ratios is presented in Exhibit 5. Note that changing the firm's debt ratio affects only its financial risk premium. As expected, the financial risk premium, the levered beta, and the expected return on GE's stock all increase with additional financial leverage.

## Application to Corporate Finance

The CAPM facilitates the examination of the impact of financial leverage on expected returns. It therefore has an important application to corporate finance. A firm's cost of equity capital, $k_E$, is the expected (or required) return on the firm's stock. If the firm cannot expect to earn at least $k_E$ on the equity-financed portion of its investments, funds should be returned to its shareholders, who can earn $k_E$ on other securities of the same risk level in the financial marketplace. The CAPM can be used by financial managers to obtain an estimate of $k_E$ and to examine the impact on $k_E$ of financial leverage.

A firm's cost of equity capital is by definition the expected return on its stock. Since the basic CAPM expression, the security market line, yields estimates of expected returns, it can also be used to estimate costs of equity capital. Similarly, the CAPM concepts and techniques relating expected returns and financial leverage can be applied in examining the impact of financial leverage on the cost of equity capital. *The results presented earlier can be applied directly simply by recognizing that $R_S$, a stock's expected return, is equal to $k_E$, its cost of equity capital.*

To apply these concepts requires as inputs the risk-free rate, $R_F$, the expected return on the market as a whole, $R_M$, the stock's beta, and the ratio of debt to equity, $D/E$. As with any CAPM application, $R_F$ can be estimated as the return on Treasury bills or bonds and $R_M$ as the expected return on the Standard and Poor's Index of 500 Stocks. Betas can be estimated by linear regression and are also published by various investment advisory services. In estimating the debt ratio, the CAPM approach assumes that market values of debt and equity are employed. By definition, market values reflect the current values of debt and equity. In contrast, book values represent values prevailing in the past when the securities were issued. In addition, betas are themselves market-determined variables. Nevertheless, for convenience, book value debt ratios are often used in practice.

To examine the relation between the cost of equity capital and financial leverage, the estimated inputs are simply plugged into the equations presented earlier. The resulting expected returns are by definition costs of equity capital. The approach demonstrates that a firm's cost of equity is positively related to the level of debt in its capital structure, and the increment to the cost of equity generated by financial leverage can be estimated in the manner described earlier.

## Conclusion

The capital asset pricing model is based upon extremely simple and clearly unrealistic assumptions. Empirical studies demonstrate that, consistent with the CAPM, there is a strong relation between stock returns and risk as measured by beta. Studies also generally support the relation between returns and financial leverage posited by the CAPM. However, these studies are by no means conclusive in establishing the validity of the CAPM. The application of the CAPM is also limited by problems associated with the model's inputs. Use of the model requires ad hoc estimates of several inputs, and the betas employed are subject to substantial estimation errors.

Thus, the CAPM should not be viewed as a wholly reliable method of estimating the cost of equity and examining the impact of financial leverage. However, in view of the deficiencies in alternative approaches, the CAPM represents a useful tool that managers may apply to an inherently difficult area of corporate finance. Finally, an alternative approach relating expected returns and financial leverage is outlined briefly in the Appendix.

---

## Appendix

The CAPM methodology described in this note incorporates the implicit assumption that the firm's cost of debt is equal to the risk-free rate. An alternative approach that relaxes this restrictive assumption is presented in this Appendix. This more general approach examines the relation between the cost of equity capital and financial leverage. This relation expressed in cost of equity terms is

$$k_E^L = k_E^U + (k_E^U - k_D) \, D/E$$

where

$k_E^L$ = levered cost of equity capital
$k_E^U$ = unlevered cost of equity
$k_D$ = cost of debt
$D/E$ = ratio of debt to equity

In this equation $k_E^U$ is the cost of equity if the firm has no debt in its capital structure. Therefore, $k_E^U$ reflects the risk-free rate and a premium for business risk. The second term on the right-hand side of the equation captures the impact of financial leverage—the financial risk premium. With additional debt, the increase in the levered cost of equity is related to the difference between the unlevered cost of equity and the cost of debt. Solving for $k_E^U$, the equation becomes

$$k_E^U = \frac{k_E^L + k_D\,(D/E)}{1 + D/E}$$

Thus, given estimates of $k_E^L$, $k_D$, and $D/E$, the firm's unlevered cost of equity, $k_E^U$, can be calculated. The value of $k_D$ will change with the degree of leverage in the firm's capital structure. Thus, the schedule of debt cost versus leverage must be known to estimate a new equity capital cost at a new debt ratio. To estimate the levered cost of equity associated with some new debt ratio, $k_E^U$, the new $k_D$, and the proposed $D/E$ can be used as inputs in the previous equation.

This alternative approach can be employed in a manner analogous to that described previously. The equations can be manipulated to yield estimates of the cost of equity associated with various debt ratios and to decompose the cost of equity into its components. The advantage of this approach is that it is not tied exclusively to the assumptions of the CAPM. Specifically, it avoids the assumption that the firm's cost of debt is the risk-free rate. The advantage of the CAPM approach is the simple methodology it provides for levering and unlevering betas.

**EXHIBIT 1**
The Relation between a Firm's Financial Leverage and the Expected Return on Its Stock

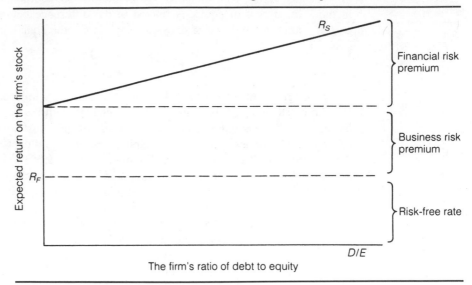

**EXHIBIT 2**
The Relation of Expected Return and Financial Leverage with the CAPM

Definitions:
  $R_S$ = stock's expected return
  $R_M$ = expected return on the market
  $D/E$ = firm's ratio of debt to equity
  $\beta^L$ = (levered) beta on the stock of a firm if $D/E > 0$
  $\beta^U$ = (unlevered) beta on the stock of the same firm if $D/E = 0$

CAPM equations:
  Security market line (SML): $R_S = R_F + \beta(R_M - R_F)$
  Levering beta: $\beta^L = \beta^U(1 + D/E)$

  Unlevering beta: $\beta^U = \dfrac{\beta^L}{1 + D/E}$

To estimate the impact of a change in capital structure:

  Step 1:   Estimate the unlevered beta.
              Given: current $D/E$ and current estimated $\beta^L$.

              Unlever the beta by solving: $\beta^U = \dfrac{\beta^L}{1 + D/E}$

  Step 2:   Estimate the levered beta associated with the new $D/E$.
              Given: $\beta^U$ from Step 1 and the new $D/E$.
              Lever the beta by solving: $\beta^L = \beta^U (1 + D/E)$

The estimated beta for the new debt ratio is then used in the SML equation to estimate the expected return associated with the new $D/E$.

**EXHIBIT 3**

Sample Analysis of the Impact on Expected Return of Financial Leverage with the CAPM, General Electric Company

---

Assumptions:

$R_M = 15\%$; $R_F = 7\%$

GE's current $D/E = .33$

Current $\beta^L_{GE} = 1.24$

Unlevering GE's beta:

$$\beta^U_{GE} = \frac{\beta^L_{GE}}{1 + D/E} = \frac{1.24}{1 + .33} = .93$$

CAPM:

|  |  |  |
|---|---|---|
| Equations: | Levering Beta | Security Market Line (SML) |
|  | $\beta^L_{GE} = \beta^U_{GE}(1 + D/E)$ | $R_S = R_F + \beta_{GE}(R_M - R_F)$ |
| Example: |  |  |
| Proposed $D/E = .00$ | $\beta^L_{GE} = .93(1 + 1.0) = 1.86$ | $R_S = 7\% + 1.86(15\% - 7\%) = 21.88\%$ |

Summary results:

| Debt Ratio | GE's Beta | GE's Expected Return, $R_S$ |
|---|---|---|
| Currently, $D/E = .33$ | 1.24 | 16.92% |
| Unlevered, $D/E = 0$ | 0.93 | 14.44% |
| Proposed, $D/E = .11$ | 1.03 | 15.24% |
| Proposed, $D/E = 1.00$ | 1.86 | 21.88% |

**EXHIBIT 4**
Sample Decomposition of Expected Return, Procter & Gamble Company and Colgate-Palmolive Company

|  | **Procter & Gamble** | **Colgate-Palmolive** |
|---|---|---|
| Unlevering betas: | | |
| Debt ratio . . . . . . . . . . . | $D/E = .25$ | $D/E = .34$ |
| Levered beta . . . . . . . . . | $\beta_{PG}^L = .90$ | $\beta_{CP}^L = 1.18$ |

$$\beta^U = \frac{\beta^L}{1 + D/E}$$

| | | |
|---|---|---|
| To unlever beta . . . . . . . . | | |
| Unlevered beta . . . . . . . . | $\beta_{PG}^U = .72$ | $\beta_{CP}^U = .88$ |

Expected return calculation and decomposition:
Assumptions: $R_M = 15\%$, $R_F = 7\%$
Definitions: $BRP$ = business risk premium, $FRP$ = financial risk premium

|  | **Procter & Gamble** | **Colgate-Palmolive** |
|---|---|---|
| Expected return decomposition: | $R_{PG} = R_F + \beta_{PG}^U(R_M - R_F) + (\beta_{PG}^L - \beta_{PG}^U)(R_M - R_F)$ | $R_{CP} = R_F + \beta_{CP}^U(R_M - R_F) + (\beta_{CP}^L - \beta_{CP}^U)(R_M - R_F)$ |
| Substituting assumed values: | $R_{PG} = 7\% + .72(15\% - 7\%) + (.90 - .72)(15\% - 7\%)$ | $R_{CP} = 7\% + .88(15\% - 7\%) + (1.18 - .88)(15\% - 7\%)$ |
| | $= 7\% + 5.76\% + 1.44\%$ | $= 7\% + 7.04\% + 2.40\%$ |
| Results: | $14.20\%$ | $16.44\%$ |
| | $R_{PG} = R_F + BRP_{PG} + FRP_{PG}$ | $R_{CP} = R_F + BRP_{CP} + FRP_{CP}$ |

**EXHIBIT 5**

Sample Decomposition of Expected Return at Various Debt Ratios,
General Electric Company

---

|  | *From Exhibit 3:* | |
| --- | --- | --- |
|  | **Debt Ratio** | **GE's Beta** |

Assumptions:

| $R_M = 15\%$ | Currently, $D/E = .33$ | $\beta_{GE}^L = 1.24$ |
| $R_F = 7\%$ | Unlevered, $D/E = 0$ | $\beta_{GE}^U = .93$ |
|  | Proposed, $D/E = .11$ | $\beta_{GE}^L = 1.03$ |
|  | Proposed, $D/E = 1.00$ | $\beta_{GE}^L = 1.86$ |

Expected return decomposition:

$$R_{GE} = R_F + BRP_{GE} \qquad\qquad + FRP_{GE}$$

$$R_{GE} = R_F + \beta_{GE}^U (R_M - R_F) \quad + (\beta_{GE}^L - \beta_{GE}^U)(R_M - R_F)$$

Example:
Proposed
$D/E = 1.00$

$$R_{GE} = 7\% + .93(15\% - 7\%) + (1.86 - .93)(15\% - 7\%)$$

$$21.88\% = 7\% + 7.44\% \qquad\qquad + 7.44\%$$

Summary results:

| **Debt Ratio** | $R_{GE} = R_F + BRP_{GE} + FRP_{GE}$ |
| --- | --- |
| Currently, $D/E = .33$ | $16.92\% = 7\% + 7.44\% + 2.48\%$ |
| Unlevered, $D/E = 0$ | $14.44\% = 7\% + 7.44\% + 0\%$ |
| Proposed, $D/E = .11$ | $15.24\% = 7\% + 7.44\% + .80\%$ |
| Proposed, $D/E = 1.00$ | $21.88\% = 7\% + 7.44\% + 7.44\%$ |

---

# Marriott Corporation: The Cost of Capital

In April 1988, Dan Cohrs, vice president of project finance at the Marriott Corporation, was preparing his annual recommendations for the hurdle rates at each of the firm's three divisions. Investment projects at Marriott were selected by discounting the appropriate cash flows by the appropriate hurdle rate for each division.

In 1987, Marriott's sales grew by 24% and its return on equity stood at 22%. Sales and earnings per share had doubled over the previous 4 years, and the operating strategy was aimed at continuing this trend. Marriott's 1987 annual report stated:

> We intend to remain a premier growth company. This means aggressively developing appropriate opportunities within our chosen lines of business—lodging, contract services, and related businesses. In each of these areas our goal is to be the preferred employer, the preferred provider, and the most profitable company.

Mr. Cohrs recognized that the divisional hurdle rates at Marriott would have a significant effect on the firm's financial and operating strategies. As a rule of thumb, increasing the hurdle rate by 1% (for example, from 12% to 12.12%), decreases the present value of project inflows by 1%. Because costs remained roughly fixed, these changes in the value of inflows translated into changes in the net present value of projects. Figure A shows the substantial effect of hurdle

**FIGURE A**
Typical Hotel Profit and Hurdle Rates

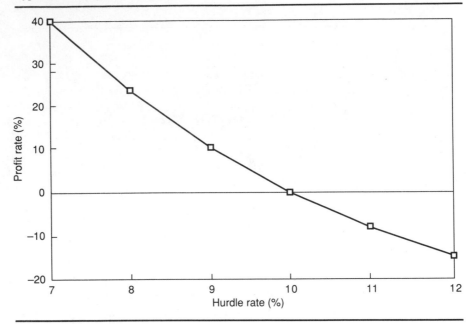

*Source:* Casewriter's estimates.

*Note:* Profit rate for a hotel is its net present value divided by its cost.

rates on the anticipated net present value of projects. If hurdle rates were to increase, Marriott's growth would be reduced as once profitable projects no longer met the hurdle rates. Alternatively, if hurdle rates decreased, Marriott's growth would accelerate.

Marriott also considered using the hurdle rates to determine incentive compensation. Annual incentive compensation constituted a significant portion of total compensation, ranging from 30% to 50% of base pay. Criteria for bonus awards depended on specific job responsibilities but often included the earnings level, the ability of managers to meet budgets, and overall corporate performance. There was some interest, however, in basing the incentive compensation, in part, on a comparison of the divisional return on net assets and the market-based divisional hurdle rate. The compensation plan would then reflect hurdle rates, making managers more sensitive to Marriott's financial strategy and capital market conditions.

## Company Background

Marriott Corporation began in 1927 with J. Willard Marriott's root beer stand. Over the next 60 years, the business grew into one of the leading lodging and food service companies in the United States. Marriott's 1987 profits were $223 million on sales of $6.5 billion. See Exhibit 1 for a summary of Marriott's financial history.

Marriott had three major lines of business: lodging, contract services, and restaurants. Exhibit 2 summarizes its line-of-business data. Lodging operations included 361 hotels, with more than 100,000 rooms in total. Hotels ranged from the full-service, high-quality Marriott hotels and suites to the moderately priced Fairfield Inn. Lodging generated 41% of 1987 sales and 51% of profits.

Contract services provided food and services management to health care and educational institutions and corporations. It also provided airline catering and airline services through its Marriott In-Flite Services and Host International operations. Contract services generated 46% of 1987 sales and 33% of profits.

Marriott's restaurants included Bob's Big Boy, Roy Rogers, and Hot Shoppes. Restaurants provided 13% of 1987 sales and 16% of profits.

## Financial Strategy

The four key elements of Marriott's financial strategy were the following:

- Manage rather than own hotel assets.
- Invest in projects that increase shareholder value.
- Optimize the use of debt in the capital structure.
- Repurchase undervalued shares.

### Manage Rather Than Own Hotel Assets

In 1987, Marriott developed more than $1 billion worth of hotel properties, making it one of the ten largest commercial real estate developers in the United States. With a fully integrated development process, Marriott identified markets, created development plans, designed projects, and evaluated potential profitability.

After development, the company sold the hotel assets to limited partners while retaining operating control as the general partner under a long-term management contract. Management fees typically equaled 3% of revenues plus 20% of the profits before depreciation and debt service. The 3% of revenues usually covered the overhead cost of managing the hotel. Marriott's 20% of profits before depreciation and debt service often required it to stand aside until investors earned a prespecified return. Marriott also guaranteed a portion of the partnership's debt. During 1987 three Marriott hotels and 70 Courtyard hotels were syndicated for $890 million. In total, the company operated about $7 billion worth of syndicated hotels.

### Invest in Projects That Increase Shareholder Value

The company used discounted cash flow techniques to evaluate potential investments. The hurdle rate assigned to a specific project was based on market interest rates, project risk, and estimates of risk premiums. Cash flow forecasts incorporated standard companywide assumptions that limited discretion in cash flow estimates and instilled some consistency across projects. As one Marriott executive put it,

> Our projects are like a lot of similar little boxes. This similarity disciplines the pro forma analysis. There are corporate macro data on inflation, margins, project lives, terminal values, percent of sales required to remodel, and so on. Projects are audited throughout their lives to check and update these standard pro forma template assumptions. Divisional managers still have discretion over unit-specific assumptions, but they must conform to the corporate templates.

### Optimize the Use of Debt in the Capital Structure

Marriott determined the amount of debt in its capital structure by focusing on its ability to service its debt. It used an interest coverage target instead of a target debt-to-equity ratio. In 1987, Marriott had about $2.5 billion of debt, 59% of its total capital.

### Repurchase Undervalued Shares

Marriott regularly calculated a "warranted equity value" for its common shares and was committed to repurchasing its stock whenever its market price fell substantially below that value. The warranted equity value was calculated by discounting the equity cash flows of the firm using the equity cost of capital for the company. It was checked by comparing Marriott's stock price with that of comparable companies using price-earnings ratios for each business and by valuing each business under alternative ownership structures, such as a leveraged buyout. Marriott had more confidence in its measure of warranted value than in the day-to-day market price of its stock. A gap between warranted value and market price, therefore, usually triggered repurchases instead of a revision in the warranted value by, for example, revising the hurdle rate. Furthermore, the company believed that repurchases of shares below warranted equity value were a better use of its cash flow and debt capacity than acquisitions or owning real estate. In 1987, Marriott repurchased 13.6 million shares of its common stock for $429 million.

## Cost of Capital

Marriott measured the opportunity cost of capital for investments of similar risk using the weighted average cost of capital (WACC):

$$\text{WACC} = (1 - \tau)\bar{r}_D(D/V) + \bar{r}_E(E/V)$$

where $D$ and $E$ are the market values of the debt and equity, respectively, $\bar{r}_D$ is the pre-tax cost of debt, $\bar{r}_E$ is the after-tax cost of equity, $V$ is the value of the firm ($V = D + E$), and $\tau$ is the corporate tax rate. Marriott used this approach to determine the cost of capital for the corporation as a whole and for each division.

To determine the opportunity cost of capital, Marriott required three inputs: debt capacity, debt cost, and equity cost consistent with the amount of debt. The cost of capital varied across the three divisions because all three of the cost-of-capital inputs could differ for each division. The cost of capital for each division was updated annually.

## Debt Capacity and the Cost of Debt

Marriott applied its coverage-based financing policy to each of its divisions. It also determined for each division the fraction of debt that should be floating-rate debt based on the sensitivity of the division's cash flows to interest rate changes. The interest rate on floating-rate debt changed as interest rates changed. If cash flows increased as the interest rate increased, using floating-rate debt expanded debt capacity.

In April 1988, Marriott's unsecured debt was A-rated. As a high-quality corporate risk, Marriott could expect to pay a spread above the current government bond rates. It based the debt cost for each division on an estimate of the division's debt cost as an independent company. The spread between the debt rate and the government bond rate varied by division because of differences in risk. Table A provides the market value–target leverage ratios, the fraction of the debt at floating rate, the fraction at fixed rate, and the credit spread for Marriott as a whole and for each division. The credit spread was the debt rate premium above the government rate required to induce investors to lend money to Marriott.

Because lodging assets, like hotels, had long useful lives, Marriott used the cost of long-term debt for its lodging cost-of-capital calculations. It used shorter-term debt as the cost of debt for its restaurant and contract services divisions because those assets had shorter useful lives.

Table B lists the interest rates on fixed-rate U.S. government securities in April 1988.

**TABLE A**
Market Value–Target Leverage Ratios and Credit Spreads for Marriott and Its Divisions

|  | Debt Percentage in Capital | Fraction of Debt at Floating | Fraction of Debt at Fixed | Debt Rate Premium above Government |
| --- | --- | --- | --- | --- |
| Marriott . . . . . . . . | 60% | 40% | 60% | 1.30% |
| Lodging . . . . . . . . | 74 | 50 | 50 | 1.10 |
| Contract services . . . . . | 40 | 40 | 60 | 1.40 |
| Restaurants . . . . . . . | 42 | 25 | 75 | 1.80 |

**TABLE B**
U.S. Government Interest Rates, April 1988

| | Maturity | Rate |
|---|---|---|
| 30-year | . . . . . . . . . . | 8.95% |
| 10-year | . . . . . . . . . . | 8.72 |
| 1-year | . . . . . . . . . . | 6.90 |

## Cost of Equity

Marriott recognized that meeting its financial strategy of embarking only on projects that increased shareholder value meant that it had to use its shareholders' measure of equity costs. Marriott used the Capital Asset Pricing Model (CAPM) to estimate the cost of equity. The CAPM, originally developed by John Lintner and William Sharpe in the early 1960s, had gained wide acceptance among financial professionals. According to the CAPM, the cost of equity or, equivalently, the expected return for equity was determined as

$$\text{Expected return} = R = \text{Risk-free rate} + \beta[\text{Risk premium}]$$

where the risk premium is the difference between the expected return on the market portfolio and the risk-free rate.

The key insight in the CAPM was that risk should be measured relative to a fully diversified portfolio of risky assets such as common stocks. The simple adage, don't put all your eggs in one basket, dictated that investors could minimize their risks by holding assets in fully diversified portfolios. An asset's risk was not measured as an individual risk. Instead, the asset's contribution to the risk of a fully diversified or market portfolio was what mattered. This risk, usually called systematic risk, was measured by the beta coefficient ($\beta$).

Betas could be calculated from historical data on common stock returns using simple linear regression analysis. Marriott's beta, calculated using daily stock returns during 1986 and 1987, was .97.

Two problems limited the use of the historical estimates of beta in calculating the hurdle rates for projects. First, corporations generally had multiple lines of business. A company's beta, therefore, was a weighted average of the betas of its different lines of business. Second, leverage affected beta. Adding debt to a firm increased its equity beta even if the riskiness of the firm's assets remained unchanged, because the safest cash flows went to the debt holders. As debt increased, the cash flows remaining for stockholders became more risky. The historical beta of a firm, therefore, had to be interpreted and adjusted before it could be used as a project's beta, unless the project had the same risk and the same leverage as the firm overall.

Exhibit 3 contains the beta, leverage, and other related information for Marriott and comparable companies in the lodging and restaurant businesses.

To select the appropriate risk premium to use in the hurdle rate calculations,

Mr. Cohrs examined a variety of data on the stock and bond markets. Exhibit 4 provides historical information on the holding-period returns on government and corporate bonds and the S&P 500 Composite Index of common stocks. Holding-period returns are the returns realized by the security holder, including any cash payment (e.g., dividends for common stocks, coupons for bonds) received by the holder plus any capital gain or loss on the security. As examples, the 5.23% holding-period return for the S&P 500 Composite Index of common stocks in 1987 is the sum of the dividend yield of 3.20% and the capital gain of 2.03%. The $-2.69\%$ holding-period return for the index of long-term U.S. government bonds in 1987 is the sum of the coupon yield of 7.96% and a capital gain of $-10.65\%$.[1]

Exhibit 5 provides statistics on the spread between the S&P 500 Composite returns and the holding-period returns on Treasury bills, U.S. government bonds, and high-grade, long-term corporate bonds.

Mr. Cohrs was concerned about the correct time interval to measure these averages, especially given the high returns and volatility of the bond markets shown in Exhibits 4 and 5. He was concerned also about which measure of expected returns should be used. Exhibits 4 and 5 present two different measures of average annual return, the arithmetic and the geometric. The arithmetic average return is the sum of the annual returns over the time period divided by the number of years in the time interval. The geometric average return is the compound average growth rate over the time interval. For example, if the return for a security were $-10\%$ in period 1 and 30% in period 2, the two averages would be

$$\text{Arithmetic average:} \quad (-10\% + 30\%)/2 = 10.0\%$$

$$\text{Geometric average:} \quad \sqrt{(.9)(1.3)} - 1 = 8.2\%$$

---

1. Cash payments are assumed to be invested in the respective securities monthly.

**EXHIBIT 1**
Financial History, 1978–1987 (millions of dollars except per share data)

| | 1978 | 1979 | 1980 | 1981 | 1982 | 1983 | 1984 | 1985 | 1986 | 1987 |
|---|---|---|---|---|---|---|---|---|---|---|
| *Summary of Operations* | | | | | | | | | | |
| Sales | $1,174.1 | $1,426.0 | $1,633.9 | $1,905.7 | $2,458.9 | $2,950.5 | $3,524.9 | $4,241.7 | $5,266.5 | $6,522.2 |
| Earnings before interest expense and income taxes | 107.1 | 133.5 | 150.3 | 173.3 | 205.5 | 247.9 | 297.7 | 371.3 | 420.5 | 489.4 |
| Interest expense | 23.7 | 27.8 | 46.8 | 52.0 | 71.8 | 62.8 | 61.6 | 75.6 | 60.3 | 90.5 |
| Income before income taxes | 83.5 | 105.6 | 103.5 | 121.3 | 133.7 | 185.1 | 236.1 | 295.7 | 360.2 | 398.9 |
| Income taxes | 35.4 | 43.8 | 40.6 | 45.2 | 50.2 | 76.7 | 100.8 | 128.3 | 168.5 | 175.9 |
| Income from continuing operations[a] | 48.1 | 61.8 | 62.9 | 76.1 | 83.5 | 108.4 | 135.3 | 167.4 | 191.7 | 223.0 |
| Net income | 54.3 | 71.0 | 72.0 | 86.1 | 94.3 | 115.2 | 139.8 | 167.4 | 191.7 | 223.0 |
| Funds from continuing operations[b] | 101.2 | 117.5 | 125.8 | 160.8 | 203.6 | 272.7 | 322.5 | 372.3 | 430.3 | 472.8 |
| *Capitalization and Returns* | | | | | | | | | | |
| Total assets | $1,000.3 | $1,080.4 | $1,214.3 | $1,454.9 | $2,062.6 | $2,501.4 | $2,904.7 | $3,663.8 | $4,579.3 | $5,370.5 |
| Total capital[c] | 826.9 | 891.9 | 977.7 | 1,167.5 | 1,634.5 | 2,007.5 | 2,330.7 | 2,861.4 | 3,561.8 | 4,247.8 |
| Long-term debt | 309.9 | 365.3 | 536.6 | 607.7 | 889.3 | 1,071.6 | 1,115.3 | 1,192.3 | 1,662.8 | 2,498.8 |
| Shareholders' equity | 418.7 | 413.5 | 311.5 | 421.7 | 516.0 | 628.2 | 675.6 | 848.5 | 991.0 | 810.8 |
| Long-term debt/ Total capital | 37.5% | 41.0% | 54.9% | 52.1% | 54.4% | 53.4% | 47.9% | 41.7% | 46.7% | 58.8% |

*Per Share and Other Data*

| Earnings per share | | | | | | | | | | |
|---|---|---|---|---|---|---|---|---|---|---|
| Continuing operations[a] | $ .25 | $ .34 | $ .45 | $ .57 | $ .61 | $ .78 | $ 1.00 | $ 1.24 | $ 1.40 | $ 1.67 |
| Net income | .29 | .39 | .52 | .64 | .69 | .83 | 1.04 | 1.24 | 1.40 | 1.67 |
| Cash dividends | .026 | .034 | .042 | .051 | .063 | .076 | .093 | .113 | .136 | .17 |
| Shareholders' equity | 2.28 | 2.58 | 2.49 | 3.22 | 3.89 | 4.67 | 5.25 | 6.48 | 7.59 | 6.82 |
| Market price (year-end) | 2.43 | 3.48 | 6.35 | 7.18 | 11.70 | 14.25 | 14.70 | 21.58 | 29.75 | 30.00 |
| Shares outstanding (millions) | 183.6 | 160.5 | 125.3 | 130.8 | 132.8 | 134.4 | 128.8 | 131.0 | 130.6 | 118.8 |
| Return on average shareholders' equity | 13.9% | 17.0% | 23.8% | 23.4% | 20.0% | 20.0% | 22.1% | 22.1% | 20.6% | 22.2% |

*Source:* Company reports.

a. The company's theme park operations were discontinued in 1984.

b. Funds provided from continuing operations consist of income from continuing operations plus depreciation, deferred income taxes, and other items not currently affecting working capital.

c. Total capital represents total assets less current liabilities.

**EXHIBIT 2**
Financial Summary by Business Segment, 1982–1987 (millions of dollars)

|  | 1982 | 1983 | 1984 | 1985 | 1986 | 1987 |
|---|---|---|---|---|---|---|
| *Lodging* | | | | | | |
| Sales | $1,091.7 | $1,320.5 | $1,640.8 | $1,898.4 | $2,233.1 | $2,673.3 |
| Operating profit | 132.6 | 139.7 | 161.2 | 185.8 | 215.7 | 263.9 |
| Identifiable assets | 909.7 | 1,264.6 | 1,786.3 | 2,108.9 | 2,236.7 | 2,777.4 |
| Depreciation | 22.7 | 27.4 | 31.3 | 32.4 | 37.1 | 43.9 |
| Capital expenditures | 371.5 | 377.2 | 366.4 | 808.3 | 966.6 | 1,241.9 |
| *Contract Services* | | | | | | |
| Sales | $ 819.8 | $ 950.6 | $1,111.3 | $1,586.3 | $2,236.1 | $2,969.0 |
| Operating profit | 51.0 | 71.1 | 86.8 | 118.6 | 154.9 | 170.6 |
| Identifiable assets | 373.3 | 391.6 | 403.9 | 624.4 | 1,070.2 | 1,237.7 |
| Depreciation | 22.9 | 26.1 | 28.9 | 40.2 | 61.1 | 75.3 |
| Capital expenditures | 127.7 | 43.8 | 55.6 | 125.9 | 448.7 | 112.7 |
| *Restaurants* | | | | | | |
| Sales | $ 547.4 | $ 679.4 | $ 707.0 | $ 757.0 | $ 797.3 | $ 879.9 |
| Operating profit | 48.5 | 63.8 | 79.7 | 78.2 | 79.1 | 82.4 |
| Identifiable assets | 452.2 | 483.0 | 496.7 | 582.6 | 562.3 | 567.6 |
| Depreciation | 25.1 | 31.8 | 35.5 | 34.8 | 38.1 | 42.1 |
| Capital expenditures | 199.6 | 65.0 | 72.3 | 128.4 | 64.0 | 79.6 |

*Source:* Company reports.

**EXHIBIT 3**

Information on Comparable Hotel and Restaurant Companies

| Company and Nature of Business | Arithmetic Average Return[a] | Geometric Average Return[a] | Equity Beta[b] | Market Leverage[c] | 1987 Revenues ($ billions) |
|---|---|---|---|---|---|
| Marriott Corporation (Owns, operates, manages hotels, restaurants, airline and institutional food services) | 10.57% | 10.01% | .97 | 41% | $6.52 |
| Hilton Hotels Corporation (Owns, manages, licenses hotels; operates casinos) | 17.16 | 14.54 | .88 | 14 | .77 |
| Holiday Corporation (Owns, manages, licenses hotels, restaurants; operates casinos) | 32.89 | 28.49 | 1.46 | 79 | 1.66 |
| La Quinta Motor Inns (Owns, operates, licenses motor inns) | −5.19 | −10.14 | .38 | 69 | .17 |
| Ramada Inns (Owns, operates hotels, restaurants) | 10.57 | −.01 | .95 | 65 | .75 |
| Church's Fried Chicken (Owns, franchises restaurants, gaming businesses) | 1.79 | −.64 | .75 | 4 | .39 |
| Collins Foods International (Operates Kentucky Fried Chicken franchise, moderately priced restaurants) | 24.32 | 19.69 | .60 | 10 | .57 |
| Frisch's Restaurants (Operates, franchises restaurants) | 45.83 | 51.66 | .13 | 6 | .14 |
| Luby's Cafeterias (Operates cafeterias) | 15.50 | 12.01 | .64 | 1 | .23 |
| McDonald's (Operates, franchises, services restaurants) | 23.93 | 22.72 | 1.00 | 23 | 4.89 |
| Wendy's International (Operates, franchises, services restaurants) | 7.76 | −.39 | 1.08 | 21 | 1.05 |

*Source:* Casewriter's estimates.

a. Calculated over period 1983–1987.

b. Estimated by ordinary least-squares regression using daily data over 1986–1987 period.

c. Book value of debt divided by the sum of the book value of debt plus the market value of equity.

**EXHIBIT 4**
Annual Holding-Period Returns for Selected Securities and Market Indexes, 1926–1987

|  | Arithmetic Average | Geometric Average | Standard Deviation |
|---|---|---|---|
| *Short-Term Treasury Bill Returns* | | | |
| 1926–1987 | 3.54% | 3.48% | .94% |
| 1926–1950 | 1.01 | 1.00 | .40 |
| 1951–1975 | 3.67 | 3.66 | .56 |
| 1976–1980 | 7.80 | 7.77 | .83 |
| 1981–1985 | 10.32 | 10.30 | .75 |
| 1986 | 6.16 | 6.16 | .19 |
| 1987 | 5.46 | 5.46 | .22 |
| *Long-Term U.S. Government Bond Returns* | | | |
| 1926–1987 | 4.58% | 4.27% | 7.58% |
| 1926–1950 | 4.14 | 4.04 | 4.17 |
| 1951–1975 | 2.39 | 2.22 | 6.45 |
| 1976–1980 | 1.95 | 1.69 | 11.15 |
| 1981–1985 | 17.85 | 16.82 | 14.26 |
| 1986 | 24.44 | 24.44 | 17.30 |
| 1987 | −2.69 | −2.69 | 10.28 |
| *Long-Term, High-Grade Corporate Bond Returns* | | | |
| 1926–1987 | 5.24% | 4.93% | 6.97% |
| 1926–1950 | 4.82 | 4.76 | 3.45 |
| 1951–1975 | 3.05 | 2.86 | 6.04 |
| 1976–1980 | 2.70 | 2.39 | 10.87 |
| 1981–1985 | 18.96 | 17.83 | 14.17 |
| 1986 | 19.85 | 19.85 | 8.19 |
| 1987 | −.27 | −.27 | 9.64 |
| *Standard and Poor's 500 Composite Stock Index Returns* | | | |
| 1926–1987 | 12.01% | 9.90% | 20.55% |
| 1926–1950 | 10.90 | 7.68 | 27.18 |
| 1951–1975 | 11.87 | 10.26 | 13.57 |
| 1976–1980 | 14.81 | 13.95 | 14.60 |
| 1981–1985 | 15.49 | 14.71 | 13.92 |
| 1986 | 18.47 | 18.47 | 17.94 |
| 1987 | 5.23 | 5.23 | 30.50 |

*Source:* Casewriter's estimates based on data from the University of Chicago's Center for Research in Security Prices.

**EXHIBIT 5**

Spreads Between S&P 500 Composite Returns and Bond Rates, 1926–1987

|  | Arithmetic Average | Geometric Average | Standard Deviation |
|---|---|---|---|
| *Spread Between S&P 500 Composite Returns and Short-Term Treasury Bill Returns* | | | |
| 1926–1987 . . . . . . . . . . . . . | 8.47% | 6.42% | 20.60% |
| 1926–1950 . . . . . . . . . . . . . | 9.89 | 6.68 | 27.18 |
| 1951–1975 . . . . . . . . . . . . . | 8.20 | 6.60 | 13.71 |
| 1976–1980 . . . . . . . . . . . . . | 7.01 | 6.18 | 14.60 |
| 1981–1985 . . . . . . . . . . . . . | 5.17 | 4.41 | 14.15 |
| 1986 . . . . . . . . . . . . . . . | 21.31 | 12.31 | 17.92 |
| 1987 . . . . . . . . . . . . . . . | −.23 | −.23 | 30.61 |
| *Spread Between S&P 500 Composite Returns and Long-Term U.S. Government Bond Returns* | | | |
| 1926–1987 . . . . . . . . . . . . . | 7.43% | 5.63% | 20.78% |
| 1926–1950 . . . . . . . . . . . . . | 6.76 | 3.64 | 26.94 |
| 1951–1975 . . . . . . . . . . . . . | 9.48 | 8.04 | 14.35 |
| 1976–1980 . . . . . . . . . . . . . | 12.86 | 12.26 | 15.58 |
| 1981–1985 . . . . . . . . . . . . . | −2.36 | −2.11 | 13.70 |
| 1986 . . . . . . . . . . . . . . . | −5.97 | −5.97 | 14.76 |
| 1987 . . . . . . . . . . . . . . . | 7.92 | 7.92 | 35.35 |
| *Spread Between S&P 500 Composite Returns and Long-Term, High-Grade Corporate Bond Returns* | | | |
| 1926–1987 . . . . . . . . . . . . . | 6.77% | 4.97% | 20.31% |
| 1926–1950 . . . . . . . . . . . . . | 6.08 | 2.92 | 26.70 |
| 1951–1975 . . . . . . . . . . . . . | 8.82 | 7.40 | 13.15 |
| 1976–1980 . . . . . . . . . . . . . | 12.11 | 11.56 | 15.84 |
| 1981–1985 . . . . . . . . . . . . . | −3.47 | −3.12 | 13.59 |
| 1986 . . . . . . . . . . . . . . . | −1.38 | −1.38 | 14.72 |
| 1987 . . . . . . . . . . . . . . . | 5.50 | 5.50 | 34.06 |

*Source:* Casewriter's estimates based on data from the University of Chicago's Center for Research in Security Prices.

# Investment Decisions

# Investment Analysis and Lockheed Tri Star

1. Rainbow Products is considering the purchase of a paint-mixing machine to reduce labor costs. The savings are expected to result in additional cash flows to Rainbow of $5,000 per year. The machine costs $35,000 and is expected to last for 15 years. Rainbow has determined that the cost of capital for such an investment is 12%.

    a. Compute the payback, the net present value (NPV), and the internal rate of return (IRR) for this machine. Assume that all cash flows (except the initial purchase) occur at the end of each year, and do not consider taxes.
*Should Rainbow purchase the machine?*

    b. For a $500-per-year additional expenditure, Rainbow can get a "good as new" service contract that essentially keeps the machine in new condition forever. Net of the cost of the service contract, the machine would then produce cash flows of $4,500 per year in perpetuity.
*Should Rainbow purchase the machine with the service contract?*

    c. Instead of the service contract, Rainbow engineers have proposed a plan to preserve and actually enhance the capability of the machine over time. By reinvesting 20% of the annual cost savings back into new machine parts, the

This case was prepared by Professor Michael E. Edleson.

Copyright © 1991 by the President and Fellows of Harvard College.
Harvard Business School case 291–031.

engineers can increase the cost savings at a 4% annual rate. For example, at the end of year 1, 20% of the $5,000 cost savings ($1,000) is reinvested in the machine; the net cash flow is thus $4,000. Next year, the cash flow from cost savings grows by 4%, to $5,200 gross or $4,160 net of the 20% investment. As long as the 20% reinvestment continues, the cash flows continue to grow at 4% in perpetuity. The formula for the present value ($V$) of an initial end-of-year perpetuity paying of $C (growing at $g$%) per period, with a discount rate of $k$%, is

$$V = \frac{C}{k - g}$$

when $k$ and $g$ are expressed as decimal fractions (e.g., .12 and .04).
*What should Rainbow do?*

2. Suppose you own a concession stand that sells hot dogs, peanuts, popcorn, and beer at a ball park. You have 3 years left on the contract with the ball park, and you do not expect it to be renewed. Long lines limit sales and profits. You have developed four different proposals to reduce the lines and increase profits:

- The first proposal is to renovate by adding another window.
- The second is to update the equipment at the existing windows.

These two renovation projects are not mutually exclusive: you could undertake both projects. The third and fourth proposals involve abandoning the existing stand.

- The third proposal is to build a new stand.
- The fourth proposal is to rent a larger stand. This option would require a $1,000 up-front investment for new signs and equipment installation; the incremental cash flows shown for later years are net of lease payments.

You have decided that a 15% discount rate is appropriate for this type of investment. The incremental cash flows associated with each of the proposals are as follows:

| | Investment | Year 1 | Year 2 | Year 3 |
|---|---|---|---|---|
| Add a new window . . . . . | −$75,000 | $44,000 | $44,000 | $44,000 |
| Update existing equipment . . | −50,000 | 23,000 | 23,000 | 23,000 |
| Build a new stand . . . . . | −125,000 | 70,000 | 70,000 | 70,000 |
| Rent a larger stand . . . . | −1,000 | 12,000 | 13,000 | 14,000 |

*Using the internal rate of return (IRR) rule, which proposal(s) do you recommend?*

*Using the net present value (NPV) rule, which proposal(s) do you recommend?*

*How do you explain any differences between the IRR and NPV rankings? Which rule is better?*

3. MBATech, Inc. is negotiating with the Mayor of Bean City to start a manufacturing plant in an abandoned building. The cash flows for MBAT's proposed plant are as follows:

| | |
|---|---|
| Year 0 . . . . . . . . . . | -$1,000,000 |
| Year 1 . . . . . . . . . | 371,739 |
| Year 2 . . . . . . . . . | 371,739 |
| Year 3 . . . . . . . . . | 371,739 |
| Year 4 . . . . . . . . . | 371,739 |

The city has agreed to subsidize MBAT. The form and timing of the subsidy has not been determined and depends on which investment criterion is used by MBAT. In preliminary discussions MBAT suggested four alternatives:

- Subsidize the project to bring its IRR to 25%.
- Subsidize the project to provide a 2-year payback.
- Subsidize the project to provide an NPV of $75,000 when cash flows are discounted at 20%.
- Subsidize the project to provide an accounting rate of return (ARR) of 40%. This is defined as

$$ARR = \frac{\text{Average annual cash flow} - (\text{Investment/No. of years})}{\text{Investment/2}}$$

You have been hired by Bean City to recommend a subsidy that minimizes the costs to the city. Subsidy payments need not occur right away: they may be scheduled in later years if appropriate.

*How much of a subsidy would you recommend for each year under each alternative?*

*Which of the four subsidy plans would you recommend to the city if the appropriate discount rate is 20%?*

4. You are the CEO of Valu-Added Industries, Inc. (VAI). Your firm has 10,000 shares of common stock outstanding, and the current price of the stock is $100 per share. There is no debt; thus the "market value" balance sheet of VAI is as follows:

Assets . . . $1,000,000    Equity . . . $1,000,000

You then discover an opportunity to invest in a new project that produces positive cash flows with a present value of $210,000. Your total initial costs for investing and developing this project are only $110,000. You will raise the necessary capital for this investment by issuing new equity. All potential purchasers of your common stock will be fully aware of the project's value and cost, and are willing to pay "fair value" for the new shares of VAI common.

*What is the net present value (NPV) of this project?*

*How many shares of common stock must be issued (at what price) to raise the required capital?*

*What is the effect of this new project on the value of the stock of the existing shareholders, if any?*

## Lockheed Tri Star and Capital Budgeting

In 1971 the American firm Lockheed found itself in congressional hearings seeking a $250 million federal guarantee to secure bank credit required for the completion of the L-1011 Tri Star program.[1] The L-1011 Tri Star Airbus is a wide-bodied commercial jet aircraft with a capacity of up to 400 passengers, competing with the DC-10 trijet and the A-300B airbus.

Lockheed management claimed that the Tri Star program was economically sound and that their problem was merely a liquidity crisis caused by some unrelated military contracts. Opposing the guarantee, other parties argued that the Tri Star program had been economically unsound and doomed to financial failure from the very beginning.

The debate over the viability of the program focused on estimated break-even sales—the number of jets that would need to be sold for total revenue to cover all accumulated costs. Lockheed's CEO, in his July 1971 testimony before Congress, asserted that this break-even point would be reached at sales of between 195 and 205 aircraft. At that time, Lockheed had only secured 103 firm orders, plus 75 options-to-buy, but management testified that sales would eventually exceed the break-even point and that the project would thus become "a commercially viable endeavor."

### Costs

The preproduction phases of the Tri Star project began at the end of 1967 and lasted 4 years, after running about six months behind schedule. Various estimates of the preproduction costs ranged between $800 million and $1 billion. A reasonable approximation of these cash outflows would be $900 million, occurring as shown in Table A.

According to Lockheed testimony, the production phase was to run from the end of 1971 to the end of 1977, with about 210 Tri Stars as the planned output. At that production rate the average production cost[2] would be about $14 million per aircraft. The inventory-intensive production costs would be relatively front-loaded, so that the $490 million ($14 million per plane, 35 planes per year) annual

---

1. Facts and situations concerning the Lockheed Tri Star program are taken from U. E. Reinhardt, "Break-Even Analysis for Lockheed's Tri Star: An Application of Financial Theory," *Journal of Finance* 27 (1972), pp. 821–838, and from House and Senate testimony.

2. Excluding preproduction cost allocations. That is, the $14 million cost figure is totally separate from the $900 million of preproduction costs shown in Table A.

**TABLE A**
Cash Flows

| Year-End | Time Index | Cash Flow ($ millions) |
|---|---|---|
| 1967 | $t = 0$ | −$100 |
| 1968 | $t = 1$ | −200 |
| 1969 | $t = 2$ | −200 |
| 1970 | $t = 3$ | −200 |
| 1971 | $t = 4$ | −200 |

production costs could be assumed to occur in six equal increments at the end of years 1971–1976 ($t = 4$ through $t = 9$).

## Revenues

In 1968 the expected price to be received from the L-1011 Tri Star was about $16 million per aircraft. Sales revenues would be booked roughly 1 year after production cost outflows. It was assumed that annual revenues of $560 million would be recognized at the end of each year from 1972 through 1977 (t = 5 through t = 10). Inflation-escalation clauses in the contracts ensured that any future inflation-based cost and revenue increases would virtually offset each other, thereby providing no incremental net cash flows.

Although revenue would not be booked until final delivery took place, Lockheed's customers would make initial cash deposits prior to the start of production. Roughly one quarter of the price of the aircraft was actually to be received 2 years prior to completion. For example, for a single Tri Star to be delivered at the end of 1972, $4 million of the $16 million selling price was to be received as a deposit at the end of 1970, leaving $12 million as cash flow expected at the end of 1972. So, for the 35 planes built (and presumably sold) in a year, $140 million of the $560 million in total annual revenue would actually be received by Lockheed as a cash inflow 2 years earlier.

## Discount Rate

Experts estimated that the cost of capital applicable to Lockheed's assets (prior to Tri Star) was in the 9–10% range. As the Tri Star project was quite a bit riskier (by any measure) than the typical Lockheed operation, the appropriate discount rate was almost certainly higher than that. Using 10% should give a reasonable (although possibly generous) estimate of the project's value.

## Break-Even Revisited

An August 1972 *Time* article reported that Lockheed (after receiving government loan guarantees) had revised its break-even sales volume: "[Lockheed] claims that it can get back its development costs [about $960 million] and start making a profit by selling 275 Tri Stars."[3] Industry analysts had predicted this (actually, they had estimated 300 units break-even volume) even prior to the congressional hearings.[4] Based on a "learning curve" effect, production costs at these levels would average only about $12.5 million per unit instead of $14 million. Had Lockheed been able to produce and sell as many as 500 aircraft, this average cost figure may have even been as low as $11 million per aircraft.

Lockheed had testified that it had originally hoped to capture 35–40% of the total free-world market of 775 wide bodies over the next decade (270–310 aircraft). This market estimate had been based on a highly optimistic assumption of 10% annual growth in air travel; at a more moderate 5% growth rate the total world market would have been only 323 aircraft. The Tri Star's actual sales performance never approached Lockheed's high expectations. Lockheed's share price plummeted from a high of about $70 to around $3 during this period. There were approximately 11.3 million shares of Lockheed common outstanding during this period. Exhibit 1 contains additional information on Lockheed's common stock.

## Value Added?

As concerns the economic viability of the Tri Star program, there are several interesting points to consider:[5]

*At planned production levels (210 units), what was the true value of the Tri Star program?*

*At a break-even production of roughly 300 units, would Lockheed really break even in value terms?*

*At what sales volume would the Tri Star program reach true economic (as opposed to accounting) break-even?*

*Was the decision to pursue the Tri Star program a reasonable one? What were the economic effects of this project on Lockheed shareholders?*

---

3. *Time,* August 21, 1972, p. 62.

4. Mitchell Gordon, "Hitched to the Tri Star—Disaster at Lockheed Would Cut a Wide Swathe," *Barron's,* March 15, 1971, pp. 5–14.

5. Ignore taxes and depreciation tax shields here. In cases near the break-even volume these would tend to offset each other nearly completely.

**EXHIBIT 1**
Monthly Prices of Lockheed Common Stock, January 1967–1974

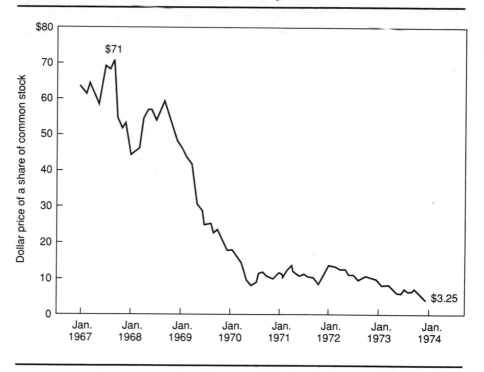

# Economy Shipping Company (Abridged)

In the spring of 1950 the controller of Economy Shipping Company, located near Pittsburgh, was preparing a report for the executive committee regarding the feasibility of repairing one of the company's steam riverboats or of replacing the steamboat with a new diesel-powered boat.

Economy Shipping was engaged mainly in the transportation of coal from the nearby mines to the steel mills, public utilities, and other industries in the Pittsburgh area. The company's several steamboats also on occasion carried cargoes to places as far away as New Orleans. All the boats owned by Economy Shipping were steam-powered. All were at least 10 years old, and the majority were between 15 and 30 years old.

The steamboat the controller was concerned about, the *Conway*, was 23 years old and required immediate rehabilitation or replacement. It was estimated that the *Conway* had a useful life of another 20 years provided that adequate repairs and maintenance were made. The book value of the *Conway* was $39,500, but the controller believed that if the company sold the boat in 1950, it would bring only around $25,000. The immediate rehabilitation costs for the *Conway* were estimated to be $115,000. The controller estimated that these general rehabilitation expenditures would extend the useful life of the *Conway* for about 20 years.

New spare parts from another boat, which had been retired in 1948, were available for use in the rehabilitation of the *Conway*. If these parts were used on the *Conway*, an estimate of their fair value was $43,500, which was their book value. Use of these parts would in effect decrease the immediate rehabilitation

---

costs from $115,000 to $71,500. It was believed that if these parts were sold on the market they would bring only around $30,000. They could not be used on any of the other Economy Shipping steamboats.

Currently, the *Conway* was operated by a crew of 20. Annual operating costs for the 20-person crew are shown in Table A.

The controller estimated that the cost of dismantling and scrapping the *Conway* at the end of its useful life after the overhaul would be offset by the value of the scrap and used parts taken off the boat.

An alternative to rehabilitating the steamboat was the purchase of a diesel-powered boat. The Quapelle Company, a local boat manufacturer, quoted the price of $325,000 for a diesel boat. An additional $75,000 for a basic parts inventory would be necessary to service a diesel boat, and such an inventory would be sufficient to service up to three diesel boats. If four or more diesels were purchased, however, it was estimated that additional spare parts inventory would be necessary.

The useful life of a diesel-powered boat was estimated to be 25 years; at the end of that time the boat would be scrapped or completely rehabilitated at a cost approximating that of a new boat. The controller did not contemplate the possibility of diesel engine replacement during the 25-year life, since information from other companies having limited experience with diesel-powered riverboats did not indicate that such costs needed to be anticipated. A general overhaul of the engines, costing $60,000 at current prices, would, however, be expected every 10 years.

After consulting the Quapelle Company and other companies operating diesel-powered boats, the controller estimated that the annual operating costs of such a boat would total $156,640 (see Table B).

Although the Economy Shipping controller had not considered the matter, at the end of the twentieth year the diesel boat would have a realizable value of $32,500 and the inventory of parts, $37,500.

Another factor the controller was considering at this time was alternative uses of funds. In the spring of 1950, Economy had sufficient funds to buy four diesel-powered boats; however, there were alternative uses for these funds. The other projects management was considering at this time had an estimated return of at least 10% after taxes. The income tax rate at the time was 48%.

What are the relevant cash flows associated with each alternative, and in

## TABLE A
Annual Operating Costs for the *Conway* and Its Crew

| | |
|---|---:|
| Wages | $110,200 |
| Vacation and sickness benefits | 1,880 |
| Social security payments | 2,400 |
| Life insurance | 1,800 |
| Commissary supplies | 15,420 |
| Repairs and maintenance | 24,400 |
| Fuel | 34,500 |
| Miscellaneous service and supplies | 12,550 |
| Total | $203,150 |

**TABLE B**
Annual Operating Costs for a Diesel-Powered Boat

| | |
|---|---:|
| Wages for a 13-person crew | $ 77,300 |
| Vacation and sickness benefits | 1,320 |
| Social security payments | 1,680 |
| Life insurance | 1,170 |
| Commissary supplies | 10,020 |
| Repairs and maintenance[a] | 21,700 |
| Fuel | 28,800 |
| Miscellaneous service and supplies | 14,650 |
| Total | $156,640 |

a. Excluding possible major overhaul of diesel engines.

what years do they occur? To simplify the calculations, use the straight-line method of depreciation. Also, make the following assumptions:

1. The diesel boat, if acquired, would be sold at the end of the twentieth year.
2. The inventory of parts for the diesel boat can be depreciated for tax purposes over a 25-year period.
3. The hull of the diesel boat ($265,000) would be depreciated over a 25-year period for tax purposes and the engines over a 10-year period.
4. The book cost of the *Conway*, including rehabilitation costs, would be depreciated over a 20-year period if rehabilitation were chosen.
5. The $32,500 residual value for the diesel boat in year 20 assumes no overhaul of the engines in year 20.

# The Super Project

In March 1967, Crosby Sanberg, manager–financial analysis at General Foods Corporation, told a casewriter, "What I learned about incremental analysis at the Business School doesn't always work." He was convinced that under some circumstances sunk costs were relevant to capital project evaluations. He was also concerned that financial and accounting systems did not provide an accurate estimate of incremental costs and revenues, and that this was one of the most difficult problems in measuring the value of capital investment proposals. Mr. Sanberg used the Super project as an example.[1]

Super was a new instant dessert, based on a flavored, water-soluble, agglomerated powder.[2] Although four flavors would be offered, it was estimated that chocolate would account for 80% of total sales.

General Foods was organized along product lines in the United States, with foreign operations under a separate division. Major U.S. product divisions included Post, Kool-Aid, Maxwell House, Jell-O, and Birds Eye. Financial data for General Foods are given in Exhibits 1, 2, and 3.

The $200,000 capital investment project request for Super involved $80,000 for building modifications and $120,000 for machinery and equipment. Modifications would be made to an existing building, where Jell-O was manufactured.

1. The name and nature of this new product have been disguised to avoid the disclosure of confidential information.

2. Agglomeration is a process by which the processed powder is passed through a steam bath and then dried. This fluffs up the powder particles and increases solubility.

Since available capacity of a Jell-O agglomerator would be used in the manufacture of Super, no cost for the key machine was included in the project. The $120,000 machinery and equipment item represented packaging machinery.

## The Market

A Nielsen survey indicated that powdered desserts constituted a significant and growing segment of the total dessert market, as shown in Table A. On the basis of test market experience, General Foods expected Super to capture a 10% share of the total dessert market. Eighty percent of this expected Super volume would come from growth in total market share or growth in the powders segment, and 20% would come from erosion of Jell-O sales.

## Production Facilities

Test market volume was packaged on an existing line, inadequate to handle long-run requirements. Filling and packaging equipment to be purchased had a capacity of 1.9 million units on a two-shift, five-day workweek basis. This represented considerable excess capacity, since 1968 requirements were expected to reach 1.1 million units, and the national potential was regarded as 1.6 million units. However, the extra capacity resulted from purchasing standard equipment, and a more economical alternative did not exist.

## Capital Budgeting Procedure

The General Foods Accounting and Financial Manual identified four categories of capital investment project proposals: (1) safety and convenience; (2) quality; (3) increased profit; and (4) other. Proposal procedures and criteria for accepting projects varied according to category (Exhibit 4). In discussing these criteria, Mr. Sanberg noted that the payback and return guidelines were not used as cutoff measures and added:

> Payback and return on investment are rarely the only measures of acceptability. Criteria vary significantly by type of project. A relatively high return might be required for a

**TABLE A**
Dessert Market, August–September 1966 Compared with August–September 1965

| Desserts | Market Share Aug.–Sept. 1966 | % Change Aug.–Sept. 1965 | |
|---|---|---|---|
| | | Share | Volume |
| Jell-O | 19.0% | 3.6 | 40.0 |
| Tasty | 4.0 | 4.0 | (new) |
| Total powders | 25.3 | 7.6 | 62.0 |
| Pie fillings and cake mixes | 32.0 | −3.9 | (no change) |
| Ice cream | 42.7 | −3.4 | 5.0 |
| Total market | 100.0% | | 13.0 |

new product in a new business category. On the other hand, a much lower return might be acceptable for a new product entry which represented a continuing effort to maintain leadership in an existing business by, for example, filling out the product line.

Super fell into the third category, as a profit-increasing project. Estimates of payback and return on funds employed were required for each such project requiring $50,000 or more of new capital funds and expense before taxes. The payback period was the length of time required for the project to repay the investment from the date the project became operational. In calculating the repayment period, only incremental income and expenses related to the project were used.

Return on funds employed (ROFE) was calculated by dividing 10-year average profit before taxes by the 10-year average funds employed. Funds employed included incremental net fixed assets plus or minus related working capital. Start-up costs and any profits or losses incurred before the project became operational were included in the first profit and loss period in the financial evaluation calculation.

## Capital Budgeting Atmosphere

A General Foods accounting executive commented on the atmosphere within which capital projects were reviewed:

> Our problem is not one of capital rationing. Our problem is to find enough good solid projects to employ capital at an attractive return on investment. Of course, the rate of capital inputs must be balanced against a steady growth in earnings per share. The short-term impact of capital investments is usually an increase in the capital base without an immediate realization of profit potential. This is particularly true in the case of new products.
>
> The food industry should show a continuous growth. A cyclical industry can afford to let its profits vary. We want to expand faster than the gross national product. The key to our capital budgeting is to integrate the plans of our eight divisions into a balanced company plan which meets our overall growth objectives. Most new products show a loss in the first two or three years, but our divisions are big enough to introduce new products without showing a loss.

## Investment Evaluation of Super Project

Exhibits 5 and 6 document the financial evaluation of the Super project. Exhibit 5 is the summary appropriation request prepared to justify the project to management and to secure management's authorization to expend funds on a capital project. Exhibit 6 presents the backup detail. Cost of the market test was included as "Other" expense in the first period, because a new product had to pay for its test market expense, even though this might be a sunk cost at the time capital funds were requested. The "Adjustments" item represented erosion of the Jell-O market and was calculated by multiplying the volume of erosion times a variable profit contribution. In the preparation of this financial evaluation form, costs of acquiring packaging machinery were included, but no cost was attributed to Jell-O agglomerator capacity to be used for the Super project, because the General Foods Accounting and Financial Manual specified that capital project requests be prepared on an incremental basis:

> The incremental concept requires that project requests, profit projections, and funds-employed statements include only items of income and expense and investment in assets which will be realized, incurred, or made directly as a result of, or are attributed to, the new project.

After receiving the paper work on the Super project, Mr. Sanberg studied the situation and wrote a memorandum arguing that the incremental approach advocated by the manual should not be applied to the Super project. His superior agreed with the memorandum and forwarded it to the corporate controller with the covering note contained in Appendix A. The controller's reply is given in Appendix B.

---

# Appendix A

# Memos to Controller

To: J. C. Kresslin, Corporate Controller

From: J. E. Hooting, Director, Corporate Budgets and Analysis

March 2, 1967

## Super Project

At the time we reviewed the Super project, I indicated to you that the return on investment looked significantly different if an allocation of the agglomerator and building, originally justified as a Jell-O project, were included in the Super investment. The pro rata allocation of these facilities, based on the share of capacity used, triples the initial gross investment in Super facilities from $200,000 to about $672,000.

I am forwarding a memorandum from Crosby Sanberg summarizing the results of three analyses evaluating the project on an

1. Incremental basis
2. Facilities-used basis
3. Fully allocated facilities and costs basis

Crosby has calculated a 10-year average ROFE using these techniques. Please read Crosby's memo before continuing with my note.

\*     \*     \*

Crosby concludes that the fully allocated basis, or some variation of it, is necessary to understand the long-range potential of the project.

I agree. We launch a new project because of its potential to increase our sales and earning power for many years into the future. We must be mindful of short-term consequences, as indicated by an incremental analysis, but we must also have a long-range frame of reference if we are to really understand what we are committing ourselves to. This long-range frame of reference is best approximated by looking at fully allocated investment and ''accounted'' profits, which recognize fully allocated costs because, in fact, over the long run all costs are variable unless some major change occurs in the structure of the business.

Our current GF preoccupation with only the incremental costs and investment causes some real anomalies that confuse our decision making. Super is a good example. On an incremental basis the project looks particularly attractive because by using a share of the excess capacity built on the coattails of the lucrative Jell-O project, the incremental investment in Super is low. If the excess Jell-O capacity did not exist, would the project be any less attractive? In the short term, perhaps yes because it would entail higher initial risk, but in the long term it is not a better project just because it fits a facility that is temporarily unused.

Looking at this point from a different angle, if the project exceeded our investment hurdle rate on a short-term basis but fell below it on a long-term basis (and Super comes close to doing this), should we reject the project? I say yes because over the long run, as ''fixed'' costs become variable and as we have to commit new capital to support the business, the continuing ROFE will go under water.

In sum, we have to look at new project proposals from both the long-range and the short-term point of view. We plan to refine our techniques of using a fully allocated basis as a long-term point of reference and will hammer out a policy recommendation for your consideration. We would appreciate any comments you may have.

To: J. E. Hooting, Director, Corporate Budgets and Analysis

From: C. Sanberg, Manager, Financial Analysis

February 17, 1967

### Super Project: A Case Example of Investment Evaluation Techniques

This will review the merits of alternative techniques of evaluating capital investment decisions using the Super project as an example. The purpose of the review is to provide an illustration of the problems and limitations inherent in using incremental ROFE and payback and thereby provide a rationale for adopting new techniques.

The alternative techniques to be reviewed are differentiated by the level of revenue and investment charged to the Super project in figuring a payback and ROFE, starting with incremental revenues and investment. Data related to the alternative techniques are summarized at the end of this memo.

## Alternative 1. Incremental Basis

**Method.**  The Super project as originally evaluated considered only incremental revenue and investment, which could be directly identified with the decision to produce Super. Incremental fixed capital ($200M) basically included packaging equipment.

**Result.**  On this basis the project paid back in 7 years with a ROFE of 63%.

**Discussion.**  Although it is General Foods' current policy to evaluate capital projects on an incremental basis, this technique does not apply to the Super project. The reason is that Super extensively utilizes existing facilities, which are readily adaptable to known future alternative uses.

Super should be charged with the "opportunity loss" of agglomerating capacity and building space. Because of Super the opportunity is lost to use a portion of agglomerating capacity for Jell-O and other products that could potentially be agglomerated. In addition, the opportunity is lost to use the building space for existing or new product volume expansion. To the extent there is an opportunity loss of existing facilities, new facilities must be built to accommodate future expansion. In other words, because the business is expanding, Super utilizes facilities that are adaptable to predictable alternative uses.

## Alternative 2. Facilities-Used Basis

**Method.**  Recognizing that Super will use half of an existing agglomerator and two thirds of an existing building, which were justified earlier in the Jell-O project, we added Super's pro rata share of these facilities ($453M) to the incremental capital. Overhead costs directly related to these existing facilities were also subtracted from incremental revenue on a shared basis.

**Result.**  ROFE 34%

**Discussion.**  Although the existing facilities utilized by Super are not incremental to this project, they are relevant to the evaluation of the project because potentially they can be put to alternative uses. Despite a high return on an incremental basis, if the ROFE on a project were unattractive after consideration of the shared use of existing facilities, the project would be questionable. Under these circumstances, we might look for a more profitable product for the facilities.

In summary, the facilities-used basis is a useful way of putting various projects on a common ground for purposes of *relative* evaluation. One product using existing capacity should not necessarily be judged to be more attractive than another practically identical product which necessitates an investment in additional facilities.

## Alternative 3. Fully Allocated Basis

**Method.** Further recognizing that individual decisions to expand inevitably add to a higher overhead base, we increased the costs and investment base developed in Alternative 2 by a provision for overhead expenses and overhead capital. These increases were made in year five of the 10-year evaluation period, on the theory that at this point a number of decisions would result in more fixed costs and facilities. Overhead expenses included manufacturing costs, plus selling and general and administrative costs on a per unit basis equivalent to Jell-O. Overhead capital included a share of the distribution system assets ($40M).

**Result.** ROFE 25%

**Discussion.** Charging Super with an overhead burden recognizes that overhead costs in the long run increase in proportion to the level of business activity, even though decisions to spend more overhead dollars are made separately from decisions to increase volume and provide the incremental facilities to support the higher volume level. To illustrate, the Division-F1968 Financial Plan budgets about a 75% increase in headquarters' overhead spending in F1968 over F1964. A contributing factor was the decision to increase the sales force by 50% to meet the demands of a growing and increasingly complex business. To further illustrate, about half the capital projects in the F1968 three-year Financial Plan are in the "non-payback" category. This group of projects comprised largely "overhead facilities" (warehouses, utilities, etc.), which are not directly related to the manufacture of products but are necessary components of the total business activity as a result of the cumulative effect of many decisions taken in the past.

The Super project is a significant decision which will most likely add to more overhead dollars as illustrated above. Super volume doubles the powdered dessert business category; it increases the Division businesses by 10%. Furthermore, Super requires a new production technology: agglomeration and packaging on a high-speed line.

## Conclusions

1. The incremental basis for evaluating a project is an inadequate measure of a project's worth when existing facilities with a known future use will be utilized extensively.
2. A fully allocated basis of reviewing major new product proposals recognizes that overheads increase in proportion to the size and complexity of the business and provides the best long-range projection of the financial consequences.

Alternative Evaluations of Super Project (thousands of dollars)

| | 1. Incremental Basis | 2. Facilities-Used Basis | 3. Fully Allocated Basis |
|---|---|---|---|
| *Investment* | | | |
| Working capital | $267 | $267 | $267 |
| Fixed capital | | | |
| Gross | 200 | 653 | 672 |
| Net | 113 | 358 | 367 |
| Total net investment | 380 | 625 | 634 |
| Profit before taxes[a] | 239 | 211 | 157 |
| ROFE | 63% | 34% | 25% |
| *Jell-O Project* | | | |
| Building | $200 × ⅔ = $133 | | |
| Agglomerator | 640 × ½ = 320 | | |
| | $453 | | |

*Note:* Figures based on 10-year averages.

a. Assumes 20% of Super volume will replace existing Jell-O business.

---

# Appendix B

## Controller's Reply

To: Mr. J. E. Hooting, Director, Corporate Budgets and Analysis

From: Mr. J. C. Kresslin, Corporate Controller

Subject: Super Project

March 7, 1967

On March 2 you sent me a note describing Crosby Sanberg's and your thoughts about evaluating the Super project. In this memo you suggest that the project should be appraised on the basis of fully allocated facilities and production costs.

In order to continue the dialogue, I am raising a couple of questions below.

It seems to me that in a situation such as you describe for Super, the real question is a *management decision* as to whether to go ahead with the Super project or not go ahead. Or to put it another way, are we better off in the aggregate if we use half the agglomerator and two thirds of an existing building for Super, or are we not, on the basis of our current knowledge?

It might be assumed that, for example, half of the agglomerator is being used and half is not and that a minimum economical size agglomerator was necessary for Jell-O and, consequently, should be justified by the Jell-O project itself. If we find a way to utilize it sooner by producing Super on it, aren't we better off in the aggregate, and the different ROFE figure for the Super project by itself becomes somewhat irrelevant? A similar point of view might be applied to the portion of the building. Or if we charge the Super project with half an agglomerator and two thirds of an existing building, should we then go back and relieve the Jell-O projects of these costs in evaluating the management's original proposal?

To put it another way, since we are faced with making decisions at a certain time on the basis of what we then know, I see very little value in looking at the Super project all by itself. Better we should look at the total situation before and after to see how we fare.

As to allocated production costs, the point is not so clear. Undoubtedly, over the long haul, the selling prices will need to be determined on the basis of a satisfactory margin over fully allocated costs. Perhaps this should be an additional requirement in the course of evaluating capital projects, since we seem to have been surprised at the low margins for "Tasty" after allocating all costs to the product.

I look forward to discussing this subject with you and with Crosby at some length.

**EXHIBIT 1**

Consolidated Balance Sheet of General Foods Corporation at April 1, 1967 (millions of dollars)

| | |
|---|---:|
| Cash | $ 20 |
| Marketable securities | 89 |
| Receivables | 180 |
| Inventories | 261 |
| Prepaid expenses | 14 |
| Current assets | 564 |
| Land, buildings, equipment (at cost, less depreciation) | 332 |
| Long-term receivables and sundry assets | 7 |
| Goodwill | 26 |
| Total assets | $929 |
| Notes payable | $ 22 |
| Accounts payable | 86 |
| Accrued liabilities | 73 |
| Accrued income taxes | 57 |
| Current liabilities | 238 |
| Long-term notes | 39 |
| 3⅜% debentures | 22 |
| Other noncurrent liabilities | 10 |
| Deferred investment tax credit | 9 |
| Total liabilities | 318 |
| Common stock issued | 164 |
| Retained earnings | 449 |
| Common stock held in treasury, at cost | (2) |
| Stockholders' equity | 611 |
| Total liabilities and stockholders' equity | $929 |
| Common stock—no. of shares outstanding at year-end | 25,127,007 |

**EXHIBIT 2**

Common Stock Prices of General Foods Corporation, 1958–1967

| | Low | High |
|---|---|---|
| 1958 | $24 | $ 39¾ |
| 1959 | 37⅛ | 53⅞ |
| 1960 | 49⅛ | 75½ |
| 1961 | 68⅝ | 107¾ |
| 1962 | 57¾ | 96 |
| 1963 | 77⅝ | 90½ |
| 1964 | 78¼ | 93¼ |
| 1965 | 77½ | 89⅞ |
| 1966 | 62¾ | 83 |
| 1967 | 65¼ | 81¾ |

**EXHIBIT 3**

Summary of Statistical Data of General Foods Corporation, Fiscal Years 1958–1967 (millions of dollars except assets per employee and figures on a share basis)

| | 1958 | 1959 | 1960 | 1961 | 1962 | 1963 | 1964 | 1965 | 1966 | 1967 |
|---|---|---|---|---|---|---|---|---|---|---|
| *Earnings* | | | | | | | | | | |
| Sales to customers (net) | $1,009 | $1,053 | $1,087 | $1,160 | $1,189 | $1,216 | $1,338 | $1,478 | $1,555 | $1,652 |
| Cost of sales | 724 | 734 | 725 | 764 | 769 | 769 | 838 | 937 | 965 | 1,012 |
| Marketing, admin., and general expenses | 181 | 205 | 236 | 261 | 267 | 274 | 322 | 362 | 406 | 449 |
| Earnings before income taxes | 105 | 115 | 130 | 138 | 156 | 170 | 179 | 177 | 185 | 193 |
| Taxes on income | 57 | 61 | 69 | 71 | 84 | 91 | 95 | 91 | 91 | 94 |
| Net earnings | $ 48 | $ 54 | $ 61 | $ 67 | $ 72 | $ 79 | $ 84 | $ 86 | $ 94 | $ 99 |
| Dividends on common shares | 24 | 28 | 32 | 35 | 40 | 45 | 50 | 50 | 53 | 55 |
| Retained earnings—current year | 24 | 26 | 29 | 32 | 32 | 34 | 34 | 36 | 41 | 44 |
| Net earnings per common share[a] | $ 1.99 | $ 2.21 | $ 2.48 | $ 2.69 | $ 2.90 | $ 3.14 | $ 3.33 | $ 3.44 | $ 3.73 | $ 3.93 |
| Dividends per common share[a] | 1.00 | 1.15 | 1.30 | 1.40 | 1.60 | 1.80 | 2.00 | 2.00 | 2.10 | 2.20 |
| *Assets, Liabilities, and Stockholders' Equity* | | | | | | | | | | |
| Inventories | $ 169 | $ 149 | $ 157 | $ 189 | $ 183 | $ 205 | $ 256 | $ 214 | $ 261 | $ 261 |
| Other current assets | 144 | 180 | 200 | 171 | 204 | 206 | 180 | 230 | 266 | 303 |
| Current liabilities | 107 | 107 | 126 | 123 | 142 | 162 | 202 | 173 | 219 | 238 |
| Working capital | $ 206 | $ 222 | $ 230 | $ 237 | $ 245 | $ 249 | $ 234 | $ 271 | $ 308 | $ 326 |
| Land, buildings, equipment, gross | 203 | 221 | 247 | 289 | 328 | 375 | 436 | 477 | 517 | 569 |
| Land, buildings, equipment, net | 125 | 132 | 148 | 173 | 193 | 233 | 264 | 283 | 308 | 332 |
| Long-term debt | 49 | 44 | 40 | 37 | 35 | 34 | 23 | 37 | 54 | 61 |
| Stockholders' equity | 287 | 315 | 347 | 384 | 419 | 454 | 490 | 527 | 569 | 611 |
| Stockholders' equity per common share[a] | $11.78 | $12.87 | $14.07 | $15.46 | $16.80 | $18.17 | $19.53 | $20.99 | $22.64 | $24.32 |
| *Capital Program* | | | | | | | | | | |
| Capital additions | $ 28 | $ 24 | $ 35 | $ 40 | $ 42 | $ 57 | $ 70 | $ 54 | $ 65 | $ 59 |
| Depreciation | 11 | 14 | 15 | 18 | 21 | 24 | 26 | 29 | 32 | 34 |
| *Employment Data* | | | | | | | | | | |
| Wages, salaries, and benefits | $ 128 | $ 138 | $ 147 | $ 162 | $ 171 | $ 180 | $ 195 | $ 204 | $ 218 | $ 237 |
| Number of employees (000s) | 21 | 22 | 22 | 25 | 28 | 28 | 30 | 30 | 30 | 32 |
| Assets per employee ($ 000s) | $ 21 | $ 22 | $ 23 | $ 22 | $ 22 | $ 23 | $ 24 | $ 25 | $ 29 | $ 29 |

*Note:* Column totals may not add exactly because of rounding.

a. Per share figures calculated on shares outstanding at year-end and adjusted for 2-for-1 stock split in August 1960.

**EXHIBIT 4**
Criteria for Evaluating Projects by General Foods Corporation

The basic criteria to be applied in evaluating projects within each of the classifications are set forth in the following schedule:

| *Purpose of Project* | *Payback and ROFE Criteria* |
|---|---|
| a. Safety and Convenience: | |
| 1. Projects required for reasons of safety, sanitation, health, public convenience, or other overriding reason with no reasonable alternatives. Examples: sprinkler systems, elevators, fire escapes, smoke control, waste disposal, treatment of water pollution, etc. | Payback—return on funds projections not required but the request must clearly demonstrate the *immediate* need for the project and the lack or inadequacy of alternative solutions. |
| 2. Additional nonproductive space requirements for which there are no financial criteria. Examples: office space, laboratories, service areas (kitchens, rest rooms, etc.) | Requests for nonproductive facilities, such as warehouses, laboratories, and offices should indicate the advantages of owning rather than leasing, unless no possibility to lease exists. In those cases where the company owns a group of integrated facilities and wherein the introduction of rented or leased properties might complicate the long-range planning or development of the area, owning rather than leasing is recommended. If the project is designed to improve customer service (such as market-centered warehouses), this factor is to be noted on the project request. |
| b. Quality: Projects designed primarily to improve quality. | If Payback and ROFE cannot be computed, it must be clearly demonstrated that the improvement is identifiable and desirable. |
| c. Increased Profit: | |
| 1. Projects justified primarily by reduced costs. | Projects with a Payback period *up to ten years* and a ten-year return *on* funds *as low as 20%* PBT are considered worthy of consideration, provided (1) the end product involved is believed to be a reasonably permanent part of our line or (2) the facilities involved are so flexible that they may be usable for successor products. |
| 2. Projects designed primarily to increase production capacity for an existing product. | Projects for a proven product where the risk of mortality is small, such as coffee, Jell-O gelatin, and cereals, should assure a payback in *no more than ten years* and a ten-year PBT return on funds of *no less* than 20%. |
| 3. Projects designed to provide facilities to manufacture and distribute a new product or product line. | Because of the greater risk involved, such projects should show a high potential return on funds (not less than a ten-year PBT return of 40%). Payback period, however, might be as much as *ten years* because of losses incurred during the market development period.* |
| d. Other: This category includes projects which by definition are excluded from the three preceding categories. Examples: standby facilities intended to insure uninterrupted production, additional equipment not expected to improve profits or product quality and not required for reasons of safety and convenience, equipment to satisfy marketing requirements, etc. | While standards of return may be difficult to set, some calculation of financial benefits should be made where possible. |

*Source:* The General Foods Accounting and Financial Manual.

* These criteria apply to the United States and Canada only. Profit-increasing capital projects in other areas in categories c1 and c2 should offer at least a ten-year PBT return of 24% to compensate for the greater risk involved. Likewise, foreign operation projects in the c3 category should offer a ten-year PBT return of at least 48%.

## EXHIBIT 5
Capital Project Request Form of General Foods Corporation

NY 1292-A 12-63
PTD. IN U.S.A.

December 23, 1966
*Date*

"Super" Facilities      66-42
*Project Title & Number*

New Request ☒   Supplement ☐

Jell-O Division - St. Louis
*Division & Location*

Expansion-New Product  ☒ A
*Purpose*  ☐ B

### PROJECT DESCRIPTION

To provide facilities for production of Super, chocolate dessert. This project included finishing a packing room in addition to filling and packaging equipment.

| SUMMARY OF INVESTMENT | |
|---|---|
| NEW CAPITAL FUNDS REQUIRED | $ 200M |
| EXPENSE BEFORE TAXES | -- |
| LESS: TRADE-IN OR SALVAGE, IF ANY | -- |
| Total This Request | $ 200M |
| PREVIOUSLY APPROPRIATED | -- |
| Total Project Cost | $ 200M |

| FINANCIAL JUSTIFICATION* | | |
|---|---|---|
| ROFE (PBT BASIS) - 10 YR. AVERAGE | 62.9 | % |
| PAYBACK PERIOD   April, F'68   Feb. F'75 <br> FROM     TO | 6.83 | YRS. |
| NOT REQUIRED | ☐ | |
| * BASED ON TOTAL PROJECT COST AND WORKING FUNDS OF | $ 510M | |

| ESTIMATED EXPENDITURE RATE | | | |
|---|---|---|---|
| QUARTER ENDING Mar. | F19 | 67 | $ 160M |
| QUARTER ENDING June | F19 | 68 | 40M |
| QUARTER ENDING | F19 | | |
| QUARTER ENDING | F19 | | |
| REMAINDER | | | |

| OTHER INFORMATION | | |
|---|---|---|
| MAJOR ☐   SPECIFIC ☐ ORDINARY | | BLANKET ☐ |
| INCLUDED IN ANNUAL PROGRAM   YES ☐ | | NO ☐ |
| PER CENT OF ENGINEERING COMPLETED | | 80 % |
| ESTIMATED START-UP COSTS | $ | 15M |
| ESTIMATED START-UP DATE | | April |

| LEVEL OF APPROVAL REQUIRED |
|---|
| ☐ BOARD   ☐ CHAIRMAN   ☐ EXEC. V.P.   ☐ GEN. MGR. |

| SIGNATURES | | DATE |
|---|---|---|
| DIRECTOR CORP. ENG. | | |
| DIRECTOR B & A | | |
| GENERAL MANAGER | | |
| VICE PRESIDENT | | |
| EXEC. VICE PRESIDENT | | |
| PRESIDENT | | |
| CHAIRMAN | | |

| For Division Use - Signatures | |
|---|---|
| NAME AND TITLE | DATE |
| | |
| | |
| | |
| | |

*(continued)*

**EXHIBIT 5** *(concluded)*

### INSTRUCTIONS FOR CAPITAL PROJECT REQUEST FORM NY 1292-A

The purpose of this form is to secure management's authorization to commit or expend funds on a capital project. Refer to Accounting and Financial Manual Statement No. 19 for information regarding projects to which this form applies.

NEW REQUEST—SUPPLEMENT—Check the appropriate box.

PURPOSE—Identify the primary purpose of the project in accordance with the classifications established in Accounting and Financial Statement No. 19, i.e., Sanitation, Health and Public Convenience, Non-Productive Space, Safety, Quality, Reduce Cost, Expansion—Existing Products, Expansion— New Products, Other (specify). Also indicate in the appropriate box whether the equipment represents an addition or a replacement.

PROJECT DESCRIPTION—Comments should be in sufficient detail to enable Corporate Management to appraise the benefits of the project. Where necessary, supplemental data should be attached to provide complete background for project evaluation.

SUMMARY OF INVESTMENT

*New Capital Funds Required*—Show gross cost of assets to be acquired.

*Expense Before Taxes*—Show incremental expense resulting from project.

*Trade-In or Salvage*—Show the amount expected to be realized on trade-in or sale of a replaced asset.

*Previously Appropriated*—When requesting a supplement to an approved project, show the amount previously appropriated even though authorization was given in a prior year.

FINANCIAL JUSTIFICATION

*ROFE*—Show the return on funds employed (PBT basis) as calculated on Financial Evaluation Form NY 1292-C or 1292-F. The appropriate Financial Evaluation Form is to be attached to this form.

*Not Required*—Where financial benefits are not applicable or required or are not expected, check the box provided. The non-financial benefits should be explained in the comments.

In the space provided, show the sum of The Total Project Cost plus Total Working Funds (line 20, Form NY 1292-C, or line 5, Form NY 1292-F) in either of the first three periods, whichever is higher.

ESTIMATED EXPENDITURE RATE—Expenditures are to be reported in accordance with accounting treatment of the asset and related expense portion of the project. Insert estimated quarterly expenditures beginning with the quarter in which the first expenditure will be made. The balance of authorized funds unspent after the fourth quarter should be reported in total.

OTHER INFORMATION—Check whether the project is a major, specific ordinary, or blanket, and whether or not the project was included in the Annual Program. Show estimated percentage of engineering completed; this is intended to give management an indication of the degree of reliability of the funds requested. Indicate the estimated start-up costs as shown on line 32 of Financial Evaluation Form NY 1292-C. Insert anticipated start-up date for the project; if start-up is to be staggered, explain in comments.

LEVEL OF APPROVAL REQUIRED—Check the appropriate box.

*Source:* General Foods.

**EXHIBIT 6**

Financial Evaluation Form of General Foods Corporation (thousands of dollars)

```
NY 1292-C   10-64
PTD. IN U.S.A.
```

| Jell-O | | | | | St. Louis | | | | | The Super Project | | | | 67-89 | | | Date |
|---|---|---|---|---|---|---|---|---|---|---|---|---|---|---|---|---|---|
| Division | | | | | Location | | | | | Project Title | | | | Project No. | | | Supplement Se. |

| PROJECT REQUEST DETAIL | 1ST PER. | 2ND PER. | PER. | PER. | PER. | RETURN ON NEW FUNDS EMPLOYED - 10-YR. AVG. | | |
|---|---|---|---|---|---|---|---|---|
| | | | | | | | PAT (C ÷ A) | PBT (B ÷ A) |
| 1. LAND | $ | | | | | | | |
| 2. BUILDINGS | 80 | | | | | A - NEW FUNDS EMPLOYED (LINE 21) | $ 380 | $ 380 |
| 3. MACHINERY & EQUIPMENT | 120 | | | | | B - PROFIT BEFORE TAXES (LINE 35) | //////// | $ 239 |
| 4. ENGINEERING | | | | | | C - NET PROFIT (LINE 37) | $ 115 | //////// |
| 5. OTHER (EXPLAIN) | | | | | | D - CALCULATED RETURN | 30.2 % | 62.9 % |
| 6. EXPENSE PORTION (BEFORE TAX) | | | | | | PAYBACK YEARS FROM OPERATIONAL DATE | | |
| 7. SUB-TOTAL | $ 200 | | | | | PART YEAR CALCULATION FOR FIRST PERIOD | - | YRS. |
| 8. LESS: SALVAGE VALUE (OLD ASSET) | | | | | | NUMBER OF FULL YEARS TO PAY BACK | 6.00 | YRS. |
| 9. TOTAL PROJECT COST* | $ 200 | | | | | PART YEAR CALCULATION FOR LAST PERIOD | 0.83 | YRS. |
| 10. LESS: TAXES ON EXP. PORTION | | | | | | TOTAL YEARS TO PAY BACK | 6.83 | YRS. |
| 11. NET PROJECT COST | $ 200 | | | | | | | |

| FUNDS EMPLOYED | 1ST PER. F 68 | 2ND PER. F 69 | 3RD PER. F 70 | 4TH PER. F 71 | 5TH PER. F 72 | 6TH PER. F 73 | 7TH PER. F 74 | 8TH PER. F 75 | 9TH PER. F 76 | 10TH PER. F 77 | 11TH PER. | 10-YR. AVG. |
|---|---|---|---|---|---|---|---|---|---|---|---|---|
| 12. NET PROJECT COST (LINE 11) | $ 200 | 200 | 200 | 200 | 200 | 200 | 200 | 200 | 200 | 200 | //////// | //////// |
| 13. DEDUCT DEPRECIATION (CUM.) | 19 | 37 | 54 | 70 | 85 | 98 | 110 | 121 | 131 | 140 | | |
| 14. CAPITAL FUNDS EMPLOYED | $ 181 | 163 | 146 | 130 | 115 | 102 | 90 | 79 | 69 | 60 | | 113 |
| 15. CASH | 124 | 134 | 142 | 151 | 160 | 160 | 169 | 169 | 178 | 173 | | 157 |
| 16. RECEIVABLES | | | | | | | | | | | | |
| 17. INVENTORIES | 207 | 222 | 237 | 251 | 266 | 266 | 281 | 281 | 296 | 296 | | 260 |
| 18. PREPAID & DEFERRED EXP. | | | | | | | | | | | | |
| 19. LESS CURRENT LIABILITIES | (2) | (82) | (108) | (138) | (185) | (184) | (195) | (195) | (207) | (207) | | (150) |
| 20. TOTAL WORKING FUNDS (15 THRU 19) | 329 | 274 | 271 | 264 | 241 | 242 | 255 | 255 | 267 | 267 | //////// | 267 |
| 21. TOTAL NEW FUNDS EMPLOYED (14 + 20) | $ 510 | 437 | 417 | 394 | 356 | 344 | 345 | 334 | 336 | 327 | //////// | 380 |

| PROFIT AND LOSS | | | | | | | | | | | | |
|---|---|---|---|---|---|---|---|---|---|---|---|---|
| 22. UNIT VOLUME (in thousands) | 1100 | 1200 | 1300 | 1400 | 1500 | 1500 | 1600 | 1600 | 1700 | 1700 | | 1460 |
| 23. GROSS SALES | $2200 | 2400 | 2600 | 2800 | 3000 | 3000 | 3200 | 3200 | 3400 | 3400 | | 2920 |
| 24. DEDUCTIONS | 88 | 96 | 104 | 112 | 120 | 120 | 128 | 128 | 136 | 136 | | 117 |
| 25. NET SALES | 2112 | 2304 | 2496 | 2688 | 2880 | 2880 | 3072 | 3072 | 3264 | 3264 | | 2803 |
| 26. COST OF GOODS SOLD | 1100 | 1200 | 1300 | 1400 | 1500 | 1500 | 1600 | 1600 | 1700 | 1700 | | 1460 |
| 27. GROSS PROFIT | 1012 | 1104 | 1196 | 1288 | 1380 | 1380 | 1472 | 1472 | 1564 | 1564 | | 1343 |
| GROSS PROFIT % NET SALES | % | | | | | | | | | | | |
| 28. ADVERTISING EXPENSE | | | | | | | | | | | | |
| 29. SELLING EXPENSE | 1100 | 1050 | 1000 | 900 | 700 | 700 | 730 | 730 | 750 | 750 | | 841 |
| 30. GEN. AND ADMIN. COSTS | | | | | | | | | | | | |
| 31. RESEARCH EXPENSE | | | | | | | | | | | | |
| 32. START-UP COSTS | 15 | | | | | | | | | | | 2 |
| 33. OTHER (EXPLAIN) Test Mkt. | 360 | | | | | | | | | | | |
| 34. ADJUSTMENTS (EXPLAIN) Erosion | 180 | 200 | 210 | 220 | 230 | 230 | 240 | 240 | 250 | 250 | | 36 |
| | | | | | | | | | | | | 225 |
| 35. PROFIT BEFORE TAXES | $(643) | (146) | 14 | 168 | 450 | 450 | 502 | 502 | 564 | 564 | | 239 |
| 36. TAXES | (334) | (76) | ( 7) | 87 | 234 | 234 | 261 | 261 | 293 | 293 | | 125 |
| 36A. ADD: INVESTMENT CREDIT | (1) | (1) | (1) | (1) | (1) | (1) | (1) | (1) | - | - | | (1) |
| 37. NET PROFIT | (308) | (69) | ( 6) | 82 | 217 | 217 | 242 | 242 | 271 | 271 | | 115 |
| 38. CUMULATIVE NET PROFIT | $(308) | (377) | (383) | (301) | (84) | 133 | 375 | 617 | 888 | 1159 | | |
| 39. NEW FUNDS TO REPAY (21 LESS 38) | $ 818 | 814 | 800 | 695 | 440 | 211 | (30) | (283) | (552) | (832) | | |

*Same as Project Request

*(continued)*

**EXHIBIT 6** *(continued)*

### INSTRUCTIONS FOR PREPARATION OF FORM NY 1292-C
### FINANCIAL EVALUATION

This form is to be submitted to Corporate Budget and Analysis with each profit-increasing capital project request requiring $50,000 or more of capital funds and expense before taxes.

Note that the ten-year term has been divided into eleven periods. The first period is to end on the March 31st following the operational date of the project, and the P & L projection may thereby encompass any number of months from one to twelve, e.g., if the project becomes operational on November 1, 1964, the first period for P & L purposes would be 5 months (November 1, 1964 through March 31, 1965). The next nine periods would be fiscal years (F'66, F'67, etc.) and the eleventh period would be 7 months (April 1, 1974 through October 30, 1974). This has been done primarily to facilitate reporting of projected and actual P & L data by providing for fiscal years. See categorized instructions below for more specific details.

**PROJECT REQUEST DETAIL**—*Lines 1 through 11* show the breakdown of the Net Project Cost to be used in the financial evaluation. *Line 8* is to show the amount expected to be realized on trade-in or sale of a replaced asset. *Line 9* should be the same as the "Total Project Cost" shown on Form NY 1292-A, Capital Project Request. Space has been provided for capital expenditures related to this project which are projected to take place subsequent to the first period. Indicate in such space the additional costs only; do not accumulate them.

**FUNDS EMPLOYED**

*Capital Funds Employed*—*Line 12* will show the net project cost appearing on *line 11* as a constant for the first ten periods except in any period in which additional expenditures are incurred; in that event show the accumulated amounts of *line 11* in such period and in all future periods.

Deduct cumulative depreciation on *line 13*. Depreciation is to be computed on an incremental basis, i.e., the net increase in depreciation over present depreciation on assets being replaced. In the first period depreciation will be computed at one half of the first year's annual rate; no depreciation is to be taken in the eleventh period. Depreciation rates are to be the same as those used for accounting purposes. *Exception:* When the depreciation rate used for accounting purposes differs materially from the rate for tax purposes, the higher rate should be used. A variation will be considered material when the first full year's depreciation on a book basis varies 20% or more from the first full year's depreciation on a tax basis.

The ten-year average of Capital Funds Employed shall be computed by adding *line 14* in each of the first ten periods and dividing the total by ten.

*Total Working Funds*—Refer to Financial Policy No. 21 as a guide in computing new working fund requirements. Items which are not on a formula basis and which are normally computed on a five-quarter average shall be handled proportionately in the first period. For example, since the period involved may be less than 12 months, the average would be computed on the number of quarters involved. Generally, the balances should be approximately the same as they would be if the first period were a full year.

Cash, based on formula which theorizes a two weeks' supply (2/52nds), should follow the same theory. If the first period is for three months, two-thirteenths (2/13ths) should be used; if it is for 5 months, two-twenty-firsts (2/21sts) should be used, and so forth.

Current liabilities are to include one half of the tax expense as the tax liability. The ten-year averages of Working Funds shall be computed by adding each line across for the first ten periods and dividing each total by ten.

**PROFIT AND LOSS PROJECTION**

*P & L Categories (Lines 22–34)*—Reflect only the incremental amounts which will result from the proposed project; exclude all allocated charges. Include the P & L results expected in the individual periods comprising the first ten years of the life of the project. Refer to the second paragraph of these instructions regarding the fractional years' calculations during the first and eleventh periods.

Any loss or gain on the sale of a replaced asset (see *line 8*) shall be included in *line 33*.

*(continued)*

**EXHIBIT 6** *(concluded)*

As indicated in the caption Capital Funds Employed, no depreciation is to be taken in the eleventh period.

The ten-year averages of the P & L items shall be computed by adding each line across for the eleven periods (10 full years from the operational date) and dividing the total by ten.

*Adjustments (Line 34)*—Show the adjustment necessary, on a before-tax basis, to indicate any adverse or favorable incremental effect the proposed project will have on any other products currently being produced by the corporation.

*Investment Credit* is to be included on *line 36-A*. The Investment Credit will be spread over 8 years, or fractions thereof, as an addition to PAT.

RETURN ON NEW FUNDS EMPLOYED—Ten-year average returns are to be calculated for PAT (projects requiring Board approval only) and PBT. The PAT return is calculated by dividing average PAT *(line 37)* by average new funds employed *(line 21)*; the PBT return is derived by dividing average PBT *(line 35)* by average new funds employed *(line 21)*.

PAYBACK YEARS FROM OPERATIONAL DATE

*Part Year Calculation for First Period*—Divide number of months in the first period by twelve. If five months are involved, the calculation is 5/12 = .4 years.

*Number of Full Years to Pay Back*—Determined by the last period, excluding the first period, in which an amount is shown on *line 39*.

*Part Year Calculation for Last Period*—Divide amount still to be repaid at the end of the last full period *(line 39)* by net profit plus the *annual* depreciation in the following year when payback is completed.

*Total Years to Pay Back*—Sum of full and part years.

*Source:* General Foods.

# Pressco, Inc. (1985)

In November 1985, Jane Rogers, a marketing representative for Pressco, Inc. was preparing a financial presentation designed to help close the sale of mechanical drying equipment to Paperco, Inc. The equipment that Ms. Rogers hoped to sell to Paperco at a price of $2.9 million would replace less efficient facilities that had been placed in service late in December 1979 by Paperco. The cost savings (exclusive of depreciation charges) which Ms. Rogers felt certain Paperco would realize from the proposed new equipment installation amounted to $560,000 per year. Of this amount, $360,000 in savings was expected to come from more efficient fuel utilization.

One year earlier, Ms. Rogers had been unsuccessful in interesting Paperco's management in this cost reduction opportunity. The customer viewed the proposed investment as moderately attractive but easily postponable at little cost to Paperco. Management was originally unwilling to commit to the purchase for this reason. Since Ms. Rogers' earlier presentation, however, new tax legislation had been rumored that would (1) eliminate the investment tax credit for new equipment;[1] (2) extend depreciation lives for new equipment; and (3) reduce the corporate tax rate from 46% to 34% beginning in 1986.

While the prospects for passage of the anticipated tax legislation were uncertain, Pressco's senior management was concerned that the basic thrust of the legislation

1. Exhibit 1 presents a chronology of changes in the tax law regarding investment tax credits from 1975 to 1985 as well as the change *anticipated* but not yet *enacted* for 1986.

might negatively affect the firm's sales of mechanical drying equipment. Ms. Rogers found this concern somewhat curious, since she had experienced an unprecedented surge in customer inquiries following the announcement of the new tax initiative. Indeed, Paperco's management suddenly expressed a quickened interest in moving forward with the purchase of the mechanical drying equipment and seemed anxious to sign a binding contract.

In preparing the economic analysis to support her sales presentation to Paperco, Ms. Rogers recalled that Paperco had utilized double-declining-balance (DDB) depreciation for assets acquired before January 1, 1981, and was using accelerated cost recovery system (ACRS) depreciation for assets acquired on or after that date (Exhibit 2). In order to be consistent with these assumptions Ms. Rogers prepared the relevant depreciation schedules for old and new equipment as indicated in Exhibits 3 and 4.

In case the new tax legislation was passed prior to the signing of a binding sales contract with Paperco, Ms. Rogers also prepared a depreciation schedule utilizing the terms of the rumored new tax legislation (Exhibit 5). Ms. Rogers was mindful of the fact that in order to reduce the economic uncertainty surrounding long-term capital investments, Congress normally grandfathers more favorable depreciation and investment tax credit schedules for projects entered into via binding contracts before new (and less favorable) tax legislation is passed. She thought this fact might have something to do with the sense of urgency shown by potential customers like Paperco.

The remaining assumptions that Ms. Rogers planned to utilize in her presentation of the investment opportunity to Paperco's management are as follows:

1. Equipment cost: $2,100,000
2. Start-up of facility, December 1986, 12 months following receipt of order, which was anticipated in December 1985
3. Equipment payment terms: 50% ($1,050,000) with order, December 1985; 50% ($1,050,000) upon start-up of facility, December 1986
4. Installation cost: $800,000; 100% upon start-up of facility
5. Paperco cost of capital: 12%
6. Depreciable life and estimated salvage value (see Table A)

**TABLE A**
Depreciable Life and Estimated Salvage Value

| Tax Reports | Facility to Be Replaced | New Facility (Existing Tax Legislation) | New Facility (Anticipated New Tax Legislation) |
|---|---|---|---|
| Equipment depreciation period . . . . . . . . . . | 10 years, DDB[a] | 5 years (ACRS) | 7 years (MACRS)[b] |
| Installation depreciation period . . . . . . . . . | 8 years, DDB[a] | 5 years (ACRS) | 7 years (MACRS) |
| Estimated salvage value at end of life . . . . . . . | $60,000 | $250,000 | $250,000 |

a. The IRS permitted taxpayers to switch from the DDB method of depreciation to the straight-line method of depreciation whenever the switch became advantageous. A switch to straight-line depreciation at the most advantageous time is incorporated in the data presented in Exhibit 4.

b. MACRS is the anticipated new depreciation system.

**7.** Facility to be replaced:

| | |
|---|---|
| Original equipment cost . . . . . . . . . | $500,000 |
| Original installation cost . . . . . . . . | $500,000 |
| Estimated market value of equipment if sold in 12 months (when displaced) . . . . | $150,000 |
| Estimated remaining physical life as of December 1985 . . . . . . . . . | 11 years |

**8.** Paperco currently paid federal income taxes at the rate of 46%. If the anticipated tax legislation were passed, this rate would be 34% beginning in 1986.

**EXHIBIT 1**
Investment Tax Credit (ITC)

IRS regulations allow a credit against tax for investment in certain depreciable property. The amount of the credit is shown in the following table:

|  | Depreciable Life (Years) | ITC Rate (%) |
|---|---|---|
| Property placed in service | 3–4 | 3⅓ |
| after Jan. 21, 1975 but | 5–6 | 6⅔ |
| before Jan. 1, 1981 | 7 and over | 10 |
| Property placed in service | | |
| on or after Jan. 1, 1981 | 3 | 6 |
| but before Jan. 1, 1983 | 5 | 8 |
| Property placed in service | 3 | 4 |
| on or after Jan. 1, 1983 | 5 | 8 |
| Anticipated new tax | | |
| legislation for 1986 | All lives | 0 |

If the equipment upon which an ITC was taken is retired before the end of its depreciable life, some portion of the ITC is recaptured by the IRS. While the entire amount of the anticipated ITC is deducted from a firm's taxes as soon as the equipment is purchased, in fact this ITC is "earned" in the sense that it cannot be recaptured by the IRS (see following schedule):

| Minimum Number of Months Property Must Be Held to Earn Credit | Cumulative ITC Earned | |
|---|---|---|
| | Property Placed in Service between Jan. 21, 1975, and Dec. 31, 1980 | Property Placed in Service on or after Jan. 1, 1981 |
| 12 | 0 % | 20% |
| 24 | 0 | 40 |
| 36 | 33⅓ | 60 |
| 48 | 33⅓ | 80 |
| 60 | 66⅔ | 100 |
| 72 | 66⅔ | 100 |
| 84 | 100 | 100 |

**EXHIBIT 2**

Depreciation Rates Permitted for Tax Purposes for Machinery and Equipment of the Type Purchased by Paperco

| | Percent of Cost to Be Depreciated in Year for Property Placed in Service | | | |
|---|---|---|---|---|
| **Year** | **Tax Legislation in Effect Prior to 1980** | | **Tax Legislation in Effect 1980–1985** | **Anticipated New Tax Legislation** |
| | 10-year life property | 8-year life property | 5-year life[a] property | 7-year life[b] property |
| 1 . . . . . . . | 20.00% | 25.00% | 15.00% | 14.29% |
| 2 . . . . . . . | 16.00 | 18.75 | 25.50 | 24.29 |
| 3 . . . . . . . | 12.80 | 14.06 | 17.85 | 17.49 |
| 4 . . . . . . . | 10.24 | 10.55 | 16.66 | 12.49 |
| 5 . . . . . . . | 8.19 | 7.91 | 16.66 | 8.93 |
| 6 . . . . . . . | 6.55 | 7.91 | 8.33 | 8.92 |
| 7 . . . . . . . | 6.56 | 7.91 | – | 8.93 |
| 8 . . . . . . . | 6.55 | 7.91 | – | 4.46 |
| 9 . . . . . . . | 6.56 | – | – | – |
| 10 . . . . . . . | 6.55 | – | – | – |
| | 100.00% | 100.00% | 100.00% | 100.00% |

a. Under the tax laws in effect in late 1985, no residual value was deducted from the amount to be depreciated. Under this law a half-year of depreciation was allowed for all equipment placed in service during a year regardless of the specific date the equipment was actually placed in service. This depreciation table is based on the 150% declining-balance depreciation method with switch to straight-line in year 3.

b. The anticipated tax legislation was expected to extend the depreciation life of equipment similar to that sold by Pressco from 5 to 7 years but permit a 200% declining-balance depreciation method with switch to straight-line in year 4.

**EXHIBIT 3**

Depreciation Expense: *New* Equipment and Installation with *No Change* in Tax Legislation or with *Grandfathering* Because of a Binding Contract (thousands of dollars)

| | Accelerated Cost Recovery System (ACRS) | | |
|---|---|---|---|
| | **Equipment** | **Installation** | **Total** |
| 1986 . . . . . . | $ 315 | $120 | $ 435 |
| 1987 . . . . . . | 535 | 204 | 739 |
| 1988 . . . . . . | 375 | 143 | 518 |
| 1989 . . . . . . | 350 | 133 | 483 |
| 1990 . . . . . . | 350 | 133 | 483 |
| 1991 . . . . . . | 175 | 67 | 242 |
| 1992 . . . . . . | – | – | – |
| 1993 . . . . . . | – | – | – |
| 1994 . . . . . . | – | – | – |
| 1995 . . . . . . | – | – | – |
| | $2,100 | $800 | $2,900 |

*Note:* Assumes installation date of December 1986 for new equipment and disposal date of December 1986 for old equipment.

**EXHIBIT 4**

Depreciation Expense: *Replaced* Equipment and Installation (thousands of dollars)

| | Double-Declining-Balance Method[a] | | |
|---|---|---|---|
| | **Equipment** | **Installation** | **Total** |
| 1979 . . . . . . | $100 | $125 | $   225 |
| 1980 . . . . . . | 80 | 75 | 155 |
| 1981 . . . . . . | 64 | 60 | 124 |
| 1982 . . . . . . | 51 | 48 | 99 |
| 1983 . . . . . . | 41 | 48 | 89 |
| 1984 . . . . . . | 33 | 48 | 81 |
| 1985 . . . . . . | 33 | 48 | 81 |
| 1986 . . . . . . | 33 | 48 | 81 |
| 1987 . . . . . . | 33 | 0 | 33 |
| 1988 . . . . . . | 32 | 0 | 32 |
| 1989 . . . . . . | 0 | 0 | 0 |
| | $500 | $500 | $1,000 |

a. See Table A, note a, regarding the switch to straight-line depreciation in the first year that this switch becomes advantageous.

**EXHIBIT 5**

Depreciation Expense: *New* Equipment and Installation with *Anticipated* Tax Legislation and *No Grandfathering* Because Contract Signed Too Late to Qualify (thousands of dollars)

| | Anticipated New Depreciation System (MACRS) | | |
|---|---|---|---|
| | **Equipment** | **Installation** | **Total** |
| 1986 . . . . . . | $   300 | $114 | $   414 |
| 1987 . . . . . . | 514 | 196 | 710 |
| 1988 . . . . . . | 367 | 140 | 507 |
| 1989 . . . . . . | 262 | 100 | 362 |
| 1990 . . . . . . | 188 | 72 | 260 |
| 1991 . . . . . . | 188 | 71 | 259 |
| 1992 . . . . . . | 188 | 71 | 259 |
| 1993 . . . . . . | 93 | 36 | 129 |
| 1994 . . . . . . | – | – | – |
| 1995 . . . . . . | – | – | – |
| | $2,100 | $800 | $2,900 |

*Note:* Assumes installation date of December 1986 and that the anticipated tax legislation is passed *before* Paperco signs a binding contract. Paperco would thus lose the 8% ITC and the 5-year ACRS depreciation schedule.

# MRC, Inc. (A)

In late March 1961, Archibald Brinton, president of MRC, Inc., was grappling with the question of whether to acquire American Rayon, Inc. (ARI). Mr. Brinton was troubled by ARI's erratic earnings record and mediocre long-run outlook. However, he recognized that MRC would benefit greatly from ARI's liquidity and borrowing capacity. He was therefore inclined to go through with the acquisition, provided ARI could be purchased at a price that promised to yield MRC an adequate return on its money.

## Background Information on MRC

MRC was a Cleveland-based manufacturing concern with 1960 earnings of $3.9 million on sales of over $118 million. The most important product lines were power brake systems for trucks, buses, and automobiles; industrial furnaces and heat-treating equipment; and automobile, truck, and bus frames. Exhibit 1 presents data on the operating results and financial position of MRC.

### Diversification Program

Upon becoming chief executive officer in 1957, Mr. Brinton had initiated an active program of diversification by acquisition. The need for rapid diversification seemed compelling. Until 1957 virtually all sales were made to less than a dozen large companies in the automotive industry, with car and truck frames accounting

---

for 85% of the $70 million sales total. As a result, earnings, cash flow, and growth were constantly exposed to the risks inherent in selling to a few customers, all of which operated in a highly cyclical and competitive market. Previous attempts at internal diversification had floundered on management's lack of expertise in markets and technologies outside the automotive area. Mr. Brinton had therefore turned to acquisitions as a means of buying up established sales and earnings as well as managerial and technical know-how. In Mr. Brinton's words, the acquisition strategy was "intended (1) to achieve related diversification and thus lessen vulnerability to technological change in a single industry; (2) to stabilize earnings and cash flow; (3) to uncouple growth prospects from the cyclical and unexciting automotive industry; and (4) to escape the constant threat of backward integration by one or more major customers." The drive for diversification had been intensified in 1959 when Chrysler announced a move toward unitized, i.e., "frameless," body construction.

By the end of 1960 the diversification campaign had resulted in five acquisitions, two of which were major transactions. Acquisition of Ross Engineering Corporation increased MRC sales by $27 million in 1957, and the purchase of Surface Combustion Corporation in 1959 added about $38 million to annual sales. The acquisition history of MRC is shown in Exhibit 2. Significantly, total sales increased almost $50 million between 1956 and 1960, despite a $30 million decline in automotive sales over that period.

## Management Structure

While the diversification program had reduced MRC's dependence on any one industry, it had also created significant strains on the company's organization structure and financial position.

As the acquisition program carried MRC into a widening variety of markets and technologies, it became increasingly apparent that the company's highly centralized decision-making processes were ill suited to the needs of a diversified corporation. By the end of 1959 it was clear the headquarters management group could not acquire or maintain detailed knowledge of all the products, markets, and technologies embraced by MRC. Since continued rapid diversification was considered imperative, the company had shifted to a highly decentralized management structure, which transferred substantial decision-making power to division managers.

In 1961 there were seven divisions. All marketing, purchasing, manufacturing, research and development, personnel matters, and accounting were handled at the division level. Each division had its own general manager (usually a vice president), who reported directly to Mr. Brinton and had the primary responsibility for the growth and profitability of his division. A division manager could get stock options and earn an annual bonus of up to 60% of his base salary, depending on the earnings and growth of his division. Divisional sales and earnings goals were formalized in an annual budget and in a rolling 5-year plan, which were formulated by each general manager and submitted each November to the head office for review by Mr. Brinton and the corporate staff.

The corporate staff provided legal, administrative, and financial support to the divisions and handled external affairs, financing, and acquisitions as well. The staff, including corporate officers, consisted of fewer than 60 people, about half of whom would be classified as secretarial and clerical.

Mr. Brinton felt that he could exercise adequate control over the decentralized organization through his power to hire and fire at the division manager level and, more important, through control of the elaborate capital budgeting system. The Appendix discusses MRC's capital budgeting procedures.

No acquisitions were made in 1960. But, by 1961, Mr. Brinton was confident that the organization was capable of smoothly assimilating new operations, and his staff had identified and opened preliminary discussions with a number of attractive acquisition prospects. However, the financial problems brought on by the strain of financing past acquisitions had become pressing.

### Finances

The acquisition campaign had been hampered from the outset by MRC's low price-earnings (P/E) multiple. Although growth was an explicit objective of the acquisition program, MRC could not exchange its shares for those of high P/E, growth companies without absorbing a stiff dilution in per share earnings. It was feared that such dilution of earnings per share would further depress the P/E ratio and thus make it still more difficult to swap stock with growth companies. Consequently, MRC had been forced to rely heavily on debt financing for most of its acquisitions.

By early 1961, MRC had largely exhausted its borrowing capacity. Between 1956 and 1960, long-term debt had risen from less than $4 million to more than $22 million. Although it appeared that capital expenditures planned for 1961 could be funded with internally generated funds, the near exhaustion of debt capacity posed a serious threat to the acquisition strategy. Discussions with commercial banks, life insurance companies, and investment bankers had made it clear that any further increases in long-term debt, without a substantial infusion of new equity, would be extremely difficult and probably impossible. Investment bankers had further pointed out that long-term lenders would probably insist on severely restricting the company's flexibility to make cash acquisitions, even if it should prove feasible to raise new debt. With MRC near its debt limit and the P/E ratio around 10 times, the entire diversification campaign was in danger of collapsing.

ARI, with its $20 million of marketable securities, appeared to provide a convenient new source of funds with which to fuel the acquisition program.

## Background Information on ARI

American Rayon, Inc., a Philadelphia-based corporation, was the third largest producer of rayon in the United States.[1] In 1960, ARI had recorded sales of $55

---

1. Rayon is a glossy fiber made by forcing a viscous solution of modified cellulose (wood pulp) through minute holes and drying the resulting filaments.

million and a pre-tax profit of $5 million, after 3 years of severe profit problems (see Exhibits 3 and 4). By early 1961 the company's stock was trading at less than half of book value on the New York Stock Exchange and top management feared that the company's new-found profitability, along with its great liquidity and a disenchanted shareholder group, would make ARI attractive to raiders. Consequently, management was seeking to arrange a marriage with a congenial partner. ARI's investment banker had brought the company to the attention of Mr. Brinton, who had expressed tentative interest in a deal.

## Acquisition Investigation

The results of MRC's investigation were mixed. On the plus side, ARI had over $20 million in liquid assets that were not needed for operations, no short- or long-term debt, and a modern central manufacturing facility. It appeared that the company could be purchased for about $40 million worth of MRC common stock. Moreover, although ARI top management was elderly, James Clinton, the 64-year-old president, was willing to stay on for 2 years after the acquisition to give MRC personnel a chance to learn the business before his retirement.

On the other hand, the longer-term outlook for the rayon industry was grim. The rayon industry had enjoyed one of the most spectacular successes in the history of American enterprise. For example, the American Viscose Corporation, which founded the industry in 1910, achieved in its first 24 years aggregate net earnings of $354 million, or 38,000% of original investment, while financing rapid expansion entirely out of earnings.[2] But rayon began to falter in the early 1950s as competing synthetics like nylon and acrylic became popular. Style and fashion shifts also made cotton more attractive. The net effect was to force production cutbacks in rayon, and by the end of the 1950s many companies, including Du Pont, had withdrawn from the rayon industry altogether.

With shrinking industry volume, ARI had experienced increasing earnings difficulties. These difficulties could be traced directly to the declining use of rayon in automobile tire cord, the market accounting for upwards of 60% of ARI's output. First tried in tire construction in 1940, the use of rayon in tire manufacture reached an annual peak around 1955.[3] With the advent of nylon cord, however, rayon's market share in tire cord began to decline. Between 1955 and 1960 rayon's share of the total tire cord market dropped from 86% to 64%, and the total poundage of rayon so used dropped 38% (see Exhibit 5).

## Prospects for ARI

It was clear to MRC management that the medium- to long-run future must hold continuing decline and eventual liquidation for ARI. If purchased, ARI could not

2. Jesse W. Markham, *Competition in the Rayon Industry* (Cambridge, Mass.: Harvard University Press, 1952), p. 16.

3. C. A. Litzler, "The Fluid Tire Cord Situation," *Modern Textiles Magazine,* September 1966, p. 20.

be expected to contribute to the MRC growth objectives, and in time it might well become a serious drag on earnings. Consequently, Mr. Brinton was somewhat leery of pushing through to an acquisition. He was not at all sure that ARI, trapped in a decaying industry, would contribute to the strategic objectives of the diversification program. He was afraid that MRC would get entangled in a dying business, and he knew that MRC management lacked the technical know-how to contribute to the profitability of ARI, should the forecasts for this business prove optimistic. Moreover, he was not at all sure that the recently overhauled organization structure could easily assimilate a company as large as ARI. In the face of these concerns, he was reluctant to move quickly, whatever the DCF-ROI (discounted cash flow–rate of return on investment) numbers might show.

However, the near-term picture, as presented by Richard Victor, vice president for mergers and acquisitions, was not entirely unappealing. Although losses were sustained in 1957 and 1958, the company had subsequently returned to profitability as a result of substantial reductions in overhead, sale or liquidation of marginal and unprofitable operations, streamlining the marketing and R&D organizations, and consolidating production in a new manufacturing facility. Based on the investigation and analysis of his staff, he estimated that ARI would be able to maintain current volume, prices, and margins through 1964, followed thereafter by annual sales declines of 10–15%. He also estimated that assumption of numerous staff responsibilities by the MRC corporate staff would add about one percentage point to ARI's before-tax profit margin. Exhibit 6 shows pro forma income statements for ARI prepared by the MRC acquisition team.

From a financing point of view, it was thought that capital spending needs over the next 6–8 years would average no more than $300,000 annually. Mr. Victor felt that, if anything, his estimates understated future profits, since he expected ARI to pick up market share as smaller companies continued to withdraw from the rayon industry.

## Valuation

At a price of $40 million, ARI looked cheap. But Mr. Brinton insisted that any acquisition undertaken by MRC must promise to yield an adequate return, as measured by its discounted cash flow–rate of return.[4] Mr. Brinton regarded an acquisition decision as a special case of the capital budgeting decision. Like a capital budgeting project, an acquisition required the commitment of economic resources, cash or common stock or debt capacity, in the expectation of realizing a future income stream. Consequently, the primary valuation procedure used in acquisitions was conceptually identical to the capital budgeting procedure (see Appendix). All outlays and all cash inflows that were expected to result from undertaking a particular transaction were projected, and the DCF-ROI was found.

---

4. This measure of effectiveness is also commonly known as the internal rate of return, the time-adjusted rate of return, and the yield.

In terms of required rates of return, acquisitions were considered to be very similar to new product introductions.

Exhibit 7 shows management's forecast of MRC's per share income for the next 3 years.

MRC's common stock had closed the day before at $14½. ARI had closed at $15.

**EXHIBIT 1**

Four Year Summary of Financial Data for MRC, Inc., 1957–1960 (millions of dollars except per share data)

| | 1957 | 1958 | 1959 | 1960 |
|---|---|---|---|---|
| *Operations* | | | | |
| Sales | | | | |
|   Automotive and transportation . . . . | $ 76.4 | $49.7 | $56.8 | $ 41.3 |
|   Capital goods . . . . . . . . . . | 30.0 | 26.0 | 27.5 | 54.3 |
|   Building and construction . . . . . . | – | – | 2.7 | 14.2 |
|   Aerospace and defense . . . . . . . | .9 | .7 | 1.8 | 8.3 |
|     Total sales . . . . . . . . . | $107.3 | $76.4 | $88.8 | $118.1 |
| Net earnings . . . . . . . . . . . | $ 5.5 | $ 3.0 | $ 4.0 | $ 3.9 |
| Depreciation and amortization . . . . . | 1.4 | 1.5 | 1.7 | 2.3 |
| Cash funds from operations[a] . . . . . . | 6.2 | 3.8 | 4.9 | 5.5 |
| Return on total capital . . . . . . . | 12.6% | 8.1% | 7.8% | 9.3% |
| Return on common equity . . . . . . | 18.4% | 8.9% | 14.3% | 13.2% |
| *Common Stock* | | | | |
| Net earnings per share[b] . . . . . . . | $ 1.73 | $ .82 | $1.18 | $ 1.16 |
| Common dividends per share . . . . . | .94 | .79 | .75 | .75 |
| Market price range (high-low) . . . . . | 13–8 | 10–8 | 15–9 | 13–9 |
| Average price-earnings ratio . . . . . . | 6.5 | 12.1 | 10.3 | 9.5 |
| Average dividend yield . . . . . . . . | 8.4% | 7.9% | 6.2% | 6.8% |
| *Financial Position* | | | | |
| Working capital . . . . . . . . . . | $ 26.9 | $22.5 | $28.7 | $ 31.3 |
| Net property, plant, and | | | | |
|   equipment . . . . . . . . . . . | 15.6 | 16.0 | 23.1 | 28.4 |
| Long-term debt . . . . . . . . . . | 4.3 | 9.6 | 16.5 | 22.7 |
| Preferred and common | | | | |
|   shareholders' equity . . . . . . . . | 39.6 | 39.5 | 40.5 | 41.6 |

a. Net earnings plus depreciation, amortization, and deferred taxes, less preferred dividends.

b. Calculated on average number of shares outstanding during the year.

**EXHIBIT 2**

Acquisition History of MRC, Inc.

| | |
|---|---|
| December 1957 . . . | Acquired J. O. Ross Engineering Corporation in exchange for 281,000 shares. |
| March 1958 . . . . . | Acquired Hartig Engine and Machine Company, Mountainside, New Jersey, for cash and notes. |
| October 1958 . . . . | Acquired Transportation Division of Consolidated Metal Products Corporation, Albany, New York, and moved operations to Owosso, Michigan, Division. |
| April 1959 . . . . . | Acquired Nelson Metal Products Company, Grand Rapids, Michigan, for cash. |
| November 1959 . . . | Acquired Surface Combustion Corporation, Toledo, Ohio, for $23 million cash. |

**EXHIBIT 3**

Five-Year Summary of Financial Data for American Rayon, Inc., 1956–1960 (millions of dollars except per share data)

| | *1956* | *1957* | *1958* | *1959* | *1960* |
|---|---|---|---|---|---|
| *Operations* | | | | | |
| Net sales . . . . . . . . . | $59.3 | $58.1 | $ 47.9 | $62.1 | $54.5 |
| Earnings before taxes . . . . . | 9.4 | (2.3) | (6.2) | 1.7 | 4.8 |
| Pre-tax profit margin . . . . . | 15.9% | – | – | 2.7% | 8.8% |
| Net earnings . . . . . . . . | $ 4.5 | $ (1.2) | $ (3.2) | $ .8 | $ 2.5 |
| Depreciation and amortization . . . | 3.9 | 4.0 | 4.1 | 4.3 | 3.3 |
| Cash funds from operations . . . | 8.4 | 2.8 | .9 | 5.1 | 5.8 |
| Return on total capital . . . . . | 5.3% | – | – | 1.0% | 3.4% |
| Return on common equity . . . . | 5.9% | – | – | 1.1% | 3.8% |
| *Common Stock* | | | | | |
| Net earnings per share[a] . . . . | $2.45 | $ (.65) | $(1.69) | $ .44 | $1.34 |
| Common dividend per share[a] . . | 3.00 | 1.75 | – | – | – |
| Book value per share[a] . . . . . | 39.68 | 39.05 | 37.37 | 37.79 | 36.42 |
| Market price range (high–low) . . | 48–37 | 24–11 | 14–6 | 13–8 | 19–9 |
| Average price-earnings ratio . . . | 17 | – | – | 23.9 | 10.4 |
| *Financial Position* | | | | | |
| Working capital . . . . . . . | $39.1 | $38.8 | $ 36.6 | $37.9 | $41.2 |
| Net property, plant, and equipment . . . . . . . . | 36.6 | 34.1 | 34.2 | 33.8 | 23.9 |
| Long-term debt . . . . . . . | – | – | – | – | – |
| Common shareholders' equity . . | 75.4 | 74.2 | 71.0 | 71.8 | 65.2 |

a. Based on 1,851,255 common shares outstanding.

**EXHIBIT 4**
Balance Sheet of American Rayon, Inc. at December 31, 1960 (thousands of dollars)

| | |
|---|---:|
| Cash | $ 2,564 |
| U.S. government securities[a] | 20,024 |
| Accounts receivable, net | 11,863 |
| | 34,451 |
| Inventories | |
| Finished goods | 4,376 |
| In process | 2,161 |
| Raw materials and supplies | 3,919 |
| | 10,456 |
| Prepaid expenses | 283 |
| Current assets | 45,190 |
| Property, plant, and equipment, net | 23,912 |
| Other | 125 |
| Total assets | $69,227 |
| Accounts payable | $ 2,863 |
| Accrued items | 1,145 |
| Current liabilities | 4,008 |
| Common stock | 26,959 |
| Retained earnings | 38,260 |
| Shareholders' equity | 65,219 |
| Total liabilities and shareholders' equity | $69,227 |

a. Carried at cost plus accrued interest, which approximates market.

**EXHIBIT 5**
Consumption of Tire Cord, 1947–1960

| | Rayon | | Nylon | | Cotton | | Total Million Pounds |
|---|---:|---:|---:|---:|---:|---:|---:|
| | *Million Pounds* | *Market Share* | *Million Pounds* | *Market Share* | *Million Pounds* | *Market Share* | |
| 1947 | 214.6 | 43% | – | – | 285.1 | 57% | 499.7 |
| 1950 | 297.0 | 64 | – | – | 165.4 | 36 | 462.4 |
| 1955 | 406.9 | 86 | 49.2 | 10% | 16.7 | 4 | 472.8 |
| 1956 | 343.0 | 83 | 58.6 | 14 | 10.6 | 3 | 412.2 |
| 1957 | 318.5 | 77 | 83.2 | 20 | 10.3 | 3 | 412.0 |
| 1958 | 253.0 | 71 | 97.9 | 27 | 7.1 | 2 | 358.0 |
| 1959 | 287.1 | 70 | 120.3 | 29 | 3.9 | 1 | 411.2 |
| 1960 | 251.3 | 64 | 138.1 | 35 | 3.1 | 1 | 392.5 |

*Sources:* 1947–55: U.S. Bureau of the Census, *Statistical Abstract of the United States—1967* (Washington, D.C.: U.S. Government Printing Office), p. 761; 1956–60: American Rayon, Inc., Proxy Statement, March 28, 1961, p. 6.

**EXHIBIT 6**

Pro Forma Income Statements of American Rayon, Inc., 1961–1967 (thousands of dollars)

| Year Ended | 1961 | 1962 | 1963 | 1964 | 1965 | 1966 | 1967 |
|---|---|---|---|---|---|---|---|
| Net sales . . . . . . . . | $55,000 | $55,000 | $55,000 | $52,000 | $48,000 | $42,600 | $40,070 |
| Earnings before taxes . . . . | 4,840 | 5,390 | 5,390 | 3,640 | 2,724 | 1,917 | 841 |
| Federal income taxes . . . . | 2,323 | 2,587 | 2,587 | 1,747 | 1,308 | 920 | 404 |
| Net earnings . . . . . . . | 2,517 | 2,803 | 2,803 | 1,893 | 1,416 | 997 | 437 |
| Depreciation . . . . . . . . | 3,000 | 3,000 | 3,000 | 3,000 | 3,000 | 3,000 | 3,000 |
| Cash funds from operations . . | 5,517 | 5,803 | 5,803 | 4,893 | 4,416 | 3,997 | 3,437 |

**EXHIBIT 7**

Three-Year Forecast of MRC Earnings, 1961–1963 (thousands of dollars except per share data)

| Year Ended | 1961 | 1962 | 1963 |
|---|---|---|---|
| Net earnings[a] . . . . . | $4,723 | $5,054 | $5,458 |
| Earnings per share[b] . . . | $ 1.46 | $ 1.59 | $ 1.74 |

a. Assumes funding for all projects tentatively approved in 1961 capital budget, but no new acquisitions.

b. Based on 2,706,896 common shares outstanding and preferred dividends of $760,000.

---

# Appendix

# Capital Budgeting Procedures of MRC, Inc.

The formal capital budgeting procedures of MRC were outlined in a 49-page manual written for use at the divisional level and entitled "Expenditure Control Procedures." This document outlined (1) the classification scheme for types of funds requests, (2) the minimum levels of expenditure for which formal requests were required, (3) the maximum expenditure which could be authorized on the signature of corporate officers at various levels, (4) the format of the financial analysis required in a request for funds to carry out a project, and finally (5) the format of the report which followed the completion of the project and evaluated its success in terms of the original financial analysis outlined in (4).

## Classification Scheme for Funds Requests

The manual defined two basic classes of projects: profit improvement and necessity. Profit improvement projects included the following:

1. Cost reduction projects
2. Capacity expansion projects in existing product lines
3. New product line introductions

Necessity projects included all projects where profit improvement was not the basic purpose of the project, such as those for service facilities, plant security, improved working conditions, employee relations and welfare, pollution and contamination prevention, extensive repairs and replacements, profit maintenance, and services of outside research and consultant agencies. Expense projects of an unusual or extraordinary character included in this class were those expenses that did not lend themselves to inclusion in the operating budget and could normally be expected to occur less than once per year.

## Minimum Amounts Subject to Formal Request

Not all divisional requests for funds required formal and specific economic justification. Obviously, normal operating expenditures for items such as raw materials and wages were managed completely at the level of the divisions. Capital expenditures and certain nonrecurring operating expenditures were subject to formal requests and specific economic justification if they exceeded certain minimum amount levels specified below.

Project Appropriation Requests (PARs) were to be issued as follows:

**Capital.**   Projects with a unit cost equal to or more than the unit cost in the following schedule shall be covered by a PAR; items with lesser unit costs shall be expensed.

| | |
|---|---|
| Land improvements and buildings . . | $1,000 |
| Machinery and equipment . . . . . | 500 |
| Tools, patterns, dies, and jigs . . . . | 250 |
| Office furniture and office machines . . | 100 |

**Expense.** Expenses of an unusual or extraordinary character that do not lend themselves to inclusion in the operating budget and could normally be expected to occur less than once per year shall be covered by a PAR.

The minimum amount at which a PAR for expense is required is $10,000.

### Approval Limits of Corporate Officers

Officers at various management levels within MRC had the authority to approve a division's formal request for funds to carry out a project subject to the maximum limitations shown below.

**Approvals.** Requests shall be processed from a lower approval level to a higher approval level in accordance with the following chart to secure the approving authorities' initials (and date approved) signifying approval. Lower approvals shall be completed in advance of submission to a higher level.

| | *Highest Approval Level Required* |
|---|---|
| Expense projects | |
|   Minimum up to $10,000 . . | Division manager |
|   $10,000 up to $50,000 . . | Corporate president |
|   $50,000 and over . . . . | Board of directors |
| Capital projects | |
|   Minimum up to $5,000 . . | Division manager |
|   $5,000 up to $50,000 . . . | Corporate president |
|   $50,000 and over . . . . | Board of directors |
| Expense and capital combinations | |
|   Required approvals shall be the higher approval level required for either the capital or expense section in accordance with the above limits. | |

### Project Appropriation Request

The formal financial analysis required in a request for funds was called a Project Appropriation Request (Exhibit A1). The key output factors in the analysis (which included the amount of the total appropriation, the discounted cash flow–rate of return on investment, and the payback period) were summarized on the opening page under "Financial Summary" for easy reference.

The PAR originated at the divisional level and circulated to the officers whose signatures were necessary to authorize the expenditure. If the project was large enough to require the approval of an officer higher than the division manager, then five other members of the corporate financial group also reviewed the proposal. This group included the controller, the tax manager, the director of financial planning, the treasurer, and the vice president of finance. These managers did not review very small projects, however, since capital items under $5,000 never reached the corporate office. Division managers could authorize these small projects on their own signature.

### Project Evaluation Report

On each PAR, the corporate controller had the option of indicating whether or not he desired a Project Evaluation Report (PER). When requested, the division manager submitted this report 1 year after the approved project was completed. The report indicated how well the project was performing in relation to its original cost, return on investment (ROI), and payback estimates.

### The Stream of PARs Reaching the Corporate Office

During 1960, MRC approved 70 PARs calling for the expenditure of more than $17 million. A sample evaluation made in 1961 of some of the projects that the board of directors had approved in earlier years is reproduced as Exhibit A2.

### Scrutinizing a PAR at the Presidential Level

In discussing capital budgeting at MRC, Mr. Brinton stated that the largest projects, involving more than a million dollars, were almost always discussed informally between the president and the division manager at least a year before a formal PAR was submitted. He said:

> Let's look at a project involving a facilities expansion. The need for a new plant addition in most of our business areas doesn't sneak up on you. It can be foreseen at least a couple of years in advance. An enormous amount of work is involved in submitting a detailed economic proposal for something like a new plant. Architects have to draft plans, proposed sites have to be outlined, and construction lead times need to be established. No division manager would submit a complete request for a new facilities addition without first getting an informal green light that such a proposal could receive favorable attention. By the time a formal PAR is completed on a large plant addition, most of us are pretty well sold on the project.

In response to the question, "What are the most significant items that you look at when a new PAR lands on your desk?" Mr. Brinton responded as follows:

> The size of the project is probably the first thing that I look at. Obviously, I won't spend much time on a $15,000 request for a new fork-lift truck from a division manager with an annual sales volume of $50 million.

I'd next look at the type of project we're dealing with to get a feel for the degree of certainty in the rate of return calculation. I feel a whole lot more comfortable with a cost reduction project promising a 20% return than I would with a volume expansion project which promises the same rate of return. Cost reduction is usually an engineering problem. You know exactly how much a new machine will cost and you can be fairly certain about how many labor-hours will be saved. On a volume expansion you're betting on a marketing estimate and maybe the date for getting a plant on stream. These are fairly uncertain variables.

On a new product appropriation, things get even worse. Here you're betting on both price and volume estimates, and supporting data can get awfully thin. Over all, I think our cost reduction projects have probably yielded higher returns and have been less risky than either plant expansion or new product proposals. They don't, of course, eat up anything like the amount of capital that the other two types of projects can require.

The third and perhaps most important item that I look for is the name of the division manager who sent the project up. We've got managers at the top and at the bottom of the class just like any organization. If I get a project from an individual who has been with the company for a few years, who has turned a division around, or shown that he has a better command of his business than anyone else in his industry, then I'll usually go with his judgment. If his business is going to pot, however, I may take a long hard look, challenge a lot of the assumptions, and ask for more justification.

Fourth, I look at the ROI figure. If the project is a large one, I have the finance people massage the numbers to see what happens to the ROI if some of the critical variables like volume, prices, and costs are varied. This is an area where knowing your division manager is enormously important. Some managers, particularly those with a sales background, may be very optimistic on volume projections. In this kind of situation you feel more comfortable if you can knock the volume down 25% and still see a reasonable return.

I haven't established formal and inviolable hurdle rates which each and every project must clear. I want to avoid giving the division people an incentive to stretch their estimates on marginal projects or, alternatively, to build in fat cushions—insurance policies—on great projects. Still, I generally look for a minimum DCF-ROI of about 12% on cost reduction proposals, 15–16% on large volume expansion projects, and 18–20% or even more on new product introductions. But these aren't magic numbers. Projects showing lower yields are sometimes accepted.

## Strategic Capital Investments

Mr. Brinton later commented on a question regarding the role of capital budgeting in overall corporate strategy:

In general, we'll invest our capital in those business areas that promise the highest return. Usually you can't afford to establish a position in a market on just the hope that a return will materialize in the future. Du Pont can afford to invest $75 million in a new fiber, but MRC can't. We can afford to invest a few million dollars in projects of this nature—and we have in areas like continuous casting and iron ore pelletizing—but most of our projects have to promise a prompt return.

**EXHIBIT A1**
Project Appropriation Request

| Division | | | Department | | | Location | | |
|---|---|---|---|---|---|---|---|---|
| Power Controls | | | | | | | | |

**Title**

Disc Brake Manufacturing Facility

| Profit Improvement | Necessity | Predicted Life | Underrun | Overrun | Starting Date | Completion Date |
|---|---|---|---|---|---|---|
| X | | 15 Years | | | July 1961 | April 1963 |

**1. DESCRIPTION AND JUSTIFICATION**

The U.S. automotive industry is experiencing a trend to the use of disc braking systems for passenger cars and light trucks. Our market research indicates this type of braking system will be widespread within 5 years and the Power Controls Division can be a major supplier of these systems if we act now to provide the required manufacturing facilities.

**2. FINANCIAL SUMMARY**

| | This Request | Previous Approved Requests | Total Project | Approval and Distribution of Copies | | | | | |
|---|---|---|---|---|---|---|---|---|---|
| | | | | Division | Date | No. | Corporate | Date | No. |
| Capital | 4,875,000 | _____ | 4,875,000 | Issued By | | | Group V.P. | | |
| Working Capital | 1,950,000 | | 1,950,000 | | | | Group V.P. | | |
| Expense | 975,000 | | 975,000 | | | | | | |
| Total | 7,800,000 | | 7,800,000 | | | | Controller | | |
| Less Salvage Value of Disposals | | | | | | | Tax Manager | | |
| Net | | | | | | | Mgr. Fin. Planning | | |
| Book Value of Disposals | | | | | | | Treasurer | | |
| Project Budgeted Amount | | | 7,800,000 | | | | Financial V.P. | | |
| Return on Investment (after Tax) | | | 16% | Division Controller | | | President | | |
| Period to Amortize (after Tax) | | | 3.6 Years | Division Manager | | | For the Board | | |
| Accounting Distribution | | | | Project Evaluation Report Required | Yes | No | | | |
| | | | | | | | | | |

**Estimated Timing of Expenditures – By Quarter and Year**

| 3/61 | 4/61 | 1/62 | 2/62 | 3/62 | 4/62 | 1/63 | 2/63 |
|---|---|---|---|---|---|---|---|
| $ 75,000 | $125,000 | $1,125,000 | $1,500,000 | $1,500,000 | $1,875,000 | $ 900,000 | $ 700,000 |

*(continued)*

## EXHIBIT A1 *(concluded)*

PRESENT VALUE OF CASH FLOWS

| YEAR | YEAR OF OPER-ATION | DISBURSEMENTS | CASH RETURNS | 15% TRIAL INTEREST RATE | | | 16% TRIAL INTEREST RATE | | | % TRIAL INTEREST RATE | | |
|---|---|---|---|---|---|---|---|---|---|---|---|---|
| | | | | Factor | PRESENT WORTH Disbursements | Cash Returns | Factor | PRESENT WORTH Disbursements | Cash Returns | Factor | PRESENT WORTH Disbursements | Cash Returns |
| 1961 | 2 Prior | 200 | | | | | 1.346 | 269 | | | | |
| 1962 | 1 Prior | 6,000 | 218 | | | | 1.160 | 6,960 | 253 | | | |
| | | | | | | Beginning of Operations | | | | | | |
| 1963 | At 1 | 1,600 | 468 | 1.000 | | xxxxxxxxxxxx | 1.000 | 1,132 | xxxxxxxxxxxx | 1.000 | | xxxxxxxxxxxx |
| 1963 | 1 | | 641 | | xxxxxxxxxxxx | | .862 | xxxxxxxxxxxx | 553 | | xxxxxxxxxxxx | |
| | 2 | | 1,792 | | | | .743 | | 1,331 | | | |
| | 3 | | 1,686 | | | | .641 | | 1,081 | | | |
| | 4 | | 1,601 | | | | .552 | | 884 | | | |
| | 5 | | 1,523 | | | | .476 | | 725 | | | |
| | 6 | | 1,473 | | | | .410 | | 604 | | | |
| | 7 | | 1,443 | | | | .354 | | 511 | | | |
| | 8 | | 1,439 | | | | .305 | | 439 | | | |
| | 9 | | 1,434 | | | | .263 | | 377 | | | |
| | 10 | | 1,432 | | | | .227 | | 325 | | | |
| | 11 | | 1,337 | | | | .195 | | 261 | | | |
| | 12 | | 1,241 | | | | .168 | | 208 | | | |
| | 13 | | 1,241 | | | | .145 | | 180 | | | |
| | 14 | | 1,241 | | | | .125 | | 155 | | | |
| | 15 | | 1,400 | | | | .108 | | 151 | | | |
| | 15 | Return Work Cap. | 1,950 | | | | .108 | | 210 | | | |
| | 15 | Residual Plant | 885 | | | | .108 | | 96 | | | |
| | 18 | | | | | | | | | | | |
| | 19 | | | | | | | | | | | |
| | 20 | | | | | | | | | | | |
| | 21 | | | | | | | | | | | |
| | 22 | | | | | | | | | | | |
| | 23 | | | | | | | | | | | |
| | 24 | | | | | | | | | | | |
| | 25 | | | | | | | | | | | |
| | 26 | | | | | | | | | | | |
| | 27 | | | | | | | | | | | |
| | 28 | | | | | | | | | | | |
| | 29 | | | | | | | | | | | |
| | 30 | | | | | | | | | | | |
| TOTALS | | 7,800 | 24,445 | | | | | 8,361 | 8,344 | | | |
| CASH RETURNS LESS DISBURSEMENTS | | xxxxxxxxxxxx | | | xxxxxxxxxxxx | | | xxxxxxxxxxxx | (17) | | xxxxxxxxxxxx | |
| DISBURSEMENTS CASH RETURNS | | xxxxxxxxxxxx | | | xxxxxxxxxxxx | | | xxxxxxxxxxxx | 1.0 | | xxxxxxxxxxxx | |

**EXHIBIT A2**
Summary of Selected Project Evaluation Reports, August 1960

| Project Number | Description | Date Approved | Project Amount ($000s) | | Rate of Return (%) | | Payback Period (years) | |
|---|---|---|---|---|---|---|---|---|
| | | | Forecast | Actual | Forecast | Actual | Forecast | Actual |
| FA-157 | Roll Forming Mill | 1/58 | $193 | $193 | 37% | 42% | 2.5 | 2.3 |
| FA-151 | Univ. Paint Mach. Unloader | 7/59 | 98 | 43 | >30 | >30 | 2.6 | 1.6 |
| FA-147 | Loading Equip. '65 Buick | 7/57 | 80 | 79 | 29 | 29 | 3.1 | 3.3 |
| P 352–51 | "V" Band Couplings Program | 8/59 | 58 | 90 | >30 | Loss | .7 | Loss |
| P 328–29 | New Gas Furnace Line | 6/56 | 495 | 491 | >50 | 43 est. | 1.0 | 1.7 est. |
| P-532 | Aluminum Die Cast Equipment | 5/59 | 86 | 86 | >30 | >30 | 2.2 | 2.0 |
| P-547 | (2) W-S #1 AC Chuckers | 7/59 | 66 | 66 | >30 | >30 | 2.0 | 1.4 |
| 64–129C | (2) W-S Chuckers | 12/58 | 116 | 114 | 12 | Loss | 5.5 | Loss |

# *Interco*

On August 8, 1988, Interco's board of directors met to discuss, among other matters, a merger proposal from City Capital Associates Limited Partnership. City Capital had offered $64 per common share of Interco on July 28, 1988, and had raised that offer to $70 per share on the morning of August 8. At this board meeting Interco's financial advisers, Wasserstein, Perella & Co., established a valuation range of $68–80 per common share of Interco and presented their evaluation of the offer. Given their valuation, Wasserstein, Perella advised the Interco board (see Exhibit 1) that the $70 per share offer was inadequate and not in the best interests of the company and its shareholders. The board of directors voted to reject the City Capital offer.

## Description of the Company

Founded in December 1911, the International Shoe Company was established as a footwear manufacturing concern and remained so until the early 1960s. In 1966 the company was renamed Interco to reflect the changing character of its business. It had grown into a major manufacturer and retailer of a wide variety of consumer products and services. Among the best-known of Interco's brands were Converse and Florsheim shoes, Ethan Allen furniture, and London Fog rainwear.

Interco's various operations were substantially autonomous and were supported by a corporate management staff in St. Louis, Missouri. The company's philosophy had historically been to acquire companies in related fields and to provide their existing management teams with the incentives to expand their businesses while relieving them of such routine support functions as financial and legal requirements. Nearly half of Interco's growth had come through acquisition. The company continually sought entities that would complement the existing Interco companies. Additional criteria used in screening and selecting acquisition candidates included the presence of highly skilled managers and products that had established leadership positions in their respective markets.

Equity analysts viewed Interco as a conservative company that was financially overcapitalized. With a current ratio of 3.6 to 1 and a debt-to-capitalization ratio, including capitalized leases, of 19.3% on February 29, 1988, Interco had ample financial flexibility. This flexibility had allowed the company to repurchase its common shares and make acquisitions as opportunities arose.

## Operating Divisions

Interco was organized into four major operating divisions:

- Apparel manufacturing
- General retail merchandising
- Footwear manufacturing and retailing
- Furniture and home furnishings

Within these four operating divisions were numerous independent companies, listed in Exhibit 2.

**Apparel Manufacturing.**   This group consisted of 11 apparel companies that designed, manufactured, and distributed a full range of branded and private-label sportswear, casual apparel, outer garments, and headwear for men and women. Apparel brands included Le Tigre, Sergio Valente, and Abe Schrader. Distribution was national in scope to department stores, specialty shops, and other retail units, including discount chains.

**General Retail Merchandising.**   This group operated 201 retail locations in 15 states. General retailing included large do-it-yourself home improvement centers, general merchandise discount stores, men's specialty apparel shops, and specialty department stores. Over the prior few years, general retail had been greatly scaled back and was now dominated largely by Central Hardware, a do-it-yourself home improvement chain that emphasized customer service and a broad selection of products.

**Footwear Manufacturing and Retailing.**   This division designed, manufactured, and distributed men's and women's footwear principally in the United States, Australia, Canada, and Mexico. The group operated 778 retail shoe stores and leased shoe departments in 42 states and in Australia. Interco's two major footwear operations, Converse Inc. and the Florsheim Shoe Co., commanded leading positions in their respective markets: athletic shoes and men's traditional footwear.

**Furniture and Home Furnishings.**  This group manufactured, distributed, and retailed quality wood and upholstered furniture and home furnishings. Furniture brands included Broyhill, Lane, Ethan Allen, and Hickory Chair. In recent years the furniture division had expanded through acquisitions and increasing profitability to dominate Interco's net income. At the end of fiscal year 1988, Interco was the largest furniture manufacturer in the world.

## Strategic Repositioning Program

Interco's goals included long-term sales and earnings growth, increased return on corporate assets, and most important, improved return on shareholders' equity. To achieve these goals, Interco took a four-pronged approach that included improving the profitability of existing operations and divesting underperforming assets, making acquisitions that had the potential for better-than-average returns and growth, and employing opportunistic financial strategies such as share repurchases and the prudent use of borrowing capacity.

With these goals established, Interco in 1984 began a strategic repositioning program aimed at improving overall corporate performance. As part of this initiative, Interco accelerated its efforts to divest underperforming assets and reposition itself in markets offering superior growth opportunities and profitability. The program resulted in a substantial change in Interco's mix of sales, as shown in Table A. In fiscal 1988 the furniture and footwear groups together accounted for 60% of corporate sales, with apparel and general retail accounting for the rest. This was a reversal of the sales distribution in fiscal 1984.

## Recent Financial Performance

Overall corporate performance for fiscal year 1988 was positive, with sales and net income increasing 13.4% and 15.4%, respectively, over 1987 levels. This performance was attributable largely to the contributions of the furniture and home furnishings and footwear groups as well as to a decrease in Interco's effective tax rate. Because of the Tax Reform Act of 1986, the company's effective tax

**TABLE A**
Percent of Sales by Operating Group, 1984 and 1988

|  | 1984 | 1988 |
|---|---|---|
| Apparel | 33% | 24% |
| General retail | 26 | 16 |
| Footwear | 21 | 27 |
| Furniture | 20 | 33 |

*Source:* Interco annual report, February 29, 1988.

rate in 1988 was 42.8% versus 47.1% in fiscal 1987. Growth in earnings moved Interco further toward its goal of a 14–15% return on equity: the 1988 ROE of 11.7% was up from 9.7% in fiscal 1987.

The furniture and home furnishings group had an outstanding year in 1988, earning an operating profit of $149.1 million versus $123.8 million in fiscal 1987 and achieving sales of $1.11 billion compared to $967.4 million in 1987. Favorable demographic trends in family formations made the outlook for this group positive despite its exposure to cyclical fluctuations in housing starts and interest rates.

Showing the largest percentage gains for fiscal year 1988, sales for the footwear group increased 34.2% and operating profits soared nearly 77%. These earnings were supported by the performance of Converse, acquired in September 1986, which had a record year in sales and earnings in 1988.

Despite multiple restructuring efforts including divestiture of underperforming assets, the apparel manufacturing and general retail divisions remained ongoing problems, largely because of a change in the nature of these businesses. In calendar year 1987 a variety of problems continued to plague the U.S. apparel manufacturing industry. Consumer spending was lower than anticipated, imports from countries with lower labor costs continued to flow into the United States, and department stores increasingly emphasized private-label goods at the expense of manufacturers of branded apparel. In response to an intensely competitive retailing industry and a drop-off in consumer spending, retailers implemented heavy promotion and deep discounting programs in 1987 and into 1988. As a result, sales had been advancing at a moderate pace, with earnings declining at a more rapid rate. Industry experts were forecasting moderate industry growth in the absence of any significant economic downturn.

Interco's general retail merchandising and apparel manufacturing groups turned in less than stellar performances in fiscal 1988. The former group's operating profits fell 3.7% on a modest increase in sales over the comparable 1987 period. The latter group earned operating profits of $20.2 million after an $11.6 million restructuring charge, compared to $47.3 million in 1987, on sales that slipped only slightly from 1987 levels.

## The Takeover Bid

Interco management and Wall Street analysts believed that the apparel group's performance would continue to weaken Interco's overall operations and cause the equity markets to undervalue its common stock. Exhibits 3 and 4 give the history of Interco's common stock prices. After the stock market crash of October 1987, Interco had accelerated its share repurchase program with the board of directors' authorization to buy back up to 5 million shares. By the end of fiscal year 1988 more than 4 million shares of common stock had been repurchased, at a cost of $152.3 million.

Given that Interco was widely viewed in the investment community as a potential takeover target, Harvey Saligman, Interco's chairman and chief executive officer, contacted Wasserstein, Perella & Co. to discuss potential defensive measures aimed at maintaining Interco's independence. To deter any unwanted third-party acquisition, the board voted on July 11, 1988, to amend Interco's shareholder rights plan, making any hostile takeover of the company prohibitively expensive. Exhibit 5 describes Interco's shareholder rights plan in more detail.

Determined to improve the return on shareholders' investment and to further deter a third-party acquisition, on July 15, 1988, Interco announced plans to restructure. The apparel group's performance for the quarter ended May 31, 1988, continued to be poor, with a 13.4% decline in sales from the comparable 1987 quarter. The proposed restructuring would involve the sale of the apparel segment, a special dividend, and/or a stock repurchase. Interco retained two investment banking firms, Goldman, Sachs & Co. and Wasserstein, Perella & Co., to explore strategic alternatives and to sell the apparel manufacturing division and possibly other assets. Saligman's proposal of such a restructuring was aimed at "narrow[ing] the focus of Interco's business and improv[ing] the price of its shares."[1]

But a takeover attempt could not be avoided. On July 27, 1988, City Capital proposed a merger with Interco. Pursuant to this proposal, City Capital offered to buy all of Interco's common shares that it did not already own at a price of $64 per share. City Capital also advised the board of its willingness to negotiate the terms of the proposal, including price. In response, the Interco board expanded Wasserstein, Perella's mandate as financial adviser. Their advisory services would now include delivering an opinion on the fairness of City Capital's offer and valuing and recommending other alternatives.[2] How much Interco was worth was a question its board of directors would have to consider in evaluating alternatives to a merger with City Capital.

City Capital Associates Limited Partnership was led by two Washington, D.C., businessmen, Steven M. Rales and his brother Mitchell. The Rales brothers had been involved in multiple acquisitions either through Danaher Corporation, a publicly owned company they controlled, or one of a variety of their other partnerships. These acquisitions had included Western Pacific Industries Inc., Chicago Pneumatic Tool Co., Mohawk Rubber Co., and Master Shield Inc. The brothers' acquisition focus had been on undervalued targets with strong market niches. With the completion of eight medium-sized acquisitions, Danaher had grown since 1981 from a small real estate trust into a diversified conglomerate of manufacturing companies. In part because of the acquisitions and the use of tax loss carry-forwards, Danaher

---

1. Francine Schwadel, "Interco Receives Bid from Rales Group for Takeover Value at $2.26 Billion," *The Wall Street Journal,* July 29, 1988, p. 4.

2. Interco had retained Wasserstein, Perella pursuant to a unique compensation contract that offered a substantial contingency fee of $3.7 million payable to Wasserstein, Perella once City Capital rescinded their offer and only if a recapitalization was completed. Wasserstein, Perella would receive $1.8 million for its services with or without this contingency fee. See George Anders and Francine Schwadel, "Wall Streeters Helped Interco Defeat Raiders but at a Heavy Price," *The Wall Street Journal,* July 7, 1990, p. A1.

Corporation's earnings had increased sixfold, from $2.9 million in 1984 to $19 million in 1987.

The Rales brothers had formed City Capital with the sole purpose of acquiring Interco. As disclosed in a Securities and Exchange Commission filing, it was their intention, after completing the acquisition, to sell Interco's apparel businesses and to consider selling parts of the footwear and general retailing businesses. In this same filing the Rales brothers indicated that they would consider paying more than $64 per common share for Interco.

On the morning of August 8, 1988, City Capital raised its offer for Interco to $70 per share and stated its willingness to increase the price per share further should a review of more detailed company information so warrant. Under the assumption of 37.5 million fully diluted shares outstanding, the offer had an indicated value of over $2.6 billion. The offer was conditional upon, among other things, the board's redemption of the newly amended rights plan or the invalidation of those rights pursuant to the proposed merger. Before raising the value of its offer for Interco, City Capital had arranged the required $2.5 billion in financing. Drexel Burnham Lambert Inc., City Capital's financial adviser, had stated that it was "highly confident" it could raise up to $1.375 billion of debt or equity for the $70 per share proposal. Additional bank financing, including a $1.1 billion credit facility arranged by Chase Manhattan Corporation, would provide the remainder of the necessary funding.

## Evaluation of Strategic Alternatives

At Interco's regular board meeting on August 8, 1988, the directors had been expected to discuss a previously announced restructuring plan that would include selling the company's faltering apparel group, paying a special dividend, and/or repurchasing shares of common stock. The sale of other divisions and further restructuring, alone or in conjunction with a recapitalization of Interco, could be used to fend off hostile raiders.

Among other alternatives that Interco had at this juncture were the options of searching for a friendly merger or leveraged buyout partner or recapitalizing the company. Under these scenarios it was assumed that key managers, including Saligman, would remain with the company.

City Capital had accumulated 8.7% of Interco's common stock, and Saligman and the board of directors had to respond to the Rales brothers' offer. Wasserstein, Perella had prepared multiple analyses since the initial $64 offer was made to evaluate the City Capital offer and to assess the value of alternatives, which included a potential friendly merger, a restructuring, and recapitalization of the company along with the sale of certain assets. Assessing Interco's value would be an important first step to any decision on City Capital's offer or any of the strategic alternatives Interco's financial advisers proposed. Historical financial statements are given in Exhibits 6 and 7. Business segment information is shown in Exhibit 8.

As financial advisers to Interco, Wasserstein, Perella prepared a number of analyses to create reference valuation ranges for the company and its common shares. Exhibits 9–13 present data and assumptions that Wasserstein, Perella relied on in providing an opinion on Interco's value. Exhibit 14 gives indexes of monthly adjusted closing prices, actual daily closing prices, and market interest rates.

At Interco's board meeting on August 8, 1988, Wasserstein, Perella informed the board that City Capital's offer of $70 per share was inadequate and not in the best interests of the company and its shareholders. This expert opinion was based on a series of analyses, including discounted cash flow analysis, comparable transaction analysis, and premiums paid analysis. The analyses produced a valuation reference range for the company of $68–80 per share (Exhibit 13). Interco's board of directors voted to reject the $70 per share bid the same day.

**EXHIBIT 1**
Board of Directors, May 16, 1988

| | |
|---|---|
| Harvey Saligman | Chairman and chief executive officer of Interco |
| Harry M. Krogh | President and chief operating officer of Interco |
| Ronald L. Aylward | Vice chairman of Interco |
| R. Stuart Moore | Vice president of Interco; president of the Lane Company, Inc., a subsidiary of Interco |
| Mark H. Lieberman | Vice president of Interco; president of Londontown, a division of Interco |
| Richard B. Loynd | Vice president of Interco; chairman of Converse, Inc., a subsidiary of Interco |
| Charles J. Rothschild, Jr. | Vice president of Interco; chairman of Megastar Apparel Group, a division of Interco |
| Zane E. Barnes | Chairman, president, chief executive officer, and director of Southwestern Bell Corporation, engaged in the general telecommunications business |
| Donald D. Lasater | Chairman, chief executive officer, and director of Mercantile Bancorporation, Inc., a bank holding company; chairman and director of Mercantile Bank National Association |
| Lee M. Liberman | Chairman, president, chief executive officer, and director of Laclede Gas Company, a gas public utility |
| Robert H. Quenon | President, chief executive officer, and director of Peabody Holding Company, Inc., engaged in coal mining and sales |
| William E. Cornelius | President, chief executive officer, and director of Union Electric Company, an electric public utility |
| Marilyn S. Lewis | Civic leader and volunteer |
| Thomas H. O'Leary | Vice chairman and director of Burlington Northern Inc., a holding company with transportation, energy, and natural resources concerns |

As of April 15, 1988, all directors, nominees, and officers of Interco as a group (24 persons) beneficially owned 1.14% of the outstanding shares of Interco's common stock.

*Source:* Notice and proxy statement, May 16, 1988.

**EXHIBIT 2**
Subsidiaries

| | |
|---|---|
| Abe Schrader Corp. | Golde's Department Stores, Inc. |
| Big Yank Corp. | Grand Entry Hat Corp. |
| Bowen Shoe Co., Inc. | Highland House, Inc. |
| Broyhill Furniture Industries, Inc. | Highland Transport, Inc. |
| Campco Holdings, S.A. | Hy-Test, Inc. |
| | |
| Campus Pacific Ltd. | Interco Subsidiary, Inc. |
| Central Hardware Co. | Keith O'Brien Investment Co. |
| Clayton Operations, S.A. | Lane Co., Inc. |
| College-Town, Inc. | Lease Management, Inc. |
| Converse Inc. | Julius Marlow Holdings, Ltd. |
| | |
| Delmar Sportswear, Inc. | L. J. O'Neill Shoe Co. |
| Ethan Allen Inc. | ORC Financial Ag |
| Factory Outlet Co. | Patriot Investment Co. |
| Fine's Men's Shops, Inc. | Queen Casuals, Inc. |
| Florsheim Inc. | Senack Shoes, Inc. |
| | |
| Florsheim Shoe Store Co. of Hawaii | Sky City Stores, Inc. |
| Florsheim Shoe Store Co.–Midwest | Stuffed Shirt Inc. |
| Florsheim Shoe Store Co.–Northwest | United Shirt Distributors, Inc. |
| Florsheim Shoe Store Co.–South | Walton Road Management Co. |
| Florsheim Shoe Store Co.–West | |

*Source:* Lotus One Source.

**EXHIBIT 3**
Common Stock History, 1986–1988

| | | | | |
|---|---|---|---|---|
| Jan. 31, 1986 | . . . | $35.125 | July 31, 1987 . . . | $51.250 |
| Feb. 28 . . . . . . | 39.000 | | Aug. 31 . . . . . | 53.250 |
| Mar. 31 . . . . . | 39.250 | | Sept. 30 . . . . . | 47.500 |
| Apr. 30 . . . . . | 39.625 | | Oct. 30 . . . . . | 36.000 |
| May 30 . . . . . | 43.500 | | Nov. 30 . . . . . | 30.000 |
| June 30 . . . . . | 47.188 | | Dec. 31 . . . . . | 32.250 |
| July 31 . . . . . | 41.375 | | Jan. 29, 1988 . . . | 37.125 |
| Aug. 29 . . . . . | 43.750 | | Feb. 29 . . . . . | 42.000 |
| Sept. 30 . . . . | 40.000 | | Mar. 31 . . . . . | 42.000 |
| Oct. 31 . . . . . | 43.750 | | Apr. 29 . . . . . | 41.125 |
| Nov. 28 . . . . . | 44.125 | | May 31 . . . . . | 43.875 |
| Dec. 31 . . . . . | 36.875 | | June 30 . . . . . | 44.750 |
| Jan. 30, 1987 . . . | 39.750 | | July 29 . . . . . | 68.500 |
| Feb. 27 . . . . . | 42.625 | | | |
| Mar. 31 . . . . . | 44.125 | | | |
| Apr. 30 . . . . . | 39.625 | | | |
| May 29 . . . . . | 40.125 | | | |
| June 30 . . . . . | 45.375 | | | |

*Source:* Interactive Data Corporation.

*Note:* Prices are adjusted for stock splits.

**EXHIBIT 4**
Daily Closing Stock Prices, 1988

| | | | | | | |
|---|---|---|---|---|---|
| May 2 | . . $40.250 | June 6 | . . $43.250 | July 11 | . . $45.250 |
| May 3 | . . 41.500 | June 7 | . . 42.000 | July 12 | . . 45.375 |
| May 4 | . . 41.000 | June 8 | . . 43.875 | July 13 | . . 46.375 |
| May 5 | . . 41.625 | June 9 | . . 43.375 | July 14 | . . 49.000 |
| May 6 | . . 40.625 | June 10 | . . 43.375 | July 15 | . . 54.375 |
| May 9 | . . 40.875 | June 13 | . . 43.500 | July 18 | . . 54.500 |
| May 10 | . . 41.750 | June 14 | . . 43.625 | July 19 | . . 58.375 |
| May 11 | . . 41.625 | June 15 | . . 42.500 | July 20 | . . 58.125 |
| May 12 | . . 42.000 | June 16 | . . 42.875 | July 21 | . . 57.875 |
| May 13 | . . 42.125 | June 17 | . . 43.625 | July 22 | . . 57.250 |
| May 16 | . . 42.250 | June 20 | . . 43.250 | July 25 | . . 58.000 |
| May 17 | . . 42.000 | June 21 | . . 43.125 | July 26 | . . 58.875 |
| May 18 | . . 41.500 | June 22 | . . 43.750 | July 27 | . . 59.375 |
| May 19 | . . 40.625 | June 23 | . . 43.625 | July 28 | . . 67.750 |
| May 20 | . . 40.625 | June 24 | . . 43.500 | July 29 | . . 68.500 |
| May 23 | . . 40.375 | June 27 | . . 43.625 | Aug. 1 | . . 68.875 |
| May 24 | . . 41.500 | June 28 | . . 44.000 | Aug. 2 | . . 67.625 |
| May 25 | . . 42.500 | June 29 | . . 44.000 | Aug. 3 | . . 67.000 |
| May 26 | . . 42.625 | June 30 | . . 44.750 | Aug. 4 | . . 67.375 |
| May 27 | . . 41.250 | July 1 | . . 44.625 | Aug. 5 | . . 68.250 |
| May 31 | . . 43.875 | July 5 | . . 45.375 | Aug. 8 | . . 72.500 |
| June 1 | . . 43.500 | July 6 | . . 44.500 | | |
| June 2 | . . 42.875 | July 7 | . . 44.625 | | |
| June 3 | . . 44.125 | July 8 | . . 45.000 | | |

*Source:* Interactive Data Corporation.

**EXHIBIT 5**
Shareholder Rights Plan

On September 23, 1985, Interco's board of directors adopted a shareholder rights plan designed to deter unsolicited takeover bids by creating the threat of substantial dilution for any person or group attempting an unfriendly merger with Interco.

The original plan was amended on July 11, 1988, by the board of directors. At that time, the directors were aware that Interco's common stock was under accumulation and were suspicious of a third-party acquisition offer for the company.[a] Changes in the purchase price per share and certain triggering provisions, otherwise known as poison pill shareholder rights, made the takeover defense more onerous. Specifically, the amended rights plan declared that it would issue a dividend of one share purchase right per share of common stock. The amended rights plan also gave the board sole discretion to lower certain triggering percentages such that the massive dilutive effects of the plan would come into play when a person or group acquired as little as 15% of the shares of Interco's stock.

At Interco's board meeting on August 8, 1988, the board approved golden parachute severance agreements for Interco's senior executives, to be triggered upon an acquisition by a third party, including City Capital. According to an SEC filing, the golden parachute severance agreements were valued at $16.3 million and covered 17 top executives at Interco. Lump sum payments, including $2.2 million to Harvey Saligman, would be made under certain conditions if the company were taken over.

a. As claimed in Civil Action No. 10111, the Second Amended and Consolidated Class Action Complaint, as filed in the Court of Chancery of the State of Delaware, New Castle County, p. 16.

**EXHIBIT 6**
Consolidated Balance Sheets at February 28/29, 1986–1988, and May 31, 1987–1988 (thousands of dollars)

| | Feb. 28, 1986 | Feb. 28, 1987 | Feb. 29, 1988 | May 31, 1987 | May 31, 1988 |
|---|---|---|---|---|---|
| Cash | $ 16,856 | $ 16,631 | $ 20,849 | $ 29,700 | $ 19,622 |
| Marketable securities | 127,341 | 63,747 | 11,033 | 57,789 | 16,366 |
| Receivables, net | 402,225 | 446,755 | 486,657 | 431,743 | 460,759 |
| Inventories | 646,866 | 733,907 | 805,095 | 786,792 | 872,135 |
| Prepaid expenses, other current assets | 22,547 | 25,614 | 35,665 | 25,622 | 44,959 |
| Current assets | 1,215,835 | 1,286,654 | 1,359,299 | 1,331,646 | 1,413,841 |
| Property, plant, and equipment | | | | | |
| Land | 26,770 | 32,266 | 32,525 | – | – |
| Buildings and improvements | 437,812 | 465,811 | 471,787 | – | – |
| Machinery and equipment | 320,256 | 364,499 | 380,402 | – | – |
| | 784,838 | 862,576 | 884,714 | 868,670 | 890,887 |
| Less: Accumulated depreciation | 343,018 | 377,226 | 405,215 | 386,762 | 412,332 |
| Net property, plant, equipment | 441,820 | 485,350 | 479,499 | 481,908 | 478,555 |
| Other assets | 99,238 | 153,383 | 146,788 | 149,170 | 146,877 |
| Total assets | $1,756,893 | $1,925,387 | $1,985,586 | $1,962,724 | $2,039,273 |
| Notes payable | – | $ 68,840 | $ 70,517 | $ 97,297 | $ 146,016 |
| Current maturities of long-term debt and capital lease obligations | $ 9,647 | 11,915 | 8,172 | 9,288 | 8,900 |
| Accounts payable and accrued expenses | 227,241 | 260,144 | 290,252 | 278,847 | 292,051 |
| Income taxes | 12,699 | 17,327 | 4,402 | 15,294 | 5,463 |
| Current liabilities | 249,587 | 358,226 | 373,343 | 400,726 | 452,430 |
| Long-term debt, less current maturities | 127,409 | 135,019 | 257,327 | 133,403 | 255,279 |
| Obligations under capital leases, less current maturities | 56,495 | 50,546 | 41,813 | 49,270 | 40,032 |
| Other long-term liabilities | 43,249 | 55,381 | 61,766 | 56,410 | 63,484 |
| Total liabilities | 476,740 | 599,172 | 734,249 | 639,809 | 811,225 |
| Preferred stock, no par value | 66,027 | 61,795 | 57,113 | 61,285 | 36,721 |
| Common stock, $3.75 stated value | 163,765 | 163,643 | 155,088 | 155,088 | 155,088 |
| Capital surplus (41,356,847 shares issued) | 104,205 | 98,246 | 44,539 | 49,149 | 32,117 |
| Retained earnings | 1,027,895 | 1,099,006 | 1,179,964 | 1,111,527 | 1,194,884 |
| | 1,361,892 | 1,422,690 | 1,436,704 | 1,377,049 | 1,418,810 |
| Less: 5,173,811 treasury shares | 81,739 | 96,475 | 185,367 | 54,134 | 190,762 |
| Shareholders' equity | 1,280,153 | 1,326,215 | 1,251,337 | 1,322,915 | 1,228,048 |
| Total liabilities and net worth | $1,756,893 | $1,925,387 | $1,985,586 | $1,962,724 | $2,039,273 |

*Source:* Interco annual reports and 10-Q reports.

**EXHIBIT 7**

Consolidated Statements of Earnings for Years Ending February 28/29, 1986–1988, and First Quarters Ending May 31, 1987–1988 (thousands of dollars except per share data)

| | Feb. 28, 1986 | Feb. 28, 1987 | Feb. 29, 1988 | May 31, 1987 | May 31, 1988 |
|---|---|---|---|---|---|
| Net sales | $2,832,384 | $2,946,902 | $3,341,423 | $781,421 | $778,107 |
| Other income | 36,140 | 32,175 | 29,237 | 6,293 | 6,864 |
| Total revenues | 2,868,524 | 2,979,077 | 3,370,660 | 787,714 | 784,971 |
| Cost of sales | 1,932,258 | 2,000,423 | 2,284,640 | 528,942 | 522,759 |
| Selling, general, administrative expenses | 681,886 | 712,861 | 799,025 | 199,145 | 201,129 |
| Interest expense | 25,523 | 28,082 | 33,535 | 7,351 | 9,179 |
| Total costs | 2,639,667 | 2,741,366 | 3,117,200 | 735,438 | 733,067 |
| Earnings before income taxes | 228,857 | 237,711 | 253,460 | 52,276 | 51,904 |
| Income taxes | 109,008 | 111,937 | 108,457 | 25,762 | 21,215 |
| Net earnings | $ 119,849 | $ 125,744 | $ 145,003 | $ 26,514 | $ 30,689 |

*Source:* Interco annual reports and 10-Q reports.

**EXHIBIT 8**
Business Segment Information for the Years Ending February 28/29, 1986–1988, and First Quarters Ending May 31, 1987–1988 (thousands of dollars)

| | Feb. 28, 1986 | Feb. 28, 1987 | Feb. 29, 1988 | May 31, 1987 | May 31, 1988 |
|---|---|---|---|---|---|
| Net sales to unaffiliated customers: | | | | | |
| Apparel | $ 907,833 | $ 817,660 | $ 813,198 | $164,339 | $138,836 |
| General retail | 461,785 | 498,324 | 532,251 | 148,138 | 149,209 |
| Footwear | 558,286 | 663,521 | 890,411 | 209,535 | 226,672 |
| Furniture | 904,480 | 967,397 | 1,105,563 | 263,409 | 263,390 |
| Total | $2,832,384 | $2,946,902 | $3,341,423 | $781,421 | $778,107 |
| Operating earnings | | | | | |
| Apparel | $ 66,716 | $ 47,269 | $ 20,240 | $ (670) | $ (247) |
| General retail | 32,085 | 40,610 | 39,101 | 14,136 | 12,498 |
| Footwear | 48,475 | 52,136 | 92,204 | 15,777 | 19,700 |
| Furniture | 105,111 | 123,766 | 149,090 | 38,319 | 32,156 |
| Total | 252,387 | 263,781 | 300,635 | 67,562 | 64,147 |
| Net of (Other income − Corporate expense − Interest expense) | 23,530 | 26,070 | 47,175 | 15,286 | 12,243 |
| Earnings before income taxes | $ 228,857 | $ 237,711 | $ 253,460 | $ 52,276 | $ 51,904 |
| Identifiable assets (year-end) | | | | | |
| Apparel | $ 456,972 | $ 465,601 | $ 425,350 | | |
| General retail | 234,004 | 248,639 | 252,195 | | |
| Footwear | 291,292 | 497,706 | 595,861 | | |
| Furniture | 618,980 | 640,106 | 688,853 | | |
| Total | 1,601,248 | 1,852,052 | 1,962,259 | | |
| Corporate | 155,645 | 73,335 | 23,327 | | |
| Total assets | $1,756,893 | $1,925,387 | $1,985,586 | | |
| Depreciation expenses | | | | | |
| Apparel | $ 11,965 | $ 12,123 | $ 12,521 | | |
| General retail | 8,294 | 9,079 | 9,681 | | |
| Footwear | 8,286 | 10,638 | 13,107 | | |
| Furniture | 20,971 | 21,675 | 26,208 | | |
| Capital expenditures | | | | | |
| Apparel | $ 13,433 | $ 8,869 | $ 9,220 | | |
| General retail | 6,169 | 8,167 | 10,735 | | |
| Footwear | 8,114 | 7,486 | 9,236 | | |
| Furniture | 27,278 | 24,720 | 36,188 | | |

*Source:* Interco annual reports and 10-Q reports.

**EXHIBIT 9**

Data and Assumptions for Valuation of Interco: City Capital Associates Limited Partnership Offer

Date: August 8,1988
Price per share: $70.00
Premium/Stock one day prior:[a] 17.9%
Premium/Stock four weeks prior: 59.1%
Premium/52-week low: 137.3%
Premium/52-week high: 17.2%
Aggregate value: $2,622.8 million
Aggregate value adj. for debt: $2,941.3 million

| | Year Ending Feb. 29, 1988[b] | Year Ending Feb. 28, 1989[c] |
|---|---|---|
| Adj. aggregate value as multiple of | | |
| Sales . . . . . . . . . . . . . . . . . . . . . . . . . | .9 | .9 |
| Operating cash flow . . . . . . . . . . . . . . . | 9.2 | 8.8 |
| Operating income . . . . . . . . . . . . . . . | 11.4 | 10.7 |
| Aggregate value as multiple of | | |
| Net income . . . . . . . . . . . . . . . . . . . . . | 18.1 | 17.0 |
| Book value . . . . . . . . . . . . . . . . . . . . . | 2.2 | 2.2 |

*Sources:* Wasserstein, Perella & Co. presentation to the Interco board of directors, August 8, 1988. Civil Action No. 10111, filed in the Court of Chancery of the State of Delaware, New Castle County, Exhibit 23.

a. Premiums based on stock prices from original July 27, 1988, offer.

b. Casewriter's note: The original source was labeled (Dec. 29), but it seems likely that the label should read, "Year Ending Feb. 29, 1988."

c. Estimate.

**EXHIBIT 10**

Data and Assumptions for Valuation of Interco: Premiums Paid Analysis, 1988

| | 1st Qtr | 2nd Qtr | 3rd Qtr[a] | Year | City Capital Offer |
|---|---|---|---|---|---|
| No. of deals[b] . . . . . . . . | 19 | 9 | 12 | 40 | — |
| Avg premium paid/Stock price | | | | | |
| One day prior . . . . . . . | 62.3% | 68.6% | 36.5% | 56.0% | 17.9% |
| Four weeks prior . . . . . | 95.5 | 91.3 | 49.9 | 80.9 | 59.1 |
| 52-week low . . . . . . . . | 159.5 | 182.8 | 181.3 | 171.3 | 137.3 |
| 52-week high . . . . . . . | 16.7 | 31.5 | 2.6 | 15.8 | 17.2 |

*Sources:* Wasserstein, Perella & Co. presentation to the Interco board of directors, August 8, 1988. Civil Action No. 10111, filed in the Court of Chancery of the State of Delaware, New Castle County, Exhibit 23.

a. Selected tender offers from July and August.

b. Wasserstein, Perella & Co. selected tender offers.

**EXHIBIT 11**
Data and Assumptions for Valuation of Interco: Analysis of Comparable Transactions

| Acquirer/Target | Announcement Date | Adjusted Aggregate Price[a] ($ millions) | Purchase Price as Multiple of [a] | | | | |
| --- | --- | --- | --- | --- | --- | --- | --- |
| | | | Net Income | Book Value[b] | Sales | Operating Income | Operating Cash Flow |
| *Furniture Manufacturing Companies* | | | | | | | |
| Masco/Henredon | June 3, 1986 | $ 260.9 | 31.6 | 2.6 | 2.1 | 20.3 | 15.8 |
| Chicago Pacific/General Mills Furniture | Aug. 12, 1986 | 89.3 | 14.1 | 1.8 | 1.0 | 12.0 | 9.9 |
| Interco/Lane | Nov. 17, 1986 | 523.7 | 19.3 | 2.8 | 1.6 | 11.1 | 9.6 |
| La-Z-Boy/Kincaid | Dec. 14, 1987 | 63.5 | 22.0 | 2.1 | .8 | 11.7 | 8.1 |
| City Capital offer | Aug. 8, 1988 | 2,941.3 | 18.1 | 2.2 | .9 | 11.4 | 9.2 |
| *Footwear Manufacturing Companies* | | | | | | | |
| Interco/Converse | July 31, 1986 | $ 202.7 | 37.1 | 1.8 | .9 | 24.7 | 18.2 |
| Reebok/Rockport | Sept. 18, 1986 | 146.1 | 30.7 | – | 1.7 | 26.0 | 23.9 |
| Reebok/Avia | March 10, 1987 | 191.0 | 40.6 | 6.7 | 2.1 | 24.6 | 23.3 |
| Moacq/Morse Shoe | June 3, 1987 | 312.5 | 2.5 | 1.8 | .5 | 13.0 | 9.2 |
| Nike/Cole Haan | Apr. 25, 1988 | 95.0 | 36.2 | – | 1.5 | 12.2 | 8.1 |
| City Capital offer | Aug. 8, 1988 | 2,941.3 | 18.1 | 2.2 | .9 | 11.4 | 9.2 |
| *Apparel Companies* | | | | | | | |
| West Point Pepperall/Cluett, Peabody | Nov. 4, 1985 | $ 551.9 | 19.6 | 1.5 | .6 | 10.6 | .2 |
| W. Acquisition/Warnco | Mar. 17, 1986 | 504.7 | 21.0 | 2.5 | .9 | 10.6 | 9.2 |
| Salant/Manhattan Indus. | Feb. 2, 1988 | 129.7 | – | 1.4 | .4 | – | – |
| Wesray/Wm Carter | Apr. 28, 1988 | 157.4 | – | 1.6 | .8 | 24.0 | 13.7 |
| City Capital offer | Aug. 8, 1988 | 2,941.3 | 18.1 | 2.2 | .9 | 11.4 | 9.2 |
| *Central Hardware Division* | | | | | | | |
| Management Group/Payless Cashways | June 24, 1988 | $1,189.4 | 22.0 | 2.3 | .6 | 13.1 | 9.2 |
| City Capital offer | Aug. 8, 1988 | 2,941.3 | 18.1 | 2.2 | .9 | 11.4 | 9.2 |

*Sources:* Wasserstein, Perella & Co. presentation to the Interco board of directors, August 8, 1988. Civil Action No. 10111, filed in the Court of Chancery of the State of Delaware, New Castle County, Exhibit 23.

a. Sales, operating income, and operating cash flow multiples adjusted for the value of net debt outstanding.

b. Book value adjusted for intangibles.

**EXHIBIT 12**

Data and Assumptions for Valuation of Interco: Discounted Cash Flow Analysis

| | Furniture Group | Footwear Group | Apparel Group | Retail Group | Total Company |
|---|---|---|---|---|---|
| Sales growth[a] | 7.7% | 6.3% | 7.1% | 7.6% | 7.2% |
| Operating margin range[b] | 13.1–14.1% | 9.1–10.4% | 6.4–7.0% | 6.5–7.5% | 9.2–10.1% |
| Capital expenditures[c] | 1 | 1 | 1 | 1 | 1 |
| Increase in working investment[d] | 12.5% | 12.5% | 12.5% | 7.5% | 11.6% |

| Discount Rate | Terminal Multiple | | |
|---|---|---|---|
| | 14.0 | 15.0 | 16.0 |
| 10.0% | $80.00 | $84.00 | $88.00 |
| 11.0 | 74.00 | 77.00 | 81.00 |
| 12.0 | 68.00 | 72.00 | 75.00 |
| 13.0 | 63.00 | 66.00 | 69.00 |

*Sources:* Wasserstein, Perella & Co. presentation to the Interco board of directors, August 8, 1988. Civil Action No. 10111, filed in the Court of Chancery of the State of Delaware, New Castle County, Exhibit 23.

a. Ten-year annual compound growth rate.

b. Projected operating margin in 1989 and in 1998.

c. As a multiple of depreciation.

d. As a percent of change in sales in 1994 forward.

**EXHIBIT 13**

Valuation Reference Range—Retain Core Companies Case (millions of dollars except per share data)

| Segment | Range | | |
|---|---|---|---|
| Furniture group | $1,525 | to | $1,750 |
| Footwear group | 775 | to | 900 |
| Total | $2,300 | to | $2,650 |
| After-tax divestiture proceeds | $ 588 | to | $ 639 |
| Net corporate adjustments[a] | (335) | to | (273) |
| Range | $2,553 | to | $3,016 |
| Per share range[b] | $68.00 | to | $80.00+ |

*Sources:* Wasserstein, Perella & Co., Inc., presentation to the Interco board of directors, August 8, 1988. Civil Action No. 10111, filed in the Court of Chancery of the State of Delaware, New Castle County, Exhibit 23.

a. Accounts for net debt, overfunded pension, and miscellaneous other assets, including real estate that could be understated.

b. Based on 37.5 million fully diluted shares outstanding.

**EXHIBIT 14**

Indexes of Monthly Adjusted Closing Prices, 1980–1988; Actual Daily Closing Prices, July–August 1988; and Market Interest Rates, August 1988

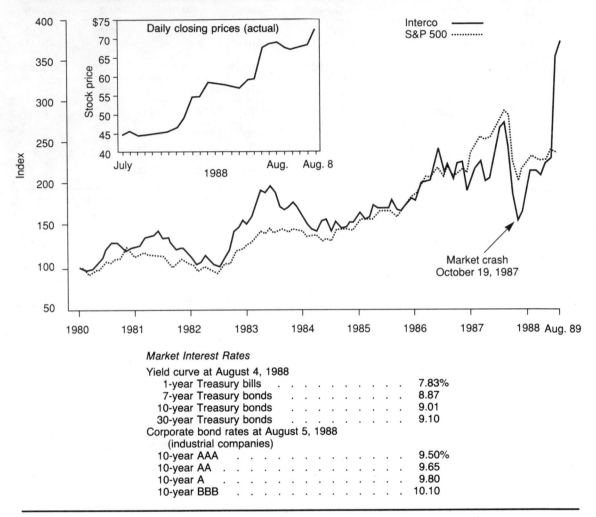

Market Interest Rates

Yield curve at August 4, 1988

| | |
|---|---|
| 1-year Treasury bills . . . . . . . . . . | 7.83% |
| 7-year Treasury bonds . . . . . . . . | 8.87 |
| 10-year Treasury bonds . . . . . . . . | 9.01 |
| 30-year Treasury bonds . . . . . . . . | 9.10 |

Corporate bond rates at August 5, 1988 (industrial companies)

| | |
|---|---|
| 10-year AAA . . . . . . . . . . . . | 9.50% |
| 10-year AA . . . . . . . . . . . . | 9.65 |
| 10-year A . . . . . . . . . . . . | 9.80 |
| 10-year BBB . . . . . . . . . . . . | 10.10 |

*Sources:* Graph—Interactive Data Corporation; table—Salomon Brothers Inc.

# E. I. du Pont de Nemours and Company: Titanium Dioxide

In May 1972 the executive committee of E. I. du Pont de Nemours and Co. convened to consider a report from the pigments department concerning the titanium dioxide market. Events had dramatically altered the economics of producing and selling titanium dioxide in the United States. Substantial excess demand had developed, causing producers to reevaluate their capacity expansion plans in this market. Du Pont's executive committee had to determine what Du Pont's response would be—and the likely reaction of its competitors—to the changed environment.

## Company Background

E. I. du Pont de Nemours and Co. (Du Pont) was a diversified manufacturer of fibers, plastics, industrial chemicals, and other specialty chemical products. In 1971 it was the seventeenth largest manufacturing corporation in the United States, with reported earnings of $357 million on sales of $3.8 billion. It was a conservatively managed company, as evidenced by its longstanding AAA bond rating and its tendency to rely on retained earnings to fund its capital expenditure programs. (A 5-year financial summary for Du Pont is provided in Exhibit 1.)

Since its founding as an explosives manufacturer in 1802, Du Pont had compiled an enviable record of growth and profitability. Historically, Du Pont had competed primarily on the basis of technological innovation and had tended to avoid cost competition in commodity markets. The rapid pace of technological development, however, and the consequent shortening of product life cycles in recent decades had forced it to defend some of its mature products more aggressively. This frequently meant improving costs and competing on the basis of price. Because its size and technological superiority usually afforded Du Pont a dominant position in the markets in which it competed, an aggressive defense of market share often gave rise to antitrust charges.

Du Pont was organized into ten industrial departments. The pigments department, the second smallest with sales of approximately $180 million in 1971, was responsible for titanium dioxide. Du Pont's involvement with titanium dioxide began with the acquisition of the Commercial Pigment Co. in 1931. By 1972, Du Pont had closed its original manufacturing facility and was operating more modern plants in Antioch, California; Edge Moor, Delaware; and New Johnsonville, Tennessee.

## Titanium Dioxide Market

Titanium dioxide ($TiO_2$) is a white chemical agent used in the manufacture of paints, paper, synthetic fibers, plastics, ink, and synthetic rubber. It acts as a whitening and opacifying agent and has no commercially satisfactory substitute.

Two principal technologies exist for manufacturing $TiO_2$: a sulfate process and a chloride process. The sulfate process produces $TiO_2$ by the digestion of low-grade titaniferous feedstocks with sulfuric acid. Although this technique does not require high-grade feedstock, it produces large amounts of ecologically hazardous wastes. In the chloride process, titaniferous feedstock reacts with chlorine in the presence of carbon to produce titanium tetrachloride, which is then converted to $TiO_2$. The chloride process can use either high-grade feedstock (rutile or synthetic rutile) or low-grade feedstock (ilmenite or lecoxene). The low-grade chloride technology (ilmenite chloride) differs from the high-grade chloride technology (rutile chloride) by requiring more chlorine per unit of output and producing more waste. However, both chloride processes produce less waste and safer waste than sulfate technology.

Domestic sales of $TiO_2$ were projected to reach 730,000 tons by the end of 1972, with a dollar value of $340 million. The volume of sales had been growing slowly at a 3% annual rate during the previous decade. Since $TiO_2$ was an ingredient in many final products with cyclical demand, its demand also tended to move with the business cycle. Based upon past experience, the volume of demand could fall by as much as 10% between the peak and the trough of a business cycle. Annual sales were projected to grow to more than 1 million tons by 1985.

$TiO_2$ prices tended to be extremely stable. Between 1963 and 1969 selling prices remained between $26 and $27 per 100 pounds. (This represented a 17% decline in real prices over the period.) After 1969, prices fell below $25, but they began recovering sharply in 1972.

## Capacity Expansion Decisions by $TiO_2$ Producers

The National Lead Co. built the first domestic $TiO_2$ plant in Sayreville, New Jersey, in 1918. This plant used the sulfate process, as did all subsequent plants built before the 1950s. Du Pont then introduced the ilmenite chloride technology at its Edge Moor plant in 1952. This facility took almost 3 years to become fully operational because of the formidable problems involved in scaling up this technology from models. As a result, although the chemical process of the ilmenite chloride method was widely known, only Du Pont possessed the operational knowledge necessary to make production economically viable.

In 1958, Du Pont again chose the ilmenite chloride process for a large plant at New Johnsonville, Tennessee. Since this plant was the largest in the industry, Du Pont realized scale economies that lowered its costs slightly below those of its competitors; however, Du Pont's decision to use the ilmenite chloride technology was based primarily on its access to ilmenite ore, not on cost savings.[1] Both the sulfate and the two chloride technologies had roughly identical per unit operating costs for plants of equivalent size.

In the late 1950s and early in 1960 large quantities of easily accessible rutile ore were discovered in the beach sands of eastern Australia. As a result, all plants built during the next decade used the rutile chloride technology, including a facility in Antioch, California, built by Du Pont in 1964.

By the early 1970s eight U.S. firms supplied over 90% of the domestic market for $TiO_2$ with imports supplying the remainder. All of these firms were diversified to varying degrees. (Exhibits 2 and 3 detail each firm's capacity, actual production, and dollar sales during 1970 to 1972 for both types of technology.)

After Du Pont, National Lead (NL) was the second largest supplier of $TiO_2$ by a wide margin; however, its share of the market fell steadily throughout the late 1960s. NL had total 1971 earnings of $23 million on sales of $925 million. It was generally less profitable than Du Pont and relied more heavily on debt to finance its growth (debt as a percentage of NL's total capital was 35% in 1971). NL was also more highly sensitive to economic fluctuations. In 1971, NL owned $TiO_2$ plants in Sayreville, New Jersey, and St. Louis, Missouri. Pigments accounted for roughly one quarter of NL's total sales and one third of its total operating profit.

## Transitions in the TiO₂ Market

Between 1969 and 1972 two major events transformed the domestic $TiO_2$ market. A sudden shortage of rutile ore developed in 1970 and 1971, and ore prices increased dramatically. When per ton prices of rutile ore rose from A$65 (Australian dollars) in the late 1960s to A$110 in 1972, the economics of the high-grade chloride technology were altered radically.

During the same period sulfate process plants were forced to make major capital expenditures to comply with newly enacted environmental protection legislation. The combined effect of these two disruptions was to significantly raise $TiO_2$

---

1. Du Pont obtained ilmenite ore from India and later from Florida. Other sources included Australia, New Jersey, and New York.

mill costs for both the sulfate and rutile chloride processes. Whereas previously Du Pont's ilmenite chloride process had only a small cost advantage over other processes, it was now significantly cheaper than the other two technologies.

Following these events, production of $TiO_2$ declined sharply as high-cost plants began to shut down. Exacerbating the supply problem, the devaluation of the U.S. dollar and the continuation of a tariff on $TiO_2$ cut imports significantly. The reduced supply of $TiO_2$ resulted in substantial excess demand and the rationing of production among users.

## Du Pont's Strategic Alternatives in TiO$_2$

Excess demand created capacity expansion opportunities for producers of $TiO_2$. Du Pont's rivals had two principal alternatives for expansion: upgrading marginally profitable sulfate and rutile chloride plants or building new ilmenite chloride plants. As Du Pont's Edge Moor plant demonstrated, this latter alternative required large-scale facilities and extensive experience to be economically viable. An optimal-scale ilmenite chloride plant would require capacity of 50,000–100,000 tons per year and would cost between $45 and $90 million. Competitors building such plants would assume the usual risks of technical failure, delayed start-ups, and so forth. But a risk of declining prices and diminished cash flow from $TiO_2$ operations also existed if many competitors simultaneously chose to add capacity and flood the market.

Du Pont recognized both the opportunities and the risks inherent in the $TiO_2$ market and took steps to formulate a strategy for coping with the changed environment. In May 1972, A. H. Geil, vice president and general manager of Du Pont's pigments department, submitted to the executive committee a report entitled "Opportunities in the $TiO_2$ Business." The report described two possible strategies in $TiO_2$ that Du Pont should consider implementing: a growth strategy and a maintain strategy.

The objective of the maintain strategy was to boost Du Pont's market share in $TiO_2$ to 45% over the next several years. The growth strategy, on the other hand, called for an aggressive response that would be designed to "provide cash for Du Pont expansion [in the $TiO_2$ market], but limit competitors' ability to expand."[2] This strategy required the integration of plans for expanding capacity through 1985, pricing $TiO_2$, and restricting the licensing of the ilmenite chloride process to improve Du Pont's competitive position in this market. Successful implementation of this strategy required that all three of these tactics be coordinated, since each independently represented a much smaller threat to competitors' expansion moves.

Forecasts of total demand for $TiO_2$, capacity costs, operating expenses, selling prices, Du Pont's market share, and Du Pont's $TiO_2$ capacity under both strategies

---

2. Federal Trade Commission, In the Matter of E. I. du Pont de Nemours & Co., Docket No. 9108, Initial Decision, September 4, 1979, p. 23.

are shown in Exhibit 4. Du Pont's market share in 1985 at the end of the capacity expansion program was expected to be almost 65% under the growth strategy compared with 45% under the maintain strategy. Forecast prices for $TiO_2$ were expected to be lower at first under the growth strategy relative to the maintain strategy as Du Pont's new capacity increased industry supply.[3] But they were expected to be relatively higher in future years because of more orderly capacity expansion. Forecast operating expenses were expected to be the same under either strategy.

The cost of new capacity was expected to be $900 per ton in 1973 and to increase as shown in Exhibit 4. Further investment in net working capital amounting to 20% of the increased sales level would also have to be made. The capital investment (other than additions to net working capital) would be eligible for a 10% investment tax credit.[4] Ongoing capital expenditure for maintenance and replacement were expected to approximate depreciation allowances over time. Thus, should $TiO_2$ production terminate at any point in the future, it was believed that Du Pont's investment in working capital and the book value of other assets could be completely recovered.

Du Pont's pre-tax operating profit margin before interest expense, but after depreciation on the new capacity, was expected to average 40% under both strategies. This was more than twice the margin that competitors building new ilmenite chloride capacity would realize at the outset. The difference resulted from Du Pont's extensive experience with this production technology and could be expected to erode over time as competitors gained similar experience.

In light of the long-term benefits and other competitive advantages associated with the growth strategy, the pigments department recommended its adoption. It noted that "a combination of factors [put] Du Pont in the unique position [of being able] to increase its share of the market by a substantial amount,"[5] and argued that such a unique set of circumstances should not go unexploited.

If accepted, the $TiO_2$ growth strategy would commit Du Pont to a massive capital expenditure program that would reach $500 million by 1985. Before reaching a decision, the executive committee had to be convinced that the relative merits of the growth strategy truly justified such an extended period of high capital expenditure.

---

3. $TiO_2$ prices forecast under the maintain strategy were essentially the same as those that would be expected to prevail even if Du Pont undertook no capacity expansion.

4. Du Pont's marginal tax rate in 1972 was 48%.

5. Federal Trade Commission, p. 16.

**EXHIBIT 1**
Five-Year Financial Summary, 1967–1971 (millions of dollars except per share data)

| | 1967 | 1968 | 1969 | 1970 | 1971 |
|---|---|---|---|---|---|
| *Income Statement* | | | | | |
| Sales | $ 3,079 | $ 3,455 | $ 3,632 | $ 3,618 | $ 3,848 |
| Net income | 314 | 372 | 356 | 334 | 357 |
| Cash flow from operations | 583 | 659 | 677 | 684 | 727 |
| Earnings per share | $ 6.73 | $ 7.99 | $ 7.62 | $ 6.86 | $ 7.33 |
| Dividends per share | 5.00 | 5.50 | 5.25 | 5.00 | 5.00 |
| Average shares outstanding | | | | | |
| (000s) | 46,158 | 46,285 | 47,076 | 47,257 | 47,281 |
| *Balance Sheet* | | | | | |
| Net working capital | $ 874 | $ 996 | $ 1,107 | $ 1,110 | $ 1,221 |
| Net property, plant, and | | | | | |
| equipment | 1,724 | 1,738 | 1,803 | 1,923 | 2,002 |
| Total assets | 3,071 | 3,289 | 3,453 | 3,740 | 3,999 |
| Total debt | 125 | 162 | 186 | 216 | 307 |
| Shareholders' equity | 2,557 | 2,697 | 2,854 | 2,964 | 3,095 |
| Total capital | 2,682 | 2,859 | 3,040 | 3,180 | 3,402 |
| Book value per share | $ 50.22 | $ 53.09 | $ 55.53 | $ 57.67 | $ 60.23 |
| Market value per share[a] | 163.25 | 162.75 | 133.38 | 113.38 | 143.75 |
| *Capital Sources* | | | | | |
| Cash flow retained | $ 308 | $ 394 | $ 423 | $ 438 | $ 480 |
| External equity financing (net) | 19 | 23 | 35 | 37 | 21 |
| Debt financing (net) | 67 | 37 | 24 | 30 | 91 |
| Total capital added | $ 394 | $ 454 | $ 482 | $ 505 | $ 592 |
| Capital expenditures | $ 454 | $ 332 | $ 391 | $ 471 | $ 454 |
| *Key Financial Ratios* | | | | | |
| Growth rate | | | | | |
| Sales | (2.5)% | 12.2% | 5.1 % | (.4)% | 6.4% |
| Profits | (19.3)% | 18.5% | (4.3)% | (6.2)% | 6.9% |
| Return on sales | 10.2 % | 10.8% | 9.8 % | 9.2 % | 9.3% |
| Return on equity | 12.3 % | 11.3% | 12.5 % | 11.3 % | 11.5% |
| Debt to total capital | 4.7 % | 5.7% | 6.1 % | 6.8 % | 9.0% |
| Current ratio | 3.2 | 3.6 | 3.6 | 3.6 | 3.5 |
| Price-earnings ratio[a] | 24.2 | 20.4 | 17.5 | 16.5 | 19.6 |
| Market value/book value[a] | 3.3 | 3.1 | 2.4 | 2.0 | 2.4 |

a. Based on midpoint of the year's trading range for Du Pont's common shares.

**EXHIBIT 2**
Production Capacity and Shipment Data for U.S. TiO$_2$ Producers, 1970–1972

| | Domestic TiO$_2$ Production Capacity by Firm (000 tons) | | | | | | Total Domestic TiO$_2$ Shipments by Firm, Including Imports[a] (000 tons) | | | | | | Total Domestic TiO$_2$ Shipments by Firm, Including Imports[a] ($ millions) | | | | | |
| | 1970 | | 1971 | | 1972 est. | | 1970 | | 1971 | | 1972 est. | | 1970 | | 1971 | | 1972 est. | |
| | Tons | % | Tons | % | Tons | % | Tons[b] | % | Tons[b] | % | Tons[b] | % | $[c] | % | $[c] | % | $[c] | % |
|---|---|---|---|---|---|---|---|---|---|---|---|---|---|---|---|---|---|---|
| Du Pont | 252 | 30% | 277 | 33% | 325 | 38% | 206 | 30% | 222 | 31% | 220 | 30% | $100 | 31% | $ 98 | 31% | $100 | 29% |
| NL Industries | 268 | 32 | 268 | 32 | 230 | 27 | 210 | 31 | 209 | 30 | 180 | 25 | 112 | 35 | 102 | 33 | 95 | 28 |
| American Cyanamid | 90 | 11 | 82 | 10 | 90 | 10 | 53 | 8 | 72 | 10 | 80 | 11 | 24 | 7 | 30 | 10 | 40 | 12 |
| SCM | 78 | 9 | 78 | 9 | 75 | 9 | 58 | 9 | 64 | 9 | 65 | 9 | 27 | 8 | 26 | 9 | 25 | 7 |
| Gulf & Western | 70 | 8 | 70 | 8 | 70 | 8 | 30 | 4 | 26 | 4 | 60 | 8 | 13 | 4 | 11 | 3 | 30 | 9 |
| Kerr-McGee | 37 | 5 | 39 | 5 | 45 | 5 | 31 | 5 | 37 | 5 | 45 | 6 | 16 | 5 | 12 | 4 | 20 | 6 |
| Sherwin-Williams | 27 | 3 | 27 | 3 | 25 | 3 | 21 | 3 | 26 | 4 | 30 | 4 | 8 | 2 | 12 | 4 | 10 | 3 |
| PPG | 18 | 2 | — | — | — | — | 9 | 1 | 10 | 1 | — | — | 4 | 1 | 4 | 1 | — | — |
| Total (U.S. firms) | 840 | 100% | 841 | 100% | 860 | 100% | 618 | 91% | 666 | 94% | 680 | 93% | $304 | 93% | $296 | 95% | $320 | 94% |
| Imports | — | — | — | — | — | — | 58 | 9 | 41 | 6 | 50 | 7 | 21 | 7 | 15 | 5 | 20 | 6 |
| Total | 840 | 100% | 841 | 100% | 860 | 100% | 676 | 100% | 707 | 100% | 730 | 100% | $325 | 100% | $311 | 100% | $340 | 100% |

*Source:* Federal Trade Commission, In the Matter of E. I. du Pont de Nemours & Co., Docket No. 9108, Complaint Counsel's Exhibits Nos. CX121A, B; CX223A, B; and CX222.

a. Excludes exports.
b. Thousands of tons shipped.
c. Dollar value of shipments.

**EXHIBIT 3**

TiO$_2$ Production by Firm and Type of Process, 1970 (thousands of tons)

| | Total Production[a] | Sulfate Process | Chloride Process |
|---|---|---|---|
| Du Pont[b] . . . . . . . . | 211 | 43 | 168 |
| NL Industries . . . . . . | 229 | 193 | 36 |
| American Cyanamid . . . . | 56 | 47 | 9 |
| SCM . . . . . . . . | 51 | 48 | 3 |
| Gulf & Western . . . . . . | 33 | 33 | – |
| Kerr-McGee . . . . . . . | 35 | – | 35 |
| Sherwin-Williams . . . . . | 19 | – | 19 |
| PPG . . . . . . . . | 10 | – | 10 |
| Total . . . . . . . . | 644 | 364 | 280 |

*Source:* Federal Trade Commission, In the Matter of E. I. du Pont de Nemours & Co., Docket No. 9108, Initial Decision, p. 11.

a. Differences between total production and total shipments (see Exhibit 2) represent adjustments to TiO$_2$ inventory.

b. Only Du Pont had chloride process production using low-grade feedstock; all others used high-grade feedstock.

**EXHIBIT 4**
TiO$_2$ Market Forecasts under Alternative Strategies for Du Pont, 1973–1985

| | Size of Market[a] (000 tons) | Cost of New Capacity ($/ton) | Pre-Tax Operating Expenses[b] ($/ton) | Growth Strategy | | | Maintain Strategy | | |
|---|---|---|---|---|---|---|---|---|---|
| | | | | Average Gross Selling Price ($/ton) | Du Pont Market Share (%) | Du Pont Capacity (000 tons) | Average Gross Selling Price ($/ton) | Du Pont Market Share (%) | Du Pont Capacity (000 tons) |
| 1973 | 752 | $ 900 | $330 | $ 540 | 35% | 350 | $ 555 | 35% | 340 |
| 1974 | 774 | 927 | 390 | 640 | 40 | 375 | 665 | 40 | 350 |
| 1975 | 798 | 955 | 460 | 750 | 47 | 400 | 760 | 45 | 360 |
| 1976 | 822 | 983 | 540 | 880 | 47 | 421 | 890 | 45 | 370 |
| 1977 | 846 | 1,013 | 580 | 950 | 51 | 443 | 955 | 45 | 381 |
| 1978 | 872 | 1,043 | 620 | 1,010 | 52 | 475 | 1,015 | 45 | 392 |
| 1979 | 898 | 1,075 | 660 | 1,070 | 52 | 505 | 1,070 | 45 | 404 |
| 1980 | 925 | 1,107 | 690 | 1,130 | 55 | 530 | 1,120 | 45 | 416 |
| 1981 | 952 | 1,140 | 710 | 1,190 | 58 | 552 | 1,170 | 45 | 428 |
| 1982 | 981 | 1,174 | 740 | 1,250 | 59 | 579 | 1,210 | 45 | 441 |
| 1983 | 1,010 | 1,210 | 770 | 1,310 | 62 | 616 | 1,270 | 45 | 455 |
| 1984 | 1,041 | 1,246 | 810 | 1,370 | 62 | 645 | 1,320 | 45 | 468 |
| 1985 | 1,072 | 1,283 | 850 | 1,430 | 64 | 685 | 1,370 | 45 | 482 |

a. Total demand for TiO$_2$ is forecast to grow at 3% annually and is not considered to be very sensitive to price.
b. Pre-tax operating expense per ton includes depreciation allowances but excludes interest expense.

531

# Southport Minerals, Inc.

## The Search for Investment Opportunity

In 1964, after 5 years of relatively low profitability, the U.S. sulfur industry entered a period of tightening supplies and rising prices. As the largest U.S. sulfur producer, Southport Minerals, Inc., enjoyed sharply increased profitability as this boom progressed (Exhibit 1, cols. 1 and 2). During this period a number of firms, including Southport, made substantial investments aimed at increasing their sulfur production in response to rising demand. In addition to its expansion in the sulfur industry, however, Southport also embarked on a major diversification program to reduce the company's dependence on sulfur, a product that accounted for nearly 90% of Southport's sales in the mid-1960s.

During that period, Southport was financially well positioned for significant diversification. The company was in a highly liquid position (Exhibit 1, col. 3) and had essentially no debt in its capital structure (Exhibit 1, col. 6). Its stock price was also rising sharply (Exhibit 1, cols. 13–14). While Southport was anxious to capitalize on its strong financial position, the firm hoped to diversify through internal means rather than through acquisitions. Unfortunately, for a number of years the firm had been unable to find attractive investment opportunities that were large enough to absorb even a fraction of its available financial resources. In 1967, however, Southport found an opportunity for a major financial commitment to develop a copper mine in Indonesia.

# Investigating the Indonesian Copper Mining Opportunity

Two events combined suddenly to provide the opportunity: First, in 1960, Southport had confirmed the existence of a major body of copper ore at an extremely inaccessible location in the Firstburg, a mountain in Indonesia.[1] At that time, however, the political climate in Indonesia was not attractive to foreign investment. By early 1967, the changed climate suggested further investigation of this copper ore body. Second, by 1967, the price of copper in world markets had risen to the point where even very low concentrate copper ores could be mined economically (see Table A).

Given these changes, Southport moved to investigate the Firstburg opportunity. The period between late 1967 and July 1968 was devoted to drilling and analyzing the extent of the deposit. By July 1968, Southport had learned that the Firstburg contained 33 million tons of ore with an average copper content of 2.5%[2] and significant traces of gold and silver.

At this point, the Bechtel Corp. (an engineering and construction firm) was asked to determine the cost and feasibility of establishing a mine site at an elevation of 9,200 ft in an uninhabited area separated from water transportation facilities by 39 miles of rain forest and 24 miles of precipitous mountain terrain. In December

**TABLE A**
Refined Copper Price, London Metal Exchange

|  | Cents/lb |
|---|---|
| 1955 | 43.9¢ |
| 1956 | 41.1 |
| 1957 | 27.4 |
| 1958 | 24.8 |
| 1959 | 29.8 |
| 1960 | 30.8 |
| 1961 | 28.7 |
| 1962 | 29.3 |
| 1963 | 29.3 |
| 1964 | 44.0 |
| 1965 | 58.6 |
| 1966 | 69.1 |
| 1967 | 51.2 |
| 1968 | 56.0 |
| 1969 | 66.3 |

---

1. The ore body was actually discovered by a young petroleum geologist on a mountain climbing expedition in 1936. The geologist's findings were published in Holland in 1939, but created no interest until the managing director of the East Borneo Co. received an exploration permit from the Indonesian government in 1959. At that point, Southport was contacted for financial and technical assistance in carrying out the exploration.

2. The copper content of the ores from U.S. mines usually ranged from .4% to 1.2%. In some African mines the copper content averaged as high as 3.0%.

1969, Bechtel reported that the proposed mining venture could be operational by the end of 1972, with a total development cost of $120 million. This amount would include construction costs, interest and insurance during construction, organizational and preoperating cost, and $4.5 million of working capital. At the mining rate projected, the ore body was expected to last for 13 years. The Firstburg deposit was sufficiently rich in copper that production costs were expected to be among the lowest in the world.

## Economics of the Proposed Venture

In evaluating the profitability of the proposed Indonesian mine, Southport's management assumed that refined copper prices would probably not fall below an average of 40 cents per pound. World copper consumption had continued to expand rapidly in the mid-1960s, in spite of significant price increases (Exhibit 2). However, the production of copper ore had not kept pace with the demand for refined copper. The results were reduced inventories of refined copper, increased use of copper scrap in the production of refined copper, and rising copper prices as well as increased interest in new sources of copper ore.

At an assumed price of 40 cents per pound for refined copper, the Firstburg investment promised the cash flows shown in Exhibit 3. When discounted at rates ranging from 6% to 30%, these cash flows produced the net present value amounts shown in Exhibit 4. To show the sensitivity of the investment returns from the project to changes in the price of refined copper, Exhibit 4 also gives the net present value of the cash flows if refined copper averaged 60 cents per pound over the life of the mine.

The Firstburg investment had attractive potential (Exhibit 4); however, the project carried some substantial risks. Not the least was the possibility of future expropriation, a problem that Southport had experienced firsthand. In 1960, Southport was caught three-quarters of the way into the development of a large mine in Cuba when the Castro government expropriated the property. As a result, Southport had to write off its $19 million equity investment.

## Negotiating a Financing Plan

The 1960 Cuban experience made Southport wary of large mining ventures in less developed and politically unstable areas of the world. Fortunately for Southport, by 1969 the governments of numerous industrialized nations had designed programs of credit guarantees to stimulate the export of products of domestic companies, or to ensure long-term sources of raw materials supply to domestic companies. These guarantee programs made it possible for Southport to insulate itself from much of the risk (both operating and political) inherent in the proposed Indonesian venture.

By late 1969, Southport had tentatively negotiated an extremely complex financing package for the Firstburg project. Specifically, Southport would form a new subsidiary, Southport Indonesia, Inc. (SI) to undertake the mining venture. To induce SI to contract to sell two thirds of the mine output to a consortium of Japanese smelters, the consortium agreed to purchase two thirds of the ore output of the mine, and to lend SI $20 million in subordinated debt at an interest rate equal to 7%. This rate was equivalent to the actual cost incurred by the consortium in borrowing the funds made available to SI. The loan would be repayable at the rate of $3.3 million per year between 1975 and 1980 (Exhibit 5, line 10). The Export-Import Bank of Japan guaranteed the repayment of this loan.

A comparable lending arrangement was worked out with a German buyer. In exchange for a contract in which SI agreed to sell one third of the Firstburg copper ore output to a German smelter,[3] this buyer agreed to purchase one third of the ore output of the mine and induced a German bank to lend SI $22 million of senior debt at 7% interest. This loan was repayable between 1974 and 1982 in escalating installments (Exhibit 5, line 9), and it was guaranteed by the Federal Republic of Germany.

Of the $120 million needed to complete the Firstburg project, $42 million was tentatively negotiated overseas; the remaining $78 million was arranged in three separate domestic transactions. A group of U.S. banks agreed to advance SI $18 million, repayable between 1974 and 1976 (Exhibit 5, line 8) at an interest rate ½% over the prime lending rate. Repayment of this senior bank debt was guaranteed by an agency of the U.S. government, the Export-Import Bank. The guarantee was possible because SI agreed to purchase $18 million of U.S.-manufactured equipment for use in the project.

A group of U.S. insurance companies agreed to lend SI $40 million, repayable between 1975 and 1982 (Exhibit 5, line 7) at 9¼% interest. Repayment of this senior debt was guaranteed by the Overseas Private Investment Corp., an agency of the U.S. government. The cost of the guarantee, 1¾% per year, raised the effective interest rate on this loan to 11%. The guarantee was possible because SI agreed to purchase $40 million of U.S.-manufactured equipment for use in the project. This purchase was in addition to the $18 million of U.S. purchases associated with the proposed bank borrowing.

Finally, SI was to be capitalized with $20 million of equity capital invested by Southport Minerals, Inc. The Overseas Private Investment Corp. guaranteed Southport Minerals' investment in SI against loss due to war, expropriation, and currency inconvertibility. To protect Southport, the capital to be supplied by each party to the proposed $120 million financing would automatically increase in the event of a cost overrun by up to 20% on a pro rata basis. Thus, the project could cost as much as $144 million before Southport would have to worry about additional financing. To further protect Southport Minerals, the Indonesian venture would be carried out by Southport Indonesia, the new subsidiary. Southport Minerals would not guarantee nor be responsible for SI's debt obligations. The proposed financing package for the complex Firstburg project is presented in simplified form in Exhibit 6.

---

3. Ore would be sold to both the Japanese and German buyers at prices quoted on the London Metal Exchange for refined copper, less prevailing world prices for smelting, refining, and transportation.

## Linking the Projected Investment Returns with the Proposed Financing Program

The tentative financing package made it possible for Southport to contemplate an investment that the company might otherwise have forgone. The financing plan created some serious problems, however, about evaluating the investment worth of the project to Southport Minerals, Inc. Four different conceptual approaches (each producing a dramatically different net present value solution) were advanced by different members of Southport's management team as the proper method for analyzing the investment worth of the Firstburg project.

### Approach 1. Discount at Southport Minerals' Cost of Capital, Ignoring Specifics of the Financing Choice

This approach was the one commonly used at Southport. It called for discounting the Firstburg project cash flows at Southport Minerals' presumed 15% cost of capital.[4] This approach ignored the specifics of Firstburg financing. Assuming a price of 40 cents per pound for refined copper, it produced a $2 million net present value for the investment proposal (Exhibit 4).

### Approach 2. Discount at a Premium above Southport Minerals' Cost of Capital, Ignoring Specifics of the Financing Choice

This approach argued that the Firstburg proposal was substantially riskier than the typical investment opportunity usually accepted by Southport Minerals. For this reason, it was argued that a higher discount rate, in the neighborhood of 20%, should be applied. At a 20% discount rate (assuming 40 cents per pound for refined copper), the project had a net present value of negative $17 million (Exhibit 4).

### Approach 3. Discount at Southport Indonesia's Cost of Capital, Taking into Consideration the Specific Financing Choice

This approach accepted the idea that the required rate of return on Southport Minerals' equity investment in SI should probably be higher than Southport Minerals' assumed 15% cost of capital. Advocates of this position argued further, however, that the Firstburg project was a ''stand alone'' investment with unique leverage opportunities. This line of reasoning suggested that given SI's proposed capital structure as of December 31, 1972, the subsidiary's cost of capital (assuming an equity cost of 20%) would be only 7.6%, as shown in Table B. At this discount rate, assuming 40 cents per pound for refined copper, the Firstburg project had a net present value of $58 million (Exhibit 4).

---

4. Since Southport Minerals' capital structure was almost 100% equity at December 31, 1969 (Exhibit 1), the company assumed that its cost of capital was the same as its cost of equity, which the company believed to be about 15%.

**TABLE B**
Southport Indonesia's Cost of Capital

| | Amount ($ millions) | % of Total Capital Structure | Pre-Tax Capital Cost | After-Tax Capital Cost | Weighted Averaged Cost of Capital |
|---|---|---|---|---|---|
| U.S. insurance company loans . | $ 40 | 33% | 11% | 6.6% | 2.2% |
| U.S. bank loans . | 18 | 15 | 7 | 4.2 | .6 |
| German loans . . | 22 | 18 | 7 | 4.2 | .7 |
| Japanese loans . | 20 | 17 | 7 | 4.2 | .7 |
| Equity . . . . . | 20 | 17 | 33 | 20.0 | 3.4 |
| Total . . . . | $120 | 100% | | | 7.6% |

## Approach 4. Discount Dividends Paid versus Equity Invested at SI's Cost of Equity

This approach argued that Southport Minerals would be totally insulated from the threat of losing more than its equity investment in SI; thus, it was inappropriate to view the investment in the project as $120 million. Southport's relevant investment was really $20 million; the relevant cash returns consisted solely of dividends paid on the equity investment. Advocates of this approach argued that cash flowing to the lenders for debt repayment created no value whatever for Southport Minerals. Cash generated through profitable operations that was not paid out as dividends had no value either, since earnings retentions could be lost in the event of expropriation.[5] According to this argument, a full partitioning of actual project cash flows to the appropriate providers of capital had to be considered in the analysis. Exhibit 7 suggests a faster paydown of debt (sum of lines 10 and 11) than that indicated in Exhibit 5 (line 11). This was true, since the loan guarantors demanded *prepayments* of debt in an amount equal to dividends whenever dividends were paid.[6] In addition, dividends were prohibited prior to December 31, 1974, and no dividends could be paid if SI's net working capital fell below $10 million. Under this set of assumptions, SI's repayments and *prepayments* on each loan would appear as shown in Exhibit 8. The net present value of the relevant cash flows (Exhibit 7, lines 12 and 13) using this logic would equal $10 million, assuming 40 cents per pound for refined copper and a 20% cost of equity. The net present values of the cash flows at other discount rates varying from 6% to 30% are presented in Exhibit 9.

---

5. The U.S. government guarantee of Southport Minerals' equity investment would cover the expropriation risk only with respect to the initial investment. It did not cover the additional equity investment created through earnings retentions.

6. In reality, the relation between debt *prepayments* and dividends was somewhat more complex. The factual situation has been simplified for clarity in the case situation.

**EXHIBIT 1**
Financial Data for Southport Minerals, Inc., 1954–1969 (millions of dollars except per share data)

| | | | | **Profitability and Financial Position** | | | | | |
|---|---|---|---|---|---|---|---|---|---|
| | (1) | (2) | (3) | (4) | (5) | (6) | (7) | (8) | (9) |
| | Profit after Tax | PAT/ Equity | Cash and Marketable Securities | Other Assets | Total Assets | Borrowed Money | Other Liabilities | Net Worth | Total Liab., Net Worth |
| 1954 . . | $10.1 | 19.9% | $ 9 | $ 57 | $ 66 | $0 | $15 | $ 51 | $ 66 |
| 1955 . . | 12.4 | 19.2 | 19 | 63 | 82 | 0 | 17 | 65 | 22 |
| 1956 . . | 13.4 | 18.9 | 19 | 69 | 88 | 0 | 17 | 71 | 88 |
| 1957 . . | 13.0 | 17.0 | 7 | 87 | 94 | 0 | 18 | 76 | 94 |
| 1958 . . | 13.1[a] | 8.8 | 70[b] | 94 | 164 | 0 | 15 | 149[b] | 164 |
| 1959 . . | 14.5 | 9.4 | 67 | 100 | 167 | 0 | 13 | 154 | 167 |
| 1960 . . | 13.2[c] | 9.4 | 64 | 140 | 204 | 0 | 63 | 141[c] | 204 |
| 1961 . . | 12.9 | 8.9 | 58 | 153 | 211 | 0 | 66 | 145 | 211 |
| 1962 . . | 12.7 | 8.6 | 59 | 123 | 182 | 0 | 33 | 149 | 182 |
| 1963 . . | 12.8 | 8.2 | 51 | 124 | 175 | 0 | 18 | 157 | 175 |
| 1964 . . | 15.3 | 9.2 | 54 | 173 | 227 | 0 | 61 | 166 | 227 |
| 1965 . . | 21.7 | 12.1 | 51 | 156 | 207 | 0 | 30 | 179 | 209 |
| 1966 . . | 32.2 | 16.4 | 63 | 176 | 239 | 8 | 35 | 196 | 239 |
| 1967 . . | 32.4 | 15.5 | 47 | 228 | 275 | 7 | 60 | 208 | 275 |
| 1968 . . | 40.4 | 17.8 | 43 | 247 | 290 | 7 | 56 | 227 | 290 |
| 1969 . . | 28.5 | 12.3 | 51 | 243 | 294 | 6 | 57 | 231 | 294 |

| | | | **Market Valuation Data** | | | |
|---|---|---|---|---|---|---|
| | (10) | (11) | (12) | (13) | (14) | (15) |
| | Earnings/ Share | Dividends/ Share | Dividend Payout Ratio | Market Value of Equity | Market Value/ Book Value of Equity | Price/ Earnings Ratio |
| 1954 . . | $ .70 | $ .42 | 60% | $ 170 | 3.3 | 17 |
| 1955 . . | .83 | .44 | 53 | 228 | 3.5 | 18 |
| 1956 . . | .89 | .50 | 56 | 236 | 3.3 | 18 |
| 1957 . . | .86 | .50 | 58 | 176 | 2.3 | 14 |
| 1958 . . | .87 | .50 | 57 | 248 | 1.7 | 19 |
| 1959 . . | .96 | .60 | 63 | 199 | 1.3 | 14 |
| 1960 . . | .88 | .60 | 68 | 235 | 1.7 | 18 |
| 1961 . . | .85 | .60 | 71 | 210 | 1.4 | 16 |
| 1962 . . | .84 | .60 | 71 | 172 | 1.2 | 14 |
| 1963 . . | .84 | .60 | 71 | 266 | 1.7 | 21 |
| 1964 . . | 1.00 | .60 | 60 | 341 | 2.1 | 22 |
| 1965 . . | 1.41 | .80 | 57 | 478 | 2.7 | 22 |
| 1966 . . | 2.08 | 1.06 | 51 | 593 | 3.0 | 18 |
| 1967 . . | 2.09 | 1.25 | 60 | 1,122 | 5.4 | 35 |
| 1968 . . | 2.61 | 1.40 | 54 | 683 | 2.0 | 17 |
| 1969 . . | 1.84 | 1.60 | 87 | 320 | 1.4 | 11 |

*Sources:* Southport Minerals, Inc., annual reports, Bank and Quotation Record.

a. Excludes extraordinary profit of $67 million from the sale of oil and gas interests.

b. In 1958, Southport's cash and net worth grew dramatically as a result of the cash sale of the company's oil and gas interests for nearly $100 million.

c. In 1960, Southport wrote off its equity investment in subsidiaries located in Cuba. Profit data exclude the effect of this extraordinary charge.

**EXHIBIT 2**

World Copper Consumption and Production by Smelter Location and Origin of Ore, 1963–1969 (thousands of tons)

| | 1963 | 1964 | 1965 | 1966 | 1967 | 1968 | 1969 |
|---|---|---|---|---|---|---|---|
| *World Copper Consumption* | | | | | | | |
| 1. United States . . | 1,580 | 1,683 | 1,855 | 2,240 | 1,595[a] | 1,707[a] | 1,914 |
| 2. Japan . . . . . | 339 | 504 | 471 | 532 | 679 | 766 | 888 |
| 3. Germany . . . . | 535 | 628 | 610 | 541 | 548 | 681 | 728 |
| 4. United Kingdom . | 615 | 698 | 717 | 653 | 567 | 594 | 603 |
| 5. All other free world | 1,408 | 1,565 | 1,593 | 1,639 | 1,481 | 1,594 | 1,749 |
| 6. Total free world . | 4,477 | 5,078 | 5,246 | 5,605 | 4,870 | 5,342 | 5,882 |
| 7. Soviet sphere . . | 850 | 955 | 995 | 1,010 | 1,070 | 1,122 | 1,211 |
| 8. Total world . . . | 5,327 | 6,033 | 6,241 | 6,615 | 5,940 | 6,464 | 7,093 |
| *World Copper Production by Smelter Location* | | | | | | | |
| 9. United States . . | 1,393 | 1,418 | 1,521 | 1,580 | 930[a] | 1,352[a] | 1,678 |
| 10. Zambia . . . . | 637 | 704 | 767 | 656 | 698 | 732 | 775 |
| 11. Chile . . . . . | 615 | 647 | 615 | 667 | 695 | 687 | 713 |
| 12. Japan . . . . . | 325 | 377 | 403 | 446 | 518 | 605 | 694 |
| 13. West Germany . . | 334 | 371 | 394 | 414 | 422 | 477 | 441 |
| 14. Canada . . . . | 361 | 398 | 422 | 410 | 478 | 499 | 431 |
| 15. Congo . . . . . | 298 | 305 | 318 | 349 | 352 | 359 | 401 |
| 16. All other free world | 710 | 712 | 730 | 846 | 851 | 928 | 947 |
| 17. Total free world . | 4,673 | 4,932 | 5,170 | 5,368 | 4,944 | 5,639 | 6,080 |
| 18. Soviet sphere . . | 752 | 858 | 903 | 968 | 1,050 | 1,108 | 1,185 |
| 19. Total world . . . | 5,425 | 5,790 | 6,073 | 6,336 | 5,994 | 6,747 | 7,265 |
| *World Copper Production by Origin of Ore[b]* | | | | | | | |
| 20. United States . . | 1,208 | 1,251 | 1,356 | 1,408 | 950[a] | 1,203[a] | 1,535 |
| 21. Zambia . . . . | 648 | 710 | 767 | 687[c] | 731 | 755 | 793 |
| 22. Chile . . . . . | 662 | 685 | 645[c] | 701 | 728 | 726 | 758 |
| 23. Canada . . . . | 462 | 487 | 510 | 508 | 603 | 633 | 573[c] |
| 24. Congo . . . . . | 298 | 305 | 318 | 349 | 353 | 358 | 399 |
| 25. All other free world | 967 | 961 | 969 | 1,098 | 1,084 | 1,168 | 1,242 |
| 26. Total free world . | 4,245 | 4,399 | 4,565 | 4,751 | 4,449 | 4,843 | 5,300 |
| 27. Soviet sphere . . | 723 | 818 | 867 | 927 | 1,009 | 1,077 | 1,160 |
| 28. Total world . . . | 4,968 | 5,217 | 5,432 | 5,678 | 5,458 | 5,920 | 6,460 |

*Source:* Yearbook of the American Bureau of Metal Statistics, 1970.

a. Between July 15, 1967, and March 30, 1968, the U.S. copper producers were on strike. Copper mining, smelting, and consumption were cut significantly during this period.

b. Some countries with copper mines exported the ore to be smelted and refined elsewhere.

c. Production was interrupted in Chile in 1965, Zambia in 1966, and Canada in 1969.

**EXHIBIT 3**

Calculations of Cash Flows Associated with the Firstburg Investment Opportunity, 1973–1985 (millions of dollars)

| | 1973 | 1974 | 1975 | 1976 | 1977 | 1978 | 1979 | 1980 | 1981 | 1982 | 1983 | 1984 | 1985 | Total |
|---|---|---|---|---|---|---|---|---|---|---|---|---|---|---|
| 1. Sales: 130 mil. lbs copper @ 40 cents | $52.0 | | | | | | | | | | | | | |
| 2. 68,000 oz gold @ $35 | 2.4 | | | | | | | | | | | | | |
| 3. .75 mil. oz silver @ $1.65 | 1.2 | | | | | | | | | | | | | |
| 4. Total sales | 55.6 | $55.6 | $55.6 | $55.6 | $55.6 | $55.6 | $55.6 | $55.6 | $55.6 | $55.6 | $55.6 | $55.6 | $55.6 | $722.8 |
| 5. Mining and milling costs[a] | 6.2 | 6.2 | 6.2 | 7.5 | 7.5 | 7.5 | 7.5 | 7.5 | 8.8 | 8.8 | 8.8 | 8.8 | 8.8 | 100.1 |
| 6. Smelting, refining, freight, and other | 13.0 | 13.0 | 13.0 | 13.0 | 13.0 | 13.0 | 13.0 | 13.0 | 13.0 | 13.0 | 13.0 | 13.0 | 13.0 | 169.0 |
| 7. Operating profits | 36.4 | 36.4 | 36.4 | 35.1 | 35.1 | 35.1 | 35.1 | 35.1 | 33.8 | 33.8 | 33.8 | 33.8 | 33.8 | 453.7 |
| 8. Depreciation and amortization | 8.9 | 8.9 | 8.9 | 8.9 | 8.9 | 8.9 | 8.9 | 8.9 | 8.9 | 8.9 | 8.9 | 8.9 | 8.7 | 115.5 |
| 9. Earnings before interest and taxes | 27.5 | 27.5 | 27.5 | 26.2 | 26.2 | 26.2 | 26.2 | 26.2 | 24.9 | 24.9 | 24.9 | 24.9 | 25.1 | 338.2 |
| 10. Taxes @ 40%[b] | 11.0 | 11.0 | 11.0 | 10.5 | 10.5 | 10.5 | 10.5 | 10.5 | 10.0 | 10.0 | 10.0 | 10.0 | 10.0 | 135.5 |
| 11. Profit after taxes | 16.5 | 16.5 | 16.5 | 15.7 | 15.7 | 15.7 | 15.7 | 15.7 | 14.9 | 14.9 | 14.9 | 14.9 | 15.1 | 202.7 |
| 12. Depreciation and amortization | 8.9 | 8.9 | 8.9 | 8.9 | 8.9 | 8.9 | 8.9 | 8.9 | 8.9 | 8.9 | 8.9 | 8.9 | 8.7 | 115.5 |
| 13. Cash flow from operations | 25.4 | 25.4 | 25.4 | 24.6 | 24.6 | 24.6 | 24.6 | 24.6 | 23.8 | 23.8 | 23.8 | 23.8 | 23.8 | 318.2 |
| 14. Return of working capital[c] | – | – | – | – | – | – | – | – | – | – | – | – | 4.5 | 4.5 |
| 15. Total cash return | $25.4 | $25.4 | $25.4 | $24.6 | $24.6 | $24.6 | $24.6 | $24.6 | $23.8 | $23.8 | $23.8 | $23.8 | $28.3 | $322.7 |
| 16. Total cash investment[d] | | | | | | | | | | | | | | $120.0 |

*Sources:* Wall Street institutional research reports; Southport Minerals, Inc., 10-K report to the SEC, 1969; casewriter's estimates.

*Note:* Based on the assumption that future world copper prices equal 40 cents per pound.

a. During the first 3 years of mining operations, costs were expected to be relatively low, as a significant portion of the copper ore at Firstburg was covered with very little overburden (non-ore-bearing material). Conventional open pit mining at slightly higher cost would be undertaken in the middle years of the mine's life. More expensive underground mining would not be necessary until the latter years of mine operation.

b. For simplicity, a 40% tax rate was assumed. Indonesia granted tax concessions making the Indonesian tax rate substantially lower than 40%. Additional taxes would be incurred by Southport Minerals in the U.S., however, on any of Southport Indonesia's earnings which were repatriated through the payment of dividends.

c. Of the $120 million in capital originally budgeted for the project, $4.5 million was for working capital.

d. Total cash investment equaled $120 million over a 4-year period: 1969, $7.5 mil.; 1970, $18.9 mil.; 1971, $42.5 mil.; and 1972, $51.1 mil.

**EXHIBIT 4**
Net Present Value of the Net Cash Flows Associated with the *Total* Investment in the Firstburg Project Calculated at Various Discount Rates

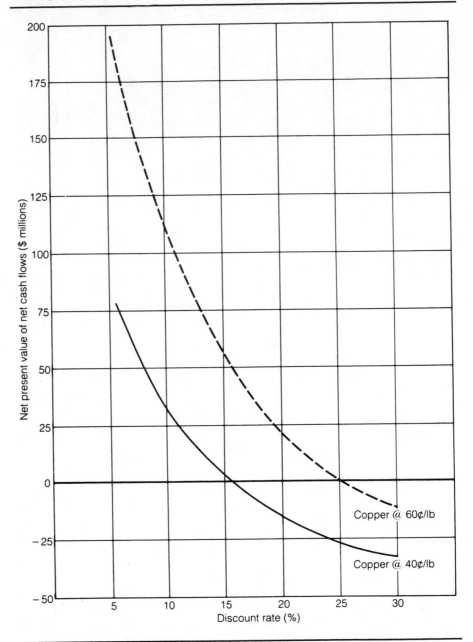

*Note:* Exhibit 3 cash flows, lines 15 and 16, discounted for the 40¢/lb copper example.

**EXHIBIT 5**

Proposed Capital Takedown Plan and Contractual Loan Principal Repayment Schedule, 1969–1982 (millions of dollars)

| | 1969 | 1970 | 1971 | 1972 | 1973 | 1974 | 1975 | 1976 | 1977 | 1978 | 1979 | 1980 | 1981 | 1982 | Total |
|---|---|---|---|---|---|---|---|---|---|---|---|---|---|---|---|
| *Capital Takedown Schedule* | | | | | | | | | | | | | | | |
| 1. Senior debt—Insurance companies | — | $ 6.7 | $17.1 | $16.2 | | | | | | | | | | | $ 40.0 |
| 2. Senior debt—U.S. banks | — | 3.1 | 7.6 | 7.3 | | | | | | | | | | | 18.0 |
| 3. Senior debt—German bank | — | 2.4 | 8.2 | 11.4 | | | | | | | | | | | 22.0 |
| 4. Junior debt—Japanese ore buyers | — | 6.3 | 5.6 | 8.1 | | | | | | | | | | | 20.0 |
| 5. Equity—Southport Minerals, Inc. | $7.5 | .4 | 4.0 | 8.1 | | | | | | | | | | | 20.0 |
| 6. Total capital | $7.5 | $18.9 | $42.5 | $51.1 | | | | | | | | | | | $120.0 |
| *Loan Principal Repayment Schedule* | | | | | | | | | | | | | | | |
| 7. Senior debt—Insurance companies | | | | | | — | $ .9 | $ 2.2 | $ 7.1 | $ 6.3 | $ 5.9 | $ 5.9 | $5.9 | $5.8 | $ 40.0 |
| 8. Senior debt—U.S. banks | | | | | | $7.2 | 6.4 | 4.4 | — | — | — | — | — | — | 18.0 |
| 9. Senior debt—German bank | | | | | | .7 | 1.4 | 2.1 | 2.1 | 2.8 | 3.2 | 3.3 | 3.2 | 3.2 | 22.0 |
| 10. Junior debt—Japanese ore buyers | | | | | | — | 3.3 | 3.3 | 3.3 | 3.4 | 3.4 | 3.3 | — | — | 20.0 |
| 11. Total repayments | | | | | | $7.9 | $12.0 | $12.0 | $12.5 | $12.5 | $12.5 | $12.5 | $9.1 | $9.0 | $100.0 |

*Source:* Southport Minerals, Inc., 10-K report to the SEC, 1969.

**EXHIBIT 6**
Loan Guarantors, Capital Providers, and Ore Buyers Involved in the Proposed Investment Project

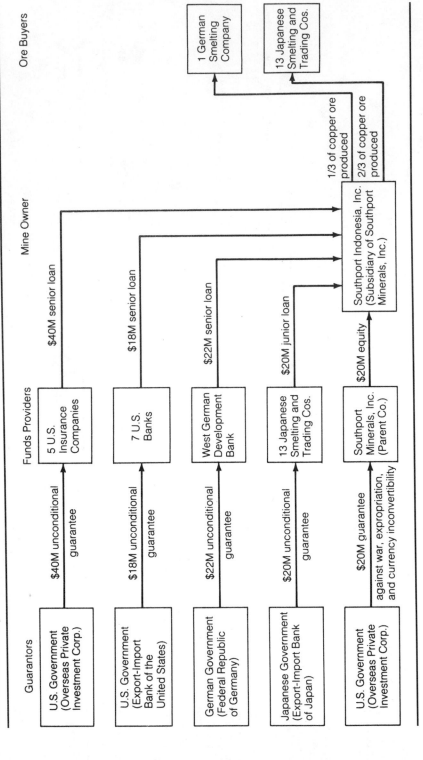

**EXHIBIT 7**

Calculation of Cash Flows (Dividends) to Southport Minerals from Its Southport Indonesia Subsidiary, 1969–1985 (millions of dollars)

| | 1969 | 1970 | 1971 | 1972 | 1973 | 1974 | 1975 | 1976 | 1977 | 1978 | 1979 | 1980 | 1981 | 1982 | 1983 | 1984 | 1985 | Total |
|---|---|---|---|---|---|---|---|---|---|---|---|---|---|---|---|---|---|---|
| 1. Earnings before interest and taxes[a] | | | | | $27.5 | $27.5 | $27.5 | $26.2 | $26.2 | $26.2 | $26.2 | $26.2 | $24.9 | $24.9 | $24.9 | $24.9 | $25.1 | $338.2 |
| 2. Interest | | | | | 8.6 | 7.2 | 6.4 | 5.3 | 4.0 | 2.3 | .6 | | | | | | | 34.4 |
| 3. Pre-tax profits | | | | | 18.9 | 20.3 | 21.1 | 20.9 | 22.2 | 23.9 | 25.6 | 26.2 | 24.9 | 24.9 | 24.9 | 24.9 | 25.1 | 303.8 |
| 4. Taxes @ 40% | | | | | 7.6 | 8.1 | 8.4 | 8.4 | 8.8 | 9.5 | 10.2 | 10.5 | 9.9 | 9.9 | 9.9 | 9.9 | 9.9 | 121.0 |
| 5. Profit after taxes | | | | | 11.3 | 12.2 | 12.7 | 12.5 | 13.4 | 14.4 | 15.4 | 15.7 | 15.0 | 15.0 | 15.0 | 15.0 | 15.2 | 182.8 |
| 6. Depreciation and amortization | | | | | 8.9 | 8.9 | 8.9 | 8.9 | 8.9 | 8.9 | 8.9 | 8.9 | 8.9 | 8.9 | 8.9 | 8.9 | 8.7 | 115.5 |
| 7. Cash flow from operations | | | | | 20.2 | 21.1 | 21.6 | 21.4 | 22.3 | 23.3 | 24.3 | 24.6 | 23.9 | 23.9 | 23.9 | 23.9 | 23.9 | 298.3 |
| 8. Working capital changes[b] | | | | | | (5.5) | | | | | | 5.5 | | | | | 4.5 | 4.5 |
| 9. Cash flow for debt repayment and dividends | | | | | 20.2 | 15.6 | 21.6 | 21.4 | 22.3 | 23.3 | 24.3 | 30.1 | 23.9 | 23.9 | 23.9 | 23.9 | 28.4 | 302.8 |
| 10. Contractually required debt repayment | | | | | 20.2 | 7.9 | 5.6 | 5.5 | 10.4 | 9.7 | 5.0 | | | | | | | 44.1 |
| 11. Debt prepayments required[c] | | | | | | 3.8 | 8.0 | 7.9 | 5.9 | 6.8 | 3.3 | | | | | | | 55.9 |
| 12. Cash available for dividend payments[c] | | | | | $ 0 | $ 3.9 | $ 8.0 | $ 8.0 | $ 6.0 | $ 6.8 | $16.0 | $30.1 | $23.9 | $23.9 | $23.9 | $23.9 | $28.4 | $202.8 |
| 13. Cash investment (equity only) | $7.5 | $.4 | $4.0 | $8.1 | | | | | | | | | | | | | | $ 20.0 |

*Sources:* Wall Street institutional reports; Southport Minerals, Inc., 10-K report to the SEC, 1969; casewriter's estimates.

*Note:* Based on the assumption that future world copper prices equal 40 cents per pound.

a. Data taken from Exhibit 3, line 9.

b. $4.5 million of the $120 million capital investment in Southport Indonesia was to be used as working capital. Since under the various loan convenants dividends could not be paid unless net working capital was at least $10 million, $5.5 million of cash flow was retained and committed to net working capital as of December 31, 1974. Since the loans were entirely repaid by December 31, 1980, these convenants became inoperative and the $5.5 million of working capital not needed to support normal operations could be paid out in dividends.

c. Under various loan convenants, no dividends could be paid until December 31, 1974, and debt prepayments in an amount equal to the proposed dividend had to be made before the dividend could be paid.

545

**EXHIBIT 8**

Schedule of Debt Amortization Required under Various Loan Agreements, 1973–1979 (millions of dollars)

| Loan Principal Repayment Schedule | 1973 | 1974 | 1975 | 1976 | 1977 | 1978 | 1979 | Total |
|---|---|---|---|---|---|---|---|---|
| *Senior Debt—Insurance Companies* | | | | | | | | |
| 1. Contractual repayment | – | – | $ .9 | $ 2.2 | $ 7.1 | $ 6.3 | $1.6 | $ 18.1 |
| 2. Prepayment | – | – | 1.3 | 7.9 | 5.9 | 6.8 | – | 21.9 |
| 3. Total amortization | – | – | $ 2.2 | $10.1 | $13.0 | $13.1 | $1.6 | $ 40.0 |
| *Senior Debt—U.S. Banks* | | | | | | | | |
| 4. Contractual repayment | – | $ 7.2 | – | – | – | – | – | $ 7.2 |
| 5. Prepayment | $ 9.1 | 1.7 | – | – | – | – | – | 10.8 |
| 6. Total amortization | $ 9.1 | $ 8.9 | – | – | – | – | – | $ 18.0 |
| *Senior Debt—German Bank* | | | | | | | | |
| 7. Contractual repayment | – | $ .7 | $ 1.4 | – | – | – | – | $ 2.1 |
| 8. Prepayment | $11.1 | 2.1 | 6.7 | – | – | – | – | 19.9 |
| 9. Total amortization | $11.1 | $ 2.8 | $ 8.1 | – | – | – | – | $ 22.0 |
| *Junior Debt—Japanese Ore Buyers* | | | | | | | | |
| 10. Contractual repayment | – | – | $ 3.3 | $ 3.3 | $ 3.3 | $ 3.4 | $3.4 | $ 16.7 |
| 11. Prepayment | – | – | – | – | – | – | 3.3 | 3.3 |
| 12. Total amortization | – | – | 3.3 | 3.3 | 3.3 | 3.4 | 6.7 | 20.0 |
| 13. Total contractual repayments | – | 7.9 | 5.6 | 5.5 | 10.4 | 9.7 | 5.0 | 44.1 |
| 14. Total prepayment | 20.2 | 3.8 | 8.0 | 7.9 | 5.9 | 6.8 | 3.3 | 55.9 |
| 15. Total debt amortization | $20.2 | $11.7 | $13.6 | $13.4 | $16.3 | $16.5 | $8.3 | $100.0 |

*Sources:* Southport Minerals, Inc., 10-K report to the SEC, 1969; casewriter's estimates.

*Note:* Based on the assumption of Southport Indonesia, Inc., paying the maximum permitted dividends at the earliest possible dates.

**EXHIBIT 9**

Net Present Value of the Net Cash Flows Associated with the *Equity* Investment in the Firstburg Project Calculated at Various Discount Rates

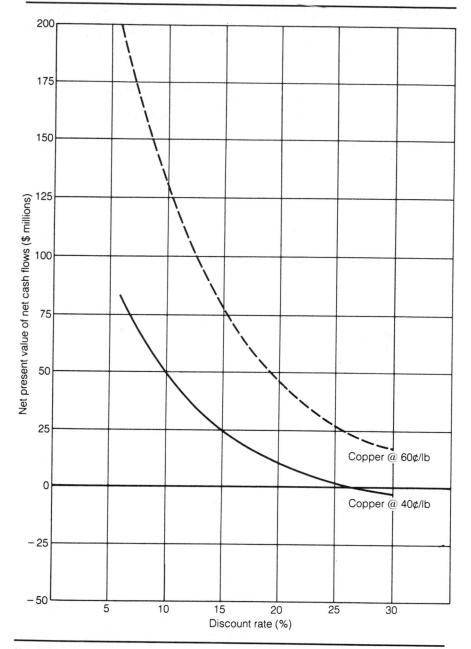

*Note:* Exhibit 7 cash flows, lines 12 and 13, discounted for the 40¢/lb copper example.

*Mergers, Acquisitions, and Restructurings*

# Cooper Industries, Inc.

In May 1972, Robert Cizik, executive vice president of Cooper Industries, Inc., was reviewing acquisition candidates for his company's diversification program. One of the companies, Nicholson File Company, had been approached by Cooper Industries 3 years earlier but had rejected all overtures. Now, however, Nicholson was in the middle of a takeover fight that might provide Cooper with a chance to gain control.

## Cooper Industries

Cooper Industries was organized in 1919 as a manufacturer of heavy machinery and equipment. By the mid-1950s the company was a leading producer of engines and massive compressors used to force natural gas through pipelines and oil out of wells. Management was concerned, however, over its heavy dependence on sales to the oil and gas industries and the violent fluctuation of earnings caused by the cyclical nature of heavy machinery and equipment sales. Although the company's long-term sales and earnings growth had been above average, its cyclicality had dampened Wall Street's interest in the stock substantially. (Cooper's historical operating results and financial condition are summarized in Exhibits 1 and 2.)

Initial efforts to lessen the earnings volatility were not successful. Between 1959 and 1966 Cooper acquired (1) a supplier of portable industrial power tools, (2) a manufacturer of small industrial air and process compressors, (3) a maker of small pumps and compressors for oil field applications, and (4) a producer of tire-changing tools for the automotive market. The acquisitions broadened Cooper's markets but left it still highly sensitive to general economic conditions.

A full review of Cooper's acquisition strategy was initiated in 1966 by the company. After several months of study, three criteria were established for all acquisitions. First, the industry should be one in which Cooper could become a major factor. This requirement was in line with management's goal of leadership within a few distinct areas of business. Second, the industry should be fairly stable with a broad market for the products and a product line of "small ticket" items. This product definition was intended to eliminate any company that had undue profit dependence upon a single customer or several large sales per year. Finally, it was decided to acquire only leading companies in their respective market segments.

The new strategy was initially implemented with the acquisition in 1967 of the Lufkin Rule Company, the world's largest manufacturer of measuring rules and tapes. Cooper acquired a quality product line, an established distribution system of 35,000 retail hardware stores throughout the United States, and plants in the United States, Canada, and Mexico. It also gained the services of William Rector, president of Lufkin, and Hal Stevens, vice president of sales. Both were extremely knowledgeable in the hand tool business and had worked together effectively for years. Their goal was to build through acquisition a hand tool company with a full product line that would use a common sales and distribution system and joint advertising. To do this they needed Cooper's financial strength.

Lufkin provided a solid base to which two other companies were added. In 1969 the Crescent Niagara Corporation was acquired. The company had been highly profitable in the early 1960s but had suffered in recent years under the mismanagement of some investor-entrepreneurs who had gained control in 1963. A series of acquisitions of weak companies with poor product lines eroded the company's overall profitability until, in 1967, a small loss was reported. Discouraged, the investors wanted to get out and Cooper—eager to add Crescent's well-known and high-quality wrenches, pliers, and screwdrivers to its line—was interested. It was clear that some of Crescent's lines would have to be dropped and inefficient plants would have to be closed, but the wrenches, pliers, and screwdrivers were an important part of Cooper's product policy.

In 1970, Cooper further expanded into hand tools with the acquisition of the Weller Electric Corporation. Weller was the world's leading supplier of soldering tools to the industrial, electronic, and consumer markets. It provided Cooper with a new, high-quality product line and production capacity in England, West Germany, and Mexico. (Information on the three acquisitions is provided in Exhibit 3.)

Cooper was less successful in its approach to a fourth company in the hand tool business, the Nicholson File Company. Nicholson was on the original "shopping list" of acceptable acquisition candidates that Mr. Cizik and Mr. Rector had developed, but several attempts to interest Nicholson in exploring merger possibilities had failed. The Nicholson family had controlled and managed the company since its founding in 1864, and Paul Nicholson, chairman of the board, had no interest in joining forces with anyone.

## Nicholson File Company

But Nicholson was too inviting a takeover target to be overlooked or ignored for long. A relatively poor sales and profit performance in recent years, conservative accounting and financial policies, and a low percentage of outstanding stock held by the Nicholson family and management all contributed to its vulnerability. Annual sales growth of 2% was far behind the industry growth rate of 6% per year, and profit margins had slipped to only one third those of other hand tool manufacturers. In 1971, Nicholson common stock was trading near its lowest point in many years and well below its book value of $51.25. Lack of investor interest in the stock was reflected in its low price-earnings ratio of 10–14, which compared with 14–17 times earnings for other leading hand tool companies. The stock was clearly selling on the basis of its dividend yield, with only limited hopes for capital appreciation. (Exhibits 4 and 5 show Nicholson's operating results and balance sheets.)

What made Nicholson so attractive was its basic competitive strength—strengths that the family-dominated management had not translated into earnings. The company was one of the largest domestic manufacturers of hand tools and was a leader in its two main product areas. Nicholson held a 50% share of the $50 million market for files and rasps, where it offered a broad, high-quality line with a very strong brand name. Its second product line, hand saws and saw blades, also had an excellent reputation for quality and held a 9% share of this $200 million market. Only Sears, Roebuck and Company and Disston, Inc., had larger market shares.

Nicholson's greatest asset, however, was its distribution system. Forty-eight direct salesmen and 28 file and saw engineers marketed its file, rasp, and saw products to 2,100 hardware wholesalers in the United States and Canada. These wholesalers in turn sold to 53,000 retail outlets. Their efforts were supported by heavy advertising and promotional programs. Overseas the company's products were sold in 137 countries through 140 local sales representatives. The company seemed to have all the necessary strengths to share fully in the 6–7% annual sales growth forecast for the industry.

## The Raid by H. K. Porter Company

Cooper was not alone in its interest in Nicholson. H. K. Porter Company, a conglomerate with wide-ranging interests in electrical equipment, tools, nonferrous metals, and rubber products, had acquired 44,000 shares of Nicholson stock in 1967 and had been an attentive stockholder ever since. On March 3, 1972, Porter informed Nicholson management of its plan to tender immediately for 437,000 of Nicholson's 584,000 outstanding shares at $42 per share in cash. The offer would terminate on April 4 unless extended by Porter; and the company was unwilling to acquire fewer shares than would constitute a majority.

Nicholson management was alarmed by both the proposal and the proposer. The company would contribute less than one sixth of the combined sales and would clearly be just another operating division of Porter. It was feared that Porter's quest for higher profits might lead to aggressive cost cutting and the elimination of marginal product lines. Nicholson's Atkins Saw Division seemed especially vulnerable in view of its low profitability.

Loss of control seemed both painful and likely. The $42 cash offer represented a $12 premium over the most recent price of the stock and threatened to create considerable stockholder interest. The disappointing performance of the stock in recent years would undoubtedly increase the attractiveness of the $42 offer to Nicholson's 4,000 stockholders. And the Nicholson family and management owned only 20% of the outstanding shares—too few to ensure continued control.

Immediately after learning of the Porter tender offer, Mr. Cizik and Mr. Rector approached the Nicholson management with an offer of help. It was clear that Nicholson had to move immediately and forcefully; the first ten days of a tender offer are critical. Messrs. Cizik and Rector stressed that Nicholson must find a better offer and find it fast. Indeed, Cooper would be willing to make such an offer if Nicholson's management and directors would commit themselves to it—now.

Nicholson was not ready for such decisive action, however, and three days passed without any decision. With each day the odds of a successful counteroffer diminished. Finally, the Cooper officers decided the risks were too great and that Porter would learn of Cooper's offer of help and might retaliate. Cooper's stock was depressed and it was possible that an angry Porter management might strike for control of Cooper. The offer was withdrawn.

By late March the situation was increasing in seriousness. Management of Nicholson moved to block the raid. It personally talked with the large shareholders and made a strong public statement recommending against the offer. But announcements by Porter indicated that a substantial number of Nicholson shares were being tendered. It was no longer a matter of whether or not to be acquired. The issue was, by whom!

Management sought to find an alternative merger that would ensure continuity of Nicholson management and operating independence. Several companies had communicated with Nicholson in the wake of the Porter announcement, but no one other than Cooper had made a specific proposal. This was largely due to their reluctance to compete at the price levels being discussed or to enter into a fight with Porter.

Finally, on April 3, agreement was reached with VLN Corporation on the terms of a merger with VLN. VLN was a broadly diversified company with major interests in original and replacement automotive equipment and in publishing. Under the VLN merger terms, one share of new VLN cumulative convertible preferred stock would be exchanged for each share of Nicholson common stock. The VLN preferred stock would pay an annual dividend of $1.60 and would be convertible into five shares of VLN common stock during the first year following the merger, scaling down to four shares after the fourth year. The preferred stock would be callable at $50 per share after the fifth year and would have liquidating rights of $50 per share. (See Exhibit 6 for a financial summary of VLN.)

Nicholson management, assured of continued operating independence, supported the VLN offer actively. In a letter to the stockholders Paul Nicholson pointed out that (1) the exchange would be a tax-free transaction, (2) the $1.60 preferred dividend equaled the current rate on the Nicholson common stock, and (3) a preferred share was worth a minimum of $53.10 (VLN common stock had closed at $10.62 on the day prior to the offer). He felt confident that the necessary majority of the outstanding common stock would be voted in favor of the proposed merger when it was brought to a vote in the fall. (Under Rhode Island law, a simple majority was sufficient to authorize the merger.)

Porter quickly counterattacked by pointing out to Nicholson stockholders that VLN common stock had recently sold for as low as $4⅝, which would put a value in the first year of only $23.12 on the VLN preferred stock. Furthermore, anyone who converted into VLN common stock would suffer a sharp income loss, since VLN had paid no common dividends since 1970.

Nicholson's stockholders were thus presented with two very contradictory appraisals of the VLN offer. Each company based its argument on some stock price, either the highest or the lowest, that would make the converted preferred stock compare favorably or not with the $42 cash offer.

## Opportunity for Cooper?

Mr. Cizik and his staff were still attracted by the potential profits to be realized from Nicholson. It was felt that Nicholson's efforts to sell to every market segment resulted in an excessive number of products, which held down manufacturing efficiency and ballooned inventories. Cooper estimated that Nicholson's cost of goods sold could be reduced from 69% of sales to 65%.

The other major area of cost reduction was Nicholson's selling expenses. There was a substantial overlap of Nicholson's sales force and that established by Cooper for its Lufkin-Weller-Crescent hand tool lines. Elimination of the sales and advertising duplications would lower selling, general, and administrative expenses from 22% of sales to 19%.

There were other possible sources of earnings, but they were more difficult to quantify. For instance, 75% of Nicholson's sales were to the industrial market and only 25% to the consumer market. In contrast, sales by Cooper's hand tool group were distributed between the two markets in virtually the exact opposite proportions. Thus, sales increases could be expected from Nicholson's "pulling" more Cooper products into the industrial markets and vice versa for the consumer market. Also, Cooper was eager to use Nicholson's strong European distribution system to sell its other hand tool lines.

The battle between Porter and VLN seemed to provide Cooper with an unexpected, second opportunity to gain control of Nicholson. Porter had ended up with just 133,000 shares tendered in response to its offer—far short of the 249,000 shares needed to give it majority control.[1] Its slate of directors had been defeated by Nicholson management at the Nicholson annual meeting on April 21. T. M. Evans, president of Porter, now feared that Nicholson might consummate the merger with VLN and that Porter would be faced with the unhappy prospect of receiving VLN preferred stock for its 177,000 shares of Nicholson stock. Mr. Evans knew that the VLN stock had been a lackluster performer and might not show any significant growth in the near term. Furthermore, the $1.60 dividend rate seemed low in relation to current market yields on straight preferred stocks of 7%. Finally, he feared that it would be difficult to sell a large holding of VLN stock, which traded in small volume on the American Stock Exchange.

On the other hand, a merger of Cooper and Nicholson would allow Mr. Evans to convert his Nicholson shares into either common stock or convertible preferred stock of Cooper. This was a much more attractive alternative, assuming that an acceptable exchange rate could be set. Mr. Evans anticipated that earnings should rebound sharply from the cyclical downturn in 1971 and felt that Cooper stock would show significant price appreciation. Furthermore, Cooper stock was traded on the New York Exchange, which provided substantial liquidity. At a private meeting in late April, Mr. Evans tentatively agreed to support a Cooper-Nicholson merger on the condition that he receive Cooper common or convertible securities in a tax-free exchange worth at least $50 for each Nicholson share he held.

Mr. Cizik was now faced with the critical decision of whether to move for control. Cooper had acquired 29,000 shares of Nicholson stock during the preceding month in the open market—in part to build some bargaining power but largely to keep the loose shares out of the hands of Porter. Still uncommitted, however, were an estimated 50,000–100,000 shares that had been bought by speculators in the hope of an escalation of acquisition offers. Another 150,000–200,000 shares were unaccounted for, although Mr. Cizik suspected that a considerable number would go with the recommendation of Nicholson management. (Exhibit 7 shows Mr. Cizik's best estimate of the distribution of Nicholson stock in early May.) His hopes for gaining 50.1% of the Nicholson shares outstanding[2] depended upon his gaining support of at least 86,000 of the shares still either uncommitted or unaccounted for.

If he decided to seek control, it would be necessary to establish both the price and the form of the offer. Clearly, the terms would have to be sufficiently attractive to secure the shares needed to gain majority control.

---

1. Porter needed 292,584 shares to hold 50.1% majority control. It already owned 43,806 shares and needed, therefore, an additional 248,778 shares.

2. Nicholson File was incorporated in Rhode Island. Under Rhode Island corporation law, a merger can be voted by shareholders holding a majority of the common stock outstanding. For reasons specific both to the laws of Rhode Island and to the Nicholson situation, dissenting stockholders of Nicholson would not be entitled to exercise the rights of dissent and would be forced to accept the exchange offer.

Mr. Cizik also felt that the terms should be acceptable to the Nicholson management. Once the merger was complete, Cooper would need to work with the Nicholson family and management. He did not want them to feel that they and other Nicholson stockholders were cheated by the merger. As a matter of policy Cooper had never made an "unfriendly" acquisition and this one was to be no exception. The offer should be one that would be supported by the great majority of the stockholders.

However, the price and the form of the payment had to be consistent with Cooper's concern that the acquisition earn a satisfactory long-term return and improve the trend of Cooper's earnings per share over the next 5 years. (A forecast of Cooper's earnings per share is shown in Exhibit 8.) The company anticipated making additional acquisitions, possibly on an exchange of stock basis, and maintenance of a strong earnings pattern and stock price was therefore important. On May 3 the common stock of Cooper and Nicholson closed at $24 and $44, respectively.

**EXHIBIT 1**

Condensed Operating and Stockholder Information, Cooper Industries, Inc., 1967–1971 (millions of dollars except per share data)

| | 1967 | 1968 | 1969 | 1970 | 1971 |
|---|---|---|---|---|---|
| *Operations* | | | | | |
| Net sales | $ 198 | $ 206 | $ 212 | $ 226 | $ 208 |
| Cost of goods sold | 141 | 145 | 154 | 164 | 161 |
| Depreciation | 4 | 5 | 4 | 4 | 4 |
| Selling and administrative expenses | 23 | 25 | 29 | 29 | 29 |
| Interest expense | 1 | 2 | 3 | 4 | 3 |
| Income before taxes and extraordinary items | 29 | 29 | 22 | 24 | 11 |
| Income taxes | 14 | 15 | 11 | 12 | 5 |
| Income before extraordinary items | 15.2 | 13.9 | 10.6 | 12.4 | 5.6 |
| Preferred dividend | 1.0 | .9 | .9 | .9 | .9 |
| Net income applicable to common stock | $ 14.2 | $ 13.0 | $ 9.7 | $ 11.5 | $ 4.7 |
| *Common Stock* | | | | | |
| Earnings per share before extraordinary items | $ 3.34 | $ 3.07 | $ 2.33 | $ 2.75 | $ 1.12 |
| Dividends per share | 1.20 | 1.25 | 1.40 | 1.40 | 1.40 |
| Book value per share | 16.43 | 17.26 | 18.28 | 19.68 | 18.72 |
| Market price | 23–59 | 36–57 | 22–50 | 22–35 | 18–38 |
| Price-earnings ratio | 7–18 | 12–19 | 9–22 | 8–13 | 16–34 |

**EXHIBIT 2**
Balance Sheet at December 31, 1971, Cooper Industries, Inc. (millions of dollars)

| | | | | |
|---|---|---|---|---|
| Cash | $ 9 | Accounts payable | $ 30 |
| Accounts receivable | 49 | Accrued taxes | 3 |
| Inventories | 57 | Long-term debt due | 5 |
| Other | 2 | Current liabilities | 38 |
| Current assets | 117 | Long-term debt[a] | 34 |
| Net plant and equipment | 47 | Deferred taxes | 4 |
| Other | 8 | Preferred stock | 11 |
| Total assets | $172 | Common equity (4,218,691 shares outstanding) | 85 |
| | | Total liabilities and net worth | $172 |

a. Maturities of long-term debt are $5.5 million, $6 million, $4 million, $2 million, and $2 million in the years 1972 through 1975, respectively.

**EXHIBIT 3**
Summary of Cooper Industries' Recent Acquisitions (millions of dollars)

| | Year Preceding Acquisition by Cooper | | | | |
|---|---|---|---|---|---|
| | Sales | Net Income | Book Value | Acquisition Price Paid | Form of Transaction |
| Lufkin Rule Company | $22 | $1.4 | $15 | $20.6 | Convertible preferred |
| Crescent Niagara Corporation | 16 | .04 | 4.9 | 12.5 | Cash |
| Weller Electric Corporation | 10 | .9 | 4.4 | 14.6 | Common stock |

**EXHIBIT 4**

Condensed Operating and Stockholder Information, Nicholson File Company, 1967–1971 (millions of dollars except per share data)

|  | 1967 | 1968 | 1969 | 1970 | 1971 |
|---|---|---|---|---|---|
| *Operations* | | | | | |
| Net sales | $ 48.5 | $ 49.1 | $ 53.7 | $ 54.8 | $ 55.3 |
| Cost of goods sold | 32.6 | 33.1 | 35.9 | 37.2 | 37.9 |
| Selling, general, and administrative expenses | 10.7 | 11.1 | 11.5 | 11.9 | 12.3 |
| Depreciation expense | 2.0 | 2.3 | 2.4 | 2.3 | 2.1 |
| Interest expense | .4 | .7 | .8 | .8 | .8 |
| Other deductions | .3 | .1 | .2 | .2 | .2 |
| Income before taxes | 2.53 | 1.85 | 2.97 | 2.42 | 2.02 |
| Taxes[a] | .60 | .84 | 1.31 | .88 | .67 |
| Net income | $ 1.93 | $ 1.01 | $ 1.66 | $ 1.54 | $ 1.35 |
| *Percentage of Sales* | | | | | |
| Cost of goods sold | 67% | 67% | 67% | 68% | 69% |
| Selling general, and administrative expenses | 22 | 23 | 21 | 22 | 22 |
| Income before taxes | 5.2 | 3.8 | 5.5 | 4.4 | 3.7 |
| *Stockholder Information* | | | | | |
| Earnings per share | $ 3.19 | $ 1.65 | $ 2.88 | $ 2.64 | $ 2.32 |
| Dividends per share | 1.60 | 1.60 | 1.60 | 1.60 | 1.60 |
| Book value per share | 45.66 | 48.03 | 49.31 | 50.20 | 51.25 |
| Market price | 33–46 | 35–48 | 29–41 | 25–33 | 23–32 |
| Price-earnings ratio | 10–14 | 21–30 | 10–14 | 9–13 | 10–14 |

a. The ratio of income taxes to income before taxes has been reduced primarily by the investment tax credit and by the inclusion in income of equity in net income of partially-owned foreign companies, the taxes for which are provided for in the accounts of such companies and not in the tax provision of Nicholson. It was estimated that the average tax rate would be 40% in future years.

**EXHIBIT 5**

Balance Sheet at December 31, 1971, Nicholson File Company (millions of dollars)

| | | | |
|---|---|---|---|
| Cash | $ 1 | Accounts payable | $ 2 |
| Accounts receivable | 8 | Other | 2 |
| Inventories[a] | 18 | Current liabilities | 4 |
| Other | 1 | Long-term debt | 12 |
| Current assets | 28 | Common stock | 31 |
| Investment in subsidiaries | 3 | Total liabilities and net worth | $47 |
| Net plant and equipment | 16 | | |
| Total assets | $47 | | |

a. Inventories in the amount of $11.8 million are priced at cost on the last in, first out method. The estimated replacement cost exceeds the carrying amounts by $9.2 million. The remaining inventories are priced at the lower of cost on the first in, first out method or market.

**EXHIBIT 6**
Condensed Operating and Stockholder Information, VLN Corporation, 1967–1971
(millions of dollars except per share data)

|  | 1967 | 1968 | 1969 | 1970 | 1971 |
|---|---|---|---|---|---|
| *Operations* | | | | | |
| Net sales | $ 45 | $ 97 | $ 99 | $ 98 | $ 100 |
| Net income | 1.97 | 3.20 | 3.20 | 1.13 | 2.98 |
| *Financial Position* | | | | | |
| Current assets | $ 25 | $ 46 | $ 49 | $ 41 | $ 46 |
| Current liabilities | 6 | 11 | 15 | 10 | 13 |
| Net working capital | 19 | 35 | 34 | 31 | 33 |
| Long-term debt | 10 | 18 | 16 | 15 | 17 |
| Shareholders' equity | 21 | 36 | 40 | 39 | 41 |
| *Stockholder Information* | | | | | |
| Earnings per share | $ .78 | $ .61 | $ .53 | $ .27 | $ .54 |
| Dividends per share | – | – | – | .20 | – |
| Shareholders' equity per share | 8.23 | 9.64 | 10.00 | 9.24 | 9.69 |
| Market price range | 6–17 | 10–18 | 7–18 | 4–10 | 5–8 |
| Price-earnings ratio | 8–22 | 16–30 | 13–34 | 15–37 | 9–15 |

**EXHIBIT 7**
Estimated Distribution of Nicholson File Company Stock

| | | |
|---|---|---|
| Shares supporting Cooper | | |
| H. K. Porter | 177,000 | |
| Cooper Industries | 29,000 | 206,000 |
| Shares supporting VLN | | |
| Nicholson family and management | 117,000 | |
| Owned by VLN | 14,000 | 131,000 |
| Shares owned by speculators | | 50,000–100,000 |
| Shares unaccounted for | | 197,000–147,000 |
| Total Nicholson shares outstanding | | 584,000 |

**EXHIBIT 8**
Five-Year Forecast of Cooper Industries' Earnings, Excluding Nicholson File Company, 1972–1976

|  | 1972 | 1973 | 1974 | 1975 | 1976 |
|---|---|---|---|---|---|
| Net income available to common stockholders ($ millions) | $ 11.0 | $ 11.9 | $ 12.8 | $ 13.8 | $ 15.0 |
| Number of shares outstanding (millions) | 4.21 | 4.21 | 4.21 | 4.21 | 4.21 |
| Primary earnings per share | $ 2.61 | $ 2.83 | $ 3.04 | $ 3.27 | $ 3.56 |

*Note:* Forecasts are casewriter's estimates.

# Gulf Oil Corporation—Takeover

On the morning of March 5, 1984, George Keller of the Standard Oil Company of California (Socal) still had not made up his mind about how much to bid. The stakes were high. For sale was Gulf Oil Corporation, the most doddering of the seven sisters. But the price was high as well. Determined to depart in dignity, Gulf management made clear that it would not consider any bid below $70 per share, a considerable premium over the $43 price at which Gulf had traded during the close of 1983, when the sale of Gulf was a remote possibility.

Bidding against Mr. Keller were some who were willing to pay $70 and more. Included in the confidential auction in Pittsburgh with Standard Oil of California were members of the Atlantic Richfield Company (ARCO) and bankers from Kohlberg, Kravis, Roberts & Co., specialists in leveraged buyouts.

Mr. Keller felt the bid from Kohlberg, Kravis was the one to beat, since it came essentially from Gulf itself. This proposal allowed Gulf to become a private firm by tendering for the shares of its public stock. The undeniable attraction of the offer lay in its preservation of the name, the assets, and the jobs of Gulf Oil, until management found a long-term solution.

The challenge from ARCO was far less threatening. If ARCO offered more than $75 per share, its debt-to-total-capital ratio would exceed 60%, an uncomfortably high level. Socal, in contrast, had a debt-to-total-capital ratio that was so low that the banks were queuing up to lend money. The banks were so anxious to lend Socal $14 billion that the potential loan was oversubscribed by 30%.

The profusion of bank credit meant that Mr. Keller could safely bid $79, $80, or even higher. The opportunities created by the acquisition were enormous, but so were the risks of betting the whole company on them. With one stroke, Socal could ensure itself access to vast quantities of high-quality light oil. Overnight, Socal could virtually double its reserves and give the next generation of management something to work with.

An appraisal of the value of the opportunities offered by the Gulf deal required, of course, an idea of how the two companies (Exhibit 1) would perform as a unit. A pro forma balance sheet (Exhibit 2) showed that the combined firm would have a considerable amount of financial leverage. While manageable in the short run, the debt would have to be reduced over the next few years.

The most direct way of accomplishing this reduction was to sell some of Gulf's assets. Another way, Mr. Keller felt, was to make use of funds Gulf currently spent on exploration and development.[1] These funds amounted to over $2 billion in 1983 (Exhibit 3). The only question was whether, by using funds that had been earmarked for the search for more oil, the long-run viability of the new enterprise would be sacrificed at the expense of financial expediency. After all, if investing in new sources of oil were worthwhile before Gulf's acquisition, it would be just as worthwhile afterwards. An opposite point of view, however, was that if Socal purchased Gulf, its reserves would be so large that Gulf's contribution to the exploratory effort could safely be discontinued.

Aside from the question of how to reduce the takeover debt there was the issue of the tax cost of the acquisition. Although the tax considerations were complex,[2] it was felt that the tax benefits and costs nearly offset each other.[3] The decision, therefore, of how much to bid depended solely upon the economic benefits of the acquisition. At times, those benefits seemed almost incalculable. As Mr. Keller said, "But it's like a 100-year mining project. A straight rate of return analysis would prevent you from doing it. The decision has to be a little glandular."[4]

---

1. Exploration and development is a time-consuming effort. For an on-shore site, it generally takes 4 years between the time the lease is acquired until the field comes on-stream. Having been developed, the field is productive for another 7–10 years.

2. Advice concerning the tax aspects of this transaction was provided by the law firm of Simpson Thacher & Bartlett.

3. It was expected that the acquisition would be structured as a liquidating sale of Gulf's assets. Under the Tax Equity and Fiscal Responsibility Act of 1982 (TEFRA), the treatment of such a sale held both benefits and drawbacks for the acquiring company. On the positive side, no gain was recognized by the acquired company on the sale of its assets. More important, the acquiring company was allowed to step up the assets to their fair market value, thereby realizing future tax benefits through higher depreciation and depletion deductions. On the negative side, certain tax deductions taken in the past by the acquired company became recaptured and had to be repaid immediately upon liquidation. For example, since Gulf used the LIFO (last in, first out) method to account for petroleum inventories, the difference between the FIFO (first in, first out) and LIFO valuations had to be treated as ordinary income and taxes paid accordingly. Also recaptured and treated as ordinary income was any depreciation in excess of the straight-line amount on real property and certain accelerated drilling costs.

4. *Fortune*, April 2, 1984, p. 22.

## The Takeover

While the seeds for Gulf's demise were sown over the course of a decade, the event that precipitated the emergency meeting in Pittsburgh on March 5, 1984, was far more recent. The decision to sell the company was made in response to a takeover attempt by Boone Pickens, Jr., the chief executive officer of Mesa Petroleum Co.

Boone Pickens had a long string of successes in targeting undervalued oil companies, beginning in 1969. In 1982, the year prior to its attempt on Gulf, Mesa tendered for two companies, Cities Service and General American Oil of Texas. In both cases, Mesa failed to gain control but made a substantial profit in reaching an accommodation with the target. In the case of Cities Service, Mesa sold back the stock it acquired through the tender for a gain of $31.5 million. In the case of General American, Mesa received $15 million for withdrawing its tender and another $42.4 million when it sold the shares accumulated in open market purchases to a higher bidder.

On August 11, 1983, Mr. Pickens and a consortium of experienced investors began purchasing shares of Gulf Oil for $39. Two months later, the Gulf Investors' Group, as the consortium called itself, had spent $638 million and had acquired about 9% of all the Gulf shares outstanding at an average cost of approximately $43 per share.

The share purchases were totally unexpected. Mesa Petroleum was a small company compared to Gulf. If Mr. Pickens intended to acquire control of Gulf, the deal would require borrowing at least $10 billion dollars, many times the magnitude of Mesa's net worth. To put the effort in perspective, 4 years before, the largest takeover was $1 billion and that involved the conglomerate United Technologies. What Mr. Pickens was attempting was as audacious as it was unprecedented.

What contributed to the surprise was the opinion of many that the time for oil mega-mergers had passed. Within a few years, Occidental Petroleum had acquired Cities Service; U.S. Steel had bought Marathon Oil; Du Pont had taken over Conoco; and Elf Aquitane had gained control of Texasgulf. The political sentiment was that these takeovers, costing tens of billions of dollars, were not in the public interest. Senator Bennett Johnston (D, La.) put the principle forcefully: "When a few merge, it's one thing, but when a whole industry is consolidating, it's a very different matter. One's a glass of wine with Christmas dinner; the other, a six-month binge."[5]

After the shock subsided, Gulf's response to the investors' group was one of indignation and outrage. The chairman of Gulf, James Lee, described the group led by Mr. Pickens as "corporate raiders" who are "cannibalizing" the company. Harold Hammer, the chief administrative officer of Gulf, said, "We've got to roll up our sleeves and hit him where it really smarts."[6] In the meantime, the investors' group raised its share in Gulf to 13.2%.

---

5. *Ibid.*

6. *New York Times,* November 5, 1983.

Mr. Pickens stated that his immediate objective was to put himself on the board of directors where he could effect changes in Gulf policy. He said he was particularly interested in forcing Gulf to spin off its domestic oil and gas properties into a royalty trust, a device he popularized and perfected at Mesa.[7] To thwart this, Gulf sought to move its corporate charter from Pennsylvania to Delaware, where Mr. Pickens would need a majority vote of the shareholders to elect alternative directors. This move, which occurred on January 18, 1984, followed a long and acrimonious proxy battle over the reincorporation. Gulf won that battle with 53% of the vote in its favor. In that contest, Gulf was heavily supported by individual investors, most of whom were personally lobbied by Gulf executives (Exhibit 4). After winning the proxy contest, Gulf felt confident that the reincorporation would deny the investors' group, with limited capital at their disposal, their only means of access to the boardroom.

On February 22, 1984, Mr. Pickens announced a partial tender offer at $65 per share. This price was within the range that the Gulf Investors' Group estimated the royalty trust shares would trade if the proposed reorganization took place, according to their December 30 presentation to the Gulf board of directors. The offer price represented a significant premium over price levels of the recent past (Exhibit 5) and the closing price of $52⅝ on the day before. To make the offer, Mr. Pickens had to borrow $300 million from Penn Central Corp., using securities of Mesa Petroleum as collateral. Even with this capital infusion, the investors' group could only afford to purchase 13.5 million shares, which would leave them far short of a majority, with 21.3% of the stock. The Pickens group, however, hoped that this show of strength would enable them to attract further financial backing.

The motives of the Pickens group were widely impugned by those sympathetic to Gulf's management. On the day of the tender offer, for instance, a local Pittsburgh paper editorialized: "Mesa chairman T. Boone Pickens, Jr., expects primarily to cash in on Gulf's golden eggs, which are in the form of vast amounts of oil and gas. After obtaining the revenue there, he plans to slaughter the goose."[8]

The tender offer precipitated a crisis at Gulf. Seeming to sense the inevitability of the outcome, Gulf decided to seek a liquidation on its own terms. James Murdy, an executive vice president of Gulf, said in a retrospective interview:[9]

> Now all of this attention put enormous speculative pressure on our stock. We saw that, and we knew we had to do the best job for all shareholders while at the same

---

7. The principal advantage of a trust was the elimination of a second layer of taxation on distributed earnings and the tax savings from the step-up in the basis of the properties. However, some past tax deductions were recaptured in the process, and the shareholders had to pay capital gains rates on the difference between the trading value of the trust units and their basis in the corporation's stock. The arrangement worked well if the corporation had a high dividend payout ratio and stockholders had a high tax basis.

8. *Pittsburgh Post Gazette,* February 23, 1984.

9. *Energy Bureau Seminar,* October 3, 1984.

time saving as much as possible for employees and others with a stake in Gulf. So when Mesa finally launched its unfair partial tender offer, our board was willing to consider selling the company to a strong merger partner rather than see Mesa steal the company.

Having made the decision to liquidate, Gulf contacted several firms—including Allied, ARCO, Socal, Sohio, and Unocal—and invited them to Pittsburgh for an unprecedented sale.

## Recent History

In 1975, Gulf lost a large portion of its reserves when Kuwait and Venezuela canceled Gulf's oil concession. In the years that followed, total reserves declined, reaching a record low in 1981. In that year, James Lee became chairman. Mr. Lee enunciated a clear strategy to reverse the decline in Gulf's competitive position. His strategy was twofold. First, he would concentrate Gulf's efforts on oil. In the past, Gulf had developed into an energy conglomerate through acquisitions of coal mines, uranium mines, and synthetic fuel plants. In the future, Gulf intended to de-emphasize these ventures, which were not notably successful. The second part of the strategy arose naturally from the first. In keeping with the renewed emphasis on oil, Mr. Lee continued to increase expenditures on exploration and development. As a result of this policy, outlays for exploration more than doubled between 1978 and 1982, and the long decline in reserves was finally arrested and reversed. He was quite explicit about his policy. In his own words, "Gulf's number one priority is to replace our domestic reserves of hydrocarbons through discoveries and acquisitions."[10]

A key phrase in this statement of purpose is "discoveries *and* acquisitions." In 1982, Gulf made an effort to acquire Cities Service. Ironically, Gulf's attempted acquisition of Cities Service involved a confrontation with Mesa Petroleum, which almost cost Mesa its corporate life. The takeover of Cities Service collapsed at the last minute, however, when the Federal Trade Commission raised several objections and Gulf withdrew its offer, causing many arbitrageurs to lose heavily.

Mr. Lee's business plan underwent a midcourse correction as a result of developments in the oil markets. Beginning in 1982 and continuing throughout 1983, the real price of oil and natural gas declined (Exhibit 6). As 1984 began, almost all experts were in agreement that, in constant dollars, the price of oil would not change for the next 10 years. Even the oil ministers of Saudi Arabia and Qatar shared this opinion.

In response to these changing fundamentals, Mr. Lee trimmed exploration expenditures significantly in 1983.[11] Even at this reduced level, however, spending

---

10. Gulf Oil Corporation, Annual Report (1981), p. 3.

11. See Exhibit 8 for a discussion of accounting policies relating to exploration and development.

for exploration in real terms equaled or exceeded that of every year before his arrival except one (Exhibit 3).

In addition to investing in discovering new sources of oil and gas, Gulf management began using the company's sizable cash flow to repurchase shares. From mid-1981 to March 1983, Gulf purchased 30 million shares of the 195 million outstanding. At that point, Mr. Lee said, "I have no philosophical problem with another bite if everything is as it is now and if our stock is as good a buy as it is now."[12]

## Mr. Keller's Decision

Mr. Keller was as aware as Mr. Lee of Gulf's lackluster showing on most measures of financial performance (Exhibit 7). Indeed, Gulf's sluggish returns and weak earnings were the chief attraction, since they suggested great opportunities for improvement. The only uncertainty facing Mr. Keller on the morning of March 5 was not whether to bid but how much to bid to be sure the opportunities didn't get away.

### EXHIBIT 1
Results of 1983 Operations, Oil and Gas Producing Activities Only (millions of dollars)

|  | Gulf | Socal |
|---|---|---|
| Revenues, oil and gas production only . . . . . | $6,503 | $5,742 |
| Less: Costs |  |  |
| Lifting costs |  |  |
| Production . . . . . . . . . . . . . . . | 911 | 1,454 |
| Wellhead taxes . . . . . . . . . . . . | 792 | 504 |
| Exploration expense . . . . . . . . . . | 594 | 758 |
| Depreciation, etc. . . . . . . . . . . . | 1,000 | 646 |
| Other operating expenses . . . . . . . . | 358 | 116 |
| Income taxes[a] . . . . . . . . . . . . . . | 1,933 | 1,368 |
| Results of operations after income taxes . . . . . | $ 915 | $ 896 |

a. Gulf's effective marginal tax rate was approximately 50%.

*(continued)*

12. Quoted in *Gulf Oil Corporation Appraisal* (John S. Herold, Inc., 1983), p. 349.

**EXHIBIT 1** *(concluded)*
Comparison of 1983 Balance Sheets for Total Corporation (millions of dollars)

| | Gulf | Socal |
|---|---|---|
| Current assets | $ 5,653 | $ 7,328 |
| Net properties | 14,090 | 14,222 |
| Investments in affiliates | 608 | 2,319 |
| Deferred charges and other assets | 613 | 141 |
| Total assets | $20,964 | $24,010 |
| Current liabilities | $ 4,756 | $ 5,117 |
| Long-term debt and capital leases | 2,291 | 1,896 |
| Deferred taxes | 2,651 | 1,960 |
| Deferred credits | – | 852 |
| Other liabilities | 355 | 79 |
| Minority interests | 783 | – |
| Total liabilities | 10,836 | 9,904 |
| Common stock | 165 | 1,026 |
| Paid-in capital | 1,095 | 871 |
| Retained earnings | 8,868 | 12,209 |
| Stockholders' equity | 10,128 | 14,106 |
| Total liabilities and stockholders' equity | $20,964 | $24,010 |
| Beta of common stock | 1.15 | 1.15 |

**EXHIBIT 2**
Pro Forma Balance Sheet, Gulf and Socal Combined (millions of dollars)

| | Offer Price of Socal for All Outstanding Gulf Shares[a] | | |
|---|---|---|---|
| | $70/Share | $80/Share | $90/Share |
| Current assets | $12,751 | $12,751 | $12,751 |
| Net properties | 29,768 | 31,421 | 33,075 |
| Other assets | 3,901 | 3,901 | 3,901 |
| Total assets | $46,420 | $48,073 | $49,727 |
| Current liabilities | $ 9,873 | $ 9,873 | $ 9,873 |
| Long-term debt and capital leases | 15,761 | 17,414 | 19,068 |
| Deferred items | 5,463 | 5,463 | 5,463 |
| Other liabilities and minority interests | 1,217 | 1,217 | 1,217 |
| Total liabilities | 32,314 | 33,967 | 35,621 |
| Stockholders' equity | 14,106 | 14,106 | 14,106 |
| Total liabilities and stockholders' equity | $46,420 | $48,073 | $49,727 |

a. Gulf had 165.3 million shares outstanding.

**EXHIBIT 3**
Exploration Cost and Reserve Data for Gulf and Socal, 1976–1983

| | Gulf | | | | | | | Socal | | | | | | |
|---|---|---|---|---|---|---|---|---|---|---|---|---|---|---|
| | Exploration Cost ($ millions) | | | Reserve Data (millions of composite bbls) | | | | Exploration Cost ($ millions) | | | Reserve Data (millions of composite bbls) | | | |
| | Expensed | + Capitalized | = Total | Begin | + Add'ns | – Prod'n | = End | Expensed | + Capitalized | = Total | Begin | + Add'ns | – Prod'n | = End |
| 1976 | $343 | $ 645 | $ 988 | 3,672 | 280 | 365 | 3,257[a] | $256 | $ 518 | $ 774 | 3,263 | 115 | 260 | 3,118 |
| 1977 | 457 | 1,175 | 1,632 | 3,257 | 326 | 338 | 3,333[b] | 250 | 640 | 890 | 3,118 | 180 | 255 | 3,043 |
| 1978 | 367 | 905 | 1,272 | 3,333 | 392 | 334 | 3,392 | 371 | 792 | 1,163 | 3,043 | 129 | 252 | 2,920 |
| 1979 | 389 | 1,223 | 1,612 | 3,392 | 127 | 367 | 3,152 | 409 | 1,194 | 1,603 | 2,920 | 345 | 261 | 3,004 |
| 1980 | 561 | 1,524 | 2,085 | 3,152 | 198 | 342 | 3,008 | 629 | 1,601 | 2,230 | 3,004 | 246 | 262 | 2,988 |
| 1981 | 688 | 2,008 | 2,696 | 3,008 | 266 | 323 | 2,951 | 862 | 2,700 | 3,562 | 2,988 | 162 | 259 | 2,891 |
| 1982 | 727 | 1,919 | 2,646 | 2,951 | 314 | 296 | 2,969 | 939 | 1,851 | 2,790 | 2,891 | 198 | 257 | 2,832 |
| 1983 | 594 | 1,595 | 2,189 | 2,969 | 359 | 290 | 3,038[c] | 758 | 1,332 | 2,090 | 2,832 | 240 | 261 | 2,811 |

a. Reduced by 330 million bbls expropriated by Ecuador.

b. Includes 88 million bbls acquired from Kewanee Industries, Inc.

c. J. S. Herold estimates that 725 million bbls in West Africa are not recoverable because of expropriation, which reduces the recoverable reserves to 2,313 million bbls.

**EXHIBIT 4**
Results of Proxy Vote on Reincorporation Proposal

| | Voting by Shares (millions) | | | |
| | For | Against | Abstain[a] | Subtotal |
|---|---|---|---|---|
| Individuals | 71.1 | 9.2 | 12.0 | 92.3 |
| Gulf Investors' Group | — | 21.7 | — | 21.7 |
| Institutions | 16.0 | 23.2 | 12.1 | 51.3 |
| Total | 87.1 | 54.1 | 24.1 | 165.3 |
| | (52.7%) | (32.7%) | (14.6%) | (100%) |

| | Percentage Voting by Category | | | |
| | For | Against | Abstain[a] | Subtotal |
|---|---|---|---|---|
| Individuals | 77% | 10% | 13% | 100% |
| Gulf Investors' Group | — | 100 | — | 100 |
| Institutions | 31 | 45 | 24 | 100 |

a. An abstention is essentially a vote against the proposal.

**EXHIBIT 5**
Trading Prices and Volumes, Gulf and Socal, 1983–1984

| | Gulf | | Socal | |
|---|---|---|---|---|
| | Price | Volume[a] | Price | Volume[a] |
| Aug. 5, 1983 . . . . . . . . . . . . . . | $37⅜ | 16,633 | $35⅝ | 21,473 |
| Aug. 12 . . . . . . . . . . . . . . | 39 | 23,955 | | |
| Aug. 19 . . . . . . . . . . . . . . | 42⅝ | 49,186 | | |
| Aug. 26 . . . . . . . . . . . . . . | 41½ | 13,737 | | |
| Sept. 2 . . . . . . . . . . . . . . | 41½ | 8,942 | 37¼ | 11,452 |
| Sept. 9 . . . . . . . . . . . . . . | 41½ | 23,020 | | |
| Sept. 16 . . . . . . . . . . . . . . | 41½ | 26,515 | | |
| Sept. 23 . . . . . . . . . . . . . . | 44½ | 31,475 | | |
| Sept. 30 . . . . . . . . . . . . . . | 42⅛ | 14,590 | | |
| Oct. 7 . . . . . . . . . . . . . . | 44⅛ | 39,708 | 35⅜ | 17,384 |
| Oct. 14 . . . . . . . . . . . . . . | 47 | 71,629 | | |
| Oct. 21 . . . . . . . . . . . . . . | 46½ | 91,278 | | |
| Oct. 28 . . . . . . . . . . . . . . | 47½ | 19,415 | | |
| Nov. 4 . . . . . . . . . . . . . . | 44½ | 39,761 | 35⅜ | 18,269 |
| Nov. 11 . . . . . . . . . . . . . . | 45⅛ | 26,660 | | |
| Nov. 18 . . . . . . . . . . . . . . | 42¼ | 56,685 | | |
| Nov. 25 . . . . . . . . . . . . . . | 43¾ | 43,358 | | |
| Dec. 2 . . . . . . . . . . . . . . | 45⅛ | 65,168 | 34⅛ | 14,356 |
| Dec. 9 . . . . . . . . . . . . . . | 43 | 15,568 | | |
| Dec. 16 . . . . . . . . . . . . . . | 42¾ | 13,879 | | |
| Dec. 23 . . . . . . . . . . . . . . | 42⅝ | 5,210 | | |
| Dec. 30 . . . . . . . . . . . . . . | 43⅛ | 10,301 | | |
| Jan. 6, 1984 . . . . . . . . . . . . . . | 46⅝ | 34,790 | 34⅞ | 9,959 |
| Jan. 13 . . . . . . . . . . . . . . | 49¼ | 51,756 | 35⅝ | 15,098 |
| Jan. 20 . . . . . . . . . . . . . . | 47 | 23,003 | 35⅞ | 16,351 |
| Jan. 27 . . . . . . . . . . . . . . | 53⅛ | 39,693 | 35½ | 15,687 |
| Feb. 3 . . . . . . . . . . . . . . | 55½ | 62,309 | 36½ | 16,680 |
| Feb. 10 . . . . . . . . . . . . . . | 57 | 48,409 | 33⅞ | 19,866 |
| Feb. 17 . . . . . . . . . . . . . . | 54 | 70,678 | 35⅞ | 13,798 |
| Feb. 24 . . . . . . . . . . . . . . | 62⅝ | 96,862 | 36⅝ | 12,775 |
| Mar. 2 . . . . . . . . . . . . . . | 69½ | 175,126 | 35¾ | 20,691 |
| Mar. 9 . . . . . . . . . . . . . . | 65⅛ | 153,597 | 34½ | 23,149 |

a. Total volume for week in hundreds of shares. All dates shown are Fridays.

**EXHIBIT 6**
Selected Market Prices, 1976–1983

| | S&P 500[a] | Oil Price per Composite Bbl[b] | Consumer Price Index | Avg. Stock Price, Seven Majors[c] | Gulf Closing Price | Gulf Dividend/ Share | Socal Closing Price | Socal Dividend/ Share |
|---|---|---|---|---|---|---|---|---|
| 1976 . . | 107.46 | $ 5.76 | 170.5 | $56.21 | $29 | $1.73 | $21 | $1.06 |
| 1977 . . | 95.10 | 7.22 | 181.5 | 45.92 | 27 | 1.83 | 19 | 1.18 |
| 1978 . . | 96.73 | 8.35 | 195.4 | 43.20 | 24 | 1.90 | 23 | 1.28 |
| 1979 . . | 105.76 | 10.63 | 217.4 | 51.89 | 35 | 2.06 | 28 | 1.45 |
| 1980 . . | 136.34 | 16.92 | 246.8 | 70.00 | 44 | 2.37 | 50 | 1.80 |
| 1981 . . | 122.74 | 22.88 | 272.4 | 51.55 | 35 | 2.65 | 43 | 2.20 |
| 1982 . . | 138.34 | 22.21 | 289.1 | 44.48 | 30 | 2.80 | 32 | 2.40 |
| 1983 . . | 164.90 | 22.42 | 298.4 | 53.03 | 43 | 2.85 | 35 | 2.40 |

a. End of year.

b. Composite amounts represent crude oil, natural gas liquids, and natural gas on a per barrel basis. Natural gas volumes are converted to crude oil equivalent barrels using a conversion ratio of 5.7 thousand cubic feet per barrel.

c. Exxon, Gulf, Mobil, Shell, Standard Oil California, Standard Oil Indiana, Texaco.

**EXHIBIT 7**
Comparison of Gulf with Industry (Seven Major Producers), 1972–1982

| | Production[a] Oil | Production[a] Gas | Earnings/ Share[b] | Return on Equity Gulf | Return on Equity Industry | Return on Assets Gulf | Return on Assets Industry |
|---|---|---|---|---|---|---|---|
| 1972 . . . . . . | 5.3% | 4.4% | 49% | 10% | 14% | 4.8% | 6.0% |
| 1973 . . . . . . | 5.0 | 4.0 | 56 | 13 | 15 | 8.0 | 8.5 |
| 1974 . . . . . . | 4.8 | 3.7 | 56 | 14 | 16 | 8.5 | 9.0 |
| 1975 . . . . . . | 4.6 | 3.6 | 52 | 10 | 12 | 5.6 | 6.5 |
| 1976 . . . . . . | 4.4 | 3.4 | 54 | 12 | 14 | 6.1 | 7.0 |
| 1977 . . . . . . | 4.3 | 3.5 | 48 | 11 | 14 | 5.3 | 6.0 |
| 1978 . . . . . . | 4.0 | 3.6 | 49 | 11 | 14 | 5.3 | 6.0 |
| 1979 . . . . . . | 3.9 | 3.5 | 44 | 16 | 21 | 7.7 | 9.0 |
| 1980 . . . . . . | 3.6 | 3.3 | 39 | 15 | 24 | 7.5 | 9.0 |
| 1981 . . . . . . | 3.2 | 3.1 | 38 | 13 | 20 | 6.0 | 8.0 |
| 1982 . . . . . . | 3.0 | 2.8 | 40 | 9 | 11 | 4.4 | 5.5 |

*Note:* The seven major producers are Exxon, Gulf, Mobil, Shell, Standard Oil California, Standard Oil Indiana, Texaco.

a. Gulf's U.S. production as percent of U.S. production of seven majors.

b. As percent of seven-company average.

**EXHIBIT 8**
Summary of Accounting Policies

**Exploration and Development**

The most significant accounting policy in the petroleum industry relates to the method of accounting for the exploration and development of oil and gas reserves. Gulf follows the "successful efforts" concept, which requires that all exploratory drilling and equipment costs be capitalized pending determination of whether the drilling is unsuccessful or successful; if unsuccessful, these costs are expensed. All other exploratory costs, including geological and geophysical costs, are charged against income as incurred. All development drilling and equipment costs are capitalized whether successful or unsuccessful.

Depreciation and depletion expenses for all capitalized costs of oil- and gas-producing properties are determined on a unit-of-production method as the reserves are produced.

# *John Case Company*

In March 1985, Anthony W. Johnson was working on a proposal to purchase the firm that employed him, the John Case Company. The Case Company, with corporate headquarters in Dover, Delaware, was a leading manufacturer of commercial desk calendars. Mr. Johnson, vice president of finance and administration, considered the company an excellent acquisition opportunity, provided the owner's asking price proved acceptable and that satisfactory financing for the transaction could be arranged.

## Background

A few weeks earlier, John M. Case, board chairman, president, and sole owner of the company, had informed his senior management group that he intended to retire from business and was about to initiate a campaign to sell the company. For several years, his physician had been urging him to avoid all stress and strain; now Mr. Case had decided to sever his business connections and devote his time to travel and a developing interest in art history and collection.

On the basis of previous offers for the company, Mr. Case had decided to ask for $20 million, with a minimum of $16 million immediately payable in cash. He thought acquisitive corporations should find this price attractive, and he believed it would be easy to dispose of the business.

Mr. Case had assured the management group that their jobs and benefits would be well protected by the terms of any sale contract that he might negotiate.

Despite his faith in Mr. Case's good intentions, Mr. Johnson had been quite apprehensive about the prospect of having his career placed in the hands of an unknown outsider. However, after some reflection, Mr. Johnson had concluded that the sale decision should be viewed as an opportunity to acquire control of a highly profitable enterprise. Purchase of the Case Company would not only ensure career continuity but also provide a chance to turn a profit in the company's equity. Mr. Johnson had realized that his personal financial resources were far too limited to allow him to bid alone for control of the company. Consequently, he had persuaded August Haffenreffer, vice president–marketing, William Wright, vice president–manufacturing, and Richard Bennink, the controller, to join him in trying to buy the company, rather than standing by while control passed to an outsider. In response to Mr. Johnson's request, Mr. Case had agreed to defer all steps to merchandise the company until he should have accepted or rejected a purchase proposal from the management group, provided this proposal was submitted within six weeks.

Because of his background in finance and his role in initiating the project, Mr. Johnson had assumed primary responsibility for assessing the profit potential of the opportunity and for structuring a workable financial plan for the acquisition. Since Mr. Case had not yet solicited bids from other potential purchasers, Mr. Johnson believed that it would be most realistic to regard Mr. Case's stated sale terms as fixed and non-negotiable.

Mr. Johnson, then, needed to determine whether he could meet the asking price and still realize a profit commensurate with the risk in this purchase. Moreover, he needed to figure out how the management group, with roughly a half million dollars among them, could finance the purchase and at the same time obtain voting control of the company.

Thus far Mr. Johnson had managed to obtain a tentative commitment for a $6 million unsecured bank term loan, and he had persuaded Mr. Case to accept unsecured notes for the noncash portion of the purchase price. He was still faced with the problem of raising close to $10 million on an equity base of $500,000 without giving up control to outsiders.

Mr. Johnson now had three weeks in which to come up with a workable financial plan or lose the deal. He was acutely aware that the life savings of his associates and himself would ride on his judgment and ingenuity.

## Description of the Company

The John Case Company was the leading producer of business calendars in the United States. The company had been established in 1920 by Robert Case (Mr. Case's paternal grandfather) to do contract printing of commercial calendars. Mr. Case had joined the organization in 1946 upon graduation from college, and in 1951 he had inherited the company.

Under Mr. Case's leadership primary emphasis was placed on controlled expansion in the established line of business. By 1984 the company, with an estimated 60–65% share of its market, had been for a decade the largest company in a small but lucrative industry. Operations had been profitable every year since 1932, and sales had increased every year since 1955. In 1984, the most recently completed fiscal year, earnings had amounted to $1,966,000 on sales of approximately $15.3 million. The return on average invested capital in 1984 was about 20%. Over the past 5 years, sales had increased at a 7% compound rate, while earnings, benefiting from substantial cost reductions, had more than doubled. Exhibits 1–3 present recent financial figures for the company.

## Products

As noted, the Case Company's principal products were commercial desk calendars. The company designed and manufactured disposable-page and flipover-page desk calendar pads in a variety of sizes. The company also sold desk calendar bases, which were purchased from outside suppliers who manufactured to Case's specifications. In 1984 standard desk calendar pads had contributed approximately 80% of net sales and 90% of earnings before taxes. Bases accounted for 10% of sales, and miscellaneous merchandise, chiefly wall calendars, accounted for the rest.

Sales were highly seasonal. Most final consumers did not start using calendars for the forthcoming year until November or December of the current year. In consequence, about 90% of Case's total shipments typically took place between June and December, with about 60% of shipments concentrated in the third quarter and 25% in the fourth quarter. Since calendar pads were dated, any merchandise remaining in stock at the end of the selling season was subject to rapid obsolescence.

## Manufacturing

The production process was relatively simple, employing widely available skills and technology. High-speed offset presses were used to print appropriate dates on paper purchased in bulk from outside suppliers; the printed sheets were then trimmed to the required sizes and stored for shipment. The entire process was highly automated and was characterized by high fixed costs, high setup costs, and low variable costs.

In spite of highly seasonal sales, the Case Company operated on level production schedules. Since the product lines were for all practical purposes undifferentiated from competing lines and the relevant production technology was well known, the capacity to sell on the basis of price, while achieving a good return on invested capital, was regarded by management as a critical success factor in the industry. Minimum production costs were therefore imperative.

Level production enabled the company to take advantage of extremely long production runs and thus to minimize down time, the investment in equipment, expensive setups, and the use of transient labor. Level production, in conjunction with the company's dominant market share, provided scale economies well beyond the reach of any competitor.

The combination of seasonal sales and level production resulted in the accumulation of large seasonal stocks. However, by concentrating the sales effort in the middle six months of the year, the Case Company was able to circumvent most of the risk usually connected with level production in a seasonal company in return for modest purchase discounts. Since customers could easily predict their needs for Case products as their budgets for the forthcoming year took shape, they were willing to place their orders well in advance of shipment. As a result, Case could manufacture against a firm backlog in the last few months of the year and thus circumvent the risk of overproducing and ending the year with large stocks of outdated finished goods.

The company maintained production facilities in nearby Wilmington, Delaware, and, through a wholly owned subsidiary, in Puerto Rico. Earnings of the Puerto Rican subsidiary, which sold all its output to the U.S. parent, were entirely exempt from U.S. taxes and until 1992 would be exempt from all Puerto Rican taxes. The tax exemption on Puerto Rican production accounted for Case's unusually low income tax rate. All Case plants and equipment were modern and excellently maintained. A major capital expenditures program, completed in 1983, had resulted in the company's having the most modern facilities in the industry. At the predicted rate of future sales growth, Mr. Wright, the chief production officer, did not anticipate any need for substantial capital expenditures for at least 5 or 6 years.

None of the company's work force was represented by labor unions.

## Marketing

As its products were nondifferentiable, Case's marketing program concentrated on providing high-quality customer service and a uniformly high-quality product. Case products were sold nationwide. Geographically the company was strongest in the Northeast, the Southwest, and the far West. Large accounts were handled by the company's five salespeople, and smaller accounts were serviced by office supply wholesalers. Roughly 10% of sales had historically gone to the federal government.

Even though the product was undifferentiated, Mr. Haffenreffer, the marketing vice president, believed that it did have some significant advantages from a marketing viewpoint. Selling costs were extremely low, as consumption of the product over the course of a year automatically generated a large replacement demand without any effort on the part of Case. About 95% of total sales generally consisted of reorders from the existing customer base, with only 5% of sales going to new customers. Historically over 98% of the customer base annually reordered Case pads and, as needed, additional Case bases. By dealing with only one source of supply, the customer was able to take maximum advantage of discounts for volume purchases. As the product was virtually immune to malfunction and the resultant customer dissatisfaction, once Case bases had been installed, the typical buyer never had any incentive to spend time and money on a search for alternative sources. Consumption of Case products was, in addition, extremely insensitive to budget cuts, economy drives, consumer whims, and the like. The desk calendar was a small-ticket but high-priority item. It was an essential in the work routines of most of its users, and it was not expensive enough to yield a meaningful reward in savings to would-be cutters. As a dated product, the desk calendar, unlike many other office products, represented a nondeferrable purchase.

## Finances

Mr. Case had been greatly influenced by his father's memories of the Great Depression, and he steadfastly refused to consider leveraging his equity in the company. Accordingly, the company operated with an all-equity capitalization. The size of the capital budget was determined by the volume of internally generated funds in conjunction with Mr. Case's decision on how much to withdraw in the form of dividends. Dividend payments had sometimes been sharply contracted to accommodate capital investment opportunities. Over the past 3 years, however, internally generated funds had been plentiful, and dividends had averaged 70% of net earnings.

Like the capital budget, the seasonal accumulation of inventories and receivables was financed from internal sources. To minimize warehousing expenses for finished goods, Case provided generous credit terms to customers who accepted early shipments. Payments for June–October shipments were not due until the end of November, although substantial discounts were offered for earlier payment. The collection period averaged 60 days. Credit experience was excellent, and generous credit terms were considered a key factor in the company's competitive success.

Although the company had not resorted to seasonal borrowing in nearly 10 years, it maintained for emergency purposes two $2 million lines of credit at major Eastern banks. Exhibit 4 shows 1984 working capital balances by month.

The Case Company's credit with suppliers was excellent. All trade obligations were promptly paid when due.

## Management

The senior management team consisted of Mr. Case plus the four individuals interested in buying the company. Transfer of ownership to the latter would not occasion much change in the de facto management of the organization. Although Mr. Case continued to exercise the final authority on all major issues of policy and strategy, over the past few years he had gradually withdrawn from day-to-day affairs and now spent much of his time in Europe and Puerto Rico. As Mr. Case had relaxed his grip on the company's affairs, he had increasingly delegated the general management of the firm to Mr. Johnson.

Compensation was generous at the senior executive level. Mr. Case drew an annual salary of $400,000; his four key subordinates received an average salary of $90,000. In addition, the four senior executives received annual bonuses which aggregated 10% of earnings before taxes and bonuses.

The members of the purchasing group were all in their thirties and early forties and among them represented close to 50 years' experience in the business. A graduate of a leading school of business administration, Mr. Johnson, aged 40, had worked for 5 years in the venture capital department of a large Eastern bank and for 2 years in his own management consulting firm before joining the Case Company.

## Company Prospects

The overall prospect was for continued growth at a steady, though unspectacular, pace. The rate of Case sales growth, management believed, was closely correlated with the rate of growth in the size of the domestic white-collar work force. Given expectations of a continuing shift of labor out of agricultural and blue-collar and into white-collar occupations, this suggested that the company should grow somewhat faster than the economy as a whole. Assuming no material changes in product lines or market share, management thought sales growth would average about 5–6% per year in the foreseeable future. Profit margins were expected to improve somewhat over the next few years, as volume expanded and an increasing proportion of new production was directed to the tax-exempt Puerto Rican facility.

### Competition

Although the commercial desk calendar industry was profitable indeed for its leading participant, it was not, in the opinion of Case management, an attractive area for potential new competitors. At present the industry was divided between Case with roughly a 60–65% share of market and the Watts Corporation, a privately held company, with an estimated 20–25% share. Watts's strength was concentrated in the Midwest and Southeast. The remainder of industry sales was fragmented among a host of small, financially weak printing shops. Case management found it difficult to imagine how a potential competitor could arrive at an economically justifiable decision to enter their market. Price was the only conceivable basis on which a new entrant could compete, but lacking the scale economies available to Case, a new entrant would necessarily be a high-cost competitor. Mr. Haffenreffer estimated that it would take a new entrant at least 3–5 years to reach break-even, assuming no retaliatory price cuts by Case. Furthermore, entering this market would necessitate a minimum capital investment of $2–4 million plus the working capital needed to support seasonal sales. On balance, it seemed unlikely that a potential competitor would brave these obstacles in the hope of grabbing a share of a $25–30 million industry with mediocre growth prospects.

Mr. Case judged that the company's financial strength, relative cost advantages, and entrenched distribution system had served to deter Watts from trying to invade any of Case's prime market areas. Similarly, he thought Case could not take away a substantial market share from Watts without risking a price war that might seriously impair margins for a protracted period.

### Unexploited Opportunities

The business plan finally approved by Mr. Case had not incorporated a diversification scheme vigorously advanced by the other members of senior management. The vice presidents had contended that the company could significantly boost both the rate of growth and level of earnings by using its cash flow and its production and distribution strengths to expand into related product lines. The proposal had called for expansion into other dated products, such as appointment books, planning books, and the like, imprinted with the name, logo, or other message of the customer, and into desk calendars similarly imprinted. Mr. Johnson had estimated that this project would require an initial capital investment of $200,000 and special product development and merchandising expenses of $900,000 spread over the first 2 years of the undertaking. It had been estimated that the new line should yield sales of approximately $1 million in the first full year of operation with a growth rate of about 40% per year in years 2–4, as the line achieved nationwide distribution and recognition. A 12–15% growth rate was anticipated in subsequent years. It was thought that this type of product line would have a profit margin before taxes of about 6%. The management group believed that the proposed line could serve as a profitable first step toward developing a full line of desktop products for commercial, industrial, and government markets.

Mr. Case had rejected the proposal on several grounds. He had observed that the proposal advocated entering a riskier line of business in which none of the management group had experience. In the proposed line of business the customer could choose among a variety of competing designs, and manufacturers had to actively generate repeat sales. He had also pointed out that the project would require a substantial investment in working capital for seasonal sales, if the new line grew as predicted. Finally, he had stated, he was quite content with his present income and, at his age, unwilling to reinvest earnings in the hope of achieving a strong position in a more competitive and less profitable business than the present one.

With Mr. Case out of the picture, the management group would have the freedom to pursue its growth program. Mr. Johnson believed that over a period of years the Case Company's growth rate could be improved significantly if earnings were reinvested in related businesses rather than disbursed as dividends. The higher growth rate would be translated into profits for management if, for instance, the faster growth allowed them to take the company public at a relatively high price-earnings ratio.

## The Purchase Proposal

Mr. Johnson recognized that a successful proposal would have to blend and reconcile the interests and goals of all parties to the transaction: the seller, the buyers, and external suppliers of finance.

The management group had determined that among them they could raise at most about $500,000 for investment in Case. Raising this amount would necessitate drawing down savings accounts, refinancing home mortgages, and liquidating positions in the stock market. Mr. Johnson was prepared to commit $160,000, Mr. Haffenreffer $140,000, and Messrs. Wright and Bennink $100,000 apiece. It had been tentatively agreed that all members of the management group would buy stock at the same price. It had also been tentatively concluded that the group would not accept a proposal that left them with less than 51% of the shares. With less than 51% of the stock the management group might not achieve the autonomy to establish corporate policy or to dispose of the company where and as they chose.

## Valuation

As mentioned previously, Mr. Johnson believed that Mr. Case's asking terms of $20 million with a minimum of $16 million in cash would remain fixed, at least until the company had been shown to a number of prospective buyers. In the past year Mr. Case had held discussions with two companies that had made unsolicited bids to purchase the company. The first offer, $15 million in cash, had come from a medium-sized firm with a diversified line of office products. It had been rejected by Mr. Case on the basis of price. The second offer had come from a highly diversified medium-sized company sporting a price-earnings ratio of more than 20 and seeking to establish a position in office products through a series of acquisitions. The final offer had come to $32 million in letter stock of the acquirer.[1] Mr. Case had found this bid extremely tempting but had been unwilling to tie up his wealth in unmarketable shares of a company with which he was not intimately familiar. The acquirer, lacking excess debt capacity and unwilling to float new stock, had backed out of the discussions.

Mr. Johnson had, in addition, assembled financial figures on the publicly traded companies he thought most comparable to the Case Company. These data are presented in Exhibit 5.

## Financing

In terms of the mechanics of the transaction, Mr. Johnson planned to effect the purchase through a new corporation in which the management group would buy 500,000 common shares at $1.00 per share. Given the management group's $500,000 versus the $20 million asking price, the biggest problem facing Mr. Johnson was how to fund the new company at all, not to mention the objective of keeping control in the management group. Mr. Johnson had managed to obtain tentative commitments for $10.5 million, including the management group's $500,000. Prior to submitting a purchase proposal to Mr. Case, however, he would have to line up commitments for the entire $20 million funds needed.

It was clear that the noncash component of the purchase price would have to

---

1. Letter stock is unregistered stock. Such stock may not be sold to the public without registration under the Securities Act of 1933, a costly and time-consuming process. Because letter stock is restricted in its transferability, it represents a relatively illiquid investment and generally sells at a discount below the price that registered stock would command in the public securities markets. When letter stock is issued in an acquisition, the acquirer generally specifies that the stock cannot be registered for a certain period of time.

be met by issuing notes with a market value of $4 million to Mr. Case. In order to maintain the maximum amount of flexibility and borrowing capacity for raising financing from outsiders, Mr. Johnson had proposed that Mr. Case take 4%, junior subordinated, nonamortizing notes. After some negotiation, Mr. Case had expressed his willingness to accept a $6 million nonamortizing, 4% 5-year note that would be junior to all other debt obligations of the newly formed corporation. The members of the management group, as well as the corporate acquirer, would have to endorse the note. It was agreed that covenants on the note would include (1) no additional debt or leases except debt incurred in the acquisition of the Case Company, short-term seasonal borrowings, or debt incurred to retire the 5-year note; (2) no dividends and maintenance of at least $3 million in working capital; (3) no changes in management or increase in management compensation; (4) no sale of Case shares by Messrs. Johnson, Haffenreffer, Wright, or Bennink as long as the 5-year note was outstanding. If the borrower should default on any terms of this note or of any other indebtedness, the junior subordinated notes would become immediately due and payable. If not promptly paid, ownership of the shares held by the management group would revert to Mr. Case. The note could be retired before maturity in whole or in part in accord with the following schedule of discounts:

| Year | Percent of Face Value |
|---|---|
| 1 . . . . . | 58% |
| 2 . . . . . | 71 |
| 3 . . . . . | 81 |
| 4 . . . . . | 96 |
| 5 . . . . . | 100 |

In his efforts to line up financing from outside sources, Mr. Johnson had succeeded in obtaining a tentative commitment for a $6 million term loan from a large Philadelphia bank known for its aggressive lending policies. This loan would be amortized over a maximum period of 6 years through annual installments. The rate would be two points above floating prime, and the borrower would have to maintain average compensating balances of 10% of the outstanding principal amount of the loan. The amount of $6 million was the maximum the bank would commit on a term basis. Lending officers of the bank had emphasized that any additional term indebtedness incurred in the acquisition of Case would have to be effectively subordinated to this loan. Exhibit 6 presents an abstract of the provisions that the bank term loan would bear. Exhibit 7 presents Mr. Johnson's forecast of Case's cash flows over the next 6 years.

Having negotiated the bank commitment, Mr. Johnson was still left with the problem of raising an additional $9.5 million. He thought that he would have to turn to venture capital sources to raise the rest of the funds needed. Based on his experience in venture finance, Mr. Johnson knew that a venture capitalist would expect to earn about 20–25% on funds. He also knew that most venture capitalists preferred to place their funds in the form of debt securities rather than common stock. The venture capitalist could generally exercise more effective control over investment through the covenants on a debt obligation than through the voting power on stock. Principal repayment on debt also provided a mechanism for a tax-free recovery of capital; this might not be possible with stock until the company had gone public. Mr. Johnson expected to have to pay an 8–9% coupon rate on any debt funds obtained from a venture capital source. The venture capitalist would probably attempt to realize the rest of the return by taking warrants to buy shares in the new corporation at $1.00, the same price initially paid by the management group. The venture capitalist would probably insist on having the option of exercising the warrants in either cash or Case debentures.

**EXHIBIT 1**

Consolidated Income Statements, 1980–1984 (thousands of dollars)

|  | 1980 | 1981 | 1982 | 1983 | 1984 |
|---|---|---|---|---|---|
| Net sales | $9,740 | $10,044 | $11,948 | $13,970 | $15,260 |
| Cost of sales | 5,836 | 5,648 | 6,994 | 8,304 | 9,298 |
| Gross profit on sales | 3,904 | 4,396 | 4,954 | 5,666 | 5,962 |
| Selling and administrative expenses | 2,216 | 2,072 | 2,470 | 3,022 | 3,274 |
| Other income, net | 40 | 108 | 70 | 128 | 120 |
| Profit before income taxes | 1,728 | 2,432 | 2,554 | 2,772 | 2,808 |
| Federal income taxes | 816 | 972 | 920 | 942 | 842 |
| Net profit | $ 912 | $ 1,460 | $ 1,634 | $ 1,830 | $ 1,966 |

**EXHIBIT 2**

Consolidated Balance Sheet at December 31, 1984 (thousands of dollars)

| | | | |
|---|---|---|---|
| Cash and marketable securities | $ 5,762 | Accounts payable | $ 654 |
| Accounts receivable | 2,540 | Accrued expenses | 366 |
| Inventories at lower of cost or market | 588 | Accrued income taxes | 246 |
| Prepaid expenses | 108 | Current liabilities | 1,266 |
| Current assets | 8,998 | Common stock ($1.00 par value) | 200 |
| Property, plant, and equipment, net | 2,110 | Retained profits | 9,716 |
| Miscellaneous assets | 74 | Shareholders' equity | 9,916 |
| Total assets | $11,182 | Total liabilities and shareholders' equity | $11,182 |

**EXHIBIT 3**
Ten-Year Summary of Operations, 1975–1984 (thousands of dollars except per share data)

| | 1975 | 1976 | 1977 | 1978 | 1979 | 1980 | 1981 | 1982 | 1983 | 1984 |
|---|---|---|---|---|---|---|---|---|---|---|
| Net sales | $7,688 | $8,356 | $8,526 | $8,790 | $9,350 | $9,740 | $10,044 | $11,948 | $13,970 | $15,260 |
| Net profit | 638 | 668 | 742 | 748 | 758 | 912 | 1,460 | 1,634 | 1,830 | 1,966 |
| Dividends | 600 | 200 | 280 | 280 | 440 | 440 | 480 | 1,220 | 1,374 | 1,480 |
| Earnings per share | $ 3.19 | $ 3.34 | $ 3.71 | $ 3.74 | $ 3.79 | $ 4.56 | $ 7.30 | $ 8.17 | $ 9.15 | $ 9.83 |
| Net profit margin | 8.3% | 8.0% | 8.7% | 8.5% | 8.1% | 9.4% | 14.5% | 13.7% | 13.1% | 12.9% |

**EXHIBIT 4**
Monthly Working Capital Balances, 1984 (thousands of dollars)

| | Jan. | Feb. | Mar. | Apr. | May | June | July | Aug. | Sept. | Oct. | Nov. | Dec. |
|---|---|---|---|---|---|---|---|---|---|---|---|---|
| Cash | $5,536 | $5,714 | $5,396 | $4,784 | $4,328 | $4,098 | $2,354 | $ 766 | $2,050 | $3,830 | $5,734 | $5,762 |
| Accounts receivable | 1,480 | 760 | 734 | 804 | 718 | 604 | 3,432 | 6,104 | 6,164 | 4,322 | 2,398 | 2,540 |
| Inventories | 1,124 | 1,666 | 2,210 | 2,752 | 3,294 | 3,838 | 2,754 | 1,670 | 526 | 588 | 608 | 588 |
| Current liabilities | (1,186) | (1,220) | (1,242) | (1,146) | (1,422) | (1,344) | (1,072) | (1,216) | (1,174) | (1,384) | (1,340) | (1,266) |
| Net working capital | $6,954 | $6,920 | $7,098 | $7,194 | $6,918 | $7,196 | $7,468 | $7,324 | $7,566 | $7,356 | $7,400 | $7,624 |

**EXHIBIT 5**
Comparative Data on Selected Companies in Related Lines of Business

| | S&P Publishing Averages | S&P 425 Industrial Stocks | DeLuther[a] | Wakefield Co.[b] | Officomp[c] | Case Co. |
|---|---|---|---|---|---|---|
| Trading market | | | OTC | OTC | OTC | — |
| Current market price | | | $22¼ | $14¾ | $29¼ | — |
| Indicated dividend yield | | | 5.5% | 8.7% | 3.7% | — |
| Price-earnings ratio | | | | | | |
| 1984 | 14.6 | 9.9 | 8.7 | 7.2 | 10.5 | — |
| 1983 | 19.6 | 11.8 | 6.4 | 5.0 | 10.2 | — |
| 1982 | 14.4 | 10.4 | 10.8 | 11.9 | 13.8 | — |
| Price range | | | | | | |
| 1984 | | | $24⅝–16¼ | $14⅞–8⅛ | $33⅛–26½ | — |
| 1983 | | | 18½–12⅛ | 11½–5⅛ | 19¾–12⅞ | — |
| Earnings per share (E) and index (I) | | | (E) | (E) | (E) | (E) |
| 1984 | | | $ 2.48 / (I) 110 | $ 1.62 / (I) 82 | $ 2.98 / (I) 177 | $ 9.83 / (I) 216 |
| 1980 | | | 2.26 / 100 | 1.97 / 100 | 1.68 / 100 | 4.56 / 100 |
| Sales (S) ($ 000s) and index (I) | | | (S) | (S) | (S) | (S) |
| 1984 | | | $16,427 / (I) 142 | $12,223 / (I) 108 | $18,608 / (I) 160 | $15,260 / (I) 157 |
| 1980 | | | 11,568 / 100 | 11,317 / 100 | 11,630 / 100 | 9,740 / 100 |
| Net earnings (N) ($ 000s) and index (I) | | | (N) | (N) | (N) | (N) |
| 1984 | | | $ 1,051 / (I) 117 | $ 501 / (I) 84 | $ 1,656 / (I) 178 | $ 1,966 / (I) 216 |
| 1980 | | | 902 / 100 | 600 / 100 | 930 / 100 | 912 / 100 |
| Net profit margins | | | | | | |
| 1984 | | | 6.4% | 4.1% | 8.9% | 12.9% |
| 1980 | | | 7.8 | 5.3 | 8.0 | 9.4 |
| Profit/Net worth | | | | | | |
| 1984 | | | 16.6% | 6.0% | 16.9% | 19.8% |
| 1983 | | | 14.2 | 5.7 | 15.0 | 19.0 |
| 1982 | | | 15.4 | 8.8 | 14.7 | 19.2 |
| Book capitalization[d] ($ 000s) | | | | | | |
| Long-term debt | | | $ 3,995 / 38.7% | $ 1,822 / 18.0% | $ 4,173 / 29.9% | — / – |
| Common stock and surplus | | | 6,318 / 61.3 | 8,298 / 82.0 | 9,783 / 70.1 | $9,916 / 100.0% |
| Total | | | $10,313 / 100.0% | $10,120 / 100.0% | $13,956 / 100.0% | $9,916 / 100.0% |
| Total market value ($ 000s) | | | $9,456 | $4,573 | $16,234 | $9,916 |
| Shares outstanding (000s) | | | 425 | 310 | 555 | 200 |

a. Producer of desk-top accessories, advertising specialty calendars, office stationery.
b. Producer of advertising specialty calendars.
c. Producer of broad line of office paper products and desk accessories.
d. All companies, December 31, 1984.

## EXHIBIT 6
Excerpts from Summary of Loan Agreement for Bank Term Loan

### Description of the Loan

*Amount.* $6 million.

*Rate.* Prime rate plus 2%, floating.[a]

*Term.* 6 years.

*Repayment.* Annual payments equal to the greater of $1 million or the sum of net profit plus amortization of goodwill and debt discounts less $200,000.

*Prepayment.* Permitted in whole or in part at any time without penalty. All prepayments to be applied to the outstanding principal balance of the loan in inverse order of maturity.

*Compensating balances.* Borrower must maintain average annual deposit balances equal to at least 10% of the outstanding principal amount of the loan.

### Conditions Precedent

Prior to the making of the loan described above, borrower must have satisfied the following terms and conditions:

*Incorporation.* Borrower must be a duly incorporated corporation authorized to undertake this borrowing and all other transactions associated with this borrowing.

*Purchase agreement.* Borrower must have entered a contract to purchase 100% of the John Case Company.

*Financing.* Borrower must have arranged firm commitments for the financing of this transaction in a manner consistent with the terms of this loan agreement.

*Equity purchase.* Messrs. Johnson, Haffenreffer, Wright, and Bennink must have committed not less than $500,000 to the purchase of common stock in the newly formed corporation that will purchase the John Case Company.

### Affirmative Covenants

During the life of this loan, borrower will adhere to the following terms and conditions:

*Financial statements.* Quarterly financial statements must be provided within 60 days of the end of the first three quarters. Audited financial statements bearing an unqualified opinion from a public accounting firm must be provided within 90 days of the end of borrower's fiscal year.

*Accounting changes.* Borrower will make no changes in its method of accounting.

### Negative Covenants

During the life of this loan, borrower will not do any of the following without written consent of the lender:

*Continuation of management.* No changes in management. Aggregate compensation to Messrs. Johnson, Haffenreffer, Wright, and Bennink not to be increased by more than 5% in any year. Present compensation to serve as a base for this computation.

*Negative pledge.* No assets to be pledged or otherwise used as collateral for any indebtedness.

*Sale of assets.* No sale of a substantial portion of the assets of the borrower. Borrower will not merge with or be acquired by any other entity.

*Acquisitions.* Borrower will not acquire any other entity.

*Capital expenditures.* Not to exceed $300,000 in any one year.

*Dividends.* In any one year restricted to after-tax profits minus all principal repayments on outstanding indebtedness.

*(continued)*

**EXHIBIT 6** *(concluded)*

*Working capital.* Not to decline below $3 million.

*Additional indebtedness.* No additional debt (including leases) with a term exceeding 1 year, unless subordinated to this loan. Any short-term debt must be retired for a period of at least 30 consecutive days in every year.

*Senior debt.* Senior debt, including all short-term indebtedness, may not exceed $10 million plus all earnings retained in the business after Dec. 31, 1985.

### Events of Default

In the event of default, this loan plus accrued interest will become immediately due and payable. The following will constitute events of default:
Failure to pay interest or principal when due.
Violation of any affirmative or negative covenant on this loan.
Bankruptcy, reorganization, receivership, liquidation.
Commission of an event of default on any other indebtedness.

a. At the time of the case, the prime rate was 10.00%.

## EXHIBIT 7
Cash Flow Forecasts, 1985–1990 (thousands of dollars)

|  | 1985 | 1986 | 1987 | 1988 | 1989 | 1990 |
|---|---|---|---|---|---|---|
| Net sales | $16,024 | $16,844 | $17,686 | $18,570 | $19,498 | $20,472 |
| Earnings before interest and taxes[a] | 3,433 | 3,640 | 3,757 | 3,608 | 3,788 | 3,976 |
| Interest expense[b] | 1,675 | 1,538 | 1,369 | 908 | 800 | 800 |
| Profit before taxes | 1,758 | 2,102 | 2,388 | 2,700 | 2,988 | 3,176 |
| Taxes | 274 | 364 | 440 | 556 | 660 | 714 |
| Profit after taxes | 1,484 | 1,738 | 1,948 | 2,114 | 2,328 | 2,462 |
| Add back: Noncash charges | 240 | 260 | 284 | 300 | 310 | 340 |
| Cash flow from operations | 1,724 | 1,998 | 2,232 | 2,444 | 2,638 | 2,802 |
| Less: Increase in working capital | 156 | 162 | 170 | 180 | 190 | 200 |
| Less: Capital expenditures | 120 | 134 | 142 | 150 | 466 | 600 |
| Available for debt retirement | $ 1,448 | $ 1,702 | $ 1,920 | $ 2,114 | $ 1,982 | $ 2,002 |
| Planned debt retirement |  |  |  |  |  |  |
| Bank loan | $ 1,448 | $ 1,702 | $ 1,920 | $   930 | $     0 | $ 2,002 |
| Mr. Case's note | 0 | 0 | 0 | 1,184 | 4,766[c] | 0 |
| Subordinated loan | 0 | 0 | 0 | 0 | 0 | 0 |
| Debt as percent of total capital | 89% | 80% | 70% | 58% | 47% | 35% |

a. Reflects elimination of Mr. Case's salary.

b. 9% coupon on subordinated loan of $6 million; 4% coupon on seller's note of $6 million; 12% rate on bank term loan; 10% rate on seasonal loan.

c. Mr. Case's note is retired from cash flow and a $2.8 million new bank term loan in 1989.

# Congoleum Corporation (Abridged)

In the summer of 1979, Thomas Cassidy, Arthur Nagle, and Anthony Grassi, officers of First Boston Corporation, were discussing with David Koester and John Uecker of Prudential Insurance Company the proposed terms for participation in the largest leveraged buyout in history. The subject of these discussions was Congoleum Corporation, a diversified firm competing in resilient flooring, shipbuilding, and automotive accessories.

Messrs. Cassidy and Nagle first approached Prudential in May 1979 to solicit interest in the concept of the buyout. The participation of Prudential, the largest institutional investor in the United States, was considered crucial to the development of a deal. Prudential did express interest. On July 16, 1979, First Boston formally proposed the purchase of Congoleum by private and institutional investors at $38 per common share. The preceding trading day, Congoleum common closed at $25.375 per share. Given 12.2 million shares outstanding, this implied an aggregate premium of $154 million. The directors of Congoleum agreed to discuss this offer and to provide some confidential information necessary to value the firm.

The next step was to agree in principle to merge Congoleum into a new holding company. This included arranging the terms and commitments for financing.

## Description of Congoleum Corporation

In 1978, Congoleum had earnings of $42 million on revenues of $576 million (see Exhibits 1 and 2). Its base of total assets was $323 million (see Exhibit 3).

The firm was active in three product market segments (see Exhibit 4): home furnishings, shipbuilding, and automotive and industrial distribution. Congoleum had no material intersegment sales.

Home furnishings products included resilient flooring targeted to the home remodeling market, and furniture and bedding for sale to the mobile home industry. The firm was one of the four largest producers of resilient flooring. The principal elements of competition were product styling, price, product performance, and service. Because of the importance of style, Congoleum produced and sold a large number of different designs and colors and introduced many new designs each year. The process for manufacturing resilient flooring was developed and patented by Congoleum. The foreign and domestic patents covering this process were due to expire from 1980 to 1987, although most would expire by 1984. The firm successfully defended its patents against infringement by three competitors, which in one case resulted in a $35 million out-of-court settlement paid by Armstrong Cork Company in 1976. Congoleum granted royalty-bearing licenses under these patents to other manufacturers, generating royalties of $17.2 million in 1978 and $13.2 million in 1977. Research and development expenditures were approximately $5 million in both 1978 and 1977.

Congoleum's shipbuilding subsidiary, Bath Iron Works (BIW), built and refurbished naval and civilian vessels. It held an excellent reputation for quality work completed within budget and on schedule. BIW had between 10 and 15 domestic competitors, most of whom were substantially larger and had poorer performances despite government support. The backlog at December 31, 1978, of $445 million included $413 million for naval ships and overhauls and $32 million for commercial ships and industrial work. This compared with a backlog of $453 million for 1977. BIW expected to fill about $225 million of its backlog in 1979. In April 1979, BIW was awarded $209 million in more naval contracts.[1] The contracts for merchant ships were fixed-price but contained escalation provisions. Naval ships were built under fixed-priced incentive contracts also containing escalation provisions. Naval contracts were subject to termination at the convenience of the government, in which case the government would pay costs incurred, termination costs, and a portion of the profit. In the last 10 years, none of BIW's contracts was terminated in this manner.

The third segment of Congoleum's business was the distribution of automotive and industrial maintenance parts. This business segment was created from Curtis Noll Corporation, which was acquired in October 1977. The products distributed were purchased from numerous suppliers. Congoleum owned patents for a code key cutter and duplicator, which it considered significant to the business of this segment. In 1978 this segment provided revenues of $115 million and operating income of $10 million (see Exhibit 4).

---

1. First Boston's offering circular noted: "Bath Iron Works does not anticipate being able to deliver any new commercial business until at least 1985 because of capacity limitations and its expectations for continued involvement in the [Navy's] FFG program."

Officers and directors owned beneficially 3.8% of the equity of Congoleum on a fully diluted basis. A portion of these shares was represented by stock options exercisable at an average price of $13.07 (see Exhibit 5). It was planned that the chairman, vice chairman, and other officers would remain with the firm after the transaction (Exhibit 5). Byron C. Radaker, chairman and chief executive officer, and Eddy G. Nicholson, vice chairman and chief operating officer, had managed Congoleum since 1975 and were credited for the company's improved performance. This was accomplished by an internal reorganization, the divestment of less profitable businesses, and the turnaround of other businesses.

## Valuation by Lazard Frères & Co

The firm of Lazard Frères & Co. was retained by Congoleum's directors to render an opinion as to the $38 per share offer. Lazard concluded, "We are of the opinion that the proposed offer of $38 per share of Congoleum is fair to the shareholders of Congoleum from a financial point of view." This analysis was based on a comparison of Congoleum's operations with its competitors, premiums paid in other recent acquisitions (see Exhibit 6), and values obtainable on liquidation (see Exhibit 7). Lazard relied on a method of valuation based on price-earnings multiples. Other information of significance in the valuation is presented in Exhibits 8 and 9.

## Description of Prudential

The Prudential Insurance Company of America was the largest institutional investor in the United States, with assets of $21 billion invested in fixed-income securities. It was regarded as the leader in privately placed investments. Of Prudential's $6 billion annual cash flow, about 60% was invested through its corporate finance department in fixed-income securities (debt securities and preferred stocks). The department's portfolio consisted of investments in more than 1,400 companies in all major industries. Loan proposals were typically analyzed by teams of three officers and approved by the senior vice president in charge of the department and by the finance committee of the Board of Directors.

Prudential's private lending included leveraged buyouts. The term of most of their private loans typically ranged from 12 to 20 years. Loan size varied from $500,000 to $250 million. The majority of the loans carried a fixed interest rate and were unsecured. Prudential's literature stated:

> On leveraged buyouts or credits for other borrowers with higher risk characteristics, our loans may include profit participation, warrants, or convertible securities in addition to a fixed interest rate.

John T. Uecker, vice president and member of the team considering First Boston's proposal, commented on financing of leveraged buyouts:

> These investments fit with our long-term portfolio strategy. We're more risk-oriented than our competitors. But we structure the deals so that the reward is consistent with

the risk we take. We always compare the terms with other buyouts we may be considering at the same time, as well as other investment alternatives we have. And we analyze the company's earnings and cash flow projections—modified by the probability of meeting them. Furthermore, we value each segment of a company on its own. Finally, we compare the returns on each type of security with those available in the market [Exhibits 10 and 11]. This is done by individual securities and then as a package. The senior debt and common stock are relatively easy to value; the junior debt is more difficult. Given the huge proportion of debt in these deals, we can view the junior notes as equity and seek an equity-type return. The alternative is to compare them to B-rated securities and look for some premium over their returns. But obtaining a high yield on junior debt is inevitably constrained by what the company can service. In these cases, we look for an equity kicker (through warrants, convertibles, and common stock) to achieve the required rate of return. In the final analysis, we're more concerned about getting an appropriate return on the total package rather than how that return gets divided up between the various securities, though we would like to see each security able to stand on its own.

About 50% of Prudential's private placement financing was proposed by investment bankers.

## Description of First Boston

First Boston Corporation was a special bracket investment banking firm. Although the firm had originated no leveraged buyouts previously, it had considerable experience with aspects of the deal: private placement financing, firm valuation, acquisitions, etc. The three officers, Thomas L. Cassidy and Arthur Nagle, both managing directors, and Anthony Grassi, vice president, developed the proposed deal. James Harpel, president of Century Capital Corporation, originally identified Congoleum as a leveraged buyout candidate and proposed that First Boston lead the negotiations. But Century Capital remained as one of the prospective equity participants. Thomas Cassidy said:

> The ability to deal effectively with people having diverse interests is extremely important in a transaction as complex as this. It may appear relatively simple after the fact. But actually it is fragile up until closing. At the beginning the interest among the participants was understandably tentative. Our first conversations with the Pru were of a conceptual nature, and the initial reaction of Congoleum management—whose involvement was very important—was "We're open to the idea, assuming you can put together the rest of the pieces and assuming the end result is in the best interests of our stockholders. . . ." The final form of the deal evolved out of a series of negotiations. Originally it was to have been a purchase of stock; it eventually evolved into a purchase of assets. Our "strip" concept was very helpful in keeping all of the institutions together. Closing the deal requires a fair amount of corporate finance capability, ingenuity, determination, and patience.

## Terms of the Proposal

Cassidy, Nagle, and Grassi proposed that a holding company be formed to buy Congoleum for an amount equivalent to about $38 per share. The buyout actually consisted of a two-step merger and sale. First, the stock of Bath Iron Works would be purchased for $92.3 million. Bath Iron Works would then be merged into the buying company. Second, the remaining net assets of Congoleum (including about $95.1 million of excess cash and the Congoleum Corporation name) would be purchased for approximately $371.3 million. The "old Congoleum" would settle its remaining liabilities and pay a liquidating dividend of $38 per share.

The purchasers would adopt the name Congoleum Corporation and proceed as a privately held firm. The assets of Bath Iron Works and Congoleum would have a tax basis equal to the amounts paid for the stock and assets, respectively, plus any liabilities assumed. Accordingly, the tax basis of the new firm would exceed its present tax basis by several hundred million dollars. This increase in tax basis could result in reduced taxable income because of increased deductions for (a) the amortization of the value of patents and patent-licensing agreements, (b) depreciation, and (c) cost of goods sold due to the write-up of shipbuilding backlog and inventories. This increase in tax basis would be available only in the event of a taxable acquisition and could not be achieved by the current stockholders. Exhibit 12 describes the allocation of the purchase premium in more detail.

The proposal provided financing of $379.6 million for the purchase in the form of bank borrowings, debt securities, and preferred and common stock. The distinctive feature of prior leveraged buyouts was that debt as a percent of total capital ranged up to 80%. Since banks typically would not allow all of that to be senior financing, the layering of the claims usually was one of the more delicate points of negotiation. David Koester, senior member of Prudential's team, said:

> We wanted all the players to share the same incentives in order to reduce any intramural warfare if trouble developed. So we insisted that the institutional investors purchase "strips," or units, containing a mixture of senior notes, subordinated notes, preferred stock, and common stock. This made First Boston's job more difficult. Previously, no leveraged buyouts had been financed in this manner. First Boston did an outstanding job assembling the players for a financing of this type and size.

Also it was proposed that First Boston, Century Capital, and the management of the new firm purchase common stock. The purchase of stock by management in the new firm was typical of leveraged buyouts. In summary, the proposed amounts to be financed by each investor and type of security were as shown in Table A.

## The Decision

At this stage of negotiation, the central issues under consideration were valuation and the appropriateness of the offering price of $38 per share.[2] Exhibit 13 shows the financial forecast on which the valuation of Congoleum was based. Exhibits 14–16 provide supporting material for the Exhibit 13 forecast.

---

2. In the cases of First Boston, Century Capital, and Congoleum management, it was also possible to augment common stock returns with other forms of compensation, such as consulting fees, stock options, and salaries guaranteed by employment contracts. As investment banker in this transaction, First Boston would be paid a fee.

**TABLE A**
Sources of Acquisition Financing (millions of dollars)

| | | |
|---|---:|---:|
| Bank borrowings . . . . . . . . . . . . . . . . . . . . | | $125.0 |
| Insurance company investor "strips" | | |
|   11¼% senior notes, principal amount | | |
|     $115,000,000 (due 1995) . . . . . . . . . . . . . | $113.6 | |
|   12¼% subordinated notes, principal amount | | |
|     $92,000,000 (due 2000) . . . . . . . . . . . . . | 89.8 | |
|   ($11.00) cumulative preferred stock | | |
|     (322,000 shares) . . . . . . . . . . . . . . . . . | 26.2 | |
|   Common stock . . . . . . . . . . . . . . . . . . . | 16.5 | |
| | | 246.1 |
| First Boston and Century Capital . . . . . . . . . . . . . | | 4.5 |
| Congoleum management . . . . . . . . . . . . . . . . | | 4.0 |
| | | $379.6 |

**EXHIBIT 1**
Ten-Year Historical Financial Data, 1969–1978 (millions of dollars except per share data)

| | 1969 | 1970 | 1971 | 1972 | 1973 | 1974 | 1975 | 1976 | 1977 | 1978 |
|---|---|---|---|---|---|---|---|---|---|---|
| Net sales . . . . . . . . . . . | $189.9 | $187.7 | $250.6 | $345.2 | $385.7 | $377.1 | $395.9 | $294.8 | $388.6 | $575.8 |
| Royalty revenues (incl. in net sales) | — | — | — | 23.4 | 4.0 | 5.5 | 7.0 | 10.1 | 13.2 | 17.2 |
| Net income . . . . . . . | 7.6 | 7.0 | 12.1 | 23.4 | 22.2 | .5 | 9.6 | 15.7 | 24.7 | 41.7 |
| Earnings per share . . . . . | $ .70 | $ .65 | $ 1.07 | $ 1.67 | $ 1.89 | $ .05 | $ .83 | $ 1.36 | $ 2.13 | $ 3.58 |
| Dividends per share . . . . | — | .02 | .09 | .13 | .20 | .27 | .27 | .33 | .40 | .67 |
| Stock price | | | | | | | | | | |
| High . . . . . . | 17.5 | 11.6 | 24.0 | 30.9 | 24.6 | 14.9 | 9.2 | 12.9 | 14.6 | 26.3 |
| Low . . . . . . | 7.5 | 3.9 | 10.1 | 20.7 | 8.5 | 2.4 | 3.0 | 8.0 | 8.8 | 12.0 |
| Working capital . . . . . | $ 35.2 | $ 49.0 | $ 53.5 | $ 69.6 | $ 88.1 | $ 92.8 | $ 81.1 | $ 76.8 | $ 78.0 | $110.1 |
| Long-term debt . . . . . | 31.7 | 42.6 | 40.0 | 42.1 | 59.3 | 74.6 | 52.3 | 16.6 | 16.1 | 14.9 |
| Net worth . . . . . . | 58.9 | 59.1 | 73.3 | 99.5 | 116.3 | 113.8 | 120.3 | 132.6 | 153.1 | 187.5 |

*Note:* Congoleum acquired Curtis Noll Corporation October 31, 1977, on a purchase basis. Its performance is consolidated with Congoleum after October 31, 1977. Certain operations were discontinued in 1976. Results for 1969 to 1975 have not been adjusted for discontinued operations.

**EXHIBIT 2**

Historical Income Statements for Years Ending December 31, 1976–1978 (thousands of dollars except per share data)

|  | 1976 | 1977 | 1978 |
|---|---|---|---|
| Net sales | $284,735 | $375,466 | $558,633 |
| Royalties[a] | 10,080 | 13,163 | 17,197 |
| Total revenues | 294,815 | 388,629 | 575,830 |
| Cost of sales | 224,028 | 285,770 | 385,851 |
| Selling and administrative expenses | 37,805 | 55,023 | 108,648 |
| Operating income | 32,982 | 47,836 | 81,331 |
| Interest expense | (2,064) | (1,734) | (1,266) |
| Miscellaneous income | 3,821 | 3,538 | 4,281 |
| Total other income and expense | 1,757 | 1,804 | 3,015 |
| Income from continuing operations before income taxes | 34,739 | 49,640 | 84,346 |
| Provision for income taxes | 17,400 | 24,900 | 42,600 |
| Income from continuing operations | 17,339 | 24,740 | 41,746 |
| Loss from discontinued operations | (19,500) | – | – |
| Patent infringement settlement | 17,885 | – | – |
| Net income | $ 15,724 | $ 24,740 | $ 41,746 |
| *Per Share* |  |  |  |
| Income from continuing operations | $ 1.50 | $ 2.13 | $ 3.58 |
| Loss from discontinued operations | (1.69) | – | – |
| Patent infringement settlement | 1.55 | – | – |
| Net income | $ 1.36 | $ 2.13 | $ 3.58 |

*Note:* These statements reflect the addition of Curtis Noll Corporation only after October 31, 1977, the date of acquisition. The acquisition was accounted for as a purchase. Restating the results of 1977 and 1976 as if Noll were included yields the following:

|  | 1976 | 1977 |
|---|---|---|
| Total revenues | $416,000 | $497,300 |
| Income from continuing operations | 19,592 | 27,725 |
| Net income | 17,977 | 27,725 |
| Earnings per share | $ 1.56 | $ 2.39 |

a. Royalties are from licenses of the company's resilient flooring patents as well as license agreements for know-how. These patents expire from 1980 through 1987, although most expire by 1984.

**EXHIBIT 3**

Consolidated Balance Sheets at December 31, 1977–1978 (thousands of dollars)

| | 1977 | 1978 |
|---|---|---|
| Cash and temporary investments | $ 12,369 | $ 77,254 |
| Receivables | 55,053 | 40,424 |
| Shipbuilding contracts in progress | 18,936 | 24,058 |
| Inventories | 73,318 | 75,258[a] |
| Other | 5,679 | 3,511 |
| Current assets | 165,355 | 220,505[b] |
| Property, plant, and equipment | 131,621 | 135,627[c] |
| Less: Accumulated depreciation and amortization | 60,472 | 64,850[d] |
| Net | 71,149 | 70,777[e] |
| Goodwill | 18,520 | 18,520 |
| Other | 11,356 | 13,250 |
| Total assets | $266,380 | $323,052[f] |
| Current maturities of long-term debt | $ 2,055 | $ 460 |
| Accounts payable | 38,391 | 41,578 |
| Accrued liabilities | 28,928 | 30,102 |
| Income taxes | 17,985 | 38,257 |
| Current liabilities | 87,359 | 110,397 |
| Long-term debt | 16,067 | 14,949 |
| Deferred income taxes and other liabilities | 9,886 | 10,221 |
| Common stock | 5,859 | 5,859 |
| Surplus | 11,846 | 11,345 |
| Retained earnings | 137,256 | 171,229 |
| Treasury stock | (1,893) | (948) |
| Net worth | 153,068 | 187,485 |
| Total liabilities and net worth | $266,380 | $323,052 |

Replacement cost data:
  a. $79,518.     d. $188,281.
  b. $224,765.    e. $93,986.
  c. $282,267.    f. $352,710.

**EXHIBIT 4**
Product Line Data, 1974–1979 (millions of dollars)

| | Year Ended December 31 | | | | | 9 Months | |
|---|---|---|---|---|---|---|---|
| | *1974* | *1975* | *1976* | *1977* | *1978* | *1978* | *1979* |
| Revenues by segment | | | | | | | |
| Home furnishings . . . . | $143 | $153 | $180 | $198 | $225 | $170 | $177 |
| Shipbuilding . . . . . . | 107 | 126 | 115 | 167 | 211 | 158 | 181 |
| Automotive and industrial | | | | | | | |
| distribution . . . . . . | 79 | 85 | 95 | 105 | 115 | 86 | 89 |
| | $329 | $364 | $390 | $470 | $551 | $414 | $447 |
| Operating income (loss) by segment[a] | | | | | | | |
| Home furnishings . . . . | $ 22 | $ 27 | $ 34 | $ 42 | $ 58 | $ 43 | $ 40 |
| Shipbuilding . . . . . . | (11) | 1 | 2 | 10 | 19 | 13 | 28 |
| Automotive and industrial | | | | | | | |
| distribution[b] . . . . . | 6 | 7 | 8 | 9 | 10 | 7 | 8 |
| | $ 17 | $ 35 | $ 44 | $ 61 | $ 87 | $ 63 | $ 76 |
| Identifiable assets by segment | | | | | | | |
| Home furnishings . . . . | $ 93 | $ 93 | $ 97 | $ 92 | $ 93 | na | na |
| Shipbuilding . . . . . . | 37 | 38 | 42 | 54 | 59 | na | na |
| Automotive and industrial | | | | | | | |
| distribution . . . . . . | 48 | 52 | 56 | 62 | 64 | na | na |
| | $178 | $183 | $195 | $208 | $216 | na | na |

na = not available.

a. Operating income does not include an allocation of interest income or expense, miscellaneous and other unallocable expenses, corporate office expenses, or provisions for income taxes.

b. The pro forma amounts for the automotive and industrial distribution segment include the results of Curtis Noll Corporation.

**EXHIBIT 5**

Management Stock and Option Ownership in Congoleum Corporation, Autumn 1979

| | Number of Shares Subject to Options and Stock Appreciation Rights | Weighted Average Exercise Price | Number of Other Shares Beneficially Owned | Total Number of Shares Beneficially Owned |
|---|---|---|---|---|
| Byron C. Radaker (Chairman, CEO) . . | 47,250 | $11.87 | 12,750 | 60,000 |
| Eddy G. Nicholson (Vice Chairman, COO) . . | 27,750 | 11.31 | 11,250 | 39,000 |
| Harry F. Pearson (Executive Vice Pres.) . . | 7,000 | 15.38 | 47,492 | 64,492 |
| All directors and officers as a group . . . . . . | 164,699 | 13.07 | 293,023 | 457,722 |

*Note:* Officers of Congoleum expected to assume equivalent positions in the new firm.

It was proposed that Radaker and Nicholson be allowed to purchase 7% and 5%, respectively, of the new firm's equity, subject to the right of the firm to repurchase the equity if their employment is terminated before 1984. Stock in the new venture was also reserved for other key employees.

Radaker and Nicholson would be employed under 5-year contracts, which specified a base salary, incentive compensation, and entitlements in the event of termination. Current and proposed compensation compared as follows:

| | Radaker | Nicholson |
|---|---|---|
| 1979 compensation . . . . . . | $370,000 | $295,000 |
| 1980 compensation per contract | | |
| Maximum . . . . . . . . . | 500,000 | 380,000 |
| Minimum . . . . . . . . . | 375,000 | 290,000 |

**EXHIBIT 6**
Data on Comparable Leveraged Buyouts and Other Acquisitions

| Company Acquired | Date | Acquisition of Stock or Assets | Premium/Price One Day Prior to Announcement | Offer as a Multiple of | | Senior Debt/ Total Debt | Sub. Debt/ Total Debt | Senior Debt/ Total Cap. | Sub. Debt/ Total Cap. |
| | | | | Net Income | Book Value | | | | |
|---|---|---|---|---|---|---|---|---|---|
| Houdaille Industries . . . . . . | 10/28/78 | S | 93% | 13.9 | 2.0 | 65.5% | 34.5% | 56% | 29.6% |
| Bliss & Laughlin . . . . . . | 8/10/79 | A | 23 | 8.7 | 1.7 | | | | |
| Carrier Corp. . . . . . . | 9/16/78 | A | 39 | 10.2 | 1.6 | | | | |
| Gardner-Denver . . . . . . | 1/22/79 | A | 46 | 12.2 | 2.1 | | | | |
| Washington Steel . . . . . . | 3/12/79 | A | 34 | 7.3 | 1.3 | | | | |
| Eltra Corp. . . . . . . | 6/29/79 | A | 25 | 11.6 | 1.5 | | | | |
| Studebaker-Worthington . . . | 7/25/79 | A | 17 | 10.7 | 1.4 | | | | |
| Marathon Manufacturing . . . | 8/13/79 | A | 13 | 11.4 | 2.1 | | | | |
| Congoleum . . . . . . | | A/S | 50 | 9.4 | 2.4 | 68.6 | 31.4 | 60.4 | 27.6 |

**EXHIBIT 7**
Valuation Based on a Breakup Price Estimated by Lazard Frères for Each Component (millions of dollars except per share data)

| | 1979 Estimated Results by Segment | | | |
| --- | --- | --- | --- | --- |
| | Home Furnishings Segment | Bath Iron Works | Automotive and Industrial Distribution | Total Corporate Consolidated |
| Operating income[a] . . . . . . . . | $56.1 | $29.0 | $11.9 | $97.0 |
| Corporate office and other[b] . . . . . | 1.1 | 1.3 | .7 | 3.1 |
| Pre-tax income . . . . . . . . | 55.0 | 27.7 | 11.2 | 93.9 |
| Taxes (48%) . . . . . . . . . | 26.4 | 13.3 | 5.4 | 45.1 |
| Net income . . . . . . . . . . | $28.6 | $14.4 | $ 5.8 | $48.8 |

| | Valuation Based on Assumed Price-Earnings Ratio | | | | | | | |
| --- | --- | --- | --- | --- | --- | --- | --- | --- |
| | Low | High | Low | High | Low | High | Low | High |
| Assumed price-earnings ratio . | 9.0 | 10.0 | 5.0 | 6.0 | 10.0 | 11.0 | | |
| Derived valuation . . . . . | $257.4 | $286.0 | $72.0 | $86.4 | $58.0 | $63.8 | $387.4 | $436.2 |
| Plus: Estimated excess cash on 12/31/79[c] . . . . | | | | | | | 95.1 | 95.1 |
| Less: Estimated long-term debt and current maturity of long-term debt on 12/31/79 . . | | | | | | | 15.6 | 15.6 |
| Less: Unfunded vested pension liabilities (as of 12/31/78) . . . . | | | | | | | 34.5 | 34.5 |
| Net breakup value . . . . . . . . . . . . | | | | | | | $432.4 | $481.2 |
| Net breakup value per share (based on 12,201,000 shares) . . . . . . . . . . . . . . . . . . | | | | | | | $35.44 | $39.43 |

a. From Congoleum's internal reporting of quarterly operating income and performance report. Operating income for the Home Furnishings segment was reduced by $2.7 million attributable to the Kinder Division. This operation has been assumed to be sold for $10 million by the end of 1979.

b. Allocated based on 1979 estimated sales (excluding $36.0 million attributable to Kinder and excluding royalty payments).

c. Total cash at year-end estimated at $103.1 million minus $8 million. Excess cash is therefore estimated at $95.1 million.

**EXHIBIT 8**

Forecast of Congoleum Operations, 1979–1981 (millions of dollars except per share data)

|  | 1979 | 1980 | 1981 |
|---|---|---|---|
| *For Year Ended December 31* | | | |
| Revenues | $596 | $680 | $737 |
| Operating income | 86 | 97 | 112 |
| Net income | 45 | 51 | 60 |
| Net income per share | $3.80 | $4.35 | $5.00 |
| Dividends per share | .90 | 1.10 | 1.30 |
| *At December 31* | | | |
| Cash and temporary investments | $ 93 | $136 | $182 |
| Working capital | 140 | 169 | 209 |
| Long-term debt | 15 | 14 | 14 |
| Stockholders' investment | 220 | 259 | 304 |

*Note:* These data are from an internal forecast by Congoleum prepared in the summer of 1978 and subsequently made available to First Boston Corp.

**EXHIBIT 9**

Financial Data on Market Segment Competitors

|  | Five-Year Expected Growth | P/E | β[a] | LT Debt % Cap. | 1979 ROE | 1982–1984 Expected Div. Yield |
|---|---|---|---|---|---|---|
| Home furnishings | | | | | | |
| Armstrong Cork | 17.5% | 5.8 | 1.00 | 18.2% | 11.6% | 3.2% |
| GAF Corp. | 14.0 | 6.0 | 1.15 | 35.0 | 10.4 | 2.6 |
| Shipbuilding | | | | | | |
| Todd Shipyards | 21.0 | 5.3 | 1.00 | 69.0 | 22.0 | 2.0 |
| Automotive and industrial distribution | | | | | | |
| Genuine Parts | 16.0 | 10.4 | .95 | 5.0 | 19.2 | 2.5 |
| General Automotive Parts | 16.0 | 9.6 | .75 | 7.0 | 19.0 | 2.4 |
| Barnes Group | 12.5 | 5.1 | .85 | 18.0 | 20.6 | 2.7 |
| Congoleum | 22.5 | 7.9 | 1.25 | 7.0 | 23.0 | 3.0 |

a. The risk-free rate was assumed to be 9.5% and the market premium 8.6%.

**EXHIBIT 10**
Average or Comparable Debt Yields by Quality, September 1979

| S&P Rating | Yield | Firm Name | Debt/Total Capital |
|---|---|---|---|
| AAA | 9.35% | | |
| AA | 9.54 | Average in category | |
| A | 9.78 | | |
| BBB | 10.49 | | |
| BB | 13.76 | Action Industries | 56.9% |
| | 11.06 | Control Data | 21.1 |
| | 11.86 | Sun Chemical | 47.6 |
| | 10.59 | Talley Industries | 43.0 |
| B | 13.32 | APL Corp. | 57.9 |
| | 12.70 | Arrow Electronics | 49.7 |
| | 11.98 | Charter Company | 50.4 |
| | 12.46 | Columbia Pictures | 41.3 |
| | 12.87 | Texas International Airlines | 51.0 |
| CCC | 16.11 | Altec Corp. | 70.8 |
| | 13.32 | General Host | 74.4 |
| | 17.22 | Grolier, Inc. | na |
| | 14.26 | LTV Corp. | 73.8 |
| | 15.02 | Rapid American Corp. | 75.7 |

na = not available.

**EXHIBIT 11**
Average or Comparable Preferred Stock Dividend Yields by Quality, September 1979

| | Yield | Firm Name | Debt/Total Capital |
|---|---|---|---|
| *Moody's Rating* | | | |
| Aaa | NR | | |
| Aa | 9.6% | Average in category | |
| A | 10.3 | | |
| Baa | 10.5 | | |
| *S&P Rating* | | | |
| BB | 10.0 | Control Data | 21.1% |
| | 10.8 | Evans Products | 36.8 |
| | 10.0 | Fairmont Foods | 39.0 |
| | 11.5 | Flexi-Van Corp. | 64.0 |
| B | 12.1 | Eastern Airlines | 68.1 |
| | 11.5 | Humana, Inc. | 72.1 |
| | 12.5 | Norin Corp. | 49.5 |
| | 12.6 | Petro-Lewis | 67.2 |
| CCC | 18.2 | Chrysler Corp. | 33.8 |
| | 11.9 | Continental Copper Steel | 45.0 |
| | 14.0 | Susquehanna Corp. | 25.3 |
| | 15.0 | United Brands | 33.3 |
| | 14.0 | Warnaco | 35.0 |
| | 13.0 | Wheeling Pittsburgh Steel | 33.7 |

NR = not rated.

**EXHIBIT 12**
Sources and Allocation of Purchase Premium (millions of dollars)

| | | |
|---|---:|---:|
| Cost of stock ($38 × 12.2 mill. shares) | $463.6 | |
| Expenses | 7.0 | |
| Purchase price | | $470.6 |
| Stockholders' investment, 12/31/78 | $187.5 | |
| Claim settlement | 3.5 | |
| Proceeds from exercise of stock options | 5.0 | |
| Estimated 1979 additions to retained earnings | 37.7 | |
| Stockholders' investment, 12/31/79 | 233.7 | |
| Less: Unfunded pension liabilities | 34.5 | |
| Adjusted stockholders' investment, 12/31/79 | | 199.2 |
| Purchase premium | | $271.4 |
| Inventory write-up from recapture of LIFO reserve | $ 4.2 | |
| Fixed assets | 83.4 | |
| Patents | 150.0 | |
| Goodwill | 33.8 | |
| Purchase premium | | $271.4 |

*Note:* After the July 16, 1979, bid First Boston retained American Appraisal Company to render a "comfort level" opinion of the fair market value of inventories as of June 30, 1979, and the shipbuilding contract backlog and patents and patent licensing agreements at December 31, 1979. Their report concluded that the net realizable value of the inventories was $83,633,000, of the backlog was $73,500,000, and of the patents and patent licensing agreements was $174,000,000. The book value of inventories at June 30, 1979, was $50,000,000. Shipbuilding contract backlog and patents and patent licensing agreements had been carried on the books at nominal values.

**EXHIBIT 13**

Income and Cash Flow Forecast for Congoleum Reflecting the Terms of the Proposed Leveraged Buyout, 1978–1984 (millions of dollars)

| | Actual 1978 | Projected | | | | | | Total 1980–1984 |
|---|---|---|---|---|---|---|---|---|
| | | 1979 | 1980 | 1981 | 1982 | 1983 | 1984 | |
| 1. Operating income (Exhibit 15) . . . . . . | $95.5 | $105.9 | $111.5 | $132.2 | $158.7 | $175.9 | $166.1 | |
| 2. Less: Corporate expenses . . . | 7.5 | 8.6 | 4.3 | 5.1 | 5.9 | 6.8 | 7.6 | |
| 3. Less: Depreciation and amortization . . . . . . . . | 6.7 | 7.5 | 35.51 | 36.26 | 37.07 | 37.95 | 21.23 | |
| 4. Earnings before interest and taxes . . . . . . . . . | 81.3 | 89.8 | 71.69 | 90.84 | 115.73 | 131.15 | 137.27 | |
| 5. Less: Interest expense, net[a] . . | (3.0) | (5.7) | 42.92 | 40.55 | 37.33 | 34.12 | 29.87 | |
| 6. Profit before taxes . . . . . | $84.3 | $ 95.5 | $ 28.77 | $ 50.19 | $ 78.40 | $ 97.03 | $107.40 | |
| 7. Less: Tax (@ 48%) . . . . . | | 45.8 | 13.80 | 24.09 | 37.63 | 46.57 | 51.55 | |
| 8. Profit after taxes . . . . . . | | $ 49.7 | $ 14.97 | $ 26.10 | $ 40.77 | $ 50.46 | $ 55.85 | $188.2 |
| *Adjustments* | | | | | | | | |
| 9. Add back: Depreciation and Amortization[b] . . . . . . | | | $ 35.51 | $ 36.26 | $ 37.07 | $ 37.95 | $ 21.23 | $168.0 |
| 10. Less: Capital expenditures . . . | | | 15.0 | 16.2 | 17.5 | 18.9 | 20.4 | 88.0 |
| 11. Less: Investment in working capital . . . . . . . . | | | 2.0 | 14.0 | 23.3 | 11.2 | 12.8 | 63.3 |
| 12. Less: Preferred dividends . . . | | | 3.5 | 3.5 | 3.5 | 3.5 | 3.5 | 17.5 |
| 13. Less: Principal repayments . . | | | 17.14 | 24.75 | 24.52 | 36.75 | 24.55 | 127.7 |
| 14. Free cash flow (to common stock)[c] . . . . . . . . | | | 12.84 | 3.91 | 9.02 | 18.06 | 15.83 | 59.7 |
| 15. Add: Dividends, interest, and principal . . . . . . . | | | 63.56 | 68.80 | 65.35 | 74.37 | 57.96 | 330.0 |
| 16. Free cash flow (to all capital) . . | | | 76.40 | 72.71 | 74.37 | 92.43 | 73.79 | 389.7 |
| 17. Less: Bank and preexisting interest and principal . . . . | | | 35.85 | 33.46 | 30.86 | 40.74 | 25.28 | 166.2 |
| 18. Free cash flow to buyout participants . . . . . . . | | | $ 40.55 | $ 39.25 | $ 43.51 | $ 51.69 | $ 48.51 | $223.5 |
| 19. Net working capital . . . . . | | $120.0 | $ 122.0 | $ 136.0 | $ 159.3 | $ 170.5 | $ 183.3 | |
| 20. Change in net working capital . | | | 2.0 | 14.0 | 23.3 | 11.2 | 12.8 | |

a. With no leveraged buyout, Congoleum's net interest expenses were expected to be, in millions of dollars, $(2.0), $(2.0), $(2.1), $(2.1), and $(3.0) over the years 1980–1984.

b. With no leveraged buyout, Congoleum's depreciation and amortization expenses were expected to be, in millions of dollars, $7.5, $8.3, $9.0, $9.9, and $10.9 over the years 1980–1984.

c. Because of covenants prohibiting dividends, these free cash flows would be reinvested (presumably in cash and marketable securities), reducing financial risk and increasing the free cash flow. Does not reflect income from the reinvestment of surplus cash.

## EXHIBIT 14
Assumptions for Financial Projections

### Corporate Expenses

$8.6 million in 1979, growing at 8% thereafter from 1980 to 1984. A savings of $5 million annually is assumed as a result of Congoleum's being a private company.

### Depreciation and Amortization

The amortization of patents was proposed as follows. Amortization of patents will be the same for book and tax purposes.

|  | Value ($ millions) | Remaining Life (years) |
|---|---|---|
| Chemical embossing process  . . . | $ 40 | 4 |
| Code key cutter  . . . . . . . . | 40 | 10 |
| Future value of U.S. royalties  . . . | 30 | 4 |
| Future value of foreign royalties  . . | 40 | 10 |
| Total  . . . . . . . . . . | $150 | |

### Depreciation of Plant and Equipment

For tax purposes, the fixed asset base will be $200.2 million. Of this, 50% is assumed to relate to plant and will be depreciated over 20 years. The other 50%, related to equipment, will be depreciated over 7 years. All subsequent capital expenditures will be depreciated over 20 years. For book purposes, the fixed asset base will be $154.0 million. The other policies above will apply.

### Interest Expense and Principal Repayments

*Bank debt.*   Assume 14% interest on principal of $120 million. Principal is to be amortized at $16.666 million annually starting in 1980.

*Senior notes.*   11¼% interest on principal of $115 million, amortized at $7,636,000 per year starting on January 30, 1981.

*Subordinated notes.*   12¼% interest on principal of $92 million, amortized at $7,636,000 per year starting on January 30, 1989.

*Covenants.*   Prohibit the payment of dividends on other than the preferred stock.

*Taxes.*   The corporate income tax rate is assumed to be 48%.

*Capital expenditures.*   Assumed to be $15 million in 1980 and increasing 8% annually thereafter.

*Minimum working capital.*   20% of nonroyalty sales. Net working capital immediately following the buyout is projected to be $120 million.

*Required cash.*   Assumed to be 2.5% of nonroyalty sales.

*Note.*   By 1980 a pattern of leveraged buyouts had emerged such that the firms were taken public again within a few years, usually when the various value-creating effects were diminished. The end of 1984 was one such horizon for Congoleum.

**EXHIBIT 15**
Projected Segment Revenue and Operating Income for Congoleum, 1979–1984 (millions of dollars)

| | Actual 1978 | Projected | | | | | |
|---|---|---|---|---|---|---|---|
| | | 1979 | 1980 | 1981 | 1982 | 1983 | 1984 |
| *Revenues* | | | | | | | |
| Home furnishings, net | $207.9 | $234.9 | $217.9 | $241.9 | $273.3 | $308.8 | $349.0 |
| Home furnishings royalties | 17.2 | 20.6 | 24.8 | 29.7 | 35.7 | 42.8 | 21.4 |
| Total home furnishings | 225.1 | 255.5 | 242.7 | 271.6 | 309.0 | 351.6 | 370.4 |
| Shipbuilding | 211.0 | 230.4 | 247.9 | 279.2 | 345.1 | 345.1 | 345.1 |
| Automotive, expediter | 78.8 | 90.6 | 104.2 | 119.8 | 137.8 | 158.5 | 182.3 |
| Automotive, conventional | 45.0 | 45.0 | 40.0 | 40.0 | 40.0 | 40.0 | 40.0 |
| Total automotive | 123.8 | 135.6 | 144.2 | 159.8 | 177.8 | 198.5 | 222.3 |
| Total revenues | $559.9 | $621.5 | $634.8 | $710.6 | $831.9 | $895.2 | $937.8 |
| *Operating Income* | | | | | | | |
| Home furnishings, net | $ 43.7 | $ 42.0 | $ 39.2 | $ 48.4 | $ 57.4 | $ 64.8 | $ 73.3 |
| Home furnishings royalties | 17.2 | 20.6 | 24.8 | 29.7 | 35.7 | 42.8 | 21.4 |
| Total home furnishings | 60.9 | 62.6 | 64.0 | 78.1 | 93.1 | 107.6 | 94.7 |
| Shipbuilding | 21.7 | 31.5 | 33.9 | 38.5 | 47.7 | 47.7 | 47.7 |
| Automotive, expediter | na | 11.8 | 13.6 | 15.6 | 17.9 | 20.6 | 23.7 |
| Automotive, conventional | na | 0 | 0 | 0 | 0 | 0 | 0 |
| Total automotive | 12.9 | 11.8 | 13.6 | 15.6 | 17.9 | 20.6 | 23.7 |
| Total operating income | $ 95.5 | $105.9 | $111.5 | $132.2 | $158.7 | $175.9 | $166.1 |

*Note:* These data are from projections made by First Boston Corporation, and assume the buyout is completed. Neither depreciation nor corporate-level expenses are reflected in operating income, nor is income from the reinvestment of surplus cash.

na = not available.

# EXHIBIT 16
Capital Structure and Debt Repayment Schedule for Congoleum, 1979–1984 (millions of dollars)

| | 1979 | Projected as of December 31 | | | | |
| --- | --- | --- | --- | --- | --- | --- |
| | 1979 | 1980 | 1981 | 1982 | 1983 | 1984 |
| *Old Debt* | | | | | | |
| 1. 7½% subordinated debentures due 1983 | $ 12.2 | $ 12.2 | $ 12.2 | $ 12.2 | $ 0 | $ 0 |
| 2. Other long-term debt | 4.24 | 3.77 | 3.32 | 3.11 | 2.86 | 2.61 |
| *New Debt* | | | | | | |
| 3. Bank term notes | $125.0 | $108.33 | $91.67 | $75.00 | $58.34 | $41.67 |
| 4. 11¼% senior notes due 1995 | 113.6 | 113.6 | 106.0 | 98.3 | 90.7 | 83.1 |
| 5. 12¼% subordinated notes due 2000 | 89.8 | 89.8 | 89.8 | 89.8 | 89.8 | 89.8 |
| 6. Preferred stock $11.00 (322,000 shares) | 26.2 | 26.2 | 26.2 | 26.2 | 26.2 | – |
| *Common Stock* | | | | | | |
| 7. Par value .10 (1,000,000 shares) | $ .1 | $ .1 | $ .1 | $ .1 | $ .1 | $ .1 |
| 8. Paid-in surplus | 24.9 | 24.9 | 24.9 | 24.9 | 24.9 | 24.9 |
| *Interest* | | | | | | |
| 9. 7½% subordinated debentures ⎫(assumed in acquisition) | | $ .92 | $ .92 | $ .92 | $ .92 | $ – |
| 10. Other long-term debt ⎭ | | .30 | .26 | .23 | .22 | .20 |
| 11. Bank term notes @ 14% | | 17.50 | 15.17 | 12.83 | 10.50 | 8.17 |
| 12. 11¼% senior notes | | 12.94 | 12.94 | 12.08 | 11.22 | 10.23 |
| 13. 12¼% subordinated notes | | 11.27 | 11.27 | 11.27 | 11.27 | 11.27 |
| 14. Total interest payments | | $ 42.92 | $40.56 | $37.33 | $34.12 | $29.87 |
| 15. Preferred dividend | | 3.54 | 3.54 | 3.54 | 3.54 | 3.54 |
| *Amortization* | | | | | | |
| 16. 7½% subordinated debentures ⎫(assumed in acquisition) | | $ – | $ – | $ – | $12.20 | $ –[a] |
| 17. Other long-term debt ⎭ | $ .46 | .47 | .45 | .21 | .24 | .25 |
| 18. Bank term notes | | 16.67 | 16.67 | 16.67 | 16.67 | 16.67 |
| 19. 11¼% senior notes | | – | 7.67 | 7.67 | 7.68 | 7.67 |
| 20. 12¼% subordinated notes | | – | – | – | – | – |
| 21. Total: Interest, principal, dividends | | 63.60 | 68.85 | 65.39 | 74.41 | 57.96 |

*Note:* Totals may not add exactly due to rounding.

a. Includes anticipated repayments as well as required repayments.

# RJR Nabisco

On October 20, 1988, Charles E. Hugel, chairman of RJR Nabisco, was appointed chairman of the Special Committee. The Special Committee (Exhibit 1) was formed to consider a proposal to purchase the company for $17 billion by a group (the Management Group) consisting of F. Ross Johnson, president and chief executive officer of RJR Nabisco; Edward A. Horrigan, vice chairman of RJR Nabisco and chief executive officer of RJ Reynolds Tobacco Company; and the investment banking firm of Shearson Lehman Hutton. At $75 per share, the buyout offer was 34% above the pre-offer price of $55.875. No details about the form of the offer were immediately available.[1] Within four days, Kohlberg, Kravis, Roberts & Co. (KKR), a firm specializing in leveraged buyouts, announced a competing tender offer for RJR Nabisco. The KKR bid was for $90 per share, or about $20.3 billion in total.

## Company Background

RJR Nabisco began as a tobacco company in 1875 and remained primarily a tobacco company until the RJR Foods subsidiary was formed after a series of acquisitions in 1967. By 1987 the company's sales had grown to $15.8 billion (Exhibit 2), and assets stood at $16.9 billion (Exhibit 3). The tobacco business included established brand-name cigarettes such as Winston, Salem, Camel, and

---

This case was prepared by Professor Richard S. Ruback.

1. The directors of RJR Nabisco viewed Mr. Johnson's consideration of a buyout as material information and disclosed the buyout proposal when it was discussed by the board.

Vantage and also products such as Planters nuts and LifeSavers candies. The business segment data in Exhibit 4 show that the tobacco business had sales of $6.3 billion and operating income of $1.8 billion in 1987.

The food products initially included Hawaiian Punch beverages, Chun King oriental foods, My-T-Fine puddings, Davis baking powder, Vermont Maid syrup, and Patio Mexican dinners. Del Monte, which was acquired in 1979, added canned goods and fresh bananas and pineapples. RJR Nabisco's food businesses expanded substantially with the 1985 acquisition of Nabisco Brands, Inc., which added brand names like Oreo, Fig and Fruit Newtons, and Chips Ahoy! cookies; Ritz, American Classic, and Quakers crackers; Nabisco Shredded Wheat cereal; Fleischmann's margarine; A-1 Steak Sauce; Ortega Mexican foods; and Milk-Bone dog biscuits. In 1987 the food businesses had sales of $9.4 billion and an operating income of $915 million.

RJR Nabisco had also entered and exited several lines of business. Sea-Land, a container-shipping company, was acquired in 1969 and divested in 1984. Heublein, Inc., a producer of alcoholic beverages and the owner of Kentucky Fried Chicken, was acquired in 1982. Kentucky Fried Chicken was sold in 1986, and the wine and spirits business of Heublein was sold in 1987. The company entered the energy business with the acquisition of American Independent Oil Company in 1970 and the U.S. subsidiaries of Burmah Oil Company in 1976. It exited the energy business by selling these assets in 1984.

Exhibit 5 contains projections for RJR Nabisco, assuming that it continued under its pre-offer operating plans. A total of nearly $10 billion in capital expenditures was projected for 1989 through 1998. The major investment in the tobacco business was extending development and test marketing of Premier, a smokeless cigarette. The company had already spent $300 million on Premier, and substantial costs would be associated with manufacturing and marketing the product. It had also approved plans to spend about $2.8 billion to modernize Nabisco's bakeries. The plans included constructing two new bakeries for $600 million each, spending $1.6 billion on the complete retrofittings of four plants, and closing five others.

## The Management Group Bid

The Management Group's strategy was to sell off RJR Nabisco's food businesses and retain its tobacco business. The strategy was based on the view that the market undervalued the strong cash flow from the tobacco business and did not fully value its food businesses because of its association with tobacco. Selling RJR Nabisco's food assets and taking the tobacco business private would eliminate the undervaluation and generate substantial gains.

F. Ross Johnson had experience selling food assets. He was CEO of Standard Brands when Nabisco acquired it to form Nabisco Brands in 1981. And he was CEO of Nabisco Brands when RJ Reynolds acquired it in 1985 to form RJR Nabisco. Furthermore, the Management Group bid occurred when the food industry was undergoing a major restructuring and revaluation. Both Pillsbury and Kraft were in the midst of takeover contests.

Grand Metropolitan PLC began a hostile tender offer for Pillsbury on October 4, 1988. Grand Met was a diversified British company that brewed and distributed beer, ale, and lager; produced and distributed alcoholic beverages; and owned and operated pubs and restaurants. Pillsbury was a diversified food and restaurant company, with popular brands such as Pillsbury Doughboy bakery items, Green Giant vegetables, and Häagen-Dazs ice cream in its food business and Burger King in its restaurant group. The $5.2 billion Grand Met bid was a 53% premium over the previous market price—about 25 times Pillsbury's net earnings and about four times the book value of common equity.[2] Pillsbury opposed the bid, and its outcome was uncertain.

Philip Morris offered to purchase all Kraft common stock at $90 per share in cash on October 18, 1988. Like RJR Nabisco, Philip Morris earned most of its profits from tobacco: its Marlboro, Benson & Hedges, and Virginia Slims cigarettes had 1987 sales of $14.6 billion and operating profits of $3.3 billion. And, also like RJR Nabisco, Philip Morris acquired most of its food assets in 1985. Philip Morris acquired General Foods with brand-name products such as Maxwell House coffee, Birds Eye frozen foods, Jell-O, Oscar Mayer meats, Ronzoni pasta, and Post cereals. Philip Morris also had brewing interests, with brands like Miller Lite, and Matilda Bay Wine Coolers. Kraft was known for such brand names as Miracle Whip, Seven Seas, and Kraft salad dressings; Kraft mayonnaise; Velveeta cheese; Parkay and Chiffon margarines; Lender's Bagels; and Breyers ice cream. The $11 billion Philip Morris offer for Kraft was a 50% premium over the pre-offer stock price and about 21 times Kraft's net earnings.[3]

Based on the prices bid for Pillsbury and Kraft, analysts estimated the value of RJR Nabisco's food businesses as follows (billions of dollars):

| | | |
|---|---|---|
| Nabisco | . . . . | $ 8–9.5 |
| Del Monte | . . . | $ 3–4 |
| Planters | . . . . | $ 1.5–2 |
| Total | . . . . | $12.5–15.5 |

Exhibit 6 contains projections for RJR Nabisco under the Management Group plan.

## The KKR Bid

Henry Kravis, a general partner of KKR, first expressed interest in organizing a leveraged buyout of RJR Nabisco at a September 1987 dinner meeting with F.

---

2. Pillsbury's 1988 net earnings per share were $2.45, excluding unusual items, and $.81, including unusual items. The difference was due to a restructuring charge of $1.64 per share. Its 1987 net earnings per share were $2.24, excluding unusual items, and $2.10, including unusual items.

3. Kraft's forecasted 1988 net income from continuing operations was $522 million. It also had income of $658 million from the sale of its Duracell battery business to KKR in 1988.

Ross Johnson. KKR had been organized in 1976 by three former executives of Bear Stearns Companies, Inc.: Jerome Kohlberg, Henry Kravis, and George Roberts. Since then, KKR had acquired more than 35 companies, paying more than $38 billion in total. KKR also completed the $6.2 billion leveraged buyout of Beatrice foods in 1986, at the time the largest completed leveraged buyout.

KKR offered to purchase up to 87% of RJR Nabisco common stock for $90 per share in cash. The remaining shares would receive securities with a value of $90 per share and terms to be negotiated by KKR and the Special Committee. KKR's $20.7 billion bid also offered $108 per share for the preferred stock of RJR Nabisco.[4] The KKR bid was conditional on approval of the merger by RJR Nabisco's board of directors.

KKR's strategy for managing RJR Nabisco contrasted sharply with the Management Group's proposal to sell all of the company's food assets. According to KKR's letter to the Special Committee:

> We do not contemplate the dismemberment of the company's operations. . . . Our present intention is to retain all of the tobacco businesses and to continue their important presence in Winston-Salem, North Carolina. We also expect to retain a significant portion of the food operations. Moreover, our financing plan does not require, nor do we intend, any presales of parts of the company.

Exhibit 7 contains projections for RJR Nabisco under the KKR operating plan.

KKR did not present specific details on financing for its offer. It had raised a $5.6 billion pool of equity capital for investments in leveraged buyouts. Also, KKR retained Morgan Stanley Group, Inc., Wasserstein, Perella & Co., Drexel Burnham Lambert Inc., and Merrill Lynch Capital Markets to assist in financing the cash portion of the buyout.

Following its bid, KKR entered into a confidentiality agreement with RJR Nabisco, giving KKR access to nonpublic material information about the company. The agreement also gave KKR the opportunity to meet with RJR Nabisco's management. Meeting them was especially important to KKR because its rival, the Management Group, had access to such information because of its position within the firm. In return for access to the information, KKR agreed not to purchase any RJR Nabisco securities, participate in a proxy contest, or advise or influence any participant in such a contest for 2 years unless it obtained approval of RJR Nabisco's board of directors.

KKR invited the Management Group to join with it in a joint bid. However, the two parties could not agree on a joint bid and abandoned the attempt on October 26, 1987. A second attempt to form a joint bid also failed, on November 3, and later that same day the Management Group announced a revised proposal to acquire RJR Nabisco. The revised bid was for $92 per share, or $21.1 billion

---

4. RJR Nabisco had 225,336,442 shares of common stock outstanding and outstanding employee stock options to purchase 3,628,414 common shares. There were 1,308,760 shares of preferred stock outstanding.

in total, and included $84 per share in cash and $8 per share in securities. Like the KKR bid, no details on the financing for the offer or the terms of the securities were available.

In addition to the bids by the Management Group and KKR, a third bid for RJR Nabisco was being considered, by groups led by Forstmann, Little & Co. and First Boston Corporation. The Forstmann, Little group had entered into a confidentiality agreement much like KKR's agreement with RJR Nabisco.

## The Auction

On November 7, the Special Committee adopted a set of rules and procedures "to determine which alternative would best serve the interests of [RJR Nabisco's] shareholders." Although not a commitment to recommend selling the company, the rules were "intended to constitute a single round of bidding. Any proposal should reflect the potential purchaser's highest offer." All bids were due by 5 P.M. on Friday, November 18. Any bid that did not conform to these rules the Special Committee would consider hostile.[5] The rules for bids included the following:

- Proposals should not be conditional on the sale of any assets of RJR Nabisco.
- Proposals should provide RJR Nabisco shareholders with a "substantial common-stock-related interest."
- Proposals should include details on financing arrangements, including commitment agreements and details of any noncash component of the offer.
- Proposals should be approved by the bidding firm's board of directors.

The board of directors and the Special Committee reserved the right to amend or terminate any of the rules, to terminate discussions with any bidder, and to reject any or all proposals.

## The Bids

On a per share basis, KKR's bid was $75 cash, $11 for pay-in-kind preferred stock, and $6 principal amount of pay-in-kind converting debt, which KKR valued at $8.[6] The debt would convert to common stock at the end of 1 year unless the holder decided to retain it. If all debt was converted into common stock, it would represent 25% of the outstanding common stock of RJR Nabisco. The cash portion

---

5. RJR Nabisco had a variety of anti-takeover provisions that could be used to oppose a hostile offer, including a supermajority provision (requiring a two-thirds vote of disinterested shareholders to approve a merger), a poison pill rights plan (which forces an acquiring firm to purchase preferred stock at a substantial premium), and Section 203 of Delaware Law (which prevents a merger within 3 years of acquiring 15% or more of a target firm).

6. Pay-in-kind securities pay dividends and coupons with additional units of the security instead of cash.

of the bid would be financed by $1.5 billion in equity, $3.5 billion in subordinated debt, and $12.4 billion in bank debt. KKR also planned on assuming the $5.2 billion of preexisting debt.

On a per share basis, the Management Group's bid was $90 cash, $6 of pay-in-kind preferred stock, and $4 of convertible preferred stock. The convertible preferred stock, as a class, could be converted into about 15% of the surviving company's equity, but it was callable by the company at any time for the face value and accumulated dividends. The cash portion of the bid would be financed by $2.5 billion in equity, $3 billion in subordinated debt, and $15 billion in bank debt. Like KKR, the Management Group planned on assuming the $5.2 billion of outstanding debt.

The First Boston group's offer involved the purchase of RJR Nabisco's tobacco business by the First Boston group and the sale of the food businesses. The food businesses would be sold for a $13 billion installment note before December 31, 1988, and a right to 80% of the net proceeds of the subsequent sale of the food businesses in excess of the installment note. RJR Nabisco shareholders would receive the proceeds from the sale of the food businesses. First Boston would purchase the tobacco business for $15.75 billion, plus warrants (valued at $2–3 per RJR Nabisco share) to acquire up to 20% of the equity of the tobacco business. On a per share basis, RJR Nabisco shareholders would receive a cash payment ranging from $98 to $110, securities valued at $5, and warrants worth $2–3. Unlike the bids by KKR and the Management Group, the First Boston proposal did not include information about its financing.

**EXHIBIT 1**

Composition of the Special Committee of the RJR Nabisco Board of Directors to Consider Offers for the Company

| Committee Member | Biographical Sketch | Common Stock Ownership (shares) |
|---|---|---|
| Charles E. Hugel, Chairman | Age 60; chairman of RJR Nabisco; president and chief executive officer of Combustion Engineering, Inc. | 750 |
| John D. Macomber, Vice Chairman | Age 60; chairman of Lasertechnics; retired chairman and chief executive officer of Celanese Corporation | 16,425 |
| Martin S. Davis | Age 61; chairman and chief executive officer of Gulf and Western, Inc. | 1,000 |
| William S. Anderson | Age 69; retired chairman and chief executive officer of the executive committee of NCR Corporation | 1,500 |
| Albert L. Butler, Jr. | Age 70; president of Arista Company; chairman of RJR Nabisco's organization, compensation, and nominating committee | 9,465 |

| Investment Bankers | Legal Counsel |
|---|---|
| Dillon, Read & Co. | Skadden, Arps, Slate, Meagher and Flom |
| Lazard Frères, Inc. | Young, Conaway, Stargatt and Taylor |

**EXHIBIT 2**
Condensed Operating and Stockholder Information, 1982–1987 (millions of dollars except per share data)

|  | 1982 | 1983 | 1984 | 1985 | 1986 | 1987 |
|---|---|---|---|---|---|---|
| Revenues | $7,323 | $7,565 | $8,200 | $11,622 | $15,102 | $15,766 |
| Operating income | 1,142 | 1,205 | 1,412 | 1,949 | 2,340 | 2,304 |
| Interest and debt expense | 180 | 177 | 166 | 337 | 565 | 489 |
| Income before income taxes | 1,012 | 1,110 | 1,353 | 1,663 | 1,782 | 1,816 |
| Income from continuing operations | 548 | 626 | 747 | 917 | 1,025 | 1,081 |
| Income from discontinued operations[a] | 322 | 255 | 463 | 84 | 39 | 128 |
| Net income | $ 870 | $ 881 | $1,210 | $ 1,001 | $ 1,064 | $ 1,209 |
| Earnings per share | $ 3.13 | $ 2.90 | $ 4.11 | $ 3.60 | $ 3.83 | $ 4.70 |
| Dividends per share | 1.14 | 1.22 | 1.30 | 1.41 | 1.51 | 1.76 |
| Closing stock price[b] | 20.40 | 24.30 | 28.80 | 31.38 | 49.25 | 45.00 |
| Price-earnings ratio[b] | 6.5 | 8.38 | 7.01 | 8.72 | 12.86 | 9.57 |
| Numbers of shares (millions)[b,c] | 281.5 | 283.2 | 258.4 | 250.6 | 250.4 | 247.4 |
| Beta[d] | .80 | .70 | .74 | 1.21 | 1.24 | .67 |

*Sources:* Company reports and casewriter's estimates.

a. Divestitures and acquisitions for 1982–1987 are as follows:

    1982  Heublein acquired for $1.36 billion.
    1983  Energy division sold for after-tax gain of $275 million.
    1984  Divestiture of transportation division completed by spinning off common stock to Sea-Land Corp. (transportation accounted for as a discontinued operation since 1983).
    1985  Nabisco Brands acquired at a total cost of $4.9 billion.
    1986  Kentucky Fried Chicken sold at after-tax loss of $39 million.
    1987  Heublein sold for after-tax gain of $215 million.

b. Year-end.

c. Figures include a 2.5-for-1 stock split effective May 17, 1985.

d. Calculated by ordinary least-squares regression using daily stock price data.

**EXHIBIT 3**
Consolidated Balance Sheets, 1986–1987 (millions of dollars)

| | 1986 | 1987 |
|---|---|---|
| Cash | $ 827 | $ 1,088 |
| Net receivables | 1,675 | 1,745 |
| Inventories | 2,620 | 2,678 |
| Other current assets | 273 | 329 |
| Property, plant, and equipment, net | 5,343 | 5,847 |
| Goodwill and other intangibles | 4,603 | 4,525 |
| Net assets of discontinued operations | 716 | — |
| Other assets | 644 | 649 |
| Total assets | $16,701 | $16,861 |
| | | |
| Notes payable | $ 518 | $ 442 |
| Accounts payable | 2,923 | 3,187 |
| Current portion of long-term debt | 423 | 162 |
| Income taxes payable | 202 | 332 |
| Current liabilities | 4,066 | 4,123 |
| Long-term debt | 4,833 | 3,884 |
| Deferred income taxes | 751 | 846 |
| Redeemable preferred stock | 291 | 173 |
| Other liabilities | 1,448 | 1,797 |
| Total liabilities | 11,389 | 10,823 |
| Stockholders' equity | 5,312 | 6,038 |
| Total liabilities and net worth | $16,701 | $16,861 |

*Source:* Company reports.

**EXHIBIT 4**
Financial Summary by Business Segment, 1982–1987 (millions of dollars)

|  | 1982 | 1983 | 1984 | 1985 | 1986 | 1987 |
|---|---|---|---|---|---|---|
| *Tobacco* | | | | | | |
| Sales | $4,822 | $4,807 | $5,178 | $5,422 | $5,866 | $ 6,346 |
| Operating profit | 1,187 | 1,150 | 1,305 | 1,483 | 1,659 | 1,821 |
| Identifiable assets | 3,219 | 3,378 | 3,812 | 4,496 | 4,822 | 5,208 |
| Depreciation | 81 | 78 | 108 | 146 | 205 | 244 |
| Capital expenditures | 238 | 383 | 527 | 647 | 613 | 433 |
| Restructuring expense | — | — | — | — | ⌐ | (261) |
| Operating profit/identifiable assets | 36.9% | 34.0% | 34.2% | 33.0% | 34.0% | 35.0% |
| *Food Products* | | | | | | |
| Sales | $2,501 | $2,758 | $3,022 | $6,200 | $9,236 | $ 9,420 |
| Operating profit | 21 | 129 | 181 | 549 | 820 | 915 |
| Identifiable assets | 1,710 | 1,761 | 2,211 | 9,598 | 9,822 | 10,117 |
| Depreciation | 51 | 56 | 68 | 195 | 376 | 380 |
| Capital expenditures | 84 | 94 | 86 | 279 | 344 | 445 |
| Restructuring expense | — | — | — | — | — | 18 |
| Operating profit/Identifiable assets | 1.2% | 7.3% | 8.2% | 6.0% | 8.0% | 9.0% |
| *Spirits and Wines* | | | | | | |
| Sales | $ 392 | $ 746 | $ 703 | $ 766 | $ 876 | — |
| Operating profit | 53 | 113 | 122 | 131 | 138 | — |
| Identifiable assets | 1,084 | 740 | 815 | 895 | 991 | — |
| Depreciation | 14 | 24 | 22 | 24 | 30 | — |
| Capital expenditures | 11 | 13 | 13 | 26 | 25 | — |
| Restructuring expense | — | — | — | — | — | — |
| Operating profit/Identifiable assets | 4.9% | 15.3% | 15.0% | 14.6% | 14.0% | — |
| *Other (Including Corporate)*[a] | | | | | | |
| Sales | — | — | — | — | — | — |
| Operating profit (loss) | $ (66) | $ (74) | $ (74) | $ (83) | $ (139) | $ (182) |
| Identifiable assets | 3,106 | 3,197 | 2,257 | 1,684 | 1,319 | 1,536 |
| Depreciation | 11 | 16 | 16 | 13 | 24 | 28 |
| Capital expenditures | 16 | 15 | 29 | 20 | 65 | 58 |
| Restructuring expense | — | — | — | — | — | (7) |
| Operating profit/Identifiable assets | −2.1% | −2.3% | −3.3% | −5.0% | −10.5% | −11.9% |

*Source:* Company reports.

a. Includes earnings on cash and short-term investments and miscellaneous discontinued operations.

**EXHIBIT 5**

Cash Flow Projections under Pre-Bid Strategy, 1988–1998 (millions of dollars)

| | 1988 | 1989 | 1990 | 1991 | 1992 | 1993 | 1994 | 1995 | 1996 | 1997 | 1998 |
|---|---|---|---|---|---|---|---|---|---|---|---|
| Tobacco sales . . . . . . . | $ 7,061 | $ 7,650 | $ 8,293 | $ 8,893 | $ 9,731 | $10,540 | $11,418 | $12,368 | $13,397 | $14,514 | $15,723 |
| Food sales . . . . . . . | 9,889 | 10,438 | 11,383 | 12,092 | 12,847 | 13,651 | 14,507 | 15,420 | 16,393 | 17,428 | 18,533 |
| Total . . . . . | 16,950 | 18,088 | 19,676 | 21,075 | 22,578 | 24,191 | 25,925 | 27,788 | 29,790 | 31,942 | 34,256 |
| Operating income (expense) | | | | | | | | | | | |
| Tobacco . . . . . | 1,924 | 2,022 | 2,360 | 2,786 | 3,071 | 3,386 | 3,733 | 4,115 | 4,534 | 4,998 | 5,508 |
| Food . . . . . | 1,079 | 1,163 | 1,255 | 1,348 | 1,459 | 1,581 | 1,713 | 1,855 | 2,011 | 2,178 | 2,361 |
| Corporate . . . . . | (350) | (287) | (279) | (296) | (314) | (333) | (353) | (374) | (396) | (420) | (445) |
| Total . . . . . | 2,653 | 2,898 | 3,336 | 3,838 | 4,216 | 4,634 | 5,093 | 5,596 | 6,149 | 6,756 | 7,424 |
| Interest expense . . . . . | 551 | 582 | 662 | 693 | 690 | 658 | 594 | 458 | 410 | 259 | −21 |
| Net income . . . . . | 1,360 | 1,498 | 1,730 | 2,023 | 2,259 | 2,536 | 2,858 | 3,251 | 3,625 | 4,094 | 4,625 |
| Depreciation, amortization, deferred taxes . . . . . | 730 | 807 | 791 | 819 | 849 | 866 | 867 | 867 | 867 | 867 | 861 |
| Capital expenditures . . . . . | 1,142 | 1,708 | 1,462 | 1,345 | 930 | 738 | 735 | 735 | 735 | 735 | 735 |
| Change in working capital . . . . . | – | 80 | 111 | 98 | 105 | 113 | 121 | 130 | 140 | 151 | 162 |
| Cash flow available for capital payments[a] . . . . . | – | $ 517 | $ 948 | $ 1,399 | $ 2,073 | $ 2,551 | $ 2,869 | $ 3,253 | $ 3,617 | $ 4,075 | $ 4,589 |

a. Cash flow available for capital payments = Net income + Depreciation, amortization, deferred taxes − Capital expenditures − Change in working capital.

**EXHIBIT 6**
Cash Flow and Capital Structure Projections under the Management Group Strategy, 1989–1998 (millions of dollars)

| | 1989 | 1990 | 1991 | 1992 | 1993 | 1994 | 1995 | 1996 | 1997 | 1998 |
|---|---|---|---|---|---|---|---|---|---|---|
| *Operating Information* | | | | | | | | | | |
| Sales | $ 7,650 | $ 8,293 | $8,983 | $9,731 | $10,540 | $11,418 | $12,368 | $13,397 | $14,514 | $15,723 |
| Operating income | 1,917 | 2,385 | 2,814 | 3,266 | 3,589 | 3,945 | 4,337 | 4,768 | 5,243 | 5,766 |
| Interest expense | 2,792 | 1,353 | 1,286 | 1,183 | 1,037 | 850 | 624 | 351 | 0 | 0 |
| Amortization[a] | 388 | 388 | 388 | 388 | 388 | 388 | 388 | 388 | 388 | 388 |
| After-tax income | (965) | 293 | 621 | 987 | 1,297 | 1,655 | 2,063 | 2,527 | 3,073 | 3,418 |
| Depreciation, amortization, deferred taxes | 777 | 725 | 726 | 735 | 749 | 754 | 758 | 763 | 769 | 774 |
| Capital expenditures | 432 | 381 | 380 | 389 | 396 | 402 | 412 | 422 | 432 | 442 |
| Change in working capital | 41 | 45 | 48 | 52 | 57 | 61 | 67 | 72 | 78 | 85 |
| Net proceeds from asset sales | 12,680 | 0 | 0 | 0 | 0 | 0 | 0 | 0 | 0 | 0 |
| Cash flow available for capital payments[b] | $12,018 | $ 593 | $ 919 | $1,282 | $ 1,594 | $ 1,946 | $ 2,344 | $ 2,797 | $ 3,332 | $ 3,666 |
| *Capital Structure* | | | | | | | | | | |
| Principal payments | | | | | | | | | | |
| Assumed debt | $ 310 | $ 375 | $ 721 | $ 816 | $ 400 | $ 728 | $ 1,854 | $ 0 | $ 0 | $ 0 |
| Bank debt | 11,708 | 218 | 198 | 466 | 1,194 | 1,217 | 0 | 0 | 0 | 0 |
| Subordinated debt | 0 | 0 | 0 | 0 | 0 | 0 | 490 | 2,510 | 3,332 | 3,327 |
| Preferred stock | 0 | 0 | 0 | 0 | 0 | 0 | 0 | 287 | 0 | 339 |
| Convertible preferred stock | 0 | 0 | 0 | 0 | 0 | 0 | 0 | 0 | 0 | 0 |
| Total | 12,018 | 593 | 919 | 1,282 | 1,594 | 1,946 | 2,344 | 2,797 | 3,332 | 3,666 |
| Year-end book values | | | | | | | | | | |
| Assumed debt | 4,894 | 4,519 | 3,798 | 2,982 | 2,582 | 1,854 | 0 | 0 | 0 | 0 |
| Bank debt | 3,292 | 3,075 | 2,877 | 2,411 | 1,217 | 0 | 0 | 0 | 0 | 0 |
| Subordinated debt | 3,000 | 3,000 | 3,000 | 3,000 | 3,000 | 3,000 | 2,510 | 0 | 0 | 0 |
| Total | 11,186 | 10,594 | 9,675 | 8,393 | 6,799 | 4,854 | 2,510 | 0 | 0 | 0 |
| Preferred stock | 1,632 | 1,938 | 2,303 | 2,736 | 3,250 | 3,861 | 4,587 | 5,162 | 2,801 | 0 |
| Convertible preferred stock | 1,035 | 1,229 | 1,460 | 1,735 | 2,061 | 2,448 | 2,909 | 3,455 | 4,105 | 4,538 |
| Common stock | 1,535 | 1,828 | 2,449 | 3,436 | 4,733 | 6,388 | 8,451 | 10,978 | 14,051 | 17,469 |
| Total | $ 4,202 | $ 4,995 | $6,212 | $7,907 | $10,044 | $12,697 | $15,947 | $19,595 | $20,957 | $22,007 |

*Note:* Figures may not add exactly because of rounding.

a. The amortization of goodwill of $338 million per year is from the proposed acquisition of RJR Nabisco at $22.9 billion, which had the book value of $7.4 billion at the end of 1988. The difference between the purchase price and book value is amortized over 40 years using the straight-line method.

b. Cash flow available for capital payments = Net income + depreciation, amortization, deferred taxes – Capital expenditures – Change in working capital + Net proceeds from asset sales.

**EXHIBIT 7**

Cash Flow and Capital Structure Projections under KKR's Strategy, 1989–1998 (millions of dollars)

| | 1989 | 1990 | 1991 | 1992 | 1993 | 1994 | 1995 | 1996 | 1997 | 1998 |
|---|---|---|---|---|---|---|---|---|---|---|
| *Operating Information* | | | | | | | | | | |
| Tobacco sales | $ 7,650 | $ 8,293 | $ 8,983 | $ 9,731 | $10,540 | $11,418 | $12,368 | $13,397 | $14,514 | $15,723 |
| Food sales | 8,540 | 6,930 | 7,485 | 8,084 | 8,730 | 9,428 | 10,183 | 10,997 | 11,877 | 12,827 |
| Total | 16,190 | 15,223 | 16,468 | 17,815 | 19,270 | 20,846 | 22,551 | 24,394 | 26,391 | 28,550 |
| Operating income (expense) | | | | | | | | | | |
| Tobacco | 2,022 | 2,360 | 2,786 | 3,071 | 3,386 | 3,733 | 4,115 | 4,534 | 4,998 | 5,508 |
| Food | 1,060 | 1,026 | 1,191 | 1,245 | 1,307 | 1,367 | 1,430 | 1,494 | 1,561 | 1,630 |
| Corporate | (219) | (158) | (167) | (176) | (185) | (194) | (203) | (213) | (224) | (235) |
| Total | 2,862 | 3,228 | 3,811 | 4,140 | 4,508 | 4,906 | 5,341 | 5,815 | 6,335 | 6,902 |
| Interest expense | 2,754 | 2,341 | 1,997 | 1,888 | 1,321 | 1,088 | 806 | 487 | 21 | 0 |
| Amortization[a] | 388 | 388 | 388 | 388 | 388 | 388 | 388 | 388 | 388 | 388 |
| After-tax income | (281) | 233 | 845 | 1,134 | 1,751 | 2,168 | 2,641 | 3,164 | 3,814 | 4,203 |
| Depreciation, amortization, deferred taxes | 1,159 | 991 | 899 | 907 | 920 | 924 | 928 | 933 | 939 | 945 |
| Capital expenditures | 774 | 556 | 555 | 572 | 586 | 598 | 618 | 638 | 658 | 678 |
| Change in working capital | 79 | 84 | 87 | 94 | 102 | 110 | 119 | 129 | 140 | 151 |
| Noncash interest expense | 206 | 237 | 312 | 366 | 0 | 0 | 0 | 0 | 0 | 0 |
| Net proceeds from asset sales | 3,500 | 2,700 | 0 | 0 | 0 | 0 | 0 | 0 | 0 | 0 |
| Cash flow available for capital payments[b] | $ 3,732 | $ 3,521 | $ 1,414 | $ 1,740 | $ 1,983 | $ 2,383 | $ 2,832 | $ 3,330 | $ 3,956 | $ 4,319 |

*(continued)*

**EXHIBIT 7** (*concluded*)

| | 1989 | 1990 | 1991 | 1992 | 1993 | 1994 | 1995 | 1996 | 1997 | 1998 |
|---|---|---|---|---|---|---|---|---|---|---|
| *Capital Structure* | | | | | | | | | | |
| Principal payments | | | | | | | | | | |
| Assumed debt | $ 310 | $ 375 | $ 721 | $ 816 | $ 400 | $ 400 | $ 2,182 | $ 0 | $ 0 | $ 0 |
| Bank debt | 3,422 | 3,146 | 693 | 924 | 1,583 | 1,983 | 629 | 0 | 0 | 0 |
| Subordinated debt | 0 | 0 | 0 | 0 | 0 | 0 | 21 | 3,330 | 149 | 0 |
| Preferred stock | 0 | 0 | 0 | 0 | 0 | 0 | 0 | 0 | 3,806 | 4,319 |
| Total | 3,732 | 3,521 | 1,414 | 1,740 | 1,983 | 2,383 | 2,832 | 3,330 | 3,956 | 4,319 |
| Year-end book values | | | | | | | | | | |
| Assumed debt | 4,894 | 4,519 | 3,798 | 2,982 | 2,582 | 2,182 | 0 | 0 | 0 | 0 |
| Bank debt | 8,958 | 5,812 | 5,119 | 4,195 | 2,612 | 629 | 0 | 0 | 0 | 0 |
| Subordinated debt | 3,500 | 3,500 | 3,500 | 3,500 | 3,500 | 3,500 | 3,470 | 149 | 0 | 0 |
| Converting debt[c] | 1,580 | 1,817 | 2,129 | 2,495 | 0 | 0 | 0 | 0 | 0 | 0 |
| Total | 18,932 | 15,648 | 14,546 | 13,172 | 8,694 | 6,311 | 3,470 | 149 | 0 | 0 |
| Preferred stock | 2,896 | 3,331 | 3,958 | 4,702 | 5,586 | 6,636 | 7,883 | 9,365 | 7,320 | 4,377 |
| Common stock | 1,219 | 1,452 | 2,297 | 3,430 | 7,676 | 9,844 | 12,485 | 15,648 | 19,463 | 23,666 |
| Total | $ 4,115 | $ 4,783 | $ 6,255 | $ 8,132 | $13,262 | $16,480 | $20,368 | $25,013 | $26,783 | $28,043 |

*Note:* Figures may not add exactly because of rounding.

a. The amortization of goodwill of $338 million per year is from the proposed acquisition of RJR Nabisco at $22.9 billion, which had the book value of $7.4 billion at the end of 1988. The difference between the purchase price and the book value is amortized over 40 years using the straight-line method.

b. Cash flow available for capital payments = Net income + Depreciation, amortization, deferred taxes − Capital expenditures − Change in working capital + Noncash interest expense + Net proceeds from asset sales.

c. Assumes converting to equity in 1993.

# Philip Morris Companies and Kraft, Inc.

John M. Richman, the chairman and chief executive officer of Kraft, Inc., concluded his October 23, 1988, letter to shareholders as follows:

> We deeply regret the dislocation and hardships that the [restructuring] plan we contemplate will cause, and we will seek to ameliorate these hardships as much as possible. We know that our shareholders, employees, customers, suppliers and communities recognize that today's situation is not of our making. Rather it is the product of current era investment policies and financial attitudes that favor short-term financial gratification over steady, long-term growth and the need to provide a sound economy for future generations.
>
> It will take several years, but with the history and traditions of Kraft and the dedication of Kraft people, we are confident that we will rebuild Kraft to the leading position it occupies today.

The letter announced a radical restructuring of Kraft in response to a hostile tender offer by Philip Morris Companies: $90 per share in cash for all of Kraft's outstanding common stock. The offer had been announced just five days earlier, on October 18, 1988.

## Kraft, Inc.

In 1987, Kraft was known for such brand names as Miracle Whip, Seven Seas, and Kraft salad dressings; Kraft mayonnaise; Velveeta cheese; Parkay and Chiffon margarines; Lender's Bagels; and Breyers ice cream. Net sales from continuing operations were $9.9 billion in 1987, an increase of 27% over 1986. Net income from continuing operations rose 11%, to $435 million. Exhibit 1 presents operating and stockholder information for Kraft from 1982 through 1987. Exhibit 2 presents balance sheet information for 1986 and 1987.

Kraft's strategy was focused on food. Its 1987 annual report stated:

> The food industry offers such diverse and rewarding opportunities that we see no purpose in running the risk of diluting our efforts or our focus with other lines of business.

This all-food strategy was in sharp contrast to its earlier diversification program. Most of the diversification occurred when Mr. Richman engineered the September 1980 merger between Kraft and Dart Industries, a $2.4 billion consumer products manufacturer. Mr. Richman, who had been promoted to chairman and CEO less than 1 year before the merger, noted that the merger brought ''diversification in one fell swoop to Kraft.'' Dart's products included Tupperware containers, Duracell batteries, and West Bend appliances. The merger was accomplished by exchanging one share of the merged company, Dart & Kraft, for each outstanding share of the two preexisting companies. Dart & Kraft was the twenty-seventh-largest company in the United States at the time of the merger. Six months later, in March 1981, Dart & Kraft acquired for $460 million Hobart Corporation, the manufacturer of KitchenAid and other food-related equipment.

Mr. Richman reversed direction and began pursuing the all-food strategy in 1986. Kraft spun off most of its nonfood businesses acquired in the Dart & Kraft merger into Premark International, Inc., on October 31, 1986. Each shareholder of Dart & Kraft received one share of Kraft common stock and a quarter share of Premark. Kraft, with sales of about $9.9 billion after the spin-off, retained its food businesses and Duracell batteries. Premark's share of Dart & Kraft included Tupperware and Hobart food service equipment, with combined sales of $1.8 billion.[1]

Kraft sold its last nonfood asset, Duracell, to Kohlberg, Kravis, Roberts & Co., a leveraged buyout firm, for $1.8 billion in June 1988. According to Kraft's 1987 annual report, the proceeds of the sale were to be used to repurchase shares and to repay debt obligations. In October 1987, Kraft authorized the repurchase of 10 million shares, and 6 million were repurchased under the authorization by year-end.

In 1987, Kraft was organized into three business segments: U.S. Consumer Food, U.S. Commercial Food, and International Food. In 1987, U.S. Consumer Food had sales of $4.5 billion and an operating profit of $593 million. U.S. Commercial Food, which included Kraft Foodservice, the second-largest U.S. food service distributor, had sales of $3 billion and an operating profit of $86.4 million. International Food had sales of $2.3 billion and an operating profit of $229.8 million. Exhibit 3 presents a financial summary of Kraft by business segment.

---

1. KitchenAid had been sold in February 1986 for $150 million.

## The Philip Morris $90-per-Share Tender Offer

On the evening of October 18, 1988, Philip Morris offered to purchase all Kraft common stock at $90 per share in cash. The offer represented a 50% premium over the $60.125 closing price on October 18. At $11 billion in total value the bid, if successful, would have been the second-largest acquisition ever completed, exceeded only by Chevron Corporation's $13.3 billion acquisition of Gulf Oil Corporation in 1984.[2]

Most Philip Morris sales and profits came from its Marlboro, Benson & Hedges, and Virginia Slims cigarettes. The company's tobacco sales increased by 15%, to $14.6 billion, in 1987. Philip Morris increased its domestic share of the cigarette market to 38% in 1987, from 37% in 1986, and 1987 operating profits were $3.3 billion. Nevertheless, consumption of cigarettes in the United States had been declining from its 1981 peak of 640 billion cigarettes. Estimated U.S. consumption for 1988 was 563 billion cigarettes. Increases in exports offset the decline in U.S. consumption, as new markets were entered, especially Japan and Taiwan. Overall, cigarette exports were predicted to increase by 15%, to 115 billion cigarettes in 1988.

Philip Morris had been pursuing a strategy of diversifying out of the tobacco business since 1969, when it acquired 53% of the Miller Brewing Company's common shares, the remainder of which it acquired in 1970. With brands like Miller, Lite, and Matilda Bay Wine Coolers, the brewing division generated sales of $3.1 billion in 1987. Philip Morris also purchased Seven-Up Company in May 1978 for $520 million. Its largest food acquisition by far was General Foods, which Philip Morris purchased in 1985 for $5.6 billion. Like Kraft, General Foods was based on brand-name products such as Maxwell House coffee, Birds Eye frozen foods, Jell-O, Oscar Mayer meats, Ronzoni pasta, and Post cereals. It had 1987 sales of $10 billion.

Philip Morris's acquisitions had mixed results. See Exhibit 4 for operating and stockholder information from 1982 through 1987. Exhibit 5 presents balance sheet information for 1986 and 1987. Exhibit 6 presents the consolidated changes in financial position, and Exhibit 7 reports line-of-business information.

Philip Morris sold its Seven-Up operations in 1986 for about book value after a $50 million write-off in 1985. General Foods' operating profit declined from $624 million in 1986 to $605 million in 1987. The 1987 operating profit represented a 9.3% return on Philip Morris's $6.5 billion investment in the food industry, including additional postacquisition investments of $868 million. Speculation was that Philip Morris might use Kraft's management team to revitalize General Foods, which had been without a chief executive officer since July 1988, when Philip L. Smith left to become chairman of Pillsbury.[3] Smith, a 22-year veteran

---

2. Kraft had 119,285,155 shares outstanding and outstanding employee stock options on 2,396,808 shares. The total number of Kraft shares purchased under the offer was therefore 121,681,963.

3. The combination also would have increased leverage with grocery stores and advertisers. In 1987, Philip Morris spent $1.5 billion and Kraft $400 million on advertising.

of General Foods, had been president and chief operating officer before its merger with Philip Morris.

The acquisition of Kraft would have made Philip Morris the world's largest food company, and it would have been a major step in the firm's strategy of reducing its dependence on tobacco and moving into the food business. As Hamish Maxwell, the chairman and CEO of Philip Morris, said in his October 21, 1988, letter to John Richman.

> Our goal is to have Kraft combine with Philip Morris to create the leading international food company. . . . Our intention is to keep Kraft's present businesses intact and for the company to be managed by Kraft executives, using your present headquarters and facilities.

Exhibit 8 contains excerpts from the letters between the two companies throughout the takeover contest.

Philip Morris proposed to finance the acquisition with $1.5 billion in excess cash and its available bank credit lines of up to $12 billion.

## Kraft's Response

On October 23, 1988, Kraft's board of directors rejected the Philip Morris bid:

> We strongly believe the $90 takeover bid . . . undervalues Kraft, for these important reasons: first, after careful analysis, our investment banker, Goldman, Sachs & Co., has advised us that the bid is inadequate; and second, our stock has been trading above the $90 offer, a clear signal that investors see the bid as low.

Kraft's response occurred when the food industry was undergoing a major restructuring and revaluation. Grand Metropolitan PLC began a hostile tender offer for Pillsbury on October 4, 1988. Grand Met was a diversified British company that brewed and distributed beer, ale, and lager; produced and distributed alcoholic beverages; and owned and operated pubs and restaurants. Pillsbury was a diversified food and restaurant company, with popular brands such as Pillsbury Doughboy bakery items, Green Giant vegetables, and Häagen-Dazs ice cream in its food business and Burger King in its restaurant group. Like Kraft, Pillsbury had just completed a major restructuring that focused the company on the food business. The $5.2 billion Grand Met bid was a 53% premium over the previous market price—about 25 times Pillsbury's net earnings and about four times the book value of common equity.[4] Pillsbury opposed the bid, and its outcome was uncertain.

The developments at RJR Nabisco were more startling. Management, in partnership with the investment banking firm of Shearson Lehman Hutton, had proposed a $17 billion leveraged buyout of RJR Nabisco on October 20, 1988. Like Philip Morris, RJR Nabisco was a tobacco and food company with brand names such as Winston and Salem cigarettes, Oreo cookies, Ritz crackers, Planters nuts, Life-Savers candies, Royal gelatin, and Del Monte fruit and vegetables. At $75 per share, the buyout offer was a 34% premium over the previous market price of

---

4. Pillsbury's 1988 net earnings per share were $2.45, excluding unusual items, and $.81, including unusual items. The difference was due to a restructuring charge of $1.64 per share. Its 1987 net earnings per share were $2.24, excluding unusual items, and $2.10, including unusual items.

RJR Nabisco, $55.875. The $75 offer was about 16 times RJR Nabisco's 1987 earnings per share of $4.70 and about three times the book value of common equity. Analysts speculated that a higher offer for RJR Nabisco was likely: its stock closed above the offer price.

Taken together, the Philip Morris bid for Kraft, Grand Metropolitan's bid for Pillsbury, and the RJR Nabisco leveraged buyout attempt by its management involved about $34 billion—an amount unprecedented in the history of the industry. Exhibit 9 examines this history, with statistics on mergers and acquisitions for food and beverage firms as well as a listing of transactions of more than $1 billion. Exhibit 10 contains historical stock prices and return-on-equity information for the food and tobacco industries.

Kraft proposed a restructuring plan as an alternative to the Philip Morris tender offer. For each share of common stock, shareholders would receive a cash dividend of $84 and a high-yield debt valued at $14, and they would retain their now highly leveraged equity interest. Kraft valued the postrestructuring stock at $12 per share and the total restructuring package at $110 per share.

Under the plan Kraft would sell some businesses for cash proceeds of about $2.1 billion after taxes. The businesses to be sold represented 45% of estimated 1988 revenues and 19% of estimated 1988 operating profits. Kraft would also reduce operating expenses. It would finance the $10.2 billion in dividend payments to shareholders with $6.8 billion in bank borrowings at a 12% annual interest rate and the $3 billion in debt with rates ranging from 12.5% to 14.75%. The $2.1 billion from asset sales would be used to pay down the bank debt.

The company planned to retain $904 million of existing debt at an average annual interest rate of 8.65%.

The debt received by shareholders would accrue interest at a 15.25% annual rate (paid semiannually), with no cash payments in the first 5 years. Interest would be paid in cash at the 15.25% semiannual rate after the fifth year. Exhibit 11 presents pre-bid sales and profit forecasts for Kraft through 1989. Exhibit 12 presents earnings and cash flow forecasts for the restructuring plan proposed by Kraft's management.

## The Stock Market Response

The price of Kraft common stock rose $10 per share, to $102, in response to the restructuring announcement. Philip Morris criticized the restructuring plan and reiterated its offer to negotiate with Kraft, which responded that "if Philip Morris or another company truly wishes to negotiate with Kraft, a simple phone call proposing a price of more than $110 is all that is necessary." Philip Morris did not increase its bid.

Uncertainty about the market value of food assets grew as Kohlberg, Kravis, Roberts entered the bidding for RJR Nabisco, with a $20.6 billion offer on October 24, 1988.

On Thursday, October 27, Kraft's common stock closed at $94.50. On Friday, October 28, Kraft's stock rose $2, closing at $96.50. Exhibit 13 contains the closing stock prices for Kraft and Philip Morris throughout the takeover contest.

**EXHIBIT 1**

Condensed Operating and Stockholder Information for Kraft, 1982–1987 (millions of dollars except per share data)

| | 1982 | 1983 | 1984 | 1985 | 1986 | 1987 |
|---|---|---|---|---|---|---|
| Revenues | $7,041 | $6,660 | $6,831 | $7,065 | $7,780 | $9,876 |
| Cost of goods sold[a] | 5,350 | 4,928 | 4,969 | 4,963 | 5,393 | 6,912 |
| Depreciation | 103 | 80 | 74 | 74 | 79 | 103 |
| Delivery, sales, and administrative expenses | 1,183 | 1,157 | 1,238 | 1,391 | 1,620 | 2,068 |
| Interest, net | 24 | (8) | 22 | 26 | 31 | 91 |
| Other income (expense)[b] | (38) | 23 | 43 | 37 | 37 | 86 |
| Income from continuing operations before taxes | 343 | 526 | 571 | 648 | 694 | 788 |
| Income taxes | 164 | 225 | 252 | 286 | 300 | 353 |
| Income from continuing operations | 179 | 301 | 319 | 362 | 394 | 435 |
| Income from discontinued operations[c] | 171 | 134 | 137 | 104 | 19 | 54 |
| Net income | $ 350 | $ 435 | $ 456 | $ 466 | $ 413 | $ 489 |
| Earnings per share | $ 2.13 | $ 2.65 | $ 3.17 | $ 3.24 | $ 3.06 | $ 3.73 |
| Dividends per share | 1.20 | 1.28 | 1.38 | 1.52 | 1.68 | 1.84 |
| Closing stock price[d,e] | 22.83 | 22.21 | 28.04 | 43.38 | 49.38 | 48.25 |
| Price-earnings ratio[e] | 11 | 8 | 9 | 13 | 16 | 13 |
| Number of shares (millions)[e] | 164 | 164 | 144 | 144 | 135 | 131 |
| Beta[f] | .72 | .55 | .69 | 1.12 | 1.18 | .74 |

*Sources:* Company reports and casewriter's estimates.

a. Cost of goods sold does not include annual depreciation.

b. Includes the cumulative effect of a change in method of accounting for income taxes of $45 million in 1987 and a nonoperating item of −$91 million in 1982.

c. Discontinued operations include Duracell, whose sale was announced in 1987, and the business of Premark International, which was spun off on October 31, 1986. Also included in discontinued operations is a $41 million gain on the sale of KitchenAid in 1986.

d. Adjusted for a 3-for-1 stock split in 1985.

e. Year-end.

f. Calculated by ordinary least-squares regression using daily stock price data.

**EXHIBIT 2**
Consolidated Balance Sheets for Kraft, 1986–1987 (millions of dollars)

|  | 1986 | 1987 |
|---|---|---|
| Cash | $ 321.5 | $ 189.0 |
| Accounts receivable | 637.6 | 763.6 |
| Inventories | 1,061.1 | 1,283.4 |
| Investments and long-term receivables | 236.2 | 178.3 |
| Prepaid and deferred items | 127.5 | 161.5 |
| Property, plant, equipment, net | 1,087.7 | 1,424.2 |
| Intangibles | 419.0 | 888.3 |
| Net assets of discontinued operations | 600.7 | 598.4 |
| Total assets | $4,491.3 | $5,486.7 |
| Accounts payable | $ 492.1 | $ 544.8 |
| Short-term borrowings | 596.4 | 645.9 |
| Accrued compensation | 148.9 | 151.2 |
| Accrued advertising and promotions | 113.7 | 132.8 |
| Other accrued liabilities | 188.4 | 245.4 |
| Accrued income taxes | 335.3 | 399.3 |
| Current portion of long-term debt | 108.5 | 37.2 |
| Current liabilities | 1,983.3 | 2,156.6 |
| Long-term debt | 237.7 | 895.3 |
| Deferred income taxes | 286.4 | 282.7 |
| Other liabilities | 185.9 | 253.7 |
| Total liabilities | 2,693.3 | 3,588.3 |
| Shareholders' equity | 1,798.0 | 1,898.4 |
| Total liabilities and net worth | $4,491.3 | $5,486.7 |

*Source:* Company reports.

**EXHIBIT 3**
Financial Summary for Kraft by Business Segment, 1983–1987 (millions of dollars)

|  | 1983 | 1984 | 1985 | 1986 | 1987 |
|---|---|---|---|---|---|
| *U.S. Consumer Food*[a] | | | | | |
| Sales | $3,718.0 | $3,781.2 | $3,911.3 | $4,016.1 | $4,518.9 |
| Operating profit | 388.1 | 446.0 | 527.3 | 545.9 | 593.3 |
| Identifiable assets | 1,450.9 | 1,615.4 | 1,309.1 | 1,807.6 | 2,509.3 |
| Depreciation | 54.0 | 50.0 | 37.6 | 36.6 | 47.4 |
| Capital expenditures | 58.0 | 71.7 | 63.1 | 93.7 | 151.2 |
| Operating profits/Identifiable assets | 26.75% | 27.61% | 40.28% | 30.20% | 23.64% |
| *U.S. Commercial Food* | | | | | |
| Sales | $1,172.7 | $1,349.3 | $1,421.0 | $1,755.8 | $3,022.0 |
| Operating profit | na | na | 61.7 | 79.5 | 86.4 |
| Identifiable assets | na | na | 291.4 | 558.9 | 914.6 |
| Depreciation | na | na | 7.6 | 8.0 | 15.3 |
| Capital expenditures | na | na | 5.2 | 17.6 | 33.7 |
| Operating profits/Identifiable assets | na | na | 21.17% | 14.22% | 9.45% |

*(continued)*

**EXHIBIT 3** *(concluded)*
Financial Summary for Kraft by Business Segment, 1983–1987 (millions of dollars)

|  | 1983 | 1984 | 1985 | 1986 | 1987 |
|---|---|---|---|---|---|
| *International Food* |  |  |  |  |  |
| Sales . . . . . | $1,769.7 | $1,707.2 | $1,733.0 | $2,007.7 | $2,334.8 |
| Operating profit . . | 165.4 | 169.4 | 145.9 | 182.8 | 229.8 |
| Identifiable assets . | 680.9 | 701.1 | 793.7 | 861.1 | 1,000.5 |
| Depreciation . . . | 19.2 | 18.9 | 20.6 | 27.5 | 34.0 |
| Capital expenditures | 37.3 | 36.2 | 39.2 | 41.7 | 48.3 |
| Operating profits/Identifiable assets . . | 24.29% | 24.16% | 18.38% | 21.23% | 22.97% |
| *Direct Selling*[b] |  |  |  |  |  |
| Sales . . . . . | $ 825.1 | $ 776.9 | – | – | – |
| Operating profit . . | 189.3 | 138.8 | – | – | – |
| Identifiable assets . | 462.7 | 488.0 | – | – | – |
| Depreciation . . . | 36.0 | 28.9 | – | – | – |
| Capital expenditures | 40.7 | 62.8 | – | – | – |
| Operating profits/Identifiable assets . . | 40.91% | 28.44% | – | – | – |
| *Consumer Products*[c] |  |  |  |  |  |
| Sales . . . . . | $1,181.0 | $1,244.8 | $ 962.5 | – | – |
| Operating profit . . | 104.7 | 118.4 | 66.9 | – | – |
| Identifiable assets . | 828.0 | 958.8 | 849.6 | – | – |
| Depreciation . . . | 26.9 | 42.9 | 34.2 | – | – |
| Capital expenditures | 43.0 | 67.9 | 47.4 | – | – |
| Operating profits/Identifiable assets . . | 12.64% | 12.35% | 7.87% | – | – |
| *Commercial Products*[d] |  |  |  |  |  |
| Sales . . . . . | $1,047.5 | $ 899.3 | – | – | – |
| Operating profit . . | 104.8 | 101.0 | – | – | – |
| Identifiable assets . | 727.6 | 556.9 | – | – | – |
| Depreciation . . . | 30.4 | 23.9 | – | – | – |
| Capital expenditures | 25.4 | 28.1 | – | – | – |
| Operating profits/Identifiable assets . . | 14.40% | 18.14% | – | – | – |

*Source:* Company reports.

na = not available.

a. Figures for 1983 and 1984 include both U.S. consumer foods and U.S. commercial foods.

b. Includes Tupperware, which was spun off to Premark International in 1988.

c. Includes Duracell, West Bend, Health Care, and KitchenAid. All assets except Duracell were sold or spun off to Premark International in 1986.

d. Includes Hobart, which was spun off to Premark International in 1986.

**EXHIBIT 4**

Condensed Operating and Stockholder Information for Philip Morris, 1982–1987 (millions of dollars except per share data)

| | 1982 | 1983 | 1984 | 1985[c] | 1986 | 1987 |
|---|---|---|---|---|---|---|
| Revenues | $11,586 | $12,976 | $13,814 | $15,964 | $25,409 | $27,695 |
| Cost of goods sold[a] | 5,046 | 5,028 | 5,170 | 5,926 | 10,495 | 10,664 |
| Excise taxes | 2,615 | 3,510 | 3,676 | 3,815 | 4,728 | 5,416 |
| Depreciation and amortization | 281 | 327 | 375 | 424 | 655 | 704 |
| Selling, administrative, and research expenses[b] | 2,125 | 2,377 | 2,467 | 3,244 | 6,061 | 7,004 |
| Equity in net earnings of unconsolidated subsidiaries | 71 | 83 | 54 | 82 | 111 | 126 |
| Interest | 246 | 230 | 273 | 308 | 770 | 685 |
| Other expense | 44 | – | 300 | – | – | – |
| Income before taxes | 1,300 | 1,587 | 1,607 | 2,329 | 2,811 | 3,348 |
| Income taxes | 518 | 681 | 718 | 1,074 | 1,333 | 1,506 |
| Net income | $ 782 | $ 906 | $ 889 | $ 1,255 | $ 1,478 | $ 1,842 |
| Earnings per share | $ 3.11 | $ 3.58 | $ 3.62 | $ 5.24 | $ 6.20 | $ 7.75 |
| Dividends per share | 1.20 | 1.45 | 1.70 | 2.00 | 2.48 | 3.15 |
| Closing stock price[d] | 30 | 35.875 | 40.375 | 44.125 | 71.875 | 85.375 |
| Price-earnings ratio[d] | 9 | 10 | 11 | 8 | 11 | 11 |
| Number of shares (millions)[d] | 252 | 250 | 243 | 239 | 238 | 237 |
| Beta[e] | 1.04 | .77 | .94 | .88 | 1.24 | .88 |

*Sources:* Company reports and casewriter's estimates.

a. Cost of goods sold does not include annual depreciation.

b. Selling, administrative, and research cost includes corporate expenses.

c. General Foods was acquired on November 1, 1985.

d. Year-end.

e. Calculated by ordinary least-squares regression using daily stock price data.

**EXHIBIT 5**
Consolidated Balance Sheets for Philip Morris, 1986–1987 (millions of dollars)

|  | 1986 | 1987 |
|---|---|---|
| Cash | $ 73 | $ 189 |
| Receivables | 1,878 | 2,083 |
| Inventories | 3,836 | 4,154 |
| Other current assets | 127 | 146 |
| Property, plant, equipment, net | 6,237 | 6,582 |
| Investments in unconsolidated subsidiaries and affiliates | 1,067 | 1,244 |
| Goodwill and other intangibles | 3,988 | 4,052 |
| Other assets | 436 | 695 |
| Total assets | $17,642 | $19,145 |
| Notes payable | $ 864 | $ 691 |
| Accounts payable | 813 | 803 |
| Current portion of long-term debt | 103 | 465 |
| Accrued liabilities | 1,967 | 2,277 |
| Income taxes payable | 557 | 727 |
| Dividends payable | 178 | 213 |
| Current liabilities | 4,482 | 5,176 |
| Long-term debt | 5,945 | 5,222 |
| Deferred income taxes | 994 | 1,288 |
| Other liabilities | 566 | 636 |
| Total liabilities | 11,987 | 12,322 |
| Stockholders' equity | 5,655 | 6,823 |
| Total liabilities and net worth | $17,642 | $19,145 |

*Source:* Company reports.

**EXHIBIT 6**

Consolidated Statements of Changes in Financial Position for Philip Morris, 1985–1987 (millions of dollars)

| | 1985 | 1986 | 1987 |
|---|---|---|---|
| *Funds Provided by* | | | |
| Net earnings | $ 1,255 | $ 1,478 | $ 1,842 |
| Depreciation and amortization | 424 | 655 | 704 |
| Deferred income taxes | 159 | 133 | 338 |
| Equity in undistributed net earnings of unconsolidated subsidiaries and affiliates | (63) | (52) | (95) |
| Total funds from operations | 1,775 | 2,214 | 2,789 |
| Increase in accrued liabilities and other payments | 1,467 | 226 | 505 |
| Working capital from sales of operations | 169 | 487 | 20 |
| Currency translation adjustments affecting working capital | 18 | 77 | 139 |
| Other, net | 211 | 210 | |
| Total funds provided | $ 3,640 | $ 3,214 | $ 3,453 |
| *Funds Used for* | | | |
| Increase (decrease) in | | | |
| Cash and receivables | $ 1,005 | $ (2) | $ 321 |
| Inventories | 1,174 | 9 | 318 |
| Other current assets | 74 | 14 | 19 |
| Capital expenditures | 347 | 678 | 718 |
| Dividends declared | 479 | 590 | 749 |
| Increase in property, plant, and equipment from income tax election | – | 508 | – |
| Investment in General Foods Corp. exclusive of $718 million working capital acquired | 4,864 | – | – |
| Other, net | – | – | 301 |
| Total funds used | $ 7,943 | $ 1,797 | $ 2,426 |
| Net funds provided (used) | $(4,303) | $ 1,417 | $ 1,027 |
| *Financing Activities* | | | |
| Increase in current notes payable | $ 149 | $ 289 | $ 189 |
| Long-term debt financing | 4,666 | 1,788 | 492 |
| Reduction of long-term debt | (326) | (3,385) | (1,534) |
| Purchase of treasury stock | (216) | (140) | (200) |
| Issuance of shares | 30 | 31 | 26 |
| Funds (used for) provided from financing activities | $ 4,303 | $(1,417) | $(1,027) |
| Increase (decrease) in working capital | $ 637 | $ (494) | $ (36) |
| Working capital (year-end) | 1,926 | 1,432 | 1,396 |

*Source:* Company reports.

**EXHIBIT 7**
Financial Summary for Philip Morris by Business Segment, 1982–1987 (millions of dollars)

| | 1982 | 1983 | 1984 | 1985 | 1986 | 1987 |
|---|---|---|---|---|---|---|
| *Tobacco* | | | | | | |
| Sales . . . . . . . | $7,821.8 | $9.094.9 | $9,802.0 | $10,539.0 | $12,691.0 | $14,644.0 |
| Operating profit . . . . | 1,475.7 | 1,647.0 | 2,141.0 | 2,441.0 | 2,827.0 | 3,273.0 |
| Identifiable assets . . . | 5,070.7 | 5,114.3 | 5,149.0 | 5,622.0 | 5,808.0 | 6,467.0 |
| Depreciation . . . . . | 97.7 | 124.7 | 151.0 | 166.0 | 200.0 | 214.0 |
| Capital expenditures . . | 498.0 | 319.9 | 163.0 | 151.0 | 191.0 | 256.0 |
| Operating profit/Identifiable assets . . . . . | 29.10% | 32.20% | 41.58% | 43.42% | 48.67% | 50.61% |
| *Food Products* | | | | | | |
| Sales . . . . . . . | – | – | – | $ 1,632.0 | $ 9,664.0 | $ 9,946.0 |
| Operating profit . . . . | – | – | – | 95.0 | 624.0 | 605.0 |
| Identifiable assets . . . | – | – | – | 7,974.0 | 8,629.0 | 9,129.0 |
| Depreciation . . . . | – | – | – | 29.0 | 167.0 | 201.0 |
| Capital expenditures . . | – | – | – | 71.0 | 395.0 | 402.0 |
| Operating profit/Identifiable assets . . . . . . | – | – | – | 1.19% | 7.23% | 6.63% |
| *Beer* | | | | | | |
| Sales . . . . . . . | $2,935.5 | $2,935.5 | $2,940.0 | $ 2,925.0 | $ 3,054.0 | $ 3,105.0 |
| Operating profit . . . . | 159.0 | 227.1 | 116.0 | 136.0 | 154.0 | 170.0 |
| Identifiable assets . . . | 2,113.7 | 2,138.9 | 1,892.0 | 1,779.0 | 1,736.0 | 1,680.0 |
| Depreciation . . . . . | 122.3 | 130.5 | 144.0 | 134.0 | 136.0 | 137.0 |
| Capital expenditures . . | 286.3 | 174.6 | 94.0 | 87.0 | 80.0 | 57.0 |
| Operating profit/Identifiable assets . . . . . | 7.52% | 10.62% | 6.13% | 7.64% | 8.87% | 10.12% |
| *Other*[a] | | | | | | |
| Sales . . . . . . . | $ 822.9 | $ 945.5 | $1,072.0 | $ 868.0 | – | – |
| Operating profit (loss) . . | (2.4) | (10.9) | 23.0 | 14.0 | $ (9.0) | $ 19.0 |
| Identifiable assets . . . | 979.4 | 1,007.3 | 1,018.0 | 643.0 | – | – |
| Depreciation . . . . . | – | – | – | – | – | – |
| Capital expenditures . . | – | – | – | – | – | – |
| Operating profit/Identifiable assets . . . . . | –.25% | –1.08% | 2.26% | 2.18% | – | – |

*Source:* Company reports.
a. Includes the Seven-Up Company, which was sold in 1986.

**EXHIBIT 8**
Correspondence During Takeover Bid Between Kraft and Philip Morris, October 1988

October 20, 1988

Mr. Hamish Maxwell
Chairman and Chief Executive Officer
Philip Morris Companies Inc.
120 Park Avenue
New York, NY 10017

Dear Hamish:

In addition to your letter requesting "negotiations" following your commencing, on Monday, a tender offer without talking to me beforehand, your lawyers and investment bankers have been barraging our advisers with similar requests. You did not see fit to discuss your takeover attempt when we were together at the Grocery Manufacturers of America meeting last Wednesday and Thursday, nor did you see fit to tell me that you were planning on filing a bizarre and baseless law suit against me and our Board of Directors on Monday.

You must have been planning your takeover bid for a long time. We intend to take our time and study the situation very carefully. We have a fiduciary duty to our shareholders and an obligation to our employees, customers, suppliers, and communities to do so. Following our study, the Board of Directors will consider the situation and determine Kraft's response. If at that time there is a purpose to be served by our meeting, we will so advise you.

Sincerely,
JOHN M. RICHMAN
Chairman and Chief Executive Officer
Kraft, Inc.

October 21, 1988

Mr. John M. Richman
Chairman and Chief Executive Officer
Kraft, Inc.
Kraft Court
Glenview, IL 60025

Dear John:

I understand and sympathize with your reaction to the events of this week. I would have preferred to discuss our offer with you prior to taking the actions we commenced. However, in the current legal environment in which we live, I accepted the advice to proceed as we did as a business decision. Our actions were designed to minimize uncertainties and delays in addressing the main issue—the economic benefits and other factors favoring the merger of Kraft with Philip Morris.

I hope you understand that any discussion of our interest in Kraft would have been premature and inappropriate when we saw each other last week at the Grocery Manufacturers of America meeting. At that time we had made no final decision to proceed with an offer and our Board had not yet approved our actions. In any event, I am hopeful you and we can now move forward in a positive and constructive manner.

I quite appreciate your need to study our offer carefully before responding to it. We have, however, seen press reports that Kraft may consider other possibilities including highly leveraged transactions that could encumber the company, operationally and financially, and which also might lead to the dismemberment of Kraft. From what I know of you and some public statements you have made, I feel sure that this is not the route you would prefer to take.

*(continued)*

**EXHIBIT 8** *(continued)*

As we have said, our goal is to have Kraft combine with Philip Morris to create the leading international food company. I repeat that our intention is to keep Kraft's present businesses intact and for the company to be managed by Kraft executives, using your present headquarters and facilities.

I believe it to be in the best interests of your shareholders and other constituencies that we avoid a prolonged struggle that could disrupt Kraft's business without adding to the value that would be realized by your shareholders.

I also believe that a meeting between us could only be helpful to you in understanding our purposes and positive thoughts concerning a combination of our two companies. . . . I want to emphasize that we are prepared to discuss all aspects of our offer.

I would be available to meet with you in Chicago at any time on short notice. I can be reached through my office if, as I hope, you see the benefits of such a meeting.

Yours sincerely,
HAMISH MAXWELL
Chairman and Chief Executive Officer
Philip Morris Companies Inc.

October 23, 1988

To: Shareholders of Kraft, Inc.

Dear Shareholder:

Kraft has an outstanding record of profitability and growth. It is a great company with great traditions, great brands, a great future, and great people who have devoted their lives to making your company what it is today.

Kraft's record of success—an increase in shareholder value, without regard to recent events, at a compound annual rate of more than 20% over the past 5 years—has been based on a strategy of balancing significant short-term returns and continued investment for long-term growth. This strategy has been working, but—frustratingly—the stock market has long been undervaluing companies which, like Kraft, sacrifice short-term profit in order to invest in long-term growth.

Last Monday, Philip Morris Companies, seeking to take advantage of this undervaluation, announced an unsolicited tender offer for Kraft at $90 per share.

We strongly believe the $90 takeover bid also undervalues Kraft, for these important reasons: first, after careful analysis, our investment banker, Goldman, Sachs & Co., has advised us that the bid is inadequate; and second, our stock has been trading above the $90 offer, a clear signal that investors see the bid as low.

Your Board of Directors has unanimously rejected the offer, and we strongly recommend that you do not tender your Kraft shares to Philip Morris.

At the same time, both your Board and company management recognize that, as a practical matter, the Philip Morris bid makes it impossible for us to go back to the situation that existed prior to the bid. Under the circumstances, your Board believes that we should take action to maximize shareholder value rather than accept an inadequate offer. Together with Goldman, Sachs we are developing a potential recapitalization plan that we believe will have a value of significantly more than $90 per share.

*(continued)*

**EXHIBIT 8** *(continued)*

The plan we are working on is intended to result in a total value estimated to be in excess of $110 per share, with a distribution in cash and securities totaling approximately $98 per share and the retention of your common stock interest, the price of which will be adjusted by the market to reflect the cash and securities distribution. Under the plan, you will receive a cash distribution and new securities, and retain your Kraft common stock. Most shareholders will have less tax to pay as a result of the distribution than if Kraft were to be acquired by Philip Morris (or anyone else) at a price that is equal to the value of the restructuring plan.

Your Board believes that this plan will enable you as a shareholder to realize present value for your shares and also continue to participate in the future of Kraft, including some exciting new product lines we have been developing.

The plan will involve the sale of some of our businesses, bank borrowings of more than $6.8 billion, and the sale of $3.0 billion of debt. We have already begun to implement some of these transactions. Goldman, Sachs has advised us that it is highly confident with respect to the placement of the debt under current market conditions. We will retain our core businesses, together with the key brands which have provided Kraft's historic strength and currently account for approximately 80% of its profitability.

Because the restructured Kraft will have more than $12.4 billion in debt and require herculean efforts by our employees, the plan will replicate the structure currently in use in sponsored leveraged buyouts by providing significant equity incentives for employees in the form of stock options and an employee stock ownership plan. This very important link between employee compensation and company performance will, we believe, ensure the enormous efforts required to make the recapitalization a complete success.

We expect that the plan will be fully developed and our Board will be able to approve it in the very near future, at which time we will announce the details. Because the plan involves very significant restructuring of our businesses and financial structure, the Board also believes you should have the opportunity to vote upon it at a special meeting of shareholders.

For your further information, on Friday, October 21, there was a series of communications with Philip Morris. Philip Morris renewed their request for immediate negotiation, stating that all aspects of their offer, including price, are open for discussion. Philip Morris said that there would be real value to them if they could conclude the agreement with us over the weekend and asked for a meeting on Saturday. We responded that if Philip Morris were prepared to offer a realistic price, we would meet on Saturday. We told Philip Morris that their $90 bid is substantially below our valuation and Goldman, Sachs's valuation and that there would be no purpose served by a meeting unless Philip Morris were prepared to start the negotiations from a price substantially greater than $90. We asked Philip Morris to tell us where they stood and told Philip Morris that if they were in the range of value that we and Goldman, Sachs believe is obtainable, we would meet with them on Saturday. Philip Morris replied that they completely disagree with our opinion of their $90 price, that they believe $90 represents full value, and they would not tell us what price they are prepared to offer. Given this attitude on the part of Philip Morris, it was clear that a meeting would not have served any purpose of Kraft and its shareholders, and we so advised Philip Morris. We also advised Philip Morris that we were not foreclosing negotiations and that if they were to offer a price that reflects the full value of Kraft, we would negotiate with them.

Since we believe that the restructuring plan will create greater shareholder value and opportunity than the Philip Morris bid or any other known alternative, it is our intention to proceed with the restructuring on an exclusive basis. However, if someone comes forward with a transaction that would be more desirable than the restructuring plan, we will negotiate and your Board will give full consideration to such a transaction.

We deeply regret the dislocation and hardships that the plan we contemplate will cause, and we will seek to ameliorate these hardships as much as possible. We know that our shareholders,

*(continued)*

**EXHIBIT 8** *(continued)*

employees, customers, suppliers, and communities recognize that today's situation is not of our making. Rather it is the product of current era investment policies and financial attitudes that favor short-term financial gratification over steady, long-term growth and the need to provide a sound economy for future generations.

It will take several years, but with the history and traditions of Kraft and the dedication of Kraft people, we are confident that we will rebuild Kraft to the leading position it occupies today.

On behalf of the Board of Directors,
JOHN M. RICHMAN
Chairman

October 24, 1988

Calvin J. Collier, Esq.
Senior Vice President and General Counsel
Kraft, Inc.
Kraft Court
Glenview, IL 60025

Dear Mr. Collier:

In light of the announcement yesterday of Kraft, Inc.'s proposed recapitalization plan, Philip Morris believes that Kraft is required to take all necessary steps to ensure that Philip Morris is given an opportunity to analyze fully Kraft's contemplated recapitalization transaction and any other proposed transaction for the sale of Kraft or any of its assets to a third party. . . .

We have a number of questions that bear on the feasibility and value to Kraft's shareholders of the announced recapitalization plan. . . .

We request that Kraft immediately supply to us specific information concerning the details of Kraft's recapitalization plan, all information concerning Kraft which may assist us in evaluating the company, and any information supplied to other third parties with respect to the sale of the company or any parts of the company.

We also request that, consistent with the responsibilities of your Board of Directors to your shareholders, Kraft not enter into, or agree to enter into, any extraordinary transaction, including a recapitalization plan, a sale of assets or securities of Kraft, or a sale of the company, or take any steps to implement any of the foregoing, until Philip Morris is given a full and fair opportunity to develop its response, and that Kraft not take any action which may diminish the value of Kraft. To that end we are today filing a motion in the Federal District Court.

Philip Morris continues to believe that, if our companies work together, a transaction can be negotiated which will achieve maximum value for Kraft's shareholders speedily and without the extraordinary disruptions to Kraft's businesses which Kraft acknowledges would be inherent in the contemplated restructuring plan.

Sincerely,
MURRAY H. BRING
Senior Vice President and General Counsel
Philip Morris Companies Inc.

*(continued)*

**EXHIBIT 8** *(concluded)*

October 25, 1988

Mr. Hamish Maxwell
Chairman and Chief Executive Officer
Philip Morris Companies Inc.
120 Park Avenue
New York, NY 10017

Dear Hamish:

I have previously advised Philip Morris of Kraft's position on your tender offer. The letter your general counsel sent to our general counsel yesterday, and the papers your lawyers filed in court yesterday, indicate that Philip Morris does not understand what Kraft is doing—or more likely, Philip Morris is pretending not to understand in order to increase its pressure tactics. Obviously it is in your interest to try to pressure Kraft and the Kraft shareholders into a transaction that benefits you at their expense. Kraft will not permit this.

Let me again make clear Kraft's position.

Kraft was not "for sale" and is not "for sale." This is no "auction" of Kraft. Philip Morris made a unilateral tender offer for Kraft. The Kraft Board of Directors rejected your tender offer. Your price is too low. Kraft has a recapitalization plan that creates far greater value for the Kraft shareholders than your inadequate offer. Kraft is submitting the recapitalization plan to Kraft shareholders for their consideration. The recapitalization will take place only if our shareholders approve it. Kraft will not pressure its shareholders, nor will Kraft permit you to stampede them. The Kraft Board is not taking action to "entrench" itself. Just the opposite, it is proceeding expeditiously to provide Kraft shareholders with a choice between your inadequate $90 bid and a better than $110 recapitalization.

As frequently happens—witness the RJR Nabisco situation—new bidders appear and old bidders raise their bids. The Kraft Board recognizes that another company or Philip Morris may offer more than $110 per share to acquire Kraft. Accordingly, the Kraft Board said that Kraft would negotiate with that company, or you, and if it, or your company, has a better transaction than the recapitalization plan, Kraft will enter into that transaction.

In other words, if Philip Morris or another company truly wishes to negotiate with Kraft, a simple phone call proposing a price of more than $110 is all that is necessary.

Please give a copy of this letter to your general counsel as our answer to his letter, and ask him to give copies to your other lawyers and financial advisers, and instruct them to stop mischaracterizing our position.

Sincerely,
JOHN M. RICHMAN
Chairman and Chief Executive Officer
Kraft, Inc.

**EXHIBIT 9**

Mergers and Acquisitions in the Food Processing and Beverage Industries, 1981–1987

| Number and Dollar Value of Mergers in the Food and Beverage Industry | | |
|---|---|---|
| | No. of Transactions | Amount Paid ($ billions) |
| 1981 | 88 | $ 4.55 |
| 1982 | 83 | 4.96 |
| 1983 | 85 | 2.71 |
| 1984 | 79 | 7.95 |
| 1985 | 105 | 12.86 |
| 1986 | 127 | 8.43 |
| 1987 | 97 | 7.75 |

Mergers in the Food and Beverage Industry over $1 Billion ($ millions)

| Bidder | Target | Year | Target's Sales | Amount Paid | Premium Percent | Price-Earnings Ratio | Multiple to Book |
|---|---|---|---|---|---|---|---|
| Philip Morris | General Foods | 1985 | $9,022.4 | $5,627.5 | 35.2% | 18.7 | 3.5 |
| RJ Reynolds | Nabisco Brands | 1985 | 5,985.0 | 4,906.4 | 31.5 | 16.7 | 4.1 |
| Nestlé S.A. | Carnation Co. | 1984 | 3,370.0 | 2,885.4 | 9.9 | 14.4 | 2.7 |
| Beatrice Foods | Esmark Inc. | 1984 | 4,120.0 | 2,508.6 | 39.5 | 15.7 | 2.5 |
| RJ Reynolds | Heublein, Inc. | 1982 | 2,140.0 | 1,302.6 | 36.5 | 13.1 | 2.7 |
| Bond Corporate Holdings Ltd. | G. Heileman Brewing Co. | 1987 | 1,173.8 | 1,083.6 | 21.6 | 23.0 | 3.2 |

*Source:* W. T. Grimm and Co., *Mergerstat Review,* 1981–1987.

**EXHIBIT 10**

Stock Price Indexes and Returns on Equity, 1982–1987

| | 1982 | 1983 | 1984 | 1985 | 1986 | 1987 |
|---|---|---|---|---|---|---|
| Stock price index (1981 = 100) | | | | | | |
| Kraft | 144.1 | 148.5 | 200.6 | 321.2 | 397.3 | 409.3 |
| Philip Morris | 128.8 | 161.2 | 190.0 | 218.3 | 368.7 | 453.0 |
| RJR Nabisco | 114.8 | 144.8 | 192.2 | 220.1 | 357.4 | 337.0 |
| Pillsbury | 133.0 | 202.1 | 256.4 | 365.4 | 413.5 | 440.8 |
| Food index | 132.9 | 161.1 | 186.9 | 297.6 | 387.4 | 398.8 |
| Tobacco index | 117.7 | 142.4 | 165.7 | 179.2 | 279.7 | 299.0 |
| S&P 500 index | 114.7 | 134.5 | 136.4 | 172.3 | 197.6 | 201.5 |
| Return on equity (ROE) | | | | | | |
| Kraft | 12.6% | 14.9% | 17.6% | 16.2% | 23.0% | 25.8% |
| Philip Morris | 21.3 | 22.4 | 21.7 | 26.5 | 26.1 | 27.0 |
| RJR Nabisco | 20.8 | 17.1 | 22.3 | 20.8 | 20.0 | 22.8 |
| Pillsbury | 16.6 | 15.0 | 17.0 | 17.3 | 16.8 | 13.5 |
| Food index | 14.3 | 17.0 | 17.9 | 18.0 | 12.0 | 12.5 |
| Tobacco index | 19.0 | 18.2 | 19.4 | 21.6 | 20.0 | 20.3 |
| S&P 500 index | 10.9 | 11.7 | 13.1 | 11.0 | 10.5 | 11.8 |

**EXHIBIT 11**

Pre-Bid Sales and Profit Forecasts for Kraft, 1988–1989 (millions of dollars)

|  | 1987 | Est. 1988 | Est. 1989 |
|---|---|---|---|
| Revenues | $9,876 | $11,200 | $12,500 |
| Earnings before interest and taxes | 834 | 950 | 1,050 |
| Interest, net | 91 | 95 | 108 |
| Income from continuing operations before taxes | 743 | 855 | 942 |
| Income taxes | 353 | 333 | 368 |
| Accounting change | 45 | – | – |
| Income from continuing operations | 435 | 522 | 574 |
| Income from discontinued operations[a] | 54 | 658 | – |
| Net income | $ 489 | $ 1,180 | $ 574 |

*Source:* Analysts' estimates.

a. Duracell was sold to Kohlberg, Kravis, Roberts & Co. for $1.8 billion on June 24, 1988. Duracell's 1987 after-tax income was $54 million, and Kraft's 1988 gain on its sale was $658 million.

**EXHIBIT 12**
Projections for Kraft's Restructuring Plan, 1989–1998 (millions of dollars)

| | 1989 | 1990 | 1991 | 1992 | 1993 | 1994 | 1995 | 1996 | 1997 | 1998 |
|---|---|---|---|---|---|---|---|---|---|---|
| Sales | $ 6,515 | $ 6,804 | $7,125 | $7,481 | $7,855 | $8,248 | $8,660 | $9,093 | $9,548 | $10,025 |
| Earnings before interest and taxes | 1,280 | 1,487 | 1,671 | 1,755 | 1,842 | 1,935 | 2,031 | 2,133 | 2,239 | 2,351 |
| Interest | 1,380 | 1,270 | 1,310 | 1,286 | 1,278 | 1,257 | 1,212 | 1,155 | 1,086 | 1,010 |
| Taxes | (39) | 89 | 148 | 192 | 231 | 278 | 336 | 401 | 473 | 550 |
| Profit (loss) after taxes from continuing operations | (61) | 128 | 213 | 277 | 333 | 400 | 483 | 577 | 680 | 791 |
| Cash flow available for capital payments[a] | 2,481[b] | 496 | 636 | 630 | 742 | 334 | 411 | 500 | 597 | 728 |
| Principal payments | | | | | | | | | | |
| Preexisting debt | 111 | 33 | 57 | 287 | 100 | 100 | 100 | 100 | 16 | 0 |
| Bank debt | 2,370 | 463 | 579 | 343 | 642 | 234 | 311 | 400 | 581 | 728 |
| Year-end book values | | | | | | | | | | |
| Preexisting debt | 793 | 759 | 703 | 416 | 316 | 216 | 116 | 16 | 0 | 0 |
| Bank debt | 4,430 | 3,968 | 3,389 | 3,046 | 2,404 | 2,170 | 1,859 | 1,459 | 878 | 150 |
| High-yield debt | 3,000 | 3,000 | 3,000 | 3,000 | 3,000 | 3,000 | 3,000 | 3,000 | 3,000 | 3,000 |
| Cram-down debt | 1,974 | 2,286 | 2,648 | 3,067 | 3,553 | 3,553 | 3,553 | 3,553 | 3,553 | 3,553 |
| Total | $10,197 | $10,013 | $9,740 | $9,529 | $9,273 | $8,939 | $8,528 | $8,028 | $7,431 | $ 6,703 |

*Sources:* Kraft and casewriter's estimates.

a. Cash flow available for capital payments = net income + depreciation, amortization, deferred taxes − capital expenditures − change in working capital + net proceeds from asset sales.

b. Includes the $2,146 million in cash proceeds from the sale of businesses in 1989.

638

**EXHIBIT 13**
Stock Prices and Market Index, October 1988

| Date | Philip Morris | Kraft | S&P 500 | Event |
|------|--------------|-------|---------|-------|
| Oct. 3 | $ 97.000 | $ 60.000 | 638.710 | |
| 4 | 98.000 | 58.500 | 637.010 | Grand Metropolitan bids for Pillsbury Company. |
| 5 | 97.375 | 59.375 | 640.020 | |
| 6 | 96.875 | 59.375 | 641.360 | |
| 7 | 100.875 | 60.625 | 654.830 | |
| 10 | 101.125 | 60.750 | 655.320 | |
| 11 | 100.750 | 60.375 | 654.680 | |
| 12 | 98.875 | 59.500 | 645.470 | |
| 13 | 99.250 | 59.250 | 648.480 | |
| 14 | 98.625 | 59.500 | 649.230 | |
| 17 | 100.000 | 60.125 | 651.460 | |
| 18 | 95.500 | 88.250 | 658.560 | Philip Morris bids $90 per share for Kraft. |
| 19 | 94.000 | 90.375 | 652.970 | |
| 20 | 99.000 | 90.250 | 666.990 | RJR Nabisco management proposes a $17 billion leveraged buyout. |
| 21 | 97.375 | 92.000 | 668.920 | |
| 24 | 97.500 | 102.000 | 665.760 | Kraft proposes its restructuring plan and Kohlberg, |
| 25 | 95.875 | 99.000 | 666.090 | Kravis, Roberts announces its bid for RJR Nabisco. |
| 26 | 95.500 | 97.500 | 663.820 | |
| 27 | 95.000 | 94.500 | 654.240 | |
| 28 | 94.750 | 96.500 | 657.280 | |

# Part IV

# Comprehensive Overview

# American Chemical Corporation

In June 1979, American Chemical Corporation announced a tender offer for any and all shares of the Universal Paper Corporation. American was one of the largest diversified chemical companies in the United States (see Exhibit 1). Universal was a large paper and pulp company (see Exhibit 2).

Universal's management opposed the takeover and, among other things, sued in federal court to have the tender offer blocked on grounds that American's acquisition of Universal would violate the Clayton Act of the U.S. antitrust laws. Both firms engaged in the production of sodium chlorate. Universal alleged that its acquisition by American would substantially reduce competition in the sodium chlorate business, particularly in the southeastern U.S. market, where the two firms were competitors. The U.S. government joined Universal in seeking a preliminary injunction to stop American's tender offer. Though it denied the allegations, American prevented a preliminary injunction by agreeing to divest its sodium chlorate plant located near Collinsville, Alabama, in the event it acquired Universal. American subsequently was successful in acquiring over 91% of Universal's shares.

In October 1979, American began looking for a buyer for the Collinsville plant. A number of potential buyers were approached, including the Dixon Corporation, a specialty chemicals company. After lengthy negotiations, Dixon agreed to purchase the net assets of the Collinsville plant from American for $12 million, subject to approval by its board of directors.

## The Market for Sodium Chlorate

Sodium chlorate ($NaClO_3$) was a chemical produced by the electrolytic decomposition of salt ($NaCl$) according to the chemical formula

$$NaCl + 3H_2O + energy \rightarrow NaClO_3 + 3H_2$$

Sodium chlorate was sold either as a white crystalline solid or in a 25% water solution.

Approximately 85% of the sodium chlorate produced in the United States was sold to the paper and pulp industries, where it was used in the bleaching of pulp. Sodium chlorate was reacted with salt ($NaCl$) and sulfuric acid ($H_2SO_4$) to produce a bleaching agent, chloride dioxide ($ClO_2$), according to the formula

$$NaClO_3 + NaCl + H_2SO_4 \rightarrow \tfrac{1}{2}Cl_2 + ClO_2 + Na_2SO_4 + H_2O$$

Chloride dioxide was the active ingredient actually used by paper and pulp producers to bleach pulp. The remaining 15% of the sodium chlorate produced in the United States was used in soil sterilants, in oxidizers for use in uranium mining, and in producing various chemicals, including sodium chlorite, potassium chlorate, and ammonium perchlorate.

Sales of sodium chlorate had grown rapidly during the 1970s from 220,000 tons in 1970 to an expected 435,000 tons in 1979 (see Exhibit 3). Sales increased by approximately 8.6% per year during the period 1970–1974 but then declined 12% in 1975 when pulp production decreased during the recession. Demand improved during the subsequent recovery, and sales grew by more than 10% per year between 1975 and 1979.

Demand for sodium chlorate from pulp producers was expected to continue increasing at 8–10% per year. While pulp production was projected to increase at a slower annual rate of about 3–4%, pulp producers' use of sodium chlorate was expected to grow more rapidly, since use of sodium chlorate (and the active ingredient chloride dioxide) helped solve their plant effluent problems. Other uses of sodium chlorate also were expected to grow at about 8–10% per year.

Capacity additions had not kept pace with sales growth during the 1970s (see Exhibit 3). Though sales had increased by over 95% between 1970 and 1979, capacity had increased by less than 70% during this period. The resulting tight markets in 1973–1974 and 1977–1978 caused a substantial improvement in profit margins between 1970 and 1979, even though production costs also increased greatly during this period. These tight markets and cost increases had caused prices for sodium chlorate to increase rapidly beginning in 1973 (see Exhibit 3).

In late 1979 there were a dozen domestic producers of sodium chlorate (see Exhibits 4 and 5). The market was dominated by large diversified chemical companies (Hooker, Pennwalt, American, and Kerr-McGee). However, a number of paper and pulp companies (Georgia-Pacific and Universal) had integrated backward into the production of sodium chlorate. In addition, two firms (Brunswick and Southern) specialized in producing sodium chlorate. The three largest producers accounted for over 55% of domestic capacity.

The majority of sodium chlorate plants were located in the southeastern United States (see Exhibit 4), where approximately two thirds of the product was consumed because of the high regional concentration of pulp and paper mills. Freight costs represented a significant portion of delivered sodium chlorate costs, and plants tended therefore to be located within 800 miles of their principal markets. Market concentration was slightly higher in the southeastern market than in the total U.S. market. The three largest producers accounted for approximately 59% of the southeastern market.

In addition to existing producers, two firms had announced plans to enter the sodium chlorate business in 1980. Union Chemicals Corporation was constructing a 40,000-ton plant in Gainsville, Georgia, and Louisiana Paper Company was building a 35,000-ton plant in Greenville, Mississippi. This increase in industry capacity was expected to reduce margins and decrease capacity utilization during 1980 and 1981. However, as sales and productive capacity achieved a closer balance, prices and margins were expected to improve once again. It should be noted that the selling price necessary to obtain a 15% return on investment on a newly constructed 40,000-ton sodium chlorate plant was estimated to be $420 per ton in 1979.

## The Collinsville Plant

American's plant in Collinsville, Alabama, had the capacity to produce 40,000 tons of sodium chlorate per year. Sodium chlorate was produced by the electrolysis of sodium chloride brine in electrolytic cells called D cells, which used graphite electrodes. The facility consisted of 20 cell tanks (or groups of cells) that were operated batchwise. They were filled with saturated brine and then electrolized to an endpoint. Graphite was consumed in the process. The resulting fluid was chemically treated to precipitate impurities, which were discarded. The remaining sodium chlorate solution was either shipped as a fluid or crystallized to a white solid.

The plant had been consistently profitable during the period 1974–1979 (see Exhibit 6). Operating profits had ranged from a low of $817,000 in 1975 to a high of $4,845,000 in 1978. Net assets had grown from $4,619,000 in 1974 to $5,414,000 in 1979. Though the ratio of operating profits to net assets had dropped to 16.9% in 1975, it equaled 90.0% in 1978 and averaged 54.3% during the 1974–1979 period.

The major cost of production was electric power. The Collinsville facility needed approximately 7,000 kilowatt hours (kwh) to produce a ton of sodium chlorate, and power costs accounted for 55–60% of manufacturing costs. Salt, graphite, and other variable costs typically represented another 20%, and labor and maintenance costs accounted for the remaining 20% of manufacturing costs.

Electric power was purchased from the Tennessee Valley Authority (TVA), whose hydroelectric power plants historically had been a source of cheap electric power. During the early 1970s, TVA's rates had been as much as 50% less than the rates of other electric utilities. However, as the region's power demands grew, TVA was finding it necessary to supplement its hydroelectric power plants with more expensive fossil fuel plants. TVA also was facing increasing pressure from consumer groups to allocate the more expensive power of fossil fuel plants to industrial users instead of residential users. As a result, the Collinsville plant's cost of power had increased from $.019 per kwh in 1977 to $.025 per kwh in 1979.

Capital expenditures at the Collinsville plant had ranged from $200,000 to $500,000 per year between 1973 and 1979 and were primarily for maintenance and pollution control. In late 1979 the plant was basically in compliance with all environmental regulations. Future capital expenditures were expected to range from $475,000 to $600,000 per year.

American had supported a research and development program that was expected to reduce costs at its sodium chlorate plants. New sodium chlorate plants increasingly were using metal electrodes (instead of graphite electrodes), which eliminated graphite costs and also reduced power needs by approximately 30%. However, the graphite electrodes at American's plants at Collinsville and Wenatchee, Washington, were not convertible at an acceptable cost to commercially available metal electrodes. American's research group therefore was working on a permanent laminate (or coating) that could be applied to the graphite electrodes in American's plants. Use of this laminate would eliminate graphite costs and was expected to reduce power needs by 15–20%. Development was approximately 40% complete and scale-up to a pilot plant was scheduled for March 1980. American expected that the laminate could be installed at the Collinsville plant at a one-time cost of about $2.25 million, which could be depreciated over a period of 10 years. Installation at Collinsville was scheduled for December 1980.

## Proposed Sale of the Collinsville Plant to the Dixon Corporation

The Dixon Corporation was a specialty chemicals company that produced a number of chemicals for sale primarily to the paper and pulp industry. Its principal products included sulfuric acid, aluminum sulfate, and liquid sulfur dioxide. As described earlier, sulfuric acid was used together with sodium chlorate to produce chloride dioxide, which was the active ingredient used to bleach pulp. Sulfuric acid also was used in the manufacture of other chemicals, steels, rayon, and detergents and in oil refining. Aluminum sulfate was used as a coagulant and purifying agent in the treatment of industrial and municipal waste. Dixon sold liquid sulfur dioxide to the paper and pulp industry for use in bleaching pulp, though it also was used to produce hydrosulfites for use in textile dyeing. The firm's principal plant was located in Calhoun, Georgia, and its sales were concentrated in the southeastern United States. Dixon's sales had grown rapidly and the firm had been consistently profitable (see Exhibit 7).

Acquisition of the Collinsville plant fit well with Dixon's strategy of supplying chemicals to the paper and pulp industry. Sodium chlorate would complement Dixon's existing product lines. Dixon already did business with some of the Collinsville plant's major customers. Sodium chlorate, therefore, could be marketed largely through Dixon's existing sales group.

In evaluating the plant's purchase, Dixon prepared the pro forma financial statements shown in Exhibit 8. These figures analyzed the plant's future profitability given its unlaminated graphite electrodes and in the absence of the operating economies that might be realized from installing laminated electrodes. Industry overcapacity was expected to push margins down in the short run. However, Dixon expected that sodium chlorate prices would increase on average at 8% per year. Power costs (per kwh) were projected to increase more rapidly, at 12% per year. Selling expenses could be reduced by marketing sodium chlorate through Dixon's existing sales force. Dixon also expected to write up the value of the Collinsville plant, which would increase its depreciation charges.[1]

As part of the sale agreement, American agreed to provide ongoing technical support to the Collinsville plant. American would keep Dixon informed concerning development of the laminated electrodes and make this technology available to Dixon. However, Dixon would have to pay for all costs associated with installation of the laminated electrodes.

The $12 million purchase price was to be financed entirely with debt capital. It was to be financed in part by privately placing $8 million in 15-year mortgage bonds with two insurance companies. These bonds would carry an 11.25% interest rate. The sinking fund provision on these bonds would retire $800,000 of bonds each year beginning the sixth year. The remainder of the $12 million purchase price was to be financed by having Dixon issue American a $4 million note to be paid off in equal amounts over 5 years. The note also carried an 11.25% interest rate.[2]

This financing package would temporarily increase Dixon's debt-to-total-capital ratio to approximately 47%. Though the firm had almost no debt immediately prior to the proposed acquisition, Dixon had relied more heavily on debt capital in the past. However, use of this much debt would initially raise the debt ratio above the firm's target debt ratio of about 35%.

---

1. Net working capital accounted for $1.4 million of the $12 million purchase price (Exhibit 6). Dixon planned to allocate the $10.6 million balance of the $12 million purchase price to the Collinsville plant. The plant would be depreciated over 10 years on the straight-line method of depreciation to a zero residual value. This relatively short life was permitted for tax purposes, since it corresponded to the anticipated remaining physical life of the plant.

2. Market interest rates were as follows:

| | |
|---|---|
| Short-term Treasury bills: | 10.5% |
| Long-term Treasury bonds: | 9.5% |
| Long-term AA corporate bonds: | 10.25% |
| Long-term A corporate bonds: | 10.75% |

# EXHIBIT 1
Financial Statements for American Chemical and Other Selected Large Chemical Companies, 1974–1978 (millions of dollars except per share data)

## American Chemical

| | 1974 | 1975 | 1976 | 1977 | 1978 |
|---|---|---|---|---|---|
| Sales | $4,828 | $4,671 | $4,805 | $5,235 | $ 5,490 |
| Net income | 323 | 198 | 212 | 251 | 349 |
| Earnings per share | $ 7.60 | $ 4.66 | $ 4.98 | $ 5.91 | $ 8.20 |
| Dividends per share | 1.00 | 1.25 | 1.50 | 1.65 | 1.80 |
| Dividend yield | 5.3% | 5.7% | 4.3% | 5.0% | 4.1% |
| Common stock prices | | | | | |
| High | $ 23 | $ 30 | $ 36 | $ 46 | $ 48 |
| Low | 10 | 17 | 21 | 30 | 32 |
| Closing | 19 | 22 | 35 | 33 | 44 |
| Closing P/E ratio | 2.5 | 4.7 | 7.0 | 5.6 | 5.4 |
| Total capitalization | $2,014 | $2,109 | $2,198 | $2,465 | $ 2,527 |
| % debt | 44% | 37% | 37% | 29% | 39% |
| % preferred stock | — | — | — | — | 20% |
| % common stock | 56% | 63% | 63% | 71% | 41% |
| Beta | | | 1.20 | | |
| Interest coverage[a] | 6.3 | 3.9 | 4.1 | 4.3 | 6.7 |
| Bond rating[b] | | | BBB/A | | |

## Allied Chemical

| | 1974 | 1975 | 1976 | 1977 | 1978 |
|---|---|---|---|---|---|
| Sales | $2,216 | $2,333 | $2,630 | $2,923 | $3,268 |
| Net income | 151 | 116 | 117 | 135 | 120 |
| Earnings per share | $ 5.43 | $ 4.17 | $ 4.52 | $ 4.93 | $ 4.25 |
| Dividends per share | 1.53 | 1.80 | 1.80 | 1.85 | 2.00 |
| Dividend yield | 6.3% | 5.4% | 4.5% | 4.5% | 7.1% |
| Common stock prices | | | | | |
| High | $ 54 | $ 42 | $ 45 | $ 51 | $ 45 |
| Low | 23 | 27 | 33 | 39 | 28 |
| Closing | 28 | 33 | 40 | 44 | 28 |
| Closing P/E ratio | 5.2 | 7.9 | 8.8 | 8.9 | 6.6 |
| Total capitalization | $1,550 | $1,839 | $1,959 | $2,279 | $2,467 |
| % debt | 28% | 34% | 33% | 36% | 38% |
| % preferred stock | — | — | — | — | — |
| % common stock | 72% | 66% | 67% | 64% | 62% |
| Beta | | | 1.43 | | |
| Interest coverage[a] | 9.2 | 5.7 | 5.2 | 5.4 | 4.9 |
| Bond rating[b] | | | A/A | | |

## Dow Chemical

| | 1974 | 1975 | 1976 | 1977 | 1978 |
|---|---|---|---|---|---|
| Sales | $4,938 | $4,888 | $5,652 | $6,234 | $6,888 |
| Net income | 558 | 616 | 613 | 566 | 575 |
| Earnings per share | $ 3.18 | $ 3.33 | $ 3.30 | $ 3.01 | $ 3.16 |
| Dividends per share | .60 | .75 | .95 | 1.15 | 1.30 |
| Dividend yield | 2.5% | 1.7% | 2.3% | 4.5% | 5.6% |
| Common stock prices | | | | | |
| High | $ 35 | $ 48 | $ 57 | $ 44 | $ 31 |
| Low | 25 | 27 | 38 | 25 | 22 |
| Closing | 28 | 46 | 43 | 27 | 25 |
| Closing P/E ratio | 8.8 | 13.8 | 13.0 | 9.0 | 7.9 |
| Total capitalization | $3,498 | $4,316 | $5,118 | $5,889 | $6,793 |
| % debt | 37% | 36% | 37% | 40% | 43% |
| % preferred stock | — | — | — | — | — |
| % common stock | 63% | 64% | 63% | 60% | 57% |
| Beta | | | 1.25 | | |
| Interest coverage[a] | 10.6 | 8.2 | 6.5 | 4.9 | 4.4 |
| Bond rating[b] | | | A/Aa | | |

## Du Pont

| | 1974 | 1975 | 1976 | 1977 | 1978 |
|---|---|---|---|---|---|
| Sales | $6,910 | $7,221 | $8,361 | $9,435 | $10,584 |
| Net income | 404 | 272 | 459 | 545 | 787 |
| Earnings per share | $ 2.74 | $ 1.81 | $ 3.10 | $ 3.69 | $ 5.39 |
| Dividends per share | 1.83 | 1.42 | 1.75 | 1.92 | 2.42 |
| Dividend yield | 6.0% | 3.2% | 3.7% | 4.8% | 5.8% |
| Common stock prices | | | | | |
| High | $ 60 | $ 45 | $ 54 | $ 45 | $ 46 |
| Low | 28 | 29 | 39 | 35 | 33 |
| Closing | 31 | 42 | 45 | 40 | 42 |
| Closing P/E ratio | 11.3 | 23.2 | 14.5 | 10.8 | 7.8 |
| Total capitalization | $4,874 | $5,085 | $5,772 | $6,127 | $ 6,394 |
| % debt | 16% | 17% | 22% | 21% | 17% |
| % preferred stock | 5% | 5% | 4% | 4% | 4% |
| % common stock | 79% | 78% | 74% | 75% | 79% |
| Beta | | | 1.22 | | |
| Interest coverage[a] | 9.5 | 4.1 | 6.0 | 6.1 | 9.5 |
| Bond rating[b] | | | AAA/Aaa | | |

## Monsanto

| | 1974 | 1975 | 1976 | 1977 | 1978 |
|---|---|---|---|---|---|
| Sales | $3,498 | $3,625 | $4,270 | $4,595 | $5,019 |
| Net income | 323 | 306 | 366 | 276 | 303 |
| Earnings per share | $ 9.35 | $ 8.63 | $10.05 | $ 7.46 | $ 8.29 |
| Dividends per share | 2.30 | 2.55 | 2.75 | 3.03 | 3.18 |
| Dividend yield | 5.9% | 3.4% | 3.2% | 5.4% | 6.8% |
| Common stock prices | | | | | |
| High | $ 70 | $ 81 | $ 100 | $ 89 | $ 60 |
| Low | 39 | 41 | 76 | 52 | 44 |
| Closing | 41 | 76 | 88 | 58 | 47 |
| Closing P/E ratio | 4.4 | 8.8 | 8.8 | 7.8 | 5.7 |
| Total capitalization | $2,396 | $2,942 | $3,349 | $3,668 | $4,115 |
| % debt | 25% | 29% | 27% | 28% | 30% |
| % preferred stock | — | — | — | — | — |
| % common stock | 75% | 71% | 73% | 72% | 70% |
| Beta | | | 1.43 | | |
| Interest coverage[a] | 11.4 | 9.1 | 8.4 | 7.0 | 6.5 |
| Bond rating[b] | | | AA/Aa | | |

## Union Carbide

| | 1974 | 1975 | 1976 | 1977 | 1978 |
|---|---|---|---|---|---|
| Sales | $5,320 | $5,665 | $6,346 | $7,036 | $7,870 |
| Net income | 530 | 382 | 441 | 385 | 394 |
| Earnings per share | $ 8.69 | $ 6.23 | $ 7.15 | $ 6.05 | $ 6.09 |
| Dividends per share | 2.18 | 2.40 | 2.50 | 2.80 | 2.80 |
| Dividend yield | 5.3% | 3.9% | 4.0% | 6.8% | 8.2% |
| Common stock prices | | | | | |
| High | $ 46 | $ 67 | $ 77 | $ 62 | $ 43 |
| Low | 32 | 40 | 56 | 40 | 34 |
| Closing | 41 | 61 | 62 | 41 | 34 |
| Closing P/E ratio | 4.7 | 9.8 | 8.7 | 6.8 | 5.6 |
| Total capitalization | $3,752 | $4,485 | $5,212 | $5,750 | $5,997 |
| % debt | 26% | 30% | 32% | 30% | 28% |
| % preferred stock | — | — | — | — | — |
| % common stock | 74% | 70% | 68% | 70% | 72% |
| Beta | | | 1.05 | | |
| Interest coverage[a] | 14.0 | 8.4 | 7.0 | 5.0 | 4.9 |
| Bond rating[b] | | | A/Aa | | |

a. Defined as EBIT/interest.
b. Standard and Poor's rating/Moody's rating.

# EXHIBIT 2
Financial Statements for Universal Paper and Other Selected Large Paper Companies, 1974–1978 (millions of dollars except per share data)

## Universal Paper

| | 1974 | 1975 | 1976 | 1977 | 1978 |
|---|---|---|---|---|---|
| Sales | $1,867 | $1,902 | $2,136 | $2,248 | $2,525 |
| Net income | 149 | 109 | 154 | 168 | 191 |
| Earnings per share | $ 3.60 | $ 2.63 | $ 3.72 | $ 4.06 | $ 4.61 |
| Dividends per share | .75 | .75 | .75 | .85 | 1.00 |
| Dividend yield | 6.3% | 3.9% | 2.5% | 2.8% | 3.6% |
| Common stock price | | | | | |
| High | $ 17 | $ 21 | $ 34 | $ 36 | $ 38 |
| Low | 10 | 12 | 18 | 24 | 26 |
| Closing | 12 | 19 | 30 | 30 | 28 |
| Closing P/E ratio | 3.4 | 7.1 | 8.1 | 7.4 | 6.0 |
| Total capitalization | $1,349 | $1,620 | $1,787 | $1,938 | $2,018 |
| % debt | 30% | 29% | 32% | 32% | 33% |
| % preferred stock | 1% | — | — | — | — |
| % common stock | 70% | 71% | 68% | 68% | 67% |
| Beta | | | 1.52 | | |
| Interest coverage[a] | 6.8 | 5.0 | 6.8 | 7.4 | 8.2 |
| Bond rating[b] | | | A/Aa | | |

## Crown Zellerbach

| | 1974 | 1975 | 1976 | 1977 | 1978 |
|---|---|---|---|---|---|
| Sales | $1,172 | $1,767 | $2,136 | $2,318 | $2,467 |
| Net income | 125 | 75 | 98 | 109 | 112 |
| Earnings per share | $ 5.06 | $ 3.01 | $ 3.88 | $ 4.34 | $ 4.39 |
| Dividends per share | 1.75 | 1.80 | 1.80 | 1.83 | 1.90 |
| Dividend yield | 7.5% | 5.1% | 4.0% | 5.6% | 6.2% |
| Common stock price | | | | | |
| High | $ 40 | $ 41 | $ 49 | $ 45 | $ 38 |
| Low | 20 | 24 | 36 | 32 | 29 |
| Closing | 24 | 36 | 43 | 34 | 31 |
| Closing P/E ratio | 4.7 | 12.0 | 11.6 | 7.8 | 7.1 |
| Total capitalization | $1,220 | $1,290 | $1,345 | $1,446 | $1,647 |
| % debt | 33% | 33% | 31% | 30% | 34% |
| % preferred stock | 1% | 1% | 1% | 1% | 1% |
| % common stock | 66% | 66% | 68% | 69% | 65% |
| Beta | | | 1.03 | | |
| Interest coverage[a] | 8.1 | 4.5 | 5.3 | 5.7 | 4.7 |
| Bond rating[b] | | | A/A | | |

## International Paper

| | 1974 | 1975 | 1976 | 1977 | 1978 |
|---|---|---|---|---|---|
| Sales | $3,042 | $3,081 | $3,541 | $3,669 | $4,150 |
| Net income | 263 | 218 | 254 | 234 | 234 |
| Earnings per share | $ 5.95 | $ 4.93 | $ 5.60 | $ 4.98 | $ 4.94 |
| Dividends per share | 1.75 | 2.00 | 2.00 | 2.00 | 2.00 |
| Dividend yield | 5.6% | 3.5% | 2.9% | 4.6% | 5.5% |
| Common stock price | | | | | |
| High | $ 56 | $ 62 | $ 80 | $ 70 | $ 49 |
| Low | 32 | 35 | 58 | 39 | 35 |
| Closing | 36 | 58 | 69 | 44 | 37 |
| Closing P/E ratio | 6.1 | 11.8 | 12.3 | 8.8 | 7.5 |
| Total capitalization | $2,207 | $2,801 | $3,093 | $3,303 | $3,407 |
| % debt | 33% | 41% | 34% | 32% | 28% |
| % preferred stock | — | — | — | — | — |
| % common stock | 67% | 59% | 66% | 68% | 72% |
| Beta | | | 1.43 | | |
| Interest coverage[a] | 11.1 | 5.4 | 5.1 | 4.7 | 5.3 |
| Bond rating[b] | | | AA/Aa | | |

## Mead Corporation

| | 1974 | 1975 | 1976 | 1977 | 1978 |
|---|---|---|---|---|---|
| Sales | $1,526 | $1,245 | $1,599 | $1,822 | $2,322 |
| Net income | 82 | 53 | 89 | 98 | 121 |
| Earnings per share | $ 3.27 | $ 2.05 | $ 3.61 | $ 4.10 | $ 5.12 |
| Dividends per share | .60 | .80 | .89 | .98 | 1.21 |
| Dividend yield | 9.2% | 6.6% | 4.4% | 4.7% | 6.8% |
| Common stock price | | | | | |
| High | $ 13 | $ 13 | $ 23 | $ 24 | $ 34 |
| Low | 8 | 9 | 12 | 18 | 17 |
| Closing | 9 | 12 | 21 | 22 | 23 |
| Closing P/E ratio | 2.8 | 5.9 | 5.8 | 5.4 | 4.5 |
| Total capitalization | $ 826 | $ 880 | $ 965 | $1,071 | $1,171 |
| % debt | 34% | 35% | 33% | 38% | 36% |
| % preferred stock | 6% | 6% | 5% | 4% | 1% |
| % common stock | 60% | 59% | 62% | 58% | 63% |
| Beta | | | 2.16 | | |
| Interest coverage[a] | 4.6 | 2.9 | 4.5 | 4.7 | 5.3 |
| Bond rating[b] | | | A/A | | |

## Kimberly-Clark

| | 1974 | 1975 | 1976 | 1977 | 1978 |
|---|---|---|---|---|---|
| Sales | $1,439 | $1,484 | $1,585 | $1,726 | $1,911 |
| Net income | 95 | 103 | 121 | 131 | 149 |
| Earnings per share | $ 4.10 | $ 4.41 | $ 5.21 | $ 5.60 | $ 6.36 |
| Dividends per share | 1.48 | 1.60 | 1.80 | 2.20 | 2.60 |
| Dividend yield | 6.5% | 4.4% | 4.1% | 5.1% | 6.4% |
| Common stock price | | | | | |
| High | $ 35 | $ 37 | $ 47 | $ 48 | $ 50 |
| Low | 19 | 24 | 36 | 37 | 39 |
| Closing | 25 | 37 | 44 | 43 | 41 |
| Closing P/E ratio | 6.1 | 8.4 | 8.4 | 7.7 | 6.4 |
| Total capitalization | $1,030 | $1,086 | $1,196 | $1,347 | $1,435 |
| % debt | 24% | 21% | 20% | 20% | 19% |
| % preferred stock | — | — | — | — | — |
| % common stock | 76% | 79% | 80% | 80% | 81% |
| Beta | | | .99 | | |
| Interest coverage[a] | 9.1 | 8.3 | 10.0 | 10.1 | 10.5 |
| Bond rating[b] | | | AA/Aa | | |

## St. Regis Paper

| | 1974 | 1975 | 1976 | 1977 | 1978 |
|---|---|---|---|---|---|
| Sales | $1,471 | $1,395 | $1,642 | $1,996 | $2,300 |
| Net income | 105 | 96 | 91 | 107 | 127 |
| Earnings per share | $ 4.76 | $ 4.27 | $ 3.82 | $ 3.36 | $ 3.94 |
| Dividends per share | 1.25 | 1.43 | 1.55 | 1.66 | 1.74 |
| Dividend yield | 7.3% | 4.5% | 4.2% | 5.6% | 6.4% |
| Common stock price | | | | | |
| High | $ 37 | $ 35 | $ 41 | $ 39 | $ 35 |
| Low | 18 | 20 | 34 | 29 | 26 |
| Closing | 19 | 34 | 39 | 31 | 28 |
| Closing P/E ratio | 4.0 | 8.0 | 10.2 | 9.2 | 7.1 |
| Total capitalization | $1,127 | $1,189 | $1,296 | $1,694 | $1,791 |
| % debt | 33% | 29% | 26% | 31% | 30% |
| % preferred stock | — | — | — | — | — |
| % common stock | 67% | 71% | 74% | 69% | 70% |
| Beta | | | 1.14 | | |
| Interest coverage[a] | 7.6 | 7.2 | 6.1 | 5.6 | 5.9 |
| Bond rating[b] | | | NR | | |

a. Defined as EBIT/interest.
b. Standard and Poor's rating/Moody's rating; NR = not rated.

**EXHIBIT 3**
Sales and Capacity of Sodium Chlorate Producers in the United States, 1970–1979

| | Sales of Sodium Chlorate (tons) | Domestic Capacity (tons) | Average Price (dollars/ton) |
|---|---|---|---|
| 1970 . . . . . . | 220,000 | 270,000 | $129 |
| 1971 . . . . . . | 260,000 | 300,000 | 136 |
| 1972 . . . . . . | 280,000 | 300,000 | 144 |
| 1973 . . . . . . | 300,000 | 320,000 | 152 |
| 1974 . . . . . . | 310,000 | 335,000 | 188 |
| 1975 . . . . . . | 270,000 | 355,000 | 243 |
| 1976 . . . . . . | 345,000 | 370,000 | 295 |
| 1977 . . . . . . | 380,000 | 385,000 | 367 |
| 1978 . . . . . . | 410,000 | 420,000 | 392 |
| 1979 . . . . . . | 435,000[a] | 455,000 | 413[a] |

a. Expected.

**EXHIBIT 4**
Domestic Producers of Sodium Chlorate

| Producer | Capacity (tons) | Plants | Capacity (tons) |
|---|---|---|---|
| Hooker Chemical Corporation . . . . | 114,000 | Columbus, Miss.[a] | 65,000 |
| | | Taft, La.[a] | 40,000 |
| | | Niagara Falls, N.Y. | 9,000 |
| Pennwalt Corporation . . . . . . . | 72,000 | Calvert City, Ky.[a] | 37,000 |
| | | Portland, Ore. | 26,000 |
| | | Tacoma, Wash. | 9,000 |
| American Chemical Corporation . . . | 65,000 | Collinsville, Ala.[a] | 40,000 |
| | | Wenatchee, Wash. | 25,000 |
| Kerr-McGee Corporation . . . . . | 63,000 | Hamilton, Miss.[a] | 33,000 |
| | | Henderson, Nev. | 30,000 |
| International Minerals & Chemicals Corporation . . . . . . . . . | 40,000 | Orrington, Me. | 40,000 |
| Olin Corporation . . . . . . . | 20,000 | McIntosh, Ala.[a] | 20,000 |
| ERCO Corporation . . . . . . . | 20,000 | Monroe, La.[a] | 20,000 |
| Universal Paper Corporation . . . . | 20,000 | Rome, Ga.[a] | 20,000 |
| Georgia-Pacific Corporation . . . . | 15,000 | Plaquemine, La.[a] | 15,000 |
| Brunswick Chemical Company . . . | 11,000 | Brunswick, Ga.[a] | 11,000 |
| Southern Chemicals Corporation . . . | 10,000 | Reigelwood, N.C.[a] | 6,000 |
| | | Butler, Ala.[a] | 4,000 |
| Pacific Eng. and Prod. Co. of Nevada . . . . . . . . . | 5,000 | Henderson, Nev. | 5,000 |
| U.S. total . . . . . . . . . . . | 455,000 | | 455,000 |
| Southeastern U.S. total . . . . . . . . . . . . . . . . . . . . . . . . . . | | | 311,000 |

a. Plants serving the southeastern U.S. market.

**EXHIBIT 5**

Financial Statements of Selected Sodium Chlorate Producers, 1974–1978 (millions of dollars except per share data)

| | Pennwalt | | | | | Kerr-McGee | | | | | Inter. Minerals & Chemicals | | | | |
|---|---|---|---|---|---|---|---|---|---|---|---|---|---|---|---|
| | 1974 | 1975 | 1976 | 1977 | 1978 | 1974 | 1975 | 1976 | 1977 | 1978 | 1974 | 1975 | 1976 | 1977 | 1978 |
| Sales | $641 | $714 | $777 | $835 | $921 | $1,550 | $1,799 | $1,955 | $2,165 | $2,072 | $859 | $1,303 | $1,260 | $1,280 | $1,364 |
| Net income | 27 | 33 | 35 | 42 | 45 | 116 | 131 | 134 | 119 | 118 | 70 | 166 | 135 | 108 | 120 |
| Earnings per share | $2.81 | $3.25 | $3.56 | $4.23 | $4.54 | $4.64 | $5.15 | $5.19 | $4.61 | $4.57 | $3.59 | $9.91 | $7.73 | $6.09 | $6.61 |
| Dividends per share | 1.24 | 1.36 | 1.54 | 2.25 | 2.05 | .85 | 1.00 | 1.19 | 1.25 | 1.25 | .57 | 1.38 | 2.10 | 2.45 | 2.60 |
| Dividend yield | 7.4% | 4.6% | 4.9% | 5.2% | 6.7% | 1.4% | 1.4% | 1.8% | 2.7% | 2.6% | 1.9% | 5.3% | 5.9% | 6.4% | 7.4% |
| Common stock prices | | | | | | | | | | | | | | | |
| High | $26 | $30 | $38 | $39 | $43 | $93 | $95 | $83 | $75 | $53 | $41 | $49 | $42 | $44 | $44 |
| Low | 15 | 17 | 27 | 32 | 32 | 47 | 60 | 61 | 45 | 40 | 21 | 31 | 33 | 35 | 34 |
| Closing | 17 | 28 | 33 | 39 | 33 | 72 | 70 | 68 | 47 | 48 | 39 | 38 | 41 | 41 | 35 |
| Closing P/E ratio | 6.0 | 8.6 | 9.3 | 9.2 | 7.3 | 15.5 | 13.6 | 13.1 | 10.2 | 10.5 | 10.9 | 3.8 | 5.3 | 6.7 | 5.3 |
| Total capitalization | $371 | $441 | $469 | $500 | $524 | $851 | $1,091 | $1,325 | $1,433 | $1,533 | $577 | $781 | $990 | $1,083 | $1,161 |
| % debt | 28% | 34% | 33% | 34% | 31% | 19% | 20% | 24% | 21% | 17% | 42% | 38% | 37% | 36% | 32% |
| % preferred stock | — | — | — | — | — | — | — | — | — | — | 10% | 4% | 2% | 1% | 1% |
| % common stock | 72% | 66% | 67% | 66% | 69% | 81% | 80% | 76% | 79% | 83% | 48% | 58% | 61% | 63% | 67% |
| Beta | | | 1.33 | | | | | 1.06 | | | | | .81 | | |
| Interest coverage[b] | 2.9 | 3.3 | 3.8 | 4.1 | 4.2 | 19.4 | 17.1 | 10.8 | 8.4 | 6.4 | 5.5 | 11.6 | 8.4 | 5.5 | 6.3 |
| Bond rating[c] | | | A/A | | | | | AA/Aa | | | | | N/A | | |

| | Georgia-Pacific | | | | | Brunswick Chemical | | | | | Southern Chemicals | | | | |
|---|---|---|---|---|---|---|---|---|---|---|---|---|---|---|---|
| | 1974 | 1975 | 1976 | 1977 | 1978 | 1974 | 1975 | 1976 | 1977 | 1978 | 1974 | 1975 | 1976 | 1977 | 1978 |
| Sales | $2,432 | $2,359 | $3,038 | $3,675 | $4,403 | $1.9 | $2.1 | $3.0 | $4.0 | $4.3 | $1.7 | $2.0 | $2.7 | $3.6 | $3.9 |
| Net income | 164 | 148 | 215 | 262 | 302 | .20 | .15 | .37 | .71 | .79 | .10 | (.05) | .28 | .74 | .73 |
| Earnings per share | $1.74 | $1.54 | $2.12 | $2.54 | $2.93 | $.40 | $.30 | $.74 | $1.42 | $1.58 | $.61 | $(.24) | $1.38 | $3.69 | $3.66 |
| Dividends per share | .47 | .49 | .70 | .83 | 1.03 | .10 | .10 | .15 | .35 | .40 | — | a | a | — | .30 |
| Dividend yield | 3.1% | 1.9% | 2.1% | 3.5% | 4.5% | a | a | a | 2.9% | 3.5% | a | a | a | 1.2% | 1.3% |
| Common stock prices | | | | | | | | | | | | | | | |
| High | $27 | $30 | $37 | $37 | $33 | a | a | a | $13 | $14¼ | a | a | a | $28 | $31 |
| Low | 13 | 16 | 26 | 25 | 24 | a | a | a | 7½ | 9 | a | a | a | 11 | 20 |
| Closing | 15 | 26 | 37 | 28 | 24 | a | a | a | 12 | 11½ | a | a | a | 25 | 23 |
| Closing P/E ratio | 8.6 | 16.9 | 17.4 | 11.0 | 8.2 | a | a | a | 8.5 | 7.3 | a | a | a | 6.7 | 6.4 |
| Total capitalization | $1,935 | $2,150 | $2,045 | $2,541 | $2,878 | $1.8 | $1.9 | $2.1 | $2.6 | $3.2 | $1.6 | $1.5 | $1.8 | $2.4 | $3.0 |
| % debt | 45% | 42% | 22% | 29% | 29% | 33% | 30% | 25% | 19% | 15% | 50% | 50% | 41% | 28% | 21% |
| % preferred stock | — | — | — | — | — | — | — | — | — | — | — | — | — | — | — |
| % common stock | 55% | 58% | 78% | 71% | 71% | 67% | 70% | 75% | 81% | 85% | 50% | 50% | 59% | 72% | 79% |
| Beta | | | 1.50 | | | | | | 1.10 | | | | | 1.20 | |
| Interest coverage[b] | 4.3 | 4.4 | 8.1 | 9.9 | 9.3 | 6.7 | 5.0 | 12.3 | 47 | 53 | 3.5 | .4 | 9.0 | 22 | 24 |
| Bond rating[c] | | | AA/Aa | | | | | NR | | | | | NR | | |

a. Stock not publicly traded.

b. Defined as EBIT/interest.

c. Standard and Poor's rating/Moody's rating; NR = not rated.

**EXHIBIT 6**
Financial Statements for the Collinsville Plant, 1974–1979 (thousands of dollars)

|  | 1974 | 1975 | 1976 | 1977 | 1978 | 1979[a] |
|---|---|---|---|---|---|---|
| *Operating Data* | | | | | | |
| Sales (tons) . . . . . | 36,899 | 30,819 | 37,464 | 40,076 | 39,790 | 38,507 |
| Average price ($/ton) . . | $ 188 | $ 243 | $ 295 | $ 367 | $ 392 | $ 413 |
| Sales . . . . . | $ 6,937 | $ 7,489 | $11,052 | $14,708 | $15,598 | $15,903 |
| Variable costs | | | | | | |
| Power . . . . . . | 2,935 | 3,395 | 4,631 | 5,530 | 6,173 | 6,759 |
| Graphite . . . . | 354 | 369 | 545 | 653 | 689 | 714 |
| Salt and other . . . . | 693 | 800 | 1,047 | 1,274 | 1,307 | 1,385 |
| Total variable costs . | 3,982 | 4,564 | 6,223 | 7,457 | 8,169 | 8,858 |
| Fixed costs | | | | | | |
| Labor . . . . . . | 590 | 608 | 646 | 739 | 924 | 1,072 |
| Maintenance . . . . | 143 | 201 | 220 | 272 | 235 | 237 |
| Other . . . . . . | 474 | 659 | 902 | 1,063 | 509 | 1,107 |
| Total fixed costs . . | 1,207 | 1,468 | 1,768 | 2,074 | 1,668 | 2,416 |
| Total manufacturing costs | 5,189 | 6,032 | 7,991 | 9,531 | 9,837 | 11,274 |
| Depreciation . . . . . | 433 | 394 | 402 | 391 | 384 | 399 |
| Selling . . . . . . | 114 | 92 | 126 | 155 | 181 | 204 |
| R&D . . . . . . . . | 105 | 154 | 207 | 274 | 351 | 429 |
| Total other costs . . | 652 | 640 | 735 | 820 | 916 | 1,032 |
| Operating profit . . . . | $ 1,096 | $ 817 | $ 2,326 | $ 4,357 | $ 4,845 | $ 3,597 |
| *Percent of Sales Ratios* | | | | | | |
| Power costs . . . . | 42.3% | 45.3% | 41.9% | 37.6% | 39.6% | 42.5% |
| Variable costs . . . . | 57.4 | 60.9 | 56.3 | 50.7 | 52.4 | 55.7 |
| Fixed costs . . . . . | 17.4 | 19.6 | 16.0 | 14.1 | 10.7 | 15.2 |
| Manufacturing costs . . | 74.8 | 80.5 | 72.3 | 64.8 | 63.1 | 70.9 |
| Operating profit . . . . | 15.8 | 10.9 | 21.0 | 29.6 | 31.1 | 22.6 |
| Accounts receivable . . | 10.1 | 10.4 | 10.2 | 9.9 | 10.1 | 10.2 |
| Inventories . . . . . | 3.7 | 7.3 | 6.2 | 4.4 | 4.1 | 4.1 |
| Accounts payable . . . | 5.8 | 6.3 | 5.6 | 5.3 | 5.1 | 5.5 |
| Net assets . . . . . . | 66.6 | 64.5 | 47.0 | 35.2 | 34.5 | 34.0 |
| *Asset Data* | | | | | | |
| Accounts receivable . . | $ 701 | $ 779 | $ 1,128 | $ 1,456 | $ 1,575 | $ 1,622 |
| Inventories . . . . . | 254 | 544 | 681 | 647 | 639 | 651 |
| Net property, plant, and equipment . . . . . | 4,066 | 3,978 | 4,003 | 3,853 | 3,964 | 4,014 |
| Total assets . . . | 5,021 | 6,301 | 5,812 | 6,956 | 6,178 | 6,287 |
| Accounts payable . . . | 402 | 472 | 619 | 780 | 795 | 873 |
| Net assets . . . . | $ 4,619 | $ 4,829 | $ 5,193 | $ 5,176 | $ 5,383 | $ 5,414 |
| Operating profit/net assets | 23.7% | 16.9% | 44.8% | 84.2% | 90.0% | 66.4% |

a. Expected.

**EXHIBIT 7**

Financial Statements for Dixon Corporation, 1975–1979 (thousands of dollars except per share data)

|  | 1975 | 1976 | 1977 | 1978 | 1979[a] |
|---|---|---|---|---|---|
| *Income Statements* | | | | | |
| Sales | $19,128 | $23,830 | $28,348 | $34,770 | $42,259 |
| Cost of goods sold | 14,085 | 16,889 | 19,950 | 24,467 | 29,185 |
| Selling and administrative | 1,952 | 2,308 | 2,824 | 3,291 | 4,436 |
| Research | 325 | 388 | 593 | 682 | 716 |
| Interest | 400 | 320 | 240 | 160 | 80 |
| Taxes | 1,125 | 1,878 | 2,285 | 2,932 | 3,818 |
| Profit after taxes | $ 1,241 | $ 2,047 | $ 2,456 | $ 3,238 | $ 4,024 |
| Earnings per share | $ 1.13 | $ 1.86 | $ 2.23 | $ 2.94 | $ 3.66 |
| Dividends per share | .20 | .30 | .40 | .40 | .50 |
| *Balance Sheets* | | | | | |
| Cash and marketable securities | $ 385 | $ 357 | $ 556 | $ 1,273 | $ 2,996 |
| Other current assets | 4,208 | 5,016 | 5,939 | 7,267 | 8,917 |
| Property, plant, and equipment | 7,436 | 7,895 | 8,354 | 8,842 | 8,918 |
| Total assets | $12,029 | $13,268 | $14,849 | $17,382 | $20,831 |
| Current liabilities | $ 2,314 | $ 2,836 | $ 3,402 | $ 4,138 | $ 5,113 |
| Debt (including current maturity) | 5,000 | 4,000 | 3,000 | 2,000 | 1,000 |
| Stockholders' equity | 4,715 | 6,432 | 8,447 | 11,244 | 14,718 |
| Total liabilities and equity | $12,029 | $13,268 | $14,849 | $17,382 | $20,831 |
| Stock price range | $ 7–14 | $ 8–22 | $ 19–30 | $ 25–40 | $ 35–45 |
| Closing stock price | 9 | 20 | 27 | 38 | 40[b] |
| Beta | | | 1.06 | | |
| Bond rating | | | NR | | |

NR = not rated.

a. Expected.

b. October 30, 1979.

**EXHIBIT 8**

Pro Forma Financial Statements for the Collinsville Plant, 1979–1984 (thousands of dollars)

| | 1979[a] | 1980 | 1981 | 1982 | 1983 | 1984 |
|---|---|---|---|---|---|---|
| *Operating Data* | | | | | | |
| Sales (tons) | 32,000 | 35,000 | 38,000 | 38,000 | 38,000 |
| Average price ($/ton) | $ 415 | $ 480 | $ 520 | $ 562 | $ 606 |
| Sales | $13,280 | $16,800 | $19,760 | $21,356 | $23,028 |
| Variable costs | | | | | | |
| Power | 6,304 | 7,735 | 9,386 | 10,526 | 11,780 |
| Graphite | 645 | 791 | 875 | 940 | 992 |
| Salt and other | 1,285 | 1,621 | 1,753 | 1,836 | 1,956 |
| Total variable costs | 8,234 | 10,147 | 12,014 | 13,302 | 14,728 |
| Fixed costs | | | | | | |
| Labor | 1,180 | 1,297 | 1,427 | 1,580 | 1,738 |
| Maintenance | 256 | 277 | 299 | 322 | 354 |
| Other | 1,154 | 1,148 | 1,179 | 1,113 | 1,153 |
| Total fixed costs | 2,590 | 2,722 | 2,905 | 3,015 | 3,245 |
| Total manufacturing costs | 10,824 | 12,869 | 14,919 | 16,317 | 17,973 |
| Selling | 112 | 125 | 138 | 152 | 168 |
| R&D | 451 | 478 | 508 | 543 | 591 |
| Depreciation | 1,060 | 1,110 | 1,160 | 1,210 | 1,270 |
| Total other costs | 1,623 | 1,713 | 1,806 | 1,905 | 2,029 |
| Operating profit | $ 833 | $ 2,218 | $ 3,035 | $ 3,134 | $ 3,026 |
| *Percent of Sales Ratios* | | | | | | |
| Power costs | 47.5% | 46.0% | 47.5% | 49.3% | 51.2% |
| Variable costs | 62.0 | 60.4 | 60.8 | 62.3 | 64.0 |
| Fixed costs | 19.5 | 16.2 | 14.7 | 14.1 | 14.1 |
| Manufacturing costs | 81.5 | 76.6 | 75.5 | 76.4 | 78.0 |
| Operating profit | 6.3 | 13.2 | 15.4 | 14.7 | 13.1 |
| Accounts receivable | 10.0 | 10.0 | 10.0 | 10.0 | 10.0 |
| Inventories | 4.5 | 4.5 | 4.5 | 4.5 | 4.5 |
| Accounts payable | 5.5 | 5.5 | 5.5 | 5.5 | 5.5 |
| Net assets | 84.5 | 65.2 | 53.7 | 47.5 | 41.8 |
| *Asset Data* | | | | | | |
| Accounts receivable | $ 1,622 | $ 1,328 | $ 1,680 | $ 1,976 | $ 2,136 | $ 2,303 |
| Inventories | 651 | 598 | 756 | 889 | 961 | 1,036 |
| Net property, plant, and equipment | 10,600 | 10,025 | 9,440 | 8,840 | 8,230 | 7,560 |
| Total assets | 12,873 | 11,951 | 11,876 | 11,705 | 11,327 | 10,899 |
| Accounts payable | 873 | 730 | 924 | 1,087 | 1,175 | 1,267 |
| Net assets | $12,000 | $11,221 | $10,952 | $10,618 | $10,152 | $ 9,632 |
| Operating profit/Net assets | | 7.4% | 20.3% | 28.6% | 30.9% | 31.4% |

*Note:* These pro forma financial statements were based on the following assumptions: (1) Continued use of *unlaminated* graphite electrodes. (2) Though excess industry capacity would hold price increases to less than an 8% annual rate in 1980, by 1984 the average annual price increase over the period 1979–1984 was assumed to equal 8%. (3) Power costs per kwh would increase 12% per year. (4) Depreciation would increase, because Dixon would have written up the value of the Collinsville plant to $10.6 million.

a. Expected.

# Dynatronics, Inc.

Ms. Liz Kraft, chief financial officer at Dynatronics, Inc., was concerned about the company's future investment and financing programs. A rapidly growing market combined with the introduction of a new product and efforts to be more responsive to customer delivery needs required considerable external financing. In April 1989, however, the company's financing opportunities were severely restricted by its current financial position.

## Background

Dynatronics was founded in Burlington, Massachusetts, in 1979 by three electrical engineers. At the outset, stock in the company was owned entirely by the three founders. Later, stock options were granted to two managers as an inducement to join the company. These options were exercised, and by 1989 the entire equity was owned by these five people in approximately equal blocks. The five also held all the top management positions and constituted the board of directors.

In the period from formation through 1988 Dynatronics enjoyed considerable success. The product line was expanded from one original product to include several lines of proprietary items sold as components. These products performed decision control, storage, and ancillary functions as components of digital systems. They were primarily produced for off-the-shelf sale to customers who used them in systems of their own design and manufacture. Company profit came principally from the sale of these proprietary products.

© 1989 by the President and Fellows of Harvard College.
Harvard Business School Case 289–063.

As the company expanded, it also began to manufacture to order a variety of special-purpose systems that applied digital techniques to computing, information handling, control tasks, and data processing. The systems were used in space equipment, navigation and positioning systems, signal processing, data converters, and a variety of other areas associated directly or indirectly with government expenditures for military and nonmilitary purposes. This business accounted for roughly one fourth of Dynatronics' sales. The company profited from the inclusion of its products in these systems, but little if any additional profit was gained by providing engineering services.

Dynatronics' proprietary products were subject to a high rate of obsolescence in an extremely competitive market. Although protected by patents, these items were always exposed to the competition of alternatively engineered products performing the same functions. Typically, the company's new products achieved about three fourths of their highest sales level in their first year. Peak volumes were reached and maintained in the second and third years. These years normally were followed by steep decay and virtual worthlessness by the sixth or seventh year. This 6- to 7-year cycle had been cut short by competitive developments for about 20% of the new products that the company had introduced during the past 10 years, and on those occasions Dynatronics had been forced to absorb substantial inventory write-offs.

The danger of being leapfrogged technically was met by unstinting expenditures on research and development to improve existing product lines and add new ones. Company officials had been successful in recruiting and holding a strong research group, and this group, supported by ample budgetary allocations, had created enviable market respect for the quality of the company's products. The five owner-managers were determined to maintain that reputation.

Over the years continuing expansion led to a number of changes in Dynatronics' internal organization. Sales outlets were established in Silicon Valley, and late in 1987 a small plant was constructed there for the design and production of systems for the aerospace industry. Earlier, production of proprietary products had been shifted from Burlington to a wholly owned subsidiary in Puerto Rico, largely because of the availability in that area of a low-wage labor force. Production operations at the subsidiary consisted almost entirely of assembling and packaging modules and allied components. Other managerial offices remained at the original site in Burlington.

In the period after 1985, rapidly widening product acceptance almost trebled the company's sales (Exhibit 1), and its investment in current assets expanded accordingly (Exhibit 2). Short-term loans, secured by the pledge of receivables, were obtained from Dynatronics' local bank to support this growing requirement. The bank had been willing to lend 85% of the face amount of the receivables, and this banking arrangement had proved generally satisfactory until early 1989. At that time an officer of the bank made it clear that Dynatronics had reached the limit of the credit line that the bank was willing to extend in the absence of some improvement in the company's capital structure. New equity would qualify Dynatronics for a larger loan, but the loan limit would no longer be increased as accounts receivable grew if the ratio of total liabilities to net worth exceeded 2.0.

As sales continued to increase in 1989, the company continued to produce earnings in approximately the same proportion to sales as in 1988, but the retention of these earnings failed to alter the bank's stand on additional financing. When approached in April, the loan officer was unwilling to extend additional credit.

He did offer to introduce Ms. Kraft to the factoring division of the bank. This division serviced higher-risk customers with accounts receivable financing. It generally set no limit on liabilities-to-net worth ratios and would lend up to 90% of the accounts receivable balances outstanding. This division of the bank would monitor Dynatronics' credit extension and accounts receivable collection activities much more closely than the bank's commercial loan department could. Because of greater risk and the extra costs involved in closer monitoring of the loan, the interest rate charged by the bank would rise from prime plus 1½% to prime plus 4% on the total loans outstanding to Dynatronics. The prime rate was currently 11½%.

## Growth Prospects

In late April, Ms. Kraft prepared the forecast shown in Table A of Dynatronics' year-end 1989 current asset position to help in assessing the company's immediate financing problems. The forecast assumed sales of $34 million and a corresponding cost-of-goods-sold figure of $20.74 million. These estimates had been employed with some confidence in projecting working capital requirements, since sales in recent months and impressions of customers' production plans for the balance of the year pointed toward continued growth. Receivables had been estimated at 22% of sales, and raw materials and work in process at a four weeks' rate of usage. Finished goods, on the other hand, had been projected at about a two-week supply.

During preceding months finished-goods inventory had been deliberately reduced in relation to sales as other cash requirements had mounted. Ms. Kraft believed that continued curtailment of investment in the finished-goods inventory was likely to be costly in terms of lost sales and competitive position. But without

**TABLE A**
Forecast of Dynatronics' Current Assets at Year-End 1989 (thousands of dollars)

| | |
|---|---:|
| Cash | $ 680 |
| Receivables . . . . . . . . . . . . | 7,480 |
| Inventory | |
|     Raw materials . . . . . . . . . . | 1,182 |
|     Work in process . . . . . . . . . | 1,721 |
|     Finished goods . . . . . . . . . | 830 |
| Prepaid expenses . . . . . . . . . | 77 |
|     Current assets . . . . . . . . . | $11,970 |

other immediate sources of funds, she felt, the stock of finished goods would have to be held to the projected level if the company were to avoid an acute cash emergency.

The marketing manager had estimated that sales of the company's current products would reach $40 million in 1990. Without major product innovation, he thought, sales could probably be maintained at that level in 1991, but if past patterns prevailed, he expected a decline of $10–12 million in 1992. The forecast for 1990 was based on the marketing group's knowledge of government appropriations for ongoing defense and aerospace programs. It could be upset by project cancellations, but these were considered highly unlikely for the projects concerned. On the other hand, the plateau and descent pattern of the more distant estimates emphasized the importance of maintaining Dynatronics' technical preeminence.

## Investment Possibilities

Ms. Kraft was under pressure to finance both the existing business lines and two opportunities for investment that might improve the projected sales pattern and its profit consequences. One investment possibility involved the introduction of a major new product line, and the other a revision of the company's finished-goods inventory control system.

The new product line, which had been under development for the past 2 years, was believed to possess technical qualities that would give it significant competitive advantages. All the items making up the line were in a late stage of development, and the line was currently scheduled for introduction at the end of the year. Market reception was difficult to gauge, but the marketing manager was confident that the line would contribute sales of at least $5 million in 1990 and $6.5 million in 1991. The line would be priced to give the same gross profit margins as the company's other products.

To put the line into production in the Puerto Rico plant required about $250,000 for specialized equipment. The plant had been built to accommodate more growth than had yet been realized, and no additional outlays were anticipated for production facilities. However, the marketing manager estimated that a budget allocation of $90,000 in addition to a normal allocation of selling, general, and administrative expenses would be needed to introduce and promote the line if it were to achieve its full potential. Additional investment in working capital would also be required to support the added sales.

The second investment possibility—that of increasing stocks of finished goods—grew out of a widespread feeling that economizing in that direction had already been pushed far beyond justifiable limits. Expediting had become commonplace in juggling production schedules, with costly consequences, and orders had been lost to competitors with disturbing frequency when customers were notified of long but necessary delivery delays. Ms. Kraft therefore had ordered a review of the company's entire inventory control system.

As a result of that study, the area of concern had been narrowed to the finished-goods segment of total inventory. Some improvements seemed possible in balancing raw material stocks, but it was not thought that this would lead to any appreciable change in the relation of total raw material inventory to production volume. Lead time required by the purchasing department and limited interchangeability of parts among product lines combined to fix the required total at roughly a four-week supply. Work-in-process inventory seemed similarly intractable. According to the production manager, allocation of shop labor, timing of lot starts, schedules, and so on, were already being decided on grounds of optimum production arrangements. Technical changes, necessitating work stoppages, often had to be introduced during the in-process stage, and therefore the production manager as well as the engineering group attached considerable value to the flexibility allowed by a four-week production period.

In contrast with its approval of current raw material and in-process control practices, the report recommended complete revamping of the system being used to determine finished-goods inventory levels. The present system was based on specific item-by-item sales forecasts for the coming quarter. Given those forecasts, goods were scheduled into production in quantities that would raise the level of existing stocks to the anticipated sales requirement. Recent financial circumstances had made it necessary to cut stocks below the target levels that would have been set in more normal circumstances, but the report's condemnation of the system was independent of that experience.

The report's criticism focused on the system's dependence on quarterly sales forecasts and the inaccuracy of such estimates. Replacement demand could be predicted with tolerable margins of error, but new orders were typically received at erratic intervals. Moreover, new orders composed a large part of the total demand for most products.

The report urged adopting a system of buffer stocks that would be set with more careful consideration of costs, returns, and risks associated with inventory maintenance. Data had been compiled on five possible inventory-to-sales ratio levels, representing substantially different inventory policies (Exhibit 3). In each case, the lost-sales estimate was derived from computer simulations (using appropriate reorder points and reorder quantities) of the demand experience of major product lines.

Since Dynatronics was currently operating with lower finished-goods stocks than those contemplated by any one of the five alternative policies, Ms. Kraft was particularly impressed by the magnitude of the lost-sales figures. She was also concerned about the inventory investment required to cut those losses by appreciable amounts. Any marked change in inventory policy would exacerbate existing financial problems.

## Financing Alternatives

While Dynatronics could gain additional financing by turning to the factoring division of the firm's commercial bank, a public offering of common stock was also an alternative. Discussions with investment bankers had led Ms. Kraft to anticipate that Dynatronics could issue up to 400,000 shares of new common

**TABLE B**
Yields on Debt Securities, April 1989

| Maturity and Bond Rating | Yield to Maturity |
|---|---|
| 90-day Treasury bills | 8.90% |
| 10-year Treasury bonds | 9.15 |
| 10-year AA corporate bonds | 10.07 |
| 10-year A corporate bonds | 10.50 |
| 10-year BB corporate bonds | 13.69 |

stock at a price of $6.50 per share. This offering price would net Dynatronics about $5.00 per share after the costs and expenses associated with the offering had been deducted. Ms. Kraft planned to review the proposed stock offering price in relation to the publicly traded stock of Dynatronics' competitors (see Exhibit 4) and in relation to Dynatronics' future prospects with and without a common stock offering. The yields on debt securities of varying credit quality in late April 1989 are shown in Table B.

An alternative to the external financing possibilities was continued reliance on the reinvestment of earnings with no payment of dividends. Ms. Kraft thought that the outlook for expansion and the profitability of contemplated funds commitments probably threw into doubt the wisdom of that policy, but she was uncertain about which investment and financing alternatives to recommend to her fellow shareholders.

**EXHIBIT 1**
Income Statements for Years Ending December 31, 1986–1988 (thousands of dollars except per share data)

|  | 1986 | 1987 | 1988 |
|---|---|---|---|
| Net sales | $9,040 | $13,860 | $26,593 |
| Cost of goods sold | 5,920 | 8,870 | 16,221 |
| Gross profit | 3,120 | 4,990 | 10,372 |
| Research and development | 1,055 | 1,455 | 2,743 |
| Selling and administrative expenses | 1,955 | 2,911 | 5,940 |
| Income from operations | 110 | 624 | 1,689 |
| Interest expense | 75 | 100 | 393 |
| Other expenses | 13 | 5 | 20 |
| Pre-tax income | 23 | 519 | 1,276 |
| Income taxes[a] | 8 | 207 | 510 |
| Profit after taxes | $ 15 | $ 311 | $ 766 |
| Earnings per share | $ .01 | $ .19 | $ .43 |

*Note:* Figures may not add exactly because of rounding.

a. After 1986, Dynatronics' effective income tax rate at the federal and state levels was 40%.

**EXHIBIT 2**

Balance Sheets at December 31, 1986–1988 (thousands of dollars)

| | 1986 | 1987 | 1988 |
|---|---|---|---|
| Cash | $ 305 | $ 400 | $ 502 |
| Accounts receivable | 1,733 | 3,150 | 5,638 |
| Inventories | | | |
|   Raw materials | 320 | 497 | 930 |
|   Work in process | 468 | 816 | 1,343 |
|   Finished goods | 610 | 736 | 1,018 |
| Prepaid expenses | 20 | 33 | 60 |
|    Current assets | 3,455 | 5,632 | 9,490 |
| Gross fixed assets | 530 | 745 | 1,343 |
| Less: Accumulated depreciation | 180 | 300 | 388 |
| Net fixed assets | 350 | 445 | 955 |
|     Total assets | $3,805 | $6,077 | $10,445 |
| Notes payable[a] | $ 960 | $2,161 | $ 4,537 |
| Accounts payable | 398 | 621 | 1,210 |
| Accrued expenses | 323 | 444 | 811 |
| Provision for taxes[b] | 23 | 200 | 303 |
| Other | 50 | 255 | 400 |
|    Current liabilities | 1,753 | 3,680 | 7,261 |
| Common stock ($.50 par value) | 795 | 820 | 900 |
| Paid in surplus | 1,215 | 1,223 | 1,164 |
| Retained earnings | 43 | 354 | 1,119 |
|     Stockholders' equity | 2,053 | 2,396 | 3,183 |
| Total liabilities and stockholders' equity | $3,805 | $6,077 | $10,445 |
| Number of shares outstanding | 1,590,215 | 1,637,805 | 1,799,365 |

*Note:* Figures may not add exactly because of rounding.

a. Secured by accounts receivable.

b. In order to avoid a penalty for underpayment of income taxes, Dynatronics made equal estimated tax payments quarterly on the 15th of April, June, September, and December of each year. The total of these four quarterly payments was required to equal *at least* the lesser of (1) 90% of the taxes that would actually be incurred in the year in question, or (2) 100% of the taxes due on income of the prior year.

**EXHIBIT 3**

Selected Financial Data on Possible Inventory Policies (thousands of dollars)

| Alternative | Inventory/ Cost of Goods Sold[a] | Total Investment in Finished-Goods Inventory[a] | Annual Sales Loss Because of Stockouts | Annual Combined Setup, Warehouse, Handling, and Insurance Costs[b] |
|---|---|---|---|---|
| Pro forma 1989 . . | 3.8% (14 days' sales) | $ 830 | $1,667 | $43 |
| A . . . | 4.9 (18 days' sales) | 1,022 | 1,267 | 53 |
| B . . . | 6.6 (24 days' sales) | 1,363 | 771 | 64 |
| C . . . | 8.7 (32 days' sales) | 1,818 | 384 | 77 |
| D . . . | 11.5 (42 days' sales) | 2,386 | 143 | 90 |
| E . . . | .0 (51 days' sales) | 2,898 | 44 | 95 |

a. Based on forecast annual cost-of-sales rate of $20.74 million for 1989.

b. Interest expense or other financing costs are not included.

**EXHIBIT 4**

Financial Data for Dynatronics and Selected Competitors, 1986–1989

| | AMP Inc. | | | | Analog Devices, Inc. | | | |
|---|---|---|---|---|---|---|---|---|
| | 1986 | 1987 | 1988 | 4/24/89[a] | 1986 | 1987 | 1988 | 4/29/89[a] |
| Sales ($ millions) . . . . . . . . | 1,934 | 2,318 | 2,670 | | 334 | 370 | 439 | |
| Earnings per share ($) . . . . . . | 1.52 | 2.31 | 2.96 | 3.10 | .51 | .40 | .80 | 1.05 |
| Dividends per share ($) . . . . . . | .74 | .85 | 1.00 | | – | – | – | |
| Closing stock price ($) . . . . . . | 36⅛ | 46¾ | 44½ | 42⅝ | 15⅝ | 11¼ | 12¼ | 11⅜ |
| Shares outstanding (millions) . . . | 108.1 | 107.5 | 108.5 | | 43.9 | 45.3 | 46.9 | |
| Book value per share ($) . . . . . | 10.50 | 12.54 | 15.10 | | 5.65 | 5.71 | 6.87 | |
| Return on equity . . . . . . . | .145 | .185 | .195 | .185 | .087 | .065 | .111 | .125 |
| Capitalization | | | | | | | | |
| Book value of debt (%) . . . . . | 4 | 5 | 5 | | 10 | 7 | 5 | |
| Book value of equity (%) . . . . | 96 | 95 | 95 | | 90 | 93 | 95 | |
| Beta . . . . . . . . . . . | | | 1.4 | | | | 1.35 | |

| | Dynatech Corporation | | | | Dynatronics, Inc. | | | |
|---|---|---|---|---|---|---|---|---|
| | 1986 | 1987 | 1988 | 4/24/89[a] | 1986 | 1987 | 1988 | |
| Sales ($ millions) . . . . . . . . | 305 | 368 | 400 | | 9 | 14 | 27 | |
| Earnings per share ($) . . . . . . | 2.10 | 2.08 | 2.05 | 2.30 | .01 | .19 | .43 | |
| Dividends per share ($) . . . . . . | – | – | – | | – | – | – | |
| Closing stock price ($) . . . . . . | 30⅞ | 19¾ | 18 | 17½ | na | na | na | |
| Shares outstanding (millions) . . . | 11.1 | 11.8 | 12.0 | | 1.6 | 1.6 | 1.8 | |
| Book value per share ($) . . . . . | 11.15 | 12.86 | 13.75 | | 1.29 | 1.46 | 1.77 | |
| Return on equity . . . . . . . | .188 | .161 | .150 | .185 | .007 | .130 | .240 | |
| Capitalization | | | | | | | | |
| Book value of debt (%) . . . . . | 25 | 22 | 18 | | 32 | 47 | 59 | |
| Book value of equity (%) . . . . | 75 | 78 | 82 | | 68 | 53 | 41 | |
| Beta . . . . . . . . . . . | | | 1.3 | | | | na | |

na = not available.

a. Security analysts' estimates for year-end earnings and return on equity (ROE) of common stock; actual data as of 4/24/89 for stock prices.

# Nova Chemical Corporation

In November 1989, Joan Donahue, vice president of finance of Nova Chemical Corporation, faced two financial decisions. One concerned the financing of a major investment to be made in new production facilities for the rapidly expanding Environmental Products Division (EPD). These new "state-of-the-art" facilities would not only improve EPD's operating margins but also provide the capacity to accommodate an expected surge in the division's sales growth over the next five years. The second concerned a possible sale of Nova's more slowly growing Industrial Products Division (IPD). An unsolicited offer to buy the net assets of IPD for $160 million had recently been received from United Chemical, Inc, a well-known basic chemicals manufacturer. The offer equaled only about half the net book value of the assets of IPD (see Exhibit 1). While Nova's management had been aware of IPD's inadequate profitability, the meager size of United's offer shocked Nova's board of directors into demanding a complete review of the value of IPD. The timing of the offer was consistent with United Chemical's history of making acquisitions during periods when earnings were expected to be under pressure in the basic chemicals industry.

The decision on the sale of IPD would markedly affect Nova's long-range financial planning. Because of the cyclical nature of the chemical industry, long-range planning had come to be accepted as a necessary and valuable activity. Each division was expected to review and update its current 5-year plan at yearly intervals as part of the company's regular budgeting routine. The plans were then sent to the headquarters financial staff to be consolidated and reviewed, and it was Ms. Donahue's responsibility to propose a matching financial plan for the company as a whole.

The plans that had been submitted for 1990–1994 showed that new financing would be required each year. The plans took into account the investment to be made in EPD's production facilities as well as previously approved investments in IPD and the Laboratory Products Division (LPD), but they did not reflect the possible sale of the Industrial Products Division (see Exhibits 2 and 3). This decision involved an amount large enough to cause substantial changes in Nova's external financing needs and thus perhaps the types of financing to be recommended. The possible sale of IPD thus had a direct bearing on the financial plan that Ms. Donahue was expected to present to Nova's directors at the December board meeting.

## Company Background

Nova had begun doing business as the Texas Chemical Company in 1951 in Brownsville, Texas. Initially the company was a basic chemicals manufacturer specializing in the production of organic chemicals. As the price of oil rose and became more volatile in the 1970s, the company began to diversify into the specialty chemicals business, supplying the rapidly growing scientific research and waste treatment markets. Product lines were added through acquisitions and, more important as time went on, through the development of a respectable in-house research and development capability. In 1975 the firm's name was changed to Nova, and 2 years later the company issued its first (and so far its only) public offering of common stock.

In 1979, Nova was formally divided into operating divisions so that management responsibilities could be more effectively defined in terms of markets and distribution channels. Three divisions were established: Industrial Products, Laboratory Products, and Environmental Products. This organization had continued. Some indication of the variety of products sold and customers served by each division in 1989 is given in Exhibit 4.

Nova's two specialty chemicals divisions (LPD and EPD) had experienced consistent growth, while the performance of its basic chemicals divisions (IPD) had been more erratic. (See Exhibit 5 for a description of the structure and 1989 outlook for the chemical industry.) While basic chemicals companies competed on price, specialty chemicals companies competed primarily on technology and service. For example, Nova's research and development group had been successful in developing several proprietary processes that enabled LPD to produce, in commercial quantities, ultra-pure chemicals for the growing scientific research market. Furthermore, the company retained these customers (over 100,000) by offering a wide range of products, superior customer service, and an inventory position that allowed LPD to ship most orders (average size: $200) on the day received.

EPD shared many of these characteristics. Enforcement of the Safe Drinking Water Act had resulted in strong growth in sales of EPD's products to municipalities, which currently represented 40% of the division's sales. Municipalities as well as industrial customers were serviced by a direct sales force composed of technical specialists in the area of waste treatment. A 10-year review of selected financial data is shown in Exhibit 6. Recent financial statements for Nova are presented in Exhibits 7 and 8.

The growth in demand for specialty chemicals had created intense competition among established manufacturers. Many were financially stronger and larger than Nova (see Exhibit 9). Additional competition had been created by the forward integration of a number of basic chemicals companies into specialty chemicals and by the entry of aggressive foreign companies. Nova's success, therefore, was probably best measured by the fact that market share had been gained in the specialty chemicals markets served by LPD and EPD.

The operating plan for LPD projected annual sales growth of about 15% for the 1990–1994 period, or approximately 21% in nominal terms assuming 6% inflation. Projected annual sales growth for EPD reflected several factors. The waste treatment market was expected to grow at a 13 percent real (19 percent nominal) rate over the 1990–1994 period. But more important, the new facilities, which would come on stream at the end of 1991, would give EPD the capacity to compete for the business of the largest customers. This had been a segment of the market that had been closed to EPD in the past due to capacity problems (see Exhibit 10).

## Capital Expenditures for the Environmental Products Division

The Environmental Products Division produced granular activated carbon, a product used to remove impurities in industrial processes and municipal water supplies. A proposal to significantly expand EDP's production facilities had been approved some months earlier, apart from the year's regular budget. Nova owned a suitable site for the plant in Mobile, Alabama. It was anticipated that plant construction and equipment installation could be completed by the end of 1991. The plant building was expected to cost $100 million and to take 1 year to build. A plant of this size could provide space for projected production growth through the year 2000. The specialized machinery needed to provide such production capacity was estimated to cost $150 million and to take an additional year to install. Approval of the project had therefore been viewed as a commitment to spend $100 million in 1990 and $150 million in 1991.

Unfortunately, a plant of this size was necessary to achieve critical scale economies in this business. There was acknowledged risk in building capacity ahead of market growth because the economic life of the equipment was most likely to be set by the pace of product technology, not by the physical durability of the equipment. For example, researchers at the University of Michigan had just announced the discovery of a highly effective clay-based product for use in the filtration of impurities. However, problems with recycling this new product remained. The fact that EPD's carbon-based product could be recycled (another important contribution of Nova's research and development group) was a major cost consideration of customers. Ms. Donahue was well aware that this development would make predicting future demand for EPD's products more difficult.

## Sale of the Industrial Products Division

One of Ms. Donahue's key decisions concerned the possible sale of IPD to United Chemical, Inc. The division manufactured and sold such basic chemicals as ethylene and propylene. Although the sale of IPD had not been under consideration prior to United Chemical's offer, Nova's president had been dissatisfied with IPD's performance in recent years. A prolonged period of price cutting was anticipated in the basic chemicals industry because of chronic excess capacity and expected modest growth in demand (see Exhibit 5). But more important, the president was uneasy about IPD's competitive position.

Unlike many of its fully integrated competitors, IPD purchased its primary raw material, petroleum, in the open market. This in itself had not been a problem, given the price and supply situation in the oil market in the 1980s. But in the mid-1980s, IPD's management had decided against a major capital investment program that would have converted IPD's plants into flexible production units capable of taking either petroleum or natural gas as feedstocks to produce ethylene and propylene. Many of IPD's major competitors had made the conversion and currently enjoyed the flexibility of switching feedstocks depending on the relative price advantage of petroleum or natural gas. The current cost of such a conversion, the industry outlook, and the projected volatility of petroleum and natural gas prices all argued against making such an investment in 1989. Thus, IPD's margins were affected not only by the cyclical nature of the basic chemicals industry but also by IPD's being unable to take advantage of natural gas prices when they were low relative to petroleum prices.

Virtually no integration existed between IPD and Nova's two other divisions. In addition to its distinctive products and customers, IPD had its own distribution channels and sales force. Because of the commodity nature of his business, the general manager of IPD believed, the company's internal accounting practices unfairly penalized the operating results of his division. Nova's research and development activities (estimated to cost $26.8 million in 1989) were centralized in a major facility in Houston, Texas. Little R&D was undertaken in areas of relevance to IPD. Nonetheless, Nova allocated corporate expenditures for R&D to each of the three divisions according to their relative sales volumes. For IPD, the $15 million charge anticipated for 1989 was substantial in relation to profits.

Ms. Donahue was aware of United Chemical's history of making opportunistic acquisitions during periods of weakness in the basic chemicals industry cycle, and she had to agree that the outlook for basic chemicals was not good. But Ms. Donahue had hoped initially to persuade United Chemical to raise its $160 million offer. That had proved impossible in the prevailing climate of low stock market price-earnings ratios for basic chemicals companies.

Consideration of the sale of IPD at the last board meeting had sparked a spirited discussion. Some board members questioned the sale of such a large part of Nova. This division represented the company's origins. Was it now to be discarded? And what were the longer-term policy implications of such an action? Alternatively, the low offer from United (which Nova believed was in excess of

IPD's liquidation value) indicated that IPD had not been a very good investment for Nova's shareholders. All members expressed concern about the effect of a sale on Nova's financial statements and stock price. For one thing, the sale of IPD for $160 million would create a $190.6 million pre-tax loss for both tax and shareholder reporting, although this loss could be taken against Nova's ordinary pre-tax income.

Nevertheless, Ms. Donahue felt that United Chemical's offer merited very serious consideration, as it would provide funds needed to finance the growth of the other two, more promising, divisions. Finally it was agreed that Ms. Donahue would present the pros and cons of a sale at the next board meeting.

## Financing Alternatives

Ms. Donahue and her staff, with the help of the firm's investment banker, had been investigating a variety of financing sources. While the financial markets had been quite volatile in the late 1980s, the situation in November 1989 was relatively calm, and improving. In line with the recent decline in Treasury rates, the bank prime rate was 10.5%, down from its recent peak of 11.5%. And yields on investment-grade corporate bonds were roughly 1 percentage point below their March 1989 levels. But in the noninvestment-grade (junk) bond market yields were unchanged or rising over the same time period (see Exhibit 11 for interest rates). While October 1989 had been a volatile month, the stock market in November had exhibited considerable strength, with the Dow Jones Industrial Average nearing its all-time high. Cyclical stocks like those of chemical companies were not in current favor, however.

In this environment of uncertain market access for low-rated firms, Ms. Donahue was forced to choose among a limited set of feasible financing options. Although she knew of firms that had been forced out of the market in recent months by unforeseen conditions, her best estimate was that at the present time the following financing options would be open to Nova:

1. Up to $100 million on a 2-year bank credit agreement at the prime rate (currently 10.5%). The balance outstanding at the end of 2 years would become payable in full at the end of the third year. This option would require (a) a compensating balance of 10% of the line; (b) a minimum working capital position (current assets less current liabilities) of $140 million; (c) a maximum ratio of total debt (short- and long-term) to net worth of 1.0; and (d) a limit on cumulative post-1989 dividends equal to 25% of cumulative post-1989 profit after taxes (excluding any loss on sale of IPD).

2. Up to $200 million issue of 15-year debentures at a coupon rate of 11.25% (BB+ rate), noncallable except for sinking fund purposes for 10 years, with fully amortizing sinking fund payments running from the sixth through the fifteenth year. Restrictions would be the same as under the bank credit agreement, with minor variations.

**3.** A single stock issue of up to $200 million at an estimated price of $22 per share, with net proceeds to the company of $21 per share.

Besides taking into account the covenants attached to these financing alternatives, Ms. Donahue was also aware of the desire of Nova's board of directors not to push below the current interest coverage ratio of 3.0.[1] Nova already had the lowest level of interest coverage among its major peer group competitors (see Exhibit 9), and the company was not anxious to explore the outer limits in this area.

Finally, Ms. Donahue had considered the possibility of a convertible debenture. However, a brief investigation revealed a weak market for such securities as of late 1989. Ms. Donahue was also interested in the financing terms she might be able to obtain on the financing options in subsequent years. Although no one could forecast the exact terms in the future, she did have some assurance that these three options would be available to Nova in future rounds of financing through 1991.

Nova had sought long-term financing twice before. In 1980 the firm had sold $100 million of 15-year, 12.5% debentures to two insurance companies. Sinking fund payments of $10 million per year began in 1985 and were scheduled to remain at that level to maturity. In 1983 the company issued $190 million of 20-year, 11.5% debentures in the public debt market. Sinking fund payments of $10 million per year were scheduled to start in 1991 and remain at that level to maturity (see Exhibit 2). The company's only other financing arrangement of importance was a $100 million line of credit with its banks. The line was subject to annual review and renewal by the banks. The line had not been drawn upon until 1988–1989, when a total of $84.5 million was taken down. That amount remained outstanding in November 1989 (see Exhibit 8).

Any financing plan would have to be consistent with management's strong concern over its share price. The family of one of the company's founders was intent on selling a substantial portion of its holdings, and a strong stock price would be an important facilitating condition.

---

1. This would exclude nonrecurring items, such as any loss that might be sustained on the sale of IPD.

**EXHIBIT 1**

Assets of Industrial Products Division, 1989 (millions of dollars)

| | |
|---|---:|
| Cash[a] . . . . . . . . . . . | $ 0 |
| Net working capital[b] . . . . . . | 98.2 |
| Net fixed assets . . . . . . . | 242.2 |
| Other assets . . . . . . . . | 10.2 |
| Total net assets . . . . . . | $350.6 |

*Note:* Figures are estimated.

a. Nova employed a centralized cash-management system administered by corporate headquarters.

b. Consists of ($ millions): accounts receivable (82.9), inventory (79.1), other current assets (10.5), accounts payable (64.2), and other current liabilities (10.1).

**EXHIBIT 2**

Pro Forma Financial Statements for Nova, Assuming Industrial Products Division Is Retained, 1989–1994 (millions of dollars)

| | 1989 | 1990 | 1991 | 1992 | 1993 | 1994 |
|---|---:|---:|---:|---:|---:|---:|
| Cash and marketable securities . . . | $ 12.5 | $ 12.5 | $ 12.5 | $ 12.5 | $ 12.5 | $ 12.5 |
| Net working capital[a] . . . . . . . | 269.1 | 281.3 | 325.5 | 371.1 | 419.2 | 470.4 |
| Net fixed assets[b] . . . . . . . . | 472.4 | 655.6 | 811.1 | 824.5 | 833.9 | 840.7 |
| Other . . . . . . . . . . . | 25.2 | 25.2 | 25.2 | 26.2 | 26.2 | 26.2 |
| Total net assets . . . . . . . | $779.2 | $974.6 | $1,174.3 | $1,234.3 | $1,291.8 | $1,349.8 |
| Bank debt[c] . . . . . . . . | $ 84.5 | $ 84.5 | $ 84.5 | $ 84.5 | $ 84.5 | $ 84.5 |
| Current portion, long-term debt . . . | 10.0 | 20.0 | 20.0 | 20.0 | 20.0 | 20.0 |
| Long-term debt . . . . . . . . | 240.0 | 220.0 | 200.0 | 180.0 | 160.0 | 140.0 |
| Stockholders' equity . . . . . . | 444.7 | 486.7 | 535.7 | 597.4 | 677.0 | 778.8 |
| Funds needed . . . . . . . . | 0 | 163.4 | 334.1 | 352.4 | 350.3 | 326.5 |
| Total capitalization . . . . . . | $779.2 | $974.6 | $1,174.3 | $1,234.3 | $1,291.8 | $1,349.8 |

a. Defined as accounts receivable + inventory + other current assets − accounts payable − other current liabilities except for borrowed money.

b. Assumes that the estimated expenditures for the Mobile plant are made in 1990 ($100 million) and 1991 ($150 million).

c. Assumes line of credit is renewed annually.

**EXHIBIT 3**

Pro Forma Income Statements for Nova, Assuming Industrial Products Division Is Retained, 1989–1994 (millions of dollars)

| | 1989 | 1990 | 1991 | 1992 | 1993 | 1994 |
|---|---:|---:|---:|---:|---:|---:|
| Sales . . . . . . . . . . | $986.2 | $1,035.5 | $1,097.7 | $1,201.6 | $1,368.6 | $1,565.2 |
| EBIT . . . . . . . . . | 116.8 | 130.2 | 144.7 | 170.6 | 208.6 | 254.8 |
| Interest expense[a] . . . . . . | 38.3 | 37.1 | 35.9 | 33.5 | 31.1 | 28.7 |
| Income before taxes . . . . . | 78.5 | 93.1 | 108.8 | 137.1 | 176.9 | 226.1 |
| Federal income taxes . . . . | 31.4 | 37.2 | 43.5 | 54.8 | 70.8 | 90.4 |
| Net income after tax . . . . . | 47.1 | 55.9 | 65.3 | 82.3 | 106.1 | 135.7 |
| Dividends (.25 × net income) . . | 11.0 | 13.9 | 16.3 | 20.6 | 26.5 | 33.9 |
| Addition to retained earnings . . | $ 36.1 | $ 42.0 | $ 49.0 | $ 61.7 | $ 79.6 | $ 101.8 |

*Note:* Figures may not add exactly because of rounding.

a. Does not include the interest expense on any new debt issues.

## EXHIBIT 4
Company Products and Customers

*Industrial Products Division*

Manufactures ethylene and propylene. Products sold to manufacturers of plastics, fibers, detergents, pharmaceuticals, adhesives, and urethanes.

*Laboratory Products Division*

Manufactures highly specialized, ultra-pure chemicals for research purposes. Customers include industrial firms, research laboratories, and universities involved in biomedical research.

*Environmental Products Division*

Manufactures granular activated carbon to remove impurities from industrial processes and municipal water supplies. Customers include manufacturers of food, pharmaceuticals, and chemicals as well as municipalities.

## EXHIBIT 5
The Chemical Industry: Structure and 1989 Outlook

Chemical products can be broken down into five categories: *agricultural chemicals* (fertilizers and pesticides); *organic chemicals* (ethylene, propylene, benzene, and styrene, which are used in plastics, fibers, detergents, pharmaceuticals, adhesives, and urethanes); *synthetics* (fibers and plastics used in packaging, construction, consumer products, automotive, and apparel industries); *industrial chemicals* (chlorine/caustic soda, industrial gases, phosphorus, and sulfuric acid used in pulp/paper, bleaching, steel, and electronics industries); and *specialty chemicals* (used for detergents, pharmaceuticals, cosmetics, paints, waste treatment, and scientific research).

Stock market analysts view the chemical industry as being made up of three types of companies: *basic chemicals companies,* which manufacture basic chemicals (agricultural chemicals, organic chemicals, synthetics, or industrial chemicals) using a variety of raw materials, including petroleum and natural gas; *specialty chemicals companies,* which manufacture specialty chemicals using basic chemicals as raw materials; and *diversified chemicals companies,* which are involved in both the basic chemicals and specialty chemicals businesses.

Basic chemicals are used in the manufacture of virtually all durable and nondurable goods. Thus the profitability of basic chemicals companies is extremely sensitive to the level of economic activity. The worldwide economic boom of the 1980s had resulted not only in strong demand for basic chemicals but also in a dramatic buildup in basic chemicals production capacity. While basic chemicals companies experienced a high rate of profitability during the 1986–1988 period, by late 1988 growth in demand had begun to fall behind growth in capacity, and prices of most basic chemicals came under pressure. Because of general economic prospects, analysts were predicting modest increases in volume of 1–2% for basic chemicals companies during the coming 3–5 years. More important, substantial additional basic chemicals capacity was to come on-stream in the next 2 years because of previously initiated capital investment programs. As a result, analysts were predicting continued downward pressure on basic chemicals prices over the next 5 years.

Manufacturers of specialty chemicals were seen as facing far better prospects in the early 1990s. The forecasted oversupply situation for basic chemicals probably meant significantly improved profit margins for specialty chemicals companies that purchased most of their raw materials from basic chemicals companies. In addition, the demand for specialty chemicals versus basic chemicals was seen as less sensitive to the level of economic activity. For these reasons, analysts were predicting growth rates in earnings of 10–15% for specialty chemicals companies in the early 1990s.

**EXHIBIT 6**

Ten-Year Financial Review, 1980–1989

| | 1980 | 1981 | 1982 | 1983 | 1984 | 1985 | 1986 | 1987 | 1988 | Est. 1989 | Nov. 22, 1989 |
|---|---|---|---|---|---|---|---|---|---|---|---|
| Sales ($ millions) . . . . . . | $750.2 | $740.2 | $760.6 | $780.3 | $802.4 | $795.5 | $755.2 | $872.8 | $962.3 | $986.2 | |
| Net income ($ millions) . . . | 30.1 | 30.3 | 31.9 | 33.5 | 36.1 | 34.1 | 32.8 | 43.1 | 47.0 | 47.1 | |
| Earnings per share . . . . . | $ 2.01 | $ 2.02 | $ 2.12 | $ 2.23 | $ 2.40 | $ 2.27 | $ 2.17 | $ 2.85 | $ 3.09 | $ 3.10 | |
| Dividends per share . . . . . | .50 | .50 | .50 | .50 | .59 | .59 | .59 | .72 | .72 | .72 | |
| Market price of common stock | | | | | | | | | | | |
| High . . . . . . . . . | $ 34 | $ 19 | $ 22 | $ 28 | $ 26 | $ 46 | $ 41 | $ 50 | $ 38 | — | — |
| Low . . . . . . . . . | 18 | 9 | 12 | 16 | 12 | 26 | 29 | 30 | 26 | — | — |
| Midpoint . . . . . . . | 26 | 14 | 17 | 22 | 19 | 36 | 35 | 40 | 32 | — | $ 22 |
| Midpoint price-earnings ratio . . | 13.2 | 6.9 | 7.8 | 9.8 | 7.8 | 16.1 | 16.3 | 14.2 | 10.3 | — | 7.1 |

**EXHIBIT 7**

Income Statements for Years Ending December 31, 1986–1989 (millions of dollars except per share data)

| | 1986 | 1987 | 1988 | Est. 1989 |
|---|---|---|---|---|
| Net sales | $755.2 | $872.8 | $962.3 | $986.2 |
| Cost of sales | 572.4 | 658.9 | 721.7 | 736.1 |
| Selling, general, administrative | 68.9 | 84.1 | 99.1 | 105.1 |
| Research and development expense | 23.1 | 23.1 | 24.2 | 26.8 |
| Interest expense | 33.6 | 32.4 | 36.8 | 38.3 |
| Other | 2.2 | 2.3 | 3.4 | 1.4 |
| Income before taxes | 55.0 | 72.0 | 77.1 | 78.5 |
| Federal income taxes | 22.2 | 28.9 | 30.1 | 31.4 |
| Net income after taxes | 32.8 | 43.1 | 47.0 | 47.1 |
| Common dividends | 8.9 | 11.0 | 11.0 | 11.0 |
| Addition to retained earnings | $ 23.9 | $ 32.1 | $ 36.0 | $ 36.1 |
| Common shares outstanding (millions) | 15.1 | 15.1 | 15.2 | 15.2 |
| Earnings per share | $ 2.17 | $ 2.85 | $ 3.09 | $ 3.10 |
| Dividends per share | .59 | .72 | .72 | .72 |
| Capital expenditures | $ 50.4 | $ 62.5 | $ 84.1 | $118.3 |
| Depreciation | 31.5 | 35.5 | 41.3 | 50.8 |

**EXHIBIT 8**

Balance Sheets at December 31, 1987–1989 (millions of dollars)

| | 1987 | 1988 | Est. 1989 |
|---|---|---|---|
| Cash and marketable securities | $ 11.8 | $ 11.7 | $ 12.5 |
| Accounts receivable | 193.7 | 211.9 | 217.4 |
| Inventory | 164.1 | 181.8 | 188.5 |
| Other | 19.9 | 20.1 | $ 20.6 |
| Current assets | 389.5 | 425.5 | 439.0 |
| Net fixed assets | 362.1 | 404.9 | 472.4 |
| Other | 24.8 | 24.9 | 25.2 |
| Total assets | $776.4 | $855.3 | $936.6 |
| Bank debt | $ 0 | $ 42.4 | $ 84.5 |
| Accounts payable | 96.4 | 105.4 | 117.3 |
| Other | 37.4 | 38.9 | 40.1 |
| Current portion, long-term debt | 10.0 | 10.0 | 10.0 |
| Current liabilities | 143.8 | 196.7 | 251.9 |
| Long-term debt | 260.0 | 250.0 | 240.0 |
| Stockholders' equity | 372.6 | 408.6 | 444.7 |
| Total liabilities and stockholders' equity | $776.4 | $855.3 | $936.6 |

EXHIBIT 9
Basic Chemicals Companies

| | Dow Chemical | | | | Du Pont | | | |
|---|---|---|---|---|---|---|---|---|
| | 1985 | 1986 | 1987 | 1988 | 1985 | 1986 | 1987 | 1988 |
| Sales ($ millions) | $10,500 | $11,113 | $13,377 | $16,682 | $29,483 | $27,148 | $30,468 | $32,917 |
| Earnings per share | $ 1.55 | $ 2.58 | $ 4.33 | $ 8.55 | $ 1.68 | $ 2.12 | $ 2.33 | $ 2.93 |
| Dividends per share | 1.20 | 1.27 | 1.43 | 1.73 | 1.00 | 1.02 | 1.10 | 1.23 |
| Common stock price | | | | | | | | |
| High | 27 | 41 | 73 | 62 | 23 | 31 | 44 | 31 |
| Low | 18 | 26 | 37 | 51 | 16 | 20 | 25 | 25 |
| Price-earnings ratio | 14.5 | 13.8 | 13.0 | 6.7 | 11.4 | 12.4 | 15.3 | 9.6 |
| Beta (1988 year-end est.) | – | – | – | 1.25 | – | – | – | 1.15 |
| After-tax return on equity | 9.2% | 14.3% | 21.6% | 33.2% | 9.7% | 11.5% | 11.9% | 13.6% |
| Capitalization (book values) | | | | | | | | |
| Long-term debt ($ millions) | $ 3,198 | $ 3,404 | $ 3,779 | $ 3,338 | $ 3,284 | $ 3,316 | $ 3,102 | $ 3,232 |
| Equity ($ millions) | 4,792 | 5,168 | 5,769 | 7,255 | 12,659 | 13,374 | 14,244 | 15,580 |
| Bond rating | A | A | A | A | AA | AA | AA | AA |
| Interest coverage | – | – | – | 10.6 | – | – | – | 7.9 |
| Shares outstanding (millions) | – | – | – | 275.3 | – | – | – | 718.45 |

| | Olin Corporation | | | | United Chemical | | | |
|---|---|---|---|---|---|---|---|---|
| | 1985 | 1986 | 1987 | 1988 | 1985 | 1986 | 1987 | 1988 |
| Sales ($ millions) | $ 1,751 | $ 1,707 | $ 1,930 | $ 2,308 | $ 6,747 | $ 6,879 | $ 7,639 | $ 8,293 |
| Earnings per share | $ 1.73 | $ 2.61 | $ 3.38 | $ 4.63 | $ 2.76 | $ 4.45 | $ 5.39 | $ 8.27 |
| Dividends per share | 1.50 | 1.53 | 1.60 | 1.70 | 2.45 | 2.58 | 2.75 | 2.95 |
| Common stock price | | | | | | | | |
| High | 38 | 53 | 56 | 60 | 55 | 82 | 100 | 92 |
| Low | 28 | 35 | 33 | 40 | 40 | 45 | 57 | 73 |
| Price-earnings ratio | 19.1 | 16.3 | 14.2 | 10.3 | 16.8 | 14.9 | 15.4 | 10.0 |
| Beta (1988 year-end est.) | – | – | – | 1.30 | – | – | – | 1.25 |
| After-tax return on equity | 5.8% | 8.9% | 11.1% | 14.3% | 6.3% | 9.2% | 10.7% | 15.6% |
| Capitalization (book values) | | | | | | | | |
| Long-term debt ($ millions) | $ 354 | $ 375 | $ 392 | $ 474 | $ 2,087 | $ 1,630 | $ 1,564 | $ 1,408 |
| Equity ($ millions) | 686 | 654 | 700 | 683 | 3,407 | 3,781 | 3,901 | 3,800 |
| Bond rating | BBB– | BBB– | BBB– | BBB– | A– | A– | A– | A– |
| Interest coverage | – | – | – | 4.4 | – | – | – | 5.6 |
| Shares outstanding (millions) | – | – | – | 20.5 | – | – | – | 68.83 |

(continued)

**EXHIBIT 9** *(continued)*
Diversified Chemicals Companies

### Air Products

| | 1985 | 1986 | 1987 | 1988 |
|---|---|---|---|---|
| Sales ($ millions) | $ 1,829 | $ 1,982 | $ 2,132 | $ 2,431 |
| Earnings per share | $ 2.34 | $ 2.33 | $ 2.84 | $ 3.90 |
| Dividends | .64 | .77 | .90 | 1.10 |
| Common stock price | | | | |
| High | 34 | 41 | 54 | 53 |
| Low | 22 | 30 | 29 | 36 |
| Price-earnings ratio | 10.6 | 14.8 | 15.2 | 11.1 |
| Beta (1988 year-end est.) | — | — | — | 1.15 |
| After-tax return on equity | 12.1% | 12.4% | 14.0% | 16.8% |
| Capitalization (book values) | | | | |
| Long-term debt ($ millions) | $ 533 | $ 708 | $ 616 | $ 667 |
| Equity ($ millions) | 1,163 | 1,100 | 1,146 | 1,272 |
| Bond rating | A+ | A+ | A+ | A+ |
| Interest coverage | — | — | — | 4.6 |
| Shares outstanding (millions) | — | — | — | 54.85 |

### Nova Chemical

| | 1985 | 1986 | 1987 | 1988 |
|---|---|---|---|---|
| Sales ($ millions) | $ 796 | $ 755 | $ 873 | $ 962 |
| Earnings per share | $ 2.27 | $ 2.17 | $ 2.85 | $ 3.09 |
| Dividends | .59 | .59 | .72 | .72 |
| Common stock price | | | | |
| High | 46 | 41 | 50 | 38 |
| Low | 26 | 29 | 30 | 26 |
| Price-earnings ratio | 16.1 | 16.3 | 14.2 | 10.3 |
| Beta (1988 year-end est.) | — | — | — | 1.30 |
| After-tax return on equity | 10.8% | 9.6% | 11.5% | 11.5% |
| Capitalization (book values) | | | | |
| Long-term debt ($ millions) | $ 280 | $ 270 | $ 260 | $ 250 |
| Equity ($ millions) | 317 | 341 | 373 | 409 |
| Bond rating | BBB– | BBB– | BBB– | BBB– |
| Interest coverage | — | — | — | 3.0 |
| Shares outstanding (millions) | — | — | — | 15.16 |

### Ethyl Corporation

| | 1985 | 1986 | 1987 | 1988 |
|---|---|---|---|---|
| Sales ($ millions) | $ 1,547 | $ 1,579 | $ 1,720 | $ 2,011 |
| Earnings per share | $ 1.02 | $ 1.25 | $ 1.44 | $ 1.91 |
| Dividends per share | .29 | .33 | .40 | .45 |
| Common stock price | | | | |
| High | 15 | 23 | 32 | 24 |
| Low | 8 | 13 | 15 | 17 |
| Price-earnings ratio | 10.8 | 14.8 | 17.3 | 11.2 |
| Beta (1988 year-end est.) | — | — | — | 1.15 |
| After-tax return on equity | 16.7% | 17.5% | 18.6% | 20.5% |
| Capitalization (book values) | | | | |
| Long-term debt ($ millions) | $ 399 | $ 408 | $ 608 | $ 608 |
| Equity ($ millions) | 801 | 942 | 958 | 1,129 |
| Bond rating | BBB+ | BBB+ | BBB+ | BBB+ |
| Interest coverage | — | — | — | 6.1 |
| Shares outstanding (millions) | — | — | — | 120.66 |

### Minnesota Mining & Mfg.

| | 1985 | 1986 | 1987 | 1988 |
|---|---|---|---|---|
| Sales ($ millions) | $ 7,846 | $ 8,602 | $ 9,429 | $10,581 |
| Earnings per share | $ 3.01 | $ 3.40 | $ 4.02 | $ 5.09 |
| Dividends per share | 1.75 | 1.80 | 1.86 | 2.12 |
| Common stock price | | | | |
| High | 46 | 59 | 83 | 67 |
| Low | 36 | 43 | 45 | 55 |
| Price-earnings ratio | 13.3 | 15.5 | 16.8 | 12.0 |
| Beta (1988 year-end est.) | — | — | — | 1.00 |
| After-tax return on equity | 17.2% | 17.5% | 18.1% | 20.9% |
| Capitalization (book values) | | | | |
| Long-term debt ($ millions) | $ 431 | $ 436 | $ 435 | $ 406 |
| Equity ($ millions) | 4,008 | 4,463 | 5,060 | 5,514 |
| Bond rating | AAA | AAA | AAA | AAA |
| Interest coverage | — | — | — | 21.0 |
| Shares outstanding (millions) | — | — | — | 222.24 |

*(continued)*

**EXHIBIT 9** (*concluded*)
Specialty Chemicals Companies

| | Avery International | | | | Engelhard Corporation | | | |
|---|---|---|---|---|---|---|---|---|
| | 1985 | 1986 | 1987 | 1988 | 1985 | 1986 | 1987 | 1988 |
| Sales ($ millions) | $ 932 | $ 1,131 | $ 1,465 | $ 1,582 | $ 2,263 | $ 2,289 | $ 2,479 | $2,350 |
| Earnings per share | $ 1.22 | $ 1.23 | $ 1.40 | $ 1.77 | $ 1.01 | $1.31 | $ 1.42 | $ 1.42 |
| Dividends per share | .31 | .35 | .41 | .47 | .48 | .49 | .52 | .54 |
| Common stock price | | | | | | | | |
| High | 20 | 24 | 29 | 26 | 22 | 22 | 29 | 22 |
| Low | 15 | 17 | 15 | 19 | 14 | 15 | 15 | 16 |
| Price-earnings ratio | 13.8 | 16.3 | 17.0 | 12.5 | 17.3 | 14.1 | 16.9 | 13.3 |
| Beta (1988 year-end est.) | – | – | – | 1.10 | – | – | – | 1.15 |
| After-tax return on equity | 15.3% | 13.9% | 12.9% | 15.3% | 8.3% | 9.5% | 8.5% | 8.4% |
| Capitalization (book values) | | | | | | | | |
| Long-term debt ($ millions) | $ 87 | $ 221 | $ 204 | $ 215 | $ 115 | $ 116 | $ 119 | $ 221 |
| Equity ($ millions) | 314 | 350 | 466 | 509 | 512 | 561 | 730 | 760 |
| Bond rating | A | A | A | A | A | A | A | A |
| Interest coverage | – | – | – | 5.8 | – | – | – | 4.2 |
| Shares outstanding (millions) | – | – | – | 44.23 | – | – | – | 44.8 |

| | Rohmand Haas | | | | Witco Corporation | | | |
|---|---|---|---|---|---|---|---|---|
| | 1985 | 1986 | 1987 | 1988 | 1985 | 1986 | 1987 | 1988 |
| Sales ($ millions) | $ 2,051 | $ 2,067 | $ 2,203 | $ 2,535 | $ 1,448 | $ 1,355 | $ 1,427 | $ 1,585 |
| Earnings per share | $ 1.94 | $ 2.50 | $ 2.85 | $ 3.46 | $ 2.57 | $ 2.93 | $ 2.91 | $ 3.05 |
| Dividends per share | .70 | .78 | .86 | 1.02 | .99 | 1.09 | 1.20 | 1.45 |
| Common stock price | | | | | | | | |
| High | 26 | 39 | 53 | 37 | 27 | 40 | 47 | 38 |
| Low | 18 | 24 | 24 | 28 | 22 | 26 | 26 | 31 |
| Price-earnings ratio | 11.3 | 12.9 | 14.3 | 9.6 | 9.5 | 11.7 | 13.6 | 11.5 |
| Beta (1988 year-end est.) | – | – | – | 1.10 | – | – | – | 1.00 |
| After-tax return on equity | 14.6% | 17.1% | 18.5% | 19.1% | 13.7% | 14.0% | 13.3% | 12.4% |
| Capitalization (book values) | | | | | | | | |
| Long-term debt ($ millions) | $ 245 | $ 278 | $ 285 | $ 288 | $ 136 | $ 96 | $ 242 | $ 240 |
| Equity ($ millions) | 936 | 1,002 | 1,053 | 1,207 | 415 | 465 | 513 | 578 |
| Bond rating | A | A | A | A | A | A | A | A |
| Interest coverage | – | – | – | 8.2 | – | – | – | 7.4 |
| Shares outstanding (millions) | – | – | – | 66.54 | – | – | – | 22.41 |

## EXHIBIT 10
Selected Financial Data by Divisions, 1986–1994 (millions of dollars)

| Sales and Profit Performance | 1986 | 1987 | 1988 | Est. 1989 |
|---|---|---|---|---|
| Industrial Products Division | | | | |
|   Sales | $512.1 | $579.1 | $599.8 | $582.2 |
|   EBIT[a] | 40.4 | 47.5 | 41.9 | 37.2 |
|   EBIT as percent of sales | 7.9% | 8.2% | 7.0% | 6.4% |
| Laboratory Products Division | | | | |
|   Sales | $104.9 | $123.0 | $136.4 | $150.6 |
|   EBIT[a] | 19.5 | 21.2 | 24.3 | 26.9 |
|   EBIT as percent of sales | 18.6% | 17.2% | 17.8% | 17.9% |
| Environmental Products Division | | | | |
|   Sales | $138.2 | $170.7 | $226.1 | $253.4 |
|   EBIT[a] | 28.7 | 35.7 | 47.7 | 52.7 |
|   EBIT as percent of sales | 20.8% | 20.9% | 21.1% | 20.8% |

| Five-Year Plan Projections[b] | 1990 | 1991 | 1992 | 1993 | 1994 |
|---|---|---|---|---|---|
| Industrial Products Division | | | | | |
|   Sales | $564.6 | $547.8 | $537.4 | $550.3 | $556.9 |
|   EBIT (.065 × sales) | 36.7 | 35.6 | 34.9 | 35.8 | 36.2 |
|   Capital expenditures | 41.6 | 31.1 | 30.0 | 30.8 | 34.6 |
|   Depreciation | 22.5 | 26.1 | 29.0 | 31.9 | 34.8 |
|   Investment in net working capital[c] | (6.9) | (2.3) | .9 | 3.2 | 4.3 |
| Laboratory Products Division | | | | | |
|   Sales | $179.5 | $214.8 | $262.1 | $319.7 | $390.0 |
|   EBIT (.18 × sales) | 32.3 | 38.7 | 47.2 | 57.5 | 70.2 |
|   Capital expenditures | 79.2 | 29.8 | 30.8 | 31.0 | 31.1 |
|   Depreciation | 14.9 | 21.0 | 23.8 | 26.4 | 29.7 |
|   Investment in net working capital[c] | 10.0 | 31.4 | 27.8 | 29.1 | 33.2 |
| Environmental Products Division | | | | | |
|   Sales | $291.4 | $335.1 | $402.1 | $498.6 | $618.3 |
|   EBIT[d] | 61.2 | 70.4 | 88.5 | 114.7 | 148.4 |
|   Capital expenditures[e] | 137.2 | 195.4 | 59.7 | 61.1 | 62.4 |
|   Depreciation | 38.0 | 53.7 | 54.3 | 55.2 | 56.8 |
|   Investment in net working capital[c] | 9.1 | 15.1 | 16.9 | 15.8 | 13.7 |

a. After allocation of all corporate expenses, including research and development.

b. Assumes annual inflation rate of 6%.

c. Defined as accounts receivable + inventory + other current assets − accounts payable − other current liabilities except for borrowed money.

d. Assumes 21% of sales in 1990 and 1991; 22% in 1992; 23% in 1993; and 24% in 1994.

e. Projected capital expenditures for this division assume that the estimated expenditures for the Mobile plant are made in 1990 ($100 million) and 1991 ($150 million).

**EXHIBIT 11**
Interest Rates, 1989

| | Jan. | Feb. | Mar. | Apr. | May | June | July | Aug. | Sept. | Oct. | Nov. |
|---|---|---|---|---|---|---|---|---|---|---|---|
| Treasuries | | | | | | | | | | | |
| 90-day . . . . . . . | 8.18% | 8.39% | 8.65% | 8.85% | 8.42% | 8.61% | 7.95% | 7.64% | 7.89% | 7.86% | 7.61% |
| 1-year . . . . . . . | 9.03 | 9.02 | 9.37 | 9.59 | 9.22 | 8.86 | 8.09 | 7.63 | 8.29 | 8.45 | 7.90 |
| 10-year . . . . . . | 9.14 | 8.98 | 9.30 | 9.28 | 9.06 | 8.60 | 8.08 | 7.81 | 8.26 | 8.30 | 7.91 |
| 30-year . . . . . . | 9.00 | 8.83 | 9.12 | 9.10 | 8.93 | 8.59 | 8.04 | 7.92 | 8.20 | 8.24 | 7.91 |
| Industrials | | | | | | | | | | | |
| AAA . . . . . . . | 9.55 | 9.58 | 9.81 | 9.66 | 9.58 | 9.00 | 8.85 | 8.84 | 8.91 | 8.81 | 8.67 |
| AA . . . . . . . | 9.93 | 9.95 | 10.18 | 10.04 | 9.82 | 9.35 | 9.15 | 9.12 | 9.17 | 9.09 | 8.95 |
| A . . . . . . . | 10.36 | 10.38 | 10.59 | 10.46 | 10.27 | 9.76 | 9.63 | 9.61 | 9.65 | 9.58 | 9.47 |
| BBB . . . . . . | 10.72 | 10.76 | 10.96 | 10.82 | 10.62 | 10.12 | 10.03 | 10.02 | 10.10 | 10.03 | 9.96 |
| BB . . . . . . . | 11.30 | 11.74 | 12.00 | 12.05 | 11.98 | 11.59 | 11.43 | 11.46 | 11.65 | 11.79 | 11.90 |
| B . . . . . . . | 11.99 | 12.47 | 12.79 | 13.16 | 13.09 | 12.73 | 12.76 | 12.76 | 12.85 | 13.30 | 13.66 |
| Bank prime rate . . | 10.50 | 11.50 | 11.50 | 11.50 | 11.50 | 11.00 | 10.50 | 10.50 | 10.50 | 10.50 | 10.50 |
| Commercial paper, | | | | | | | | | | | |
| 3-month . . . . . | 9.10 | 9.05 | 9.82 | 10.00 | 9.68 | 9.40 | 9.05 | 8.25 | 8.65 | 8.83 | 8.48 |

# Appendixes

# Appendix A

## Tax Table

This table has been prepared for use in connection with cases in this book. It is not a complete statement of applicable rates, and it should not be used as a reference for general purposes.

Federal Tax Rates on Corporate Income and Payment Dates

| Income Years | Rate[a] | Income Years | Rate[a] |
|---|---|---|---|
| 1946–1949 . 38% | | 1965–1967 | 48 % |
| 1950 . . . 47 | | 1968–1969[c] | 52.8 |
| 1951–1953[b] 52 | | 1970[c] . . | 49.2 |
| 1954–1963 . 52 | | 1971–1978 | 48 |
| 1964 . . . 50 | | 1979–1986[d] | 46 |
| | | 1986– . . | 34 |

a. Rate applicable to top bracket of tax, excluding the excess profits tax, when in effect.

b. Excess profits tax also in effect for part or all of year.

c. Includes special surcharge.

d. For 1984 through 1986 the top bracket rate on taxable income between $1,000,000 and $1,405,000 was 51%. See text.

The 52% rate in effect from 1951 through 1963 consisted of a normal tax of 30% of taxable income and a surtax of 22% of taxable income in excess of $25,000. The 50% rate in effect in 1964 consisted of a normal tax of 22% and a surtax of 28%. The 48% rate in effect from 1965 through 1974 consisted of a normal tax of 22% and a surtax of 26% on taxable income in excess of $25,000.

In addition, in 1968 a special surcharge of 10% was imposed, making the effective rate for that year 52.8%. This rate held for 1969, but the special surcharge was phased out gradually by quarters during 1970 so that the overall effective rate for that year was 49.2%, and by 1971 the rate was again 48%.

For tax years ending after 1974 and before 1979 the normal tax rates were 20% on the first $25,000 of taxable income and 22% on taxable income over $25,000. The surtax rate was 26% on taxable income over $50,000. For tax years beginning after 1978 the taxable income of corporations was subject to graduated tax rates.

Corporate Graduated Tax Rate, 1979–1986

| Amount of Taxable Income ($000s) | Applicable Tax Rate | | |
|---|---|---|---|
| | *1979–1981* | *1982* | *1983–1986* |
| Zero–25 . . . . . . . . | 17% | 16% | 15% |
| Over 25–50 . . . . . . . | 20 | 19 | 18 |
| Over 50–75 . . . . . . . | 30 | 30 | 30 |
| Over 75–100 . . . . . . . | 40 | 40 | 40 |
| Over 100 . . . . . . . | 46 | 46 | 46 |

For taxable years beginning after December 31, 1983, the benefit of the graduated rates on corporations with taxable income in excess of $1 million was phased out by imposing an additional 5% tax on the portion of taxable income over $1,000,000 and up to $1,405,000. Thus, the tax rate on income in this bracket was 51%. For taxable income in excess of $1,405,000 the tax rate dropped back to 46%. The effect of this provision was to impose a flat 46% rate on all corporations with taxable incomes in excess of $1,405,000.

The Tax Reform Act of 1986 reduced the top corporate tax rate from 46% to 34%, effective July 1, 1987, for corporations with taxable incomes in excess of $335,000. Graduated rates, from 15% to 39%, applied to corporations with taxable incomes of less than $335,000.

Since 1950 corporate income tax payments have moved closer to current payment. Beginning in 1950, payments were gradually accelerated until in 1954 they were brought entirely within the first half of the year following the tax liability. The Revenue Acts of 1954 and 1964 and the Tax Adjustment Act of 1966 set up even more accelerated schedules. Through 1967, all tax liabilities up to $100,000 were payable in equal amounts on March 15 and June 15 of the year following the tax liability. The Revenue Act of 1968 provided for a gradual acceleration of tax payments for corporations with tax liabilities of less than $100,000 as well as for corporations with tax liabilities of more than $100,000. Tax liabilities over $100,000, for companies on a calendar year, were payable according to the following schedule. For 1967 through 1982, if the actual tax liability for the year exceeded the amount of estimated tax payments made on this liability during the year, the balance had to be paid in equal installments on March 15 and June 15 of the following year for corporations filing their tax returns on a calendar year basis.

For taxable years beginning after December 31, 1982, the entire balance had to be paid when the return was due, March 15 of the following year for corporations filing on a calendar year basis.

Corporate Tax Liabilities, 1949–1967 and After

| Income Year | Percentage Paid in Income Year [a] | | | | Percentage Paid in Following Year [b] | | | |
|---|---|---|---|---|---|---|---|---|
| | Apr. 15 | June 15 | Sept. 15 | Dec. 15 | Mar. 15 | June 15 | Sept. 15 | Dec. 15 |
| 1949 | — | — | — | — | 25 | 25 | 25 | 25 |
| 1950 | — | — | — | — | 30 | 30 | 20 | 20 |
| 1951 | — | — | — | — | 35 | 35 | 15 | 15 |
| 1952 | — | — | — | — | 40 | 40 | 10 | 10 |
| 1953 | — | — | — | — | 45 | 45 | 5 | 5 |
| 1954 | — | — | — | — | 50 | 50 | — | — |
| 1955 | — | — | 5 | 5 | 45 | 45 | — | — |
| 1956 | — | — | 10 | 10 | 40 | 40 | — | — |
| 1957 | — | — | 15 | 15 | 35 | 35 | — | — |
| 1958 | — | — | 20 | 20 | 30 | 30 | — | — |
| 1959–1963 | — | — | 25 | 25 | 25 | 25 | — | — |
| 1964 | 1 | 1 | 25 | 25 | 24 | 24 | — | — |
| 1965 | 4 | 4 | 25 | 25 | 21 | 21 | — | — |
| 1966 | 12 | 12 | 25 | 25 | 13 | 13 | — | — |
| 1967 and after | 25 | 25 | 25 | 25 | — | — | — | — |

a. These are percentages of the estimated tax liability on income of the current year.

b. These are percentages of the tax liability on income of the previous year.

# Appendix B

## Note on Investment Tax Credit*

Most recently repealed by the Tax Reform Act of 1986, a tax credit subsidy for business purchases of capital goods was first enacted by the U.S. Congress in 1962. Its purpose was twofold. First, the United States was emerging from a small economic recession in 1961, and it was hoped that the credit would encourage business spending for new plants and equipment. While the primary goal of the credit probably was to bolster a sagging economy, it also promised a substantial secondary benefit. For a number of years trade groups from numerous basic American industries had complained that European producers with lower labor costs and more modern physical facilities were slowly exporting more and more of their production to the United States. It was hoped that a tax subsidy encouraging new investment in capital goods would allow American producers to modernize their facilities and reduce their costs enough to be more competitive in the U.S. market with European producers.

Between 1962 and 1968 the investment credit underwent several revisions. It was "permanently" repealed (there had been a temporary suspension in 1966) by the Tax Reform Act of 1969. Because of a continuing business recession and rising unemployment in 1971, the investment tax credit was reenacted in the Revenue Act of 1971 under the name "job-development credit." As the law stood after reenactment, a purchaser of "Sec. 38"[1] property could deduct from federal income

---

* This note has been prepared for use in connection with cases in this book. It is not a definitive statement, and it should not be used as a reference for general purposes.

1. For purposes of the credit, "Sec. 38" property is defined as all depreciable property (not including buildings) used as an integral part of (a) manufacturing, (b) mining, (c) production, and (d) furnishings of services such as transportation, energy, water, and sewage disposal.

tax liability 7% of the cost of new "Sec. 38" property in the year it was purchased, as long as the property had an expected useful life of 7 years or more. For property with a life of 5 to 7 years the credit was equal to two thirds of this 7%, and for property with a useful life of 3 to 5 years the credit was equal to one third of 7%. Property with a useful life of less than 3 years did not qualify for the credit. (Under the old investment tax credit repealed in 1969, the required lives were 1 year longer; that is, the upper limit was 8 years and the lower limit was 4 years.)

The investment credit was increased from 7% to 10% for qualified business property acquired and placed in service after January 21, 1975. Since 1975 a variety of additional tax credits have been enacted to stimulate such activities as increasing expenditures on research; the clinical testing of certain drugs; the production of fuel from nonconventional sources; alcohol used as fuel; contributions to employee stock ownership plans (ESOP); the targeted jobs credit; and outlays for designated "energy property." Many of these credits have since been abolished or curtailed; in any event, they are far too specialized to be discussed in this brief summary statement.

The Tax Reform Act of 1984 created a new concept—the general business credit. It combined the available investment credit (both the regular and energy credits), targeted job credit, alcohol fuel credit, and ESOP credit into a single, general business credit (including any carrybacks and carryovers). For "Sec. 38" property depreciated on a 5-year accelerated cost recovery system (ACRS), the credit was 10%; for a 3-year recovery period, the credit was 6%.

Exhibit 1 of the Pressco, Inc. (1985) case spells out some of the technical provisions of the investment tax credit as they existed at the time of this case, just prior to the enactment of the Tax Recovery Act of 1984.

The investment tax credit (or general business credit) represents a direct credit against the total income tax liability. For a company with a 46% marginal tax rate, a tax credit of $100,000 can save as much in income taxes as a $217,391 deduction from pre-tax income. Taxpayers who have a total tax liability of $25,000 or less in a given year are allowed to credit up to 100% of the liability. For those whose tax liability exceeds $25,000 the limit on the credit is $25,000 plus the following percentage of the liability in excess of $25,000:

| | |
|---|---|
| 1979 . . . . . . | 60% |
| 1980 . . . . . . | 70 |
| 1981 . . . . . . | 80 |
| 1982 . . . . . . | 90 |
| 1983–1985 . . . . | 85 |
| 1986 and after . . . | 75 |

Any credit that cannot be used in a given year may be carried back or forward to offset the tax liabilities of other years. In 1986 unused credits could be carried back for 3 years and forward for 15 years.

The Tax Reform Act of 1986 terminated the regular investment tax credit for virtually all otherwise qualified property placed in service after December 31, 1985. Exceptions include "transition" property (e.g., property placed in service after 1985 but acquired under a written contract that was binding prior to December 31, 1985), certain qualified progress expenditures, and qualified timber property. The latter category continues to be eligible for a 10% investment tax credit. The other two categories of qualified property are eligible for an investment credit at the following rates:

| | |
|---|---|
| 1986 . . . . . . | 10.00% |
| 1987 . . . . . . | 8.25 |
| 1988 and after . . . | 6.50 |

The carrying forward of unused investment credits was also reduced, but not terminated, for years after 1986.

It cannot safely be assumed that the repeal of the investment tax credit will long endure. As noted, this credit has been repealed (even "permanently" repealed) in earlier years only to be reenacted under the pressure of the next business recession.

# Appendix C

## Present Value Tables

# TABLE C1
## Present Value of $1

| Periods until Payment | 1% | 2% | 2½% | 3% | 4% | 5% | 6% | 8% | 10% | 12% | 14% | 15% | 16% | 18% | 20% | 22% | 24% | 25% | 26% | 30% | 40% | 50% |
|---|---|---|---|---|---|---|---|---|---|---|---|---|---|---|---|---|---|---|---|---|---|---|
| 1 | 0.990 | 0.980 | 0.976 | 0.971 | 0.962 | 0.952 | 0.943 | 0.926 | 0.909 | 0.893 | 0.877 | 0.870 | 0.862 | 0.847 | 0.833 | 0.820 | 0.806 | 0.800 | 0.794 | 0.769 | 0.714 | 0.667 |
| 2 | 0.980 | 0.961 | 0.952 | 0.943 | 0.925 | 0.907 | 0.890 | 0.857 | 0.826 | 0.797 | 0.769 | 0.756 | 0.743 | 0.718 | 0.694 | 0.672 | 0.650 | 0.640 | 0.630 | 0.592 | 0.510 | 0.444 |
| 3 | 0.971 | 0.942 | 0.929 | 0.915 | 0.889 | 0.864 | 0.840 | 0.794 | 0.751 | 0.712 | 0.675 | 0.658 | 0.641 | 0.609 | 0.579 | 0.551 | 0.524 | 0.512 | 0.500 | 0.455 | 0.364 | 0.296 |
| 4 | 0.961 | 0.924 | 0.906 | 0.888 | 0.855 | 0.823 | 0.792 | 0.735 | 0.683 | 0.636 | 0.592 | 0.572 | 0.552 | 0.516 | 0.482 | 0.451 | 0.423 | 0.410 | 0.397 | 0.350 | 0.260 | 0.198 |
| 5 | 0.951 | 0.906 | 0.884 | 0.863 | 0.822 | 0.784 | 0.747 | 0.681 | 0.621 | 0.567 | 0.519 | 0.497 | 0.476 | 0.437 | 0.402 | 0.370 | 0.341 | 0.328 | 0.315 | 0.269 | 0.186 | 0.132 |
| 6 | 0.942 | 0.888 | 0.862 | 0.837 | 0.790 | 0.746 | 0.705 | 0.630 | 0.564 | 0.507 | 0.456 | 0.432 | 0.410 | 0.370 | 0.335 | 0.303 | 0.275 | 0.262 | 0.250 | 0.207 | 0.133 | 0.088 |
| 7 | 0.933 | 0.871 | 0.841 | 0.813 | 0.760 | 0.711 | 0.665 | 0.583 | 0.513 | 0.452 | 0.400 | 0.376 | 0.354 | 0.314 | 0.279 | 0.249 | 0.222 | 0.210 | 0.198 | 0.159 | 0.095 | 0.059 |
| 8 | 0.923 | 0.853 | 0.821 | 0.789 | 0.731 | 0.677 | 0.627 | 0.540 | 0.467 | 0.404 | 0.351 | 0.327 | 0.305 | 0.266 | 0.233 | 0.204 | 0.179 | 0.168 | 0.157 | 0.123 | 0.068 | 0.039 |
| 9 | 0.914 | 0.837 | 0.801 | 0.766 | 0.703 | 0.645 | 0.592 | 0.500 | 0.424 | 0.361 | 0.308 | 0.284 | 0.263 | 0.225 | 0.194 | 0.167 | 0.144 | 0.134 | 0.125 | 0.094 | 0.048 | 0.026 |
| 10 | 0.905 | 0.820 | 0.781 | 0.744 | 0.676 | 0.614 | 0.558 | 0.463 | 0.386 | 0.322 | 0.270 | 0.247 | 0.227 | 0.191 | 0.162 | 0.137 | 0.116 | 0.107 | 0.099 | 0.073 | 0.035 | 0.017 |
| 11 | 0.896 | 0.804 | 0.762 | 0.722 | 0.650 | 0.585 | 0.527 | 0.429 | 0.350 | 0.287 | 0.237 | 0.215 | 0.195 | 0.162 | 0.135 | 0.112 | 0.094 | 0.086 | 0.079 | 0.056 | 0.025 | 0.012 |
| 12 | 0.887 | 0.788 | 0.744 | 0.701 | 0.625 | 0.557 | 0.497 | 0.397 | 0.319 | 0.257 | 0.208 | 0.187 | 0.168 | 0.137 | 0.112 | 0.092 | 0.076 | 0.069 | 0.062 | 0.043 | 0.018 | 0.008 |
| 13 | 0.879 | 0.773 | 0.725 | 0.681 | 0.601 | 0.530 | 0.469 | 0.368 | 0.290 | 0.229 | 0.182 | 0.163 | 0.145 | 0.116 | 0.093 | 0.075 | 0.061 | 0.055 | 0.050 | 0.033 | 0.013 | 0.005 |
| 14 | 0.870 | 0.758 | 0.708 | 0.661 | 0.577 | 0.505 | 0.442 | 0.340 | 0.263 | 0.205 | 0.160 | 0.141 | 0.125 | 0.099 | 0.078 | 0.062 | 0.049 | 0.044 | 0.039 | 0.025 | 0.009 | 0.003 |
| 15 | 0.861 | 0.743 | 0.690 | 0.642 | 0.555 | 0.481 | 0.417 | 0.315 | 0.239 | 0.183 | 0.140 | 0.123 | 0.108 | 0.084 | 0.065 | 0.051 | 0.040 | 0.035 | 0.031 | 0.020 | 0.006 | 0.002 |
| 16 | 0.853 | 0.728 | 0.674 | 0.623 | 0.534 | 0.458 | 0.394 | 0.292 | 0.218 | 0.163 | 0.123 | 0.107 | 0.093 | 0.071 | 0.054 | 0.042 | 0.032 | 0.028 | 0.025 | 0.015 | 0.005 | 0.002 |
| 17 | 0.844 | 0.714 | 0.657 | 0.605 | 0.513 | 0.436 | 0.371 | 0.270 | 0.198 | 0.146 | 0.108 | 0.093 | 0.080 | 0.060 | 0.045 | 0.034 | 0.026 | 0.023 | 0.020 | 0.012 | 0.003 | 0.001 |
| 18 | 0.836 | 0.700 | 0.641 | 0.587 | 0.494 | 0.416 | 0.350 | 0.250 | 0.180 | 0.130 | 0.095 | 0.081 | 0.069 | 0.051 | 0.038 | 0.028 | 0.021 | 0.018 | 0.016 | 0.009 | 0.002 | 0.001 |
| 19 | 0.828 | 0.686 | 0.626 | 0.570 | 0.475 | 0.396 | 0.331 | 0.232 | 0.164 | 0.116 | 0.083 | 0.070 | 0.060 | 0.043 | 0.031 | 0.023 | 0.017 | 0.014 | 0.012 | 0.007 | 0.002 | |
| 20 | 0.820 | 0.673 | 0.610 | 0.554 | 0.456 | 0.377 | 0.312 | 0.215 | 0.149 | 0.104 | 0.073 | 0.061 | 0.051 | 0.037 | 0.026 | 0.019 | 0.014 | 0.012 | 0.010 | 0.005 | 0.001 | |
| 21 | 0.811 | 0.660 | 0.595 | 0.538 | 0.439 | 0.359 | 0.294 | 0.199 | 0.135 | 0.093 | 0.064 | 0.053 | 0.044 | 0.031 | 0.022 | 0.015 | 0.011 | 0.009 | 0.008 | 0.004 | 0.001 | |
| 22 | 0.803 | 0.647 | 0.581 | 0.522 | 0.422 | 0.342 | 0.278 | 0.184 | 0.123 | 0.083 | 0.056 | 0.046 | 0.038 | 0.026 | 0.018 | 0.013 | 0.009 | 0.007 | 0.006 | 0.003 | 0.001 | |
| 23 | 0.795 | 0.634 | 0.567 | 0.507 | 0.406 | 0.326 | 0.262 | 0.170 | 0.112 | 0.074 | 0.049 | 0.040 | 0.033 | 0.022 | 0.015 | 0.010 | 0.007 | 0.006 | 0.005 | 0.002 | | |
| 24 | 0.788 | 0.622 | 0.553 | 0.492 | 0.390 | 0.310 | 0.247 | 0.158 | 0.102 | 0.066 | 0.043 | 0.035 | 0.028 | 0.019 | 0.013 | 0.008 | 0.006 | 0.005 | 0.004 | 0.002 | | |
| 25 | 0.780 | 0.610 | 0.539 | 0.478 | 0.375 | 0.295 | 0.233 | 0.146 | 0.092 | 0.059 | 0.038 | 0.030 | 0.024 | 0.016 | 0.010 | 0.007 | 0.005 | 0.004 | 0.003 | 0.001 | | |
| 26 | 0.772 | 0.598 | 0.526 | 0.464 | 0.361 | 0.281 | 0.220 | 0.135 | 0.084 | 0.053 | 0.033 | 0.026 | 0.021 | 0.014 | 0.009 | 0.006 | 0.004 | 0.003 | 0.002 | 0.001 | | |
| 27 | 0.764 | 0.586 | 0.513 | 0.450 | 0.347 | 0.268 | 0.207 | 0.125 | 0.076 | 0.047 | 0.029 | 0.023 | 0.018 | 0.011 | 0.007 | 0.005 | 0.003 | 0.002 | 0.002 | 0.001 | | |
| 28 | 0.757 | 0.574 | 0.501 | 0.437 | 0.333 | 0.255 | 0.196 | 0.116 | 0.069 | 0.042 | 0.026 | 0.020 | 0.016 | 0.010 | 0.006 | 0.004 | 0.002 | 0.002 | 0.002 | 0.001 | | |
| 29 | 0.749 | 0.563 | 0.489 | 0.424 | 0.321 | 0.243 | 0.185 | 0.107 | 0.063 | 0.037 | 0.022 | 0.017 | 0.014 | 0.008 | 0.005 | 0.003 | 0.002 | 0.002 | 0.001 | | | |
| 30 | 0.742 | 0.552 | 0.477 | 0.412 | 0.308 | 0.231 | 0.174 | 0.099 | 0.057 | 0.033 | 0.020 | 0.015 | 0.012 | 0.007 | 0.004 | 0.003 | 0.002 | 0.001 | 0.001 | | | |
| 40 | 0.672 | 0.453 | 0.372 | 0.307 | 0.208 | 0.142 | 0.097 | 0.046 | 0.022 | 0.011 | 0.005 | 0.004 | 0.003 | 0.001 | 0.001 | | | | | | | |
| 50 | 0.608 | 0.372 | 0.291 | 0.228 | 0.141 | 0.087 | 0.054 | 0.021 | 0.009 | 0.003 | 0.001 | 0.001 | 0.001 | | | | | | | | | |

**TABLE C2**
Present Value of $1 Received Annually

| Periods to Be Paid | 50% | 40% | 30% | 26% | 25% | 24% | 22% | 20% | 18% | 16% | 15% | 14% | 12% | 10% | 8% | 6% | 5% | 4% | 3% | 2½% | 2% | 1% |
|---|---|---|---|---|---|---|---|---|---|---|---|---|---|---|---|---|---|---|---|---|---|---|
| 1 | 0.667 | 0.714 | 0.769 | 0.734 | 0.800 | 0.806 | 0.820 | 0.833 | 0.847 | 0.862 | 0.870 | 0.877 | 0.893 | 0.909 | 0.926 | 0.943 | 0.952 | 0.962 | 0.971 | 0.976 | 0.980 | 0.990 |
| 2 | 1.111 | 1.224 | 1.361 | 1.424 | 1.440 | 1.457 | 1.492 | 1.528 | 1.566 | 1.605 | 1.626 | 1.647 | 1.690 | 1.736 | 1.783 | 1.833 | 1.859 | 1.886 | 1.914 | 1.927 | 1.942 | 1.970 |
| 3 | 1.407 | 1.589 | 1.816 | 1.923 | 1.952 | 1.981 | 2.042 | 2.106 | 2.174 | 2.246 | 2.283 | 2.322 | 2.402 | 2.487 | 2.577 | 2.673 | 2.723 | 2.775 | 2.829 | 2.856 | 2.884 | 2.941 |
| 4 | 1.605 | 1.849 | 2.166 | 2.320 | 2.362 | 2.404 | 2.494 | 2.589 | 2.690 | 2.798 | 2.855 | 2.914 | 3.037 | 3.170 | 3.312 | 3.465 | 3.546 | 3.630 | 3.717 | 3.762 | 3.808 | 3.902 |
| 5 | 1.737 | 2.035 | 2.436 | 2.635 | 2.689 | 2.745 | 2.864 | 2.991 | 3.127 | 3.274 | 3.352 | 3.433 | 3.605 | 3.791 | 3.993 | 4.212 | 4.330 | 4.452 | 4.580 | 4.646 | 4.713 | 4.853 |
| 6 | 1.824 | 2.168 | 2.643 | 2.885 | 2.951 | 3.020 | 3.167 | 3.326 | 3.498 | 3.685 | 3.784 | 3.889 | 4.111 | 4.355 | 4.623 | 4.917 | 5.076 | 5.242 | 5.417 | 5.508 | 5.601 | 5.795 |
| 7 | 1.883 | 2.263 | 2.802 | 3.083 | 3.161 | 3.242 | 3.416 | 3.605 | 3.812 | 4.039 | 4.160 | 4.288 | 4.564 | 4.868 | 5.206 | 5.582 | 5.786 | 6.002 | 6.230 | 6.349 | 6.472 | 6.728 |
| 8 | 1.922 | 2.331 | 2.925 | 3.241 | 3.329 | 3.421 | 3.619 | 3.837 | 4.078 | 4.344 | 4.487 | 4.639 | 4.968 | 5.335 | 5.747 | 6.210 | 6.463 | 6.733 | 7.020 | 7.170 | 7.325 | 7.652 |
| 9 | 1.948 | 2.379 | 3.019 | 3.366 | 3.463 | 3.566 | 3.786 | 4.031 | 4.303 | 4.607 | 4.772 | 4.946 | 5.328 | 5.759 | 6.247 | 6.802 | 7.108 | 7.435 | 7.786 | 7.971 | 8.162 | 8.566 |
| 10 | 1.965 | 2.414 | 3.092 | 3.465 | 3.571 | 3.682 | 3.923 | 4.192 | 4.494 | 4.833 | 5.019 | 5.216 | 5.650 | 6.145 | 6.710 | 7.360 | 7.722 | 8.111 | 8.530 | 8.752 | 8.983 | 9.471 |
| 11 | 1.977 | 2.438 | 3.147 | 3.544 | 3.656 | 3.776 | 4.035 | 4.327 | 4.656 | 5.029 | 5.234 | 5.453 | 5.938 | 6.495 | 7.139 | 7.887 | 8.306 | 8.760 | 9.253 | 9.514 | 9.787 | 10.368 |
| 12 | 1.985 | 2.456 | 3.190 | 3.606 | 3.725 | 3.851 | 4.127 | 4.439 | 4.793 | 5.197 | 5.421 | 5.660 | 6.194 | 6.814 | 7.536 | 8.384 | 8.863 | 9.385 | 9.954 | 10.258 | 10.575 | 11.255 |
| 13 | 1.990 | 2.468 | 3.223 | 3.656 | 3.780 | 3.912 | 4.203 | 4.533 | 4.910 | 5.342 | 5.583 | 5.842 | 6.424 | 7.103 | 7.904 | 8.853 | 9.394 | 9.986 | 10.635 | 10.983 | 11.348 | 12.134 |
| 14 | 1.993 | 2.478 | 3.249 | 3.695 | 3.824 | 3.962 | 4.265 | 4.611 | 5.008 | 5.468 | 5.724 | 6.002 | 6.628 | 7.367 | 8.244 | 9.295 | 9.899 | 10.563 | 11.296 | 11.691 | 12.106 | 13.004 |
| 15 | 1.995 | 2.484 | 3.268 | 3.726 | 3.859 | 4.001 | 4.315 | 4.676 | 5.092 | 5.576 | 5.847 | 6.142 | 6.811 | 7.606 | 8.559 | 9.712 | 10.380 | 11.118 | 11.938 | 12.381 | 12.849 | 13.865 |
| 16 | 1.997 | 2.488 | 3.283 | 3.751 | 3.887 | 4.033 | 4.357 | 4.730 | 5.162 | 5.668 | 5.954 | 6.265 | 6.974 | 7.824 | 8.851 | 10.106 | 10.838 | 11.652 | 12.561 | 13.055 | 13.578 | 14.718 |
| 17 | 1.998 | 2.492 | 3.295 | 3.771 | 3.910 | 4.059 | 4.391 | 4.775 | 5.222 | 5.749 | 6.047 | 6.373 | 7.120 | 8.022 | 9.122 | 10.477 | 11.274 | 12.166 | 13.166 | 13.712 | 14.292 | 15.562 |
| 18 | 1.999 | 2.494 | 3.304 | 3.786 | 3.928 | 4.080 | 4.419 | 4.812 | 5.273 | 5.818 | 6.128 | 6.467 | 7.250 | 8.201 | 9.372 | 10.828 | 11.690 | 12.659 | 13.754 | 14.353 | 14.992 | 16.398 |
| 19 | 1.999 | 2.496 | 3.311 | 3.799 | 3.942 | 4.097 | 4.442 | 4.844 | 5.316 | 5.878 | 6.198 | 6.550 | 7.366 | 8.365 | 9.604 | 11.158 | 12.085 | 13.134 | 14.324 | 14.979 | 15.678 | 17.226 |
| 20 | 1.999 | 2.497 | 3.316 | 3.808 | 3.954 | 4.110 | 4.460 | 4.870 | 5.353 | 5.929 | 6.259 | 6.623 | 7.469 | 8.514 | 9.818 | 11.470 | 12.462 | 13.590 | 14.877 | 15.589 | 16.351 | 18.046 |
| 21 | 2.000 | 2.498 | 3.320 | 3.816 | 3.963 | 4.121 | 4.476 | 4.891 | 5.384 | 5.973 | 6.312 | 6.687 | 7.562 | 8.649 | 10.017 | 11.764 | 12.821 | 14.029 | 15.415 | 16.185 | 17.011 | 18.857 |
| 22 | 2.000 | 2.498 | 3.323 | 3.822 | 3.970 | 4.130 | 4.488 | 4.909 | 5.410 | 6.011 | 6.359 | 6.743 | 7.645 | 8.772 | 10.201 | 12.042 | 13.163 | 14.451 | 15.937 | 16.765 | 17.658 | 19.660 |
| 23 | 2.000 | 2.499 | 3.325 | 3.827 | 3.976 | 4.137 | 4.499 | 4.924 | 5.432 | 6.044 | 6.399 | 6.792 | 7.718 | 8.883 | 10.371 | 12.303 | 13.489 | 14.857 | 16.444 | 17.332 | 18.292 | 20.456 |
| 24 | 2.000 | 2.499 | 3.327 | 3.831 | 3.981 | 4.143 | 4.507 | 4.937 | 5.451 | 6.073 | 6.434 | 6.835 | 7.784 | 8.985 | 10.529 | 12.550 | 13.799 | 15.247 | 16.936 | 17.885 | 18.914 | 21.243 |
| 25 | 2.000 | 2.499 | 3.329 | 3.834 | 3.985 | 4.147 | 4.514 | 4.948 | 5.467 | 6.097 | 6.464 | 6.873 | 7.843 | 9.077 | 10.675 | 12.783 | 14.094 | 15.622 | 17.413 | 18.424 | 19.523 | 22.023 |
| 26 | 2.000 | 2.500 | 3.330 | 3.837 | 3.988 | 4.151 | 4.520 | 4.956 | 5.480 | 6.118 | 6.491 | 6.906 | 7.896 | 9.161 | 10.810 | 13.003 | 14.375 | 15.983 | 17.877 | 18.951 | 20.121 | 22.795 |
| 27 | 2.000 | 2.500 | 3.331 | 3.839 | 3.990 | 4.154 | 4.524 | 4.964 | 5.492 | 6.136 | 6.514 | 6.935 | 7.943 | 9.237 | 10.935 | 13.211 | 14.643 | 16.330 | 18.327 | 19.464 | 20.707 | 23.560 |
| 28 | 2.000 | 2.500 | 3.331 | 3.840 | 3.992 | 4.157 | 4.528 | 4.970 | 5.502 | 6.152 | 6.534 | 6.961 | 7.984 | 9.307 | 11.051 | 13.406 | 14.898 | 16.663 | 18.764 | 19.965 | 21.281 | 24.316 |
| 29 | 2.000 | 2.500 | 3.332 | 3.841 | 3.994 | 4.159 | 4.531 | 4.975 | 5.510 | 6.166 | 6.551 | 6.983 | 8.022 | 9.370 | 11.158 | 13.591 | 15.141 | 16.984 | 19.188 | 20.454 | 21.844 | 25.066 |
| 30 | 2.000 | 2.500 | 3.332 | 3.842 | 3.995 | 4.160 | 4.534 | 4.979 | 5.517 | 6.177 | 6.566 | 7.003 | 8.055 | 9.427 | 11.258 | 13.765 | 15.372 | 17.292 | 19.600 | 20.930 | 22.396 | 25.808 |
| 40 | 2.000 | 2.500 | 3.333 | 3.846 | 3.999 | 4.166 | 4.544 | 4.997 | 5.548 | 6.234 | 6.642 | 7.105 | 8.244 | 9.779 | 11.925 | 15.046 | 17.159 | 19.793 | 23.115 | 25.103 | 27.355 | 32.835 |
| 50 | 2.000 | 2.500 | 3.333 | 3.846 | 4.000 | 4.167 | 4.545 | 4.999 | 5.554 | 6.246 | 6.660 | 7.133 | 8.304 | 9.915 | 12.233 | 15.762 | 18.256 | 21.482 | 25.730 | 28.362 | 31.424 | 39.196 |

# TABLE C3
## Future Value of $1 at End of Period n

| Periods until Payment | 1% | 2% | 2½% | 3% | 4% | 5% | 6% | 8% | 10% | 12% | 14% | 15% | 16% | 18% | 20% | 22% | 24% | 25% | 26% | 30% | 40% | 50% |
|---|---|---|---|---|---|---|---|---|---|---|---|---|---|---|---|---|---|---|---|---|---|---|
| 1 | 1.010 | 1.020 | 1.025 | 1.030 | 1.040 | 1.050 | 1.060 | 1.080 | 1.100 | 1.120 | 1.140 | 1.150 | 1.160 | 1.180 | 1.200 | 1.220 | 1.240 | 1.250 | 1.260 | 1.300 | 1.400 | 1.500 |
| 2 | 1.020 | 1.040 | 1.051 | 1.061 | 1.082 | 1.103 | 1.124 | 1.166 | 1.210 | 1.254 | 1.300 | 1.323 | 1.346 | 1.392 | 1.440 | 1.488 | 1.538 | 1.563 | 1.588 | 1.690 | 1.960 | 2.250 |
| 3 | 1.030 | 1.061 | 1.077 | 1.093 | 1.125 | 1.158 | 1.191 | 1.260 | 1.331 | 1.405 | 1.482 | 1.521 | 1.561 | 1.643 | 1.728 | 1.816 | 1.907 | 1.953 | 2.000 | 2.197 | 2.744 | 3.375 |
| 4 | 1.041 | 1.082 | 1.104 | 1.126 | 1.170 | 1.216 | 1.263 | 1.361 | 1.464 | 1.574 | 1.689 | 1.749 | 1.811 | 1.939 | 2.074 | 2.215 | 2.364 | 2.441 | 2.520 | 2.856 | 3.842 | 5.063 |
| 5 | 1.051 | 1.104 | 1.131 | 1.159 | 1.217 | 1.276 | 1.338 | 1.469 | 1.611 | 1.762 | 1.925 | 2.011 | 2.100 | 2.288 | 2.488 | 2.703 | 2.932 | 3.052 | 3.176 | 3.713 | 5.378 | 7.594 |
| 6 | 1.062 | 1.126 | 1.160 | 1.194 | 1.265 | 1.340 | 1.419 | 1.587 | 1.772 | 1.974 | 2.195 | 2.313 | 2.436 | 2.700 | 2.986 | 3.297 | 3.635 | 3.815 | 4.002 | 4.827 | 7.530 | 11.391 |
| 7 | 1.072 | 1.149 | 1.189 | 1.230 | 1.316 | 1.407 | 1.504 | 1.714 | 1.949 | 2.211 | 2.502 | 2.660 | 2.826 | 3.186 | 3.583 | 4.023 | 4.508 | 4.768 | 5.042 | 6.275 | 10.541 | 17.086 |
| 8 | 1.083 | 1.172 | 1.218 | 1.267 | 1.369 | 1.478 | 1.594 | 1.851 | 2.144 | 2.476 | 2.853 | 3.059 | 3.278 | 3.759 | 4.2998 | 4.908 | 5.590 | 5.961 | 6.353 | 8.157 | 14.758 | 25.629 |
| 9 | 1.094 | 1.195 | 1.249 | 1.305 | 1.423 | 1.551 | 1.690 | 1.999 | 2.358 | 2.773 | 3.252 | 3.518 | 3.803 | 4.436 | 5.160 | 5.987 | 6.931 | 7.451 | 8.005 | 10.604 | 20.661 | 38.443 |
| 10 | 1.105 | 1.219 | 1.280 | 1.344 | 1.480 | 1.629 | 1.791 | 2.159 | 2.594 | 3.106 | 3.707 | 4.046 | 4.411 | 5.234 | 6.192 | 7.305 | 8.594 | 9.313 | 10.086 | 13.786 | 28.925 | 57.665 |
| 11 | 1.116 | 1.243 | 1.312 | 1.384 | 1.540 | 1.710 | 1.898 | 2.332 | 2.853 | 3.479 | 4.226 | 4.652 | 5.117 | 6.176 | 7.430 | 8.912 | 10.657 | 11.642 | 12.708 | 17.922 | 40.496 | 86.498 |
| 12 | 1.127 | 1.268 | 1.345 | 1.426 | 1.601 | 1.796 | 2.012 | 2.518 | 3.138 | 3.896 | 4.818 | 5.350 | 5.936 | 7.288 | 8.916 | 10.872 | 13.215 | 14.552 | 16.012 | 23.298 | 56.694 | 129.75 |
| 13 | 1.138 | 1.294 | 1.379 | 1.469 | 1.665 | 1.886 | 2.133 | 2.720 | 3.452 | 4.364 | 5.492 | 6.153 | 6.886 | 8.599 | 10.699 | 13.364 | 16.386 | 18.190 | 20.175 | 30.288 | 79.371 | 194.62 |
| 14 | 1.150 | 1.320 | 1.413 | 1.513 | 1.732 | 1.980 | 2.261 | 2.937 | 3.798 | 4.887 | 6.261 | 7.076 | 7.988 | 10.147 | 12.839 | 16.182 | 20.319 | 22.737 | 25.421 | 39.374 | 111.12 | 291.93 |
| 15 | 1.161 | 1.346 | 1.448 | 1.558 | 1.801 | 2.079 | 2.397 | 3.172 | 4.177 | 5.474 | 7.138 | 8.137 | 9.266 | 11.974 | 15.407 | 19.742 | 25.196 | 28.422 | 32.030 | 51.186 | 155.57 | 437.89 |
| 16 | 1.173 | 1.373 | 1.485 | 1.605 | 1.873 | 2.183 | 2.540 | 3.426 | 4.595 | 6.130 | 8.137 | 9.358 | 10.748 | 14.129 | 18.488 | 24.086 | 31.243 | 35.527 | 40.358 | 66.542 | 217.80 | 656.84 |
| 17 | 1.184 | 1.400 | 1.522 | 1.653 | 1.948 | 2.292 | 2.693 | 3.700 | 5.055 | 6.866 | 9.277 | 10.761 | 12.468 | 16.672 | 22.186 | 29.384 | 38.741 | 44.409 | 50.851 | 86.504 | 304.91 | 985.26 |
| 18 | 1.196 | 1.428 | 1.560 | 1.702 | 2.026 | 2.407 | 2.854 | 3.996 | 5.560 | 7.690 | 10.575 | 12.375 | 14.463 | 19.673 | 26.623 | 35.849 | 48.039 | 55.511 | 64.072 | 112.46 | 426.88 | 1477.9 |
| 19 | 1.208 | 1.457 | 1.599 | 1.754 | 2.107 | 2.527 | 3.026 | 4.316 | 6.116 | 8.613 | 12.056 | 14.232 | 16.777 | 23.214 | 31.948 | 43.736 | 59.568 | 69.389 | 80.731 | 146.19 | 597.63 | 2216.8 |
| 20 | 1.220 | 1.486 | 1.639 | 1.806 | 2.191 | 2.653 | 3.207 | 4.661 | 6.728 | 9.646 | 13.743 | 16.367 | 19.461 | 27.393 | 38.338 | 53.358 | 73.864 | 86.736 | 101.72 | 190.05 | 836.68 | 3325.3 |
| 21 | 1.232 | 1.516 | 1.680 | 1.860 | 2.279 | 2.786 | 3.400 | 5.034 | 7.400 | 10.804 | 15.668 | 18.822 | 22.574 | 32.324 | 46.005 | 65.096 | 91.592 | 108.42 | 128.17 | 247.06 | 1171.4 | 4987.9 |
| 22 | 1.245 | 1.546 | 1.722 | 1.916 | 2.370 | 2.925 | 3.604 | 5.437 | 8.140 | 12.100 | 17.861 | 21.645 | 26.186 | 38.142 | 55.206 | 79.418 | 113.57 | 135.53 | 161.49 | 321.18 | 1639.9 | 7481.8 |
| 23 | 1.257 | 1.577 | 1.765 | 1.974 | 2.465 | 3.072 | 3.820 | 5.872 | 8.954 | 13.552 | 20.362 | 24.891 | 30.376 | 45.008 | 66.247 | 96.889 | 140.83 | 169.41 | 203.48 | 417.54 | 2295.9 | 11223. |
| 24 | 1.270 | 1.608 | 1.809 | 2.033 | 2.563 | 3.225 | 4.049 | 6.341 | 9.845 | 15.179 | 23.212 | 28.625 | 35.236 | 53.109 | 79.497 | 118.21 | 174.63 | 211.76 | 256.39 | 542.80 | 3214.2 | 16834. |
| 25 | 1.282 | 1.641 | 1.854 | 2.094 | 2.666 | 3.386 | 4.292 | 6.849 | 10.835 | 17.000 | 26.462 | 32.919 | 40.874 | 62.669 | 95.396 | 144.21 | 216.54 | 264.70 | 323.05 | 705.64 | 4499.9 | 25251. |
| 26 | 1.295 | 1.673 | 1.900 | 2.157 | 2.773 | 3.556 | 4.549 | 7.396 | 11.918 | 19.040 | 30.167 | 37.857 | 47.414 | 73.949 | 114.48 | 175.94 | 268.51 | 330.87 | 407.04 | 917.33 | 6299.8 | 37877. |
| 27 | 1.308 | 1.707 | 1.948 | 2.221 | 2.883 | 3.734 | 4.822 | 7.988 | 13.110 | 21.325 | 34.390 | 43.535 | 55.000 | 87.260 | 137.37 | 214.64 | 332.95 | 413.59 | 512.87 | 1192.5 | 8819.8 | 56815. |
| 28 | 1.321 | 1.741 | 2.000 | 2.288 | 2.999 | 3.920 | 5.112 | 8.627 | 14.421 | 23.884 | 39.204 | 50.066 | 63.800 | 102.97 | 164.84 | 261.86 | 412.86 | 516.99 | 646.21 | 1550.3 | 12348. | 85223. |
| 29 | 1.335 | 1.776 | 2.046 | 2.357 | 3.119 | 4.116 | 5.418 | 9.317 | 15.863 | 26.750 | 44.693 | 57.575 | 74.009 | 121.50 | 197.81 | 319.47 | 511.95 | 646.23 | 814.23 | 2015.4 | 17287. | |
| 30 | 1.348 | 1.811 | 2.098 | 2.427 | 3.243 | 4.322 | 5.744 | 10.063 | 17.449 | 29.960 | 50.950 | 66.212 | 85.850 | 143.37 | 237.38 | 389.76 | 634.82 | 807.79 | 1025.9 | 2620.0 | 24201. | |
| 40 | 1.489 | 2.208 | 2.685 | 3.262 | 4.801 | 7.040 | 10.286 | 21.725 | 45.259 | 93.051 | 188.88 | 267.86 | 378.72 | 750.38 | 1469.8 | 2847.0 | 5455.9 | 7523.2 | 10347. | 36119. | | |
| 50 | 1.645 | 2.692 | 3.437 | 4.384 | 7.107 | 11.467 | 18.420 | 46.902 | 117.39 | 289.00 | 700.23 | 1083.7 | 1670.7 | 3927.4 | 9100.4 | 17046. | 46890. | 70065. | | | | |

# Index of Cases